The Separation of

The Rise and

Bengali Muslim Nationalism

The Separation of East Pakistan

The Rise and Realization of Bengali Muslim Nationalism

Hasan Zaheer

Karachi
Oxford University Press
Oxford New York Delhi
1995

Oxford University Press, Walton Street, Oxford OX2 6DP

Oxford New York
Athens Auckland Bangkok Bombay
Calcutta Cape Town Dar es Salaam Delhi
Florence Hong Kong Istanbul Karachi
Kuala Lumpur Madras Madrid Melbourne
Mexico City Nairobi Paris Singapore
Taipei Tokyo Toronto

and associated companies in

Berlin Ibadan

Oxford is a trade mark of Oxford University Press

First published by Oxford University Press, Pakistan, 1994
This edition in Oxford Pakistan Paperbacks, 1995

ISBN 0 19 577592 9

Printed in Pakistan at
Mas Printers, Karachi.
Published by
Oxford University Press
5-Bangalore Town, Sharae Faisal,
P.O. Box 13033, Karachi-75350, Pakistan.

*Dedicated to former East Pakistan
where Shahnaz and I spent some
of the happiest years of our life, with
our children Guriya and Abbas,
(Farrukh was born later)
and my youngest brother, Mehdi.*

Contents

	page
List of Abbreviations	*ix*
Preface	*xi*
Prologue	*xxvii*

Part I: Muslim Bengal and Pakistan

1. The Search for Identity 1936–1947	3
2. Two Turbulent Decades: August 1947–March 1969	13
3. Enforcing the Federation: March 1969–March 1971	108

Part II: Army Action, Civil War, and Separation

4. Restoring the Authority	163
5. Making of the Government in Exile	178
6. Economic Consequences: East Pakistan	185
7. Economic Consequences: Pakistan	214
8. The Politics of International Relief and Refugees	237
9. India, the World, and the Crisis	273
10. West Pakistan's Responses	322
11. War, Surrender, and Separation	353
Epilogue	426

page

Appendices:

1 Letter of R. G. Casey, Governor of Bengal, to Viscount Wavell, Viceroy and Governor-General of India, dated 17 December 1944 . 437
2 Letter of H. S. Suhrawardy to Liaquat Ali Khan dated 21 May 1947. 441
3 Letter of H. S. Suhrawardy to Liaquat Ali Khan dated 21 May 1947. 445
4 Hindu-Muslim Pact for Bengal. Reproduced from *Civil and Military Gazette,* Lahore, 24 May 1947. 446
5 Letter of H. S. Suhrawardy to Liaquat Ali Khan, Prime Minister of Pakistan, dated 11 June 1948. 448
6 Letter of H. S. Suhrawardy to Liaquat Ali Khan, Prime Minister of Pakistan, dated 8 July 1948. 453
7 Letter of Liaquat Ali Khan, Prime Minister of Pakistan, to H. S. Suhrawardy dated 13 July 1948. 454
8 Letter of H. S. Suhrawardy, Prime Minister of Pakistan, to Ataur Rahman Khan, Chief Minister East Pakistan, dated 17 April 1957. 455
9 Notification of 2 April 1971, deputing a team of central government officers to East Pakistan. 456
10 Chittagong and Chalna Ports Operations April–November 1971. 457
11 Operations of commercial bank branches in East Pakistan as on 7 May 1971. 462
12 Statement showing currency chests looted as in early May 1971. 463
13 Statement showing damage to major bridges on the Pakistan Eastern Railway as on 26 May 1971. 464
14 Statement showing damage to major road bridges in East Pakistan as in May 1971. 466
15 Minutes of the Meeting of the Constitution (Cornelius) Committee held on 26 May 1971 at the President House. 467

Notes and References 472

List of Important Persons Involved in the Management of the East Pakistan Crisis in 1971 505

Index 507

Maps between pages 214 and 215

Abbreviations

ADP	Annual Development Programme
CAD	Constituent Assembly Debates
CALD	Constituent Assembly (Legislature) Debates
CMLA	Chief Martial Law Administrator
COP	Combined Opposition Parties
CSP	Civil Service of Pakistan
DAC	Democratic Action Committee
DCMLA	Deputy Chief Martial Law Administrator
DMI	Director Military Intelligence
DMLA	Deputy Martial Law Administration
EBCP	East Bengal Communist Party
EBCP (M-L)	East Bengal Communist Party (Marxist-Leninist)
EBDO	Elective Bodies (Disqualification) Order
EBLAP	East Bengal Legislative Assembly Proceedings
EBR	East Bengal Regiment
EC&EAD	Economic Co-ordination and External Assistance Division
EPAP	East Pakistan Assembly Proceedings
EPCP	East Pakistan Communist Party
EPCP (M-L)	East Pakistan Communist Party (Marxist-Leninist)
EPR	East Pakistan Rifles
EPRTC	East Pakistan Road Transport Corporation
EPSL	East Pakistan Students' League
EPSU	East Pakistan Students' Union
GDP	Gross Domestic Product
IAF	Indian Air Force
ICRC	International Committee of the Red Cross
IRC	International Red Cross
ICS	Indian Civil Service
ISI	Inter-Services Intelligence
ISPR	Inter-Services Public Relations
LCTs	Landing Craft Types

LFO	Legal Framework Order 1970
MLA	Martial Law Administrator
NAD	National Assembly Debates
NAP	National Awami Party
NDF	National Democratic Front
PAF	Pakistan Air Force
PDM	Pakistan Democratic Movement
PER	Pakistan Eastern Railway
PIA	Pakistan International Airlines
PLD	Pakistan Legal Decisions
PRODA	Public Representative Offices (Disqualification) Act
PSO	Principal Staff Officer to the President
RTC	Round Table Conference
TCP	Trading Corporation of Pakistan
VCGS	Vice Chief of General Staff
WSAG	Washington Special Action Group

Preface

'We send our best officers to East Pakistan,' said Sir Eric Franklin C.B.E., Establishment Officer, government of Pakistan, as I was ushered into his office in the barracks within the Assembly compound behind the main building one afternoon in October 1956 in Karachi. Looking up from the papers in front of him, which were obviously my confidential reports, he motioned me to sit down, offered me tea, and informed me that 'therefore we are posting you there.' This was the end of probation after two years training in the Civil Service of Pakistan (CSP), which included about ten months in the elegant civil service academy at Lahore, district assignments in East Pakistan for six months, and a six-month course in public administration at the University of Oxford and other institutions in the UK. After this glamorous training, a posting to the backwaters of East Pakistan, so far away from the glitter of Lahore and Karachi, was depressing. Somewhat flattered by the compliment of the Establishment Officer at that time, over the years I learnt that such gracious remarks usually preceded an unpleasant and unwanted posting or similar eventuality.

In those days, the government machinery was better organized than it is now, and the officers did not have to hang around waiting for placement. Soon after the Establishment Division's notification, the East Pakistan government communicated my appointment orders as subdivisional officer Chapai Nawabganj, while I was still at Karachi. Where was Chapai Nawabganj? No one in the Establishment Division had heard of the place. So I went to Saddar to buy a map of East Pakistan, and traced the railway route to it, which went up north from Dhaka, came down to the River Jamuna to cross the ferry, continued south for some distance, turned again to the north, and finally terminated at Chapai Nawabganj on a small branch line at the end of the railway system, right on the western border with India.

A few days later I left for Dhaka. In the mid-1950s, the journey was by the Super-Constellation aircraft, one of the latest at the time. It was noisy, bumpy, and tiring, and took more than six hours. I reported to Eden Buildings, the provincial secretariat, and booked the train seat to my headquarters. The train left at 9 p.m. from Dhaka, and a little after midnight arrived at Jagannathganj Ghat station, which was a sprawling shunting yard on the sandy bank of the River Jamuna; there was a change-over to a steamer for crossing the river. Since the contours of the river bank, criss-crossed by small channels, shifted with the seasons, there were no permanent platforms to board or disembark from the trains. The passengers and loaders jostled through ankle-deep sand to the gangway of the huge steamer. Its first class deck had a spacious and comfortable lounge and a baroque dining-saloon which served sumptuous meals. It took a few hours to cross the mighty river, and then on to the train again on the other bank at Sirajganj Ghat. After travelling the whole day, the terminal station of the mainline, Amnura, was reached at about 9 p.m. It was pitch dark. There was no electricity, only stationary and moving patches of light from the kerosene oil lamps. Changing to the branch line, I reached Chapai Nawabganj at about midnight. I anxiously peered at the dimly-lit platform from the window over the milling passengers, searching for anyone who might have come to receive me. There was only one first class compartment in the train, hooked on to it just for me, and I saw my reception committee, headed by the senior magistrate and illuminated by gaslight, hurrying towards it. A barefoot constable was clearing a path for them on the crowded platform. I was escorted to the only mechanical vehicle, a Second World War vintage Willy's jeep, parked amongst the bullock carts.

The policy at the time was that every CSP officer should serve three years in his own province, a minimum of three years in the Wing other than that of his domicile and after that in the Centre or in any of the provinces. This inter-Wing policy was an important element of the cadre rules of the Civil Service of Pakistan which was recruited, trained, and controlled by the central government, but members of which served in various provincial governments as well as at the Centre. Through training and service in various parts of the country, it was hoped that the central cadre of senior administrators, based on competitive merit and representing all regions but owing allegiance to none, would provide a strong linkage between the Centre and the provinces through its *esprit de corps*. These objectives were achieved to a certain extent. Of all the classes, those of the Civil Service of Pakistan of the two Wings were the only ones which were socially and professionally integrated. They respected each other even while disagreeing on sensitive regional issues in official forums. The relationship was so deep-rooted that it still survives among those of that generation. The inter-Wing transfer policy, however, did not work properly because the officers of both the Wings resisted it. From the batch inducted into the Civil Service each year, Establishment Division allocated some officers to the Wing other than their own, while others were posted initially to their own province of domicile. The former had to stay in the province of their postings much longer because the latter, particularly those hailing from the Punjab, managed to avoid their turn of being posted to East Pakistan to relieve their batch-fellows after three years; I had to stay for more than five years in East Pakistan for these reasons. The initial allocations were regarded as arbitrary and led to general protests. In 1957, Prime Minister Suhrawardy ordered, as a principle, the posting of the entire batch of West Pakistani CSP officers who had completed their training that year, to East Pakistan, and of all Bengalis to the West Wing without any exception. This was the only way that a wholesome system could have been sustained. In the short period that he was in office, Suhrawardy could apply the principle to one year's batch only. After him, no government could enforce it, and in Ayub's time it was considerably diluted.

I had gone to East Pakistan at a time when the Awami League had just come into power in the province. Its workers were young and aggressive, and there were occasional differences of opinion on administrative matters with them or the party members of the national and provincial assemblies, which is quite natural under the parliamentary system. In most such cases, I was supported by the provincial government against them. But in general it was a harmonious and productive relationship between the ruling party and the administration. At the central and provincial levels there were East-West tensions and controversies, but they all seemed far away; one read about them occasionally in the newspaper statements of the politicians. At the day-to-day human level there was a well-developed feeling of Pakistani nationalism among all classes. Even the prosperous Hindu middle classes were a part of mainstream community life. Generally, they co-operated with the administration, and played a leading role in social, educational, and charitable projects. At the working level, it was an organized administrative system where it was taken for granted that orders would be carried out loyally in letter and spirit. It was, as it seems now in the light of its later militant transformation, a remarkably peaceful, unarmed, and cultured society. The number of even licensed arms was very small, relative to the population, and they were mostly for sporting guns; prohibited bore arms were unheard of. Revolvers were few. There was smuggling on a modest scale to and from India, and that of cattle from India was even encouraged officially. Major crimes were few, and murders still fewer. I remember very few cases in which the investigation officers asked for police remands of the accused. The incriminating weapon in offences of physical violence was usually a sharp but rusted knife. My criminal case work was mostly confined to private complaints, usually related to trespass on land, occasionally leading to grievous injuries. Private litigation, expensive to the parties, was otherwise harmless. Very few of these cases were pursued to the end; at some fairly early stage, they were compounded. Litigation was part of the culture, and even the district and subdivisional officers, in their capacity as heads of the governing committees of social, cultural, and educational institutions, would at any one time be defending themselves as respondents in a few civil cases filed by public-spirited citizens. There was nothing personal in it. It was just that the plaintiff saw a point of principle differently from the administrative head. On the whole, there was a harmonious working relationship between the people and the administration. I could thus fully devote myself to developmental activities. Coming from a distant region and speaking Bengali poorly, I travelled night and day in the most remote corners of the subdivisions and districts, and never for a moment did I and my wife feel that we were strangers. The local people and all my officers treated me as one of them, and looked up to me, as they did to all district officers, with respect, expecting justice and compassion. The only way one made a reputation in the district was by doing one's job well, identifying oneself with the local community, and serving the people: which region one came from did not matter. The Bengalis had a very enlightened but demanding view of what public service was. They would not spare deviations from judicious conduct by the officers, or suffer their arrogance and allow themselves to be pushed around. There would be a flood of petitions against the errant officer to the authorities, and the campaign would be pursued until the government was forced to take notice. But they were extremely generous with their love and respect to those officers, irrespective of their origin, who were considerate and showed concern for their welfare.

I served in East Pakistan in the districts and the Secretariat in middle positions, eventually becoming deputy commissioner of Jessore before returning to West Pakistan in early 1962. It was the most peaceful and satisfying period of my career.

Ten years later, in May 1971, when I was again posted to East Pakistan, I came to a different world in Dhaka. This time I was part of what the Bengalis regarded as the West Pakistani occupation forces. I was not regarded as one of them, or for them. I was specially called to East Pakistan after the army action; I was living in exclusive premises guarded by a West Pakistani police force; I could not move after dusk without an escort and there was no question of going out of the city. They would not judge me by my individual performance, but by the conduct of those who were 'regaining control' of the province. This was the most depressing period of my career.

In Dhaka I had plenty of time to ponder over the sea change of the peaceful Bengali province into an intolerant and ferocious armed camp, and still more on the ongoing events. The idea of this study took birth in those unhappy days. Originally, I had planned it to cover only Yahya's years, preceding the fall of Dhaka. But going over the initial draft chapters on the events of 1971, I felt that to understand why those events took place, it was necessary to analyse them in the historical perspective of the genesis of Pakistan, and, in greater detail, that of the East–West relationship during the quarter of a century of their union. The debate about the separation of East Pakistan is confounded by self-serving, righteous, and motivated explanations such as political versus military defeat, Yahya's drinking habits, Bhutto's not attending the Assembly session in March, or not accepting the Polish resolution in the Security Council before the fall of Dhaka. None of these explain how the polarization reached the point where the Bengali prime minister-designate would even refuse to come to the capital of the country to meet the West Pakistani head of state to discuss the arrangements for transfer of power to him, demand to be left alone to govern his own province, and dissociate his province from the other units of the Federation. The organic process of disintegration in modern nation-states arises from the accumulation of perceived grievances and a sense of injustice, repression, and hopelessness; it takes a long time to reach breaking-point. This study attempts an objective analysis of the issues which bedevilled East–West relations during their unstable union and which created such alienation between the people of the two Wings that final separation became inevitable. An outline of the thesis and a plan of this study are described below.

Part I of the book analyses the rise of Bengali Muslim nationalism in three periods: (i) 1935 to August 1947; (ii) August 1947 to March 1969; and (iii) March 1969 to March 1971. In the first period, the different interpretations of three covenants of the Muslims of the subcontinent, entered into in 1940, 1941, and 1946, for a separate Homeland, and the Bengali Muslims' assertion of an identity distinct from the Muslims of the other regions of India have been examined. The selection of the cut-off point of 1935 has been determined with reference to the introduction of provincial autonomy under the Government of India Act 1935, and the Indian Muslims' search for a constitutional formula which adequately safeguarded their interests. Indeed, the distinctive social and cultural development of Bengali Muslims, unaffected by the Muslim renaissance movements of northern India, could be traced to a much earlier date. But going back any further would have rendered the study unwieldy, since it is essentially concerned with the separation of Bengali Muslims from West Pakistan after their having lived together for twenty-five years.

The second period, August 1947 to March 1969, covers two decades of fragile union. The first ten years of independence demonstrated the incompatibility of the two Wings. The Federation of Pakistan as it came into being in August 1947 with the major federating units a thousand miles apart, separated by a hostile country, and each in every way different from the other, was a tenuous state structure. The Bengalis demanded that these peculiar characteristics be recognized in the new constitutional framework by the grant of a large degree of autonomy to East Pakistan. The Quaid-i-Azam had underlined the importance of constitution-making, the crux of which was the relations of the federating units with the Centre, by assuming the presidentship of the Constituent Assembly. He did not live long enough to bring about the resolution of East–West issues which were emerging, and which were forcefully brought to his notice during his visit to Dhaka in March 1948. His immediate successor, Liaquat Ali Khan, did not realize that the unity and solid base of the new state depended on a mutually acceptable relationship between the two Wings and not on the Objectives Resolution and rhetoric about Islam. Nevertheless, he should be given credit for persuading the Bengalis to give up their numerical majority in the central legislature, which they started with in 1947, and agree on parity of representation between the two Wings. This remained the only anchor in the turbulent relationships until mindlessly snapped by Yahya Khan. Perhaps Liaquat Ali Khan was the only leader, after the Quaid-i-Azam, most suited to bring the East and West Wings together in a viable state structure. After him, constitution-making ceased to be a national issue to be resolved by the consensus of all the federating units; the exercise became a purely regional fight between the Punjab and Bengal.

The Punjabi leadership would not concede provincial autonomy which would have somewhat diluted the issue of representation at the Centre. It refused to accept the numerical majority of Bengalis by virtue of population. It did not even accept parity of representation at the Centre until its apprehensions of East Pakistan's collusion with the smaller provinces of West Pakistan, under such an arrangement, were allayed by the formation of One Unit, much against the wishes of the latter. By a peculiar logic, any constitutional formula opposed to the wishes of the power centres was termed as anti-state and anti-Islamic. The Bengali leadership, on the other hand, was parochial and xenophobic even in matters which served the larger interests of their region. The Bengali intelligentsia turned the persecution complex, from which the middle classes suffered, into a virtue. Instead of exerting themselves, and inducing the people to profit from the tremendous economic opportunities which independence had offered to East Pakistan, no less than to the West Wing, they took the easy course of blaming outsiders for all their ills. They complained of backwardness and neglect of their region, but labelled as exploiters those who came there to take up the slack in business and industry.

To contain the non-conformist tendencies of Bengali politics, the central leadership resorted to manipulation and repression of the popular forces to prevent their representation in the power structure of the Centre and East Pakistan. Bengali Muslim nationalism had emerged as a powerful force even before Independence. Their charismatic leader Suhrawardy, who had led Bengal into Pakistan in the elections of 1946, was not allowed to assume the parliamentary leadership of the East Pakistan Assembly in August 1947. Instead, the amenable Nazimuddin, who had no base among the masses, was elected Chief Minister under instructions of the central leadership. Liaquat Ali Khan, who regarded Suhrawardy as a rival, got him disqualified from the membership of the Constituent Assembly, and Nazimuddin externed him from East Pakistan. The victimization of opponents became, from the early formative period of Pakistan, part of the political culture, to be resorted to by the ruling party quite routinely as an instrument of governance. After Nazimuddin, the central government leadership, in 1951, nominated Nurul Amin; even the formality of election of its leader was not allowed to the provincial parliamentary party which was becoming radicalized on provincial issues.

The East Pakistan Assembly was elected in 1947, before Independence, on a franchise which did not give voting rights to more than fifteen per cent of the population. The ruling Muslim League party avoided elections when its term expired in 1951. After two extensions to its life by the Provincial Assembly itself, and a third one by the Constituent Assembly, provincial elections were held in March 1954. At that time more than thirty-six of its seats were vacant and the ruling party, not sure of its popularity, had avoided holding by-elections. In the ensuing general elections the ruling Muslim League got only nine seats out of the total Muslim seats of 237 in a House of 309 members. It was spared the humiliation of not even being given the status of a separate party in the House by an independent member joining it to make up the minimum membership of ten. The Chief Minister, Nurul Amin, was defeated by a wide margin, by an unknown student. The Muslim League had got just twenty-seven per cent of the votes cast.

The Muslim League government in the Centre, instead of accepting the United Front which had secured sixty-four per cent of the votes and 223 Muslim plus some minority seats, and instead of opening communication channels with the new Bengali leadership, tried to circumvent the election results by undemocratic methods both in the province and at the Centre. The new provincial government reluctantly allowed to be formed was dismissed after a short duration under emergency provisions of the Constitution. Later, various destabilization measures were adopted to divide the United Front, driving the militant nationalist forces to unite under the banner of the Awami League.

At the Centre, in 1954, the total number of seats of the Constituent Assembly was seventy-nine. The Assembly was brought into being by the 3 June Plan and the Indian Independence Act. Its main task was to frame the Constitution, but it also acted as a legislative body under the Government of India Act 1935. No life span was prescribed for the Assembly. During more than seven years, from August 1947 to October 1954, as a constitution-making body it held fifteen sessions of only 116 days, with an average sessional attendance of 37 to 56 members. The members included central ministers, provincial governors, chief ministers, provincial ministers, and even ambassadors serving abroad, and other holders of offices of profit. Early in 1947, the Assembly had amended the Government of India Act 1935 to delete the provisions relating to the disqualification of the members holding offices of profit. Whenever a casual vacancy occurred, usually because of natural causes, the provincial assembly would elect one of its member to it. By 1953 it had become a rotten body. The independent Press, *Nawa-i-Waqt* and *The Pakistan Times* among others, was calling for its dissolution in the latter half of 1953. Suhrawardy and other opposition leaders had been making similar demands more vigorously even earlier. The popular dissatisfaction with its performance and competence spurred the Constituent Assembly to speed up constitution-making. As against the average of one to eight days that it devoted to this task in the first fourteen sessions of its life, it laboured for twenty-eight days in the fifteenth session before adjourning at the end of 1953. Prime Minister Muhammad Ali Bogra refused to reorganize the Assembly by inviting the new representatives from East Pakistan. Instead, he accelerated its efforts to present the nation with a *fait accompli*. Meeting for thirty-one days in the sixteenth session in 1954, by the time it was dissolved by Ghulam Muhammad in the last week of October, the Constituent Assembly had practically finalized the draft Constitution in spite of widespread protests in public forums about its validity.

The dismissal of the Constituent Assembly was widely welcomed, particularly in East Pakistan. The Federal Court did not restore the unrepresentative and self-perpetuating Constituent Assembly. Whatever the purists may say, the only constitutional way to create a representative and democratic body to frame a Constitution, acceptable to all parties and regions, appeared to be the dismissal of this body by the civilian head of state. This Ghulam Muhammad did, though for his own reasons. Its replacement by a representative institution was made possible by the Federal Court which denied constitution-making powers to the Governor-General, who tried to assume them through the Emergency Powers Ordinance, and compelled him to set up an elected body for the purpose.

The second Constituent Assembly represented the new Bengali realities; out of forty Bengali seats in it, the Muslim League got only one. The Assembly met in July 1955 and finalized the Constitution in January 1956 with the explicit and implied agreement of all the popular parties of East Pakistan. For the first time, there was a genuine feeling of participation in national affairs among all classes of Bengalis. Much of the credit for this consensus document goes to Suhrawardy who made the Awami League accept it in spite of the strong reservations of its dominant radical elements. If the old Assembly had been restored, there would have been bloodshed in East Pakistan.

The second decade of independence, 1958–1969, saw the beginning of the end of united Pakistan. The abrogation of the 1956 Constitution destroyed the inter-Wing consensus on the constitutional framework of the Federation. To the Bengalis, it was a betrayal by West Pakistanis of the compromise which, though unsatisfactory from their point of view, they had accepted under pressure from Suhrawardy, for the sake of unity. Ayub sought support for his regime from the conservative political elements of Bengal which no longer had any power base. This led to a reaction among the popular parties. Their relatively modest autonomy demands of the 1950s were superseded by the underlying radical tendencies. They now came to the fore in the succinct form of the Six Points, which envisaged a confederation of the two Wings.

The third period of the union, presided over by General Yahya, spans the two years from March 1969 to March 1971. At this time it had become urgently necessary to negotiate structural changes in the East–West relationship to maintain the unity of the country. Yahya had neither the patience, nor the vision, nor the mandate for such a complex task. During the decade of Ayub's dictatorial regime, dissent was suppressed and all kinds of hurdles were placed in the path of political interaction between the two Wings. The controlled media and the West Pakistan leadership kept public opinion ignorant of the rise of defiant and militant Bengali nationalism. The conventional view among the West Pakistan intelligentsia about inter-Wing issues in 1970 was no different from what it had been in the early 1950s: they were all creations of Hindus, Indian agents, and communists who were misleading the emotional Bengalis. The best that could be hoped for in 1970 was a negotiated compromise for a loose federal arrangement, essentially in the spirit of the Six Points. But Yahya rushed headlong into dismantling unilaterally the few agreed points of the 1956 Constitution which had survived its abrogation, like parity of representation and One Unit, and then thoughtlessly proceeded to promulgate the Legal Framework Order. West Pakistan, however, was not prepared to accept anything near the Six Points. Neither Bhutto nor Yahya was in a position to concede confederation as was demanded by the Awami League in March 1971. If they had accepted it, Bhutto would have been demolished by the rightist and religious parties, and the intelligentsia in general, and Yahya would have been deposed by the army junta.

Part II of the book deals with the rapid process of the dissolution of the Federation in the last nine months of its life, following the 25 March army action. The titles of its eight chapters suggest the nature of the disastrous consequences of the use of force to resolve an intractable political problem. The army action would have made some sense if it had had a political objective. But it was allowed to drift into a mindless operation for the final solution of Bengali Muslim nationalism. It is not clear whether Yahya, or his generals fully comprehended the nature of the crisis that the country was plunged into by their policies. There is no evidence that they did. The generals determined the conduct of the army operation in East Pakistan, and influenced the direction of the regime's political stances, but the consequences of these policies were left to the

President to deal with. Yahya himself was inclined to the use of force in case of difficulties, and he seemed to be quite clear, as he admitted when everything around him was crashing, that he had to show to the people of West Pakistan that he fought to the last to keep the country together. He showed some willingness, under American pressure, to hold negotiations with the Awami Leaguers in India, and when India had left no doubt of its aggressive intentions. But he could not bring himself to reverse the bloody process set in motion on 25 March 1971 and resume contacts with Mujib who, it is just possible, might have been more receptive in the immediate post-operation period. Anthony Mascarenhas in *Bangladesh: A Legacy of Blood* (cited in chapter 5) has quoted Mujib (p. 5) telling him in London on 8 January 1972, on his way to Bangladesh from Pakistan, that he was 'going to keep some link with Pakistan'. It was, of course, out of the question in the circumstances of the times. Mujib was quite in the dark about the happenings in East Pakistan during the nine months he was in jail. But it does show that he had some sort of linkage in mind even after the army action, though of the kind that would not have been acceptable to West Pakistan before the fall of Dhaka.

Yahya was overwhelmed by the consequences of his own policies, and became a hostage to his own tough rhetoric. Living in a hazy make-believe world, he seemed to have convinced himself that the army could not fail to control the situation, and, in the last resort, the Americans would somehow bail him out. The generals did not disagree with him on the first point, and Nixon and Kissinger never made clear to him the strict limits of their personal support.

Finally, the study leads to the conclusion that, given the degree of alienation by the late 1960s, it was in the interest of peace and prosperity of the people of both the Wings to go their separate ways, either under a confederation, or as independent sovereign states. Invoking Islam was neither necessary nor sufficient to sustain the unity of Pakistan. The issues were secular and not religious, and they had to be resolved in the spirit of tolerance, justice, fairplay, and mutual accommodation by the political leadership. Above all, a federal state requires equal and genuine participation of all the regions in the conduct of national affairs. These conditions are necessary at any time to run the state, but they were required in a still higher degree in united Pakistan with its two parts so far apart and so diverse. There is no evidence that they would have been forthcoming in the future, any more than they were visible in twenty-five years of union.

A few words about the sources of material on which the study is based. Chapters 3 to 11 are based almost entirely on unpublished oral or documentary sources. In Dhaka, in May 1971, I was appointed Member Provincial Planning Board, a post created specially for the co-ordination of economic and other matters, arising from the crisis, with other agencies within East Pakistan, and with the central government and foreign agencies and governments. I was, in this position, both a participant in and an observer of the inner workings of the crisis management. Apart from the plethora of papers that came my way, I maintained a diary, copious notes, and memoranda about the events and the developing situation, personally experienced or learnt from conversations with army and civil officers of all ranks in Dhaka. In the twilight period of vanishing authority, immediately before and after the surrender, the offices in the Governor House and in the cantonment were no longer sanctums. Gone were the smartly-uniformed messengers and *jawans* guarding their doors. The Eastern Command complex of offices was occupied by the Indian army, and its underground operations room presented the sad spectacle of defeat. Newspapers, file covers, and burnt, half-burnt, and undamaged papers were littered in various premises. In the general confusion following the disappearance of authority, I remained on the look-out for papers and was rewarded for my pains as the chapters relating to the period would show. The material collected during my stay in Dhaka in 1971 was supplemented and illuminated, over the subsequent years, by more documents and interviews and conversations with those who held key positions during that period. In April 1971 a special cell, headed by Muzaffar Hussain, was created in the central government as a focal point to deal expeditiously with matters relating to the East Pakistan crisis. I am grateful to Muzaffar Hussain for giving me access to his papers. Most of this material I had brought over to West Pakistan over a period of six months. Some I had deposited with a colleague in Dhaka in the last days before its fall, which he later sent to me. Some, obtained after the surrender, including the daily diary of the POW camp in India, were smuggled through the prison guards.

Chapter 1 is based on published documents. A large portion of Chapter 2 is based on unlisted, unpublished, and forgotten official reports and papers which were identified during the blind search for relevant material in dusty, dingy, and unlikely places. In addition, material for this chapter was obtained from interviews with relevant personalities, and the notes kept by me of conversations about significant events in the country's history, and my own experiences and impressions of them.

As far as possible I have quoted sources for what has been stated in the text. But in some cases information and papers were provided on condition of confidentiality. In others, the events and their background have been reconstructed from such varied sources over a long period that they cannot be attributed to any one in particular. But all such material has been checked from more than one source.

I am most grateful to Professor W. H. Morris-Jones of the Institute of Commonwealth Studies, University of London, who read early drafts of some of the chapters of Part II. His comments gave me new insights and great encouragement to persist with the project. He was always very generous with his time, in correspondence and meetings during my visits to London over the years. He, of course, is in no way responsible for the content or the style of the book.

I am also thankful to Professor Gustav F. Papanek, whose seminar courses I had attended during my post-graduate studies at Harvard University, and who is now Director, Asian Program in the Institute for Economic Development, Boston University, for his comments on some of the draft chapters and encouragement to complete the book. Thanks are also due to Dr Nawab Haider Naqvi, Director, Pakistan Institute of Development Economics, who read some draft chapters and gave his comments. Needless to say, neither of them bears any responsibility for what I have said in the book or the way I have said it.

I am grateful to Professor Zawar Hussain Zaidi of the School of Oriental and African Studies, London, now Editor-in-Chief Quaid-i-Azam Papers, for supplying a number of documents relevant to my study which has enriched the presentation.

I am grateful to Dr Abdus Sattar, Director-General, Pakistan Computer Bureau for lending me a word processor and arranging instruction by one of his staff, Mr Mahbub, in its use. It opened up a new world of writing to me and greatly lightened the laborious task.

I thank Major-General Nazir Husain, Surveyor-General of Pakistan for getting the East Pakistan maps prepared by Mr Ahmed Yar in his organization.

I am grateful to Ms Ameena Saiyid, Managing Director, Oxford University Press, Pakistan, for making this publication not only possible but a very agreeable venture to me. A dynamic professional, she has been, throughout the preparatory period of publication, most accommodating in meeting my requests about the various aspects of the production of the book. I am also thankful to Ms Sabiah Askari, Senior Editor, Oxford University Press, Pakistan.

The inquiries from numerous friends and colleagues about how the book was progressing and when it was coming out always gave me pleasure and boosted my morale. I hope it does not disappoint them.

Lastly, I must gratefully mention the patience (and perhaps occasional impatience) of my family—my wife, Shahnaz, and my children, Guriya, and Farrukh and Abbas—when I was at the writing-table on weekends, holidays, and in my spare time, for as long as they now remember. Shahnaz, on whom the burden of my preoccupation mainly fell, I knew was proud of what I was doing, though, like a good wife, lest it go to my head, she never said so to me or in my presence. She ensured that I had peace and quiet, and a separate study. Farrukh and his wife Nausheen, both computer buffs, developed a compatible program for the index, after a series of complicated conversions from the original OUP disks. But for their persistence and ingenuity, the book would have taken even longer to finish. Others supported me in various ways; Salim and Mehdi helped me with secretarial services from time to time over the seemingly unending period. At times they all must have wondered whether the work would ever be completed. Guriya's children, Mahvish, Zain, and Maheen grew up with this book. As they always saw me busy writing it, they thought this was what all grandfathers were supposed to be doing all the time. It was a delight to see their excitement when I told them that the book was finished, and that very soon they would be able to show it to their friends on sale at the corner bookshop.

Islamabad
October 1993

Hasan Zaheer

Prologue

16 December 1971. Hotel Inter-Continental, Dhaka.

The rising sun cleared the pre-dawn mists. It was a sparkling sunny morning of clear blue skies, typical of the mild winter season in Bengal. For the first time in a fortnight, it was quiet and seemed a normal working day. Yesterday, the Indian Army Commander had ordered a cease-fire for twenty-four hours to allow Lieutenant-General Niazi to accept the surrender terms by 9.00 a.m. today. This ultimatum had been extended by a few hours at the request of the Pakistani Commander.

I had an early breakfast in the coffeeshop on the ground floor. It was crowded with representatives of the International Committee of the Red Cross (ICRC) and foreign voluntary organizations, UN officials, and foreign correspondents. They all seemed very happy and relieved over the impending surrender, and the emergence of Bangladesh. The erstwhile Governor of East Pakistan, his ministers, and twenty-five West Pakistani civil officials had also come to the hotel two days earlier, after they had found themselves abandoned in the city. The hotel was accepted as a neutral zone by the belligerents including the *mukti bahini*. In the last few days, organized government had ceased to exist. Dhaka had become a ghost city controlled by unidentified roaming marauders.

The West Pakistanis were an odd lot in the jovial atmosphere. The foreigners, the Bengali waiters, and the chef at the snacks counter were all congratulating each other on the liberation of Bangladesh. It was not a very congenial morning for enjoying the pleasure of lingering over the breakfast table in the well-appointed, cosy coffeeshop, filled with the aroma of fried eggs, sausages, toast, tea, and coffee.

I returned to my room on the eleventh floor and looked out of the window at the panoramic view of the city, lost in the memory of the years I had served in this land. On the shimmering hazy horizon, the skyline was punctuated by the spiralling smoke of smouldering buildings or, perhaps, military dumps. The roads were deserted and vehicular traffic was absent. The silence was eerie in the bright daylight after a fortnight's continuous screeching of low-level aerial bombardment, boom of artillery, and the chattering of automatic weapons.

My room at the back of the hotel looked down on the adjacent building of Radio Pakistan. At about 9.30 a.m., seemingly from nowhere, a small group of teenagers started converging on the building, shouting anti-Pakistan slogans. Failing to force open the gates, they climbed over the compound wall and ran inside towards the Pakistan flag flying on the roof. The West Pakistani police guard came out from their quarters which were in a small barrack behind the main building, pulling up their trousers, buttoning their tunics, and uncertainly aiming their rifles in the general direction of the running boys. The policemen were in a panic; they were alternately trying to stop the crowd from entering the premises and taking cover against possible assault. The mob, however, did not try to harm them. Their immediate target was the Pakistan flag. Two boys climbed on to the roof, hauled down the flag, and raised a small Bangladesh flag, which one of them pulled out from inside his vest. At this, a loud cheer went up and the crowd, which by now had swelled and gathered outside the compound on the road, also raised full-throated slogans.

At about 10 a.m. the representatives of the ICRC called a meeting in the dining-room of the Bengali and West Pakistani residents of the hotel. We were informed that the ICRC and the UN agencies had been helping the Indian and Pakistani Commanders to communicate with each other and that the surrender was imminent. The ICRC representative explained the salient features of the various Geneva Conventions whereby the West Pakistanis would enjoy the protection of the occupying power, that is India, as civilian internees, but the Bengalis would not be eligible for such immunity from the new government of Bangladesh. At this, some Bengali ministers broke down, while others protested. These ministers had been branded as collaborators and renegades by the *mukti bahini* and warned of dire consequences to their persons, relatives, and property. Some of them left the hotel during the night to seek safety elsewhere.

By noon, the deserted roads had come alive with cheering crowds. Inter-Continental was the centre of attraction for the idle spectators as well as the heavily-armed *mukti bahini*. Some of the *bahini* personnel wanted to enter the hotel with their weapons, but they were prevented from doing so by the ICRC officials.

At about 1 p.m., while we were having lunch, there was some commotion outside in the lobby. Foreign journalists hurriedly left their lunch, excited whispers passed around the tables, and the news spread that the Indian army had entered Dhaka and an Indian colonel was meeting the ICRC officials in the dining-room. We quickly finished our meal and went to the lobby where the *mukti bahini* and Indian army personnel were sitting. In the gallery leading to the parking area, past the shopping arcade, the hotel residents were peering over each others' shoulders at the side entrance. There was a jungle of TV and still cameras there, all poised to capture the historic moment of the arrival of the Indian army. The West Pakistanis were advised to remain in their rooms.

Our eleventh floor provided a wide-angle view of the happenings down below. Since we had rooms on both sides of the corridor, we had the advantage of overlooking all sides. At about 2 p.m. the Indian army personnel carriers and tanks were seen coming from the direction of Tangi. They stopped at the crossing of Mymensingh and Minto Roads; two tanks, one at each pillar, were parked at the hotel gate. The soldiers got down and, in a rather leisurely manner, took up positions alongside the entrance and boundary wall. They were mostly Sikhs. The crew of the tanks and some other personnel walked into the compound of the bungalow at the opposite corner on Minto Road. The Indians were welcomed by the inmates of the house and the women garlanded them. Trays of sweetmeats and food were brought out by young girls and distributed to the soldiers.

At the back, a group of Bihari *razakars* was seen marching past on Mymensingh Road towards Mohammadpur, shouting *Pakistan Zindabad*. The armed mob seemed to be stunned at this brashness and, miraculously, they went past unmolested.

A little later, a Pakistan army truck full of *jawans*, while passing through the same route on the way to the cantonment, was stopped by an armed band. The *jawans* left the carrier and took up positions on the footpath behind the trees and whatever other cover they could find. The truck was burnt by the shouting mob. At this, the *jawans* broke cover and, in twos and threes, fanned out in different directions. One group of four or five was guided to Minto Road by some good-natured spectators. Suddenly, there were bursts of machinegun fire from an unknown direction. The Indian soldiers who were enjoying the hospitality of the bungalow, and others who were outside on the road proudly accepting the goodwill gestures of the public, took up positions. They returned the fire in the direction from which it had come. Later, we learned that an Indian captain had been killed in the brief exchange.

Meanwhile, the Pakistani soldiers on Minto Road were encircled by the *mukti bahini.* The civilian spectators among the crowd were not unfriendly but they were enjoying the discomfiture of the *jawans.* Sobhani, who was on the front lawn of the hotel loaded with his cameras, went to the boundary wall and shouted to the *jawans* to come back to Mymensingh Road and then go to the cantonment. Indian soldiers also came forward now from their positions and escorted them back to the main road. A massacre was narrowly avoided.

In the lengthening shadows of the winter afternoon, all roads in Dhaka were leading to the Ramna Maidan and the Hotel Inter-Continental. Teenagers lugging automatic weapons heavier and larger than themselves, women in bright saris, old and young men with children on their shoulders, rickshaws, cycles, scooters, and cars with horns blaring were all milling around the hotel. Trucks unloaded armed *muktis,* who spread out in the crowd. Some went for the cars parked on Minto Road, and smashed open their doors. In no time, all the vehicles had mysteriously disappeared. The crowd was tumultuous but somewhat restrained, only occasionally raising slogans against Pakistan, directed at the West Pakistani residents.

In Ramna Maidan, near the Race Course pavilion, the surrender ceremony was taking place in the gathering darkness. We could only see the distant silhouettes of people against the gaslights.

An air of total abandon and liberation pervaded the city as far as the eye could see. It was homecoming for the freedom-fighters and release from nine months of fear, tension, and confinement for the ordinary citizen. The surging humanity revelling in the achievement of its separate destiny had spoken: it was a verdict against the twenty-four year history of repression, obscurantism, and disregard of the people's will, and on the futility of the use of force in resolving national issues.

An unhappy chapter in the history of the Muslims of South Asia had ended. A new one had begun, redeeming the covenant entered into by the Muslims of the subcontinent at the Lahore Session of the All-India Muslim League on 24 March 1940, and reiterated in 1941 at the Madras Session, to create separate 'Muslim Free National Homelands'. On this day the second Muslim Homeland had emerged: a new nation was born.

PART I

Muslim Bengal and Pakistan

CHAPTER 1

The Search for Identity

1936–1947

The emergence of Bangladesh on 16 December 1971 was the culmination of the struggle of Bengali Muslim nationalism, launched in the mid-thirties, to establish a separate identity of its own; not only distinct from the Hindu majority of the province but also from their co-religionists of the other regions of India. It was submerged in the whirlwind of the Pakistan movement of the Muslims of the subcontinent for some time. But a hardcore nationalist element which had emerged as an organized entity in the early 1940s, and had gained strength during the general elections of 1946, was determined to secure the rights and identity of Muslim Bengal.

In Bengal, the two main Muslim parties in 1936, preparing for provincial elections under the Government of India Act 1935, were the United Muslim Party led by Nawab Habibullah of Dhaka and the Krishak Proja Samity led by A. K. M. Fazlul Huq. The former was a recent creation representing the landed, commercial, and urban bourgeois interests. Apart from Khawaja Nazimuddin and his brother Khawaja Shahabuddin who belonged to the founding Nawab family, Huseyn Shaheed Suhrawardy was the moving spirit behind the Muslim Party. The Samity was non-communal and represented peasant interests.[1] Fazlul Huq wielded considerable influence in rural Bengal but was not averse to taking advantage of opportunities as they came along, communal or secular.

The tussle between the Nawab of Dhaka and Fazlul Huq for domination of provincial politics threatened to divide the Muslims in the coming elections. In August 1936, a conference of Muslim factions of all shades of opinion had failed to resolve the differences. M. A. H. Ispahani invited Mohammad Ali Jinnah to visit Bengal to revitalize the All-India Muslim League and bring the various Muslim parties under it. After a great deal of persuasion and bargaining, the League Parliamentary Board was set up to select candidates for the elections. This Board consisted of forty-eight members, representing all the Muslim parties, plus four nominees of Jinnah. Fazlul Huq, however, refused to merge the identity of his Proja Samity with the Board and objected to the nomination of four non-Bengali businessmen by Jinnah.[2] He said that 'he would not tolerate the non-Bengali trading community of Calcutta to control the destiny of Bengal Muslims.'[3] In September, a few months before the elections, Jinnah removed Fazlul Huq from the Parliamentary Board.

The League emerged as the second largest party after the Congress in the Bengal Legislative Assembly. Its success was due to the rising consciousness of the Muslim middle classes about their identity and rights against the domination of the Hindus. Fazlul Huq had defeated Nazimuddin but had to seek the co-operation of the League to form a coalition ministry. Seeing the upsurge of the masses towards the League, he joined it soon after, and became the President of the provincial Muslim League with Suhrawady as Secretary.[4] The Samity was forgotten for the time being, and Fazlul Huq became one of the All-India Muslim League leaders.

The Muslim League had rejected the federation scheme of the Government of India Act of 1935 in its twenty-fourth session at Bombay in April 1936, but had decided that 'the Provincial Scheme of the Constitution be utilized for what it is worth.'[5] The working of provincial autonomy was, however, found unsatisfactory by the Muslims of the minority provinces. The Patna Session of the Muslim League, held in December 1938, accordingly authorized its President to formulate suitable proposals, as alternatives to the Government of India Act of 1935, with a view to safeguarding the interests of the Muslims of India.[6]

In March 1939, the Muslim League Working Committee appointed a committee, under the presidentship of Jinnah, 'to examine various schemes propounded by those who are fully versed in the constitutional developments of India and other countries, and those that may be submitted thereafter to the President, and report to the Working Committee.'[7] The Committee had nine members including Nazimuddin from Bengal.

In 1938–9, a number of schemes, envisaging a partition of India or regrouping of the provinces into zones of Hindu and Muslim majorities under a loose federation, were put forward by Muslim academics and political leaders of the Muslim minority provinces, the Punjab and Sindh. Among the schemes for the division of India, the one proposed by two professors from Aligarh University—Dr Syed Zafarul Hasan and Dr Afzal Qadri—gained wide publicity and seemed to have greatly influenced the final draft of the Lahore Resolution. According to this scheme, British India was to be divided into three independent, sovereign states–the predominantly Muslim states of north-west India and Bengal, and a Hindu state comprising the rest of India. At about the same time, in 1939, Nawab Sir Muhammad Shah Nawaz Khan of Mamdot, President of the Punjab Provincial League proposed the division of India into five countries, each embracing contiguous Muslim and Hindu majority areas, but linked in a confederation. Sir Sikandar Hayat Khan of the Punjab and Sir Abdullah Haroon of Sindh, who were members of the League committee which was considering the various constitutional proposals, produced their own schemes. Sir Sikandar's scheme envisaged an All-India federation of regional federations of seven zones, demarcated on the basis of contiguous Hindu and Muslim areas. Sir Abdullah Haroon proposed a division of India into two separate federations, having a majority of Hindus and Muslims respectively; the Muslim federation was to comprise the north-western part of India and Kashmir only.[8]

By early 1940, the League Committee had completed its examination of the various proposals and the Working Committee in its meeting on 4 February decided to propose a separate homeland for Muslims in the forthcoming session of the All-India Muslim League in March.[9]

The twenty-seventh session of the All-India Muslim League commenced on 22 March 1940 at Lahore. Fazlul Huq led the Bengal League delegation which included Suhrawardy. On the same date, the Working Committee, in which Bengal was represented by Nazimuddin and Abdurrahman Siddiqui, met and prepared a draft resolution 'regarding the future Constitution of India' for submission to the Subjects Committee. In the Subjects Committee, which was formed to draft resolutions to be placed before the open sessions, Suhrawardy, who had reached Lahore earlier than Fazlul Huq, acted as the spokesman of the Bengali Muslims. He opposed any idea of an All-India federation and subscribed to the idea of a separate homeland but argued that 'each of the provinces in the Muslim majority areas should be accepted as a sovereign state and each province should be given the right to choose its future Constitution or enter into a commonwealth with a neighbouring province or provinces.'[10]

On 23 March, the famous Lahore Resolution was moved in the open session by Fazlul Huq as leader of the biggest Muslim majority province.[11] It envisaged demarcation of geographically contiguous units into regions 'which should be so constituted, with such territorial adjustments as may be necessary, that the areas in which the Muslims are numerically in a majority, as in the North-western and Eastern Zones of India, should be grouped to constitute Independent States in which the constituent units shall be autonomous and sovereign'. The Resolution authorized the Working Committee 'to frame a scheme of constitution in accordance with these basic principles, providing for the assumption finally, by the respective regions, of all powers, such as defence, external affairs, communications, customs, and such other matters as may be necessary.'[12]

The interpretation of the Lahore Resolution has remained a subject of controversy ever since its adoption, because of its internal contradictions and subsequent application in terms of a single Muslim state. On a plain reading of the text, the Resolution does not convey the concept of a single Muslim state. In the third paragraph, the Resolution speaks of 'Independent States' of the group of areas in which the Muslims are numerically in a majority and in which the constituent units shall be autonomous and sovereign. The term 'constituent unit' seems to imply a federation, but the units in the federation are not sovereign. The fifth paragraph again refers to the assumption by the respective regions (not one region) of all sovereign powers. In the annual session at Madras in 1941 the Muslim League Constitution was amended by incorporating a slightly modified version of the Lahore Resolution. Instead of just 'grouped' of para 3 of the Resolution, the word 'together' was added after it. The aim and object of the Muslim League thus became:

> The establishment of completely Independent States formed by demarcating geographically contiguous units into regions which shall be so constituted, with such territorial adjustments as may be necessary, that the areas in which the Mussalmans are numerically in a majority, as in the North-Western and Eastern zones of India, shall be grouped together to constitute Independent States as Muslim Free National Homelands in which the constituent units shall be autonomous and sovereign;. . .[13]

This amended version in the Muslim League Constitution emphasized, if anything, the establishment of more than one Independent State. The Independent States, in plural, were mentioned twice, further strengthened by the plural 'Free National Homelands'. The addition of 'together' to the 'grouped' governed the clause of Muslim majority areas of the zones and merely emphasized the federative nature of the Independent States encompassing each zone. Alternatively, if, through hindsight, it is interpreted that the idea was to group together the Independent States then, by virtue of the constituent units being sovereign and autonomous, the linkage could only be confederal and not federative.

The idea of a single Federal Muslim State, comprising the north-western and eastern zones came to acquire legitimacy only through popular perception of the Lahore Resolution. It was not borne out either by the text of the Resolution or the thinking of the founding fathers, as reflected in their speeches and the political literature of the period preceding or immediately following the passage of the Resolution. No objection was raised, from any quarter, to the idea of more than one Muslim Homeland. Perhaps the League leaders themselves were not very clear, in 1940, about the shape of the Muslim Homeland they were demanding. There were differences of opinion abut the concept of the Homeland—should it be separate from India or linked with a loose All-India federation? To ask for the division of the subcontinent at the time, was plunging into the dark and it was only through further evolution of thought and in the light of political developments that the precise definition of 'homeland' emerged in 1946 and even then it was objected to by a vocal minority of the Eastern zone, as we shall see later.

In a remarkable consensus, the Muslims of Bengal of all shades—leftists, urban bourgeoisie, landlords, peasants, and radical students—joined together under the banner of the Muslim League to achieve the goal of a Muslim Homeland. There was, however, a basic difference in the approach of the Muslims of Bengal and the Muslims of the minority provinces and the Punjab towards the nature of the Homeland. To the Muslim intellectuals of northern India, influenced by the Aligarh school of thought, the demand for Pakistan was the culmination of the Muslim renaissance movement initiated by Sir Syed Ahmed Khan in the latter half of the nineteenth century. In their thought-processes, it was to safeguard the religious, cultural, and political rights of the Muslims of the entire subcontinent. They assumed a cultural and linguistic unity of Muslims which was not there. For the Muslims of Bengal, economic emancipation from Hindu domination was the immediate and tangible consideration in the pursuit of a separate Homeland. To them, Pakistan meant achieving state power to redress the injustices inflicted by Hindu dominance since the advent of the British, more than one and a half centuries earlier. As regards the Bengali language and culture, the Muslims had no problems with Hindus. They could share them and did not have to go to northern India for their cultural inspiration.[14]

* * *

In September 1941, Fazlul Huq was forced to resign from the League, on the question of membership of the National Defence Council, set up by the Viceroy. In a defiant letter of resignation, he attributed his ouster to the machinations of the Muslim leaders of the minority provinces and vowed; 'I will never allow the interest of the thirty-three million Muslims of Bengal to be put under the domination of any outside authority, however eminent it may be.'[15]

Towards the end of 1943, Abul Hashim succeeded Suhrawardy in the key organizational post of Secretary of the Provincial Muslim League. Abul Hashim was a secular Bengali nationalist, who enjoyed the support of students and was greatly influenced by communist ideology and organizational techniques. He announced his determination to free the Muslim middle classes from the domination of 'reactionary elements' like the Nawab family, Maulana Akram Khan, and the Ispahanis (all Muslim Leaguers).[16]

In 1943 Nazimuddin became the Chief Minister of Bengal, but due to the tussle between the Provincial League, which was controlled by Suhrawardy and Abul Hashim, and the Parliamentary Party, he was defeated in the Assembly in March 1945. At about the same time, the Provincial Parliamentary Board was set up to select League candidates for the forthcoming Central and Provincial Assemblies elections. The Suhrawardy group won a majority on the Board, in spite of the fact that the composition of membership, prescribed by the central League leadership, favoured the conservative group of Nazimuddin.[17] This was a crucial victory for the radical nationalist elements.

In the general elections held in November 1945 for the Central Assembly, and in March 1946 for the Bengal Assembly, the Muslim League bagged all the Muslim seats in the former and 439 out of 494 Muslim seats in the latter.[18] Such was the authority and appeal of Jinnah and the Muslim League that seven non-Bengalis, including three non-residents, were elected to the Central Assembly from Bengal.[19]

Suhrawardy became the Chief Minister of Bengal in April 1946. But he was distrusted by the Central League leadership and in spite of being the chief executive of the biggest Muslim majority province, he was not included in the Working Committee of the All-India Muslim League. During the critical period, 1945-7, Bengal was represented in this highest policy-making body of the League by Maulana Akram Khan, Nazimuddin, or Ispahani.[20] None of them represented the new realities of Bengal politics.

In April 1946, the Muslim League called a Convention of all the newly-elected League legislators in Delhi. Bengal was represented in the Convention, among others, by Suhrawardy and Abul Hashim. Assam was represented by Maulana Abdul Hamid Bhashani.[21]

The Subjects Committee of the Convention met on 8 April, and discussed the draft resolution which defined the north-eastern and north-western zones, and laid down that the two zones would form part of an independent and sovereign state of Pakistan. Abul Hashim objected to the proposed draft on the ground that it amounted to an amendment of the Lahore Resolution of 1940. He argued for a separate independent state in the north-eastern zone, as a state with two distant zones, separated by a hostile country, could not be a viable proposition; its defence would be impossible and two such zones could never be integrated into a whole.[22]

Abul Hashim was ruled out of order, and on 9 April the

Convention unanimously passed the Pakistan Resolution. He was, however, articulating the strong feelings of a hardcore militant constituency of Muslim Bengal which commanded electoral and street power. Suhrawardy, who had moved the Resolution and made an emotional speech about Muslim solidarity, had to assuage the sentiments of the radical group. At the conclusion of the Convention, he observed that at that moment, the question was Pakistan and Hindustan and 'once this is conceded, it will be for the Pakistan State to define the status of its constituent units. The units should, as far as possible, be workable units and should conform to the conditions of linguistic and cultural affinities.'[23]

According to Kamruddin, Jinnah assured Abul Hashim that the Resolution was not meant to amend the Lahore Resolution, but only to have a separate Constituent Assembly from that of Hindustan in order to prepare one or two Constitutions on the basis of the Lahore Resolution. A few months later, Kamruddin further states, at the time of the next Council session in Bombay, Jinnah again assured the Bengal League members, who met him in a deputation, that the Lahore Resolution was not amended. 'The [Lahore] Resolution,' Jinnah said, 'would be before the Pakistan Constituent Assembly and as a sovereign Body it would be the final arbiter of the country's Constitution.'[24]

This seems to be the position, because the Muslim League Constitution which had incorporated the Lahore Resolution (with the plural 'States') as its aim and object in 1941, was not amended, following the Pakistan Resolution of 1946. The Muslim League membership forms continued to carry the same aim and object of 'Independent States in which the constituent units shall be autonomous and sovereign', even as late as March 1947.[25] Abul Hashim seemed to have had a point about the constitutional ambiguity of the Pakistan Resolution, though perhaps in the atmosphere of the times there would have been no problem in amending the League Constitution also in a session of the All-India Muslim League.

The last session of the Council of the All-India Muslim League in united India, was held in Delhi on 9–10 June 1947, to endorse the Mountbatten Plan for the partition of India.[26] Abul Hashim opposed the partition of Bengal, and called it a betrayal of the Lahore Resolution.

The Muslim leadership of Bengal had no clear conception of

what would constitute the Eastern State of Pakistan. In December 1944, R. G. Casey, the Bengal Governor, had reported to the Viceroy 'that the conception of "Eastern Pakistan" held by Nazimuddin (and so, I imagine, by the Muslim League in Bengal) is not the standard idea of a Muslim State. He paints the picture of a wholly autonomous sovereign state with a bare Muslim majority of population in which Muslims and Hindus would live in amity' Nazimuddin's belief that 'he may get the Hindus to agree to the idea of an independent Eastern Indian State', suggested to the Governor 'that his support for Pakistan is a bargaining counter.'[27]

As the partition of Bengal became a real possibility, within the context of the division of India in early 1947, the Bengal Muslim leaders were divided between what the Calcutta District Muslim League, in a memorandum to Jinnah, called the 'Divisionists' and the 'Unionists'. The former wanted division of Bengal, and were led by Akram Khan, Hamidul Haq Choudhury, and Nurul Amin. The Suhrawardy and Abul Hashim group wanted to keep a united, independent Bengal. Nazimuddin, typically, remained undecided and supported one group or the other at various times.[28]

In February 1947, Abul Hashim secretly discussed with Sarat Chandra Bose, a veteran Bengali Congress leader, plans for mobilizing a movement for Sovereign Bengal. These plans, which became public, led to a furore in the Hindu Press against the proposal. In April and May, Suhrawardy and Abul Hashim frantically tried to work out an agreement with the willing Congress leaders, and also publicly pleaded with the Hindu intelligentsia for a united Bengal. Trying to convince the Hindus of his *bona fides*, Suhrawardy said 'that he has visualized Bengal all along as a sovereign Independent state and not a part of any Union.'[29] He also stressed that 'the cry for the partition of Bengal is nothing but an attempt to get the rich prize of Calcutta and thus deprive the Muslims of trade and commerce.'[30] Abul Hashim said that the Lahore Resolution 'never contemplated the creation of any Akhund [united] Muslim State.'[31]

On 26 April, Suhrawardy met Mountbatten, the Viceroy, and told him 'that given enough time he [Suhrawardy] was confident that he could get Bengal to remain as a complete entity . . . [and] that he could get Mr Jinnah to agree that it need not join Pakistan if it was prepared to remain united.' Mountbatten said he was 'against splitting India up into many units'; he favoured keeping

Bengal 'as one economic unit' but was not very encouraging about its sovereign status, with its own army and as a member of the Commonwealth, which was what Suhrawardy was envisaging.[32] In the third week of May, an agreement was reached for a United Bengal between Suhrawardy, Abul Hashim, Fazlur Rahman, and Abdul Malek on the League side, and Bose and two other Congress leaders. The agreement was subject to the approval of the high commands of the two parties.[33] On 21 May, Suhrawardy sent the draft agreement to Liaquat Ali to obtain the approval of the Quaid-i-Azam before the announcement of the 3 June Plan.[34] He followed it up on the same day with a five-page letter to Liaquat Ali to 'once more impress upon the Quaid-i-Azam . . . the terrible disaster that will overwhelm Bengal, and particularly the Muslims of Bengal, if Bengal is partitioned.' He pointed out that 'the Lahore Resolution visualized Independent Sovereign States of those areas where the Muslims are in a majority.'[35] The conservative League leadership never forgave Suhrawardy for his efforts to keep Bengal united, for sound economic reasons, though the Quaid-i-Azam had reportedly given his blessings to it.[36] Gandhi, Nehru, Patel, and the Hindus, in general, were all opposed to the idea, and nothing came of it.

CHAPTER 2

Two Turbulent Decades: August 1947–March 1969

THE FIRST DECADE 1947–1958

Consequent upon the partition of Bengal, Nazimuddin was elected leader of the Parliamentary Party and took over as the Chief Minister[1] of East Pakistan.[2] In the contest for leadership, Nazimuddin was supported as against Suhrawardy by the Central League leadership which distrusted the latter because of his involvement with the independent Bengal movement, and his association with Gandhi to bring about communal harmony in India. Abul Hashim and his group remained neutral because of misunderstandings that had developed between them and the Suhrawardy Ministry.[3]

In order to understand the conflicts that developed later between the East and West Wings, it is necessary to analyse the regionalist forces operating in the Eastern province in the early years and the responses of the ruling class to their demands. The indigenous elements which made up regional politics consisted of the pro-Pakistan Bengali nationalists, Hindus, and communists. The student class was the main instrument through which this politics was articulated.

Even before Partition, Abul Hashim and his workers had shifted their activities to Dhaka, after Suhrawardy had refused to support Abul Hashim in the latter's bid for the presidentship of the Bengal Provincial League.[4] Soon after the achievement of Pakistan, the nationalist and leftist elements, which had earlier thought it expedient to join the Muslim League, resigned from it and started organizing themselves in separate groups. A group of League workers and intelligentsia met in Dhaka in July 1947 and formed the East Pakistan People's Freedom League, with a programme of economic emancipation, and also issued a manifesto. This was followed by a conference of the youths of East Pakistan and the setting up of the Democratic Youth League, which remained active in agitational politics in East Pakistan as a communist front organization until it was liquidated by the government.[5] The rightists were no less active; young Islamist professors and students of Dhaka University set up, on 1 September 1947, a militant cultural body called the *Tamaddun Majlis,* which played a leading role in the language agitation.[6]

There were various economic and psychological reasons why the Bengali Hindus felt insecure and found it difficult to adjust to the new reality of the Muslims of Bengal holding state power independently of them. Firstly, through various socio-economic measures, the East Pakistan government sought to change the hinterland status of the province and to remove the economic domination of the Hindus. The most important step in this direction was the East Bengal State Acquisition and Tenancy Act passed in 1950.[7] It abolished the landholding system introduced by the Permanent Settlement Regulation of 1793, and deprived the absentee Hindu landlords of their economic base in East Pakistan. The East Bengal Transfer of Agricultural Land Act, passed at the same time, restricted the sale of lands, which stopped the transfer of capital to West Bengal.[8] The East Bengal (Emergency) Requisition of Property Act empowered the government to requisition houses and buildings for official purposes. Most of the houses and buildings in urban areas belonged to the Hindus. The East Bengal Rent Control Act placed a ceiling on the rents that could be charged by the landlords who again were mostly Hindus. All these and other socially necessary measures, though not aimed as such, necessarily affected the affluent Hindu classes by depriving them of their capital assets, or curtailing the incomes from them. Secondly, the emphasis on the Islamic character of the new State gave the Hindus a feeling of alienation from mainstream politics. A prominent Hindu member of the Provincial Assembly felt 'that I have become impotent due to the pernicious theory of party politics based on religion.'[9] Thirdly, the Hindu middle class, as the dominant socio-economic group for a century and a half, had developed contempt towards the Muslims of Eastern Bengal and found it difficult to adjust psychologically to their rule.[10]

The urban population, the educated community, the landed interests, and the bureaucracy of Bengal were predominantly Hindu at the time of Independence. The Muslim-majority area of Eastern Bengal was merely a hinterland of Hindu-dominated West Bengal. In the early period following Partition the Hindu vested interests in East Pakistan and Calcutta believed that Partition would not be sustainable because of the immense difficulties that the province was facing, and, in any case, the borders would be soft to allow traditional economic ties to operate.[11] Accordingly, every move for the integration of the economy, politics, and administration of the new country, which necessarily meant distancing from the traditional Calcutta links, was interpreted and distorted by the Hindu leadership as depriving East Pakistan of its rights, and a diversion of its resources for the benefit of 'outsiders'. But, by and large, the Muslim middle classes had a love-hate feeling towards the corresponding Hindu classes; there was a deep cultural affinity between them. Having achieved state power to redress the economic and other imbalances, the Muslims had no difficulty in co-operating with the Hindu minority in the political, social, and cultural fields. In accepting the Hindus in the mainstream of community life, they were not being anti-Pakistan, or totally under the influence of the Hindus, as used to be alleged by the Pakistani establishment. They were good Muslims and patriotic Pakistanis, but their approach to public life was liberal and secular. There was no Islamic extremism in the East Wing to divide and detract the people from the real issues. Deep down all groups and parties, including a considerable section of the Muslim League, cherished a concept of Pakistan in which the East Wing enjoyed full economic, political, and cultural autonomy.

The communist influence in Eastern Bengal dated back to the peasant movement of the 1930s and 1940s, led by the Communist Party of India.[12] In 1947, the Communist Party of Pakistan was set up and a majority of Bengali communists opted for East Pakistan, although Muslim membership in the Party was only five per cent of the total.[13] According to intelligence reports, the activities of the Party in East Pakistan were organized and led by the old guard deputed from or located in Calcutta. The Party forged close links with, and infiltrated the opposition groups. It exploited local grievances and the difficult economic situation, by organizing strikes and uprisings in different parts of the province, and attempted to create general disaffection against the central and provincial governments. The communist activities reached their climax in the language riots in February 1952, after which the government took serious action against the Party. In July 1954 it was banned in East Pakistan, but it continued to exert influence through front organizations among students and workers, and through infiltration of regular political parties like the Awami League and the Ganatantri Dal.[14]

The interaction of the Muslim nationalists, the Hindus, and the communists was mainly through the medium of the student community. All the divergent political forces tried to secure the support of students in the pursuit of their objectives. As a class, the students were not anti-Pakistan, but by their negative attitude and under the influence of extra-academic elements, they frequently paralysed urban life and overwhelmed the democratic institutions. The successive governments in East Pakistan became hostage to the vagaries of student politics.

The West-dominated ruling class of early Pakistan never really tried to understand the Bengali point of view. From the inception of Pakistan, it developed a self-righteous state of mind which ignored the objective political realities of East Pakistan. The Pakistani establishment, which was a conglomerate of the Punjab political leadership, the old League leadership of NWFP, migrant League leaders of Muslim minority provinces in India, and the senior Punjabi and *Mohajir* civil servants, passionately believed (a) in a strong central government; (b) that Urdu, as the symbol of unity and Islamic ideology, should be the only state language of the country; (c) that the opposition groups in East Pakistan were generally subversive, influenced and instigated by the Hindus and communists; and (d) that the defence of East Pakistan depended on the strength of the armed forces in West Pakistan, for which resources should be allocated even at the cost of overall social and economic development. These narrow premises, and others in a similar vein, coupled with a sense of racial and cultural superiority in the West Pakistani elite, prevented the evolution of a dynamic and equal relationship between the two Wings. The dominant ruling class suffered from a siege mentality. Any demand of East Pakistan which deviated from the dogma was regarded as a conspiracy and a threat to Islamic ideology and the integrity of the country.

The role of Bengali leaders in the East Pakistan and central governments and the permanent services, in the early years of Pakistan, needs special mention. The ruling Bengali group belonged to the conservative faction of the Bengal Provincial League which, it will be recalled, had lost the Parlimentary Board elections to the radicals in 1945. The League ministers, both in the province and at the Centre, owed their position to the non-Bengali Prime Minister and not to their provincial party base.[15] They were in no position to take a firm and principled stand against the central government on issues agitating the minds of their compatriots.

The top and middle positions in the East Pakistan Secretariat were filled by officers of the old Indian Civil Service, who all belonged to other provinces. They served the province well during difficult circumstances, but the Chief Minister and the Ministers accepted their advice without bringing any political dimension to it. In the Central Secretariat at Karachi, there was no Bengali secretary out of a total of thirteen; only one joint secretary out of nineteen; and four deputy secretaries out of fifty-nine.[16] No thought was given to this serious gap which could have been filled by promoting able and experienced Bengal provincial service officers. The old civil service cadre rule, which reserved senior posts in the central and provincial governments for members of the Indian Civil Service, was adopted for the new Civil Service of Pakistan. It could have been relaxed in favour of Bengali provincial service officers, at least on a one-off basis to ensure regional balance.

The result of the weakness of the ruling Bengali leadership and the unassimilated higher echelon civil service was that the Muslim League government in East Pakistan never developed an identity, or the dynamics of a responsive government. It became merely a backwater extension of the central government, and failed to provide any check and balance to the thoughtless policies of the Centre in the formative years, which created lasting bitterness between the two Wings.

The dissensions among the Muslim League stalwarts in the provinces, which came to the fore immediately after Independence, led to the decline of the only national organization and the rise of regionalist opposition groups. The weakness of the League stemmed from its failure to transform itself from the opposition role of the spokesman of the Muslims of the subcontinent to that of a national party attending to the urgent task of welding diverse regional and communal interests into an integrated nation-state.[17] An example of this failure was provided in the last meeting of the All-India Muslim League Council, held at Karachi on 14 and 15 December 1947, in which Suhrawardy pleaded for opening League membership to all communities to bring them into mainstream national politics. Sardar Abdur Rab Nishtar thought that, by this proposal, 'our two friends [the other secularist was Mian Iftikharuddin, President, Punjab Muslim League] want to finish the League. I say if the League exists, Islam exists, Musalmans exist.' He was supported by Liaquat Ali Khan, and Suhrawardy was outvoted.[18] The East Wing had a Hindu minority which was twenty-five per cent of its population, and this kind of parochialism injected a rigidity into national politics which did not help the intergration of the two Wings.

In East Pakistan the emergence of an opposition was more rapid and organized. There was already dissatisfaction in an articulate section of the Provincial League at the election of Nazimuddin as Chief Minister. Suhrawardy, who exercised considerable influence over the burgeoning radical elements in the body-politic of East Pakistan, had stayed back in Calcutta after losing to Nazimuddin. But his supporters in the East Pakistan Assembly continued to oppose the government within the League forum. Suhrawardy kept up a lengthy correspondence with Liaquat Ali Khan, during the period April to July 1948, criticizing the Nazimuddin government for its handling of the communal situation, and for its placing restrictions on his activities in East Pakistan. In his letter to the Prime Minister, dated 11 June, Suhrawardy claimed that 'even when the majority of the members were against Nazimuddin, I refused even to set foot in Dacca, although I was begged to do so; and I only went there after the Quaid-i-Azam had fixed the Ministry firm in the saddle, and the party that was supporting me had accepted my advice to support the Nazimuddin Ministry and even to join it, if offered.'[19]

The protestations of Suhrawardy did not impress the Prime Minister. The government of East Pakistan did not allow him to address public meetings and externed him from the province in June 1948. Earlier, on 18 May, he was deprived of his membership of the Constituent Assembly.[20] Suhrawardy continued to seek the Prime Minister's intervention with the East Pakistan government.

On 13 July, referring to their meeting, Liaquat Ali Khan finally informed Suhrawardy that the action taken against him 'was a matter entirely for the Provincial Government and I could not interfere in their administration.'

In February 1948, the restructuring of the Pakistan Muslim League was undertaken. The exercise proved divisive and led to widespread splits in all the provinces. Chaudhry Khaliquzzaman, the Chief Organizer, had decided to strengthen the groups in power, irrespective of their democratic credentials and the grievances of the dissident elements. The party no longer had any commitment to pursue nor any national causes to espouse. Henceforth, it became a peripatetic king's party, with the sole objective of conferring legitimacy on dubious power groups.

In East Pakistan, the appointment of Maulana Akram Khan as the provincial organizer led Bhashani and his supporters to break away from the League. In a convention of political workers on 24 June 1949, attended by Bhashani, Fazlul Huq, and other League leaders, a new party called East Pakistan Awami Muslim League was formed, with Bhashani as President. So important was the support of students, even to the veteran political leaders, that Sheikh Mujibur Rahman, a student leader at that time in jail, was appointed Joint Secretary of the party. The manifesto of the party included mainly provincial issues like nationalization of the jute trade, Bengali as the state language, and the holding of general elections on the basis of adult franchise.[21]

Suhrawardy, whose supporters had joined the Awami Muslim League, tried to bring it within the framework of a national party. In March 1950, he called a convention of political workers, at which a new party called the All-Pakistan Awami Muslim League was formed, with himself as the President and Chief Organizer.[22] In December 1952, he called a convention of the three anti-Muslim League parties of NWFP, Punjab, and East Pakistan at Lahore. Except the East Pakistan Awami Muslim League, which had a solid political base, it was a motley gathering of adventurist and opportunist elements. The divergent political forces and culture of the two Wings became quite apparent in the efforts to build a progressive national party. The new party which emerged from the convention avoided the mention of the burning national issues which were agitating East Pakistan, to keep a semblance of an all-Pakistan character. For the time being, a sort of loose affiliation of the provincial parties was accepted under the umbrella of the new party, All Pakistan Jinnah Awami Muslim League, with the East Pakistan Awami Muslim League keeping its separate name, identity, and programme.[23]

Within a year, differences arose in the leadership on organizational and national issues. Mamdot and his Punjabi supporters objected to the nomination of East Pakistan Awami League members to the Working Committee of the Jinnah Awami Muslim League, as they did not accept the former as part of the parent body. They also took exception to the East Pakistani demands for complete autonomy, Bengali as the state language, and a single chamber legislature elected on population basis.[24] Bhashani warned that 'whatever may be our relationship with Mr Suhrawardy', he would not tolerate any interference by the Jinnah Awami Muslim League; the conditions in the two Wings were completely different and the concept of provincial autonomy should be applicable to party organization also.[25]

In West Pakistan there were dissensions, defections, and mutual expulsions of leaders from the Jinnah Awami Muslim League. By 1953, Suhrawardy's attempt to synthesize the politics of the two Wings through an indigenous national organization, reflecting post-Independence realities, had failed.

In East Pakistan, on the other hand, the Awami League had emerged as a well-organized and disciplined opposition party. In July 1953, in a largely-attended session, its Council approved the party's manifesto and unanimously elected Bhashani as President and Mujibur Rahman as General Secretary. At the top of the list in the manifesto was provincial autonomy, leaving only defence, foreign affairs, and currency to the Centre, and Bengali as the state language.[26]

* * *

Broadly speaking, during the first decade of Independence, there were three main areas of conflict in the East-West relationship. They were the status of Bengali, constitution-making, and economic centralism. The question of the status of Bengali was resolved by the mid-1950s, but, in the process, the controversy had left permanent scars on the national polity; no consensus could ever be reached on constitutional and economic issues, both of which boiled down to the single demand for complete provincial autonomy.

The Status of Bengali

The dynamic process of national integration, generated by the euphoria of a separate homeland was disrupted barely three months after Independence, by the language controversy. It started from the Pakistan Educational Conference called by the Bengali Minister of Education, Fazlur Rahman, at Karachi in November 1947, to reform the educational system on the lines of 'Islamic ideology'. The representatives of East Pakistan attending the Conference opposed Urdu as the only national language.

In February 1948, a Hindu member of the Constituent Assembly moved an amendment in the Assembly rules to allow Bengali to be used in the House along with Urdu. Liaquat Ali Khan opposed the motion on the ground that 'Pakistan has been created because of the demand of a hundred million Muslims in this subcontinent and the language of a hundred million Muslims is Urdu. . . . It is necessary for a nation to have one language and that language can only be Urdu and no other language.'[27]

The demand for Bengali as one of the state languages gathered the spontaneous support of the Bengali civil servants, academics, students, and various groups of the middle class. Several members of the Provincial Assembly, including some ministers, were reportedly active in supporting the movement. By the end of February 1948, the controversy had spilled over on to the streets. The East Pakistan Student League, founded in the first week of January by Mujibur Rahman, was in forefront of the agitation. A Committee of Action of the students of Dhaka University, representing all shades of opinion—leftists, rightists, and centrists—was set up in the first week of March with the objective of achieving national status for Bengali. At this stage, the political parties or the members of the Provincial Assembly were not openly involved in the movement.

The climax was reached on 11 March, when a student demonstration was baton-charged and a large number of students were arrested. The situation grew worse in the days that followed. The Quaid-i-Azam was due to visit Dhaka from 19 March. The provincial government became nervous and Nazimuddin under pressure of widespread agitation, the impending visit of the Governor-General, or perhaps because of his conviction of the genuineness of the demand, sought the help of Muhammad Ali Bogra to enter into negotiations with the Committee of Action. An agreement was signed by Nazimuddin with the Committee which, *inter alia,* provided that (1) the Provincial Assembly shall adopt a resolution for making Bengali the official language of East Pakistan and the medium of instruction at all stages of education; and (2) the Assembly by another resolution would recommend to the central government that Bengali should be made one of the state languages.[28] The resolution making Bengali the official language and the medium of instruction in East Pakistan was moved and passed by the Assembly, but the other one addressed to the Centre was not moved by the ruling party.[29]

The Quaid-i-Azam's visit to East Pakistan in the third week of March was marred by the language controversy. He felt that Nazimuddin had accepted the demands of the students under duress, and the resolutions of the Provincial Assembly were not binding on the central government. In an address to a Bengali audience he declared that while the language of the province could be Bengali, the 'State language of Pakistan was going to be Urdu and no other language. Any one who tries to mislead you is really an enemy of Pakistan.'[30] There was a disturbance at the Dhaka University convocation when the Quaid declared that Urdu would be the only state language. He also met the members of the Committee of Action and tried to persuade them of the necessity of having one national language; the students were not convinced.

The controversy temporarily cooled down after the visit of the Quaid-i-Azam, but he was unable to resolve it. The stray notes of his Dhaka visit, jotted down by the Quaid in his notebook, make it plain that he was given a one-sided briefing on the issue. Apparently the notes are of the points made by the officials, League leaders, and others who met him. But some of them may be the Quaid's own immediate reactions also. It would, however, be safe to deduce from them that he was given a picture which depicted the demand for Bengali as one of the two state languages as nothing more than a conspiracy of disgruntled League leaders, the Hindus, the communists, and the anti-Pakistan elements in Calcutta.[31]

In a move to neutralize the Suhrawardy group, which was alleged by Nazimuddin to be behind the language movement, Muhammad Ali Bogra and Tafazzul Ali were offered jobs in the government by the Quaid-i-Azam before he left Dhaka. The former was made an ambassador, and the latter a provincial minister.[32]

The Quaid-i-Azam was suffering from a terminal disease at the time. He was also under tremendous pressure of the problems of setting up the new State. Neither his health nor time permitted him to apply his political wisdom to the language issue and to question the half-truths presented to him. In the Lucknow session of the All-India Muslim League in 1937, when a resolution proposing Urdu as the language of Muslim India and the official language of the Muslim League was moved, it was strongly opposed by the Bengali delegates. The Quaid-i-Azam had intervened, and the final version of the resolution had only asked that 'wherever the Urdu language is the language of the area, its unhampered use and development should be upheld, and where it is not the predominant language, adequate arrangements should be made for teaching it as an optional subject.'[33]

The uncompromising attitude of the central government on Bengali was based on wrong premises. As a matter of fact, soon after Independence, changes had been effected, in response to popular demands, in the syllabii of the schools and colleges of East Pakistan to make them Pakistan and Islam-oriented.[34] The adamant stand of West Pakistan created an adverse reaction among the Bengalis, and even those who could read and speak Urdu refused to acknowledge it. The 1951 Census had recorded 8.8 million literate persons in East Pakistan, of whom 6.4 million were Muslims. Of the latter, 3.3 million or 10 per cent of the total Muslim population belonged to the exclusive category of those able to read the Holy Quran. Those able to speak Urdu, on the other hand, were recorded as one per cent. The East Pakistan Superintendent of Census reported that because of the language agitation in the province at the time of enumeration, the number of persons who could speak Urdu was possibly understated. The Census Commissioner, noting a correlation in other regions between the ability to read the Arabic of the Holy Quran and the ability to read Urdu, also doubted that only one per cent could read Urdu against ten per cent of Bengali Muslims able to read the Holy Quran.[35] Immediately after the emergence of East Pakistan, the 'deliberate imposition of Arabic words upon the Bengali language and literature by the new enthusiasts was not resented at first. A possibility had thus opened up for the people of East Pakistan to drift further away from those of West Bengal and forge a stronger link with those of West Pakistan.' A survey of undergraduate and post-graduate students in Dhaka conducted in 1957 'showed that although Bengali was the mother tongue of 93 per cent of them, 35 per cent of these Bengali students could read, write and speak in Urdu.'[36] If Urdu had not been insisted upon so vehemently, it was likely that in the natural course of events a common language, although with different scripts, would have been evolved.

The protagonists of Urdu, however, proceeded with the task of Islamizing the Bengali language with evangelical fervour. If it was not possible to replace it by Urdu, the next desirable solution was to change its script from Devnagri to Persian or Arabic. But the most grotesque suggestion was to make Arabic the national language of Pakistan. The idea emanated from the non-Bengali Education Secretary of East Pakistan, F. A. Karim, adopted by the Bengali Central Minister for Education, Fazlur Rahman and caught the imagination of the Punjabi Governor Firoz Khan Noon.[37] In 1952, twenty-one centres of the Central Ministry of Education were teaching Bengali in Arabic script in East Pakistan, about which the Chief Minister pleaded ignorance, although education was a provincial subject. Such was the insensitivity of the ruling party to popular issues that the East Pakistan Muslim League Council also recommended Arabic as the state language.[38] This was not acceptable even to the West Pakistan intelligentsia.

The Interim Report of the Basic Principles Committee, published in September 1950, had provided for Urdu as the only national language. There was an immediate reaction in East Pakistan against the proposals of the Report, of which language was only one item of the package. It would have remained so to be resolved as part of an overall agreement in the Constitution between East and West Wings, had Nazimuddin, as Prime Minister, not focused on it in an unwise statement in an emotionally-charged atmosphere.

The second language agitation started on 28 January 1952, the day following Nazimuddin's reiteration in a public meeting of the Quaid-i-Azam's views on the national language. The students of Dhaka University, in a protest meeting, attacked the Prime Minister and the provincial ministers and Chief Minister as stooges of West Pakistan. They accused the Prime Minister of going back on the agreement of 1948, and the following day formed a Committee of Action representing all shades of student organizations. From 30 January, a series of strikes was called in the university and colleges, and processions were taken out in the city. The Urdu-speaking students did not join the boycott of classes which resulted in ethnic clashes on the campuses.

This time the Awami League and other opposition parties and leaders decided to give the lead to the movement. According to intelligence reports, in a secret meeting called by the Awami League on 30 January, which was attended by a number of communist front as well as other organizations it was agreed that the agitation could not be successfully carried by the students alone. To mobilize full political and student support, it was decided that the leadership of the movement should be assumed by the Awami League under Bhashani. An all-party convention was held in Dhaka on 31 January, presided over by Bhashani and attended by prominent leaders like Abul Hashim and Hamidul Haq Choudhury. A broad-based Committee of Action, headed by Bhashani and representing the entire political and student opposition power was set up. The Committee, in its meeting on 3 February, on the suggestion of Abul Hashim decided to call a province-wide strike on 21 February and defy the government ban, if imposed, on processions and demonstrations.

The entire province was in a state of uprising against the central and East Pakistan governments. The intelligence agencies were reporting in full the militant build-up of the agitation. Neither the provincial government nor the Prime Minister registered the political implications of the crisis, and treated it as purely a law and order matter. And to meet it, an order banning processions within the limits of Dhaka city was issued in the evening of 20 February by the district administration under instructions of the provincial government.

On 21 February, small processions from various parts of the city started converging on Dhaka University. By noon, several thousand persons had gathered in the University compound. Inflammatory speeches were made from loudspeakers fitted inside the medical college hostel, and batches of persons started coming out from the University compound to defy the ban. While this was going on, a small procession of girls coming towards the trouble spot was stopped by the police. At this, the students rushed out from inside the university and medical college and joined the girls' procession by breaking the police cordon; they proceeded towards the Assembly building which was in session at the time. The police used tear-gas to stop the procession; having failed to stop it, they fired a few rounds. One student died on the spot, two later died in hospital.[39]

The Provincial Assembly met at its usual hour, at 3.30 p.m., shortly after the police firing. In the highly emotional atmosphere of the House, the League members were as much affected by the killing of the students as the opposition; many of them joined the opposition in denouncing the government. On the following day, the Chief Minister tried to mollify the members by moving a motion recommending to the Constituent Assembly that Bengali should be one of the state languages of Pakistan.[40] The motion was unanimously passed. But for the first time a number of Muslim members voted in favour of the amendments moved by the opposition, which so far had consisted of the Hindu Congress members only. The split in the Muslim League became formalized when some members demanded a separate bloc from the Speaker; the Awami League had attained the status of an opposition parliamentary party.[41]

Firoz Khan Noon, the Governor of East Pakistan, in a report to the Prime Minister, five days after the police firing, interpreted the event as a 'blessing in disguise because it has brought to the surface the most dangerous nefarious designs of our enemies' which, he was glad to inform the Prime Minister, had failed. In the opinion of the Governor, the language issue was the conspiracy of 'clever politicians and disruptionists from within the Muslim community and caste Hindus and communists from Calcutta as well as from inside Pakistan.' The object, the Governor concluded, was to set up a provincial government under Fazlul Huq who 'would have danced to the tune of Calcutta Hindus.'

In subsequent reports to the Governor-General and the Prime Minister, Firoz Khan Noon continued to repeat this conspiracy theory to explain the language movement. But on 28 February, he felt compelled to report to the Prime Minister that he did not think 'that you can get out of it without accepting Bengali as one of the State Languages but it must be Bengali written in Arabic script'. In support, the Governor quoted some obscure precedents from history; he was told that during the time of the Mughal Governor, Shaista Khan, Bengali was written in Arabic script. He had even found some Bengali books in the Dhaka museum written in that script.[42]

The police firing on 21 February sealed the fate of the Muslim League in East Pakistan for all time to come. At the time, the Assembly was in its budget session (the financial year in those days ended in March). The Governor immediately prorogued it as otherwise he apprehended that 'there would have been great excitement and more trouble created even on the floor of the House.' The Muslim League ministers and leaders could not go to any part of the province. The newspapers giving the government's point of view were not allowed by the students to be distributed in the districts. The government arranged to drop pamphlets from the air throughout the province. A number of Muslim League members resigned from the Assembly and the remaining ones were critical of the government. The budget had to be passed by the Assembly, unless Governor's rule were imposed and the Assembly and the ministry were dissolved. The dissolution would have been regarded as success of the movement, which was directed against the Muslim League ministry. Eventually, under great apprehensions and uncertainities whether the members would attend the session if the Assembly was summoned and, if so, whether the ministry would get majority support of the Parliamentary Party, the meeting was called in the last week of March and the budget was passed.

The events of 21 February changed the course of East–West relations. That the language movement was much more than a conspiracy of anti-Pakistan elements was amply demonstrated when, in the provincial elections of March 1954, the Muslim League was practically wiped out. Eventually, Bengali was accepted as one of the state languages in May 1954, but Bengal politics, henceforth, became more and more regionalist. A *Shaheed Minar* (Martyr's Monument) was erected at the site of the firing as a symbol of Bengali resistance to West Pakistan domination, and, ever since, the day is commemorated every year.

Constitution-making

The controversies that arose during constitution-making were broadly of two categories. One was in respect of the Islamic character, and the other pertained to the status of East Pakistan *vis-à-vis* the central government and West Pakistan.

On 7 March 1949, the first step towards the framing of the Constitution was taken, when the Objectives Resolution 'embodying the main principles on which the Constitution of Pakistan is to be based' was moved in the Constituent Assembly by the Prime Minister.[43] The notable feature of the Resolution was that it sought to combine the concepts of a modern state with the general principles of a pristine Islamic State, principles which were susceptible to more than one interpretation. The Hindu members of East Pakistan expressed serious apprehensions about the status of non-Muslims in the proposed Islamic State. They quoted orthodox interpretations of Islam, which were being preached by the religious parties, and expressed fears that eventually it would be the orthodox *ulema* and not the enlightened and liberal school, represented by Liaquat Ali Khan and other western-educated League leaders, that would prevail if the Objectives Resolution were passed. Referring to the Resolution which prescribed that the 'State will exercise authority within the limits prescribed by Him [God]', a Hindu member, for example, asked 'What are those limits, who will interpret them? Dr Qureshi or my respected Maulana Shabbir Ahmad Osmani? In case of difference, who will interpret?'[44] And this difference, between the orthodox and modernist approach, surfaced during the debate itself. Referring to the orthodox interpretation of the eligibiltiy of non-Muslims to hold high offices, the same member observed: 'if some non-Muslim wants to be the President of the State, he will not be able to do so.'[45] To this, Liaquat Ali Khan responded by specifying the Islamic State as one 'which is established in accordance with this [Objectives] . . . Resolution'; in such a state, the Prime Minister said, it would be 'absolutely wrong' to say that a non-Muslim cannot be 'the head of administration under a constitutional government.'[46] But Maulana Shabbir Ahmad Osmani did not exactly think so; according to him:

> The Islamic State means a state which is run on the exalted and ex-

> cellent principles of Islam . . . [it] can be run only by those who believe in those principles. People who do not subscribe to those ideas may have a place in the administrative machinery of the State but they cannot be entrusted with the responsibility of framing the general policy of the State or dealing with matters vital to its safety and integrity.[47]

Liaquat Ali Khan, while moving the Objectives Resolution, claimed that, since it provided for the exercise of the power and authority of the State 'through the chosen representatives of the people', the Resolution naturally eliminates any danger of the establishment of a theocracy.' Little did he realize the opening that the Resolution was giving to the obscurantists and what the Munir Report called 'political brigands and adventurers, even non-entities', to exploit the name of Islam in mundane political affairs and jolt the foundations of the State from time to time.[48] None of the three covenants of the Muslims of the subcontinent, which spelled out the unanimous demand for a separate Muslim Homeland, or Homelands—the Lahore Resolution of 1940, the Madras Resolution of 1941, and the Pakistan Resolution of the Legislators' Convention of 1946—or the debates leading to these resolutions had mentioned anything about an Islamic State. Over the years, the Resolution proved a perennially divisive point of reference in the polity of Pakistan.

The Objectives Resolution had a number of negative effects on East–West relations. Firstly, it prevented the assimilation of twenty-five per cent of the minority population of the East Wing into the mainstream politics of the country. Secondly, it enabled the vested interests to use Islam as an argument in political controversies, thus preventing the natural process of inter-Wing integration; joint electorates, Urdu, and a strong centre were sought to be justified on Islamic grounds. Thirdly, the religious parties, which assumed an importance quite out of proportion to their electoral strength, distorted the democratic process by insisting on Islam rather than the commonality of interests as the sole basis of unity of the nation.

On 12 March, the day the Objectives Resolution was adopted, the Basic Principles Committee was constituted by a resolution of the Constituent Assembly, to report on the main principles on which the Constitution of Pakistan was to be framed in the light of the Objectives Resolution. The Committee consisted of the Bengali President of the Assembly and twenty-four members, of whom only seven were from Bengal, including three Hindus, although East Pakistan had a majority in the Assembly.[49]

On 28 September 1950, the Prime Minister presented the Interim Report of the Basic Principles Committee to the Constituent Assembly and simultaneously moved for postponement of its consideration.[50] Its publication raised a storm of protest in East Pakistan. The main issues which agitated the East Wing were: (a) the constitution and powers of the central legislature; the East Wing objected to the bicameral legislature, in the upper house of which its representation would be equal to the smallest unit, and for the lower house of which the composition had not been indicated. Since it was recommended that both houses should have equal powers and, in case of a dispute, a joint session of both the houses was to take a decision, the Bengalis apprehended that their existing majority in the central legislature would be reduced to a minority or, at best, whittled down to parity; (b) the relations between the federation and the provinces, particularly the three lists of subjects proposed to be allocated for the purpose of legislation to the central legislature, provincial legislatures, and concurrently to both of them; on the basis of these lists, and other provisions pertaining to the powers of the central government, the Bengalis' perception was that 'there will be a unitary Central Government' and 'they will be made a colony of Pakistan';[51] and (c) Urdu was recommended as the only state language.

Immediately after the publication of the Interim Report a body known as the Central Committee for Democratic Federation was set up in East Pakistan to organize a movement against its recommendations. It was sponsored by the Awami League. A convention of political leaders and workers was held in November 1950 'in which the demands of East Pakistan were formulated in an alternative proposal based on the Lahore Resolution of 1940.' The convention proposed that (a) there should be a United States of Pakistan, consisting of the Eastern and Western regions with a parliament elected on the basis of equal representation from each region under a joint electorate system; (b) the central subjects should be only defence and foreign affairs provided that (i) there should be two units of Defence Forces with two Regional General Officers Commanding in the East and the West under Supreme Command at the Federal Capital; (ii) the Regional Defence Force should be raised from and manned by the people of the respective regions; (iii) there should be a Regional Foreign Affairs office in the Eastern Region; and (c) the Federal Government should impose taxes only on some specified items; new items for taxation could be added with the consent of the regions.[52] The Six Points of the Awami League, which led to the breakup of Pakistan, with all its nuances, were more or less the reformulation of this Bengali position.

Liaquat Ali Khan failed to realize the significance and strength of the regionalist forces in East Pakistan. An independent candidate had defeated the Muslim League in the provincial by-election and the radical forces had demonstrated their street power during the language riots and other agitations. Even the East Pakistan Muslim League Working Committee, in a meeting held in October 1950, had criticized the Interim Report and asked for basic modifications, in line with the special geographical position of East Pakistan. In the Provincial League Council meeting, also attended by Liaquat Ali Khan, some members termed the Interim Report as 'terribly anti-Bengali'.[53] The response of the Prime Minister to the strong feelings of East Pakistan, and the orthodox religious elements who thought that the Interim Report did not go far enough to establish a pure Islamic State, was to move the Constituent Assembly again on 21 November to postpone the consideration of the Interim Report.[54]

Liaquat Ali Khan, after the withdrawal of the Interim Report, proposed to the Muslim members of the Constituent Assembly from East Pakistan, including Fazlul Huq, parity of representation between the two Wings, and this was unanimously accepted by them.[55] But no attempt was made to achieve a broad national consensus. The contentious issues between the East and West Wings, which were holding up constitution-making, were never brought out in public forums; 'The debate was behind closed doors, and the public and non-League members of the Assembly had to wait until the official ranks had been dragooned into line.' The facade of unanimity thus achieved through pressures 'bred bitter resentment', and did not last beyond the doors of the committee rooms.[56]

On 22 December 1952, after a lapse of two years, the final report of the Basic Principles Committee was presented to the Constituent Assembly by Prime Minister Nazimuddin. The Committee, as before, recommended a bicameral legislature for the Centre, but with the difference that the lower house, with equal representation of the two Wings, was to have all the powers; the upper house 'will enjoy only the privilege of recommending revision in hasty legislation' by the lower house.[57] There was no mention of the state language in the report.

The proposal to give all authority to the lower house was not acceptable to the Punjabi central and provincial leadership. It was thought that, in spite of parity, Punjab might be overwhelmed by alliances between East Pakistan and the smaller provinces of West Pakistan. As a result of the Punjabi campaign against the report, its consideration in the Constituent Assembly was postponed, but it had a reaction in East Pakistan. The Chittagong District Muslim League demanded confederation between East and West Pakistan.[58] The Awami League and the religious parties of East Pakistan reiterated their demand for a unicameral legislature on the basis of population, leaving only defence, foreign affairs, and currency with the Centre.[59] Confederation as a way of keeping the two Wings together found an echo in the Central Assembly, during debates on the Basic Principles Committee Report. Mian Iftikharuddin from the Punjab actually moved an amendment in the Report to replace the term 'Federation' with 'Confederation.'[60]

Time was running out for the moderate political forces, with a national platform, in power in the Centre and the provinces, to finalize a reasonably workable Constitution. Nazimuddin should have drawn realistic conclusions from the language riots of February 1952 about the popular base of regionalist parties in East Pakistan. His lack of judgement and his naivete led to crises which proved disastrous both for East–West relations and the country as a whole. His untimely statement had led to language riots in East Pakistan, which eliminated forever the moderate political forces from the Bengal polity. In West Pakistan, he failed to control the religious parties, which started the movement against the Ahmadis with the connivance of the ambitious Punjab Chief Minister, and paved the way for martial law in Lahore and for his own dismissal.

The Constituent Assembly met on 1 January 1953, for discussion of the Report of the Basic Principles Committee. The record of the Assembly proceedings of this date shows an extraordinary lack of government leadership. The President of the Assembly asked the members' opinion on whether they would like to have more time to study the Report. The Hindu Congress member from East

Pakistan, Sris Chandra Chattopadhyaya, opposed any postponement and observed that the Bengalis were clamouring for the Constitution and, in case of further delays, 'They would say that we are not the real representatives of the people, because we were not, they say, elected by adult franchise, and let there be fresh elections.' He pleaded for consideration of the Report; 'if there is any omission or anything wrong, let new people come and let them amend it [the Constitution] according to their own liking.'[61] This was the lone sane voice in the Assembly. Mian Iftikharuddin referred to his note of dissent and claimed that three other Punjab members had also given minutes of dissent, although in the record these three were shown to have signed the Report.[62] The government side was conspicuous by its low-key presence in the House and silence during the debate over the document, for which Nazimuddin as the leader of the ruling party had been claiming so much credit only about a week earlier.

Muhammad Ali succeeded Nazimuddin in April and, on 7 October, he presented a compromise formula of federal representation. It provided for a majority for East Pakistan in the lower house, but parity between East and West in the combined upper and lower houses. The Islamic provisions were also diluted to make the Islamization gradual. The Constituent Assembly for the first time took up parawise consideration of the Basic Principles Committee Report on a day-to-day basis; from 7 October to 14 November, 140 paragraphs, which covered practically all the controversial issues, had been passed by the Assembly. At this stage, the momentum of the compromises was broken by an unwise adjournment to enable the East Pakistani members to campaign for the forthcoming provincial elections.

The year 1954 witnessed traumatic political changes. In the provincial elections of East Pakistan held in March, the Muslim League was practically wiped out by the United Front. It was not a very firm alliance, because of the heterogenous character of the parties, but somehow held together until the elections for the negative aim of defeating the Muslim League. The major parties constituting the Front were the Awami League, led by Suhrawardy, Bhashani, and Mujibur Rahman; the Krishak Sramik Party, led by Fazlul Huq; Ganatantri Dal, a leftist party; and Nizam-i-Islam Party, a religious party of East Pakistan, committed to introducing an Islamic order in the country.[63] In spite of frictions, jealousies between the leaders, and divergence in ideological outlook, all the opposition parties subscribed to the 21-point programme. The two main points directly related to the constitutional framework were (a) to make Bengali one of the state languages; and (b) 'In accordance with the historic Lahore Resolution, to secure full and complete autonomy and bring all subjects under the jurisdiction of East Bengal, leaving only Defence, Foreign Affairs, and Currency under the jurisdiction of the Centre. Even in the matter of defence, arrangements shall be such as to have the Headquarters of the Army in West Pakistan and the Headquarters of the Navy in East Bengal and to establish Ordnance Factories in East Bengal with a view to make East Bengal self-sufficient in the matter of defence, and convert the present Ansars into full-fledged militia.'[64]

The Awami League, which represented the organized Bengali nationalism in the urban and rural areas, emerged as the largest single party. The Muslim League got only ten seats, and most of its leaders including the Chief Minister, were defeated. Fazlul Huq was elected leader of the Parliamentary Party and he was sworn in as Chief Minister of East Pakistan on 3 April. The law and order situation in East Pakistan, which was bad even before the United Front ministry, further deteriorated during its brief tenure. The central government attributed this to the influence of the communists in the ruling parties of the United Front. This view was strengthened by the opposition of the Awami League and other United Front parties to the United States' military aid to Pakistan. Fazlul Huq's controversial statements to the foreign Press and in Calcutta, regarding provincial autonomy and the division of the subcontinent, did nothing to allay the suspicions of the establishment about the *bona fides* of the United Front.

Soon after the elections, the United Front had asked for the dissolution of the Constituent Assembly and the resignation of its Bengali members, who had been elected by the previous Assembly. Talks between Fazlul Huq and the Prime Minister and the central ministers about the Constitution, particularly the relationship of East Pakistan with the Centre, proved fruitless. According to the Prime Minister, Fazlul Huq 'had categorically declared that his ultimate goal was "independence" of East Pakistan, and he was prepared to "concede" Foreign Affairs, currency and defence to the Central Government only temporarily.'[65] The United Front ministry was dismissed on 29 May and the provincial administration was taken over by the central government. The reason given for resorting to this extraordinary measure was mainly the ministry's failure to maintain law and order; Fazlul Huq was called 'a self-confessed traitor to Pakistan' by the Prime Minister.[66]

Undeterred by the non-cooperation of the government of East Pakistan, and ignoring the verdict of the people of that Wing, Muhammad Ali resumed the task of constitution-making at the point at which it had been left off in November of the previous year. The sixteenth session of the Constituent Assembly was called on 14 March which continued its sittings with short intervals until 21 September, when it finally passed the Basic Principles Committee Report.[67] Moving an amendment to the Report to confine the powers of the federal government only to defence, foreign affairs, and currency, it was left to a Hindu opposition member to remind the House that 'it has been declared by the people of East Bengal that the members sitting here do not represent the views of the people of East Bengal and they have no right to speak on their behalf.'[68] But the tauntings of the opposition had no effect on the Muslim League members of East Pakistan, who continued with the process of constitution-making in complete disregard of democratic norms.

The Punjabi leadership, however, was quick to realize the implications of the fundamental change brought about in the polity by the defeat of the Muslim League in East Pakistan, and the unanimous vote in favour of provincial autonomy. The solid block of Bengalis in the Parliament could easily woo the smaller provinces and thus dominate the Punjab. The Punjab had agreed with the Muhammad Ali formula of representation on the basis of understanding among the Leaguers; the new breed of Bengali politicians was not likely to be as accommodating in their approach as the Muslim League. On 15 September, when the Constituent Assembly was in the final stages of adopting the Report of the Basic Principles Committee, the Punjab Chief Minister, Firoz Khan Noon, sprang a surprise by proposing a zonal sub-federation of the provinces of West Pakistan. The debate that followed was heated and bitter. A Bengali member accused the Punjab Chief Minister of trying to keep East Pakistan 'in a perpetual minority', and 'to have to his breast all the other Provinces so that they may not go away from his iron embrace to any other view point.'[69]

Members from the smaller provinces and East Pakistan vehemently opposed the Punjab proposal; the Punjabi members supported it. The Assembly refused to consider it, and continued with the business of constitution-making.

It seemed obvious that, in the absence of the recently-elected Bengali representatives in the Assembly and agreement of the Punjab, the attempt to impose the Constitution was going to lead to some sort of crisis. The government members themselves seemed to have some inkling or premonition of reaction from the Governor-General. This appears to be the explanation for two surprise legislative measures introduced on 20 and 21 September in great secrecy and urgency. They were (a) repeal of the Public and Representative Offices (Disqualification) Act of 1949 (PRODA); and (b) an amendment of the Government of India Act of 1935. The former enactment, under which holders of public offices could be tried for corruption, and, on conviction, debarred from seeking any elective office, had been used in the past rather selectively to settle scores with political opponents. Proceedings under the Act could be initiated only by the Governor-General and reportedly, at the time, action against some of the politicians including the members of the Assembly, was being comtemplated. The second legislative measure was intended to take away the powers of the Governor-General to dismiss the Prime Minister, which powers he had exercised in the case of Nazimuddin, although a provision to this effect was being incorporated in the new Constitution also. In the debate on the two bills, introduced by a non-official member, the government played no role, except for the Law Minister who only helped to refine the drafts of the enactments; each of the bills was hastily enacted the day it was moved.[70] Having passed the constitutional framework and the two enactments, to protect it against the vagaries of the Governor-General, the Constituent Assembly was adjourned till 27 October for taking up the Constitution Bill.

On 24 October, the Governor-General issued a Proclamation, declaring a state of emergency and dissolving the Constituent Assembly on the ground that it, 'as at present constituted, has lost the confidence of the people'.[71] There is no doubt that the Assembly had perpetuated itself for seven years, during which period most of its members had ceased to represent anyone. But Ghulam Muhammad, the Governor-General, was no great lover of democracy. His real intention was to impose a Constitution of his own. This is clear from the Emergency Powers Ordinance, issued on 27 March 1955, after the favourable judgment of the Federal Court in Tamizuddin Khan's case, in which the Governor-General's action was challenged. By virtue of this Ordinance, 'the Governor-General not only claimed the power of making by order such provisions as appeared to him to be necessary or expedient for the Constitution of Pakistan' but also 'repealed or amended certain provisions of the existing Constitution', and excluded the jurisdiction of the courts in respect of any matter arising out of the Proclamation of Emergency issued simultaneously with the Ordinance.[72] Having failed to get their way in the Constituent Assembly, the 'Punjabi central leadership, represented by the Governor-General and others', thought that the only way to protect the rights of Punjab was to impose the Constitution through executive orders.[73] The Federal Court, however, foiled this attempt at constitutional dictatorship and by its judicious pronouncements prevented the Governor-General from assuming supra-legal powers. The interpretation of law in the famous cases of Tamizuddin Khan and Usif Patel by the Federal Court had threatened a total breakdown of the legal and constitutional framework of the country. The Federal Court, presided over by Chief Justice Muhammad Munir, however, forced the Governor-General to restore the democratic process according to the guidelines given by it.

The judgment of the Federal Court, indirectly upholding the dissolution of the Constituent Assembly, has been criticized ever since for setting a bad precedent.[74] What is usually not mentioned is the enthusiasm with which the Governor-General's act was hailed by the politicians both in East and West Pakistan.[75] Ironically, the dissolution of the Assembly, which opened up the prospects of offices for its constituent parties, both in the Centre and East Pakistan, also led to splits in the United Front; the leaders of the two major parties tried to gain the favour of the Governor-General. Suhrawardy, who had supported the dissolution of the Assembly, was promised prime ministership of a future coalition ministry by the Governor-General, Ghulam Muhammad.[76] In December, he was given a seat in the 'cabinet of talents' of Muhammad Ali, which was sworn in on 24 October. But the Prime Minister, who had the support of the United Front, inducted a nominee of Fazlul Huq in the cabinet in January 1955, to counterbalance Suhrawardy. Neither of the two leaders of the United Front consulted each other about participation in what was the Governor-General's cabinet. The factional tussles reached breaking point after the release of Mujibur Rahman, General Secretary of the Awami League, from jail in January 1955, when an attempt was made to oust Fazlul Huq from the parliamentary leadership of the United Front in April.[77] The split was not on any principles—they all agreed on the 21-point programme—but was actuated by greed for power and personality clashes between Fazlul Huq and Suhrawardy.

The Commander-in-Chief of the Pakistan Army, General Ayub Khan, who was Defence Minister in the new cabinet, presented a paper to the cabinet on the 'present and future problems of Pakistan'. He insisted that 'The first thing is to unify West Pakistan' and 'pressed very hard for it and initiated the process of merger of the provinces'.[78] In fact, the idea was an old one. As far back as December 1947, Sir Archibald Rowlands, in a report to the Quaid-i-Azam on the economic prospects of Pakistan, had said: 'I personally think that on grounds of economy, both in terms of money and of administrative manpower, there is in fact a great deal to be said for such an amalgamation (of West Punjab, Sind, the NWFP and Balochistan to be christened West Pakistan), but I recognize that such a solution is politically impossible, at least in the immediate future'.[79] In the turmoil of 1954, however, the economic and administrative benefits were not the main considerations, though they were the ostensible arguments given by the central government. The immediate significance of integration was in meeting the looming threat of Bengali domination.

The Constituent Assembly Order 1955, which sought to bring into existence a new legislature, provided parity of representation between the two Wings. The previous Assembly had had a Bengal majority and, although the principle of parity had been accepted by the Muslim League, the United Front parties had as yet not explicitly agreed to the formula. All of them announced a boycott of the elections to the new Constituent Assembly. The central leadership tackled each of the two major East Pakistan parties separately. As regards the Awami League, the government offered to allow Bhashani to return to Pakistan, and Suhrawardy, who already had a stake in the regime as a minister with a reasonable prospect of prime ministership, persuaded the Awami League Working Committee to accept parity and take part in the elections. Fazlul Huq of Krishak Sramik was easily persuaded to fall in line by the restoration of the United Front Ministry in East Pakistan, with his nominee as Chief Minister, in June 1955.

In early July 1955, the first session of the second Constituent Assembly was held. In a House of 80 members, the Muslim League was the largest single party with 25 seats (all except one of Muhammad Ali from West Pakistan), followed by the United Front, 16, and Awami League, 12; the remaining seats were distributed among minor parties and independents.[80] On 7 August, Iskandar Mirza became the Acting Governor-General. Muhammad Ali, who had obstructed the appointment of Iskandar Mirza, had to go. Negotiations between the Muslim League and the Awami League failed because of the opposition of Fazlul Huq to Suhrawardy as prime minister, and the offer of the United Front to compromise on the 21-point programme and otherwise co-operate without insisting on the leadership of the coalition party. Accordingly, Choudhury Muhammad Ali, a former civil servant who had been a minister in every government since 1951, was elected leader of the Muslim League Parliamentary Party and became the Prime Minister of the League-United Front coalition. Suhrawardy went into opposition to incur the odium of opposing the constitutional proposals with which he had been closely associated.[81]

The first legislative item passed by the Assembly was the enactment of the Establishment of West Pakistan Act in September. The sordid manner in which the integration of West Pakistan was brought about is well known. The bill was opposed by the Awami League, although Suhrawardy as Law Minister had helped draft it. But the coalition government had no difficulty in getting it through; the Assembly had no choice but to give *ex post facto* approval to it.

The draft Constitution was ready when the Constituent Assembly was dissolved, but the few controversial points had to be renegotiated with East Pakistan. On 3 November, I. I. Chundrigar, the Law Minister, reported to the cabinet on four issues which required decision. They were (a) the distribution of powers between the provinces and the Federation; (b) whether the elections should be joint for all communities, or separate for the Muslims and the minorities; (c) the language of the Federation and the provinces, and for what period, if any, English should be retained for official use; and (d) Islamic provisions, and the form in which they should be incorporated in the Constitution. The matter was placed before the subcommittee appointed by the Coalition Party, under the chairmanship of the Prime Minister. East Pakistan was represented by Fazlul Huq and two members of his party, one religious leader of little consequence, and two Hindu members.[82] No effort was made to achieve a broad consensus by associating the Awami League. A suggestion made at a later stage by the Awami League to formulate the Constitution in an all-party conference was not accepted by the Prime Minister.

The draft Constitution Bill was presented to the Constituent Assembly on 9 January 1956. So far as East–West relations were concerned, the distribution of powers in the three lists of subjects—Federal, Provincial, and Concurrent—was the main issue. These lists in the Government of India Act of 1935, the Interim and Final Reports of the Basic Principles Committee, and as they appeared in the 1956 Constitution, show no substantive difference, except that in the last one the Railways were allocated to the provinces and the subjects not appearing in any one of the lists were also given to the provinces. Other provisions governing the relations between the Centre and the provinces were almost the same as proposed earlier; the overriding control of the Centre was ensured through the peacetime provisions, like the power of the federal government to issue directives to the provinces, appointment of the governors, and control over senior civil service appointments in the provinces. In times of grave emergency, the President could issue a Proclamation of Emergency and exercise all the provincial executive and legislative powers; the existence of the emergency itself was to be determined by the President. The only structural change brought about by the 1956 Constitution was the integration of West Pakistan. Bengali was accepted as one of the state languages, and the question of electorates was to be decided later in consultation with the provincial assemblies of East and West Pakistan.

The draft Constitution evoked severe criticism from the Awami League, Ganatantari Dal, which was a component of the United Front, and the intelligentsia in general in East Pakistan. Bhashani, in a public meeting in Dhaka on 15 January, threatened secession if the Centre did not meet the demands of East Pakistan.[83] In the

Awami League Working Committee meeting held on 21 January, attended by the party office-bearers of all the districts also, it was decided to move amendments to the Constitution Bill to incorporate in it regional autonomy, parity in all political, economic, and financial matters, and joint electorates. In case these amendments were not accepted, the Awami League members were to withdraw from the Assembly before the final voting. The Working Committee also called for an all-party conference to resolve the differences.[84] The Working Committee of Krishak Sramik Party also met on 15 January to formulate its proposals for full provincial autonomy, and parity in all matters between the two Wings, and decided to place them before the Constituent Assembly.

Choudhury Muhammad Ali rejected the Awami League demand for an all-party conference, which was endorsed by Fazlul Huq also. Later, Suhrawardy as Prime Minister maintained that he 'and the gentleman who led the United Front Party [Fazlul Huq] together made a prayer to the Prime Minister [Choudhury Muhammad Ali] to suspend the sitting [of the Constituent Assembly] for only two or three days for the purpose of thrashing out' the controversial matters but 'the Prime Minister refused to give that time'.[85] Choudhury Muhammad Ali knew that, sitting together in a meeting, the East Pakistan parties would confront him with a solid front as they were doing now in public statements. Separately, he could and did bring round Fazlul Huq and his party to support his constitutional proposals. The United Front leadership had obtained a good price for its co-operation; its ministry in East Pakistan was sustained by the central government, in spite of a doubtful majority in the Provincial Assembly, it was sharing power in the central government, and, as it turned out later, Fazlul Huq had the promise of the governorship of East Pakistan after the passage of the Constitution.

The Awami League leadership was no less opportunist and keen for power. In August of the previous year, it had tried hard to strike a bargain for a coalition with the Muslim League. But the unconditional offer of Fazlul Huq to coalesce with the Muslim League as against the Awami League, which wanted the prime ministership, deprived the latter of the opportunity to secure power. The Bengali middle classes and Suhrawardy, shrewd politician that he was, realized that regional autonomy, which restricted the Centre only to defence, foreign affairs, and currency, was not practical politics. It could, however, be a bargaining point for obtaining parity with West Pakistan in economic, financial, and all other matters. This was feasible to a great extent, and a compromise with the Awami League, a substantial section of which was under the influence of Suhrawardy, on these lines perhaps would have resulted in a unanimous Constitution.

The quality of the representative character of the two major East Pakistan parties and their leaders—Fazlul Huq and Suhrawardy—was quite different. Fazlul Huq had emerged as a leader of the Bengal peasantry in the 1930s. His influence was personal, and the status of his party kept changing with what he perceived as better prospects elsewhere, as we have seen above during the pre-Independence period. He was 83 years old at this time and out of touch with the urban middle classes and students who set the political pace in East Pakistan. The Awami League, on the other hand, represented a wide spectrum of assertive Bengali urban classes, all of whom were agreed on regional autonomy and a distinct identity for East Pakistan. Before the split and breakaway of Bhashani in 1957, there were three main elements in the party. They were Marxists, nationalists somewhat left of the centre, and students of both kinds. Bhashani, who led the Marxists, was a mixture of peasant, religious, and Marxist. He never took part in elections, and avoided the responsibilities of working within the constitutional framework. He was always ready to exploit the difficulties of the government of the day, including that of the Awami League, and remained a negative factor in Pakistani politics from 1947 to 1971. Suhrawardy, suave, cosmopolitan, and sophisticated was the antithesis of Bhashani, and the two remained at loggerheads in the party until the departure of the latter. In between was Mujibur Rahman, an ardent Bengali nationalist who wielded power and was a disciple of Suhrawardy. Suhrawardy, although opposed by Bhashani in party forums on national issues, almost always carried the day. He was the only Bengali leader who could influence the extreme nationalist elements, and bring them round to a workable position. The three Awami League leaders, Suhrawardy, Bhashani, and Mujibur Rahman, commanded massive political power, without which no viable agreement with East Pakistan was possible.

The Pakistani political culture has never appreciated the virtues of consensus in securing enduring settlements of basic issues. Choudhury Muhammad Ali could have sought, and perhaps obtained, the co-operation of Suhrawardy in the formulation of constitutional proposals with which the latter had been associated in the previous government. Suhrawardy had drafted the Establishment of West Pakistan Bill, although by the time it came before the Parliament he had gone into the opposition and opposed it. Later, when he was Prime Minister, he strongly resisted attempts to dismember the One Unit and also declared that 98 per cent of provincial autonomy had been guaranteed by the Constitution. But in February 1956, the Constitution Bill was pushed through against all opposition in the Assembly, and processions and demonstrations in East Pakistan, and was finally passed on 29 February. The Awami League walked out before the final voting, followed by the majority of the Hindu members, Ganatantari Dal, and the Azad Pakistan Party.

The Constitution came into effect on 23 March, but East–West relations remained strained as before. The Awami League continued to consolidate its position in East Pakistan, under the stormy leadership of Bhashani and the organizational skills of Mujibur Rahman, on the slogan of provincial autonomy. Nevertheless, it was under the new Constitution that the Awami League assumed power both in the Centre and in East Pakistan in September; Suhrawardy became the Prime Minister and Ataur Rahman Khan the Chief Minister. Both the governments were coalitions, but in both, the Awami League was the dominant partner. For the first and last time, East Pakistan gained a sense of participation in the power structure.[86]

Suhrawardy was a man of prodigious energy and an experienced administrator. He dominated the government machinery but, more importantly, he introduced a refreshing change in national politics by throwing open to public debate the controversial issues of the pro-Western foreign policy, defence pacts, and electorates. On each one of them, Suhrawardy boldly faced the opposition in his own party forums, in the Parliament, or in the provincial legislatures, and used political skill to obtain a favourable mandate. The Muslim League governments had never spelled out the foreign or domestic policy issues in the parliamentary or party forums for a free and open discussion to mould public opinion and derive a popular mandate on them.

The first item on the agenda of the Suhrawardy government was the principle of electorates, which was to be determined by an Act of Parliament after ascertaining and considering the views of the provincial assemblies. This needed to be taken up early to start preparations for elections under the new Constitution. As was anticipated, the East Pakistan Assembly passed a resolution in favour of joint electorate on 1 October, by a vote of 159 to one with 84 abstentions.[87] The West Pakistan Assembly, however, recommended separate electorates. The Muslim League members of the West Pakistan Assembly, with the inherited convictions of the pre-Independence period, thought that the Hindu influence would be aggravated in East Pakistan by joint electorate. They were supported by the Jamaat-i-Islami and other religious parties which mounted a campaign outside the Assembly against joint electorate. The situation was also complicated by 'floating members', whose only commitment was to the power alignments of the day. A formula was devised to prescribe separate electorate in West Pakistan and joint in East Pakistan, and an Act on these lines was enacted by the National Assembly on 11 October, after two days of bitter debate.[88] A parliament consisting of one half of the members elected jointly by all classes of the population, and one half representing separate religious communities would have been a constitutional absurdity. Suhrawardy was eventually successful, in April 1957, in persuading his coalition partner, the Republican Party, to agree to joint electorate in West Pakistan. This enabled the election machinery to be put in motion, and implementation of the new Constitution.

'The Maulana [Bhashani] is making our life miserable. He has started a relentless campaign against the government and is determined to discredit us in all possible manners . . . In the circumstances, I thought it proper to quit office and made the proposal yesterday in an emergent meeting of the working committee . . .' Thus wrote the Chief Minister of East Pakistan to Suhrawardy on 13 May 1957. The immediate cause of Ataur Rahman Khan's complaint was the threat of the President of the Awami League to go on hunger strike and start a province-wide agitation against his party's government, unless the prices of rice and other commodities were reduced immediately. Instead of allowing the party to consolidate itself in power to achieve its objectives, Bhashani did everything to destabilize it by taking extreme positions on regional autonomy, pro-Western foreign policy, and defence pacts, and by demanding instant solutions.

In February 1957, in the Awami League Council meeting held at Kagmari, the contest between Bhashani and Suhrawardy over foreign policy remained inconclusive. The Council merely reiterated its previous resolution opposing pacts and alliance. At the same time it almost unanimously signified its support to the party's continuation in office with the central coalition.[89] The session of the Council drew considerable publicity, not only because of the decor of its stage and premises with the pictures of a motley group of world leaders, but also by the statement of Bhashani 'that a stage might come in the future if the grievances of East Pakistan were not redressed, when the people of East Pakistan might feel inclined to say *Assalam Alaikum* [goodbye]' to Pakistan.[90] On 3 April, an unofficial resolution inspired by Bhashani, demanding full regional autonomy, except defence, foreign affairs, and currency, for East Pakistan, was unanimously approved by the East Pakistan Assembly. There were some moderate speeches during the debate which pleaded with members to give the Constitution 'a fair trial and implement it to the fullest degree', and warned that otherwise 'there will soon be no Constitution, no Government, no Parliament to talk about.' But since Bhashani had asked for 'active support of all parties in the legislature . . . for regional autonomy of an undiluted and revolutionary type', not many, including those in the government, were willing, outside the Assembly, to face the consequences of a more balanced approach.[91]

The resolution was typical of Bhashani's technique of championing the extreme form of an issue, using extra-constitutional means to mobilize public opinion, and forcing his adversaries to do the same. He used it very effectively in 1971 against Mujibur Rahman. But Suhrawardy had a stature and calibre of a different order. He took no serious notice of the resolution of the East Pakistan Assembly and called it a 'political stunt'. 'The Constitution,' he said, 'provided enough powers to the Provinces.'[92] Bhashani continued to harass the provincial government on passing issues, by threatening to resort to various pressure tactics, as the Chief Minister complained in the letter quoted above. The showdown, which had become inevitable by mid-1957, came in the Awami League Council meeting held on 13 June, over

Suhrawardy's pro-Western foreign policy and defence pacts. The Council approved Suhrawardy's stand by a heavy majority; of the 750-odd councillors attending the special session, only 25 opposed Suhrawardy's foreign policy when the motion was put to vote.[93] Earlier, he had obtained an overwhelming mandate for his foreign policy from the Parliament also, in the preceding February.[94]

Bhashani reacted to his defeat by entering into consultations with the leaders of the newly-founded Pakistan National Party, which was a combination of three provincial parties of West Pakistan—the Azad Pakistan Party of Mian Iftikharuddin, the Red Shirts of Khan Abdul Ghaffar Khan, Sind Awami Mahaz of G. M. Syed—and some other minor groups. In July, he called a convention of Democratic Workers in Dhaka and formed his National Awami Party, which was joined by the Pakistan National Party.[95] Bhashani with his leftist followers resigned from the Awami League. We will hear more of them in 1971.

The Awami League's tenure of power in the central government was the only period in the history of East–West relations which was free from bitterness between the two Wings. The contentious issues of autonomy and parity were frozen, and the Constitution of 1956 was, more or less, accepted by public opinion in East Pakistan as the framework within which further redress of their grievances would be sought. Preparations for elections were afoot, and it could be hoped that free and fair elections would give birth to a viable political order.

It was ironical that the Suhrawardy Government should have been undermined by its coalition partner, the Republican Party, on the issue of One Unit. The One Unit, as described above, was the brainchild of the West Pakistani establishment and was a condition precedent to the passage of the Constitution in the Parliament. It was the foundation on which the whole edifice of the 1956 Constitution was built. To undo the integration now would have meant a reopening of the entire range of controversial matters which were settled, or at least frozen, for the time being. There is no doubt that in bringing about the integration of West Pakistan, coercive measures were used and the voting in the legislature of the minority provinces on the issue was not free and fair. The issue of One Unit therefore, remained alive in the West Pakistan Assembly which, by virtue of its illegitimate birth, had become a disgraceful representative body even by Pakistani standards. The unprincipled behaviour of its members, rapidly shifting loyalties, and the cynical manipulations of the President, Iskandar Mirza, and his nominee Governor Mushtaq Ahmad Gurmani are beyond the scope of this study, but are well documented elsewhere. At the time we are discussing, September 1957, by a series of permutations and combinations of party strength, the Republican Party had found it necessary to seek the support of the Pakistan National Party in order to keep itself in power. The latter party was a combination of parties, as mentioned above, which were rooted in the provinces. Those belonging to the minority provinces of Sindh and the NWFP had, in particular, all along opposed the merger of their identities in the province of West Pakistan. Their Assembly strength, which normally would have been considered insignificant, acquired, for the ruling Republicans, crucial importance as casting votes. This vital position was used by the Pakistan National Party to force the Republicans to support a resolution for the dismemberment of One Unit, which was passed by the West Pakistan Assembly on 17 September, by a majority of 170 to four votes. The Muslim League, which had sponsored and brought into existence the One Unit in the previous year, remained neutral in the voting.[96]

Suhrawardy was strongly opposed to the breakup of West Pakistan; the Republicans withdrew their support from the coalition ministry, and Suhrawardy was asked by Iskandar Mirza to resign. His request to let him try to obtain a vote of confidence from the Parliament was rejected by the President. No prime minister in the parliamentary history of Pakistan was voted out or voted in by the parliament; they were appointed, dismissed, or made to resign by the head of state, who, in each case, happened to be non-Bengali.

On the face of it, it appears rather strange that Suhrawardy should be made to quit on his strong support for One Unit, which was the creation of the Punjabi establishment, the President, and the Commander-in-Chief—the real power pillars of the State. And it was no secret that the Republicans were the creatures of the President. How and why would they undermine Suhrawardy on an issue to which the establishment was so totally committed? The fact of the matter is that Suhrawardy was never trusted by any one of these power elements. He had advocated land reforms, which had alienated the Punjabi power group, and his government had taken certain steps to rectify the economic imbalance between the two Wings, which hit the Punjabi and *Mohajir* vested interests.[97] His secular outlook and representation of Bengali nationalism, even though of a federalist kind, made him suspect in the eyes of influential West Pakistani groups who always attributed progressive Bengali politics to Hindu machinations.[98] President Mirza did not like Suhrawardy because the latter had an independent power base in East Pakistan, and he and his party were not amenable to the influence of the President as other politicians were. Suhrawardy was perhaps going too fast towards the holding of elections, and the political process was taking a turn which would interfere with Mirza's plans to scuttle the parliamentary system, a year later. Ayub, ignorant of the code of the legal profession, considered that Suhrawardy, as defence counsel in the Rawalpindi Conspiracy trial, had done great harm to the army by 'harsh and undignified cross-examination of the army officers' and was, therefore, 'no friend of Pakistan.'[99]

In the remaining one year of the first decade of independence, there were two more prime ministers. President Iskandar Mirza continued to make and unmake governments in the Centre and East Pakistan through unscrupulous politicians.[100] During his tenure of three years and two months as constitutional head of state, he appointed and dismissed, or made to resign, five prime ministers, and, through his nominee governors, six ministries in East Pakistan, and three chief ministers in West Pakistan.[101]

Economic Centralism

British India was governed under the unitary system until the Government of India Act of 1935, which provided for a federation and a modicum of provincial autonomy. The federation part was not put into operation but the provincial governments, elected on a narrow franchise, worked for a number of years before 1947. The relations of these provincial governments with the government of India were not those of constituent units with the federal government; they exercised limited powers under a centralized system. Matters of high finance, involving fiscal and monetary policies, foreign exchange, and international trade remained the exclusive preserve of the central government. Neither the political leadership, nor the civil servants who assumed the management of Pakistan's economy had any experience of the economic and financial stresses and strains of the federal system. They inherited the centralized model of government and, quite unconsciously, adopted it for Pakistan without making adjustments for the geographical and political realities of the East Wing. This tendency received early suppport from a former British official of the government of India, Sir Archibald Rowlands, who was called by the Quaid-i-Azam to advise the new state on economic matters. In December 1947, when the government of Pakistan was still in the process of being put together and the financial system was yet to be organized, Sir Archibald opined that 'If Pakistan is to be strong, it must be strong at the Centre.' Accordingly, he recommended the transfer of some sources of revenues from the provinces to the Centre, placing industrial development on the central list of subjects, and setting up of a strong planning organization at the Centre. He did realize that the creation of a strong Centre might 'be opposed by some political interests', but this, he thought, would 'be founded on an inadequate appreciation of the issues involved'.[102] The financial recommendations of Sir Archibald were put into effect in a very short time by the government of Pakistan.

The major economic grievances of Bengal against the central government, in the first decade of Pakistan, can be grouped under three areas of public policy: (a) division of revenues between the Centre and provinces; (b) jute and foreign exchange; and (c) development planning. Each one of them was criticized on the ground of centralism, and used as an argument for provincial autonomy and ultimately for the Six Point formula.

(a) Division of Revenues:

On 21 March 1951, during discussion of the central budget for 1951–2 in the Constituent Assembly, Nurul Amin accused the central government of adopting dubious methods to encroach on provincial revenues. Firstly, the statutory share of the provinces in the proceeds of income tax had been withheld since the inception of Pakistan, without changing the law. Secondly, the constitutional provision regarding the share of East Pakistan in the jute export duty was unilaterally amended in its own favour by the central government, without consulting the provincial government. Thirdly, the administration of the provincial sales tax, which was an expanding source of revenue for the East Pakistan government, was taken away by the Centre. Thus, deprived of its legitimate sources and shares of revenue, the East Pakistan government was running into deficits. Nurul Amin also demanded that population should be the basis of distributing the windfall surplus earned by the central government; East Pakistan had been allocated 25 million rupees out of 80 million rupees.[103] The Chief Minister was fully supported by all the Bengali members.

Ghulam Muhammad, who had been Finance Minister since the inception of Pakistan, took the Bengali accusations as a personal affront, which they probably were meant to be. In reply, on 24 March, he accepted that the Centre had 'encroached on the provincial fields', but claimed that it was done with the concurrence of the provinces. Immediately after Independence, he recalled, in a meeting in November 1947, inaugurated by the Quaid-i-Azam and attended by the chief ministers, on an appeal of the central government, it was unanimously agreed that the Centre may appropriate the provincial share of income tax and take over the administration of sales tax. But the Finance Minister had no satisfactory explanation for amending constitutional provisions regarding the provincial share in the jute export duty, without consulting the East Pakistan government and, in violation of the pre-Independence arrangement, limiting it to a ceiling of Rs 35 million. Ghulam Muhammad's argument was that these 'encroachments' were necessitated by the high cost of defence, which, he admitted, was 'quite out of proportion with our resources at the time', continued to claim a major portion of revenues, and was likely to remain so until 'we are stronger'.[104] He told the Bengali members that East Pakistan was poor, and 'the bulk of the revenues of the Centre today is derived from West Pakistan . . .'[105] In an airy manner, which the Bengalis always resented, Ghulam Muhammad sympathized that 'Eastern Pakistanis have their difficulties, psychological difficulties, complexes and as a matter of history they were badly treated before Partition.'[106] He also rejected the population principle for distribution of grants to the provinces.[107]

Earlier, in the last week of February during the budget discussion in the East Pakistan Assembly, the members had accused the Bengali representatives in the Centre and the East Pakistan government of being 'diffident in putting forward our legitimate claims to the central government and getting our dues.

They appear to be afraid of the Centre.'[108] Nurul Amin, therefore, had to press the Bengal case a little more vehemently than was usual with the Muslim League members of East Pakistan. On 25 March speaking on the demand for custom duty, he rebutted the Finance Minister's statement that East Pakistan was not earning enough and quoted official statistics from a central government publication to prove otherwise. In round figures, during the years 1948–9 and 1949–50, East Pakistan exported goods worth Rs 1254 million and Rs 597 million as against its imports of Rs 231 million and Rs 214 million respectively; during the same years, West Pakistan exports amounted to Rs 526 million and Rs 518 million as against its imports of Rs 648 million and Rs 632 million respectively. It was clear, Nurul Amin claimed, that 'what was earned in East Pakistan was spent here in West Pakistan', and he blamed the Centre's policies of import licensing and foreign exchange allocation for this situation.[109]

Eventually, on the intervention of Liaquat Ali Khan, the suggestion of Nurul Amin for an expert examination of the issue was accepted by the government of Pakistan over the objections of Ghulam Muhammad.[110] In consultation with the East Pakistan government, Sir Jeremy Raisman, a British expert, was invited in July to examine the existing allocation of revenues between the Centre and the provinces and 'suggest any changes, if necessary, in order to ensure an equitable allocation of revenues.'[111] The recommendations of Sir Jeremy, submitted in December, were accepted as an Award by both the central and East Pakistan governments and were given effect from the financial year 1952–3. The East Pakistan government felt that, on the whole, 'substantial, though not full, justice has been done to the case of East Bengal.'[112] The revenue deficit of the East Pakistan budget came down to Rs 7 million in 1952–3, as against Rs 40 million in 1951–2.[113] The Award cooled tempers temporarily, but the 'continuous drain from East Pakistan', perceived by the Bengalis, remained a perpetual issue to embitter the relations of the two Wings.

(b) Jute and Foreign Exchange:

Before Partition, East Pakistan produced 73 per cent of the jute of the subcontinent, but 75 per cent of the exportable raw jute was pressed into bales in India, and the province did not possess a single jute mill.[114] By the end of 1950, jute contributed 45 per cent of the total export earnings of Pakistan.[115] The main consumer of jute was India, which was also the supplier of essential goods to East Pakistan. Trade with India was thus vital to East Pakistan. These centuries-old economic relationships were disrupted by the strained political relations between India and Pakistan, mainly caused by matters which did not concern East Pakistan. In the long run, it diversified the economy of East Pakistan and made it independent, instead of continuing as a hinterland. In the short run, the process of adjustment was painful.

The irreversible economic break with India came in September 1949, when Pakistan refused to devalue, following devaluation of the sterling by the United Kingdom. India, which had devalued its rupee, did not accept the par value of Pakistan currency and trade between the two countries came to a halt. The immediate effect of non-devaluation on the jute economy of East Pakistan was disastrous and remained a sore point with Bengalis for a long time. The jute season had just begun with a weak tendency in prices, because India had not lifted the committed quantity of 5 million bales during 1948–9. 'On the 19th September when devaluation of sterling was announced the market was disturbed and the jute trade came practically to a standstill due to Government of Pakistan decision to maintain the value of her rupee at the existing level . . . The prices offered being uneconomic, the growers generally held back sellings.'[116] The magnitude of the fall in prices was variously stated by the Bengali members in the Provincial and National Assemblies to highlight the adverse effects of the Centre's decision. In the following years, the non-devaluation was more openly criticized as a mechanism to appropriate Bengal resources for the benefit of West Pakistan. There is no doubt that non-devaluation caused a lot of misery and the East Pakistan economy suffered a deep recession. To counter the adverse consequences on the jute trade, the central government 'set up a Jute Board to keep the position under constant review and to step in to make purchases on Government account should this be necessary. The National Bank of Pakistan was also brought into being in advance of the due date of its establishment to help finance the jute crop.'[117] Although the Finance Minister claimed success for these measures, the fact was that they failed to mitigate the sufferings of the growers in the immediate period. The minimum support prices of jute fixed by the government were 28 per cent less than those ruling before devaluation.[118] The Jute Board set up in October could not possibly extend support coverage to any significant number of growers within a few months; up to the middle of March 1950, it had purchased only about 11000 maunds at minimum prices.[119] In subsequent years, the Jute Board developed into a competent specialized institution and helped stabilize the volatile jute regime.

The Bengalis alleged that all the arguments in favour of non-devaluation worked for the benefit of West Pakistan at the cost of East Pakistan. It was argued against devaluation that it would fuel inflation and retard industrial development by making consumer and capital goods more expensive, while exports, being entirely agricultural raw materials, were not susceptible to any expansion by currency device. The debate continued long after the event and the eventual devaluation of the rupee in 1955. On the whole, while the Bengali grower suffered badly in the medium term, East Pakistan benefited in the long run due to the diversification of its raw jute outlets and its progressive processing and manufacturing into higher value added products. Starting with a nil position at the time of Independence, by 1958 East Pakistan was producing about 200,000 tons of jute goods, consuming a million bales.[120] The gains to West Pakistan were enumerated by Amjad Ali, the Finance Minister, in 1956: he attributed the industrial development in the West Wing to private investors who earned through export and import and ploughed back the profits into textiles.[121] The phenomenon was due to cheaper import of capital goods, with consequent lower import duties, and huge profits accruing from import licensing in an overvalued currency, both situations arising from non-devaluation of the rupee.

During the budget debate in 1956, Amjad Ali revealed that the non-devaluation in 1949, alleged to have been deliberately taken 'to drain the wealth of East Pakistan', was against the advice of both the Ministry of Finance and the Governor of the State Bank. The decision, he insinuated, was taken on the advice of Fazlur Rahman, the Bengali Commerce Minister.[122] Mujib disowned his compatriot by the derisive comment that 'He (Fazlur Rahman) is and was a Muslim Leaguer.'[123]

(c) Development Planning:

In pre-Independence India, investment decisions were, by and large, left to private enterprise in regard to direction and location. The government did undertake infrastructure works like the railways, roads, and irrigation canals, but they were mostly on strategic considerations. There was no attempt at centralized or regional planning to ensure equitable development in all parts of the subcontinent. It was shortly before the end of the Second World War that a Department of Planning and Development was created in the government of India and the provincial governments were asked to prepare projects for execution, after the War, with the loans and grants of the central government.

Early in 1948, the government of Pakistan set up a Development Board, a Planning Advisory Board, and an Economic Committee of the Cabinet, 'to co-ordinate development plans, recommend priorities', and make periodic reports to the Cabinet on the progress of development projects.[124] A Six-Year Development Programme, covering the period July 1951 to June 1957, was approved by the government in November 1950. The Programme was not a plan in the usual sense, but only a collection of 67 updated schemes or new projects, mostly in outline. No attempt was made to ensure regional equity in its composition, but it was recognized that 'Eastern Pakistan was a part of the Eastern Front and suffered from the scorched-earth policy as well as the effects of war.' The railway system, 'which was reduced to scrap by the intensive use and lack of repairs during the period of army occupation' was quoted as an example.[125]

The performance of the East Pakistan government during the first five and a half years of independence was extremely poor. Up to 1952–3, out of the total development expenditure of Rs 1880 million in the public sector by the central and provincial governments, East Pakistan incurred only Rs 235 million. Funds were not the problem, because during the four years, 1948–9 to 1951–2, out of its allocation of Rs 117 million from the central government development loans of Rs 361 million, East Pakistan drew only Rs 25 million; during the same period the Punjab drew Rs 187 million against its allocation of Rs 160 million.[126]

The government of Pakistan was well aware of the problems of the East Wing from the beginning. The Economic Appraisal Committee, of which Fazlur Rahman, the Bengali Minister for

Economic Affairs, was the Chairman, reported in March 1953 that it was 'struck by the slow progress' in East Pakistan, and recommended to the central government the provision of 'greater guidance and assistance to them [East Pakistan government] in the matter of planning and implementation of development schemes.'[127]

The concern for the East Wing was reiterated in the First Five Year Plan, which covered the period 1955–60. The authors of the Plan claimed that one of its distinctive feature was 'the strong emphasis placed on rapidly increasing the developmental effort in East Pakistan.'[128] But differences of opinion arose on the allocation of resources between East and West Pakistan. The Economists' Report on the Draft Plan, which emerged from a conference of leading economists of the country convened by the Planning Board in June 1956, noted that out of the total programme of Rs 9230 million, East Pakistan was allocated Rs 3000 million, West Pakistan Rs 3500 million, and the Centre, including Karachi, Rs 2730 million. The Report, signed by eleven economists including five Bengalis, found that most of the development expenditure of the Centre would be located in West Pakistan, and urged the central government to increase its expenditure in East Pakistan to the maximum possible extent. Unlike the later reports of the panel of economists on successive five-year plans, the Report on the First Plan was given a unanimous colour in its formulation. But the dissatisfaction of the Bengali representatives on the resource allocation to the East Wing comes out clearly when, recognizing the non-availability of feasible schemes and the good intentions of the Planning Board, the Report gives its firm view 'that East Pakistan should be brought to the same level of development as West Pakistan within the shortest possible time.'[129]

As a result of discussions at the levels of politicians and experts, the Planning Board revised the financial allocations, and projects totalling Rs 300 million already received from East Pakistan were included in the Plan and a reserve of Rs 700 million was kept for schemes to be prepared later for various sectors. Eventually, the revised Plan came up for approval before the National Economic Council in February 1957. The attention of the Council was focused on the regional allocation of resources. It noted that in the first two years of the Plan period, actual performance was below the level envisaged in the Five-Year Plan, 'so that reinforced efforts would be needed to achieve the Plan targets in respect of the three year phase.'[130] What emerged from the Council—which was presided over by Suhrawady, and included the Chief Minister, three provincial ministers, and two central ministers of the Awami League—was a higher proportion of allocation to East Pakistan to make up for the lag of the two previous years. But West Pakistan's share was further increased. In the revised Plan for the remaining three years, 1957–60, East Pakistan's share in the total public expenditure was increased from 32 per cent of the total in the draft Plan to 46 per cent, and West Pakistan's share went up from 38 per cent to 48 per cent; the central government's share was reduced from 29 per cent to only 6 per cent of the total public outlay on development.[131] The Council, however, buttressed the inequality of regional allocation by stating that 'no reliable estimate of resources available for development can be made for periods longer than a year', and the annual development programme would be the instrument of continuous review and adjustment of the Plan in the light of availability of resources, feasible schemes, and capacity for implementation.[132] Thus, with a higher share of the total resources than before, the prospect of getting more from the reserve fund, and the opportunity to press its case for higher allocations in the annual development programme, a working agreement on public sector development was arrived at between East Pakistan and the Centre under Prime Minister Suhrawardy.

While the public sector plans were being formulated, discussed, and revised, private enterprise in West Pakistan proceeded to fill the vacuum caused by the migration of Hindus in trade, banking, industry, and other fields. The visible and rapid rate of industrial progress in Karachi and other parts of West Pakistan caused bitterness and heart-burning among the Bengalis. They charged the central government with neglect and deliberate adoption of policies to divert East Pakistan resources for the development of West Pakistan. This charge was not wholly justified. The fact of the matter was that the Bengali middle classes had failed to take advantage of the tremendous opportunities offered by the departure of Bengali Hindu businessmen. They failed to exert themselves to learn new trades, and did not develop entrepreneurial flair as the locals and migrants from India did all over West Pakistan. There was no indigenous capital or enterprise in East Pakistan to set up industries or take over the trade. Yet, when one of the few Muslim business houses, the Ispahanis, which had always had all its interests in Bengal, undertook jute marketing in the difficult circumstances following the non-devaluation decision, one member asked in the East Pakistan Assembly, 'What business have they to come here?'[133] On the other hand, the Chief Minister of East Pakistan complained that he had failed to attract industrialists from West Pakistan to subscribe 51 per cent of the capital in a cotton-spinning mill sponsored by the provincial government, and could not get a technical manager to prepare the project.[134] Another member thought 'that there has been a conspiracy of capitalists not to invest' in the industrial development of East Pakistan.[135] But the xenophobia that was freely expressed by the local leadership from public forums was not conducive to a favourable investment climate. The 'exploitation' syndrome took a violent turn in the killings of the non-Bengali management of the Chandragona Paper Mills, and ethnic rioting in the Adamjee Jute Mills in 1954. The United Front leadership did nothing to create a suitable environment for industrial development. On the other hand, there were no such inhibitions in West Pakistan; Ghulam Muhammad, the Finance Minister, made the point that some people 'brought large sums of money with them [from India]. All that flows here [in West Pakistan] and could have flown also to East Bengal but for the policies adopted by certain Ministers . . .'[136]

The two Wings were one country. Unless they were treated as two economies, industrialization in the first phase had to be, as a matter of survival, on a 'first come first served' basis as far as the issue of sanctions, release of foreign exchange, and choice of location were concerned. East Pakistanis missed the opportunities by not coming forward themselves, and not encouraging 'outsiders' to undertake their development. In the alternative, the logic of the Bengali grievances was two economies and a confederation between the two Wings. In the 1950s it was a bit too early for East Pakistan to seriously press its demands in such stark terms but, looking back, this seems to be the route which the frustrations of the East Wing were taking. Perhaps this might have come about through the constitutional process if it had been allowed to take its normal course.

THE SECOND DECADE 1958–1969

On 7 October 1958 at 10.30 p.m., the President, Iskandar Mirza, issued a Proclamation abrogating the Constitution of 1956, under which he had been elected to the office of the Head of State and which he had sworn to 'preserve, protect and defend'.[137] The Proclamation mentioned the failure of the parliamentary governments to tackle food shortages and smuggling, and referred to the 'irresponsible criticism' of foreign policy, some politicians 'talking of bloody revolution', 'threats and cries of civil disobedience', and 'disgraceful scenes enacted recently in the East Pakistan Assembly'. Without elaborating on his own role in making and unmaking political alignments, the President lamented that he did his 'utmost to work the Constitution in a democratic way', and 'laboured to bring about coalition after coalition, hoping that it would stabilize the administration'. For all these reasons, and because 'traitors and unpatriotic elements . . . [were] attacking the Head of State . . . to achieve their ultimate purpose', the President concluded 'that a vast majority of the people no longer have any confidence in the present system of Government . . .' He declared his intention to 'devise a Constitution more suitable to the genius of the Muslim people,' and to submit it ' to the referendum of the people'.[138]

The abrogation of the Constitution of 1956, and the assumption by the army of the role of the custodian of West Pakistani interests, permanently impaired the East–West political balance. Up to this point, the political leadership of the two Wings could meet and bargain on a level of equality in the national forum of the Parliament. Compromises could be reached through political attrition and lure of offices, if not occasionally also by a sense of realism injected through timely threats by unseen powers working in the background. But henceforth, the nature and direction of national politics would be determined by the diktat of the army leadership. It would lay down neat solutions of complicated problems, and freely resort to coercive measures to mould the muddled polity to its own thinking. The politics of consensus and participation would be at a discount, and free-wheeling debate on national issues would be considered dangerous to the regime, and therefore to the stability of the State. The East Wing would thus be confronted with the formidable combination of the Punjab-dominated army and Punjabi politicians, both having, by and large, the same views about East–West relations. The Constitution of 1956 was a reasonable working document, which all the political parties of East and West Pakistan were willing to give a try through participation in general elections under it. Over time, through the electoral process and political interaction, one could have expected it to continue to reflect compromises on the still unsettled issues of provincial autonomy and One Unit, in the light of the changing political strengths and alignments of the various parties. The point is that no chance was given to the Constitution which it had taken nine years to frame, and the biggest virtue of which was a working acceptance of it by the representative leadership of both East and West Pakistan. The misdemeanours and the failure to solve the inherent economic problems attributed to the politicians, though serious in themselves, were generally of a kind usually found in newly independent countries. The question arises why Iskandar Mirza took the drastic step of abrogating the constitutional process which was on the take-off point through the first general elections. To understand the Proclamation of 7 October, it is necessary to trace the role of the army in the country's politics in the first decade of Independence. This has an important bearing on East–West relations, which went all the way downhill from October 1958 onwards.

* * *

The interaction of the army with the political leadership started with the ill-advised tribal raid to liberate Kashmir in late 1947. The effort failed, but the Maharajah of Jammu and Kashmir got an excuse to accede to India on 26 October 1947, and to invite the Indian forces to take over the State. The Pakistan army, which was still being commanded by British officers at senior levels, was inevitably drawn into the conflict to stop the Indians from overrunning the portions of the State under Pakistani occupation. By November 1948, the Indian army was ready for a general offensive to capture the Pakistan-held areas of Bhimber–Mirpur, Poonch, and Muzaffarabad–Kohala. The General Headquarters (GHQ) submitted alarming assessments to the government of Pakistan of India's capability to achieve its objectives. The fall of Bhimber–Mirpur and Muzaffarabad or Kohala would have given

India the strategic advantage of overcoming the major obstacles of the rivers Ravi, Chenab, and Jhelum, posing a direct threat to the security of Pakistan itself. In July, Nehru informed the British Prime Minister that although they knew of the direct involvement of the Pakistan army in the Kashmir operations, any use of the Pakistan air force would lead to a general war between the two dominions. The British Prime Minister warned Liaquat Ali Khan to desist from bringing the Pakistan air force into action. In case this was done, he informed him, all British officers would be withdrawn from the belligerent dominions, which in the case of Pakistan would have meant a paralysis of the entire armed forces. It thus became impossible to use even the meagre resources available to neutralize the Indian army build-up. Based on the army's own pessimistic appreciations of the military situation, and the political judgement on the prospects of a solution through the United Nations, the government of Pakistan agreed to a cease-fire on 1 January 1949, and an agreement on the demarcation of a cease-fire line was reached in July. That was the end of the UN efforts, but the cease-fire agreement enabled Pakistan to retain the Azad Kashmir territory which was important to buttress the national frontiers of Pakistan.

The Kashmir cease-fire decision, like the subsequent ones in other wars, was criticized in the army circles as ill-timed. The political government was blamed for bungling the operations and then agreeing to the cease-fire. The political leadership was indeed guilty of involving Pakistan in the Kashmir operation by letting loose an indisciplined horde, without sufficient planning and with the national army still commanded by British officers who were not under the orders of the government of Pakistan so far as hostilities with India were concerned. Perhaps a more realistic approach to the two major political parties of Kashmir, rather than entirely depending on the fragmented internal rebellion initiated by one and the tribal raid from Pakistan, would have been a more legitimate and fruitful means for ensuring the accession of Kashmir to Pakistan. However, any suggestion that, after the induction of the Indian forces, the Pakistan army could have withstood the Indian offensive in Kashmir or in the general war was more in the realm of romance than hard realities.

The next encounter of the army with the civilian leadership was in what is generally called the Rawalpindi Conspiracy. It was initiated in July 1949 by Brigadier (later Major-General) Akbar Khan and his ideologue wife. They established contacts with officers of various ranks and in different commands, the Communist Party, and perhaps the Russians. The preparations were interrupted by the deputation of Akbar Khan to a course in the UK in January 1950, but resumed after his return in August. The final meeting of the conspirators was held on 23 February 1951, at the house of Akbar Khan in Rawalpindi, in which he explained the following plan. On the night of 3–4 March, the Prime Minister was expected to be in Rawalpindi. At midnight, Major-General Akbar Khan, who was now the Chief of General Staff, would send a military contingent to arrest the Prime Minister, the Commander-in-Chief, the General Officer Commanding 7 Division Rawalpindi, and a number of other high ranking civil and military officers. Simultaneously, all the Divisional Commanders would be summoned by Akbar Khan to Rawalpindi on the grounds of an emergency. The Karachi operation was to be carried out by Air Commodore Janjua, if necessary, with the help of Brigadier Latif Khan from Quetta. The Prime Minister was to be forced to announce on Radio Pakistan the resignation of his government, and handing over of power to a military council consisting of Akbar Khan as C-in-C army, Janjua C-in-C air force, and the existing naval chief, who was not a collaborator. To cater for failure, arrangements were made to fall back on the base in Hazara Valley, where a nucleus people's army was proposed to be raised, to carry on the revolutionary struggle. In the latter part of February, an inspector of the Criminal Investigation Department of the NWFP police reported the details of the conspiracy to the provincial government, and swift action was taken under orders of the central government to arrest the ringleaders and a large number of civilian and army suspects. Ultimately eleven army officers of the ranks of major-general to captain and four 'revolutionaries', Mrs Nasim Akbar, Faiz Ahmed Faiz, Sajjad Zaheer, and an absconder, Muhammad Hussain Atta, were charged before the Special Tribunal.[139] Sajjad Zaheer was the General Secretary of the Communist Party of Pakistan.[140]

The conspiracy was aimed against the 'corrupt and inefficient civilian government', and not directly related to the setbacks in Kashmir, though that was used in recruiting collaborators, most of whom did not care for the communist ideology. The announcement regarding the conspiracy and the arrest of the army officers, most of whom had fought in Kashmir and were considered heroes in the Punjab, by, the Prime Minister on 7 March created a sensation and a romantic halo round them. In a statement to the Constituent Assembly on 21 March, Liaquat Ali Khan revealed that the plan of the conspirators envisaged the setting up of a government 'patterned on the Communist model, but under military domination.'[141]

Ayub Khan, who had taken over as C-in-C on 17 January 1951, said that his predecessor General Gracey did mention something to him about a 'Young Turk' party in the army, but 'was not very explicit', and only told him that 'there were some peculiar people like Akbar Khan'.[142] General Gracey knew much more than he told Ayub. Brigadier Francis Ingall, Commandant Pakistan Military Academy, who for a while held additional charge of Station Commander Abbottabad, gives this account of what he conveyed to the British C-in-C:

> One day Latif [Brigadier, one of the accused in the conspiracy] invited me to a dinner party at his house . . . [The other guests] were mostly young officers from the front [Kashmir], including a well-known major-general and an air vice-marshal . . . [The conversation] became increasingly political; in fact, some of the sentiments I heard being expressed were downright subversive. Uncomfortably, I turned to my host and told him I would have to leave if this sort of talk continued . . . [and told them] It was my duty as Station Commander in Abbottabad to report such subversion to General Gracey . . . [But Latif insisted that Ingall should stay, saying] 'that no one in authority understands how strongly we feel about the situation in Kashmir—least of all General Gracey. We asked you here tonight so that you would indeed report all you have heard to the Chief' . . . The following morning I went to Rawalpindi to see the Chief, and in my presence he telephoned the PM in Karachi to recount all that I had reported . . . At first the Government's response was restrained. The officers were warned and told not to continue with their plot. But they went ahead just the same.[143]

Ayub in his account of the conspiracy, although critical of the conspirators, is sympathetic to the motives of Akbar Khan in overthrowing the civilian government: 'we had a government which failed to discharge its functions properly . . . Akbar Khan's aim was to establish a tidier form of government'.[144] The event provided a good opportunity to eliminate the officers who were not very enthusiastic about Ayub's appointment: 'We examined the antecedents of officers and got rid of the doubtful ones'.[145] In the general state of suspicion and fear that followed in the army after the discovery of the conspiracy, it was easy for Ayub Khan to carry out these purges and build up a loyal cadre of officers.

The first direct intervention of the army in civil affairs came in March 1953. At the end of February, the religious parties started a movement demanding that the Ahmadis, who claimed to be Muslims, should be declared a minority outside the pale of Islam, they should be debarred from holding high offices of state, and the Ahmadi Foreign Minister, Zafarullah Khan, should be removed. The Objectives Resolution of March 1949, the recommendations of the Report of the Basic Principles Committee presented by Nazimuddin in December 1952 regarding Islamic provisions (they included the setting up of a body of religious scholars to vet the Islamic validity of legislative measures) and the general rhetoric of the politicians about Islam created an atmosphere in which fanatics thrived. Nazimuddin, being a religious man himself, was not willing to take firm timely action against the leaders of the agitation, though he refused to accept their demands. The Punjab Chief Minister, Mumtaz Daultana, not a very religious man, saw an opening for the realization of his higher ambitions in the movement, and actually promoted it. The Punjab government did not prosecute the religious leaders for their unlawful activities and, motivated by narrow political considerations, allowed them a free run of the province to preach and instigate violence. In the absence of firm action at the provincial level, the district officers facing daily the brunt of the anger of frenzied mobs felt unsure of the degree of severity with which punitive measures were to be applied to curb the increasingly militant movement. The Cabinet Secretary, in a report to the Cabinet after visiting the Punjab in the first week of March, agreed with its top administrators that the prevailing civil disorder was the result of the slogan of an Islamic State, which had given undue importance to the *mullahs*, and to the continued weakness of the provincial government in dealing with the agitation. The Prime Minister was paralysed and was sending frantic messages to the Governor-General, who was in Jeddah, to come back.

At 2.30 p.m. on 6 March, the army was asked to take over Lahore. The statement later filed by the central government before the Commission, headed by Chief Justice Muhammad Munir, to inquire into the disturbances, gave an account of the events of the morning of 6 March leading to the decision to impose immediate martial law in Lahore. While the Cabinet was considering the Punjab situation, the Chief Minister rang up the Prime Minister at 11 a.m. and informed him that the situation in Lahore had gone out of control, and that the provincial government wanted to announce acceptance of the demands of the agitators. The Chief Minister asked for immediate approval from the central government for entering into negotiations with the leaders of the movement. He was asked to wait for further instructions. Soon after, at 11.45 a.m., the Governor of the Punjab rang up and, agreeing with the assessment of the Chief Minister about the Lahore situation, hinted that the city might be handed over to the army. Confronted with the situation which both the political head of the provincial administration, the Chief Minister, and the representative of the central government, the Governor, considered beyond their control, the Cabinet directed Iskandar Mirza, the Defence Secretary, to issue instructions to Major-General Azam Khan, the General Officer Commanding, to declare martial law in Lahore, and to the Commander-in-Chief to get ready to do the same in other districts, if later considered necessary. Iskandar Mirza was now in charge of the situation.[146]

The handing over of Lahore to the army and the making of the civil administration subordinate to it brought about a qualitative change in the former's status in national affairs. The political leadership, by its ineffective, irresponsible, and inept handling of the situation, had allowed power to slip away from its hands forever. Martial law continued for some time after the city had come back to normal, and General Azam issued a number of martial law orders, in respect of matters which had nothing to do with his terms of reference to restore peace in Lahore. In the light of subsequent developments, the Lahore martial law looks like a full-dress rehearsal of the country-wide Martial Law of 1958.

The dismissal of Nazimuddin and the nomination of his successor by the Governor-General, rather than by the Muslim League Parliamentary Party, which acquiesced in both the actions, moved the focal point of power to the army which was content to operate, for the time being, through the head of state. The belated attempt of the ruling party in September 1954 to retrieve its position through an amendment in the Interim Constitution Act to curtail the powers of the Governor-General backfired.[147] The dissolution of the Constituent Assembly, the formation of the 'cabinet of talents', the integration of West Pakistan into one unit were all part of the blueprint prepared by Ayub Khan in early 1954.[148] The concept of 'controlled democracy' worked out by Ayub was quite congenial to Ghulam Muhammad and Iskandar Mirza, both of whom in any case depended on army support to keep themselves in power. The Commander-in-Chief had been keeping the political situation under close watch since the Lahore martial law, not yet sure of the right moment to strike. Meanwhile, he tested the ground by joining the reformed cabinet of Muhammad Ali as Defence Minister for a brief period. His direct observation of the lack of depth and moral basis of the political order convinced him that 'the people were completely fed up with the state of affairs and desperately wanted a change'.[149]

There was yet another tussle between the army and the political leadership, this time in East Pakistan. In a meeting held by the Muslim League Prime Minister, Ismail Ibrahim Chundrigar, on 12 December 1957 and attended by the Awami League Chief Minister of East Pakistan and the Commander-in-Chief, among others, it was decided to hand over the ten-mile border belt of East Pakistan to the army to stop the smuggling of essential commodities, particularly rice, to India. The measure, called 'Operation Close Door', was put into effect from 20 December under the overall control of the General Officer Commanding, East Pakistan. The army, navy, and air force were deployed, and all the central and provincial anti smuggling agencies working within a ten-mile border belt were placed under the army. The Chief Minister was reluctant to induct the army, and was particularly against giving it jurisdiction well inside the hinterland up to ten miles. The civilian agencies had special anti-smuggling powers within a five-mile border belt. The army's insistence on controlling ten miles excluded a large part of the province from the control of the civilian government. On 16 December, Firoz Khan Noon had taken over as Prime Minister, at the head of a new coalition which included the Awami League. Soon after the start of the operation, there were allegations of high-handedness and corruption against the army and naval officers employed on anti-smuggling duties. Tensions developed between the civil administration and the army authorities over jurisdiction, and the scant regard of the latter for civil laws. In January 1958, the Prime Minister was faced with serious criticism, within the coalition party, of seizures and searches without proper warrants and other arbitrary actions of the army well inside East Pakistan. Iskandar Mirza strongly supported the army demand for an extended border belt of ten miles. The General Officer Commanding pressed for still greater control over the civilian agencies which he wanted recruited and trained on army lines. Ultimately, in a blaze of public controversy in the provincial Press, and under pressure from the coalition party, the army was withdrawn in April.[150] With the bigger plan of a complete take-over of the country in the offing, the army was not interested in continuing to involve itself in petty bickering with the civilian government.

There were four consequences of the army's interaction with civil affairs as described above. Firstly, in the immediate formative period, the Kashmir dispute, on the battleground and in the United Nations forums, absorbed all the energies of the central government leadership to the neglect of the crucial economic and political problems of East Pakistan. Kashmir was not an issue in which the East Wing felt involved; for the Bengalis it was a far-off and perhaps unnecessary war which was draining their resources. The armed stand-off in Kashmir was inevitably enlarged into a permanent security threat to the whole country; the nation had to find ever-increasing resources to keep pace with the armed strength of its hostile neighbour, both in terms of size and technology. In the first budget of seven months, the defence allocation accounted for 80 per cent of the gross revenues of the central government.[151] In subsequent years, it remained of the order of 55 to 60 per cent on revenue account alone.[152] Including the allocations under capital head and some of the expenditure hidden in civil estimates, the resources pre-empted by defence were a significant proportion of the gross domestic product. In addition, military aid amounting to $ 171 million was received from the United States during the period ending June 1957. But during approximately the same period, only four per cent of the total defence expenditure was being incurred in East Pakistan.[153] The income-generating effect of the location of defence expenditure is a part of the wider controversy of transfer of resources from East Pakistan, which will be discussed later. Here it may be noted that the social and political strains, which manifested themselves in a perpetual state of protests and agitation in East Pakistan, were to a large extent due to extreme poverty and hardships aggravated by the diversion of resources for a non-productive sector. Secondly, the internal resources not being enough to achieve the twin objectives of an adequate deterrence to ensure the territorial integrity of Pakistan and maintain its claim on Kashmir, foreign policy was directed to the search for military aid. In the mid-fifties, at the height of the Cold War, this meant alignment with the anti-Russian policies of the United States in the region. There was a strong reaction in East Pakistan to Western military aid and Pakistan's accession to regional military pacts in order to contain communism. The foreign policy as such, and the commitments involved in the military pacts were never debated or approved by the Parliament. After Liaquat Ali Khan, foreign policy became the preserve of the non-political centres of power dominated by the army. The pro-Western policy never received the support of the people of Pakistan, who did not consider communism or Soviet Russia a threat. Their security concerns related to Indian hostility. The divergent perceptions of security threats of the Western powers and Pakistan, however, coincided in the regional pacts; Pakistan was able to get military aid to meet its security threats, and the United States thought it was arming an ally who would be available in case of its own needs. By 1957, however, the Americans were having second thoughts about the commitments of military aid made in October 1954. In January 1957, President Eisenhower called military aid to Pakistan 'the worst kind of plan and decision we could have made. It was a terrible error, but we now seem hopelessly involved in it'.[154] In December, the US Ambassador in Pakistan reported: 'At the present time Pakistan military expenditure absorbs approximately 65 per cent of the government tax revenues. The drain on the economy is such that US aid . . . only serves to maintain precarious living standards, and it . . . is difficult for the man in the street to appreciate a benefit which has to be measured in almost negative terms.' The military programme, the Ambassador continued, 'is based on a hoax, the hoax being that it is related to the Soviet threat.' The Pakistan 'concentration on India is such that a considerably larger Pakistan arms program would not yield a division for use to the West within the Baghdad Pact area.' Yet, in the same dispatch, after severely criticizing Pakistan's demands for more military aid, the Ambassador cautions against being seen 'withdrawing our support from those elements which . . . are currently our closest friends and supporters', and recommends that 'it is imperative that the review of the Pakistan military establishment be conducted *by and with* Mirza and General Ayub and at all costs *not against them'* (emphasis original).[155] Thirdly, the sheer size and command over resources made the army establishment an autonomous and secretive organization, not open to any scrutiny by the government, Parliament, or public opinion. It thus became a self-reliant institution, capable of taking independent political initiatives.[156] Fourthly, a succession of weak and short-duration prime ministers after Nazimuddin, owing their existence to the non-political head of state, consolidated the status of the army as a distinct and dominant political entity in the person of Ayub Khan. He continued to get extensions in the five-year tenure of his office; the last one was given in June 1958. Cultivating an image of a professional army officer in the British tradition, reluctant to interfere in political matters, and emerging more confident after every political crisis, Ayub Khan acquired the halo of the man on the white charger, waiting for the call to rescue his country from chaos.

* * *

In July 1958, in an all-party conference, which was boycotted by the Muslim League, it was decided to shift the date of general elections from November to 15 February 1959.[157] In West Pakistan, Abdul Qayyum Khan, the Muslim League President, adopted reckless tactics to overawe the government and his opponents. He talked of revolution and rivers of blood, paraded the uniformed national guards in party processions and meetings, and, above all, he made Iskandar Mirza the target of his criticism. The other parties reacted to the threats hurled in the intemperate speeches of Qayyum Khan, and the likely use of a private army of national guards by the Muslim League in the elections. Suhrawardy threatened to organize a uniformed volunteer corps of the Awami League. Accordingly, an ordinance was issued in September, which had the effect of banning the Muslim League national guards.[158] The Muslim League, however, was in no mood to restrain itself. In East Pakistan, the Provincial Assembly was the scene of violence and disgraceful behaviour by the members. On 23 September, the police had to be called into the chamber to control the rioting members. In the free-for-all, the ailing Deputy Speaker was hit by one of the flying objects which were being hurled and reportedly succumbed to injuries received from it.[159]

The political atmosphere, vitiated by violence and the irresponsible utterances of the politicians, was further complicated by the insurrection of the Khan of Kalat in September 1958. Although the Khan had strongly supported the Pakistan movement and had acceded to Pakistan in 1948, he was reported to be actively promoting the Greater Balochistan movement. His contacts with India, Iran, and Afghanistan were known, but his activities posed no serious problem to the government of Pakistan until the end of 1957, when the Commissioner of Kalat started sending disturbing reports of an overt change in the attitude of the Khan and his followers towards the Pakistan authorities. It was reported that the Khan was working for the restoration of Kalat State as a nucleus of Greater Balochistan, outside the Federation of Pakistan. In July 1958, the Khan on his way to Europe stayed with the President, and met the Prime Minister in Karachi. On his return, the movement gathered momentum; the Pakistan authorities were defied and the pro-government tribesmen and their *sirdars* and relatives were instigated to join the Balochi cause. By mid-September the Khan was flying a new flag which was not the recognized old flag of the State, and the region was reported to be in the grip of rebellion. Ultimately, in early October, the Khan and some of his relatives were arrested and the movement died down. The timing of the rebellion did not go unnoticed; it was generally believed that Iskandar Mirza had staged it to justify his Proclamation of 7 October.[160]

The real cause of concern to Ayub Khan and Iskandar Mirza, and to the establishment, was the political trends that had been emerging since the passage of the Constitution in 1956. By the middle of 1958, it was possible to deduce the post-election scenario. In East Pakistan the Awami League under Suhrawardy was expected to sweep the polls; Fazlul Huq was too old, and his party, Krishak Sramik, was without any leadership of stature. The East Pakistan Muslim League had long ceased to be of any consequence, and the extreme leftist parties, including Bhashani's, were too fragmented to put up a credible electoral fight. The

Awami League rank and file were opposed to everything that the establishment stood for; it wanted full regional autonomy, reduction in defence expenditure, a non-aligned foreign policy, and so on. Its leadership was aggressive and less open to the kind of blandishments which worked fairly satisfactorily with Fazlul Huq and his party. The Awami Leaguers represented the new generation of Bengali leadership which did not shrink from talking of secession, if full autonomy and parity in every field were not conceded to East Pakistan. In the budget session of the Constituent Assembly (Legislature) in March 1956, the Bengali members had warned of the consequences of maintaining the *status quo* in East–West relations. The following selected quotations from their speeches will show the extent of the alienation of the Bengali leadership from West Pakistan in the late 1950s.

> East Pakistan is far away from the rest of the country and as such it must have its establishment of army, navy and air force, by which it can face any emergency . . . The major portion of the revenues of the Central Government has been allotted for the defence of the country . . . If the fate of the common man is not improved, what is the good of improving the condition of the armed forces?[161]

> I want a categorical assurance from the Government that some concrete measures will be announced and put into effect for the maintenance of parity . . . [otherwise] a time may come when there may be a parting of ways.[162]

> . . . Pakistan actually came into existence on the voluntary association of the two Wings of Pakistan . . . There cannot be any association or union between two grossly unequal partners . . . some day you will find—it will not take much time—that East Bengal is drifting further away from West Pakistan . . . you cannot starve the people by saying that we must have first our military strong . . . why do you create such situations or conditions for which such a large sum will be necessary [for defence]?[163]

> Let me give this warning in very clear terms that unless . . . you give up this out-moded and exploded theory of defending East Pakistan from West Pakistan, you will lose us and we will all die before you are able to give us any help from here . . . the entire force for the defence

> of East Bengal must be raised within East Bengal and the money you are spending here [West Pakistan] for the purpose of defence must be shared also by the people of East Bengal.[164]

> Probably my friends of West Pakistan think that if any money is spent for the industrial development of East Bengal, the money will go to the winds because some of them think that how long will East Bengal continue with them . . . East Bengal people are politically conscious; they know how to fight and get their rights.[165]

> What justification can they have for East Pakistan to remain in Pakistan if you continue to pursue a policy to the detriment of East Bengal people in questions of defence or industry or commerce . . . If you do not seriously make an attempt to solve this problem, you will have to face a very bad day . . . Muslim League has died in East Pakistan and anybody who might come from East Bengal . . . will not allow you to ignore East Pakistan any more.[166]

The Awami League was expected to win the elections on the emotional slogan of Bengali nationalism which, with all its ramifications, would call for a new set of relationships between the East and West Wings. The political prospects in West Pakistan were no less discouraging. Qayyum Khan was openly criticizing Mirza and drawing considerable crowds in the Punjab and Karachi, where the Muslim League was in a position to win a good number of seats. But if it came into power it was likely to be more radical, and not amenable to the traditional concerns of the existing establishment. In the smaller provinces, the regionalist parties were likely to gain electoral strength on the issue of One Unit. The unanimous block of Bengalis, no matter what party they belonged to, aligned with the radicals and regionalists of West Pakistan, would represent an independent political power not susceptible to extraneous influences. The prospect of Mirza continuing as President of Pakistan, under post-election alignments, was doubtful. Without an effective head of state, who would share its concerns and act as a buffer between it and the politicians, Ayub felt that the army, as an institution, would be subjected to political pressures and regional pulls, and he might find it difficult to obtain sufficient resources to meet its growing requirements.

* * *

In the above context, the American connection was an important factor in the decision to abrogate the constitutional process, which was threatening the pro-West power centre; 'US relationships [are] so important to Pakistanis that complete non-involvement [of the US is] impossible.'[167] As early as January 1955, the US State and Defence Departments were discussing the relative merits of Mirza and Ayub as possible successors to Ghulam Muhammad as Governor-General. The State Department regarded Mirza as 'more competent than General Ayub'. But the Chairman Joint Chiefs of Staff, who had recently visited Pakistan, considered Ayub as 'the best man', and thought that 'as far as honesty and directness is concerned, Mirza was no match for General Ayub.'[168] In March the US intelligence agencies expressed satisfaction that 'political power in Pakistan has been openly assumed by a small group of British-trained administrators and military leaders centring around Governor-General Ghulam Muhammad and his two principal associates, Generals Iskandar Mirza and Ayub Khan . . . [and] Although East Pakistani provincialism will continue to pose serious problems, we do not believe that separation will become a major threat.'[169] In the controversy regarding the quantum and pace of committed military assistance, in June the US Ambassador strongly recommended that the State Department strengthen the position of the 'group who have held power in Pakistan for the past two years [and who] are more favourable to the US and free world interests than any possible alternative in sight.' Although in the new Constituent Assembly, the Ambassador added, the ruling group would retain the 'central position', this was likely to be somewhat diluted because of the need 'to strike a bargain with non-Muslim League elements', and any slow-down in delivery of military hardware 'might seriously impair the ability of the group to influence the Assembly.'[170] In August the US Ambassador was keen that Suhrawardy should join the cabinet of Chaudhury Muhammad Ali, and conveyed the message to Mirza and Suhrawardy; he knew that Suhrawardy was the only political leader who could sell the pro-West policy to the people, particularly in East Pakistan. The Ambassador must have been disappointed, but in the State Department satisfaction was expressed that 'The combination of General Mirza and Chaudhury Muhammad Ali represents a top leadership very friendly to the United States.'[171] When Suhrawardy became Prime Minister in September 1956, he toed the pro-West line. But Mirza was not satisfied and told the American Ambassador and the UK Deputy High Commissioner, in a joint meeting, that the 'government [of Suhrawardy] countenanced constant criticism of the US, and the previous government had not displayed any guts in explaining foreign policy and so far Suhrawardy [was] not doing any better.' Mirza informed the envoys that he had warned Suhrawardy that if he tampered with foreign policy or 'meddled with the military', and 'if Suhrawardy double-crossed him in these respects he, Mirza, too could play dirty and Suhrawardy would have a revolution on his hands.' The diplomats understood that Mirza very much intended to be in control of the country when he told them 'that he [Mirza] hoped our governments would understand if he had [to] take drastic action.'[172] In November 1956, the US intelligence estimate was that the Suhrawardy government might last for six months or more, and 'If Mirza cannot preserve his dominance over the government by ordinary means, he would almost certainly exercise his emergency powers to rule by decree.' The same report considered Mirza's dominance over the government an assurance of 'a modicum of stability.'[173] In May 1957, the US Embassy showed concern over 'recent signs [of] a continuing tendency of Mirza [to] fall back on President's rule as a solution to conditions he considers unsatisfactory.' At this time, Mirza was thinking of dismissing the Awami League government in East Pakistan. The Embassy thought that Presidential rule in East Pakistan would be interpreted as US support for 'Punjab tyranny and victimization [of] their province.' It might also be taken to mean that in Pakistan the representative system could not coexist with expanded military strength. The Embassy wanted to take up the matter with Mirza, but, significantly, the State Department did not agree; it said it 'would prefer at present not to make the suggested representations to Mirza' as it might be construed as interference in the internal affairs of Pakistan.[174]

Both Mirza and Ayub, as 'guardians' of the integrity of the country—which they equated with the army and pro-American policy—considered elections a dangerous exercise in the prevailing political situation, which was rapidly getting out of their control. Ayub gave the impression that he took the initiative and put the President on notice 'to act to save the country from ruination.'[175] According to one source, Mirza held a meeting with Ayub and some other generals at Nathiagali on 22–5 June 1958, to review the political situation. It was decided that in the next three months Mirza would try to bring it under 'control'. Mirza, at the time, planned to bring Muzaffar Ali Qizilbash to head the Muslim Leauge, which manoeuvre, however, failed.[176] Whatever the truth about this meeting, Mirza was not making a secret of his dissatisfaction with the Constitution, the political system, and the politicians. He could not be averse to any suggestion of sweeping away the political process and bringing in army rule, though not in the way it turned out, with his ouster.

* * *

Ayub Khan had prepared a heavy political, economic, and social agenda for rebuilding Pakistan. There were many positive elements in his programme such as the Family Laws, the Indus Basin Treaty, the emphasis on economic development, and a secular approach to social and political issues. The weakness of his regime arose from its defiance of popular opinion, until it was too late. The discussion of the policies and events which have a bearing on East–West Pakistan relations are divided into two distinct periods of the rise and fall of Ayub Khan; the rise from October 1958 to September 1965, and the fall during the subsequent years to March 1969.

I. October 1958–September 1965

Ayub Khan's first priority, as one would expect, was to demolish the old political order and humiliate its practitioners, and then to erect a new power structure for governing the country. Political parties along with representative institutions were abolished by the Proclamation of 7 October itself. Student bodies, because they were politically-oriented, particularly in East Pakistan, came within the purview of the ban on politics. In November, the elected local bodies were also dissolved; any institution with a representative character was suspect in the eyes of the regime. Simultaneously, a number of politicians were detained and charged under security laws and martial law regulations. The main political targets of the military regime were the National Awami Party and the East

Pakistan Awami League; both these parties were committed to the breakup of One Unit, and to regional autonomy and an independent foreign policy. A large number of leftist workers and intellectuals suffered imprisonment and lost their means of livelihood. In East Pakistan, Bhashani and a number of former central and provincial ministers, members of the assemblies, and several other leaders and workers of the Awami League were detained. Most of them were released after a few months. But activists like Mujib and Bhashani remained in detention intermittently.

To create a new order, longer term measures debarring the politicians from staging a comeback were necessary to make place for an apolitical leadership. For this purpose, on 7 August 1959 a comprehensive law, the Elective Bodies (Disqualification) Order, known as EBDO, was issued. Under Article 5 of the Order (a) public servants who had been removed from service on any charge other than inefficiency; (b) persons who had ever been served with an order under the Security of Pakistan Act or a similar law relating to an act prejudicial to the defence, external affairs, or the security of Pakistan; (c) persons found guilty by the Federal Court or High Court or a tribunal under PRODA; and (d) persons convicted of any offence, and sentenced to more than two years imprisonment stood debarred from being candidates or members of an elective body, until 31 December 1966.[177] The sweeping nature of this provision can well be gauged by the fact that a number of repressive laws barring the jurisdiction of the courts had been enacted since 1947 and freely used by the central and the provincial governments against their opponents. It is estimated that about 6,000 persons, half of them from East Pakistan, stood disqualified under Article 5 of EBDO.[178]

The top leadership of the leading parties which escaped the provisions of Article 5 were dealt with under Articles 7 and 8. Under Article 7, any person served with a notice could opt to retire from politics until 31 December 1966, in which case further proceedings against him were dropped. In case this option was not exercised by the respondent, an inquiry would be instituted under Article 8 and, if found guilty, he would be disqualified up to December 1966. Article 5 had considerably reduced the task, and only a small number were left to be dealt with through judicial proceedings. The total number of persons disqualified under

Articles 7 and 8 was only 78: 30 from East Pakistan, of whom 19 opted for voluntary retirement and 11 were adjudged guilty.[179]

Under EBDO, three tribunals were appointed, one for each of the two provinces and one at the Centre, to inquire into cases referred to them by the government. Each of the tribunals was presided over by a judge of the High Court and included two members, one a serving army officer and the other a retired civil officer. For preliminary investigations, to identify the persons against whom references would be made, inquiry committees were set up at the Centre and in the provinces, the former headed by a minister and the latter by the respective martial law administrators, with civil officers as members.[180] The Bengalis disqualified under the three Articles of EBDO included the top Awami League leadership, of whom Suhrawardy and Mujib were the most prominent. There were only a few Muslim Leaguers, and those too not the leading ones. Since it was the government which decided against whom to proceed, and very few of those proceeded against were exonerated by the tribunals, the cleansing process reflected the ideological and personal prejudices of the regime.

Soon after the de-politicization process was set in motion, steps were taken to erect a new constitutional structure. The foundation was laid with the Basic Democracy Order, issued on 7 October 1959, which provided for various tiers of local bodies. The country was divided into single-member units of 1,000 to 1,500 voters (adults, male and female), each one of which was required to elect one member. These units were grouped together to form union councils in rural areas and town or union committees in urban areas. The total number of councillors, called Basic Democrats, was fixed at 80,000—40,000 in each of the two Wings.

The Basic Democracy elections were completed by early January 1960. Ayub Khan, who was astute enough to realize that he had to acquire legitimacy by some kind of popular means, decided 'that before the election results of Basic Democracies were announced, I should take the opportunity of seeking a vote of confidence from the 80,000 Basic Democrats . . .'[181] Accordingly, the Presidential (Election and Constitution) Order 1960 was issued whereby 'if a majority of the votes cast declare confidence in the President', Ayub Khan 'shall be deemed thereby both to have been given authority . . . for the making of a Constitution and also to have been elected President of Pakistan . . . to hold office thence forward and for the first term of the office of the President under that Constitution.'[182] In the ensuing referendum the ballot paper contained only two squares of 'Yes' or 'No'; against 'Yes' was the photograph of Ayub Khan, against 'No', a patch of solid blue. The voting results announced on 15 February 1960 were what they were designed to be: 75,084 for Ayub Khan and 2,829 against him.[183] The Basic Democrats owed their privileged existence to the regime; they could hardly be expected to vote otherwise.

On 17 February, after being sworn in as the 'first elected' President of Pakistan, Ayub Khan appointed a Constitution Commission under Justice Muhammad Shahabuddin of the Supreme Court. The Commission was asked to submit, after examining the 'progressive failure of parliamentary governments in Pakistan', constitutional proposals to secure 'a firm and stable system of government'.[184] The members of the Commission—five from each Wing—were mediocre personalities from business and the legal profession. The Chairman, Justice Shahabuddin, was an eminent judge and known to be a man of high integrity.

The Commission had begun its onerous task in inauspicious circumstances. Two months before it was set up, President Ayub had made clear his views about the future constitutional framework, pre-empting the recommendations of the Commission. It would be a unitary government, with no political parties, no provincial assemblies, only one indirectly elected national assembly, and so on.[185] The responses to the questionnaire of the Constitution Commission, issued in April 1960, evoked controversies. Chaudhury Muhammad Ali's response was a scathing criticism of martial law and the presidential sytem. Similarly, the statements of nine *ulema* and thirteen 'representative' organizations of East Pakistan submitted to the Commission were critical of the military regime. All this material was widely publicized in the Press and for a time it seemed as if the debate would intensify. To contain it, the regime declared public discussion of constitutional proposals an offence and thereafter the Commission conducted its proceedings in camera.

The Commission submitted its Report in May 1961. The scant respect shown by Ayub Khan and other leaders of the regime to the Commission's independent character had adversely affected its credibility among the intelligentsia. Conscious of this popular perception, the Commission, as a 'preliminary point' of the Report, somewhat defensively asserted that the Chairman had accepted office on the distinct understanding that the Commission would be 'unfettered in the due discharge of its functions', and gratefully quoted the assurance of the President that the Commission 'enjoys full freedom and full powers to make such recommendations as it deems proper for the country.' Although tendentious official pronouncements continued to be made, the Report maintained that it had reached its 'conclusions independently, and to the best of our judgement, on the material furnished in the answers to the questionnaire and in the statements made before us.'[186] Going through the Report after thirty years, its methodology appears dubious and its conclusions superficial.

The Commission's methodology of assessing public opinion regarding the system of government consisted of (a) a 35-page questionnaire of 40 questions, including 16 annexures, two of which contained excerpts from the works of English-speaking constitutional experts: not surprisingly only about 6,269 responded to this formidable document out of the 21,000 members of the public to whom it was issued; (b) the oral evidence of 565 persons who appeared for interviews before the Commission; and (c) 'informal discussions with several persons whom he [the Chairman] met socially'.[187] This, and the personal views of the members, were the basis of the Commission's recommendations for the government of a country of 90 million people, 51 to 54 per cent of whom were of the age of 20 years and above.[188]

The detailed recommendations of the Commission are not relevant to this study. The important part is the basic change from the parliamentary to the presidential form of government recommended by it, which coincided with the wishes of the regime. The striking feature of the Report is the superficial discussion of the regional issues which had bedevilled the constitution-making process for nine years. It sought to support its recommendations by the number of responses in their favour in the questionnaire, and by the witnesses. But the Commission's statistical analysis was misleading because it did not indicate the regional breakup of its opinion survey. Thus, for example, it was stated that only 41 per cent of the replies to the questionnaire and 23 out of 229 witnesses questioned on the subject supported a weak Centre with defence, foreign affairs, and currency.[189] But to which region did these witnesses belong? The feelings about One Unit in minority provinces were all too well known, and even in West Pakistan a random sampling could not have given such a result. In East Pakistan, the intelligentsia were unanimous about full regional autonomy. The evidence, such as it was, should have been sifted more carefully by the Commission to determine the regional margin of support for its recommendations. And even on the showing of the Commission's opinion survey, 51 per cent were in favour of a parliamentary system of government.[190] As recommended, the presidential system, in the circumstances prevalent at the time, meant concentration of power at the Centre, in the hands of a West Pakistani, for the coming five years at least: in the provinces, the governors appointed by the President 'shall have, in provincial matters [executive and legislative], powers similar to those of the President subject to the latter's control and directions'.[191] For ten long years the Constitution could not be framed because the Bengalis had demanded full regional autonomy, some times bordering on secession, and representation on population basis, both of which were not acceptable to West Pakistan. After a series of crises, a framework was produced which, with all the defects of a compromise document, represented a working consensus on the system of government. The Commission, after fifteen months of deliberations on highly controversial issues, proposed a system which, instead of synthesizing the positions of the two Wings, denied participation to East Pakistan even to the extent that they had enjoyed under the old order. In so doing, the Commission ignored the principles laid down by itself for the framers of a Constitution: 'One is that the scheme devised should be workable and the other that those for whom it is intended should be prepared to make it work.'[192] History showed that the presidential system fulfilled neither of the two criteria. When it was thrown out by popular agitation, the limited consensus which had been achieved in 1956 was no longer available to build bridges between the two Wings.

Perhaps it is unrealistic to be too critical of the Commission. In the overwhelming atmosphere of military rule, which influenced all institutions of state to varying degrees, one way or the other, it was inevitable that it should reach the conclusions that it did. Ayub was still riding the crest of a wave of popularity and he had made clear his views. Political parties were banned, the political leaders behind bars, or under threat of imprisonment, and public debate on constitutional matters effectively curbed. To be fair to the Commission, however, it may be mentioned that it tried to design a package of checks and balances to mitigate the dangers of the presidential system. It is not necessary for our purpose to go into them, because they were not addressed to the particular concerns of East Pakistan where even an embellished presidential system posed a threat to its autonomy and its participation in the decision-making of the central government.

Ayub 'made detailed comments on its [the Commission's] Report for the guidance of a Committee of the Cabinet' set up under Manzur Qadir, the Foreign Minister and a renowned lawyer, to examine the recommendations.[193] The Bengali Law Minister, Muhammad Ibrahim, withdrew from the proceedings of the Committee and stayed back in Dhaka.[194] Ultimately, after long deliberations and occasional acrimonious internal debates, the Constitution was promulgated on 1 March 1962. The constitutional structure that finally emerged revolved round the President. All executive authority was vested in him. He was given wide financial powers. He appointed his own Council of Ministers; the Defence Minister was to be a person who had held the rank of Lieutenant-General, or its equivalent in the Navy or Air Force, unless the portfolio was held by the President himself. The provincial governor and his council of ministers were to be appointed by the President, as indeed were all the other key officers of the State. The ministers were not members of the central or provincial legislatures. The President could remove the governors and ministers for misconduct, and initiate proceedings to disqualify them from holding public offices. The President and the members of the National and Provincial Assemblies were to be elected by the electoral college of Basic Democrats. All legislation passed by the National Assembly required the assent of the President who, in case of persistent differences, could refer the issue to a referendum of the electoral college. The President could also dissolve the National Assembly. The Constitution provided only one list of subjects for legislation by the National Assembly, leaving the residuary powers to the provincial legislatures. But the National Assembly could legislate on all matters, if the national interest so demanded, in relation to the security of Pakistan including the economic and financial stability of the country; planning or co-ordination; or the achievement of uniformity in respect of any matter in different parts of Pakistan. Whether such a national interest had emerged was to be determined by the President. Propounding his views on 'the nation's propensities to chaotic politics', Ayub Khan advised the people of Pakistan: 'Here are some of my ideas on the [Constitution] which have in them the fire of my heart; give them a trial for your own good.'[195]

After the initial stunning effect of martial law, political activities had re-emerged in various forms. In East Pakistan, the two main student organizations, the Students League and the Students Union, backed by the Awami League and the National Awami Party respectively, were used as vehicles of protest by their principals. On 30 January 1962, Suhrawardy was arrested in Karachi, on his return from a tour of East Pakistan, for 'anti-state activities.'[196] In East Pakistan the arrest was followed by province-wide student riots during February and March of 1962. Mujib and other Awami League leaders were arrested. In the middle of April, Dhaka University was closed down. The student demands now covered not only the repeal of the objectionable clauses of the University Ordinance, which was the original cause of unrest, but also political matters like the release of political detenus and, significantly, a guarantee of civil liberties.[197] These demands were supported by the Dhaka High Court Bar Association and the intelligentsia in general.

As a prelude to constitutional rule, elections to the National and Provincial Assemblies were held in April–May. In spite of the constitutional prohibition on any association of political parties with the elections, many old politicians, not disqualified by EBDO, and relatives of those who were, participated in them. The pressure to revive political parties was exerted from all directions in the very first meeting of the National Assembly on 9 June. To pre-empt any embarrassing move by the opposition, an official Political Parties Bill was drafted on 30 June. It was introduced in the National Assembly and passed into Act on 14 July. The Opposition staged a walkout as a protest against its restrictive provisions.[198]

The major political elements of East and West Pakistan rejected the political framework of Ayub Khan and initially refused to revive the parties under it. The leaders of the two Wings became united on the common demand for the restoration of democracy in the country. On 24 June, nine prominent Bengali leaders, including the disqualified ones, representing such diverse political parties as the Muslim League, Krishak Sramik Party, the Awami League, Nizam-i-Islam, and the National Awami Party issued a manifesto demanding a constituent assembly elected on the basis of adult franchise to frame a Constitution. They opposed the revival of political parties because 'under the Constitution of 1962 there was no room for political activity' and the 'real leaders of the people [EBDOed politicians] had been debarred from "joining" the political parties'.[199] Suhrawardy, after his release from detention on 19 August, persuaded thirty-five party leaders, including nineteen from East Pakistan, representing the whole spectrum of politics, to meet at Lahore in September to chalk out a common objective. In the meeting, while there was a difference of opinion on the revival of parties, a consensus was reached on the single objective of democratization of Ayub's Constitution, by suitable amendments, to be pursued from a common platform. The extreme positions of a constituent assembly to frame a new Constitution and the breakup of One Unit pressed by the delegates of the smaller provinces of West Pakistan were avoided. On 5 October, Suhrawardy announced the formation of the National Democratic Front (NDF), which called itself a 'movement', and not a political party.[200]

The political ferment created by the alliance of opposition forces and the revival of the Jamaat-i-Islami and other political parties, all demanding restoration of democracy, led the Ayub regime to take containment measures. The public meetings of Suhrawardy and other NDF leaders organized at Lahore and Gujranwala to mobilize public opinion were disrupted by the police and its hirelings. The Press, a substantial segment of which had been brought under direct government control, was used to discredit the National Democratic Front as communist-inspired and subversive. More effective were the two Ordinances issued on 8 January 1963, designed to confuse the NDF leadership; one provided for appeal by the EBDOed politicians to the President for waiving their disqualification, and the other amended the Political Parties Act to include the Front within the definition of a political party, which debarred the EBDOed politicians from any kind of association with it. 'The government also announced that twenty-one persons had applied for pardon, but it did not divulge the names. All this created such a stink that the government did not dare to place the ordinance before the legislature for confirmation and it lapsed.'[201] The rumours about leaders who had asked for pardon served the government purpose of creating distrust among the political leadership, and of destroying reputations.

The other measure, that of treating the National Democratic Front as a political party, served its purpose of preventing the EBDOed politicians of East and West Pakistan from coming together. On 27 and 28 January 1963, simultaneous meetings of the NDF were held at Karachi and Dhaka. All the major parties of East Pakistan, including the Muslim League, which was not revived in East Pakistan, decided to continue to operate from the platform of the Front and to set up a committee to organize it at the district and lower levels. The Karachi meeting took a dramatic turn, and was termed as a 'conspiracy' by the government which prosecuted the participants for sedition.[202] The regime's strategy was to deny a common forum to the politicians of East and West Pakistan, keep West Pakistan free from political activities, and allow East Pakistan leaders a certain latitude within their own province. The Nawab of Kalabagh, Governor of West Pakistan, applied standard feudal tactics to harass the opposition by prosecuting its leaders on flimsy grounds and reinforcing the pressure by such informal misuse of state power as disruption of their public meetings by the police, intimidation of the owners of printing presses, forcing them not to print opposition newspapers, etc.[203] In East Pakistan, his counterpart Monem Khan gave the same treatment to the opposition but methods were somewhat modified to suit the local culture. Both the Governors enjoyed the full confidence of Ayub.

The regime's measures to prevent the emergence of a grand national alliance through a formal organization of the partyless National Democratic Front were largely successful. But this was not the only reason for the Front's fade-out. There were internal differences among the politicians, whether the alliance should be of the properly constituted political parties or individual political leaders. Suhrawardy's argument that the parties would find it difficult to agree to a common national programme had some merit but was also self-serving. The EBDOed leaders would have had no place in the parties; in their individual capacity in the partyless alliance, although hit by the amended Political Parties Act, they would still be the leaders of the defunct parties. On the other hand, he was proved right when, on their revival, the political parties, particularly those of East Pakistan, shed their national character and became champions of provincial interests. Suhrawardy's departure for Europe in March for medical treatment removed from the scene the only national leader of stature who could have held the East and West Pakistan politicians together in a workable national alliance. The dominating view of West Pakistan was in favour of revival of parties, and some of them, like the Council Muslim League and Jamaat-i-Islami, had already been revived; others were on the verge of it. In July–August, in East Pakistan the Awami League, the National Awami Party, Krishak Sramik Party, and the Muslim League discussed their merger into a new formally-constituted National Democratic Party. But Suhrawardy saw too many difficulties of programme and leadership in the formation of a new party of such diverse and antagonistic elements. The National Democratic Front continued to remain the focal point of political activities in East Pakistan, where it became more a provincial organization than the organ of the national forum envisaged by Suhrawardy.[204]

But tensions were building up among the East Pakistan parties over the lead, which each one was trying to take from the other. Mujib was getting restive and wanted to revive the East Pakistan Awami League to propagate the party's own programme; to Suhrawardy he expressed 'doubts that national unity and national integration will solve the problems of East Pakistan.'[205] Suhrawardy died on 5 December. Mujib now succeeded in persuading the Working Committee to revive the East Pakistan Awami League, which was done towards the end of January 1964. He became the General Secretary and the driving force of the party. In a meeting on 25 January, the party demanded provincial autonomy with only defence, foreign affairs, and currency with the Centre, under a federal parliamentary system, direct elections on adult franchise basis, and the repeal of EBDO.[206] In June, an eleven-point manifesto was formulated which, in addition, called for long-term planning based on two economies of East and West Pakistan to remove disparity.[207] The party launched a vigorous campaign through meetings, demonstrations, and extensive tours to mobilize public opinion. Ayub's response to the Awami League's militant nationalism was detention and prosecution of Mujib and some other leaders under various laws, at frequent intervals, and generally restricting their activities.

The National Awami Party was a loose organization of leftists and provincialists which had been formed in 1957 mainly by the dissident Awami Leaguers of East and West Pakistan. In East Pakistan, Bhashani was the moving spirit of the party. He had joined the National Democratic Front, although his support for the movement had become lukewarm after meeting Ayub and leading a semi-official delegation to China in the latter half of 1963. In February 1964, under pressure from the revivalist groups of East and West Pakistan, the party decided to revive itself. In July, the party issued a thirty-six point manifesto which included demands for full regional autonomy, leaving only defence, foreign affairs, and currency with the Centre, dissolution of One Unit, and restoration of the previous boundaries of West Pakistan provinces, direct elections on adult franchise basis, independent foreign policy, etc.[208]

The dynamics of constitutional rule had compelled Ayub Khan himself to overcome his aversion of political parties. In September 1962, his civilian ministers sponsored a convention of political workers and leaders of the old Muslim League at Karachi, and out of it emerged a splinter party, which came to be called the Convention Muslim League. Efforts were made by Ayub Khan's supporters to win over the front-rank Leaguers, but most of them stayed away from the regime and formed a parallel organization, called the Council Muslim League, under the presidentship of Nazimuddin. In May 1963, Ayub Khan formally joined the Convention League, which had been shaped under his advice, and in December he accepted its presidentship. The office-bearers of the party were nominated from the ranks of political adventurers and retired bureaucrats of dubious antecedents who depended entirely on the support of the administration for party work, and who derived immense benefits from their positions. There were tussles between the Governors' favourites and the central party leadership. Ayub Khan himself never took the party very seriously; he made no secret of his faith in his own charisma and state power exercised principally through his two ruthless Governors.[209]

The adverse effect of the revival of parties on the National Democratic Front, as a body representing all shades of opinion, became apparent when the government presented the Electoral College Bill in the National Assembly in March 1964. Although all parties were against indirect elections through the electoral college of Basic Democrats as proposed in the Bill, they failed to mobilize themselves on the common forum of the NDF. In East Pakistan the revived parties, the Awami League, the National Awami Party, and Nizam-i-Islam Party formed an *ad hoc* body called the All-Party Committee of Action for Adult Franchise and Direct Elections. But in the absence of a common forum of all political elements of the two Wings, the protest failed to make any impression and the ruling party easily weaned away the opposition members to obtain a two-thirds majority to pass the Bill in the National Assembly.

The forthcoming elections for the basic democracies (electoral college), the President, and the Assemblies, again galvanized the opposition leaders to join together to confront the regime on the minimum programme of restoration of democracy. In July, representatives of the Council Muslim League, the Awami League, the National Awami Party, Nizam-i-Islam Party, and Jamaat-i-Islami met at Dhaka and formed an alliance called the Combined Opposition Parties (COP). The East and West Pakistani leaders of these parties, all properly constituted with their own manifestos, agreed on a nine-point programme, which included the demands for a democratic Constitution and 'provincial autonomy, consistent with the integrity of Pakistan, with parity at the Centre.' The National Awami Party agreed not to press the controversial issues of One Unit and independent foreign policy for the sake of unity. The regional autonomy demand was also expressed in mild terms in the manifesto.[210]

* * *

The Presidential election of 1965 was the first challenge Ayub faced from the political forces of the country. The opposition sprang a surprise on the regime by nominating Miss Fatima Jinnah, sister of the Quaid-i-Azam, as its presidential candidate. Ayub Khan, who was expecting a walk-over in the elections because of the absence of a credible opposition candidate suddenly faced a mass upsurge in favour of Miss Jinnah. In a direct election based on adult franchise, there is no doubt Miss Jinnah would have won both in East and West Pakistan. Even in the 80,000 strong electoral college, she probably would have won if the elections had been held under a neutral administration. The immense influence of the district administration over the Basic Democrats, and the extensive use of government resources in the election campaign proved decisive in ensuring Ayub's success in the presidential election held on 2 January 1965.

Though Ayub's supporters did not realize it at the time, the victory left a deep scar on the credibility of the President. The pre-election campaign had initiated the typical syndrome of the emperor having no clothes. The contest was bitter and the politicians, for the first time, openly said what they thought of Ayub and his system. The long processions and mammoth meetings of the opposition were more spontaneous, in public eyes, than those of Ayub Khan.[211] In any case, the votes obtained by Miss Jinnah, 47 per cent in East Pakistan, 26 per cent in West Pakistan, and 36 per cent of the total valid votes polled, were not such as to sustain the larger-than-life image of Ayub cultivated during the previous seven years.[212] The fact that Ayub expressed satisfaction on getting only 63 per cent of the votes was indicative of how serious the challenge from the opposition candidate was.[213]

In a post-election analysis of voting, the Ministry of Information identified the anti-regime sectors of public opinion: they were the refugees of Karachi, minority communities, industrial labour, and those who genuinely believed in civil rights and democracy. In a meeting held by Ayub Khan on 17 January, attended, among others, by the two Governors, his advisers attributed the poor showing to the conduct of officials and of those who enjoyed the financial patronage of the government. Typically, it did not occur to any one to highlight the dissatisfaction of East Pakistan, expressed through 47 per cent negative votes against the regime, and the need to give serious thought to this message. The decision that followed was, therefore, more of the same: further checks of the loyalty of the officials and of those enjoying government patronage.[214]

The defeat of Miss Jinnah led to the disintegration of the COP. In East Pakistan, it entered into an electoral alliance with the National Democratic Front for elections to the National and Provincial Assemblies. The opposition managed to win only a small number of seats; in the National Assembly, the constituents of the COP formed an 18-member United Parliamentary Party under the leadership of Nurul Amin. Similar parliamentary parties were formed in the Provincial Assemblies. In all cases the number was too small to make any impact on the government.[215]

* * *

Ayub Khan's exhortations to eschew provincialism and politics—the two being synonymous to him—initially applied to all national problems. His analysis of East Pakistani politics, unfortunately, never went beyond the usual West Pakistani theory of conspiracy of communists and Indian agents. But he showed a better understanding of the Bengali economic grievances and, in meeting them, overruled the West Pakistan establishment. What he failed to appreciate was that the logic of East–West Pakistan relations demanded the resolution of both the economic and the political issues. The result was that although Ayub Khan did more for the economic development of East Pakistan than any previous government, this had no impact on Bengali grievances. A lesser effort in a genuine participatory political process would have led to much more goodwill between the two Wings.

The burning economic question was the disparity in the per capita incomes of East and West Pakistan in the latter's favour, and its widening trend. The panel of economists on the Second Five Year Plan had worked out the per capita money income of West Pakistan at about 30 per cent higher than that of East Pakistan in 1957–8.[216] Mahbubul Haq, who was a member of the panel, subsequently estimated the disparity at 18 per cent in 1951–2; it had widened to 29 per cent in 1959–60. The visible difference in the living standards in the two Wings, however, was greater than indicated by relative money incomes because of the higher purchasing power of a rupee in West Pakistan. Adjusting for lower prices in West Pakistan in respect of certain basic commodities, Haq put the real income disparity between West and East Pakistan as high as 60 per cent in 1959–60. With adjustments over a wider range of commodities, he maintained, it might be higher still.[217]

The Bengalis argued that the widening disparity was due to a higher rate of investment in West Pakistan, made possible by the exchange control and import licensing policies of the central government. All foreign exchange earned by Pakistani nationals had to be surrendered to the central government at the official rate, which was lower than the free market price; all imports were licensed at the official rate, without specifying the destination. During the period 1948–60, East Pakistan exported more than it imported and the surplus foreign exchange was utilized in West Pakistan, which imported more than it exported. In terms of rupees, the East Pakistanis got less than the market price of foreign exchange. But the West Pakistanis earned windfall profits by using the overvalued foreign exchange for imports. On the other hand, East Pakistan imported more from West Pakistan than it exported to it and paid higher prices for West Pakistani manufactured goods than the international prices because of the tariff protection to local industries. Over the decade, East Pakistan enjoyed a net surplus, taking both international and interregional trade into account; this net surplus, it was argued, represented the transfer of real resources to West Pakistan. According to a Ministry of Finance study, from 1948–9 to 1959–60, this net surplus amounted to Rs 1,730 million.[218] The report of the Bengali members of the Finance Commission, described later, multiplied it to Rs 2,600 million to reflect the free market value of foreign exchange.[219] Haq's estimate of this transfer of real resources was about Rs 210 million per annum in the pre-First Plan period and Rs 100 million in the First Plan period.[220]

More important than the transfer of East Pakistan's own resources was the allocation of a major share of foreign aid and loans to West Pakistan. Of the total developmental aid (including US Technical Assistance) of Rs 5,420 million up to June 1960, 62 per cent was allocated to West Pakistan, 17 per cent to East Pakistan, and 21 per cent was unallocable to the regions.[221] Assuming 'that the distribution of foreign aid and loans, and foreign exchange reserves should have been equal in the two regions on a per capita basis', Haq estimated that, all told, the annual implicit transfer of resources was of the order of 4 to 5 per cent of East Pakistan's income to West Pakistan, and this rate of transfer increased during the First Plan period.[222]

The effects of this influx of outside resources in West Pakistan were reflected in the investment levels of the two Wings. In the public sector, during the period 1947 to 1960, the central and provincial development expenditure in East Pakistan was roughly 24 per cent of the total, and on an average 75 per cent of the total investments of semi-autonomous bodies were located in West Pakistan.[223] In the private sector, during the same period, capital issues in West Pakistan amounted to Rs 3,030 million, as against Rs 850 million only in East Pakistan;[224] during the period 1951 to 1960, 72 per cent of the total import of machinery on private account was in West Pakistan.[225]

The official debate on interregional economic issues during Ayub's regime started from the panel of economists set up to advise the Planning Commission, on the Second Five Year Plan (1960–5). The Bengali members on the panel were the old generation moderate economists who had been representing East Pakistan on the expert bodies of the central government since the early 1950s. The Report of the panel, submitted in August 1959, following past practice, termed itself 'unanimous', but its section on regional balance brought out deep differences. The West Pakistanis asserted that, taking into account the contribution for the maintenance of the central government and defence expenditure, surplus on interregional trade, and net supply of services such as banking, insurance, etc., there had been a net transfer of resources from West to East Pakistan.[226] The Bengali members enumerated past neglect and the rising trend of economic disparities. Agreeing with both the views, the panel recommended 'that the Government *must* commit itself to maintaining at least a certain minimum rate of growth in *each region*' (emphasis original).[227] To achieve this aim, 'some sacrifice of the rate of growth in West Pakistan' would be necessary and 'the present form of federal government has to undergo a change'.[228] This was a long way from the defensive approach of the same Bengali economists in the panel on the First Five Year Plan when they had emphasized 'that the rate of development in West Pakistan should [not] be slowed down to enable East Pakistan to catch up with West Pakistan'.[229]

Ayub Khan's initial approach to economic development ignored interprovincial issues. It was reflected in the Second Five Year Plan (1960–5) which, unlike the First Five Year Plan, made no specific mention of East Pakistan in the discussion of its objectives, size, and strategy. Interwing disparity was relegated to the last chapter of the Plan document as a side issue, at par with the less developed areas of West Pakistan. Its authors considered inequalities inevitable 'during the earlier phases of economic growth' and, rather offhandedly, concluded that it was neither possible to lay down achievable growth rates in the two provinces, nor 'to predict an equalization of income levels between the two provinces, or project a precise reduction in their income disparity over a given period'.[230] Accordingly, no East–West breakup of allocations was given in the original Plan approved in June 1960 or in its revised estimates approved in June 1961.

In August 1961, the Ministry of Finance, under the direction of the President, prepared a study summarizing the available data on 'Comparative appraisal of the economic progress made in East and West Pakistan since Independence', and on 'certain aspects of interwing economic relationships'. The study, entitled 'Report on Economic Relations between East and West Pakistan', concluded that the national income estimates of the Central Statistical Office did 'not provide an adequate basis for judging the rate of growth in the two Wings. But, in its 70 pages with sixteen annexures covering another 107 pages, the Report produced an impressive breakdown of East–West figures in respect of agriculture, industry, public finance, foreign aid, balance of payments, interwing trade, and the movement of capital. All indicators showed that East Pakistan had not received its fair share of national resources and was lagging behind West Pakistan because of this.[231] The Report confirmed what had been so far only *ad hoc* or intuitive judgements of economic disparities. It was not published but became an internal source document for official debates.

On 18 October 1961, in a speech at Dhaka, Ayub referred to the 'feeling prevalent in East Pakistan that there had been less development there than in West Pakistan', and conceded that to some extent the complaint was justified. He promised that 'to make up the leeway', the development in East Pakistan would be accelerated, and announced the setting up of a Finance Commission to determine an equitable allocation of resources between the two provinces.[232] The ten-member Commission was notified on 19 December. It concluded its acrimonious deliberations on 16 January 1962, with three dissenting reports—the Chairman's Report, the West Pakistani Report, and the Bengali Report.[233]

The Bengali Report based its recommendations on the particular terms of reference which asked the Commission to recommend 'the principles which should govern the allocation to the Provinces of resources at the disposal of the Centre, . . . keeping particularly in view the requirements of planned economic development'. 'Planned economic development' was interpreted to mean the removal of disparity within a time-frame. To achieve this objective, it was demanded that the developmental resources, comprising foreign and domestic loans and foreign grants, including technical assistance, as well any savings from non-developmental expenditure, should be distributed between East and West Pakistan on the basis of population, weighted by the inverse ratio of per capita income. Assuming a disparity of 25 per cent, the allocation for East Pakistan was worked out at 67.5 per cent of the total developmental resources. Regarding non-developmental resources of taxes, it was recommended that the provincial shares be divided on the basis of population. A point was also made of income and employment benefits resulting from central government expenditure, of which only about one-fifth was being incurred in East Pakistan. Constitutional guarantees were asked for (a) for the removal of interwing disparity in 25 years; (b) for the suggested formulae of allocation of resources; and (c) for an annual and five-yearly full-scale review of the progress of the achievement of these objectives.

Both the West Pakistan Report and the Chairman's Report opposed the Bengali demands. The former thought that since the allocation of resources had to be related to the development plans approved by the government from time to time, 'it would be inappropriate for the Commission to specifically indicate any particular ratio in which the resources should be distributed between the two Wings'. The latter recommended postponing the issue to the Third Plan period for which a new Finance Commission was likely to be set up, after the promulgation of the new Constitution but before the close of the ongoing Plan period.

The Report of the Finance Commission of 1962 was a landmark in the polarization of East and West Pakistan relations at the official level. The Bengali representation in the Commission was dominated by the new generation of civil servants and academics. The key departments in the provincial government were headed by Bengali CSP officers of middle seniority who had gained the experience and confidence to press their point of view in the forums of the central government against their senior West Pakistani colleagues. A number of Bengali economists, with doctorates from American universities, were serving in various semi-governmental institutions. In the absence of political representation, the economic leadership of East Pakistan had been taken over by these professionals who influenced the decision-making of the central government and provided intellectual input in the formulation of the Six Points of the Awami League.[234]

To neutralize the growing political pressure from East Pakistan, Ayub took some positive measures in the economic field. In the first half of 1962, the three central statutory bodies responsible for industries, railways, and water and power, which together accounted for a major portion of central government development expenditure, were bifurcated and placed under the two provincial governments; they were the Pakistan Industrial Development Corporation, the Pakistan Railway Board, and the Water and Power Development Authority. The provincial governments were handed over all the development projects of these bodies located in their territories. The provincial governments were also delegated enhanced powers for sanctioning development schemes. Following the Finance Commission Report, East Pakistan's demand for the assignment of central tax revenues on the basis of population was conceded; under the new arrangements effective from 1 July 1962, 54 per cent of the divisible pool, consisting of 70 per cent of sales tax (30 per cent to be distributed on incidence basis) and the total amount of other taxes and duties, was allocated to East Pakistan. Under the old arrangements, the entire amount generated from sales tax was shared on incidence basis and, in other tax revenues, East Pakistan's share was 45 per cent.[235]

To further placate the Bengalis, the disparity issue was given explicit recognition in the new Constitution promulgated on 1 March 1962, and effective upon the withdrawal of Martial Law from 8 June. According to Article 145 of the Constitution, the primary object of financial, commercial, and economic policies, and economic development was removal of per capita income disparities between the provinces; the national resources (including foreign exchange) were accordingly to be 'used and allocated in such manner as to achieve that object in the shortest possible time'. The National Economic Council was required to submit a report every year to the National Assembly 'on the results obtained and the progress made in the achievement' of this objective; under Article 144, the National Finance Commission was required to submit a five-yearly report on the same subject. The constitutional commitment to the removal of disparity was not confined to the one-time formulation of five-year plans; it was to govern the ongoing economic management of the country.

In pursuance of this guideline, the share of East Pakistan in public sector development expenditure rose from 26 per cent in 1949–50 and 36 per cent in 1959–60 to 50 per cent in 1963–4.[236] In 1964–5, for the first time, the gross budget allocations of Rs 2,050 million for East Pakistan were higher than the Rs 1,950 million for West Pakistan; in addition, East Pakistan was allocated Rs 250 million for its rural works programme as against Rs 150 million for West Pakistan.[237] A number of other measures were taken to accelerate development in East Pakistan; the import duty on machinery and spare parts was 7.5 per cent in East Pakistan compared to 12.5 per cent in West Pakistan; practically the whole of East Pakistan enjoyed a tax-holiday for periods of between four to six years as against two to four years in West Pakistan; and the import of cement from West Pakistan was liberally subsidized.[238] As a result of these deliberate measures, the annual compound rate of growth in East Pakistan, during the period 1959–60 to 1964–5, rose to 5.4 per cent, as against 5 per cent in West Pakistan, and compared to 1.9 per cent during the preceding ten years.[239] Yet, on average, the disparity in per capita incomes during the Second Plan period, according to the May 1966 Report on Inter-Regional Disparities, remained the same as it was in 1959–60. This, and the subsequent Reports of 1967 and 1968, could only defend the government by pointing out that the widening trend had been contained.[240]

II. September 1965–March 1969

The Third Five Year Plan (1965–70) was released in June 1965, in the euphoric atmosphere of the successful implementation of the Second Plan. It was formulated within the framework of the 20-Year Perspective Plan, which aimed at quadrupling the gross national product and doubling the per capita income of 1964–5 in 1984–5. It was also planned that parity in the per capita income of the two provinces should be achieved by 1984–5. Anisur Rahman, the Harvard-educated Bengali economist and a propounder of the two-economies thesis, lauded the Third Plan as 'the first plan where the problem of regional disparity has found a precise quantitative expression' and which highlighted 'the need for bold and positive steps to boost private investment in East Pakistan'.[241] It was indeed a bold and imaginative document, projecting an increase of 40 per cent in the regional income of East Pakistan, and 35 per cent for West Pakistan (compared with the actual growth of 30 and 28 per cent respectively in the Second Plan). To meet the physical targets to achieve this growth, out of the total Plan outlay of Rs 52,000 million (Rs 30,000 million public and Rs 22,000 million private), East Pakistan was allocated Rs 27,000 million (Rs 16,000 million public and Rs 11,000 million private).[242]

The basic assumptions of the Third and Perspective Plans were 'continued availability of foreign assistance on an expanding scale and the ability of the country to convert a substantial part of additional incomes into resources for development.' The Indo-Pakistan war in September 1965 shattered both these expectations. Foreign assistance declined by 25 per cent, and defence expenditure claimed Rs 5,500 million more than the Plan projection as a result of this war, and the subsequent need for replacing free equipment under US military assistance. The fall-out of the ill-advised war was heavier on East Pakistan than on West Pakistan. The average annual growth of the gross provincial product of East Pakistan during the Plan period (1965–6 to 1969–70) was a mere 4 per cent, which was not only much below the Plan target of 7 per cent but even less than the Second Plan period. West Pakistan, however, in spite of being the war zone exceeded the target growth rate—6.4 per cent against 6 per cent. The explanation for this phenomenon lay in (a) the distribution of reduced developmental resources between Plan and non-Plan public sector programmes; and (b) private investment. The Plan size of the public sector development expenditure was reduced by 30 per cent and, within the reduced amount, the share of East Pakistan was kept at 52 per cent of the total as had been envisaged. But the expenditure on the Indus Basin Works, which was outside the Plan, was kept intact; including this item in West Pakistan's allocation, the share of East Pakistan came down to about 45 per cent of the total public sector expenditure. In addition, 74 per cent of the private investment during the Plan period took place in West Pakistan. The total investment size (public and private) in East Pakistan during the Third Plan period thus amounted to only 38 per cent of the total. Whatever the explanation, the natural result of this pattern of allocation of national resources was a worsening in East–West per capita income disparity from 36.40 per cent in 1964–5 to 45.60 per cent in 1969–70.[243]

* * *

The impact of the war on East–West political relations was more immediate and no less disastrous. The decision to escalate the armed confrontation with India by sending infiltrators to Indian-occupied Kashmir was a purely West Pakistan decision. East Pakistan was inclined to improve relations with India in order to reduce the defence burden, and had never felt strongly about Kashmir. The war sharpened East Pakistan's sense of vulnerability and isolation in case of an external threat. The Bengalis had always had serious reservations about the defence policy which maintained West Pakistani domination in the armed forces, and deployed the bulk of them on the western fronts. During the budget debate in the National Assembly in March 1956, this policy was strongly criticized by the Awami League and other Bengali members.[244] In December 1956, the Awami League Chief Minister had protested against a statement of the Commander-in-Chief that East Pakistan could not be adequately defended. But Suhrawardy, as Prime Minister, presumably after getting a clarification from Ayub Khan, informed the Chief Minister that what the Commander-in-Chief had meant was that the strategic defence of East Pakistan rested on the Lahore front; 'If that holds, East Pakistan is safe as it has remained so far.' The persistent demand of Bengalis for the location of naval headquarters in East Pakistan was also not accepted by the armed forces for 'administrative reasons'.[245] The weakness of this national strategy was exposed by the war. The Lahore front was held by the skin of the teeth. The widely-held view, both in West and East Pakistan, was that it was the Chinese threat to activate the Sino-Indian border that checked the Indians from taking advantage of the defencelessness of the East Wing.

All the political parties condemned the Indian aggression and supported the war efforts during its duration. But differences in the security and political perceptions of the two Wings re-emerged in the aftermath of a controversial cease-fire and the peace agreement signed with India at Tashkent on 10 January 1966. The exaggerated claims of success against India propagated by the official channels did not match with the government's acceptance of a cease-fire without achieving the war aim of liberating Kashmir. The Tashkent Declaration led to widespread protests by the students and all the political forces of West Pakistan. But it was welcomed by the political leaders of East Pakistan, including Mujib and Bhashani, and by the Bengalis in general. On 5 February, on the initiative of the West Pakistani opposition parties, an All-Pakistan National Conference of Opposition parties was held at Lahore to discuss the Tashkent Declaration. Mujib called for peaceful settlement of international disputes and demanded full autonomy, on the basis of the Pakistan Resolution, which he interpreted in terms of the Six Points for East Pakistan.[246] The West Pakistani leaders refused to discuss the Six Points and, in protest, Mujib withdrew from the conference.

The Six Points summarized the long-standing grievances of the Bengalis. There was nothing new in them; they were the same that had been made as far back as 1950 in the convention of political workers sponsored by the Awami League, and repeated in various forums by the Bengali leaders since then. But the nineteen-year history of conflicts and perceived exploitation of their land had lent credibility to them in the eyes of the people of East Pakistan. Mujib, on his return from the conference, was elected President of the East Pakistan Awami League. The party mobilized mass support for its programme and embarked on a militant course of Bengali nationalism from which it refused to budge. The Six Points in a very short time gained overwhelming popular support and it became difficult for any Bengali leader to oppose or suggest any modification to them. The National Awami Party initially criticized them as a bourgeois programme, but nevertheless had to incorporate the Points in its own twelve-point manifesto.[247]

Ayub's response to the challenge posed by the Bengali nationalists was shortsighted, even in terms of his own survival. The government machinery projected the Six Points to discredit the entire opposition, which included a large number of moderate and liberal elements. On 16 March, Ayub declared that the 'six-point programme of the Opposition is aimed at achievement of their dream of "greater sovereign Bengal" which will spell disaster for the country and turn East Pakistanis into slaves.'[248] Ayub failed to comprehend the threat to the federal structure posed by the Six Points, which were becoming the rallying cry of Bengali nationalism. Instead of building a national consensus to neutralize and accommodate the regional demands within the federal system, he resorted to the usual techniques of the detention of opposition leaders of both East and West Pakistan, a media campaign questioning their patriotism, and placing restrictions on their activities.

After the National Conference, on 30 April five parties forged a new alliance called the Pakistan Democratic Movement (PDM). Apart from the federal parliamentary form of government, its eight-point programme included regional autonomy, leaving only defence, foreign affairs, and currency with the Centre; removing disparity between East and West Pakistan in all respects within ten years; shifting naval headquarters to East Pakistan; and appointing a defence council with an equal number of members from East and West Pakistan. The Bengali leaders, Nurul Amin and others, who signed the agreement belonged to the moderate National Democratic Front. Mujib, who was invited to join the alliance, rejected the compromise programme. Bhashani's party was excluded from the Pakistan Democratic Movement as it had been from the National Conference. In early 1968, his National Awami Party had split into two factions, corresponding to the rift in the international communist movement: Bhashani became the President of the pro-Beijing faction and Abdul Wali Khan the President of the pro-Moscow faction. Bhashani called the Pakistan Democratic Movement alliance reactionary, but the Wali Khan group was inclined to join it. Thus, the exclusion of the two Bengali leaders, Mujib and Bhashani, who in their persons and parties represented the mainstream politics of East Pakistan, rendered the PDM an alliance without any national character. The Six Points had created a rift in the ranks of the opposition parties which, up to that point, had been able to agree, to a large degree, on regional autonomy within a federal system.

In January 1968, the government disclosed the Agartala Conspiracy to separate East Pakistan through a revolt, which was to have been armed and financed by India. Mujib, who was already in jail, and thirty-four civil and military personnel were implicated in it. The evidence of the involvement of Mujib in the conspiracy was only circumstantial and it is not certain what the court verdict would have been. More relevant, in the light of subsequent developments, was the government's failure to discredit Mujib, the Awami League, and the Six Points in East Pakistan by the charges of conspiracy with India. The Bengali view on the allegations was that they were not true, and reflected the usual West Pakistani animosity towards popular Bengali causes and leaders. But there was a significant section of opinion which was not averse to seeking even Indian assistance in obtaining freedom from the domination of West Pakistan. The Indian connection in East Pakistan was not so fatal to the political leaders as it was in the West. The Conspiracy trial, accordingly, made no impression on the Bengali intelligentsia, and even if the accused had been convicted by the Special Tribunal, which was set up to try the case, it would not have dented the image of Mujib. In fact, the Conspiracy trial boosted his stature among the Bengalis. The Indian involvement with Mujib and the Awami League leadership was not unlikely; there was evidence of it in the events of 1971. Indeed, it would have been surprising if the Indian intelligence had not kept itself in touch with the militant nationalist elements of East Pakistan. There are always conspiracies against undemocratic regimes which persistently deny to the opposition entry into the power structure. With no hope of bringing about change from within and enjoying popular support, the dissidents may be driven to despair and fail to distinguish between the actions of the government and the integrity of the state. This is not to justify treason but to highlight the fact that absolute regimes are harmful to the unity of the nation.

* * *

By the last quarter of 1968, the Ayub regime had reached the end of the road. It stood alone against the political forces of East and West Pakistan which had now assumed a new character with the addition of some personalities of the establishment itself. They, unlike the traditional parties, were not averse to defying government bans and taking to the streets. None of them—Zulfikar Ali Bhutto, the erstwhile Foreign Minister of Ayub, Asghar Khan, the former chief of the Pakistan Air Force, and S. M. Murshed the former Chief Justice of the Dhaka High Court—had received political training through representative institutions. They captured the imagination of the people, who had for so long been deprived of any self-expression, by openly criticizing Ayub with an insider's knowledge. Their entry into the opposition camp was well-timed. By 1968, the regime had lost much of its force and glitter, and its architect was a sick man. Bhutto, who formed the Pakistan People's Party in late 1967, eventually became the dominating political force of West Pakistan during the events leading to the secession of East Pakistan. Of the other two, S. M. Murshed faded out with the movement against Ayub Khan, and Asghar Khan became the wandering soul of Pakistan politics.

The movement against Ayub Khan started with a seemingly isolated clash between the police and students on 7 November 1968 at Rawalpindi. By 13 November, it had gathered such momentum that the government thought it necessary to arrest seven members of the People's Party, including Bhutto, five of the National Awami Party (Wali Khan group), including its President, Abdul Wali Khan, and two of the Council Muslim League. In the event, Bhutto's arrest was a big mistake. It accelerated the tempo of the movement in West Pakistan and caused it to spread to the simmering East Wing in early December. The three major student bodies, the East Pakistan Students League and two factions of the East Pakistan Students Union, had earlier joined together and set up the Students Action Committee with the explicit blessings of the Awami League and the National Awami Party (Bhashani group).[249] The Committee issued an eleven-point programme which incorporated the manifestos of the two political parties, in addition to specific student grievances.[250] The alliance was confined to East Pakistan student bodies, with no link with West Pakistan.

The old politicians took some time to realize the intensity and depth of the movement. In the first week of January 1969, the national executive of the moribund Pakistan Democratic Movement met in Dhaka and announced a boycott of the forthcoming elections, which were due to be held before March 1970. It demanded, among other things, direct elections on adult franchise basis, full powers for the directly-elected assemblies, and restoration of civil rights.[251] Negotiations were entered into with other parties to make the alliance more broad-based. On 8 January, the constituent parties of the Pakistan Democratic Movement, the East Pakistan Awami League, the National Awami Party (Wali Khan Group), and Jamiat-Ulema-i-Islam formed a new alliance called the Democratic Action Committee (DAC) to achieve 'full and complete democracy'.[252] The National Awami Party (Bhashani Group) and the newly-formed Pakistan People's Party did not join the national alliance. Bhutto announced that he would contest the presidential elections, if there was no candidate from East Pakistan. During the preceding months, he had been drawing large crowds, in spite of the government's attempts to suppress him, and he was largely successful in establishing his independent identity, much to the chagrin of the older parties. Bhutto had grown up under the dazzling one-man rule of Ayub Khan, which admitted of no sharing of power. Even though increasingly inflexible in his demands, Mujib, unlike Bhutto, felt quite at home in sitting down with his contemporaries. Bhashani was a rival of Mujib for the leadership of East Pakistan and depended on his agitational methods to assert it.

Meanwhile, the anti-Ayub agitation had been gathering a momentum of its own since November 1968, in which month there were four deaths and one thousand arrests. In the following months, casualties escalated: December 1968, 11 deaths and 1,530 arrests; January 1969, 57 deaths, 4,710 arrests, and 1,424 injured in street clashes; February 1969, 57 deaths, 100 arrests, and 412 injured; March 1969, 90 deaths, 356 arrests, and 490 injured.[253] The army was being frequently called out in Dhaka and other major cities to handle the situation, which was sliding beyond the control of the civil authorities. Ayub's position in the army itself was rapidly eroding. I remember a meeting of senior civil and army officers at about this time, addressed by him, on the current situation. There was not much in the speech, except the usual diatribe against the opposition. But the atmosphere was instructive. The army officers were talking and laughing during the briefing by the Interior Minister (a naval officer of the rank of Lieutenant-General) before the arrival of the President. When one of the civilian ministers, who was being accused at the time of profiteering, entered the hall, the army officers hissed audibly. Ayub Khan was a shadow of his former radiant presence; he looked strained and haggard. The audience were not assured by the pathetic figure that Ayub cut that he would be able to meet the challenges of the time.

At long last, after more than two months of rioting and killings, on 5 February Ayub Khan invited the Democratic Action Committee for negotiations. The delay had demonstrated the effectiveness of the street power commanded by the political forces, and had strained the discipline of the law-enforcing agencies. The initiative now lay with the opposition. The DAC put forward preconditions for negotiations, and the government proceeded to comply with them. Prohibitory orders on public meetings were withdrawn, and the ban on certain newspapers and curbs on the Press were lifted. The emergency which had been imposed at the time of Indo-Pakistan war was revoked on 17

February and, thereafter, political prisoners, including Bhutto and Wali Khan, were released. The main hurdle to negotiations was eventually removed when the government agreed to release Mujibur Rahman and withdraw the Agartala Conspiracy case. The West Pakistani politicians had rightly insisted on it, because no resolution of the crisis was possible without credible Bengali representation in the negotiations.

The dialogue between the government and the Democratic Action Committee was initially limited to two points—the introduction of a federal parliamentary form of government, and direct elections on adult franchise basis. But Mujib changed the somewhat cordial atmosphere that was emerging from the conciliatory measures of Ayub Khan. Before coming to the conference, in a public meeting in Dhaka on 22 February, he demanded representation on population basis in all spheres, election of a new sovereign parliament on the basis of direct adult franchise, and full regional autonomy on the basis of the Six Points and, for West Pakistan, a sub-federation with autonomy for its provinces.[254] On the day the conference met, Bhutto and Bhashani, who had refused to attend it, signed an agreement demanding restoration of democracy, establishment of Islamic socialism, withdrawal from military pacts, and opposition to imperialism, etc.[255] The relevancy of these points at this stage was questionable. The first was well within sight through negotiations with Ayub Khan. The other two were policy issues which, following the restoration of democracy, had to be dealt with in accordance with the popular mandate of the elected government. The only peaceful course of action at this stage would have been to have direct elections on adult franchise basis for setting up a parliamentary form of government and to leave all other issues to be decided by the elected representatives.

With Mujib's obduracy on the Six Points, and Bhutto and Bhashani breathing blood and fire on the streets in the major cities of the two provinces, the atmosphere was hardly congenial for a peaceful transition to a democratic government. The plenary session of the Round Table Conference (RTC) was held on 26 February and adjourned to 10 March without any substantial discussions. In the meeting of the Democratic Action Committee, held at Lahore on 6 March to evolve an agreed brief for negotiations with Ayub Khan, Mujib stuck to his demands for representation on the basis of population, dismemberment of One Unit, but, above all, implementation of the Six Points. On the West Pakistan side, there was a divergence of views. Some wanted to go ahead with the elections with Ayub Khan as President during the transitory period, after the demands for a parliamentary system and direct elections had been accepted. Others suggested a revival of the 1956 Constitution. The religious parties were more concerned with the repeal of the Family Laws than with the constitutional framework. The moderates were put on the defensive by the extremists in and outside the Democratic Action Committee; the latter charged them with collusion with the government. On the whole, the DAC retained a formal consensus on the parliamentary form of government and direct elections, based on adult franchise. An informal consensus also seemed to have emerged on replacing One Unit by a sub-federation of provinces and full regional autonomy within a federal system. But no agreement could be reached on East–West relations as formulated by the Awami League.

The impasse of the pre-1956 Constitution period had reappeared with a vengeance. The West Pakistan leaders, individually and collectively, had neither the stature nor the popular base to negotiate a package compromise with Mujib. In the 1950s, there was the forum of an elected Assembly and the responsibility of resolving issues fell on the leadership of the ruling party. After a decade of suppression of interaction between the leaders of different regions and ideologies, the politicians had lost whatever little sense of responsibility they had had. Bhutto, at this stage, was more concerned with building up his position than with wider national issues. Later, after the elections in 1970, when he emerged as the spokesman of West Pakistan, it was too late: Mujib had by then become the Messiah of East Pakistan, beyond the need or desire for national consensus. In early 1969, the Awami League was still not certain of its overwhelming electoral support and Mujib was not perhaps expecting the Six Points to be accepted *in toto*.[257] Under the circumstances, it was only Ayub who could still provide leadership in the resolution of East–West Pakistan issues. If he had not delayed the initiative for negotiations by two months, during which the extremist forces came out on the streets and gained confidence, perhaps a constitutional change-over to a parliamentary government might have been possible. The elected representatives of the two Wings would then have been in a better position to work out a deal among themselves; the presence of an outside power tempted the politicians to raise their stakes. Even later, in March, Ayub Khan could, on behalf of West Pakistan, concede some Bengali demands to get the Awami League to agree to transitory arrangements for holding elections. Although Bhutto was trying to prevent a constitutional compromise under the auspices of Ayub Khan, in which he was likely to be marginalized, he had not yet attained the stature which could make any unanimous agreement arrived at, at the RTC, unworkable. But Ayub Khan remained passive during the conference, and did not come up with any formula to resolve the crisis which, after all, had resulted from the abrogation of the constitutional process and his imposition of Martial Law in 1958.

On 10 March the RTC reconvened and, after four days of discussions, Ayub Khan accepted the two demands for a parliamentary system and direct elections. But for Mujib the basic issue was 'that under the existing constitutional arrangements (based on parity) the Bengali basic interests have consistently suffered in the absence of effective political power'; for him the 'adoption of the Federal scheme presented in the Six-points Programme is an essential pre-requisite for the achievement of a political solution for the problems of the country'. The transition to a parliamentary government could be effected only within the framework of an East–West compromise. The agitation continued and the crisis deepened. Mujib, dissatisfied with his West Pakistani colleagues' response to his demands, withdrew the Awami League from the alliance immediately after the RTC ended on 13 March. The Democratic Action Committee, the last of the series of attempts to find common political ground between East and West Pakistan, was also dissolved on the same day.

During the RTC, every evening Ayub held lengthy discussions with his advisers, Altaf Gauhar, Manzur Qadir, and others. These consultations would continue well past midnight, and Ayub would get tired and leave them to go to bed. He was worn out, betrayed by the army which was his base and strength, and besieged with conflicting advice. It was proposed that a government of opposition leaders be formed. But how to find those willing to join it? Manzur Qadir suggested Mujib should be appointed Prime Minister and actually included this in the draft of the final address of the President to the conference. But there was no way to achieve a consensus of West Pakistan politicians on it.[258] There were those who would not even attend the conference to find a way to bring about a democratic system. It was more important to them to build their personal standing by agitating on the streets, tearing up the fabric of the country. In the chaotic state of politics, there was no responsible national leader who could seize the initiative to negotiate a peaceful way out of the crisis. With the President under seige, and the politicians at daggers drawn with each other, it was futile to expect any national solution from the RTC. Ayub had lost the initiative and those who had placed him in power had already decided to replace him.

Yahya Khan, Commander-in-Chief of the Pakistan Army, played a crucial role during the crisis in February and March. In Islamabad and Rawalpindi, in those days, the widespread disturbances and the proceedings of the RTC were the main topics of conversation at social gatherings. Everyone in the establishment circles agreed that Ayub Khan had to go. The army officers made no secret of their dissatisfaction with the President who had done so much for them. Not that they thought anything was wrong with the authoritarian system. Their animosity arose from a combination of jealousy of the civilian bureaucracy which occupied key positions, contempt at their having lost control of national affairs, and, above all, a desire to directly take over and set things right. They made it clear that they would bail the country out from the turmoil on their own terms, without Ayub Khan and his civilian bureaucracy. The army's withdrawal of support to Ayub Khan was reflected in two ways. Firstly, it was less than enthusiastic in handling the violent agitations against the regime in the big cities. Secondly, it refrained from strengthening Ayub Khan's hands in negotiations with the politicians. During the RTC it was thought that a hint to Mujib by Yahya Khan that a political deadlock might lead to martial law would instil a sense of realism in him. In the meeting that was arranged for the purpose, however, Yahya Khan feigned indifference and told Mujib that he had nothing to do with the negotiations and it was for the government and politicians to resolve the problems.

The preparations for the army take-over had been set in motion at least from the middle of March, if not earlier. In early March, a colleague invited me, along with eight or ten civil servants, to his house, to meet the head of military intelligence over a cup of tea. The conversation naturally centred on the current situation. Everyone criticized the political failings of the Ayub regime, though it was agreed that economic progress had taken place in the last decade. The brigadier did not talk much, but we all did, which obviously was the purpose of the meeting. The exercise was repeated with a cross-section of the bureaucracy. It was a sort of opinion poll by the army to back up its decision to topple Ayub Khan. The fact that the army was so openly discussing the President's shortcomings in official circles was itself indicative of its intentions.

Brigadier (later Major-General) M. I. Karim has given the following account of the events leading up to the imposition of Martial Law. About the middle of March, Brigadier Karim was asked by Major-General S.G.M.M. Peerzada, Adjutant-General of the Pakistan Army, to keep himself available in the GHQ for an unspecified purpose which, the latter said, would be clear in the next two or three days. On 19 March, Karim was informed that a decision had been taken to impose martial law on 23 March and a team of officers was set up to draft the necessary regulations, orders, and related instruments. General Peerzada was not sure whether Ayub Khan would willingly hand over power or if the army would have to mount an operation on its own. Ayub Khan was wavering and wanted martial law only in the disturbed areas. But Yahya Khan had made it clear that the situation could be brought under control only by an army take-over and the imposition of martial law throughout the country, and that Ayub Khan would have no place in it. Although Ayub Khan had earlier agreed to transfer power to the army, some politicians were trying to persuade him, till the last moment, to follow the Constitution and hand over power to the Speaker. The army was getting impatient and eventually Ayub Khan submitted to it. The tape of the speech, handing over power to Yahya Khan, recorded by Ayub was taken in custody by the army. Karim was deputed to carry it to Karachi, to ensure its translation and broadcast on the national hook-up of Radio Pakistan which, due to technical reasons, could only be done from there. As a double check, a duplicate copy of the tape was taken by General Shaukat Raza to Karachi by a special flight. The traditional Joint Services Parade on 23 March, which was observed as Pakistan Day, was cancelled, as originally it had been intended that the army take-over be announced on this date. Meanwhile, martial law regulations and instructions had been dispatched to the Army Commanders at Lahore, Karachi, and Dhaka. Karim was met by Vice-Admiral Ahsan at Karachi airport, and both of them went to the house of the Army Commander where personnel from Radio Pakistan were called. Translations of the speech were made, and Karim personally supervised the broadcast.[259]

Curiously, at this advanced stage of preparations for the army take-over, and only three days before it actually materialized, Ayub appointed new governors in West and East Pakistan on 20 and 21 March respectively. After the failure of the Round Table Conference, the army had decided to assume power and was not prepared to give more time to Ayub Khan to retrieve the situation by changes in his administration. This was borne out by the fact that immediately after the departure of Ayub Khan, twenty-five Martial Law Regulations and four Orders were published. Another fourteen Regulations were issued in the month of April, in addition to the Provisional Constitutional Order.[260] Obviously, the preparations for the take-over had been going on in the GHQ for quite some time.

CHAPTER 3

Enforcing The Federation

March 1969–March 1971

For eleven years, Ayub Khan had ruled the country with the sanction of the army. Having lost that support, he now handed power back to the source from which he had derived it. On 24 March 1969 in a letter to General Yahya Khan, Commander-in-Chief of the Pakistan Army, he requested him 'to take over full control of the affairs of country'. On 25 March Ayub made his last address to the nation. The same day, Yahya assumed power as Chief Martial Law Administrator (CMLA) and Commander of all the armed forces of Pakistan and placed the whole country under martial law; the Constitution of 1962 was abrogated. The Chief of Staff Army, Lieutenant-General Abdul Hamid Khan, the Commander-in-Chief Air Force, Air Marshal Nur Khan, and the Commander-in-Chief Navy, Vice-Admiral S. M. Ahsan were appointed Deputy Chief Martial Law Administrators (DCMLA).[1] On 14 April, the Provisional Constitution Order was issued whereby, subject to the supremacy of martial law, the State of Pakistan was to 'be governed as nearly as may be in accordance with' the Constitution of 1962, but without its provisions of Fundamental Rights and the courts' powers to enforce them. The same Order, which was given retrospective effect from 25 March, also made Yahya Khan President of Pakistan.[2]

To evaluate the course of events leading up to the army action in March 1971 and the subsequent secession of East Pakistan, it is necessary to describe in some detail the style and content of the government of the Yahya regime.

The martial law regime operated through the civil administration which was allowed to be carried on by the civil servants, under the direction and control of army officers placed at strategic points in the administrative hierarchy. In political and other areas of national concern, decision-making power lay in some unstructured consultative forum in the GHQ or Martial Law Secretariat. No record of the process through which fatal decisions were arrived at was ever kept. But there could not be any doubt that Yahya Khan, who had assumed absolute civil and military powers, was the focal point of the regime, ultimately responsible for all its crucial decisions. The immense powers conferred by the late Constitution on the President could now be exercised unhindered even by its limited institutional checks and balances. The civilian administration, because of the limits set on it by inherent legal and administrative norms, however, could not meet the objectives set for itself by the regime. But as CMLA, Yahya Khan could and did issue the most outrageous regulations, violating all canons of natural justice and human rights, beyond question by any authority in the country.[3]

For the purpose of martial law administration, the country was divided into two zones, A and B, corresponding to the provinces of West and East Pakistan. The civil and military authorities of each zone were placed under a Martial Law Administrator (MLA), who was the local Army Commander. The MLA, in turn, divided the zone into sectors, each under a military officer as Sub-Administrator of Martial Law over the corresponding civil functionary. The MLA in the early period exercised the powers of the Governor also. Thus, in the province he exercised absolute powers of the same kind as enjoyed by the President and the CMLA at the Centre, limited only by such subjective checks as the latter might care to apply.

At the Centre, on 3 April, a Council of Administration was set up, consisting of the President and the CMLA as Chairman, and the three DCMLAs. It started as an informal decision-making forum to lay down broad lines of policy. Its meetings were attended by General Peerzada and sometimes also by two civilians, the Cabinet Secretary and the Secretary to the President. Subsequently, when specific issues came before it, differences of opinion developed between Nur Khan and others over the former's populist posture.[4] Nur Khan's political judgement did not match his ambitions. The Central Secretariat very soon realized that he was going at a tangent to the regime and speculation was rife that he would not last.

M. M. Ahmed relates the following:

> Nur Khan was thoughtlessly pursuing changes in labour laws including uniform wages throughout the country. I opposed [this] and pointed out that this would retard industrial development because wages in various regions had been determined by their peculiar conditions. It would be a setback to the development of East Pakistan if its wages were equated with Karachi or West Pakistan.
>
> I remember a meeting on labour policy held by Nur Khan with me and Ghulam Ishaq Khan at Chaklala. After the discussions, Ishaq asked for the agreed points to be recorded. Nur Khan said, 'Why? Don't you trust me?' Ishaq paused, looked at him and said, 'Frankly, sir, no.'
>
> In the Cabinet meeting discussion on wages, Yahya supported me. At another time and on another matter, Yahya in disgust asked me to get Nur Khan off his back.[5]

Nur Khan's waywardness precipitated organizational changes in the administration. In August, he was shifted as Governor of West Pakistan where he behaved still more independently and lasted only a few months. To balance the removal of the Air Chief, Ahsan was appointed Governor East Pakistan, which office he held until March 1971. Both these officers were retired from service and, with their appointments as heads of civil administration, the offices of the MLA and the Governor were separated. The regional Army Commander continued as Martial Law Administrator. At about the same time, Yahya Khan appointed a council of eight ministers, four from each of the two provinces, all of mediocre ability in their respective fields. They were three washed-out politicians, two retired bureaucrats, one retired general, one educationist, and an executive of a multinational company. Soon thereafter, two close advisers of the regime were also inducted into the council; they were G. W. Choudhury, a Bengali professor of political science who was nominally given the portfolio of Communications, and former Chief Justice A. R. Cornelius, who became the Minister of Law. It was by no means a cabinet of talents, or representative of anything. Except Choudhury and Cornelius, the others had hardly any access to the President. Choudhury's appointment created a minor crisis, described by Peerzada:

> We were short of one nominee from East Pakistan. A Bengali minister rang up and said he and his colleagues were perturbed over the rumours of Choudhury's inclusion in the Cabinet and invited me to dinner to discuss the matter. They told me that Choudhury was not acceptable to them because he was a government informer when he was teaching in Dhaka University. I conveyed this to the President who flared up and asked me to give an alternative Bengali name in three days. I could not give him a name and anyway he liked Choudhury very much and wanted him in the Cabinet.[6]

According to Colonel Hasan, Choudhury was associated with the regime from the very beginning and was brought to the notice of Yahya Khan by Karim in consultation with Mujib: Mujib, Sabur Khan, and Justice Abdus Sattar were consulted about the Bengali members of the Cabinet.[7]

The nerve centre of the regime was located in the Headquarters (HQ) or Secretariat of the CMLA, which was manned by army officers. It started operating from the premises of the erstwhile President's Secretariat from the first day of martial law. The head of the CMLA HQ was Lieutenant-General Peerzada; 'Two days before take-over, Yahya Khan called me and asked to be ready to act as Principal Staff Officer (PSO) to him. I said I hoped it was for a short while. Yahya Khan said, "yes, for a very short while". After joining as PSO my contacts with army officers in the GHQ were minimal and purely official'. Under Peerzada there were two brigadiers (both of them later generals): Brigadier Martial Law Affairs, Rahim Khan, and Brigadier Civil Affairs, M. I. Karim. The former dealt with all matters relating to martial law, Intelligence agencies, political activities, and the ministries of home affairs, communication, health, and education. The latter, a Bengali officer, handled all the other ministries and divisions. Each one of these brigadiers had a number of army officers working under him. Colonel Hasan, of the Judge Advocate Office of the GHQ, was the legal expert in the CMLA Secretariat; he remained associated with the drafting of all the legal and constitutional instruments of the regime and the political negotiations relating to them.

The President's Secretariat consisted of two wings, Personal and Public. The Personal side under the Military Secretary, who managed Presidential engagements, tours, household, etc., continued as before. On the Public side, the Secretary to the President dealt with all the papers received from the ministries and submitted them to the President. In his later years, Ayub Khan had had a principal secretary who was relieved after Yahya Khan took over; but M. Qayyum, a CSP officer, continued as Secretary to the President. Describing his situation soon after martial law, Qayyum said:

> The two Brigadiers showed me a note suggesting reduction of my staff which they submitted to the PSO who asked me why I had agreed to the disbandment of my outfit. He then called the two Brigadiers and rejected the proposal. In early April the PSO issued orders that I would mark all civil files to him and would not see the President without first informing him and thereafter giving a report to the PSO about the meeting. In the beginning all civil papers passed through me but later I was taken out from the distribution list of the intelligence reports and the foreign office telegrams. Some sensitive files were directly dealt with by the PSO and I came to know of them only accidentally.[8]

Outside the CMLA Secretariat at the central level, the core of the regime included General Hamid Khan, and Major-General Ghulam Umer. Hamid was the closest adviser of Yahya Khan, both shared convivial tastes and a long friendship. Yahya Khan had made him a full General and delegated almost all the powers of the Commander-in-Chief to him. A National Security Council, headed by the President and including service chiefs, provincial governors, some ministers and secretaries, and heads of various intelligence agencies was set up. Umer was appointed Secretary of the Council and also the head of the newly-created National Security Division of the government of Pakistan. It was staffed mostly by army officers. The corporate role of this body remained dormant. Umer, explaining its objectives, says:

> I had suggested the National Security Council as a forum to discuss national issues in totality and to develop coherent policies on them. One or two meetings were held but nothing thereafter. Peerzada thought I was trying to establish a superbody. But my Division concerned itself with various situations including the political situation. Ataur Rahman Alvi [of Standard Bank] was also handling political affairs directly on behalf of the President.[9]

The officers of the GHQ were also assigned to civilian tasks on an *ad hoc* or regular basis. At the provincial level, there were

Martial Law Administrators and Governors, all belonging to the Armed Forces. They ruled the provinces through military advisers and functionaries, of whom Major-General Farman Ali was the most important man on the staff of the Governor of East Pakistan. About 125 military officers, directly, and 300 indirectly, were administering the martial law regime; but 'the impact of their involvement was much more than these numbers indicate . . . they started influencing people and events behind the scenes by ready cash and promises of a share in political power.'[10]

The quality of the regime's management of national affairs reflected the parade-ground style of Yahya Khan. He was reported to have said:

> I made no particular attempt to know how to run a government. I exercised my trained mind: for 32 years I had been in the army and various appointments including the highest, controlling lakhs of people, knowing their mind, knowing the problems and administratively sorting them. So I thought running the country was no different from running the army.

An adviser who was closely associated with the decision-making process of the regime recalled that 'a feature of President Yahya's administration which may be common to all authoritarian rulers was that entering into any kind of argument with the President was impossible. At the most one could briefly speak one's mind always in guarded language and leave the idea to take effect if it could'. Others have spoken of the pride Yahya Khan took in his skill in handling the politicians. Criticizing the non-serious way of Yahya Khan's working, Umer says:

> There was no institutionalized body of advisers. It was suggested that the President allocate subjects to each one of us who would study it in depth and the President might hold top-level meetings to decide matters. But what generally used to happen was that in the evening gatherings of Yahya Khan some issue would come up and whoever happened to be present, some provincial Governor or a senior army general, would participate in discussions.

The picture is perhaps overdrawn but indicative of Yahya Khan's cavalier handling of state affairs.

In his first broadcast of 26 March 1969, Yahya Khan, echoing the Martial Law Proclamation of 1958, promised first 'to bring back sanity' to the country. The so-called insanity was only the popular agitation against a repressive regime. Since constitutional channels for bringing about a change were blocked, popular expression was bound to result in defiance of the law. If there was any breakdown of law and order, it was because of Ayub Khan's failure to cope with the consequences of his own long undemocratic rule, which strengthened extremist forces in East Pakistan. Martial law could be justified, if at all, by Ayub's inability to transfer power to the elected representatives within the framework of East Pakistan's demands. The new regime's only mandate was, therefore, to find a democratic way to keep the country united. Yahya Khan either missed the point or was insincere (some said both) in declaring the restoration of a constitutional government as his sole aim when he made a sound, clean, and honest administration a precondition for transfer of power to the elected representatives. Peerzada says that, although he had severed all connections with the GHQ, 'the President, as Commander-in-Chief, used to meet the principal and other senior army officers in conferences in the GHQ and socially in the messes. Whenever Yahya came back from such meetings, he admonished me not to be soft in civilian matters and in such a hurry to transfer power. The army wanted him to be tough in civilian affairs'.

On 10 April in a Press conference Yahya Khan announced the regime's manifesto: the administration was to be cleaned up, educational problems were to be addressed, experts were working on a fair wage policy, agriculturists' problems would be resolved, a committee to ensure reasonable prices of essential commodities had been set up, political activities would be allowed at an appropriate time, and regional autonomy was to be decided by the people's representatives.[11] Karim recalls a number of teams of economists, political scientists, and management experts set up in the CMLA Secretariat to study the various problems. We used to hear about them in those days but their composition or terms of reference were never notified.[12] It did not appear to be a regime in a hurry to transfer power to the elected representatives. Being an observer on the premises and, to an extent, a participant in the system, M. Qayyum's view was that the army was planning for a long-term role in the government. This did not necessarily mean martial law for an indefinite period. Apparently, the idea was to ensure some kind of army guardianship of the elected government when it came into being, with Yahya Khan as President.

The CMLA Secretariat, as a deliberate policy, projected itself not as a part of the government as such, but a 'paramount power', to ensure that the civil government worked properly. The army junta, believing that Ayub was misled by civil servants, avoided close association with them for fear of similar 'contamination'. The process of consultation and the informal working relationship necessary in governmental working were absent between the civil and army functionaries during Yahya regime. The principal form of interaction was terse orders from the latter to the former. The two Brigadiers assumed the position of super-secretaries of the government in respect of the ministries and divisions assigned to them.[13] The PSO acquired the *de facto* status of Prime Minister and, as such, was not to be approached routinely by the secretaries, except perhaps by a few like the foreign secretary. In civilian circles, Peerzada's image was that of a vain, remote, and formidable officer but a man of integrity. He says he scorned politics: 'Farman and Umer were political creatures. I never believed in their political manipulations. My view was strictly professional—hold fair elections, transfer power, and get out.' M. M. Ahmed, Deputy Chairman of the Planning Commission, was the only senior civil servant who, in the beginning, had access to the President as Adviser on economic matters. But later, Karim says, Yahya wanted to bring some East Pakistani economists who, together with A. Rab, the Bengali Secretary for Planning, and M. M. Ahmed were to deal with economic affairs to ensure a regionally equitable system.

The severe warning to 'every member of the administration' in the March broadcast of Yahya Khan had a debilitating effect on the civil bureaucracy. In the Secretariat, the officers were demoralized, and very little serious work was done. The names of certain senior civil servants had appeared in the Press as under investigation. Their worst fears came true when in June, they were asked to fill in a statement of about ten pages, regarding their assets since their birth, and even earlier! Anonymous and pseudonymous petitions from disgruntled elements against senior officers were entertained and made the basis of suspending 303 civil servants under Martial Law Regulation No. 58, entitled 'Removal From Service (Special Provisions) Regulation'. They were asked to show cause, without any statement of allegations or their source, why they should not be dismissed. No one expected to get a fair hearing from the martial law authorities. Top civil servants were humiliated by the wide publicity of the unsubstantiated charges given by the government in the media and by the committees of junior army officers set up to pass judgment on their cases. Army officers did not come within the purview of this accountability, though many of them enjoyed shady reputations. Eventually, all the suspended officers were either dismissed or compulsorily retired. The hardship and the deep sense of injustice generated by the summary proceedings totally alienated the bureaucracy, which was in any case marginalized by the martial law administration. The bureaucracy, thereafter, remained a passive critic of the regime, whose setbacks evoked sardonic jokes and derisive comments in civilian circles.

* * *

In the third week of April, Yahya started talks with political leaders in Lahore and Dhaka to resolve the East–West deadlock. Choudhury, alongwith Karim and Hasan, was also meeting the politicians on behalf of the President to ascertain the common ground between the two Wings. There was a considerable body of opinion, particularly in West Pakistan, in favour of the revival of the 1956 Constitution to avoid the reopening of controversial regional issues. The three mainstream political leaders of West Pakistan, Pakistan People's Party's (PPP) Chairman Bhutto, head of the West Pakistan Jamaat-i-Islami Mian Tufail Muhammad, and the Council Muslim League President Daultana, supported the revival of 1956 Constitution.[14] The venerable Bengali convenor of the Pakistan Democratic Party, Nurul Amin, and its West Pakistani leader Nasrullah Khan also supported the 1956 Constitution. Nurul Amin also suggested a bicameral legislature with a lower house on the basis of population and the upper house with parity of representation of the two Wings.[15] Bhashani suggested an all-party conference to reach a consensus on the Constitution, and on issues such as regional autonomy and One Unit. Mujibur Rahman demanded a referendum on the questions of One Unit, regional autonomy, and representation on the basis of population. Both Mujib and Bhashani opposed any revival of the 1956 Constitution; Mujib also rejected the bicameral legislature formula.[16]

On 28 November Yahya Khan announced that general elections would be held on 5 October 1970 under a legal framework to be evolved by him. He elaborated four possible mechanisms through which power could be transferred to representative institutions: (i) an elected constitutional convention which would dissolve itself after producing a Constitution; (ii) revival of the 1956 Constitution; (iii) framing a Constitution and holding a referendum on it in the country; or (iv) a provisional legal framework on the basis of a consensus among political leaders. He gave reasons for rejecting the first three, and decided to give his own provisional Constitution for the purpose of bringing into existence a National Assembly to frame a Constitution.[17] The objections to the first course of action as being too cumbersome, involving two elections and a delay in transfer of power, and to the third as being undemocratic were generally acceptable. But the second option deserved more serious consideration. Its merit was that a working draft Constitution would have been available to accommodate the Bengali demands within the framework of a federal structure, keeping controversial points to a minimum. Yahya Khan never made any serious attempt to persuade the Bengali leaders to agree to the revival of the only consensus document produced by the two Wings. At this stage he had the leverage to pressurize the politicians to reach a consensus on the critical issues between East and West Pakistan.

In the same broadcast of 28 November Yahya Khan identified three main constitutional issues connected with the mechanism of transfer of power. They were: One Unit, representation of the two Wings on population basis, and the relationship between the Centre and the provinces. During his tours of various parts of the country, Yahya said, he had found general agreement 'amongst different sections and groups of people' for the restoration of the system of separate provinces in West Pakistan and acceptance of the principle of one man one vote, instead of parity between the two Wings. On the third question, of the extent of regional autonomy, no such consensus was found, and Yahya contented himself with a pious hope that the people of the two Wings would work out a satisfactory relationship to live together as equal and honourable partners. On 30 March 1970 the Province of West Pakistan (Dissolution) Order and the Legal Framework Order were promulgated.

The Legal Framework Order (LFO) was a confused document.

Some of its provisions were to be incorporated by the National Assembly in the Constitution; some laid down transitional arrangements for elections; other were Rules of Procedure of the National Assembly. Its main features were: (i) the National Assembly was to consist of three hundred and thirteen members; three hundred directly elected on adult franchise basis, and thirteen seats reserved for women, to be filled by the elected members of respective provinces. Both kinds of seats were allocated on the basis of the Population Census 1961; East Pakistan thus got 169 seats, and the remaining 144 seats were distributed among the four provinces and the Centrally Administered Tribal Area of West Pakistan; (ii) the National Assembly would be summoned, after the general elections, to frame a Constitution for Pakistan on such a date and at such a place as the President thought fit; (iii) the extent of regional autonomy was not specified but it was mentioned as one of the Fundamental Principles of the Constitution for the guidance of the constitution-makers that 'the Provinces shall have maximum autonomy, that is to say maximum legislative, administrative and financial powers but the Federal Government shall also have adequate powers including legislative, administrative and financial powers . . .' This convoluted definition was not very enlightening nor, as we shall see later, was it meant to be; (iv) The National Assembly was required to complete Constitution-making within a period of 120 days, failing which it would stand dissolved; (v) The Constitution Bill as passed by the National Assembly was to be authenticated by the President: in case of the President's refusal, the National Assembly would stand dissolved; (vi) The crucial question of the voting procedure in respect of the Constitution Bill, whether it should be passed by a simple majority or by a special procedure, was left to be decided by the Assembly itself.[18] The majority party was thus given the power to decide that the Constitution Bill should be passed by a simple majority and not by a consensus of all the federating units.

The pre-election decisions of Yahya Khan between November 1969 and March 1970, leading up to the promulgation of the Legal Framework Order, proved fatal. The unilateral undoing of One Unit and of the principle of parity of representation between the two Wings betrayed Yahya Khan's lack of political judgement and his ignorance of the constitutional history of Pakistan. The significance of these two issues lay in their being parts of a package which had sought to reconcile the East Pakistani demand for greater regional autonomy with Punjabi fears of Bengali domination. It was negotiated by the elected representatives of East (other than the Awami League) and West Pakistan and incorporated in the 1956 Constitution. A working interregional consensus subsequently emerged. Suhrawardy persuaded the Awami League, in spite of its reservations on the extent of autonomy offered , to accept the compromise document, and the party assumed offices both in the Centre and in East Pakistan and agreed to participate in the general elections under it. West Pakistan had reneged on its commitments by the abrogation of the 1956 Constitution and, clearly, a new covenant had to be negotiated to concede much greater political control to the Bengalis over their own and national affairs. In the changed atmosphere, both the One Unit and parity had to go. But the two issues could not be considered in isolation. They had to be part of an overall political settlement between the two Wings. One Unit was not directly related to Bengali concerns, but the acceptance of the basic change in electoral representation in Bengal's favour deprived Yahya Khan and the West Pakistan elected representatives of any leverage for working out a federal formula somewhere between the autonomy granted in the 1956 Constitution and the Six Points. Peerzada says that Yahya Khan had made up his mind, at an early stage, to do away with One Unit and the principle of parity, and to introduce the principle of one man one vote. Unless these issues were resolved in the LFO, Yahya Khan thought, the politicians and the people at large would have no faith in the general elections. In his 28 November broadcast, he said he had found a consensus on these issues among a cross-section of people, which had reinforced his 'initial reaction that these matters should not become election issues'. One may well ask why not. What was wrong with obtaining a popular mandate on national issues? In a meeting when Yahya Khan announced his decision to dissolve One Unit, Cornelius said that he suggested a referendum but the President was allergic to this device.

In the event, the difficulties with the LFO arose not perhaps so much by what was explicitly conceded but by what was kept vague and open for the politicians to decide in the National Assembly. The process of the formulation of the Order is instructive. Choudhury claims that the 'initial draft was prepared by Peerzada and myself with a very small group of aides and with the utmost secrecy . . . the "inner cabinet" consisting of Yahya, General Hamid, General Peerzada, two provincial Governors and two zonal MLAs, used to have lengthy discussions. The civilian cabinet—including the Law Minister, Justice Cornelius—was completely bypassed.'[19] Hasan says that he and Cornelius were brought into the consultative process on the LFO at a somewhat later stage and that they objected to the clause relating to voting procedure as drafted by Choudhury. It was suggested that constitutional matters should be subject to the concurrence of a three-fourth majority of the total membership of the Assembly and twenty-five per cent of the members of each federating unit. But Choudhury prevailed and the original provision was retained in the final draft. Hasan also recalls that the original draft had spelled out the extent of provincial autonomy but at a certain stage Choudhury deleted it. Karim confirms that the subject of provincial autonomy was discussed and a decision taken about its extent, but it did not appear in the LFO. Hasan participated in five or six meetings on the drafting of the LFO in March 1970 attended by Peerzada, Choudhury, Cornelius, M. M. Ahmed, and himself. M. M. Ahmed says that the LFO was never discussed in any Cabinet meeting, and adds, 'I might have been a member of some Committee, but I do not recall making any significant contribution in its [LFO's] drafting. Choudhury was the main architect of the LFO. He was very close to Yahya.' No minutes of these discussions were taken and the papers were kept by Choudhury. Only after a decision had been taken on the main issues was the draft handed over to the Law Ministry for giving it legal shape. Cornelius recalled a meeting of Yahya with a group of ministers, in which he and some others expressed doubts about the absence of a special voting procedure to pass constitutional matters and the limit of 120 days on constitution-making. But the President adhered to his views.

The final draft was examined on the technical side in the Ministry of Law, and Cornelius placed it for formal approval before the Council of Ministers. Peerzada defends the LFO which, he says, was not intended to be a Constitution covering all issues: 'Whereas One Unit, parity and one man one vote were relatively simpler issues requiring yes or no, the question of provincial autonomy was more complex. It was a purely political issue and could not have been decided by diktat. After all everything could not be taken care of [in the LFO]. We could not act God.'

The two major issues, the quantum of provincial autonomy and the voting procedure for passing the Constitution, which were not defined in the LFO, later proved insoluble. It appears that Yahya, on his own or under the influence of Choudhury, had concluded at an early stage that Mujib was the key figure in East–West relations and was keen to avoid confrontation with him at any cost. He had been meeting Mujib during visits to Dhaka and was otherwise in regular communication with him through Presidential emissaries. Karim claims that he was Yahya's main link with Mujib. Ahsan, Umer, Farman Ali, and other leaders of the regime frequently met the Bengal leader to discuss current affairs or to transmit messages. But so far as the LFO was concerned, it was Choudhury who seemed to have obtained Mujib's blessings at every stage. Choudhury has narrated the drafting process of the LFO and the additions and deletions that were made to accommodate Mujib: 'Yahya's plan conceded all the demands put forward by Mujib . . . He [Yahya] merely expressed a pious hope that on constitutional matters there would be a consensus of opinion from various parts of the proposed federation.'[20] The generals were, however, not prepared to accept verbal assurances and insisted on the explicit provision of a 60 per cent vote of the total membership of the proposed legislature in constitutional matters. Choudhury recounts that the 60 per cent provision was there in the draft LFO when 'it was put before the Cabinet just one day before its announcement' but 'At the eleventh hour, by most skilful manouevring, Yahya dropped the clause from the plan . . . [it] came as a pleasant surprise to many in East Pakistan.'[21] Similarly, Mujib did not want provincial autonomy to be defined in the LFO and, despite the serious reservations of his advisers, Yahya agreed to keep the issue open. Choudhury refers to the evidence of Mujib's bad faith brought to Yahya's notice during the same period by the intelligence agencies, and blames Yahya as a non-serious administrator for not retracing his steps.[22] But neither did Choudhury reconsider the advice he was tendering.

Yahya was indeed a vain person, not given to deep reflection on complicated matters. Like Ayub, having a formidable army at his command, he could not imagine in the heyday of his regime that the political situation could ever go out of his control. He could visualize three scenarios in ascending order of confrontation with the Bengalis: first, the most optimistic situation forecast by all the intelligence agencies was that no single party would gain an absolute majority in the National Assembly. This would enable the regime to manage a coalition of reasonable parties and personalities. Second, if such a coalition did not emerge, or if it did prove recalcitrant, the President could exercise his powers to reject the Constitution framed by the National Assembly; the Assembly would then stand dissolved and fresh elections could then be indefinitely postponed. Third, as a last resort, martial law could be revived with full force, if the first situation did not materialize and the second option was found impractical. Indeed, as we shall see later, by allowing himself to be left with only the third option and the tragic results that followed, Yahya showed himself to be a poor manager of men and affairs.

In a presentation in late January 1970, before a meeting of Yahya, General Hamid, General Umer, General Sahibzada Yakub Khan, General Tikka Khan, General Peerzada, Admiral Ahsan, and others, Choudhury argued that 'our [his and Yahya's] whole approach . . . was based on expectations of a reasonable attitude from Mujib as well as others and therefore no step should be taken to precipitate a crisis'. A number of participants opposed this soft approach towards Mujib and wanted specific limits on provincial automony in the LFO.[23] Karim remembers the same or a similar meeting at about this time, and says that the consensus that was arrived at therein was neither recorded nor implemented as such. The generals eventually went along with whatever Yahya wanted, but Karim recalls their misgivings and mutterings that 'we should not mess up this time'.

The West Pakistan leaders showed no pronounced reaction to the decision to replace parity by representation on population basis as announced in the 28 November broadcast, or later on the absence of safeguards against the Six Points in the LFO when it was issued in March 1970. Perhaps by the latter date the election campaign had gained momentum and the politicians were concentrating more on the immediate objective of winning seats rather than thinking of the wider issues that would confront them after the elections. Before its promulgation, the draft of the LFO, according to Karim, was shown in strict confidence to some leading politicians: 'I took the draft to Fazlul Quadir Choudhury, and Ahsan and Yakub Khan were asked to show it to Mujibur Rahman'. Peerzada, who was known to be close to Bhutto, had kept the latter informed of the main provisions of the LFO. Bhutto subsequently insisted that he had reservations about the LFO and gave three reasons why he did not publicly press them: firstly, after a few speeches he found that the public was not reacting to his criticism of the Order; secondly, most of the leaders had not only accepted the arrangements but had in fact welcomed them; and thirdly, if he had insisted on a more comprehensive provisional Constitution, his rival parties would have turned round on him saying that he was against the electoral process and wanted Yahya to give an undemocratic Constitution. The fact is that, unlike Mujib, no West Pakistani leader was sure of his popular base and none of them felt confident enough to take a stand on national issues before the elections. The traditional parties distrusted Bhutto and his party programme and, still thinking in terms of the conventional framework of national politics, thought they would be able to counter him by collaborating with their Bengali counterparts. But ten years of Ayub's rule had fragmented national politics and the Bengal polity had become completely regionalized. Henceforth, the politicians of East and West Pakistan could only meet as adversaries and not as partners.

* * *

Political activities were allowed from 1 January 1970, though the enactment laying down the legal framework for elections was announced three months later. Cornelius and some ministers had advised that, in the charged atmosphere, political activities should not be allowed so early in the electoral process but Yahya did not agree. The election prospects perceived by the regime in early 1970 have been described by Umer as follows:

> The conclusion was that no single party would be able to get an absolute majority. As the election campaign progressed it became clear that the Awami League would be confined to East Pakistan and People's Party to West. Jamaat-i-Islami might be able to get stray seats in both the Wings but the number would be small. In the circumstances Muslim League was considered as the only national party which might win a sizeable number of seats in both the Wings provided its three factions

> combined. It may still not be the largest party but its presence will be conducive to a positive atmosphere. The President met the heads of the three factions—Qayyum, Daultana, and Fazlul Quadir but they wanted to stay separate although they were persuaded to talk. It was then suggested that all these three leaders should be replaced by Nurul Amin as the head of a unified Muslim League. Alternatively, it was proposed that the three leaders should agree to joint candidates and joint election campaign. But all efforts to bring them together failed. [The regime therefore decided to patronize Qayyum and his Muslim League.] Yahya met Bhashani several times in mid-1970 through Ataur Rahman Alvi, a bank manager close to Yahya, and tried to bring about a Qayyum-Bhashani electoral alliance. Any alliance with other leftists was not acceptable because they were too violent. Jamaat-i-Islami supported the regime but they were not included in the alliance efforts. Their support was of a different kind.

The reluctance of Daultana and Fazlul Quadir to merge their factions into one unified Muslim League was due to the special relationship which Qayyum had from the beginning developed with the regime. He had the blessings of the National Security Division and the intelligence agencies and was closely associated with two stalwarts of the regime, Muzaffar Ali Qizilbash, the Finance Minister, and General Sher Ali, the Information Minister in the Yahya Cabinet. The two old Leaguers appreciated that in a unified League Qayyum was thus bound to occupy the commanding position. Qayyum, however, was a poor choice as a balancing national force. His reputation was mainly based on his repressive but efficient rule as Chief Minister of the NWFP but he was not a mass leader of national stature. Nevertheless, with the backing of the intelligence agencies he was able to put together an organization of disparate elements and fielded 131 candidates in the elections, half of them in East Pakistan, where he was much weaker than in the West.

To finance its electoral preferences, the administration resorted to arbitrary and shady methods. The Convention Muslim League had substantial funds available, collected during the Ayub era, to fight the elections. On 12 June while the election campaign was at its height and after its refusal to merge into a unified Muslim League, a Martial Law Order was issued which provided that no person could operate the accounts of the Convention Muslim League funds except in accordance with the orders issued by the

Chief Martial Law Administrator.[24] By this arbitrary edict the Yahya government obtained control of substantial funds and deprived the recalcitrant Convention League and its Bengali President of whatever advantage they had. Considerable amounts were diverted from these funds to finance the candidates of the Qayyum League and other favourites of the intelligence agencies. The Director, Intelligence Bureau, taking advantage of his position and the freewheeling style of the Yahya government, was alleged to have collected more than Rs 4 million—a great deal of money in those days—from ten leading industrialists and businessmen of the country by giving the impression that the President wanted funds to help the candidates of different political parties. The contributors, according to the prosecution, were asked to deposit indicated amounts in bank accounts opened under fictitious names, all of which were operated by Director using signatures of non-existent persons. During police investigations, one of the accused intelligence officers named senior army officers serving in East Pakistan and political leaders and workers to whom cash, transport, and other materials were distributed, under orders from the Director, for election purposes. Some of these alleged beneficiaries were not traceable while others denied having received anything; only a few political workers admitted receiving some transport, loudspeakers, etc.[25]

* * *

In East Pakistan during the election campaign of 1970 there were two mass political forces. One was represented by the Awami League led by Mujib, and the other consisted of the leftist groups of whom Bhashani was the most effective spokesman. The Awami League under Mujib had mobilized the urban and rural middle classes to gain freedom from the domination of West Pakistani capitalists and the military and civil bureaucracies which, it was felt, would always be the position under the federal system. Its manifesto of Six Points was aimed at a confederal arrangement with West Pakistan, though it did not explicitly say so until the last stage of constitutional negotiations, as we will see later. But internally the party programme did not envisage any radical transformation of class structure after the achievement of autonomy. In the struggle for its main objective of regional autonomy, the Awami League's approach was basically political. Its cadre of workers were not trained for an armed struggle. The party's plans, in case of failure of the political process, called for a mass movement against the government, and subversion of the loyalties of the Bengali element in the established institutions of the armed forces and the bureaucracy to Pakistan.

There was, however, a militant element in the Awami League which believed in socialism as the solution to the poverty in East Pakistan and which argued that only in an independent East Bengal or Bangladesh would it be possible to set up a socialist order. The nucleus of this group was formed in 1962 at Dhaka University, and it had obtained control of the East Pakistan Students League (EPSL) which, along with the pro-Beijing East Pakistan Students Union (EPSU), had played a leading role in the presidential elections of 1966 and in the agitation against Ayub in 1969. Until the emergence of Bangladesh it posed as an integral part, though a radical one, of the Awami League. Other leftists gave priority to a revolutionary class struggle of the masses which, they argued, was being jeopardized by encouraging the secession of East Pakistan under bourgeois leadership and chose to boycott the elections. But the radicals in the Awami League regarded elections as a step towards the final goal of independence and threw themselves wholeheartedly into the campaign under its bourgeois leadership. The election campaign enabled it to organize the party cadres of thousands of urban educated youth for mass contact in the villages. By 6 June 1970 the group had drafted a declaration of independence and prepared the design for a new national flag. On 12 August, six months prior to the elections, the Central Committee of the EPSL adopted a resolution for a *Swadhin Samajtantrik* Bangladesh (Independent Socialist Bangladesh).[26]

Mujib's entire career was based on student politics. He had himself founded the EPSL in 1948 and, in all his struggles against the West Pakistani establishment, he had skilfully deployed the students. It is inconceivable that he did not know the designs of this radical group within the Awami League which, after the emergence of Bangladesh, identified itself, in 1972, as a separate party, the *Jatyo Samajtantrik Dal* or JSD (Socialist National Party) and proved Mujib's nemesis. In 1970, however, it was a useful instrument in his hands. The dedication and organization of the radical leaders and workers were available to the Awami League for winning the elections. In dealing with West Pakistan, the militant posture of the group could be utilized as an argument for Mujib's inability to adopt a moderate stand. The debate continues, as it used to during the East Pakistan crisis, whether Mujib was really a hostage to the radicals in his party. It is difficult to imagine a mass leader of Mujib's standing and political experience as a helpless man. His own speeches during the election campaign were no less radical than those of the hardliners of the party. He announced that the ensuing elections were 'his last fight to achieve the rights of Bengal through peaceful means' and warned that 'if the Six Point demands were not fulfilled through elections, he would again call the heroic people of Dhaka to join him in the struggle and give blood once again.'[27] He condemned the Legal Framework Order but said he and his party had 'decided to participate in elections [under it] as they considered elections a referendum on regional autonomy on the basis of the six-point programme.'[28] The strain of regional belligerence in Mujib's election campaign became increasingly perceptible as the polling dates approached. Privately, before the elections, he was assuring Yahya that the Six Points were his bargaining position. Karim recalls a meeting between Yahya and Mujib at Dhaka in which the latter's speeches on the Six Points were brought up. Mujib, referring to the 1954 elections, said, 'Look we are politicians. At the time there was a lot in the nature of the six points, but nothing happened'. This was a plausible answer to the concern of the regime and had the intended soothing effect for the time being. But post-election developments showed that the extreme position of Mujib was not mere rhetoric.

During the period 1970–71, the Awami League was not the only political force in East Pakistan. Apart from the radical group within it, there were two broadly identifiable (with reference to their source of ideological inspiration—Moscow or Beijing) leftist streams wielding considerable influence in the militant and defiant political atmosphere of the day. The pro-Moscow NAP of Wali Khan, headed by Professor Muzaffar Ahmed in the East Wing, had decided to participate in the elections but it did not command much popular support and its revolutionary zeal was of a lower order. For the Soviet Union, the Indian support for Mujib, which was becoming obvious by 1970, was a sufficient safeguard of its position in the political set-up likely to emerge after the elections.

It was therefore supporting the Muzaffar NAP and the Awami League in equal measure.[29]

The Bhashani NAP, which was the repository of pro-Beijing left forces including Maoists, had split when Bhashani initially decided to participate in the elections. Four major pro-Beijing groups, varying in strength and divided more by the personalities of their leaders than by clear-cut policies, were operating during this period in East Pakistan. Muhammad Toaha, General Secretary of Bhashani NAP, and Abdul Haq, General Secretary of the peasant organization, *Krishak Samity,* also led by Bhashani, differed with their leader and left him to form the East Pakistan Communist Party (Marxist-Leninist) or EPCP (M-L). In terms of field work, contacts with intellectuals and students, and propaganda, this was the most important group.[30] It favoured armed struggle to change the existing order, but opposed any nationalist struggle that might divide Pakistan.[31] The other important faction of Abdul Matin–Alauddin Ahmed, which had formed the East Bengal Communist Party (EBCP), 'argued that the independence of East Pakistan achieved under the leadership of a worker-peasant alliance was the correct strategy for socialism in the region.'[32] It had some support in the trade unions in Chittagong and was reported to have considerable influence in Pabna, the home district of Matin. The Zafar–Memon group, which operated underground, claimed the credit for being the first to demand an independent socialist East Bengal, and was totally committed to a militant course. An extreme fringe faction led by Siraj Sikdar was 'believed to be rather active in the coastal district of Barisal . . . and is said to spend a lot of time studying Mao-thought.'[33] All these pro-Beijing groups accepted the need for an armed uprising to change the established order, did not believe in the constitutional process, and distrusted Mujib.

All classes of Bengalis were imbued with nationalist fervour generated by the election campaign. The academic and bureaucratic leadership was as much committed to the achievement of complete autonomy as the political leaders on the hustings. In May, the Panel of Economists on the Fourth Five Year Plan (1970–75) submitted two reports, one each from the representatives of East and West Pakistan. The former included professional economists and civil servants. The West Pakistan Report complained that the Bengalis 'were starting from certain rigid political parameters, and were not willing to give due consideration to the very real economic problems which would be faced by West Pakistan if a very sudden and sharp further reduction in the investment ratio of that Wing were to take place.'[34] The Bengali members began their Report with the statement that under the new Constitution, 'centre–province relationships as well as the perspectives and objectives of development planning itself may undergo changes—even fundamental changes.' Accordingly, while presenting a conceptual framework of the Bengali position, they rejected the main premises of the draft Plan in respect of East–West economic relations. They said that they were unable to communicate with their West Pakistani colleagues 'as to the urgency of removal of disparity at a rate which is meaningful in the situation of today.'[35] Karim says that Colonel Choudhury, Staff Officer of Peerzada, told him that he had read a top secret paper of M. M. Ahmed, suggesting that it was time for a friendly separation of the two Wings rather than elections, and warning of serious economic consequences for the entire country otherwise. And Umer recalls that even before the elections, Yahya had started saying that West Pakistan had to be saved.

M. M. Ahmed denies that he was against East Pakistan and, referring to the heated debate on the Fourth Five Year Plan in mid-1970, says

> I tried my best to remove the impression that I was against the Bengalis. But what they were demanding was impossible. The West Pakistan growth could not be arrested to increase allocations to East Pakistan. In any case 40 per cent of the Plan resources were committed for ongoing projects which could not be abandoned. Moreover, the foreign aid was negotiated on the basis of total projects of the country and their feasibility. Indiscriminate allocation to East Pakistan was not going to help us in getting foreign aid for half-baked and uneconomic projects.
>
> The Bengalis wanted to postpone the Fourth Plan which was due to start from 1 July 1970. They were expecting political changes in the forthcoming elections and new relationships between the centre and East Pakistan. I opposed the postponement of the Plan which had been drafted through a long-drawn-out process, and waiting for the induction of a new government would have meant a delay of two years in introducing it. As a compromise, I suggested that the plan may be approved but with only one year's allocations for the two

wings; the elected representatives may determine inter-wing allocations for the remaining four years.

After a whole day's meeting on the Plan, at the end the Bengalis demanded additional allocation by way of, as they said, rounding up of the figures. I didn't agree. They were already given 60 per cent of the Plan allocations and there was no justification for further increase. Next day Peerzada sent me a note suggesting some changes in the allocations approved on the previous day. I didn't agree and said that changes in the decisions already made could only be effected by the President or the Cabinet on a fresh summary.

The election to the National Assembly, which were originally planned for 5 October, were eventually held on 7 December. The results authenticated the polarization of the two Wings: in East Pakistan the Awami League captured 160 out of the 162 directly–elected seats, and in West Pakistan the People's Party won 81 out of 138 seats. The Awami League was in an absolute majority in the Assembly. 'The senior generals', Karim says, 'were shocked, and one corps commander termed the results a disaster. They were obsessed with the attitude of the Awami League towards the Army'. On a personal note, the generals apprehended that Colonel M. A. G. Osmany would be the defence minister in an Awami League government and that he would revenge himself on the senior officers who had blocked his promotion and forced his retirement from the army. M. Qayyum related that in the Cabinet meeting after the elections Yahya gave a tongue-lashing to the Director Intelligence Bureau, Rizvi, who had all along been reporting that no single party would gain an absolute majority. Umer admits that the real strength of the Awami League was not correctly understood by him, 'we knew they would win a large number of seats but never thought they would win by such a number as they did.'

The regime might have been gloomy about the results but immediately after elections there was a degree of optimism among the West Pakistani intelligentsia about the revival of the political process, and a general acceptance of the Awami League's right to form the government. But Mujib's tone did not change after his overwhelming success when everyone in West Pakistan was desperately waiting to hear some softening words from him as the Prime Minister-elect of the country. The climax was reached on 3 January 1971, when in a mammoth public meeting at the Race Course in Dhaka he declared that 'None would be able to stop us framing a Constitution on the basis of the Six-Point programme' and administered an oath somewhat to this effect to the newly-elected members of the National and Provincial Assemblies.[36] On the following day, 4 January, Mujib implicitly ruled out any negotiations for compromise by saying that the Bengalis had given their verdict and that the members of the National Assembly 'had no right to change the Six-Point formula.'[37] These assertions of Mujib had to be taken more seriously now that he was under no compulsion to score points against his opponents. Karim relates that the Race Course meeting upset Yahya and 'he asked me to explain the Six-Points, which I did. Yahya exploded and said "This man (Mujib) is talking nonsense. He is talking sedition."' Karim pointed out that 'Mujib had all along been talking like this during the election campaign but you never said anything.' Yahya replied, 'But he had told me this was a political thing but now he is serious about them.'

The post-election scene witnessed the accentuation of nationalist fervour in East Pakistan. The election results were seen not as the success of a single party as such but the victory of Bengali nationalism. Bhashani, who seemed to have been bypassed by the overwhelming success of the Awami League and the segmentation of his NAP, raised the demand for a sovereign independent East Pakistan in January 1971. He regarded the Awami League victory as the people's verdict for a separate East Pakistan and threatened to start a mass movement if the Awami League resiled from it. But many people termed the demand a new-fangled one to embarrass Mujib in the constitutional negotiations.[38] The old leftists accused Bhashani of 'creating a demand for secession merely to divert the attention of the masses of East Pakistan' and 'protecting the interests of the petit bourgeoisie of East Pakistan, almost in the same way as Mujib.'[39] The Toaha-Haq group termed the call for an independent East Pakistan a 'diversionary move' and did not regard 'secession as an issue in itself.'[40] Bhashani had correctly assessed the post-election situation to regain his power base by articulating a popular sentiment. Ayub Khan's ten years of absolute rule, the mass upsurge against it, and the cyclone disaster had transformed 'the entire mental make-up of the people of East Pakistan. The new forces which have been suddenly let loose cannot be contained or even restrained within the existing framework nor even perhaps within the scope of Mujib's six-point programme.'[41]

By the first week of January, the majority leaders of the two Wings, Bhutto and Mujib, were in open confrontation. Bhutto was asking for a federal system with 'viable and feasible regional autonomy' and consensus of all the federating units in its making, and at the same time warning 'that no Central Government could either be formed or function without the co-operation and support of the People's Party.'[42] Mujib was insisting that 'his party alone was competent to form the government both in the Centre and in Bangladesh', but determined to undermine the Centre by implementing his Six Points.[43] To bring order to the political situation, Yahya invited Mujib to Rawalpindi for discussions; but Mujib declined to meet the President in the capital. It was given out by the Awami League that Mujib would not come to West Pakistan. Karim thinks that Mujib's followers had no faith in his intellectual integrity and apprehended that either their leader would be detained in West Pakistan or that he would succumb to the blandishments of the West Pakistanis. Umer says that he went to Dhaka and requested Mujib to come to Rawalpindi and assured him of all the respect and protection due to a future Prime Minister. When Mujib did not budge, Umer sought the intervention of Khondkar Mushtaque Ahmed, a senior Awami League leader, who thought that Mujib was afraid that he would be killed in West Pakistan. In February, Karim was sent again to invite him, but all assurances of safety and welcome failed to persuade Mujib to change his mind. The explanations for this extraordinary behaviour of the future Prime Minister can be either that he was genuinely afraid of entrusting himself to the military regime, or that he wanted to convey to the West Pakistani establishment that henceforth Dhaka would be the centre of power, or that he was not interested in being the head of the goverment of united Pakistan which, he might have thought, he would never be allowed to remain. More likely it was a combination of all these elements.

Yahya visited Dhaka in the second week of January. He had two meetings with Mujib. The private meeting of the two, without aides, on 12 January was recriminatory. Karim relates the following dialogue:

Yahya, referring to the Race Course oath-taking, asked: Sheikh Sahib what is this you have done?

Mujib: This is my bargaining point. I have fought for Pakistan. I am not going to secede from it. But I want to assure you Mr President that we are going to demand certain rights—economic and also resource distribution.

Yahya: I am working for that. That is why I gave one man one vote. That is what I want. I have said so in so many of my statements. There is no problem about that.

Mujib: But you said you won't agree to these things in the Constitution.

Yahya: No, my chaps are working out something and I will show it to you before it is announced and if you have anything to say we can discuss it.[44]

Yahya's own version of the meeting, according to Choudhury, was pessimistic. They both congratulated each other; Mujib on winning the elections and Yahya for having held them. The dialogue went something like this:

Yahya: Unfortunately you have emerged leader of a political party which does not have a single seat in West Pakistan. There, Mr Bhutto has emerged leader of the majority party. You talk to him and then inform me of the results of your talks.

Mujib: No, Sir. This is a democracy. As leader of the majority party, I will form the Government.

Yahya: You are most welcome but you must also think of the whole of Pakistan.

Mujib: Yes, West Pakistan leaders come and see me.

Yahya: Mr Bhutto did not come here.

Mujib: Not Mr Bhutto, but other people come and see me.

Yahya: What others, my friend? They belong to defeated parties of West Pakistan. It is an understanding to be able to live together with all the federating units.

Mujib: Whoever wants to talk, he may come to me.

Yahya: You are the leader of the biggest party. You go and talk.

The following day there was a formal meeting of the principals and their aides. Mujib was accompanied by Tajuddin Ahmed, Nazrul Islam, Kamruzzaman, Khondkar Mushtaque Ahmed, and Mansur Ali. Yahya's team included Peerzada and Ahsan. Peerzada recalls the pleasant atmosphere in which the meeting took place. Yahya and Mujib congratulated each other; Mujib on winning the election and Yahya on holding free and fair elections in spite of being a military officer. Yahya then gave a fatherly pep talk, referring to the LFO and the necessity of amending the Six Points, which were beyond the federal concept. Peerzada was hopeful after the meeting that the Six Points could be negotiated and watered down. According to Admiral Ahsan, after the Awami League leaders had given a presentation of the Six Points and answered the questions raised by the President, the following exchange took place:

Mujib: Sir you now know what the Six Point programme is. Please tell me what objections you have to this programme.

Yahya: Sheikh Sahib I have nothing against the Six Point programme but you will have to carry the West Pakistan leaders with you.

Mujib: Of course, Sir. Kindly call the Assembly as soon as possible. I suggest 15 February. You will see that I will obtain not only a simple majority but almost two-thirds majority.

Ahsan: With an absolute majority in the Assembly the Awami League can bulldoze their Constitution without bothering about West Pakistan's interests.

Mujib: No, no. I am a democrat and the majority leader of all Pakistan. I cannot ignore the interests of West Pakistan. I am not only responsible to the people of East and West Pakistan but to the world opinion. I shall do everything on democratic principles. To begin with I hope you will arrive in Dhaka three or four days before the Assembly session. I will show you our draft Constitution. If you find objections, I will try to accommodate your wishes. As the leader of the majority party, I will propose a draft of the President's address to the Assembly. I will express my gratitude to you in the Assembly for restoring democracy. Then we shall go through all the process of a democratic Parliament. We will have the subjects committee, we will discuss the issues and find acceptable formulas inside and outside the Assembly.

After further discussion on the methodology of constitution-making:

Mujib: Sir, my party intends to elect you as the next elected President of Pakistan. This is a great honour and we think you fully deserve this for restoring democracy in the country.

Yahya: I am a simple soldier. I will go back to the barracks or go home. I will exercise my fundamental right.

Mujib: No sir, we will not allow you to turn down this honour. When the Nation demands your services you cannot refuse.

In a more serious vein Yahya stressed the necessity of the Awami League working closely with the majority party of West Pakistan, the Pakistan People's Party. Mujib replied: 'I will certainly seek the co-operation of the People's Party and also the other parties of West Pakistan.' He went on to say: 'I do not wish to impose any solution to the problems of West Pakistan Provinces. I realize they cannot have nor do they need the same extent of autonomy as East Pakistan. I am prepared to help if required but I will not interfere with any arrangements the West Pakistan leaders themselves wish to make.'

Mujib also complained of the East Pakistan government taking vital decisions without consulting the elected representatives. Yahya asked Ahsan to suggest, in consultation with the Awami League, interim arrangements to associate the elected representatives with the administration of the central government. Tajuddin Ahmed and Dr Kamal Hossain were appointed to liaise with the Governor.

The same evening in the President House some army officers suggested that the President should not only be elected but should also remain the actual Commander-in-Chief or Supreme Commander of the Armed Forces and should not be a mere figurehead.

By all accounts these meetings, although not altogether disappointing, did not resolve the conflicting positions. Mujib was non-committal about any compromise on the Six Points and only talked in general terms, and insisted on calling the Assembly session. Yahya made no serious attempt to pin him down to specific amendments in the Six Points. Mujib was evasive about his assurances given to Yahya in private meetings before the elections that he would show the Awami League's draft Constitution to him beforehand. The best Yahya could extract was Mujib's willingness to talk to Bhutto. With the mounting pressure in East Pakistan for the holding of the Assembly session, and no agreement over East-West-Centre relations in sight, it was politically inept to declare Mujib the future Prime Minister on 14 January before Yahya left Dhaka.[46] Yahya was not bound to commit himself regarding the formation of a government under Mujib before the Constitution had been framed. In fact, his statement gave the public a wrong impression of broad agreement between Yahya and Mujib on key issues. Yahya's problem was that he did not think through his position and proceeded in an *ad hoc* manner all along. He could have either gone along entirely with Mujib and called the Assembly session demanded by him and allowed the political process to work itself out, or, if he thought that the Six Points were beyond the federation, immediately after the elections he should have brought the politicians together under his auspices and used whatever leverage he was still left with to negotiate a compromise. He adopted neither one nor the other course. Having brought about the unintended state of East–West confrontation, Yahya could not withdraw from the scene, leaving the politicians to sort out the intractable issues. By his shortsighted policies he had left little for the West Pakistan politicians to bargain with Mujib.

Yahya went to Larkana on 17 January for hunting, as a guest of Bhutto. Peerzada, who accompanied him, recounts the visit:

> To see Bhutto after Mujib at Larkana or elsewhere was logical. Yahya enjoyed *shikar* and discussed current politics also. In one of the meetings Bhutto philosophized 'Mr President, there are three parties to power transfer—the majority party of Mujib, the majority party of West Pakistan (the People's Party), and the Army.' Yahya snubbed him 'Zulfi, don't put me on this three-legged stool. I have done my duty.' Yahya then elaborated his discussions with Mujib and advised that there was only one party and that was the majority party emerging from the elections. Any bargaining by West Pakistan should be done with Mujib. Yahya further said that he would encourage *all* political parties [emphasis by Peerzada] to hold preliminary talks about the constitutional position in keeping with the LFO.[46]

Bhutto has given his account of the meeting with his guests. Apart from Peerzada, Yahya had brought with him his close friend General Hamid, and one or two other generals. On arrival, Yahya with his usual joviality said that he had purposely brought Hamid to dispel Bhutto's impression that the generals were hostile to him. Later, Yahya referring to his Dhaka meetings told the host and others: 'I had very good discussions in East Pakistan and the Six Points were explained to me. I think it is quite possible to have a Six-Point Constitution. Even in Australia, foreign trade is in the hands of the Provinces.' Bhutto observed that the President had not given careful thought to the implications of the Six Points. While it might be possible to have a settlement if Mujib compromised on two points, foreign trade and foreign aid and taxation, in their totality the Six Points were bound to lead to secession. Continuing, Bhutto said that while he would personally prefer to sit as leader of the opposition, he could not allow Mujib to take the posts of both prime minister and president. By convention, nominations to the two posts should be made by the majority parties of the respective Wings. In the alternative, Bhutto suggested a grand coalition of the two Wings. Yahya said this was what he had suggested to Mujib.

It is easy to imagine that, given the deep suspicions about Mujib's Six Points, Bhutto's articulation of the dangers arising from them to the country and the army itself must have created a deep impression on the generals. Karim thinks that in the Larkana meeting 'Bhutto made known to Yahya in a very subtle way that the army leadership was with him on the East–West issue. It also created suspicions in Bengali minds of a combination of the army and Bhutto to deprive East Pakistan of their electoral victory.' Yahya's choice of Bhutto's own home as the venue for political negotiations, while enjoying the lavish hospitality of the rival leader, was impolitic in the highly sensitive atmosphere of the times. The President was expected to be seen carrying on serious negotiations on critical national affairs with rival political leaders in an even-handed manner. With Mujib, the meetings were strictly according to the presidential protocol of timings and venue at the President House. In Larkana, the political negotiations were carried on in circumstances which could be interpreted as a friendly get-together of the generals and Bhutto, presided over by the President, discussing West Pakistan's strategy to counter the designs of the Bengalis.

Bhutto's role as the sole spokesman of West Pakistan was not as unanimous as that of Mujib in respect of East Pakistan. The People's Party had won 62 seats out of 82 in the Punjab, 18 out of 27 in Sindh, 1 out 25 in the NWFP (including the Tribal Areas) and none in Balochistan, a total of 81 out of 138 seats in West Pakistan.

It had secured only 42 per cent of the total valid votes polled in the Punjab and Sindh each; 14 per cent in NWFP; and about 2 per cent in Balochistan.[47] Bhutto's claim rested on his being the leader of the largest single party in West Pakistan and his ability to mobilize the masses on populist slogans. But he was handicapped in fighting the case of federation *vis-à-vis* Mujib, not only by the partisan politics of 57 West Pakistani elected representatives of other parties, but also by the threat of defection of some of his own party members. He made no attempt to develop a consensus of the West Pakistan parties on constitutional issues. While not suited by his political training and temperament to build bridges with his opponents, he was intelligent enough to realize that in the open session of the National Assembly he might not be able to retain his West Pakistan majority.

A People's Party delegation visited Dhaka from 27 January for three days and held a series of meetings with Mujib and other Awami League leaders. Bhutto has given the following version of these discussions. He told Mujib that although the 'general impression of the people of West Pakistan was that the Six Points spelt the end of Pakistan', he was 'prepared to go as far as possible to meet the essential demands of the Six Points.' 'To assess and prepare public opinion in West Pakistan', however, Bhutto 'requested a reasonable length of time before the convening of the National Assembly.' Mujib, however, was 'intractable' and wanted the earliest possible session of the National Assembly, not later than 15 February.[48] Mujib briefed Ahsan in the presence of General Yakub Khan and General Farman Ali about the inconclusive talks with Bhutto, but informed them that there would be another meeting with the People's Party for more detailed discussions. Meanwhile, Mujib asked the Governor and the Generals to press Yahya for an early session of the National Assembly.

On his return, Bhutto met Yahya on 11 February and told him that the Awami League had already prepared its draft of the Constitution which it would no doubt get passed by the Assembly. He assumed, without sufficient evidence, that the Awami League sought to impose constitutional obligations of intolerable financial burdens on the West Pakistan provinces to compensate East Pakistan for past inequities. He advised Yahya not to call the Assembly session until he (Bhutto) had completed his discussions in the West Wing, held public meetings in the main cities, and made one more attempt to negotiate a settlement with Mujib. For this process to be completed, he asked Yahya to announce a date for the Assembly session sometime towards the end of March.[49] It is not clear what change Bhutto could have brought about during this period in the situation as it had developed. He had already met some of the party leaders of West Pakistan and, in any case, he had about two months to forge an alliance in West Pakistan. His own party leaders, by and large, followed his lead and no time was needed for discussions with them. As for the public meetings, complicated constitutional issues could not be settled by demagoguery in mass meetings. The delay in calling the Assembly had already created suspicions among the Bengalis who were getting impatient; the law and order situation was taking a turn in which peaceful meetings of the Assembly might become difficult to hold in Dhaka. The polarization was becoming stronger and, as more and more West Pakistani leaders were visiting Dhaka and meeting the Awami League leaders, Bhutto's own claim to be the sole upholder of the federation was losing credibility. There was nothing to be gained by continuing the suspension of the democratic process, as far as the unity of the country was concerned.

Yahya must have realized the futility of any more procrastination when he announced on 13 February that the National Assembly would meet on 3 March. On 15 February Bhutto announced in Peshawar that the People's Party would not attend the Assembly session unless it was made clear to him and his party men that there would be some amount of reciprocity from the majority party, either publicly or privately. He then went on to make some indiscreet remarks about the 'jeopardy which he and his party members would put themselves in by going to East Pakistan in the present state of affairs.' Referring to the other West Pakistani leaders who might be attending the session he threateningly said 'but they will have to come back also.'[50] But who could have given the guarantees that Bhutto was demanding? The LFO, which was accepted by all the parties who had participated in the elections, had conceded the right to frame the Constitution to the simple majority. There was no constitutional way to get round this fact.

Bhutto's decision not to attend the Assembly evoked criticism even from the opponents of the Awami League in East Pakistan. In

West Pakistan, except the Qayyum Muslim League and the People's Party, all other parties had decided to attend the Assembly. The leader of one such party made the sensible remark that if the majority party was unreasonable, they would walk out from the Assembly.[51] This was the course adopted by the Awami League as a dissident party when the Constituent Assembly had adopted the Constitution in 1956. They fought within the system and eventually agreed to work under it. But what Bhutto was asking for was outside the system and could only be resolved by extra-constitutional measures.

Bhutto was called to Rawalpindi by Yahya on 19 February and they had a five and a half hour meeting.[52] On 20 February the LFO was amended so that any member of the National or Provincial Assembly could resign even before he had taken the prescribed oath and assumed the office of member. Bhutto had earlier taken from every elected member of the People's Party a letter of resignation from the Assembly to which he had been elected. In terms of the original LFO, this letter had no value unless the member first attended the Assembly session and took oath. The amended LFO allowed an elected member to resign his seat before the first meeting of the Assembly, by a notice in writing under his hand to the Chief Election Commissioner. Bhutto could thus forward the resignation letters of any of his party men who, in defiance, tried to attend the forthcoming session of the Assembly This unusual legal provision must have been made only in pursuance of a definite plan to strengthen Bhutto's hands to control his party members. But why would Yahya go out of his way to accommodate Bhutto? Later, when Bhutto made the alternative demand for the removal of the limit of 120 days for the completion of constitution-making as a condition for his attending the session, Yahya refused to agree on the ground that since the LFO was agreed to by all the parties, any amendment of it on the demand of one party would create complications with others. The argument was rather thin; the LFO had been amended a number of times and the removal of the time limit was not likely to be objected to by the Awami League because, according to Bhutto, their draft Constitution was ready for enactment by the Assembly. Yahya again seemed to be providing an alibi to Bhutto.

On 22 February, Yahya called a conference of the Governors and MLAs; Hamid, Peerzada, and others were also present. Yahya brought up the political deadlock on the Assembly session. Sahibzada gives this account of the meeting:

> The opinion was generally but not unanimously against any postponement of the Assembly session. But Yahya seemed to have made up his mind. I and Ahsan requested for a private meeting. The President left the Cabinet room and took me, Ahsan, Hamid, and Peerzada to the side-room. I and Ahsan explained the very serious consequences of any postponement. Yahya wanted to impose open-sword martial law to roll back the political situation to what it was in 1969. We said it was impossible now. He was adamant but said he would further discuss it next morning. That night I could not sleep and drafted a letter to Peerzada for the President bringing out the full implications of postponement and re-introduction of naked martial law. Both I and Ahsan were staying in the East Pakistan House and in the morning I showed this handwritten letter to Ahsan who endorsed it. We went to the President's Secretariat and I gave this handwritten letter to Peerzada who read it and remarked, 'it will create trouble.' But he did not say whether he agreed with its contents or not. Meanwhile, the buzzer came from the President and we were ushered into his office. Peerzada placed my letter before the President who read it once and then again. Yahya was a bit shaken but stuck to his views. He thought 'a whiff of the grapeshot' would do the trick and reimposition of the rigours of martial law would create no problems. We could not convince the President. He remained adamant regarding postponement unless Mujib could be persuaded to make concessions on the Six Points to enable Bhutto and other West Pakistan leaders to attend the Assembly session. But we dissuaded him from re-introducing the naked martial law. Peerzada during all this time did not say a word. We were asked to inform Mujib on 28 February about the postponement. On 28 February Ahsan, myself, and Farman met Mujib, who was accompanied by Tajuddin, in the Governor House. Mujib was perturbed when told about the postponement. He asked Tajuddin to go out and then said that he would be in serious trouble with his extremists. He pleaded that if postponement was inevitable, a fresh date may be announced simultaneously. We promised to convey his views to the President and did this in a series of signals, urging postponement to a definite date and again warned Rawalpindi of the serious consequences if this was not done. I and Ahsan frantically tried to contact the President and also communicated our views in the strongest terms to Peerzada and General Hamid.

Peerzada was in favour of postponement as he told me: 'If the

National Assembly had not been postponed and met as earlier announced on 3 March I have no doubt the Awami League would have declared independence.'

The decision to postpone the National Assembly meeting is regretted, in retrospect, by the West Pakistani intelligentsia as a tragic decision which led to the breakup of Pakistan. A considerable body of opinion holds Bhutto responsible for it. Two aspects of the situation, as it had emerged in the last week of February, need to be highlighted to put the controversy in its proper perspective. It may also be mentioned in passing that, at the time these momentous decisions were taken, they were not criticized by the Press or the intelligentsia of West Pakistan in the manner in which they are now, with the acquired wisdom of hindsight. In fact, most of the vocal classes and forums hailed them and welcomed the army action eventually taken in the last week of March. The opposition to Yahya came from Admiral Ahsan and the generals serving in East Pakistan who were more realistic than the generals in Rawalpindi. In their courageous stands they got no support from any quarter and in West Pakistan at the time were even condemned as traitors for pleading peace and harmony between the two Wings of the country.

The first aspect relates to the consultative process by which Yahya arrived at the decision to postpone the Assembly session *sine die*. Yahya was initially dismayed at the election results and the post-election behaviour of Mujib, but after his discussions with the Awami League leadership at Dhaka in the second week of January, he seems to have regained his confidence. In a buoyant Press conference immediately after these meetings he called Mujib—the only time he did so—the future Prime Minister of Pakistan. He saw no harm in the Six Points. But in Larkana he faced the combination of the political and military leadership of West Pakistan, which thought differently. Mujib's failure to tone down his public statements on the Six Points, his refusal of the repeated invitations to come to Rawalpindi, and the unwillingness to show the Awami League draft Constitution which he had promised before the elections, weakened Yahya's credibility in the regime leadership. He could no longer overrule or ignore his advisers' latent suspicions, now more openly expressed. According to Umer, he now spoke more frequently of saving West Pakistan. The sequence of events immediately before the decision to postpone the Assembly indicates a pattern. In early February, after receiving from Bhutto a report of his meetings with Awami League leaders, Yahya sent Karim to Dhaka to invite Mujib to Rawalpindi. Mujib refused. Yahya was furious and asked Ahsan to read and then hand over the following message to Mujib in the presence of the MLA: 'Convey to Mujib that I am very dissatisfied with his refusal to accept my invitation to visit Rawalpindi. If he does not arrange to come to Rawalpindi as soon as possible he will be entirely responsible for the serious consequences which will follow.' Although Yahya agreed to withdraw the message on Ahsan's persuasion, it does show the degree of estrangement between the principal spokesmen of the two Wings. About Bhutto's call for postponement of the Assembly session, Hasan relates: 'Bhutto called me up from Peshawar late in the evening of 14 February because he was not getting Peerzada and said that he was proposing postponement of the Assembly and wanted confirmation of the President whether he should proceed. I conveyed this to Peerzada who rang up Yahya and confirmed to Bhutto.' The linkage between the five and a half hour Bhutto–Yahya meeting on 19 February and the amendment in the LFO on 20 February, which enabled Bhutto to strengthen his control over recalcitrant party men, is too obvious to be missed. During the Governor's Conference two days later, Ahsan found the atmosphere in Rawalpindi one of crisis and military intervention. All this shows that Yahya's thought-processes had started transforming after the Larkana meeting. The pressures exerted by Bhutto and the hawkish generals and the continued truculence demonstrated by Mujib led Yahya to seriously consider the re-imposition of naked-sword martial law to regain control over the situation. It is alleged that there was an understanding between Bhutto and the central army leadership to prevent the Awami League from implementing the Six Points, which it would have if the National Assembly had been allowed to meet. The course of political affairs after the Larkana meeting lends credence to the convergence of the army's perceptions with Bhutto's of the dangers posed by the Awami League to the integrity of Pakistan.

The second aspect pertains to the substantive question whether the martial law regime was prepared to accept the new financial, economic, and administrative structure envisaged by the Six Points. It may safely be assumed that the Constitution framed by the

Assembly would have been substantially based on the Six Points as far as East Pakistan was concerned. The Awami League's original manifesto had envisaged Pakistan 'as a Federation granting full autonomy on the basis of the six-point formula to *each* of the federating units' (emphasis added). However, in the post-election discussions, it was conceded by the Awami League that West Pakistan provinces might follow different constitutional arrangements. The analysis of the Six Points that follows is therefore with reference to East–West relations.

Point number one, relating to the federal parliamentary system based on direct adult franchise and representation on population basis in the federal legislature, had already been conceded. The remaining five points envisaged a fundamental change in the centre–provinces relationship. Point number two restricted the Federal Government only to foreign affairs, defence, and currency; the latter two, in turn, were circumscribed by the conditions set forth in the other four points. Even under foreign affairs, foreign economic relations were sought to be provincialized. Point number three provided either separate currencies for the two Wings or a single currency with separate federal reserve systems for each Wing. The single currency under the proposed arrangements was only symbolic; the procedure in each case was to prevent free movement of capital between the two Wings. The Bengali grievance that West Pakistani capitalists were taking the profits away to West Pakistan had a basis, but was not wholly true. There is no denying that, but for the enterprise of non-Bengalis, there would have been very little industrialization in East Pakistan, and internal and foreign trade would have continued to remain in the hands of Calcutta capitalists. In the industrial sector alone, six non-Bengali industrialists with assets in East Pakistan (Adamjee, Dawood, Bawany, Ispahani, Amin, and Karim) controlled over 40 per cent of the total assets, 32 per cent of production in the large manufacturing sector, and 81.5 per cent of the jute industry of the country. Three houses (Adamjee, Ispahani, and Amin) accounted for 69.1 per cent of the total jute manufacture, Adamjee alone holding the major share of 49 per cent. Out of the six industrial houses, four had their entire holdings in East Pakistan in 1961. Each of the other two houses (Adamjee and Dawood) had about 50 per cent of their total net assets located in East Pakistan. A comparative study of 1961 and 1970 shows that, except for a few changes in relative rankings in terms of value of assets and dispersal of holdings, the top houses remained the same over the decade.[54] The heavy stakes of non-Bengali capitalists in East Pakistan no doubt emerged from the windfall profits they made, but the growth in their assets showed that most of these earnings were being ploughed back into East Pakistan. The big business houses, the degree of concentration of wealth in them, and the kind of windfall profits which enabled them to increase their capital assets were the same in both the Wings. Reforms were needed at the national level. Point number three only sought to regionalize monopoly capitalism by subjecting the non-Bengali capitalists to such conditions as were applicable to foreign investors. Point number four entrusted all taxation powers to the provinces; the Federal Government to be provided with 'requisite revenue resources for meeting the requirements of defence and foreign affairs . . . on the basis of a ratio to be determined by the procedure laid down in the Constitution.' This revenue assignment was to be consistent 'with the objective of ensuring control over the fiscal policy by the Governments of the federating units.' The defence budget would thus be subject to the the fiscal policy of East Pakistan, which was bound to be at variance with the security threat perceptions of the West-dominated army. Point number five sought separate accounts of the foreign exchange earnings of each federating unit under the control of the respective province; the requirements of the federal government to be met by the federating units on the basis of a formula incorporated in the Constitution. This Point also gave powers to the regional government to negotiate foreign aid and trade within the framework of the foreign policy of the Federal Government. With no consensus on foreign policy, it was difficult to conceive a coherent foreign aid and trade approach by the two Wings. The substantial defence requirements of foreign exchange were likely to be subjected to the same scrutiny by the East Pakistan government as the total budget before agreeing to any contribution. Point number six empowered East Pakistan to maintain a militia or para-military forces under the control of its government. This provision would enable East Pakistan to become self-sufficient in defence in terms of its own perceptions of threats from across the borders. The East Pakistan government was not, therefore, likely to be very responsive in financial terms to the competitive state of preparedness with India that was always demanded by the Pakistan army.[55] The Bengalis in general were not deeply committed to the Kashmir problem and the Awami League was inclined towards good relations with India. They had always had serious reservations, particularly after the 1965 War, about the army's strategy of defending East Pakistan not on their own soil but by powerful thrusts on the western borders of India. Singly and in totality, points three to six would have necessitated a fundamental restructuring of foreign and defence policies of a kind which no West Pakistani leadership drawing its strength from the Punjab, and least of all a Punjab-dominated military regime, could possibly accept.

The Six Points were never referred for official examination to bring out their full implications and to develop alternative proposals to accommodate Bengali demands within a viable federal structure. This had become necessary after the elections, when they had become the official policy of the majority party. Yahya did not clinch the issue when the Awami League leaders made a presentation of the Six Points to him in January. He had not briefed himself to ask the Bengali leaders informed and intelligent questions about the shape of the federation that would emerge from the implementation of their formula. Indeed, a day before these meetings, according to Ahsan, Peerzada was searching for a copy of the Six Points. The Awami League, backed by professional economists, had issued detailed explanations of its programme from time to time and made light of the dangers perceived in West Pakistan to the integrity of the country through complete regional autonomy. In the party literature on the subject, six-point autonomy was sought to be justified with reference to the concept of regional autonomy of the British Cabinet Mission Plan of 1946 and the autonomy envisaged in the Lahore Resolution of 1940.[56] The West Pakistan media and academic circles regarded the Six Points as just a dangerous slogan. There appeared to be little realization of the emergence of new political forces which required a re-ordering of the established system and a new national compact among the major federating units. Umer recalls some vague and casual thinking about the Six Points:

> One point of view was not to discuss the Six Points in detail. Many on the civil side thought that Bengal was a liability. M. M. Ahmed, V. A.

> Jaffery, and perhaps Ghulam Ishaq Khan carried out an exercise and concluded that the Six Points will be suicidal for West Pakistan. But the subject was never formally brought up for consideration in the cabinet or before the President.

According to the rules of procedure, the Planning Commission or the Ministry of Finance could initiate formal examination of a sensitive political issue like the Six Points only under instructions from the President, and not on their own. M. M. Ahmed confirms that the 'Six Points were never examined in depth at the official level. They were not taken seriously before the elections, as Mujib had given an understanding to Yahya that they were merely bargaining points.'

The position that emerges from the above analysis of the various factors in the February situation is that Bhutto, in opposing Mujib and the Six Points, was really articulating the stand of the West Pakistani establishment. His refusal to go to the National Assembly had the full support of Yahya and the Rawalpindi generals. It would not be fair to blame Bhutto for the postponement of the National Assembly session unless it is conceded that the Six Points were acceptable to the army, the establishment, and to West Pakistan in general. If the Six Points were acceptable to Yahya then he need not have postponed the Assembly session. The Army could have easily ensured the security and attendance of such West Pakistani members as were willing to attend the session, Bhutto's threat of dire consequences notwithstanding. But Yahya gave no assurance of security of the person of the political leaders who intended to attend the session. He rather flippantly told them, when they came to see him after Bhutto's Lahore speech of 28 February 'when your legs are broken, you tell me and then I will do something.'[57] In fact, Yahya seems to have used Bhutto to get out of the situation created by his thoughtless decisions. Bhutto, on the other hand, used Yahya to build himself up as the sole leader of West Pakistan and earned the permanent odium of forcing the postponement of the Assembly, leading to the secession of East Pakistan. Bhutto could have as effectively adopted the democratic path of attending the session and using the Assembly floor for whatever he wanted to project. In the last resort, he could have walked out after showing that he had exhausted all constitutional means to maintain the integrity of Pakistan.

As had been predicted by 'men on the spot', all hell was let loose in Dhaka after the radio announcement of the postponement of the Assembly session in the early afternoon of 1 March. There were processions, strikes, and riots. The Awami League became the *de facto* government of the province. The same evening Ahsan was relieved and Yakub Khan was asked to take over. Yakub Khan urged the President to come to Dhaka. Yahya refused, but on 4 March in a telephonic conversation with Yakub Khan, agreed to announce a new date for the Assembly. This concession was too late by three days. Mujib was now demanding the immediate setting up of a provisional government. Yahya turned down the demand, saying, 'some other President would have to give this concession.' Seeing the violent reaction in East Pakistan, Yahya, on 4 March belatedly called an all-party conference to meet at Dhaka on 10 March. Except the People's Party, all the leaders refused the invitation. Yakub Khan thought that the course of events was leading towards military intervention which, in his opinion, would have disastrous consequences and he submitted his resignation on 5 March. The same evening in a broadcast Yahya announced the next date of the Assembly session—25 March. Hardline generals were appointed to handle the deteriorating situation. Peerzada says, ' Yahya suddenly decided in Karachi, on 2 or 3 March, to appoint Lieutenant-General Tikka Khan as Governor and MLA East Pakistan. I knew in Karachi he was in contact with Bhutto but I cannot say definitely that the selection was made on his advice. But it was not on my advice. Lieutenant-General Amir Abdullah Khan Niazi was appointed Commander Eastern Command, on the advice of General Hamid. Both of them were of low calibre.' Earlier, in the last week of February, Yahya had dismissed his cabinet to tighten the grip of the army on the administration; only Cornelius and Choudhury were retained as advisers. Meanwhile, men and material were being rushed to reinforce the Eastern Command. The army's contingency plan, in case of military action and suspension of political activities, called Operation Blitz, was updated some time in February, cleared with the HQ CMLA, and communicated to all the formation commanders. By the time Yahya decided to go to Dhaka in mid-March to hold political negotiations, the army had reached an advanced stage of preparation to regain control of East Pakistan if called upon to do so.

As the crisis in the East deepened, Yahya seemed to be getting closer to Bhutto. Important decisions in the aftermath of the postponement were preceded by publicized meetings of the two.[58] Yahya was carrying on a long-distance dialogue with Mujib also, over the telephone. But these conversations were ineffectual and abrasive: Mujib saying 'Are you the President of West Pakistan only?' And Yahya retorting 'Are you the Prime Minister of East Pakistan only?' Mujib was bitter, and in a tense mammoth public meeting on 7 March demanded: immediate lifting of Martial Law, transfer of power to the elected representatives, return of troops to the barracks, and an inquiry into the firing by the army which had resulted in killings.[59] The writ of the government of Pakistan was no longer applicable in East Pakistan and the state of siege was becoming a *de facto* secession. Yahya could no longer evade the moment of truth. He sent a personal message to Mujib not to precipitate matters and to await his arrival in Dhaka.

Yahya met Bhutto in Karachi on his way to Dhaka on 14 March and, the same afternoon in a public meeting, Bhutto proposed transfer of power to the majority parties of East and West Pakistan in their respective Wings. The parliamentary parties of West Pakistan strongly criticized Bhutto for suggesting the division of Pakistan.[60]

Yahya arrived in Dhaka on 15 March. Following is a day-to-day account of the final efforts to bring about a negotiated settlement to keep Pakistan united.[61]

Soon after his arrival, on 15 March Yahya called a meeting of the Governor and senior officers of the armed forces, posted in East Pakistan, in the President House, to review the political and law and order situation. The air force officer opposed any military intervention.

The first meeting between Yahya and Mujib was held on the morning of 16 March and the second round on 17 March, both without aides.[62] No minutes of these one-to-one meetings were kept and the working procedure, Hasan says, was that 'after the Sheikh left, Peerzada used to be called in and thereafter, according to the directions given to him by the President, the PSO would brief us. Such briefings formed the basis of our discussions with the Awami League team.' Mujib made it clear to Yahya that East Pakistan could not live with West Pakistan on the old basis any more. He demanded withdrawal of martial law and immediate transfer of power to the elected representatives, at both the provincial and central levels. Yahya agreed to the transfer of power and a martial law Regulation was drafted providing for the suspension of the martial law operation and setting up of a council of ministers from amongst the elected representatives to aid and advise the Governor in the performance of his functions.

In the evening of 17 March, teams of the President and the Awami League met to discuss the modalities of transfer of power. The Awami League team comprised Kamal Hossain, Tajuddin, and Nazrul Islam. The President's team maintained that lifting of martial law without an instrument ratified by the National Assembly would create a legal vacuum in which anything could happen. The Awami League team, however, insisted on withdrawal of martial law and rejected the proposed mechanics of transfer of power through the Martial Law Regulation. The meeting adjourned without any agreement.

On the morning of 19 March, Mujib met Yahya again and reiterated the demands made in the previous meetings. The same evening, the two teams met and went over the issue of the withdrawal of martial law. The President's team argued that in case the Martial Law Proclamation of 25 March 1969 was revoked, the instrument setting up the central and provincial governments would be legally void; Yahya Khan was President by virtue of being the CMLA. But these legal niceties failed to convince the Awami League team. Tajuddin responded that it was a political issue and should be resolved in a political manner, and Kamal Hossain saw no problem in Yahya divesting himself of the powers of the CMLA and assuming the title and powers of the President.

Cornelius, who had examined the question of the withdrawal of martial law, had in the meantime been summoned to Dhaka. His conclusion, which he had earlier submitted to the President, was that, under the existing conditions, martial law, giving sanction to the federal structure as incorporated in 1962 Constitution, was the sole source of central authority and could not be withdrawn without proper constitutional arrangements. After the meeting of 19 March Peerzada, Cornelius, and Hasan jointly recommended to the President that (i) central and provincial cabinets be set up; (ii) the National and Provincial Assemblies be invested with legislative powers as provided in the 1962 Constitution; and (iii) martial law organizations like courts, administrators, etc., be abolished in East

Pakistan but the office of the CMLA be kept intact. After some hesitation and despite the strong objections of military authorities, Yahya agreed to the proposals and asked Cornelius to resolve the legal problem. Accordingly, a Martial Law Regulation on these lines was drafted.

On 20 March a full-dress meeting of the President and Mujib and their aides was held. Yahya asked Cornelius to explain the necessity for the retention of martial law until the ratification of constitutional arrangements by the National Assembly. While Cornelius was doing so, Tajuddin interrupted and said, 'what is he talking about? It has been agreed between our leader and the President that martial law will be lifted altogether.' Cornelius pointed out that the Assembly was going to meet only a few days later, on 25 March, and the lifting of martial law might be postponed until the members had taken oath to abide by the terms of the Proclamation and the interim Constitution given by it. Mujib did not agree and said, 'No, no. You do not understand. This is a political matter.' The Awami League insisted on an immediate withdrawal of martial law and undertook to bring a West Pakistani constitutional expert, A. K. Brohi, to support their stand. The President said that he must consult West Pakistan leaders on the issue. In the meanwhile, it was decided that the teams should work out an amended 1962 Constitution of a parliamentary form of government in the Centre and provinces, and the terms of a Proclamation through which it might be promulgated. The idea was to ascertain the views of the Awami League on other issues involved in the transfer of power. It was also decided in this meeting, on the suggestion of Mujib, to set up two committees of the elected representatives, one at Dhaka of East Pakistani members and the other at Islamabad of West Pakistani members; each to formulate constitutional proposals in respect of its Wing. The proposals of the two committees would then be debated in the National Assembly to frame a Constitution acceptable to both the Wings.

During the next two days, Cornelius and Hasan prepared a number of working drafts of a Proclamation, accommodating as far as possible the view point of the Awami League. M. M. Ahmed was summoned from West Pakistan to advise on financial provisions. But on 21 March, Mujib and Tajuddin in an unscheduled meeting with the President said that they no longer wanted a representative government at the Centre which may be run by the President, if he so wished with the help of advisers; Mujib only wanted the Provincial Assemblies to be summoned and vested with complete legislative powers. This was a very significant development. The Awami League was already in full control of the province. Its extremists were openly talking of independent Bangladesh. There were strong rumours that foreign powers had promised financial and political support to an independent East Pakistan, provided it could be brought about legally. In the highly volatile circumstances prevailing in East Pakistan, therefore, Cornelius was concerned that even a very short interregnum, during which the country was without any central authority, might be used for declaring independence. He also considered it dangerous for West Pakistan, where the Tribal Areas enjoyed virtual independence. But Yahya told Cornelius that he did not care about the legal niceties and had no objection to the withdrawal of martial law through Proclamation, if it was acceptable to the West Pakistan leaders.

The Awami League had, by now, clearly indicated that it was not interested in national issues or concerned with the problems of West Pakistan. Its demands, which were confined to the status of East Pakistan, were: (i) restoration of civil government in East Pakistan within a week or so under a governor chosen by the Awami League; (ii) martial law to be lifted totally as soon as the governor took office—totally, because otherwise it would not have a completely free hand in East Pakistan; (iii) an interim Constitution based on the 1962 Constitution with amendments, to be given through a Proclamation; the interm Constitution to incorporate the Six Points in so far as East Pakistan was concerned; and (iv) the President to continue as such under an agreement to be signed by the leaders of all parties and to also be the C-in-C of the armed forces.

A new draft Proclamation was prepared by Cornelius and Hasan in the light of the Mujib–Yahya meeting of 21 March. Meanwhile, Yahya had sent for West Pakistan leaders, who had started arriving in Dhaka and who met the President separately on 19 March. Bhutto arrived on 21 March with a large team and met Yahya the same evening. Yahya briefed Bhutto on Mujib's proposals, and the discussions held so far with the Awami League. Yahya informed him that he had told Mujib that the Awami League proposals would be subject primarily to the concurrence of Bhutto and preferably of the other West Pakistan leaders also and that he intended to obtain this consent in writing from the leaders.

With some difficulty Yahya managed to prevail upon the two leaders to meet jointly with him on the morning of 22 March. In the presence of Yahya, the two leaders remained stiff and formal and no substantive discussions were held. But when they went outside, according to Bhutto, they had a heart-to-heart talk on the lawn of the President House. Immediately after the departure of Mujib, Bhutto conveyed to Yahya his strong reservations about the Awami League's proposals.[63] Mujib was now opposed to any meeting of the National Assembly sitting for the whole country. Bhutto requested that the Presidential Order summoning the National Assembly on 25 March should be rescinded. A proposal to refix the session for 2 April to endorse the Proclamation was not accepted by the Awami League.

Faced with a deadlock, Yahya now turned to the politicians and on the same day, 22 March, called a meeting of the West Pakistan leaders other than those of the People's Party. The meeting was attended by Wali Khan, Mufti Mahmud, Sardar Shaukat Hayat, Daultana, and Mir Ghous Bux Bizenjo. Peerzada describes the proceedings: 'Yahya Khan informed the meeting that a Proclamation was being issued to lift martial law. It was perhaps Daultana who objected to this procedure and said it should not be done except through the National Assembly which may be called for fifteen minutes if only to approve the Proclamation. Not all the leaders spoke on the urgent issues in the meeting. Wali Khan confined himself to a few jocular remarks. In response to the objections of the leaders, Yahya asked them to go to Sheikh Mujib and persuade him to attend the National Assembly which had already been called for 25 March. They went to the Sheikh and came back to inform Yahya that Mujib had refused to back down from his four points. Yahya asked them, "What should I do now?" They said, "You are the President. Do your duty".'

22 March was a hectic day for the President and his staff. By the afternoon, a working draft of the Proclamation was delivered to Tajuddin and Bhutto. The same evening, at 6 p.m., the President's team, which now included M. M. Ahmed besides Peerzada, Cornelius, and Hasan, met Bhutto who was accompanied, among others, by J. A. Rahim, Mahmud Ali Kasuri, and Mubashir Hasan.

The People's Party raised the same objection to the lifting of martial law through Proclamation without ratification by the National Assembly as was being made by Cornelius. They made the following points: (i) the Proclamation should either be endorsed by the National Assembly or should be announced immediately but made effective after ratification by the Assembly. Alternatively, the Proclamation should keep the office of the CMLA intact; (ii) in the absence of legal sanction, the terms of the Proclamation would not be binding and there would be no legal bar to a unilateral declaration of independence by the Awami League; (iii) what would the status of the LFO be after the Proclamation? (iv) sufficient safeguards should be incorporated to meet the expenditure on central subjects in case East Pakistan was to contribute its share on a percentage basis; (v) authority to vary the Third Schedule of the 1962 Constitution should be restricted to modification of the Schedule and not extend to the amendment of the relevant Article or modification of all the items of the Schedule including those agreed to be administered by the Centre, like defence; (vi) it should be provided that when the reports of the two committees were presented in the combined sitting of the National Assembly, no measure would be deemed passed unless approved by a majority of the members of each Wing; and (vii) the National Assembly should first sit as a single body before the two House Committees were set up.[64]

The People's Party delegation said that they had done their duty by highlighting the implications of a Constitution based on the Six Points. They, however, expressed their willingness to go along with the broad agreement embodied in the draft Proclamation, subject to the rectification of legal lacunae left by the withdrawal of martial law and clarifications sought during discussions, even though they were not in full agreement with some of its features.

Three meetings were held between the President and Awami League teams to thrash out the details of the Proclamation; the question of the modality of its promulgation was still not decided. The first meeting was on the morning of 23 March. The President's team expected to discuss the draft circulated by them the previous day, which incorporated the agreed points and which was the basis of discussion with the People's Party. But the Awami League team, for the first time, produced their own twenty-six page draft and insisted that that should be the basis of discussions. Peerzada protested that this would create complications because the People's Party might reopen the discussions by producing their draft. However, the meeting proceeded with the study of the Awami League draft. Since the President's team wanted time to go through it, the meeting was postponed to 6 p.m.

The two drafts were poles apart in their concepts and assumptions.[65] The President's team's draft tried to accommodate the Bengali demands within the existing system; the Awami League draft sought to restructure the Centre–East Pakistan relations on a completely new basis. The detailed discussions that took place in the second meeting on the same day in the evening accordingly led nowhere. The Awami League draft consisted of two parts; one, of the Proclamation proper, which incorporated the Six Points, and the other a Schedule which contained ancillary amendments to the 1962 Constitution to give effect to the system envisaged in the first part. There were some loose ends in the Awami League draft, perhaps deliberately left there for bargaining, but essentially the scheme was devised to establish a confederation of two independent states, and at the end the Awami League team said so. Its main features were: (i) martial law should stand revoked in a province with effect from the day on which the provincial governor took his oath of office and in any case at the expiry of seven days from the date of the Proclamation; (ii) as against 49 Central subjects in the third Schedule of the 1962 Constitution the Awami League provided only 12 in its draft. Of these only two were of a substantive kind and even they were formulated in a truncated form as 'Defence of Pakistan' and 'Foreign Affairs, excluding Foreign Trade and Aid'. In the original third Schedule, under 'Defence', there were five sub-items relating to the armed forces, all of which were excluded, leaving a number of areas relating to defence vague, and capable of different interpretations. Similarly the seven related items under Foreign Affairs were eliminated. It was suggested that the minimum necessary within the concept of one country was 'Foreign Affairs including foreign policy aspects of Foreign Trade and Aid' and not the formulation of the Awami League. The draft also provided for the appointment of separate trade representatives abroad and independent foreign borrowings without reference to the Centre; (iii) the Centre had no power of taxation whatsoever, even for its limited subjects. It was suggested that either the Centre should be given powers to levy taxes to the extent of its needs through its own agencies or through the East Pakistan government or that there should be a constitutional provision for East Pakistan to make an agreed percentage contribution to the central expenditure and that this contribution should be made charged expenditure in the East Pakistan budget; (iv) there would be a separate Reserve Bank of Bangladesh under the control of the Bangladesh legislature. It was pointed out that it would not be possible to set up a separate central bank by 9 April. A new organization of the State Bank of Pakistan, a new law of exchange control, the replacement of Pakistan securities with East Pakistan securities, etc. were complicated matters and could not be completed in a fortnight. It was suggested that the Proclamation should merely incorporate the concept instead of giving the deadline of 9 April. The President's team also suggested a Federal Reserve Board to co-ordinate the credit policies of the two Wings; (v) it was provided that there would be two Constituent Conventions, one of the elected members of Bangladesh and the other of West Pakistan. They would meet on 9 April and prepare Constitutions for their respective Wings within 45 days. These Conventions were different from the House Committees earlier decided. The members of the Conventions were allowed to take oath before the Chief Election Commissioner instead of in the National Assembly. In short, the central government had no authority or consultative role in the affairs of the 'State of Bangladesh' (the term used for East Pakistan in the Awami League draft).

The Awami League team refused to budge on any of the points. The third and last meeting was on 24 March when the Awami League team came up with an amendment to its draft which took it even beyond the Six Points, the first of which had said that the character of the government of Pakistan shall be federal. It amended its draft now to read 'After the Constitutions of the State of Bangladesh and States of West Pakistan have been framed . . . the President shall summon a meeting of the National Assembly, at which all the members shall sit together as a sovereign body for the purpose of framing a Constitution for the Confederation of Pakistan'; the previous day the term used had been 'the whole of Pakistan'. The question of legal lacunae was no longer relevant; the Awami League had expressed its intentions of doing what the

President's team had apprehended they would, in the absence of a legal cover for central authority. The President's team protested. Cornelius said the amendment was in conflict with the entire draft which was for a federal system, and suggested the term 'Union of Pakistan' instead of 'Confederation'. But the Awami Leaguers refused and said the change had been made under the orders of Mujib.

There is conflicting evidence whether the teams had agreed to meet again to further discuss the amendments proposed by the President's team and to finalize the draft. The White Paper has quoted the press statement of Tajuddin after the meeting of 24 March that they had nothing more to say and there was no need for any further meeting. Cornelius said he had fixed a meeting with Kamal Hossain for the following day in order to go over the ancillary provisions of the 1962 Constitution for incorporation in the Proclamation. But after the meeting, Peerzada conveyed the President's order to Cornelius that the West Pakistani officials who were in Dhaka for talks should leave on 25 March. Hasan also says that the next meeting was fixed for 25 March at 4 p.m. but he was asked to postpone it to 26 March. He went to Dhanmandi with an escort to inform Mujib who remarked, 'Hasan Bhai, they are playing dirty.' Tajuddin later asserted that there was no breakdown of talks and after the meeting on 24 March 'where Mr. M. M. Ahmed passed on his amendments, a call was awaited from General Peerzada for a final session where the draft could be finalized.' He maintained that Yahya never indicated in the January or March meetings what part of the Awami League programme was totally unacceptable to him.[66] Kamal Hossain asserts that their draft contained nothing new. It was only a clean copy incorporating the points discussed and agreed to up to that point, except for the term 'Confederation' which, he says, was negotiable between Yahya and Mujib. In fact, as a matter of tactics, he said, he had all along refused to give any paper and had asked the President's team to produce a draft of the agreement. Kamal Hossain regards the new draft version of the proceedings as a conspiracy and attributes it to the 'mischief' of Peerzada.[67]

On 24 March Bhutto met Yahya and Peerzada. That night, according to Bhutto, an emissary took Ghulam Mustafa Khar to meet Mujib who proposed that Bhutto should become Prime Minister of West Pakistan and leave East Pakistan to him.[68] On 25

March at 4 p.m., Bhutto and his team were briefed on the proposals of the Awami League. They again opposed the lifting of martial law. The negotiations were over. Hasan saw Peerzada and Yahya leaving, purportedly for a party in the Eastern Command, and found 'everything in the President House kept in place as if the President was staying. At about 11 or 11.30 p.m. a lieutenant-colonel entered and took over the President House premises and told Hasan that army action would start at 12 midnight.'

In the Yahya scheme of things, military action was the ultimate fallback position if the Awami League did not come round to an acceptable compromise. All the top generals were in Dhaka during the negotiations and watching the situation carefully. Peerzada says:

> During the hectic period of March 15 to 25 March Yahya was not only holding political negotiations. In between he was visiting army installations and meeting army officers in the cantonment. Like other times after every visit and meeting with army officers he came back with a more aggressive attitude towards political settlement and with an over-simplified view of the army's capability to control affairs. He was heavily influenced by the top brass that he need not or should not concede too much to the politicians.

M. M. Ahmed recalls his role in the negotiations and gives the following impressions, long after the event (in 1993):

> In March during negotiations with the Awami League, Peerzada called me to Dhaka to help regarding financial provisions of the new Constitution. I tried to avoid [this] and suggested A. G. N. Kazi in my place but Peerzada insisted on my presence.
>
> I was of the view that the Centre should retain the powers of taxation although the entire collection from East Pakistan may be given over to them. Similarly, I was opposed to the regionalization of foreign aid which was an adjunct of foreign policy. Then there was the question of meeting the central government expenditure. It was likely that with all heads of taxation with it, East Pakistan would be reluctant to contribute to defence to the extent that was desired by the central government. I also pointed out that after all as the majority party the Awami League would control the central government also and as such it seemed to be fighting against itself.
>
> My impression is that they were willing to concede on most of these points. But on 23 March, Mujib came to meet the President with

> Bangladesh flag flying on the car. He could have had a Pakistani flag also. As he entered the gate there was an exchange of hot words with the Military Secretary who strongly protested against the Bangladeshi flag entering the President House.
>
> On one of these days the President was to go to the cantonment but he was informed that the Awami Leaguers had blockaded the roads. The President waited on the lawn until the route was cleared. He refused to use a helicopter. I think these things made him angry with the Awami Leaguers.
>
> Yahya used to meet Hamid, Umer, Mitha and other generals regularly in the cantonment during this period.

In mid-March the operational plans for the internal security of East Pakistan were hastily revised to update them to the realities of the times. As against the earlier plan, which assumed loyalty of the Bengalis in civil and army establishments, the new plan called 'Searchlight' accepted that 'the Awami League had widespread support even amongst the E.P. [East Pakistan] elements in the Army.' The operation, therefore, 'has to be with great cunningness, surprise, deception, and speed combined with shock action.'[69] Apparently, the army was confident of meeting all these pre-conditions and of regaining control of the province even against violent opposition from all sections of the 75 million Bengalis.

Major-General Farman Ali and other senior army officers in Dhaka were involved in the political developments in the province and seemed to have a fairly good idea of the magnitude of the task of re-establishing central government authority in Dhaka and other parts of the province. As earlier on other issues, there was a difference of opinion about the feasibility of army action between the East Pakistan and GHQ generals. Farman claims:

> I was against the army action. Local commanders were against it. But the West Pakistan generals were for it. For three days it was discussed what to do with Mujib; should he be taken alive or killed. One section was for killing him. Till the twenty-first, we did not know whether action will be taken. On the twenty-second, Tikka informed us to be ready.

Part II

Army Action, Civil War, and Separation

CHAPTER 4

Restoring the Authority

Twenty-four hours after the army had moved to regain control of East Pakistan from the Awami League, Yahya Khan informed the nation that the political negotiations had failed. On 26 March 1971 at 8 p.m. in a radio broadcast from Rawalpindi, he gave a brief resume of his efforts to arrive 'at some reasonable solution', blamed Mujib for his 'obstinacy, obduracy, and absolute refusal to talk sense', accused him of treason, reaffirmed that 'it is the duty of the Pakistan Armed Forces to ensure the integrity, solidarity, and security of Pakistan', and informed the people of Pakistan that he had 'ordered them [the army] to do their duty and fully restore the authority of the Government [in East Pakistan].' All political activities were banned, but the Awami League was 'completely banned as a political party'.[1]

In the aftermath of army action, both the Awami League and the Yahya regime held each other responsible for bad faith and resort to arms. The government of Pakistan alleged that by 24 March the Awami League's preparations for an armed uprising and declaration of an independent state of Bangladesh had reached an advanced stage. It had thus become a purely military question who should strike first—the Pakistan army or the Awami League. Although Yahya denounced Mujib as traitor in his broadcasts of 26 March and 28 June, the details of the Awami Leagues plans to secede were not revealed until much later when the 'White Paper on the Crisis in East Pakistan' was published by the government of Pakistan on 5 August. Tajuddin and the other Awami Leaguers, on the other hand, claimed that there was no breakdown in negotiations and the army action was an act of treachery which forced them to go into exile, resist the Pakistan army, and declare independence.[2]

According to Umer, the Awami League was proceeding within

the framework of its three alternative contingency plans to secure the independence of East Pakistan with Indian assistance. By 20 January, as it was not getting its way in the negotiations, it was preparing to launch plan two in order to achieve its objective. Information was coming in, Umer says, of the Awami League plan but the situation was allowed to assume serious proportions; 'we pushed ourselves into the 25 March military action' by not taking appropriate measures in the earlier stages. Peerzada says, 'During the negotiations, I used to wonder whether the Awami League was playing according to a preconceived plan. Since then I have reasons to believe that what they called "contingency plans" in case of failure of negotiations were nothing but a conspiracy already hatched, to secede.'

The details of the Awami League's contingency plans were produced by the prosecution in the evidence of Bengali army officers during the trial of Mujib in August. These plans and the activities relating to them are described below.[3]

In 1967 the Awami League had set up cells to give practical shape to the Six Point programme. Dr Nurul Islam headed the economic cell and Colonel Osmany the military cell. In November 1970, Mujib, although sure of sweeping the polls, apprehended that the martial law regime would not transfer power on the basis of the Six Points to his party. He directed Osmany to prepare detailed plans to meet such a situation and motivate all Bengalis in the armed forces, para-military forces, and other organizations of uniformed personnel to join the liberation struggle when the call was given.

The cells were actively monitoring the situation after the elections. In the meeting of the economic and political cells, in early January 1971, Tajuddin informed the participants that the US Ambassador had called on Mujib and had categorically told him that the US would not be in a position to help him if the Pakistan army undertook to suppress the Awami League movement. The Ambassador advised Mujib to come to an agreement with the West Pakistan leaders, to which Mujib had replied that he would not compromise on principles. It was the consensus of the meeting that the Pakistan army would not be able to suppress the entire people of East Pakistan; Indian support, international pressures affecting economic and military aid, and the long rainy season would all militate against the Pakistan army and a Vietnam-like situation would emerge.

Meanwhile, Osmany had started contacting serving and retired Bengali military officers. He convened a meeting of about twenty army officers, including one retired major-general, in January 1971, in the officers' mess of 2 East Bengal Regiment at Joydebpur. The others were a brigadier and some colonels, majors, and captains. Osmany presented three plans to the meeting. Plan One pertained to the defence services policy of the Awami League, in case there was a peaceful transfer of power to it after the elections; the armed forces would be reorganized to rectify the adverse ratio of Bengalis in them and also to eliminate chances of martial law in future. Plan Two laid down details of armed resistance after declaration of the birth of independent Bangladesh, if power was not transferred to the Awami League and its success in the elections was sought to be crushed. The rebel forces, to be called *mukti bahini,* would be raised from the Bengali elements of the various armed forces, volunteers, and ex-servicemen. The Awami League members of the Assemblies would assist the rebel force in logistics. The province would be demarcated into six sectors for operational purposes. The targets for occupation in each sector would be aerodromes, ammunition and petrol dumps, communication centres, power stations, and Pakistan army command headquarters. Details of scorched-earth measures were also laid down to obstruct the Pakistan army operations. Plan Three catered for the failure of liberation forces to retain occupation of Bangladesh against the offensive of the Pakistan army. In such a situation, all sector commands would retreat across the borders to India. The road link bridges, etc. would be destroyed during retreat. A long-drawn resistance would be organized with the assistance of India on the military, diplomatic, and political fronts. Osmany informed Tajuddin that he had already had meetings with the Indians, along with Awami League leaders, and was assured of full help in terms of the plans. Duties were assigned to various officers, and the next meeting was held in early February to finalize operational details on the basis of the assignment reports of the various officers. In the middle of March Osmany held a small meeting to discuss the disruption plans and to convey the decision of the Awami League high command that Plan Two would be in operation from 10 p.m. on 26 March.

The neat and accurate details of the contingency plans, corresponding to what actually happened after the army action, spelled out in the confessional statements of the Bengali officers may give rise to some doubts about their complete veracity. But in their broad outline they seem to be confirmed by events and by other sources. Firstly, the co-ordinated response to the army action indicated a fair degree of pre-planning of resistance. There were simultaneous uprisings of Bengali elements in the army, paramilitary forces, and police all over the province. Indian assistance was readily forthcoming on the borders; key points were occupied; most of the Awami League leadership left for India, and no time was lost in declaring an independent Bangladesh. The prompt resistance in different directions, in fact, showed a better co-ordination than the Pakistan army action, which was taken without adequate diplomatic, political, or even military preparations. Secondly, Mujib and other Awami League leaders admitted after the emergence of Bangladesh that they had contingency plans in case the army decided to use force.[4] Thirdly, the International Commission of Jurists, otherwise hostile to the Yahya regime, commenting on the Awami League plans given in the White Paper observed that, although the 'source of this information is not given, but it seems inherently probable, as well as being consistent with subsequent events, that there would have been a contingency plan of this nature.'[5]

In Dhaka on the night between 25 and 26 March, the army operation was planned to start at 1 a.m., after the President's plane had entered West Pakistan air space. By this time all threshold preparations, detailed in the revised security plan called 'Searchlight', like troop movements to target areas in the city, switching off of the telephone exchanges, etc. were to be completed. But due to the resistance that the Awami League workers offered to the troops moving out of the cantonment at about 10 or 11 p.m., the essential ingredients of the plan, 'cunningness, surprise, and deception', were lost.

During March, even before the army action, there were defections and desertions of Bengalis from the military units and the East Pakistan Rifles (EPR), a paramilitary force. The first target of the army in the city was therefore the disarming of Bengalis in the various forces. EPR personnel were disarmed in their HQ at Peelkhana at 2.30 a.m. after some resistance in which both the army and EPR personnel suffered casualties. Some EPR personnel managed to escape with their weapons. The two thousand-strong

Dhaka reserve police was disarmed at 3 a.m. They also suffered casualties in resisting the army. The Dhaka University campus, which was regarded as the centre of the Bengali resistance, was attacked at 2 a.m. According to army circles, after stiff resistance with rifles and shotguns, the hostel, which was the hotbed of 'rebellion', was finally 'secured' at 5 a.m.[6] Curfew was imposed on the entire city and the army attacked the previously-marked strongholds all over the city.

Major-General Farman Ali was the executor of the Dhaka part of 'Searchlight'. He succeeded in 'shock action' by concentrated and indiscriminate firing on target areas, but failed to arrest the maximum number of student and political activists, particularly the sixteen leaders listed in the plan.[7] Farman's version is:

> We were not allowed to start operations before the President's plane had reached the Karachi reception zone which was 1 or 2 a.m. This affected the planned movement of the troops to the city. The departure was supposed to be secret but the Bengali group-captain present at the airport informed Mujib. At that time all the Awami League leaders were with Mujib and I straight away wanted to go and detain them. But I was not allowed to do so at that time. The military personnel who were detailed later did not recognize the wanted persons. The police could have been helpful but it was no longer available.

A commando platoon arrested Mujib from his house at 1.30 a.m. His guards resisted, and one of them was killed. Kamal surrendered the following day. In the ferocity of the army action and indiscriminate killings and arrests, even the moderate elements did not feel safe. Except these two, the Awami League leadership thus left for India either from fear or design. The process of the emergence of Bangladesh, which had become inevitable by now, would have been different if the elected leadership had remained available for negotiations and not lost their political freedom of action by going to India.

Roedad Khan, Secretary Information, who had recently been appointed to this post, was called to Dhaka in the middle of March but he was not put in the picture to handle the foreign and domestic media. Colonel Siddique Salik, an officer of the Inter-Services Public Relations (ISPR), was the spokesman of the regime. The ISPR did not bother much about its public relations and the need to cultivate foreign journalists. Roedad came to know of the army action at about 10 p.m. at a dinner from a foreign correspondent who received a call from his contact and announced to the guests and the host that 'The fun has started. Tanks are rolling.' When Roedad reached the cantonment, Salik told him, 'we have got the big fish', meaning Mujib. But the immediate problem was that all the Bengali staff of Radio Pakistan had disappeared. With some difficulty, a non-Bengali *moulvi* was traced to recite the Holy Quran to start the morning service on 26 March and an army officer read the news.[8]

From early March, the East Pakistan crisis had attracted the attention of the world media and Hotel Inter-Continental was full of foreign newsmen representing the most powerful newspapers, news agencies, and radio and television networks of the western world. In the late evening of 25 March while the excitement was at its highest pitch at the doubtful prospects of some compromise, there came a sudden clampdown on journalistic activities. An army detachment came to the hotel, took up positions at the gates and confined the newsmen within the premises. There was no explanation or briefing by any spokesman of the army about the extraordinary happenings. The journalists were naturally keen to go out and see things for themselves but some of them who did try were pushed back by the commanding officer; 'I can handle you. If I can kill my own people, I can kill you,' shouted the young captain ordering the journalists back to the hotel. But it was not necessary to go out to know what was happening. The Bengali contacts of the foreign correspondents in different parts of the city kept them informed of what was happening for two to three hours after the action had started until the telephone exchange was switched off. It was also visible from the upper storeys of the hotel; the night presented a deadly shadow play of light and sound of the fire-power of a modern army. The city skyline was one continuous arc of fireworks.

The foreign correspondents could not be removed from East Pakistan until 27 March and the 'shock action' envisaged in the initial offensive took place in full view of the world news media. On 27 March in the early morning, the foreign journalists were bundled into army trucks and under heavy armed guard taken to the airport. Their baggage and bodies were thoroughly searched there for written material and photographs, some of which were confiscated. In some cases the process was repeated at Karachi before they left Pakistan. Eye-witness accounts of the indiscriminate army operation during one day and two nights, and the treatment meted out to twenty-five foreign newsmen, were reported in the *New York Times* of 28 March[9] and by UPI Hong Kong on 29 March.[10]

This humiliation of the representatives of the world media was indicative of the haphazard nature of the army action. Uptil then the foreign Press had not been against the regime and there was no occasion to be so boorish towards them. It was necessary to explain to them the government's case, the reasons for the breakdown of political negotiations, the necessity of taking some action to restore law and order, and the programme for their departure. The mindless handling of the world's powerful media was only slightly less catastrophic than the army action itself. They did not forget or forgive this treatment and Pakistan's case suffered immensely in the world opinion-making forums for the next nine months. Tikka was beyond understanding these matters. The ISPR, whose job it was to ensure good public relations, remained inactive and allowed the army to get a bad name all over the world. It was unfortunate that even Farman, who had established a rapport with the foreign correspondents, did not intervene.

The number of people killed in the Dhaka operation remained unknown but the Bengali sources claimed they were in thousands. A still larger number left the city for the anonymous safety of villages. But the army faced a very difficult situation in the outlying districts and interior areas due to the rebellion of the Bengali elements in various armed forces. Out of approximately 17,000 EPR personnel, only 4,000 could be disarmed. The rest decamped with their arms to join the rebels or go home. Most of the provincial police defected with arms, wireless, and other equipment. All the Bengali troops and officers either deserted with arms or resisted the disarming of their battalions. In Chittagong, 8 East Bengal, East Bengal Regimental Centre, and the trainees of 9 East Bengal, which was in the process of being raised, rebelled on the night of 25–26 March. 4 East Bengal located at Brahmanbaria and Shamshernager defected; one of its companies at Comilla, however, was disarmed. The battalion moved to the Sylhet area where Major Khalid Musharaf was organizing the resistance force. 2 East Bengal HQ at Joydebpur rebelled on the night of 28–29 March and decamped with all the arms, ammunition, and equipment. Two companies of

3 East Bengal, located at Ghoraghat and Gaibanda in North Bengal, defected and moved towards Hilli. The battalion less these two companies was disarmed at Saidpur. 1 East Bengal, which had the reduced approximate strength of two companies because it was due to move to West Pakistan, was located at Chandpur. It was ordered to Jessore where it was disarmed after some resistance; some of its personnel succeeded in escaping with arms and ammunition. 10 East Bengal was the National Service battalion and had been recently raised; there were desertions in it between 3 and 25 March, the remaining trainees were sent on leave and the battalion was rendered ineffective.

The Pakistan army's plans had not envisaged the nature and magnitude of the resistance that it encountered in actual operations. In Chittagong city, fierce battles between the army and rebel units and police raged from 26 March to 4 April. Both the navy and the air force were used to reduce rebel strongholds and even after eight days there were pockets on the surrounding hills and in the suburbs, which were eliminated only over a period of time. The army columns sent from major cantonments to relieve the beleaguered garrisons or occupy district headquarters were ambushed by the rebels, both sides suffering casualties. On 28 March the road column coming from Comilla was held up thirteen miles short of Chittagong by rebel opposition. A Special Service Group column sent on the night of 28–29 March from the Chittagong area to link up with the Comilla Column was ambushed and suffered casualties which included its commanding officer. In Sylhet town the rebels had entrenched themselves in the district courts and circuit house buildings and were eliminated on 9 April. The garrison in Rajshahi was surrounded by rebel forces and troops had to be lifted by helicopter to strengthen the besieged battalion. The air force was also used to strafe the rebel points on the outskirts of Rajshahi. By 12 April the major portion of the province was still in rebel hands. Army columns moving to occupy major cities had met with reverses at various places and suffered heavy casualties. It was not until early May that the army could claim all district and subdivisional headquarters and major towns cleared of the rebels.[11] There were still some pockets of resistance, particularly in areas close to the border but mopping-up operations were being pursued with vigour. The hostile elements were eliminated, had gone underground, or had been driven across the borders. The government of Pakistan felt confident enough to allow a team of selected foreign correspondents to visit East Pakistan from 6 May onwards.

In securing the occupation of the province, the Pakistan army had to fight all the way to reach every part of it. And even then the Chittagong Hill Tracts and Cox's Bazar were outside its control. At the end of May, it had reached the limits of its capability. Further efforts to retain, in the coming months, what had been achieved, stretched the army to breaking-point. The physical occupation of the administrative centres and major cities by no means signified the restoration of the authority of the central government over the province in any integrated sense. The rebellion was all-pervasive, even if not everywhere overt, and the army's efforts to install civil administration in occupied places proved futile. Civil administration does not resort to coercive powers in its day-to-day functioning; its writ is largely based on the moral authority it enjoys by the acquiescence of the people. In a state of rebellion by almost the entire population, it cannot function. Only military rule can sustain the occupying authority in these circumstances. Thus, clearing the towns and cities of the rebels, as the army termed its occupation—implying that only a handful were resisting it—was meaningless. The occupation of the towns and countryside lasted, somewhat precariously, only as long as the troops stayed on. As the liberation struggle took the form of guerrilla activities in urban and rural areas and Indian military pressures were built up on the borders, it was difficult to determine who controlled the vast interior outside Dhaka and Chittagong.

Nevertheless, the East Pakistan martial law authorities proceeded with the reconstruction of the provincial administration, to maintain control of the area cleared of the rebels by the army. This was sought to be done by removing the disloyal elements in the bureaucracy (all Bengali civil servants were suspect, some more than others), and inducting reliable West Pakistani officers in key positions. The Bengali police was severely depleted by defections and those that remained could not be relied upon. Thus, not only the senior officers but the subordinate ranks including the constables, who were recruited locally and liable to serve only in their home districts, were also brought from West Pakistan, mostly the Punjab, and posted in the totally alien interior areas of East Pakistan. A martial law regulation was issued to enable the central government to transfer these policemen to East Pakistan. At a later stage, they were also used in army operations, for which they had no training.

In the first week of May, Lieutenant-General Tikka Khan, Governor, Martial Law Administrator and, for some time, Commander of all the armed forces in East Pakistan asked for top level changes of the Bengali Chief Secretary and the Inspector-General of Police. The army authorities suspected both of them of collaboration with the Awami League in the pre-26 March period. In addition, the central government was asked to depute fourteen West Pakistani civil and police officers of district and divisional rank. The Governor reported that six deputy commissioners, one deputy inspector-general of police, and two superintendents of police were missing, and the conduct of three deputy commissioners and two superintendents was under investigation. 'Missing' in those days could mean anything: crossed over to India or killed (never determined by whom). The fifteen West Pakistani officers notified for posting to East Pakistan represented strongly against their transfer. Their pleas were not accepted but they were informed that most of them would be posted in Dhaka which, they were assured, was a safe place. A similar assurance was given about Chittagong where it was considered necessary to post a West Pakistani divisional commissioner.

I was one of the fifteen West Pakistani officers ordered to report to Dhaka. My selection was due to my previous experience of having served in East Pakistan for six years. Pakistan International Airlines (PIA) used to run one service between the two Wings in those days. Leaving Karachi at 1.30 a.m., I and a few colleagues reached Dhaka at 8.30 a.m., after six and a half hours, via Colombo, on 17 May. As we disembarked, the plane was encircled by soldiers. Some PIA ground staff stood at the foot of the gangway to guide the passengers to the lounge. The whole place was deserted and with the fixed machine-guns and patrolling soldiers gave the impression of being under imminent threat of attack. The passengers were herded into the lounge, the doors of which were closed except for the one leading to the custom and immigration shed, which was guarded by a sentry. A nervous and somewhat fearful Bengali protocol officer, whom we knew from our previous posting, came in and mournfully welcomed us. We listened in silence to his outpourings about the sorry state of affairs in the

Secretariat and the city, and the arrogance of the army officers who would not let him receive us properly as distinguished visitors. After about an hour, we queued into the immigration and custom hall where, under the supervision of an army officer, our luggage was inspected and antecedents checked as if we had come to a foreign country.

In the evening I and Akhlaque Hussain, a West Pakistani colleague, went out to meet our Bengali friends. The pervading fear and nervousness in their homes told us more of what had happened and was still happening than the stories they related to us. The gates of the sprawling bungalows, usually open, were tightly shut, and were opened only after we had identified ourselves. The state of fear and demoralization of the very senior officers, their wives, and children was shocking. Each one had horrifying stories to tell about atrocities, insecurity of women's honour, and directly or indirectly being affected by the army operation.

The following day, on 18 May, I reported to the Secretariat. It looked desolate with hardly a public visitor around. Akber S. Ahmed, Deputy Secretary of the Services Department who should have normally informed me of my posting was himself in a state of shock. He had lived through the upheavals of the Awami League agitations and the army action and was desperately trying to get away from the province. Shafiul Azam, the Chief Secretary, was not available that day due to a family tragedy, which was indicative of the ghastly state of affairs.[12]

Later the same day, I went to see Major-General Farman Ali who was Deputy Martial Law Administrator and designated Major-General-in-charge Civil Affairs. He was the kingpin of civil administration in East Pakistan and remained so till the fall of Dhaka. He had his office in the Governor House. He gave a casual briefing on the situation in a somewhat aggrieved manner, giving the impression that he and the officers on martial law duties 'to help' the civil administration were carrying a great burden in East Pakistan as a patriotic duty. This was the usual refrain of the army officers posted in East Pakistan in May and June. The atmosphere in the martial law offices in the Governor House was cheerful and confident. Unlike the Civil Secretariat, there was a horde of visitors waiting to see concerned officers for permits (various kinds of permissions were required under martial law orders) and other favours.

Colonel S. D. Ahmed (later Brigadier), who sat next door to Farman, was an exception to the general run of army officers in Dhaka. He had no illusions about the army's capability to hold on to East Pakistan. During the violent days of the army crackdown, he had saved a number of Bengalis including Rahman Sobhan, the firebrand theoretician of the Awami League, whom, I was told, he helped to escape from East Pakistan. He was living in an elegant suite on the top floor of the Governor House and there was provision for excellent food and drinks. Colonel Ahmed was generous and lavish in his hospitality, but irreverent to authority, particularly to his austere boss, Tikka Khan. He gave me firsthand accounts of the grisly army operation. During the short period that he was in Dhaka, after my arrival, I saw life in the cantonment, which was an island of peace and comfort surrounded only a few furlongs away by a bleak, silent, and fearful city. In the daily round of evening and late-night parties, nothing was found missing. There was no lack of confidence, no regrets over the unfortunate happenings, and no doubts about the future among the officers. They did not envisage political moves for reconciliation in any foreseeable future.

Having successfully directed the army operation, General Tikka Khan focused his energies on civil administration, which he gathered in his own person and reduced to directives on all and sundry subjects. The General undertook to tackle all military and civil problems with earnestness and a genuine conviction in his ability to solve them. He held interminable meetings every day with departmental secretaries, heads of various agencies, and other officials, cajoling them to restore normalcy in their respective spheres. The labour leaders, mill managements, owners and operators of river vessels and road transport, executives of oil companies, and bankers, etc. would all be called to the Governor House where Tikka Khan would deliver a harangue and exhort them to still greater efforts and threaten them with martial law. In between, he would rush to Chittagong and Khulna to reactivate the ports, and to other places like Bogra to assess the losses to public treasuries. Immense energy and resources were dissipated in chasing phantoms; repairing roads and railways which were be struck again at the same or other places, changing the traditional pattern of traffic from land to river without adequate resources, organizing a new police force of loyal elements which were not available, eliminating the rebel elements which could not be wished away, movement of food without sufficient transport, restoring the banking system with no takers of credit, resuming industrial activities in the absence of labour and management, etc., etc. At the end of the day, lengthy progress reports would be sent to the CMLA Secretariat, summarizing the efforts of the Governor and the MLA to restore the authority of the government. Going through these reports, one is struck by the awesome responsibility assumed by Tikka Khan and the other generals, but still more by the fact that it did not seem to bother them at all. The CMLA Secretariat at Rawalpindi could have formed a more objective view of the hopelessness of the situation from these reports but in the euphoria of April–June nothing seemed beyond the capability of the army.

By July, the pattern of guerrilla activities in the occupied areas, on the borders, and particularly in the north and south of Dhaka had emerged with devastating effect. The main trouble area at this time was the hilly border with Tripura and Assam which provided a suitable terrain to the insurgents for operations at minimum cost. The main railway lines were suspended. At Feni, south of Comilla, the major bridge which provided the rail link between Chittagong and Dhaka and Sylhet, was out of commission. Other road and rail bridges remained out of use.[13] Reprisals were being carried out by the army on the villages nearest to the site of sabotage. Vehicular traffic on the Comilla–Brahamanbaria road, such as it was, was occasionally fired upon, and a portion along the frontier had been evacuated to deal effectively with the guerrillas coming from across the border. In the Sylhet sector the roads were mined by the rebels and the tea gardens along the border were being shelled. In the interior there were pockets of insurgents. The Madhupur forest preserve in the Mymensingh district, to the north of Dhaka, was the scene of an army operation against the remnants of East Bengal regiments. The supporters of the pro-Beijing EPCP (M–L) were active in Naokhali district which at this time of the year was inaccessible by road. In Dhaka itself there were bomb explosions. The army, stretched to the maximum chasing the faceless enemy, had raised a militia, called *Razakars,* of the local non-Bengalis to guard vital installations.

The skirmishes on the borders with the Indians, and army operations in the countryside had remained in low key during the monsoon period. But by August India had stationed two army corps (eight divisions) with air support on the borders. In addition, the Indian Border Security Force had been increased from eighteen to more than thirty battalions. The guerrilla force was being trained in fifty training centres 'established in West Bengal and Tripura for the young, mostly Hindu, boys who volunteer to leave the refugee camps to serve with the *Mukti Fouj* [liberation army]'. About 40,000 guerrillas were under training to operate in East Pakistan as soon as the monsoon was over and to swoop down on the heels of the Indian army's advance into East Pakistan.[14]

The widespread insurgency in the province during the monsoon was brutalizing the Pakistan army and getting it deeper and deeper into the morass of guerrilla fighting in an effort to retain its authority. Being involved in chasing the shadows within, it became complacent about the preparations being made across the border to force the issue after the rainy season was over. In the briefings of the army officers to the visiting central government officers, some of which I attended, the situation was described as a stalemate in which the urban areas would be held by the Pakistan army and the countryside by the rebels for an indefinite period. The foreign Press was generally predicting a war between India and Pakistan by the end of the year. Recounting the formidable problems faced by the Pakistan army in East Pakistan in August, one seasoned correspondent was impressed by 'their self-confidence in retaining their delicate and difficult defensive role'.[15]

The subversive activities, which had remained sporadic and in low key during the monsoon, flared up from the middle of August all over the province. Leaflets and posters threatening bloody attacks on government offices and the collaborators appeared all over Dhaka before Independence Day, 14 August. City life, which had come round to something like working level, relapsed. As the date neared, security precautions were intensified and the city looked more desolate. Army jeeps with mounted automatic weapons patrolled the city. Bomb explosions and machine-gun chattering became the normal evening sounds of Dhaka. The Independence Day programmes drawn up by the authorities were disrupted. On the night of 14 August at 10 p.m. our Guest House was attacked by machine-guns, seemingly from all sides, the attack lasting for half an hour. The police guard responded by firing volleys blindly into the dark foliage around the building from its well-lighted positions on the boundary walls. There were similar attacks at other places the same night.

The guerrilla activities of the rebels in the end proved very effective in keeping the army on the run and allowing it no respite. From the latter half of August the rebels carried the fight to the heart of the major cities and the key installations. Four Pakistani supply vessels were sunk in August, 'including the simultaneous sinking of two vessels in Chittagong harbour by limpet mines, thereby seriously interrupting the flow of soldiers and military supplies from West to East Pakistan.'[16] The *mukti bahini* claimed to have captured twenty-three steamers and launches with their cargo of arms, ammunition, foodgrains, and essential commodities. On 4 November, a loaded oil-tanker capsized at the Chittagong Burmah Eastern jetty as a result of three successive explosions.[17] Large areas of Dhaka city went without water for nine hours when the Siddhirganj power plant was damaged by an explosion on 3 November. Three separate explosions damaged all four generators at the station and the entire industrial belt of Dhaka, Tangi, and Narayanganj was without power for fourteen hours. The television transmission station located in the heart of the business district of Dhaka was damaged by an explosion on 20 October. On 11 November a bomb exploded in the busy shopping centre of Baitul Mukkarum, killing five people. Water was running short in Dhaka city and there were frequent breakdowns of power due to sabotage of the far-flung transmission lines or power plants. Apart from the sophisticated acts of sabotage, there were assassinations of pro-Pakistan leaders. In mid-October, Monem Khan was shot dead in his house. Similar killings were reported from the interior of people who dared to co-operate with the administration.

Dhaka was a ghost city in October–November. The army had moved to the borders. Large numbers of people were leaving the city. Every day one could see bullock-carts loaded with families and their possessions moving towards the outskirts. The acts of sabotage became more daring. Bomb blasts, automatic weapons, and stray firing were the only sounds heard from early evening throughout the night. Social intercourse with our Bengali colleagues had dried up. Their worries and uncertainties were greater than ours. By the time war started in the third week of November, hardly anything was left worth fighting for.

CHAPTER 5

Making of the Government in Exile

On the morning of 26 March, a group of Bengali radio personnel stopped the broadcasts of Chittagong radio station, which was relaying martial law orders from Dhaka. They set up *Sadhini Bangla Biplobi Kendra* or Free Bengal Revolutionary Radio at Kalurghat, where the Chittagong radio transmitter was located, and started broadcasting directly from there, rallying people to defy the Pakistan army.[1] Two declarations of the independence of Bangladesh were made from this rebel radio. One was on 26 March at 2.30 p.m., purportedly coming from Mujibur Rahman himself and reported as such in the Indian Press, but actually a message read out by a local Awami Leaguer on behalf of Mujib.[2] The second declaration, which got much wider publicity, was by Major Ziaur Rahman, who declared independence in his own name at 7.30 p.m. on 27 March.[3] Subsequently, Mujib confirmed that he had declared independence on 26 March before his arrest.[4]

The elected leadership of the Awami League, which had crossed over to India in the last week of March, took prompt measures to give legitimacy and a structure to the resistance movement. On 10 April, the Proclamation of Independence Order was issued in the name of the elected representatives of East Pakistan. The Order, which was published in the Indian Press on 18 April was given retrospective effect from 26 March and confirmed the earlier declaration broadcast in the name of Mujib. The justification for the declaration of independence ran like this: the freely-elected representatives were summoned to meet on 3 March to frame a Constitution, but 'the Assembly so summoned was arbitrarily and illegally postponed for an indefinite period' and 'while still conferring with the representatives of people of Bangladesh,

Pakistan authorities declared an unjust and treacherous war . . . ; the elected representatives of Bangladesh, therefore, 'honour bound by the mandate given to us by the people of Bangladesh whose will is supreme duly constituted ourselves into a Constituent Assembly, and having held mutual consultations, declared, and constituted Bangladesh to be a sovereign people's Republic.'[5] The number or names of the elected representatives who subscribed to this Proclamation was not indicated. On 10 April in a radio broadcast, Tajuddin, 'on behalf of the government of Bangla Desh headed by Sheikh Mujibur Rahman', announced that an army was being built around the nucleus of professional soldiers from the Bengal regiments and the EPR. He announced the demarcation of East Pakistan into six operational commands—Sylhet/Comilla, Chittagong/Noakhali, Mymensingh/Tangail, Faridpur/Barisal, Khulna/Patuakhali, and North Bengal—and named the commander of each one of them.[6] They were all former Pakistan army officers and already operating on their own in the assigned sectors. In fact, the reason given for their appointment was the successes achieved by them up to that time within their respective zones. The purpose of this announcement was to bring the conventional and other forces under the control of the Awami League leadership through a unified command structure; Colonel Osmany was formally appointed commander-in-chief of the Bangladesh *Mukti* Force a few days later.

Two days later, on 13–14 April, 'following protracted deliberations at a meeting of National Assembly members and top Awami League leaders', a cabinet of the government of Bangladesh was announced.[7] On 17 April, a ceremony was held, in a village in Meherpur subdivision of Kushtia district, within a mile of the Indian Border Security Force's outpost, to announce the Democratic Republic of Bangladesh. The place was about eighteen miles north-west of Chuadanga town, which had been occupied by the Pakistan army only a day before after fierce resistance during which it was also bombed by the air force. To give maximum publicity to the cause of liberation, the function was held on the soil of East Pakistan, in the presence of two dozen foreign Press and television correspondents.[8] The formation of the provisional government of Bangladesh sought to create a focal point for a co-ordinated struggle to liberate East Pakistan and attract the attention of the world community to it.

The bloody operation that followed the army action of 25–26 March galvanized the whole political spectrum of East Pakistan, leftists of all hues, and the extremist and moderate bourgeois nationalists, into participating in the struggle for the liberation of East Pakistan. Even the pro-Beijing leftists who until the army action were condemning independent Bangladesh as a nationalist bogey and a diversion from the class struggle were compelled to join, because of the popular upsurge, the mainstream politics of liberation.

Soon after 26 March, two loose coalitions of political groups emerged as centres of resistance to the Pakistan army. One was led by the Awami League and included the East Pakistan Communist Party (EPCP), the National Awami Party (headed by Professor Muzaffar Ahmed), and the East Pakistan National Congress (representing the Hindus).[9] The alignment with the two pro-Moscow parties, which had no electoral strength or trained cadres in the field, was rather symbolic, intended to demonstrate the broad-based nature of the Awami League-led struggle. The Congress had more or less merged its identity in the Awami League by fully supporting the latter's candidates in the elections. This political coalition of moderates enjoyed the backing of the Indian government as against the revolutionary front of the liberation struggle. The insistence of India on political negotiations with the Awami League leadership to solve the East Pakistan crisis, discussed elsewhere, imparted legitimacy and authority to the Awami League government in exile. This was publicized to be located in Mujibnagar, somewhere in East Pakistan, but its secret location was actually No. 8 Shakespeare Saran in Calcutta. The acting president, the prime minister, and all other functionaries worked together in this building in close collaboration with the Indian government. Only Osmany was reported to be conducting operations from various places in East Pakistan or on the border. The public address of the exiled government was No. 9 Circus Avenue, the former Pakistani consulate building, which was named the 'Mission of the Government of the People's Republic of Bangladesh'. The Indian government had opened an office in Calcutta to liaise with the Bangladesh government. India had tried hard to obtain diplomatic recognition of the Bangladesh government from various countries, especially Yugoslavia. But no country was willing to take this step. Although the Bangladesh and Indian spokesmen claimed that the Awami Leaguers had brought 600 million rupees from East Pakistan, it was clear that the government of India was providing substantial financial aid to maintain the paraphernalia and style of the government in exile and its multifarious activities in East Pakistan and in foreign countries. The East Pakistanis working abroad were also reportedly sending donations to the provisional government.[10]

The other centre leading the resistance was a coalition of revolutionary groups which formed the National Liberation Struggle Co-ordination Committee in April. These groups committed to 'East Bengal armed struggle against the West Pakistani dictatorship and for an independent socialist East Bengal' were: NAP led by Bhashani; Maoist East Bengal Communist Party (EBCP) reported to be active in the Rajshahi, Chittagong, Pabna, Jessore, and Kushtia districts; the Maoist Co-ordinating Committee of Communist Revolutionaries, centred in Dhaka; and several student, peasant, and workers' unions. The National Liberation Committee, on 1 June, called for a united military struggle along with the Awami League and other resistance groups. These two liberation fronts between themselves claimed resistance forces of 50,000 to 100,000 guerrillas in mid-October, in addition to about 10,000 to 15,000 regular troops of the Bengal regiments and the EPR.[11]

The EPCP (M–L) was operating on its own in certain areas especially in Noakhali district. Throughout the East Pakistan crisis in 1971, the People's Republic of China had supported the Yahya regime, opposed the Bengali secessionists, and criticized India for interfering in the internal affairs of Pakistan. In July, the contradiction posed by China's stand caused disagreements in the EPCP (M–L) and led to the split of Toaha–Huq group. Huq considered that 'the entire confrontation was the product of Indian expansionism backed by the Soviet Union with the sole intent of destroying the territorial integrity of Pakistan.' Toaha agreed with the role of India and the Soviet Union but 'remained ambivalent about whether to support a movement of national independence led by the Awami League.' He established his base in the Noakhali–Chittagong area under a new banner called East Bengal Communist Party (M–L) and ultimately adopted the strategy of fighting both the bourgeois liberation forces and the Pakistan army. Huq retained the original party with the appellation 'East Pakistan', and offered to co-operate with Pakistan authorities against 'imminent Indian aggression, if only the army would stop its brutal attacks on the people.'[12]

The set-piece engagements with the Pakistan army undertaken by the *mukti bahini* in the first flush of rebellion, with the blessings of the Indian authorities, had resulted in heavy casualties. In July, it led to mutual recriminations among the various exiled groups and an acrimonious debate in the Bangladesh command and the Indian Press.[13] In the positional warfare attempted by the rebel elements against the Pakistan army, the elements of Bengal regiments had provided the main defence and those of the EPR had held the flanks; the volunteers, *Ansars* and *Mojahids,* were deployed on patrolling and arranging supplies. Taliapara in Sylhet, the home village of Colonel Osmany, Commander of the rebel forces, was the rebel training centre for which the instructors and logistic support came from India. This hastily-organized resistance structure, however, proved unequal to the well-armed professional Pakistan army. Only 3,000 men out of 6,000 of the five Bengali battalions and 8,000 out of the 17,000 men of the EPR had survived, escaped, or opted to join the resistance.[14]

These professionals provided the hard core of the *mukti bahini* under the command of Colonel Osmany, as the military arm of the Bangladesh government. Augmented by some recruitment in the ranks, and with the help of the Indians, these Bengali remnants of the Pakistan army were regrouped into two brigades with headquarters in the Indian border states of Assam and Tripura. One of the brigades, commanded by Khalid Musharaf, had its headquarters at Agartala and was called K-Force. The other was commanded by Ziaur Rahman with its headquarters in the north in Assam and named Z-Force.[15] The Awami League leadership was seriously concerned about the possible radicalization of the liberation struggle and its take-over by the revolutionary parties, if the *mukti bahini* did not show results quickly. This was possible only by heavy reinforcement of the *mukti bahini* which India in its own national interests started providing on a massive scale at a later stage. Given the revolutionary activities of the Naxalites in West Bengal, India was not unaware of the dangerous potential of the revolutionaries having a free run throughout Bengal. It could hardly afford 'a Vietnam at the doorstep' and took vigorous political and diplomatic steps, before resorting to war, to finally resolve the East Pakistan crisis.

The fears of the Awami League government were justified, but the danger of radicalization and losing control over the liberation movement was not only from the leftists. The ultra-nationalist officers of the *mukti bahini* were highly critical of the strategic approach of the high command and its dependence on India for its success. Two former Pakistan army officers who had escaped from West Pakistan, Abu Taher and Muhammad Ziauddin, were the main dissidents and proponents of an alternative strategic approach. They opposed the use of Indian territory for bases and insisted that the exile government and its military headquarters should be located on the soil of Bangladesh. Instead of regular military formations, they argued, the trained military personnel should be dispersed into the countryside 'to raise and train guerrilla brigades drawn from the peasantry to start a People's war' which 'in their view was the only road to a military victory where Bangladeshis—not Indians—would defeat Pakistan. This group remained categorically opposed, as a result, to Indian military intervention.'[16]

The diverse resistance forces represented by 'official' *mukti bahini* and the dissident group within it, the communist guerrillas of Matin's EBCP, Toaha's EBCP (M–L), Huq's EPCP (M–L), Bhashani's NAP, and other leftist elements, unorganized civilian armed bands owing allegiance to no party, and 'the private armies of bandit elements such as Kader Siddiqui in Tangail', were all dependent on India, one way or the other, for bases, sanctuaries, and arms. But it was not easy for India to sustain a dominant position for its protégé, the Bangladesh government, in the chaotic battlefield that East Pakistan had become. Both the Indian government and the Awami League leadership were afraid of the communists, particularly the pro-Beijing elements. Thus, while the National Liberation Struggle Co-ordination Committee called for unity with the Awami League, the latter was not very keen to welcome the revolutionaries as partners. Khondkar Mushtaque, the Bangladesh Foreign Minister, in an interview in July said that China was supporting Yahya to destroy the Awami League and that the Bangladesh government was not allowing recruitment of communists in the *mukti bahini* which was confined to the followers of the Awami League. Of late, however, he added, members of the pro-Moscow NAP had been allowed to join the guerrilla forces.[17] Many volunteers were rejected by the Bangladesh command after careful screening when they were found to hold extreme left-wing political views; these 'appear to have found their way to separate Naxalite camps where Maoism is the accepted creed.'[18]

The ideological turmoil and factionalism of the liberation movement resulting from the nationalists, ultra-nationalists, and different factions of leftists fighting parallel to or against each other reached a stage by October when 'a new force—Mujib Bahini—composed mainly of students loyal to Sheikh Mujibur Rahman . . . began to be sent in from Calcutta to counter the growing influence of leftists forces in Bangladesh. The East Bengal Labour Movement (part of the National Liberation Struggle Committee) reported armed encounters with the Mujib Bahini in its newspaper of October 1971. Meanwhile, ordinary *Mukti Bahini* (liberation army) commanders, supposedly under Awami League leadership but emanating from Bangladesh, were reported to be more radical . . .'[19]

The indigenous Bangladesh liberation struggle, torn by internal dissensions, would probably have remained a fragmented and ineffective movement for a long time to come had India not provided the overwhelming political and military leadership to bring it to a successful conclusion.

CHAPTER 6

Economic Consequences: East Pakistan

On 2 April 1971, HQ CMLA issued a notification constituting a special team led by Muzaffar Husain, Secretary National Assembly, to 'proceed to Dacca [Dhaka] on Monday, April 5th, in order to assist and advise the Martial Law Administrator Zone "B" and facilitate coord [co-ordination] with the Central Government.'[1] The censored Press, and the government-controlled television and radio had been reporting complete normalcy in Dhaka and other places since the start of the army operation. The urgent dispatch of a special team was the first indication to the civil officials in Rawalpindi/Islamabad that the take-over by the army in East Pakistan was not as smooth as had been expected and the economic life of the province had been disrupted to the extent that special measures were required to revive it.

The ten-member team arrived in Dhaka on 6 April. They were escorted by the army from the airport to the Governor House. The following day they were shifted to Hotel Inter-Continental which, the local martial law authorities said, was the only safe place in the city for the members to stay.[2]

Against this backdrop of insecurity in the capital, the team members proceeded to study the economic situation. They held discussions with Farman Ali, the Chief Secretary, and other senior civil officers. None of them went out of Dhaka to see the conditions on ground; indeed, they could not move freely even in the city which remained deserted during the day and under strict curfew during the night. There were no communications between Dhaka and even the districts reported 'cleared' by the army; most of the main towns were still held by the rebels. There were no means to ascertain either the ground position of the physical infrastructure like roads, railways, rivercraft, food, and other storage-godowns and power stations, etc., or the number of government functionaries still in position at various places. Nevertheless, the team, on the basis of whatever little information could be obtained, completed its task within a week and submitted a comprehensive document titled 'Report of the Special Team on the Revival of Economic Activity in East Pakistan', with a covering summary, to the Cabinet Division on 19 April.[3]

The special team report brought out, in considerable detail, the total breakdown of the economic framework in East Pakistan, in the first week of April. Describing the report as only a 'preliminary assessment' of the prevailing economic situation in the province, the team indicated the critical areas for priority attention and recommended measures to expedite revival of economic activities. The report, however, made it clear that unless two interconnected conditions were met, none of the suggested measures was likely to produce results. They were: (a) improvement in the general law and order situation, to create a 'sense of security and confidence among the people'; and (b) 'restoration of all the important transport and communication links.' While (b) was dealt with at length, and measures were suggested to activate the transport and communication sector, the team found itself 'unable to offer any meaningful comments or advice on the law and order situation.'

The state of the major sectors of the East Pakistan economy depicted in the report is described below.

1. Transport and Communication:

The two ports, Chittagong and Chalna, were so congested that their operation had come to a halt. At Chittagong port, about 200,000 tons (including 165,000 tons of foodgrain) of cargo were piled up in the godowns and on the plinths. Another twenty-five to thirty ships, with a similar tonnage, were awaiting unloading.

The team made three short and medium-term recommendations for the clearance of Chittagong port. The first was to bring into operation the food silo at the port as soon as possible; it was nearing completion but had been delayed due to the departure of the Japanese technicians after the army action. The second measure envisaged greater reliance on riverine transport for the movement of cargo to its destinations. Of the total estimated riverine transport capacity of 110,000 tons in the province, only about 40,000 tons could be utilized at Chittagong port in the rough weather of April and May by the coasters and sea-going barges. But these craft were not available; the crews had run away and the vessels had been hidden away in far-off creeks and islands by the owners. It was recommended that these vessels be requisitioned and moved in convoys, with adequate protection against the rebels, to the required destinations. The third recommendation was to augment the riverine transport capacity by immediately purchasing forty-five second-hand coasters, ferries, shallow draught vessels, and oil-tankers.

The critical situation of Chittagong port had been brought to the notice of the President earlier, in the first week of April. To prevent further accumulation, the Ministry of Defence had issued instructions that (i) cargo ships awaiting unloading at Chittagong should be redirected to Karachi; and (ii) all Chittagong-bound cargo ships on the high seas and at other points should, until further orders, continue to be diverted to Karachi. The diverted ships off-loaded about 150,000 tons of cargo at Karachi but many East Pakistan-bound ships proceeded to nearby foreign ports, such as Colombo, Singapore, Rangoon, and Penang, and unloaded about 100,000 tons. Arrangements were later made, at considerable cost, to retrieve this stranded cargo.

The Pakistan Navy, which was in charge of the port, had reported the desperate situation to the Economic Adviser on 15 April. It informed him that most of the port craft and equipment, like tugs, cranes, pilot vessels, etc. were immobilized, and all the transit sheds and warehouses were filled to capacity. Nothing was moving out by rail or road, and even the inland river transport, which in normal times carried only fifteen per cent of the total imports, was not available; a few coasters seized by the navy were being operated by its personnel for transport of defence material to Narayanganj. The navy recommended immediate purchase or charter of coasters and the opening up of road and rail links.

The team did not think that the railway could be restored to its earlier role as the main carrier of the region in the short or even medium term. Its network, the report erroneously concluded, was more susceptible to sabotage than road and water transport. By 15 April, only two or three very short railway sections were in operation, and all the main lines were out of commission. The team, however, hoped that it might be possible to make the roads operational as soon as the law and order situation was brought under control. On this hopeful assumption it recommended that the government-owned East Pakistan Road Transport Corporation (EPRTC) should open a trucking division with 4,000 trucks and also procure an additional fleet of 1,500 buses.

The inter-wing telephone and telegraphs links had been disconnected by the army for 'security' reasons. The teleprinter equipment was heavily damaged and only half the lines were in operation. It was recommended that the required equipment, which was being manufactured in West Pakistan, be brought over to restore the affected lines for private commercial purposes. The telephone, telegraph, and postal services within the province, however, were completely disrupted. The receiving and relaying equipment at different places were the special target of the rebels and there was no way to restore internal communications in the short-run. Postal services, as such, had ceased to exist and nothing could be done to revive them under the prevailing circumstances.

2. *Industrial Activities:*

Industrial production which was already at its lowest in early March, came to a complete stop after 26 March. In the first week of April practically all the factories were closed. The team identified the following problems faced by the industries. Firstly, there was the all-pervading insecurity of life and property and, consequently, a loss of confidence in all kinds of productive endeavour among trade, banking, and industrial circles. A large number of industrial establishments in East Pakistan were owned by West Pakistanis, and were operated by non-Bengali managers and technicians; most of them had left in March and were not likely to return until things had settled down. Secondly, the skilled and unskilled Bengali labour had also run away, after the army action, from the urban industrial areas to the collective security of their home villages. Thirdly, because of the breakdown in transportation and communication, there were no prospects of the raw materials reaching the factories, or of clearance of goods produced for local sales and export to West Pakistan or foreign countries. Fourthly, the team came across a few cases in which the non-availability of essential maintenance spares had resulted in the closure of factories. The most important such case was the Ghorasal Fertilizer Factory; the Japanese technicians, who were waiting for some essential spares to restart it, had left the country immediately after the army action. Lastly, the team found that, since business was at a standstill, the banks had restricted credit facilities which hampered whatever little of the industrial and trade activities remained. Export consignments were lying in the ports, the exporters' funds were blocked, interest charges were accumulating, and normal transactions remained suspended.

It was not only that there were no owners, managers, and workers to run the industrial units, but the infrastructure, other than transport and communication, was also in shambles. The Tangi and Kanchan industrial areas of Dhaka were reported to be without power. Gas supply to these areas had been cut off by the Titas Gas Company on 4 April as the major portion of the pipeline and the gas fields were in rebel hands. The Tangi industrial area was also experiencing an acute water shortage. The shortage of furnace, kerosene, and diesel oils was being felt. The Eastern Refinery at Chittagong had been closed for more than a month, although its storage tanks had more than one and a half month's requirement of crude oil, and two tankers were awaiting unloading.

The report recommended eighteen measures for the resumption of industrial production; six of them emphasized the obvious necessity of the restoration of the infrastructure by the government. Some of them sought to build up the confidence of the Bengali workers, through exhortations on television and radio, to return to work. For the management, the inducements recommended were: liberalization of bank credit, release of adequate foreign exchange for urgent imports, relaxation of import regulations in respect of critical items, deferment of custom duties on machinery and industrial raw materials, levy of excise duties on actual production instead of rated capacity, and moratorium by the government-owned financial institutions on repayment of loans. It was also recommended that ten to fifteen operators from Karachi refineries should be flown in to complete the maintenance of the Eastern Refinery, for which it had been shut down before the March disturbances, and to restart production.

3. Internal, Inter-Wing, and International Trade:

Export sales of jute and jute goods, which accounted for forty-three per cent of the total export earnings of Pakistan, were at a standstill in early April. At the end of February, 24,000 tons of jute consignments were lying at Chalna and 4,000 tons at Chittagong. There was practically no movement of jute during March from secondary markets in the interior to the baling centres and ports. Due to the hold-up of consignments at ports, disruption of the banking system, and stoppage of jute movement from the interior, the exporters and traders were experiencing a financial squeeze. The East Pakistan economy was based on the export of jute and jute products. Its stoppage had depressed growers' prices and the incomes of a large number of people in the cash sector of the economy. Consequently, there were serious apprehensions of famine in the rural areas due to lack of purchasing power.

Inter-wing trade had also come to a standstill for the same reasons as the foreign trade. In 1969–70, imports to East Pakistan from West Pakistan amounted to Rs 1,667 million, and its exports, mostly manufactures, to West Pakistan were valued at Rs 916 million. About 75 per cent of East Pakistan's tea production was consumed in the West Wing. Of the 147 tea estates, 126 were situated in Sylhet district which was still under the control of rebels. No one, at the time of the team's visit, knew how many were working. It was estimated that the production in 1971, even after the restoration of law and order, might not be more than 40 to 50 per cent of the previous year's crop of 69 million lbs. Thus, the normal deficit of 10 million lbs, which was met by imports, would increase to 45 to 50 million lbs. East Pakistan also supplied to West Pakistan 80 per cent of the latter's consumption of safety matches, nearly all the jute bag requirements, and newsprint. Substantial payments on account of supplies made from West Pakistan had remained frozen due to the Awami League ban, during March, on inter-wing transactions. Similarly, the tea exporters had not received payments from buyers in West Pakistan since February. The stoppage of inter-wing trade hurt West Pakistan more because it now had to import some of its requirements against foreign exchange and find alternative markets for its goods. In East Pakistan, all activities in any case had come to a standstill and goods supplied by West Pakistan were neither required nor could be imported due to transport difficulties.

4. Banking and Credit:

The head offices of major commercial banks and the State Bank of Pakistan were located in Karachi. During March, until the army action, the Awami League had restricted their operations to the receipt of deposits, limited payments, and inter-bank clearances within East Pakistan. By early April, the banks in Dhaka had reopened for normal business but the position of outlying branches and their cash holdings was not known.

The team considered monetary expansion the main instrument for the revival of economic activities in East Pakistan. Although the immediate problem was non-availability of labour, power, gas, water, etc., it apprehended that, after normalization, credit was likely to become a constraint. In February, commercial deposits and advances were equal in East Pakistan but by April the latter had exceeded the former due to the withdrawal and transfer to West Pakistan of deposits amounting to Rs 200–250 million. It was suggested that the State Bank of Pakistan should lend this amount to the eastern banking system and the normally strict criteria for advances to industry and trade should be relaxed. The West Pakistani private banks, however, were not likely to relax commercial criteria and incur risks. They were more likely to use the State Bank assistance to improve their deposits/advances ratio, which had deteriorated in March. To ensure liberal offerings of credit to the private sector, and in the priority areas of jute, textile, and interregional and foreign trade, the team suggested that part of the State Bank assistance should be extended through government-owned financial institutions.

At this time, one of the worries of the government was the fate of the chests of new currency which used to the maintained in district treasuries, under the Deputy Commissioner, by the State Bank of Pakistan to meet the cash requirements of the economy. The total amount of money in these chests in the province, at the time of the army action, was Rs 3,620 million. Details of the looting of this money will be given later.

5. Collection of Central Revenue:

While the proposals of the team for the revival of the East Pakistan economy involved considerable outlay of local currency and foreign exchange, the province itself had ceased to generate any resources to undertake any part of the recommended programme. The central government revenues from East Pakistan, on account of custom duties, sales tax, and excise, had dwindled to almost nothing. The Custom House, Chittagong, had stopped functioning from 2 March although the staff remained present and some branches continued working. Immediately after the army action, both the Bengali and West Pakistani staff deserted their posts. At the time of the team's visit, some preventive staff had returned but there was hardly anyone in the appraisal department, which assessed and collected the duties. But there was no work for the appraisers; in spite of various relaxations of procedure and demurrage charges, no bills of entry were being filed by the importers. As a result of the stoppage of industries, the position of excise duties was no better. Against the normal monthly receipt of Rs 50 million under this head, the collection in March and early April was negligible.

6. Provincial Finances:

The Annual Development Programme (ADP) of East Pakistan, for 1970–1, was Rs 3,079 million. The province's own contribution to it was fixed at Rs 154 million from the surplus of its revenue budget which did not materialize due to floods, cyclone, and political disturbances. The balance was to be financed by central government assistance and foreign aid. The non-availability of the provincial contribution, and shortfall in the utilization of foreign aid for the same reasons, had reduced the size of the ADP. A suggestion by Muzaffar Husain to scale down the central government contribution also by suspending the implementation of major projects like the machine tool factory, petro-chemical complex, etc. was not accepted by the Bengali Chairman of the Planning Board because of another pressing demand.

The provincial ADP and the portion of the central government ADP located in the province were important to East Pakistan, where public sector investment played the key role in generating employment and economic activities. In 1970–1, private investment, which was mostly non-Bengali, had suffered a further setback due to political uncertainties and the anti-West Pakistani feelings. While in the urban sector credit expansion was necessary for economic revival, in the rural areas recession in the jute trade necessitated injection of purchasing power to enable the people to buy food. The instrument for this process was the rural works programme which comprised small labour-intensive development schemes in these areas. In the reduced ADP, therefore, a higher provision had to be made for this programme and the original central government assistance could not be brought down proportionately.

The Bengali officials also proposed a twenty-five per cent increase in the following year's ADP, which was then under discussion. This, they said, was necessary to finance the ongoing works and for repair and rehabilitation of transport, communications, and various other damages resulting from army action and rebel activities. The financial impact of the damages, however, was not confined to the provincial field. It was also exerting severe pressure on the finances of central agencies operating telecommunications, ports, etc. in East Pakistan. With internal generation of resources limited to West Pakistan and very little prospect of foreign aid, the options of the government of Pakistan in dealing with the East Pakistan crisis were becoming more and more restricted.

Nothing was known of the cash balances of the government of East Pakistan, held with the State Bank for its current expenditure, in the second week of April. The last available position was dated 26 February, when it had had a balance of only Rs 5.25 million. No returns were, as yet, coming from the seventeen district treasuries and the National Bank of Pakistan, where it was doing the treasury work. The team recommended the immediate release of Rs 300 million by the central government to enable the East Pakistan government to meet its day-to-day expenditure.

* * *

On 21 April, the report of the special team came before the Weekly Meeting of the President. The institution of 'Weekly Meeting', which did not necessarily meet every week, had come into being after the dissolution of the Council of Ministers in February. It was chaired by the President and dealt with purely administrative and economic matters originating from various ministries. The PSO and the cabinet secretary attended all the meetings. Other participants were from amongst the two advisers, deputy chairman Planning Commission, and the secretaries to the government, depending on the subjects on the agenda. Its deliberations and decisions were based on the technical papers submitted by the ministries and properly recorded. In the economic sphere, for example, the worsening economic situation and other consequences resulting from the East Pakistan crisis were brought up from time to time by the concerned ministries but the causative factors were not touched upon. As the crisis continued to escalate beyond the control of the army, the senior civil servants criticized the regime in private conversations for persisting in its barren policies. But in the available channels of officials reports and forums, like the Weekly Meeting, they refrained from giving independent advice. The basic administrative and political directions were determined in informal and unidentified recesses of the Yahya regime, and the senior civil servants passively followed them.[4]

The Weekly Meeting to discuss the report of the special team was attended by two advisers, deputy chairman Planning Commission, and sixteen secretaries, of whom two were Bengalis. Muzaffar Husain presented the major policy recommendations of the report, involving allocation of funds, for decisions to be taken at the Meeting. Most of the other recommendations, he informed the Meeting, fell within the jurisdiction of the East Pakistan government which was taking action to implement them; on some matters, involving relaxation in procedures, etc., action was nitiated on the spot by the concerned member of the team. In the discussion that followed, no mention was made of the continuing rebel activities. Law and order was a provincial subject; at the Centre, the Ministry of Home Affairs was responsible for the internal security of the country. In the aftermath of army action, law and order had been submerged in the overall army offensive to regain control of the province. In the battlefield conditions, the word of the army commander was law, and transcended even the authority of martial law. The provincial government, as such, was somewhere in the shadows; the province was under *de facto* military administration. Consequently, the internal security of East Pakistan was no longer within the purview of the Ministry of Home Affairs, which could communicate only with the provincial government. Although the Bengali Secretary, Home Affairs, was present at the Meeting, he was as much in the dark about the happenings in East Pakistan as the other civilians.

It was necessary to consider the diversion of substantial resources, recommended in the report, in the overall perspective of the country's capacity to sustain the open-ended cost of the East Pakistan policy. One would have expected the Economic

Adviser and the secretaries of economic ministries to ask for a briefing on the state and extent of control of the province, the security conditions in Dhaka, and the likely time-frame for the restoration of normalcy. None of them, however, raised these issues. The civilian head of the Ministry of Defence was present but had nothing to contribute to the discussions. The President, who presumably was keeping himself abreast of the developing crisis, did not deign to enlighten the participants, and the Principal Staff Officer, who acted as the *de facto* Prime Minister, remained a disinterested observer of the proceedings.

The key recommendations of the team involved substantial financial outlays by the government of Pakistan which really meant diversion of resources from West Pakistan. The structural readjustment of the relative roles of the various modes of transport proposed in the report suggested that the team did not consider its programme as a one-time effort; it expected the state of insecurity to continue. It thought that this traditional pattern, which had developed over decades, could be reversed just by purchasing more coasters without developing the extensive ground facilities and surveying and organizing new routes, hitherto served by other modes. Someone, in fact, did point out during discussions that the utilization of even the existing riverine transport was limited by insufficient terminal facilities at the inland river-ports. Moreover, the assumption that riverine transport was more secure than other modes betrayed ignorance of the nature and magnitude of rebel activities; the rivers proved as insecure as the roads and railways. The difference was that the latter two modes were permanently put out of commission due to blasting of bridges, culverts, and ferries, while river movement was subjected to continuous attacks. In suggesting this transport strategy, as in other spheres, the civilians were influenced by the thinking of the military authorities who, in April, thought they could move mountains; the military administrators had no concept of the financial, social, and political costs of their policies.

The allocation of resources for rehabilitation generated an abrasive debate in the Meeting. It was argued that, during the non-cooperation movement in March, deposits were transferred from the West Pakistani banks to the two regional banks incorporated in East Pakistan. The West Pakistani banks were, thus, left with local loans without the support of deposits and were understandably reluctant to incur any more liabilities which were not commercially justified. Generally, the recommendations of an administrative nature were approved by the Meeting. But it was directed that most of those having financial implications should be taken up with foreign aid, for which the donor countries had to be approached. Others, which required local currency from the budget, foreign exchange from available resources, and bank credit were either approved in principle, subject to further scrutiny by the Ministry of Finance, or only partially accepted.

The report and its consideration at the presidential level galvanized the central ministries into giving high priority to the economic problems of East Pakistan. The civil servants were no less optimistic, at this time in April, than the army, that the latter would be able to regain complete control over the province very soon; things would settle down and it would be possible to normalize East Pakistan.

From the beginning of May the military authorities allowed the inter-wing movement of civilians by PIA. Senior central government officers started visiting East Pakistan to take stock of the state of affairs in their respective spheres. As the army regained control of the district headquarters and outlying areas, the full magnitude of the destruction was pieced together from the reports of the re-established administrative channels.

* * *

Kafiluddin Mahmood, Additional Secretary, Ministry of Finance visited Dhaka in the third week of May. On his return, he reported that although the various incentives recommended by the special team had been extended, there was little prospect of the revival of trade and industry due to the continued disruption of the transportation system and the inadequacy of physical inputs. Of more immediate concern to the Ministry of Finance was the state of the banking system and the currency chests. Mahmood obtained data compiled by the State Bank about them which, though incomplete, was disturbing. As on 7 May, out of 1,150 branches of twelve commercial banks and the Agricultural Development Bank, information was available only in respect of 658, of which 535 were working and 123 had closed down. The closure of the bank branches authorized to deal in foreign exchange had affected the remittances from Pakistanis abroad, and foreign trade. As regards the fifty-six currency chests maintained in the district treasuries and the branches of National Bank and State Bank, fourteen had been looted, twenty-two were intact and nothing was known about twenty till 15 May. The recorded amount in the fourteen plundered chests about which information was available was Rs 353.82 million. The exact amount of moneys stolen was not known, but the State Bank official feared it might be well over Rs 200 million. The biggest loss was reported from the State Bank branch at Bogra which had a substantial stock of the higher denomination notes of Rs 500.[5] The President, in a Press conference on 24 May, disclosed that the government estimate of the looted amount from treasuries and the banks was Rs 600 million; the accounting was going on and the final figure might be higher still.[6] There were dark rumours about these thefts and large transactions in the unofficial foreign exchange market in West Pakistan.

In the second week of May, the Central Industries Secretary, after meeting the businessmen and visiting the industrial areas of Dhaka and Khulna during his one-week stay, reported a slight improvement in the industrial situation. His impression (he does not mention any survey on the ground in his note) was that about twenty-five to thirty per cent of the factories had started production in single shift at much less than their capacity, about the same number had opened but were not yet in operation, and the remaining ones were completely closed. Jute factories in Narayanganj and Khulna were in partial production and one of the two units of newsprint factories was in operation. About twenty five to forty per cent of industrial labour was reporting for work but the technicians and supervisory staff were mostly absent.

In this ravaged state of the industrial sector, the Secretary made two curious recommendations. One was the suspension of labour laws and giving a free hand to the managements to screen out the workers who had been giving them trouble in the past and the 'possible saboteurs contaminated by the Bangla Desh movement'. The Secretary, who had served in East Pakistan, ought to have known that screening on the grounds suggested by him would eliminate almost the entire Bengali industrial labour force. Any such move would also deter the very small numbers who were coming forward to resume work in the urban areas. Another similar suggestion was the raising of an industrial security force of 4,000 to 5,000 ex-servicemen at the cost of the industrialists to protect the mill premises and staff and labour colonies at Dhaka, Narayanganj, Chittagong, and Khulna. The regular police force had been depleted to an extent where the lower ranks had to be commandeered from West Pakistan and the factory owners were incurring losses due to shutdowns and facing a severe cash squeeze. There were a few more suggestions of a similar, impractical kind made by the Industries Secretary. The trade channels for distribution of goods, he recommended, should be 'revamped by scrapping the Hindu wholesalers and district agents and replacing them with Muslims'. He assumed that Muslims of the 'patriotic' kind would be available to take over the entire distribution system of goods and services in the province. The Secretary also proposed some short- and long-term solutions to the internal transportation problems. In the short-term, it was suggested that the inland waterways should be developed and two canals should be dug to provide short and reliable trunk-water routes between Khulna and Narayanganj, and Chittagong and Chandpur; the longer-term measure was an alternative road alignment from Feni, or just south of Feni, to Chandpur and to Dhaka away from the border—just how far to be safe from guerrillas, he did not specify.[7] Such simplistic solutions were typical of the administrative wisdom of the day, both civil and military.

While the transportation system was providing an intractable problem, costly efforts to activate the fixed installations were creating distortions of their own. The Eastern Refinery in Chittagong was brought into operation at considerable cost in the last week of April by personnel airlifted from West Pakistan along with equipment. But soon its production had to be curtailed because the products were not moving to consumption points. The West Pakistani staff, however, was kept there to keep it running at an uneconomic level. In the second week of May, the gas supply was restored to the Dhaka–Narayanganj area but the industries dependent on it remained closed for other reasons. Khulna Shipyard had a hundred per cent staff and sixty per cent workers on the day the Industries Secretary visited it. But it had no raw materials, although it could build small vessels for defence and civilian use, for which a worldwide search was going on.

* * *

In the first week of April, the representatives of the World Bank and aid-giving countries in Islamabad had asked M. M. Ahmed for information about conditions in East Pakistan. In a note recorded on 4 April, Ahmed formulated two major issues on which the donor countries/agencies were seeking information : (a) when their technicians/advisers could resume operations in East Pakistan; and (b) whether any of the programmes would require modifications in its content or time horizon. At that time the Economic Adviser had asked the special team to discuss the matter with the army authorities in Dhaka.

The East Pakistan government was actually keen to resume development work to show to the world that the province was normal. In early May, the Governor informed the central government that foreigners based in Ghorasal, Dhaka, Chittagong, and Khulna could return to their projects from 15 May onwards, and elsewhere from 1 June. About 400 foreigners were working on aided projects, including the more important ones of power and fertilizer, which were at advanced stages of completion when abandoned in March. It was necessary to complete them to save huge financial losses, avert damage to machinery and equipment, and supplement the rehabilitation efforts. This was possible only if the foreign consultants and contractors who had been working on them resumed their work. Moreover, during a survey of damages to installations, priority areas like the distribution of food were emerging. The normal process of development planning was no longer relevant, except for the ongoing projects very near completion; more important was the repair of existing installations and ensuring their continued operation. For this also the help of the foreign experts or suppliers was necessary.

One such critical sector was the foodgrain silos. The World Bank was financing the construction of four foodgrain silos which were in the final stages of completion at the time of the army action. The US consultant firm and the German contractors were persuaded to resume work. But here the administrative priorities came in conflict with the security concerns of the intelligence agencies which did not give clearance to two experts of these firms. The reason was the hostile firsthand accounts that were fed by the foreign nationals working in East Pakistan to the western media. On the other hand, in some cases the foreign experts refused to return on moral grounds. Ghorasal Urea factory was on trial production when the Japanese technicians had left in late March. In spite of repeated requests to them to return and complete special and maintenance repairs, they did not do so, because the Japanese trade unions had decided not to do any work in East Pakistan. The government had little choice but to bring in foreign experts to complete the projects and also help in repairs and rehabilitation of the damaged installations. Many such contradictions of priorities were emerging in the day-to-day efforts to deal with the crisis in East Pakistan.

In the first week of June, a ten-member IBRD/IMF mission visited East Pakistan to prepare a report for the forthcoming meeting of the consortium of donor countries later in the month. The meeting was to decide the quantum of economic assistance for the following year and Pakistan's request for rescheduling of debts. The recommendations of the mission were going to determine the decisions of the donor countries on both the issues. The mission members started arriving in Dhaka from 30 May. Elaborate preparations were underway to arrange their visits to various places and institutions, etc. A day before the arrival of the mission, the Economic Adviser deputed Zafar Iqbal to brief Tikka Khan and others in the provincial administration about the approach to be adopted in discussions with the mission.

I. P. M. Cargill, Director of the South Asia department of the World Bank was the leader of the mission. He arrived in Dhaka on 6 June, called on the Governor on the following day, visited a few places in the interior, and held a final meeting with the Governor and senior officers on 10 June. He was no stranger to the subcontinent and its culture. As an ICS officer he had served in Sindh for a few years after Independence. In the World Bank he had been dealing with Pakistan and visiting it regularly for a number of years. It was no use painting an unrealistic picture to him about the affairs of the province. Even a casual visitor could see that things in Dhaka were not normal in any way. The city was generally deserted during the day and under curfew during the night. A large number of shops appeared to be permanently closed from the gathered dust and fungus on the shutters and locks; some of them were sealed. The city would be plunged into darkness intermittently as the transmission towers on the grid system were blown up by the insurgents; the Inter-Continental Hotel was without electricity on 3 and 4 June. Bomb explosions and shootings would reverberate during the night. All these visible and audible guerrilla activities would be intensified during the visits of Bank missions and foreign dignitaries. In fact, a foreigner could get complete information in the hotel from its staff and the room bearers who acted as the couriers of the rebels to the foreign guests.

The Governor hosted a dinner for the Bank mission on 6 June. While drinks were being served in the drawing-room of the Governor's House, sounds of bomb explosions, which did not seem to be very far off, were heard at regular intervals. This was while each one of us, the Pakistani officials, had got hold of one or two members of the mission and were arguing for our rehabilitation programmes and the bright future that we envisaged for economic revival. By the time we had moved to the dining-table, shooting had been added to the bomb explosions and the chatter of machine-gun fire almost drowned the polite conversation and both we and our guests found it hard to keep it up. We avoided looking at each other and tried to finish the meal as soon as possible. The incongruity of the situation was overwhelming; well-dressed people eating in a civilized manner off the finest china and sparkling silver and crystal under the sound and fury of death and destruction. No one knew the location of these happenings but obviously they were deliberately timed and placed for the benefit of the World Bank officials. The dinner was over at about 10 p.m. and all of us departed in a cacophony of howling dogs, explosion of bombs, and rapid firing of machine-guns. The city roads gave a weird feeling with not a moving thing in sight but persistent sounds of shooting, seemingly coming nearer, or so one imagined in the eerie atmosphere, driving at reckless speed to one's destination. Yet, on the following morning and subsequently in the meeting on 10 June, Tikka Khan insisted that everything was normal. I could not help admiring his aplomb, arising from simplicity, or honest conviction, or the former leading to the latter.

The final working session of the Bank mission was held on 10 June in the largish teak-panelled office of the Governor. The meeting was attended by four members of the Bank Mission including Cargill, and six Pakistani officials including myself, A. M. S. Ahmad, and Zafar Iqbal, with the Governor presiding. A summary of the observations of Cargill and Tikka Khan, based on notes and a partial transcript recorded by me during the meeting, is given below.

As we were settling down at the conference table, Cargill mockingly remarked, addressing no one in particular that he and his colleagues went everywhere they wanted to go but their visits to some places must have caused deep anxiety (to the Governor because of the disturbed state in those areas). The meeting started, without much ceremony, with the caustic comments of Cargill on the concept of a return to normalcy. He rebutted any claim to it, because the disruption had not been a one-time event. The present situation was the inevitable consequence of army action, he said, which was continuing, and to talk of a return to normalcy was meaningless. Statistics on the number of industries working, or the number of people who had returned to government offices carried no conviction in the present situation. What mattered, he emphasized, was what people were doing or feeling. Given the nature of the terrain, the administration was faced with an extremely difficult task in maintaining law and order, moving food stocks, and arranging shipment of exports. The integrated transport system was not working fully and Cargill was sceptical of the turn-round figures of coasters given to him. The situation reminded him of Europe during the Second World War (the Governor butted in to mention the *Quit India* Movement, without realizing the implications). The feeling of uncertainty, Cargill continued, had paralysed the people with fear, which was a formidable constraint on the revival of economic activities. Perhaps a lower profile of the army might inspire some confidence among the people. He felt that very little thinking had apparently been done on this psychological factor. The physical constraints, like lack of credit, were accepted, but the banks would require security and guarantees for advances made by them. 'Jute was not grown for eating, it was for selling', but *farias* and *beoparis* were afraid to go to the interior with money, and transport was not available. Cargill emphasized that a martial law regulation would not solve this problem (the Governor protested that there was no martial law regulation, only a directive to the State Bank regarding credit. One of the mission members pointed out that it amounted to the same thing). Available resources, Cargill observed, were not going to meet all top priority needs. Rehabilitation of transport, communication, and other sectors meant a set-back to development. There appeared to be no recognition of the paucity of resources on the part of the government.

Tikka Khan, who had prepared himself well for the meeting, reacted in his staccato style, rattling off statistics from his thick, loose-leaf diary and reiterated the 'normalcy' theme. He told the Bank mission 'the money is yours' and they would no doubt decide about the nature and quantum of assistance but communications had to be restored and coaster vessels procured to facilitate the movement of jute for which there was plenty of demand and 'the world is crying for it'. The mills were not getting jute and the carry-over 'will go from 1 million to 1.8 million bales'. The tea industry was right on the border; British managers had been abducted and Indian propaganda was maligning his administration. Newsprint mill production had increased to seventy tons per day. He claimed that Mymensingh and other places had been cleared; all methods, through martial law and civil authorities, were being adopted to remove fear, and Dhaka was eighty per cent normal. The Governor blamed the rebels for hampering his efforts and creating fear. Things, however, were improving, Tikka Khan insisted, and normalcy should be measured with reference to the situation prevailing before 25 March. The fear and uncertainties were there, but they were due to the activities of the rebels and Indian propaganda. The Governor hoped that by 1 September all these difficulties would be over.

Cargill agreed that there might be cogent non-commercial reasons for running the mills but such measures in an extraordinary situation had financial implications. If the mills could not dispose of their products, they would run out of cash very soon. The government's own resource position was weak; taxes were levied on profits but no profits could be expected under the circumstances.

The meeting, which lasted for about two hours, ended in an inconclusive and somewhat abrasive atmosphere. There was little doubt in anyone's mind, except the Governor's, that the Bank mission was not going to be very sympathetic in its recommendations to the Aid Consortium meeting.

The same day, the Governor sent a somewhat optimistic report to the Economic Adviser in a telegram of four foolscap-pages. The record of discussions as conveyed was, strictly speaking, not incorrect; about half of it covered what the Governor had said. But it did not accurately reflect the rejection by the Bank mission of the claims and optimism of the Governor. Typically, the docile

Press followed the same misleading line for domestic consumption. In *Dawn* of 17 June, Cargill was reported to have said that 'The Martial Law Administration in the Eastern Wing is busy conducting a rehabilitation survey and a clear picture of the actual requirements for rehabilitation would be known *in a couple of months*' (emphasis added). It was given this misleading headline: 'Cargill optimistic about aid resumption—complete understanding on economic situation'. The optimism was more on the part of sub-editor than the shrewd leader of the World Bank mission.

The Aid to Pakistan Consortium met in Paris on 21 June and Cargill gave a verbal presentation of the highly critical findings of the mission. The Bank did not recommend commitments of new economic aid, but the donor governments represented in the meeting expressed willingness to participate in a humanitarian relief programme in East Pakistan under UN supervision.[8]

About three weeks later, the written report of the mission was leaked out and dramatically splashed in the Western and Indian Press. Robert Macnamara, President of the World Bank, was reported to be inclined to forbid its internal distribution, but when accused of 'suppressing' the truth he eventually agreed to its circulation to the Directors.[9] It was also reported that he had decided to expunge the controversial parts of the report from the Bank's official records. (This has not been done.) However, Macnamara in a letter to Yahya Khan, expressed regrets over the unauthorized publication of the Bank/IMF mission report.[10]

The report of the mission, apart from its underlying aversion to the military administration in East Pakistan and its failure to highlight the role of the insurgents in destructive activities, was not far from the truth in its conclusions. It noted four effects of the army action on the economy of East Pakistan. The first was the destruction of property in cities, towns, and villages—selectively by the insurgents and indiscriminately by the army. The second was major damage inflicted by the rebels on the transport and communication networks in the early days of the conflict. The third was the considerable loss of vehicles and vessels to the economy either by their being taken away to India, hidden by the operators, or requisitioned by the army for its use. The fourth element in the situation emphasized by the mission was the general atmosphere of fear and uncertainty. The mission had this to say about this aspect:

> Perhaps most important of all, people fear to venture forth and, as a result, commerce has virtually ceased and economic activity generally is at a very low ebb . . . It appears that this is not just a concomitant of the Army extending its control into the countryside and the villages off the main highways, although at this stage the mere appearance of military units often suffices to engender fear. However, there is also no question that punitive measures by the military are continuing; even if directed at particular elements (such as known or suspected Awami Leaguers, students, or Hindus), these have the effect of fostering fear among the population at large. At the same time, insurgent activity is continuing. This is not only disruptive in itself, but also often leads to massive Army retaliation. In short, the general atmosphere remains very tense and incompatible with the resumption of normal activities in the province as a whole.[11]

There is no doubt that the all-prevading atmosphere of fear, resulting from an absence of the rule of law and the absence of any forum to which recourse could be had by a citizen for relief against excesses of the functionaries of state, was the single most important barrier in restoring normalcy. Although Tikka Khan in the meeting with the mission admitted the need for removing fear, his actions did not really show that he believed in it. The *ad hoc* and superficial administrative measures to meet the crisis, of which the recommendations of the Industries Secretary mentioned above were a sample, led the mission to conclude that 'there was little understanding among the authorities concerned of the complexity of the problem of economic revival and consequently neither a programme to aid recovery nor effective management'.

The army operation, which was claimed as a success in May, achieved nothing more than an unstable stalemate. The army was unable to ensure normal economic life against the activities of insurgents and a hostile population, but was unwilling to initiate pacification measures. The various elements of the basic infrastructure, destroyed or disrupted during the course of fighting in April, continued to be vulnerable to still more depredations. Normalcy in any credible sense remained beyond reach, despite the mobilization of considerable human and material resources to repair and rehabilitate the major physical assets. The geography of the deltaic region also contributed to the failure of these efforts. East Pakistan is divided into two distinct regions by the River Jamuna in the upper reaches, and the River Padma in the lower.

This riverine barrier, of many miles at places, had created eastern and western economic zones, each with its peculiar features. They were linked by two rail ferries and one road ferry. The provision for transport, power, and many other facilities was made on the basis of each zone's separate requirements. The repair and rehabilitation of the two systems consequently entailed duplication of time and effort.

The state of the major systems—transportation and power—in the two zones and their continuous deterioration during the period April to November is described below.

Port Operations

The transport system of East Pakistan radiated from and converged on the two ports, Chittagong and Chalna. Chittagong handled the bulk of the province's imports; in 1969–70 it had handled 4.20 million tons of imports and 0.6 million tons of exports.[12] Chalna mainly catered to the export of jute and jute goods, and the import requirements of the western zone; in 1969–70 it handled a million tons of each.[13] In normal times the daily average movement of cargo out of Chittagong port was about 9,000 to 10,000 tons, of which 75 per cent was by rail, 16 per cent by river, and 9 per cent by road.[14] As will be seen from Appendix 10 on port operations, the daily average unloading at the beginning of May at Chittagong was about one-fourth of the level of 1969–70; it reached about 60 to 70 per cent of the previous year's level in September and October (Table 1). The high level was mainly accounted for by the concentrated efforts of the administration for the import and distribution of foodgrains. The railway's share of the much lower quantities moving out of the port had come down considerably, without a corresponding increase in the capacities of other modes of transport (Table 1A). This resulted in an accumulation of ground balance at Chittagong port, which, on average during May to November, remained much above the 200,000 tons reported by the special team in April (Table 1B). It would have been still higher but for the silo which was brought into operation, emergency requisitioning of buildings in the city for use as godowns, and the dumping of private cargo in the local sports stadium.

The average number of port employees and dock labour daily in attendance remained about 50 to 60 per cent of the normal strength during May to November. But neither the unloading nor the attendance at the port, much below the normal level as these indicators were, truly reflected the turmoil in the interior of the province. It was the very small quantity of cargo, consisting mainly of essential food and relief goods, moving out of the port up-country which showed the extent of the disruption of organized life in East Pakistan.

In early May, steps were initiated to retrieve the East Pakistan cargo which had been unloaded in foreign ports. The authorities of these ports were threatening to dispose of this cargo and heavy demurrage charges were accumulating. Most of the consignees were private parties who did not come forward with the necessary documents. With remarkable efficiency, an inventory of the stranded cargo at various foreign ports was built up with the help of local shipping agents, the commercial banks, and the director-general ports and shipping. Even while the information was being compiled, ships were chartered and programmed to lift the identified cargo, at considerable expense, from 20 May. Like many other isolated commendable efforts during the East Pakistan crisis, the retrieval operation not only served no useful purpose but also somewhat added to the problems. The retrieved cargo put pressure on the reduced handling capacities of the two ports at a time when food shipments were lagging behind the arrival schedule that had been worked out by the special team. The Chittagong port authorities had asked the port and shipping directorate to transship only such East Pakistani cargo lying at Karachi which was destined for Chittagong proper. The retrieved cargo, when it arrived, merely added to the congestion of the port. Neither the private parties nor the government agencies came forward to take deliveries of their consignments. Instructions were issued by the provincial government to its agencies to clear their goods from the port by 15 June. But there were problems. Firstly, the government agencies and departments had no funds to clear the material and equipment; secondly, there was no way to transport this material to the places where it was required; and thirdly, since work on development projects was suspended, the agencies were not pushed about delivering the material to the sites. Under the circumstances, all efforts were directed to the removal of the cargo to various parts of the city, which merely added to the problems of the administration.

Chalna port, on the other hand, was more manageable because the imports and exports handled by it were more balanced. Moreover, movement from and to the port was linked with riverine transport, unlike Chittagong which mainly catered for imports and was connected with the road and rail systems. It will be seen from Appendix 10 that, from July, Chalna port was working very near to its normal level. That was why most of the foodgrain imports were diverted to it.

Railways

The Pakistan Eastern Railway (PER) had a route mileage of 1,777 with a large number of major and minor bridges and culverts per track mile. In the eastern zone the system was meter-gauge and divided by the River Brahmaputra into two; one sub-system was the main line from Chittagong to Sylhet and the other branched off halfway on this section at Akhaura to Bhairab Bazar which was the junction station for main lines from Chittagong to Mymensingh in the north, and Chittagong to Dhaka and Narayanganj in the south-west. The western system consisted of both broad-gauge and meter-gauge. The zonal systems, connected at two points by big steamer ferries on the River Jamuna, transshipping goods and passengers from one bank to the other, were the mainstay of the economy. They were integrated into a complicated network, involving transshipment not only through river ferries but also from one railway gauge to the other, and connecting the ports with the hinterland through feeder riverine services. A disruption at any one major point was likely to derange the network.

Immediately after the army action on 26 March, the railway system had ceased to operate. Thereafter, the first pair of trains was run on the suburban services between Dhaka and Narayanganj on 8 April. On 26 May, the Divisional Superintendent, Paksey division, reported to the Railway Commissioner, who was deputed by the central government to survey the position, that five sections in the western zone, all running close to the western or northern borders with India, were inoperative due to damaged track, bridges, and signalling and communication systems. As a result of these closures, the report said, the direct line between Khulna and the northern areas of Rangpur, Dinajpur, and Bogra districts was suspended, and the link with Rajshahi was at best tenuous. The majority of the employees, on the open line and in the workshops, were Biharis and they had either dispersed to safer places or stopped coming out from their colonies since early March. Transshipment at Santahar from broad-gauge to meter-gauge was suspended because of the absence of labour and staff; this had resulted in a shortage of fuel oil. The technical cadres were depleted both at higher and middle level, and 70 per cent of the inspecting and supervisory staff, the backbone of the railway system, were not reporting for duty. No salaries had been paid even at the divisional headquarters; in the outlying sections the field staff had not been paid for the previous three months.

Typically of the spurious reporting of the times, the provincial Transport Department informed Muzaffar Husain, in a note covering the same period as the report of the Divisional Superintendent, that 'in the West Zone rail communication has been restored almost over the entire area excepting the section Santahar–Parbatipur'. It was a misleading statement. Of the six patchy train services quoted to support it, three originated from the same station to three different destinations on the same line and were practically one service; one was a branch line; one was a long diversion from the main broad-gauge line to meter-gauge involving transshipment of freight; and one was a shuttle service as and when permitted by military authorities. The situation on the ground was that no goods trains were being run because of the inoperative gaps on the main line.

In the eastern zone the situation was worse. Yet, in the same departmental note referred to above, it was asserted that 'in the Eastern Zone railway communication has been restored over the entire area' adding, as an afterthought, 'excepting Akhaura–Dhoomghat, Akhaura–Shahjibazar and Kishoreganj–Gauripur–Mymensingh sections'. The closure of these sections had rendered all the main lines of the eastern zone, Chittagong–Mymensingh–North Bengal, Chittagong–Sylhet, Chittagong–Dhaka, and Dhaka–Sylhet, inoperative.

The railway system of East Pakistan had thus ceased to be a viable national carrier of goods and even passengers over any significant distance. The severest blow to the system was the demolition of about sixteen major bridges on the main lines by the rebels.[15] The selection of target bridges (mostly of a span of 40 feet and over) and the nature of the damage inflicted showed a high degree of professionalism in the use of explosives. These were only the more important and seriously damaged crossings; there were other minor bridges and culverts all over the system similarly affected. Of these sixteen bridges, nine were on the Chittagong-Sylhet section which ran very close to the border with India. Difficulties in mobilizing men and material on sites and hostile actions from across the border continued to disrupt the repair work on these bridges throughout the period April–November, or fresh damage was inflicted on the repaired or hitherto unaffected structures. Intermittent artillery barrages and attacks from the Indian side were particularly directed at the Belonia bulge to prevent the repair of the two vital bridges of Feni and Dhoom on the main line from Chittagong up-country. Success in repairing these two bridges would have been a breakthrough in activating port operations and a major portion of the railway system. Repairs on the other seven or eight major bridges, which were away from the border, proceeded more smoothly and, by the end of May, five of them had been temporarily restored to traffic. But they were of little significance without the strategic link-up with Chittagong.

Roads

The province had a trunk-road system of about 2,000 miles connected by as many as twenty-five steamer ferries. In addition, there were numerous country-boat ferries all over the province, on feeder roads maintained by local bodies. The large number of bridges and culverts and the compacted earth embankments to raise the road above flood-level made the highway system highly vulnerable to sabotage; the former could be blasted and the latter cut to render the network inoperable for bulk freight movement.

As with the railway, the most extensive damage was on the eastern side. The intensity of the damage was in proportion to the proximity of the alignment to the border. In the last week of May, the Additional Chief Engineer of the provincial highway department reported severe damage to ten major road bridges.[16]

Of these, five were on the Chittagong–Sylhet highway, four within the short stretch from Companiganj to Shaistaganj at points nearest to the border, and one at a similar point in the south at Suvapur; three of the five were completely destroyed. Of the other five bridges, two between Dhoom, on the main Chittagong–Comilla road, and Ramgarh, in the Chittagong Hill Tracts, were destroyed. In the central region two bridges—one on the Mymensingh–Tangail road and one on the Mymensingh–Kishorganj road—were damaged. Two more, one on the Dhaka–Comilla section, and one in the western zone were also tampered with. No repair to these bridges had been started by May because of the advent of the monsoon.

Serviceability of the roads, however, was not the only problem. Out of about 9,000 freight vehicles in the province, approximately 1,000 were reported to have been damaged or taken across the border to India. In early May, the provincial administration was following up the proposal to open a freight division in the EPRTC with 4,000 trucks. There were, however, serious doubts about the capability of the EPRTC to handle a fleet of this size. In any case, no resources were in sight for an investment of this magnitude. By the end of May, the provincial government had also realized the futility of its efforts to restore land transport.

Riverine Transport

The vulnerability of the rail and road systems had led the central and provincial governments to concentrate efforts and resources on acquiring riverine vessels. The substitution of railway by river routes required augmentation of the river transport fleet and a survey and organization of new routes to reach places hitherto covered by other modes. To restore the normal level of 9,000–10,000 tons of goods daily dispatched up-country from Chittagong port, and assuming the railway's share to be 2,000–3,000 tons, water transport was assigned a daily outward tonnage of 4,500–5,500 though this did not fully make up the railway shortfall. The existing seagoing coaster fleet comprised twenty-three vessels of which only seventeen were in service at any one time, the remaining being under repairs and maintenance. With a better turn-round, this fleet could at best clear only about 1,500–2,000 tons of cargo per day from Chittagong port.

To restructure the transportation system of the province in favour of water transport, it was necessary to augment the existing fleet of seagoing barges and coasters, and to acquire the landing craft types (LCTs) capable of crossing the Bay of Bengal. It was estimated that on the basis of the existing fleet's performance, 40–50 coasters would be required to carry the traffic assigned to water transport. Accordingly, a worldwide search for coasters, and credits to finance their purchase from the secondhand market to ensure ready deliveries, was launched in early May. The aid-giving countries accepted the need for riverine vessels but only on humanitarian grounds for food and relief distribution and not by way of restructuring the regional transportation system, necessitated by army action. They did not trust the assurance of the government of Pakistan that the assistance provided by them would be used only for civilian purposes. The UK government agreed to the utilization of one of its existing credit lines to Pakistan to finance the purchase of five coasters, but within the framework of an international relief effort. In case no such arrangement was feasible, it was willing to finance the commercial charter of the vessels, provided (i) they were manned by British civilian crews; and (ii) the use made of the vessels could be checked by monitoring their logs. These conditions were not acceptable to the government of Pakistan. Similarly, the Dutch government approved the purchase of three coasters from Holland from its credit line after considerable diplomatic efforts and written guarantees from the Pakistan government about their use. Eventually, a number of coasters were donated but mostly on a charter basis under strict supervision and as part of the international relief effort, as will be seen in a later chapter.

Power

In May, during the President's budget conference in Karachi some industrialists complained about the power shortage as a constraint in the revival of industries in East Pakistan. The President 'desired that quick action should be taken to overcome the reported power shortage.' The Planning Commission deputed the chief of its power section to East Pakistan to survey the position. The report showed widespread damage to 6,300 miles of transmission and distribution lines of the grid systems in the east and west zones. In the eastern grid, ten transmission towers on the 132 KV line were blown up between Karnaphuli and Siddhirganj; of these, seven were between Comilla and Chittagong along the border, making this section inoperative. The Dhaka–Comilla–Sylhet sector, fed by the natural gas power stations at Siddhirganj, Ashuganj, and Shahjibazar, snapped into darkness when the third tower between Comilla and Siddhirganj was blown up on 28 June. A tower between Siddhirganj and Dhaka was also damaged, but the section was in operation. In the western zone the grid substation at Ishurdi was out of commission and the 132 KV Khulna–Bheramara interconnector was being served by the local power stations at these two places. A large number of 66/33 KV secondary transmission lines had also been damaged in both the zones. In some localities of the main cities, the distribution system had been burnt down. The grid systems had ceased to operate and most of the places were somehow being provided power by local generation and at lower voltages. At the same time, the power consumption, sixty per cent of which was accounted for by industrial consumers, had gone down considerably. The peak demand in June, which occurred now in daytime instead of the evening hours as in normal times, was only about fifty per cent of the maximum demand recorded in October 1970.

The report made the usual recommendations for relocating the transmission lines away from the border, repair of the damaged towers, and tightening of security to prevent further sabotage. The President was informed of this dismal state; as usual, he directed that the recommendations 'should be vigorously followed.'

CHAPTER 7

Economic Consequences: Pakistan

The dismal East Pakistan economic situation brought out in the Weekly Meeting on 21 April necessitated some immediate containment measures by the government of Pakistan, to preserve national solvency. In the last weeks of April, May, and June, in a series of Presidential Meetings, detailed papers were presented by the economic ministries on various aspects of the prevailing economic situation and projections for the coming year.[1]

On 24 April, a special meeting was called by the President to review the foreign exchange budget for the year July 1970–June 1971 and to consider the proposals of the Ministry of Finance to arrest the deteriorating balance of payments situation. To implement these proposals, the Ministry of Commerce, at the same meeting, submitted two summaries for the restriction of imports and for giving more incentives to exports.

The foreign exchange reserves had shown a continuous declining trend since March 1970. The Yahya regime, convinced that Ayub's downfall was due to his preoccupation with development, showed scant regard for economic realities and drifted into a spree of populist policies. The poor economic management was reflected in the continuous fall in foreign exchange reserves during its tenure; they went down by Rs 892 million, from Rs 1,667 million in March 1970 to Rs 775 million in March 1971.[2] At this time, short-term liabilities against letters of credit alone stood at Rs 1,240 million. But these reserve figures included capital assets like gold and foreign securities which are not liquidated to meet current demands. The 'own reserves' position of the freely available foreign exchange to cover current expenditure was reported to the meeting by the Ministry of Finance as follows.

1970:	Rs in millions	1971:	Rs in millions
1 July	408.50	31 January	–168.60
1 August	320.70	28 February	–124.10
1 September	266.00	1 April	–89.40
1 October	178.60	14 April	–98.20
1 November	56.10		
1 December	36.40		

The negative 'own reserves' showed that current expenditure was being met by liquidating capital assets or by foreign commercial loans at high interest rates (because of the poor credit rating of Pakistan arising from its reserve level), or both.[3]

The foreign exchange budget for the year approved in June 1970 had provided for an excess expenditure of Rs 520 million over the projected receipts against the advice of the Ministry of Finance. There was a strong feeling in certain quarters at that time that unnecessarily large reserves had been accumulated by starving the economy of essential and much-needed imports. Moreover, it was expected that by October 1971 the multiple exchange rate policy would be revised to attract IMF assistance. Negotiations were also under way with the World Bank and the IMF for debt rescheduling. Although not a very prudent approach, the Ministry of Finance reluctantly accepted the depletion of the reserves implied by the deficit, hoping to recoup this by these external supports. The position was reviewed in December 1970 and since the earnings had not shown a promising trend in the first six months, it was decided to curtail expenditure to keep the deficit at the original level.

In December, the physical exports during 1970–1 were projected to be 8.5 per cent higher than in 1969–70. Exports from West Pakistan were well ahead of the target up to April and, for the whole year, were likely to be 17 per cent more than the previous year by June. In East Pakistan, however, the year had started with a set-back due to cyclones and floods but the export shortfall was more or less made up by February. The disturbances and the army action in March changed the situation completely. Most of the jute used to be shipped during January–May, following the export contracts concluded during October–December. The Ministry of Commerce made a guesstimate of a maximum export of Rs 230 million and a minimum of Rs 100 million from East Pakistan during

April–June although, in the prevailing circumstances, even the lower figure was an optimistic projection.

About sixty per cent of the foreign exchange earnings available with the government was allocated to defence and debt servicing; the former had the highest priority and the latter obligation was fixed. The tightening-up measures, therefore, related to the squeezing of civilian public and private sectors. The major impact was on civilian imports which were categorized into four lists, each with its own exchange rate. The goods included in the first two lists, called the 'free list' and the 'licensable list', were importable at the cheapest official rate of exchange at Rs 4.76 to a US dollar. The former, financed exclusively by foreign aid and barter, was confined to those few items, mostly raw materials and capital goods, which had been agreed to with the aid-giving countries, and included in the barter agreements. Due to the stoppage of foreign aid, funds for this list had dried up. Some very essentials items like crude oil and petroleum products, textbooks and medicines, and a few items of special interest to East Pakistan were included in the 'licensable list' which was financed through government resources. The third, 'cash-cum-bonus list', included a wide range of industrial raw materials and consumer goods. In this category, half the foreign exchange was provided at the official rate and the other half had to be purchased by an importer from the market at the ruling price. During July–December 1970 this composite import rate of exchange, on an average, was Rs 9.14 to a dollar.[4] The fourth category was the 'bonus list' which included consumer goods and some raw materials. It was financed by bonus vouchers which represented the pool of freely-traded foreign exchange, fluctuating at rates considerably higher than the official rate, allowed to exporters. During the same period the effective import rate on pure bonus worked out at Rs 13.52 to a dollar.[5]

In the light of the April estimates of foreign exchange receipts, the Ministry of Finance informed the meeting of its inability to finance any imports from government resources. In the revised import policy for the remaining few months of the year, therefore, both the licensable and cash-cum-bonus lists, except for a few items, were suspended, and almost the entire imports were shifted to the bonus list. The severe impact of costlier imports on the cost of production of locally-manufactured goods and the general price level was recognized, but at the time the greater anxiety was to avoid default on debt and other foreign liabilities. The best that could be done to mitigate to some extent the impact of costlier imports on the domestic economy was to reduce or abolish tariffs on selected items of an essential nature.

In spite of all these economy measures, the available foreign exchange was not enough to cover the curtailed expenditure and other obligations. Three measures, one in-house and two external, were suggested for replenishing resources in the short term. The internal measure suggested by the Ministry of Commerce was to increase rates of bonus on some fast-moving export items and on remittances from Pakistanis living abroad. It was argued that these enhanced rates would induce the exporters to find alternative markets for West Pakistani manufactures which were formerly exported to East Pakistan. Moreover, with the bulk of the imports on the bonus list, unless the bonus voucher pool was increased the pressure of demand on it would make the imports still more costly.

One of the important foreign exchange earners affected by the East Pakistan crisis was the foreign remittances. During July–December 1970, these had fallen by thirty-five per cent compared to the same period the previous year. In February and March 1971, they were only about one-third of the average monthly flow for the first six months of the year. It was argued by the Ministry of Commerce that the remittances had been diverted to unofficial channels due to the rumours about the devaluation of the Pakistani rupee. Then there was the total disruption of the communication and banking system in East Pakistan. The branches of commercial banks in Sylhet, where most of the Pakistani expatriates hailed from, had direct telecommunication links with the UK for remitting funds. This system was no longer operative. But a more important reason, reported by the Pakistan High Commission, was the pressure of the very active Bangladesh lobby in the UK on their compatriots to contribute to its funds and not to send their remittances through official channels.

The enhancement of bonus rates was not considered feasible for various technical and other reasons by the meeting. The proposed increases, it was pointed out, would further widen the gap in the terms of trade between agriculture and manufactures, and introduce yet another exchange rate, violating the commitment made to the IMF. In any case, it was argued, the exports from

West Pakistan were doing fairly well and the overall fall in the country's foreign exchange earnings in physical exports and invisibles were due to the conditions in East Pakistan which were not responsive to economic incentives.

Immediate relief to tide over the crisis was accordingly sought from external sources. The expectations of IMF support and debt rescheduling were not likely to be fulfilled due to the hostility in the donor countries and the unhelpful attitude of international financial institutions in the post-army action period. Exchange reforms could not be undertaken as the expected financial support from the IMF and the Consortium countries to back them was not forthcoming. For debt rescheduling, the World Bank had refused to take any initiative and had suggested bilateral negotiations with the creditor countries. The meeting authorized the Ministry of Finance to enter into immediate negotiations with the major creditors for an outright moratorium on debt service payments for at least six months, during which negotiations would also be started on long-term debt rescheduling. The desperateness of the situation was underlined by inserting an alternative to the outright moratorium in the negotiation brief. It was to ask the creditor countries to accept payment in local currency (guaranteed against changes in the exchange rate) for a specified period.

The second external measure approved by the meeting was to negotiate short-term loans from friendly Muslim countries and foreign banks. In course of time, Saudi Arabia and Abu Dhabi extended short-term credits of \$ 50 million and \$ 10 million respectively, and Kuwait gave a grant of \$ 2 million.

Meanwhile, due to the precarious reserve position, speculation was rife in business circles about the devaluation of the rupee. This was affecting exports and investment decisions and also leading to larger foreign exchange payments than normal. The Ministry of Finance wanted to issue a firm denial but for inexplicable reasons the meeting directed that it should be in a low key.

Yet another urgent issue brought up in the same meeting of 24 April by the Ministry of Commerce was the disruption of inter-Wing trade, which was creating shortages of essential goods in West Pakistan. During the first eight months of 1970–1, trade between the Wings was more or less normal. The two Wings being part of the same country, the importers did not carry any inventory and the movement of stocks was regulated on a current consumption basis, with short delivery periods. The disruption of trade in March and April, therefore, soon manifested its adverse effects in West Pakistan; in the East Wing, imports of any kind had ceased to have any economic significance in the overall crisis. The main items which West Pakistan was likely to run short of were tea, newsprint, and jute goods. West Pakistan consumed about 65 million lbs. of tea, which was roughly equal to the output of East Pakistan; about 12 million lbs was programmed for import during 1970–1. Internal tea trading had come to a standstill due to disturbances in the producing areas of Sylhet and the dislocation of transportation from there to Chittagong, where auctions used to be held. From 28 April efforts were being made by the martial law authorities to start the auctions to bring the existing stocks to the market, but the prospects, in the absence of supplies from Sylhet, were uncertain. The production in that season, April to December, was expected to be about thirty per cent less than the normal, leading to an increase in the import bill of about Rs 40 to 50 million. Arrangements were made to import newsprint on government account, although, in the meantime, the Khulna mill had started production and a consignment was already on its way. Jute manufactures were badly required as packing material for sugar, tobacco, etc., but since the mills in East Pakistan were closed, even the position of ready stocks which could be exported to West Pakistan was not known. It was decided that the Trading Corporation of Pakistan (TCP), a public-sector trading organization, should undertake inter-Wing trade where normal private channels had dried up.

Meanwhile, there were no funds to meet the debt-service payments falling due in May and, for the first time in its history, Pakistan was faced with the ignominy of defaulting on its international obligations. The IMF had rejected an application for an emergency drawing for the specific purpose of meeting these obligations. Having exhausted all avenues for mobilizing convertible funds, the government of Pakistan at the end of April advised the creditor countries that circumstances had compelled it to suspend conversion in foreign currencies of debt-service payments of official credits, falling due during the period starting from 1 May, for a period of six months. The moratorium was applied only to the government-to-government credits; payments due on credits of international agencies and on those contracted outside consortium pledges in consortium countries and, in case of non-consortium countries, credits contracted outside government agreements, were not covered by it. All payments on due dates were made in rupees to the creditor countries' special accounts in the State Bank of Pakistan and guaranteed against changes in the exchange rate.[7] The sum covered by the moratorium was reported to be $ 30 million.[8] Meanwhile, in pursuance of the Weekly Meeting decision, the Pakistan government requested a special session of the World Bank's Aid-to-Pakistan Consortium to discuss its proposal of a six-month moratorium on repayment of foreign loans, pending long-term rescheduling. The discussions on the subject with the Bank mission, which visited Pakistan on 2–5 May, were inconclusive. It was announced that M. M. Ahmed would visit Washington on 7 May to pursue the matter with the Bank, the IMF, and the US Government.[9] M. M. Ahmed failed to obtain any relief from the aid-giving countries and agencies. He recalls:

> In May 1971, I had gone to the US with a letter from Yahya to Nixon. The meeting with Nixon in the Oval was satisfactory. He was sympathetic and directed someone present during the meeting to take up the issues mentioned by me with the western governments. But with the World Bank and the International Monetary Fund (IMF) it was not possible to cut any ice. Macnamara [Bank President] gave me a sheaf of reports and newspaper cuttings describing the atrocities of army action. He showed his helplessness to convince his Board which was opposed to any aid to Pakistan. Managing Director of the IMF was more candid, and said 'I can't go against my masters' wishes', when I took up the postponement of debt repayment with him. Both of them strongly highlighted the adverse public opinion against Pakistan and refused to extend any relief.

* * *

About a month later, in the last week of May, the Planning Division and the Ministries of Finance and Commerce submitted four summaries on the economic situation, which were discussed in the President's Weekly Meeting on 2 June. The reports analysed various macro indicators of economic performance during the period July 1970 to March 1971. These, read with the April summaries discussed above, brought out the stark economic consequences of the regime's policies in East Pakistan.

The first summary of the Ministry of Finance on the 'Budgetary and Monetary Situation' depicted the prevailing picture of internal resources, external assistance, development outlays, balance of payments, and the monetary situation. Table 1 summarizes the total resource position of the central government.

Table 1: **Central Government Resources (1970–1971)**

	1970–1 Estimates (Rs in millions)	
	January	May
A. Internal Resources		
(i) Tax receipts	6,980	5,990
(ii) Non-tax receipts	2,060	1,850
(iii) Net capital receipts	363	226
(iv) Total (i) + (ii) + (iii)	9,403	8,066
(v) Provinces' share in taxes	1,550	1,411
(vi) Revenue expenditure	5,216	5,486
(vii) Total (v) + (vi)	6,766	6,897
(viii) Net Surplus available for development (iv) – (vii)	2,637	1,169
B. External Resources		
(ix) Rupee generating aid	1,640	1,307
(x) Total rupees availability (viii) + (ix)	4,277	2,476
(xi) Project aid	1,612	1,170
Total resources (x) + (xi)	5,889	3,646

The January estimates of total central revenue receipts (including some new taxes imposed in that month) for the year 1970–1 had gone down by Rs 1,337 million in May; the revenue expenditure, on the other hand, had increased by Rs 270 million due to unforeseen grants to East Pakistan for flood and cyclone relief, extra subsidy to PIA after the ban on flights over India, and concealed defence expenditure. The net availability of internal resources for development in May had come down, due to these factors, to about 44 per cent of the January estimate of Rs 2,637 million. External assistance, which had accounted for about 55 per cent of the development resources, was reduced by about 24 per cent. The reduction in project aid did not have an immediate impact because, under the circumstances, new projects were not likely to be taken up by aid-giving agencies; even the funds in the pipeline could not be utilized due to the paucity of matching local currency. Of more immediate consequence were the commodity loans which augmented the government's budgetary resources through the sale of goods imported under it. The generation of Rs 1,640 million from this source, based on the commitments made in the 1970 Consortium meeting, was reduced to Rs 1,307 million because the donor countries avoided signing any loan agreements after March.

In January, East Pakistan's contribution to the total central revenues, under the four heads shown in Table 2, as estimated for the year 1970–1 on the basis of past trends, stood at 23 per cent, and West Pakistan's at about 77 per cent. In the first eight months the actual collections were below normal in East Pakistan due to floods, cyclone, and political agitations; from March onwards, they practically ceased. In the prevailing conditions, the estimates of the Ministry of Finance regarding anticipated collections from the eastern region up to June had no basis, and all those present in the meeting knew it. Even on this unrealistic reckoning, however, East Pakistan's contribution came to no more than 16 per cent; in the next year, with no prospect of the pacification of the region, the situation was going to be worse. In spite of the backwash of the East Pakistan crisis, which affected its industrial production and other economic activities, resilient West Pakistan generated about 84 per cent of the central tax revenues in 1970–1.

The poor revenue collection in East Pakistan evoked a banal discussion in the meeting on the defects of the existing taxation system of the country. None of the secretaries or advisers mentioned the political causes of the total breakdown of the system in the eastern region. Kazi defended the estimation technique of the Ministry of Finance which, he maintained, had proved fairly accurate, within very narrow error margins, during the past years. The explanation for the variation between the receipt estimates and actual collections, he asserted, had to be focused on factors other than the inherent defects of the tax system. These 'other factors', which affected all sectors of the economy analysed in the summary were, however, not pursued in the discussions.

***Table 2:* Central Revenue Receipts from Major Heads**

	1970–1 (Rs in millions)			
	January Estimate 1970–1	Collections up to March	Anticipated up to June	Revised Estimates 1970–1
Customs	1,811	1,328	352	1,680
East Pakistan	493	293	7	300
West Pakistan	1,318	1,035	345	1,380
Excise	2,921	1,920	530	2,450
East Pakistan	697	430	nil	430
West Pakistan	2,224	1490	530	2,020
Income Tax	1,282	690	320	1,010
East Pakistan	200	50	10	60
West Pakistan	1,082	640	310	950
Sales Tax	783	560	140	700
East Pakistan	193	130	nil	130
West Pakistan	590	430	140	570
Total	6,797	4,498	1,342	5,840
East Pakistan	1,583	903	17	920
West Pakistan	5,214	3,595	1,325	4,920

The shortfall in the availability of rupee resources adversely affected the size of the development programme and the financial assistance for its implementation which had been committed by the central government to the provinces. The annual development programme for 1970–1 was budgeted at Rs 6,980 million. Table 3 shows the mode of its financing.

***Table 3:* Financing of the ADP (1970–1971)** (Rs in millions)

	Total Programme	Project Aid	Provinces' Surplus	Central Financing
Centre	1,800	550	—	1,250
East Pakistan	3,080	650	260	2,170 (1,960)
West Pakistan	2,100	400	370	1,330 (1,220)
Total	6,980	1,600	630	4,750 (4,430)

[Figures in brackets are net of cut]

Apart from project aid and the provinces' own surpluses, the central government was committed to financing the balance of the provincial programmes. The East Pakistan government, instead of contributing any surplus, was in a deficit of Rs 360 million, but West Pakistan had a surplus of Rs 260 million. The rupee resources of the central government had gone down from the estimated Rs 4,277 million to Rs 2,476 million, as shown in Table 1. In April, the Ministry of Finance was compelled to apply a cut of 10 per cent in its commitments to the provinces.

The reduction in the central government development assistance was resented by the West Pakistan provinces which, unlike East Pakistan, were fully geared to implement their programmes. The Punjab Governor addressed the Deputy Chairman, Planning Commission, in early May to protest against the cut, demanding that the matter be placed before the President. The Planning Division had accordingly brought up a summary, in the Weekly Meeting on 2 June, highlighting the shortfalls in the implementation of the development programme. The Ministry of Finance stated in its summary that, on the basis of the latest resource estimates of Rs 2,476 million, to sustain even the reduced financial commitment of Rs 4,430 million, deficit financing of the order of Rs 1,960 million would have to be resorted to. As discussed later, this, added to the other pressing demands, would raise the deficit financing to an unprecedented level.

The Ministry of Finance was criticized for releasing development loans to the provinces in the first and second quarters on the basis of the budgeted programme rather than the actual physical implementation. Since rupee allocation was related to the budgeted project aid and the latter was lagging behind, it was suspected by the participants that the major portion of cash development loans had been diverted by the provincial governments to meet their revenue deficits. The suspicions were particularly directed towards East Pakistan, whose governments were generally regarded in the central secretariat as somewhat irresponsible in the utilization of central allocations. Kazi accepted that the Ministry of Finance had not exercised strict control over the development releases but this, he maintained, was not possible due to the declining cash balances of the provinces. Meanwhile, unbudgeted and *ad hoc* allocations were being demanded for the rehabilitation of East Pakistan's economy and the ever-increasing needs of defence. Development, as such, had become irrelevant; the problem was to maintain the existing level of economic activities.

In another summary, the Planning Division presented a review of the economic growth during 1970–1. According to the latest exercise carried out just before the meeting, the Planning Secretary informed the Meeting that the implemented development programme would not exceed Rs 5,000 milllion as against the budgeted figure of Rs 6,980 million. It estimated a growth of 2.8 per cent in the GDP over the previous year which, with a population increase of about 3 per cent per annum, meant a decline in per capita income for the first time in the preceding ten years. In fact, even the figure of 2.8 per cent was dubious as the Ministry of Finance was not sure even of a development programme of Rs 4,430 million. The Planning Secretary, however, consoled the meeting with the observation that 'in view of the exceptional situation created by the natural and political calamities in the current year, even maintaining last year's level of GDP could be considered satisfactory'.

Reverting to the same summary of the Ministry of Finance, mention may be made of the two other items covered by it, the foreign exchange projections and the monetary situation.

The Ministry of Finance had worked out a rigorous projection of foreign exchange receipts and payments for the following five months, May–September; the situation could not be foreseen with reasonable certainty beyond this time-frame. Based on actual shipments of exports during the period March–July, payments for which were likely to be received within two months, invisible earnings, and the outstanding receivables expected to be realized by September, the estimated availability of free foreign exchange for this period was placed at Rs 1,400 million. As against this, the absolute minimum liabilities to be met during the same months amounted to Rs 2,170 million as follows:

(i)	80 per cent of the outstanding commitments at the end of April:	Rs 940 million
(ii)	75 per cent of fresh commitments made during May–June:	Rs 270 million
(iii)	public and private sector invisible payments during May–September:	Rs 530 million
(iv)	debt servicing May–September:	Rs 430 million

During discussions on the precariousness of the foreign exchange position, Kazi again had to defend himself against insinuations of mismanagement. He reminded the meeting of the strong advice of the Ministry of Finance against a deficit foreign exchange budget and the depleting of reserves. Some of the immediate measures for replenishing resources and postponing liabilities had already been taken after the April meetings described above. Meanwhile, the meeting noted some hopeful signs in the arrest of the declining trend of the reserves; for the last three months they had been more or less stagnant at an average level of Rs 500 million.

The economic picture was rounded up in the Ministry of Finance's summary by an analysis of the monetary regime of the country, which was under great pressure generated by the burdens of the East Pakistan crisis. The changes in the composition and magnitude of the monetary assets and their causative factors pointed to a grave threat to the financial stability of the country.

The changes in the eight-month period of 1970–1 and the factors which caused them are shown in Table 4.

***Table 4:* Changes in Monetary Assets** (Rs in millions)

	July-February 1970–1	July–February 1969–70
Currency in Circulation	+ 1,179	+ 619
Demand Liabilities	+ 450	+ 472
Time Liabilities	– 263	+ 515
Other Deposits	– 11	+ 10
Post Office Savings Bank	+ 81	+ 25
Change	+ 1,436	+ 1,641
Causative Factors		
Private Sector	+ 1,002	+ 1,291
Government Sector	+ 1,131	+ 294
Foreign Sector	– 579	+ 19
Other Items	– 118	+ 37
Change	+ 1,436	+ 1,641

During 1970–1, monetary assets increased at a slower pace than in the corresponding period for the previous year: Rs 1,436 million as against Rs 1,641 million. But there was a significant change in the composition of the assets. The currency in circulation rose by Rs 1,179 million compared with about half the rate during the same period in 1969–70. A considerable part of this expansion was effected through withdrawal of time deposits from scheduled banks. The figures for March and April had not been compiled at the time because of non-availability of data from East Pakistan, but the incomplete information available had shown heavy withdrawals from the banks. The shift in preference for currency was mainly attributable to the uncertain political conditions and the radical manifestos of the political parties, which included nationalization of banks.

The slower pace of monetary expansion in the first eight months of 1970–1 was not the result of sound financial management by the Ministry of Finance. The causative analysis showed that it was mainly due to the deficit in the balance of payments; the foreign sector contracted by Rs 579 million, during the period July 1970 to February 1971, because of the widening gap between stagnant foreign exchange earnings and the rising liabilities for imports, debt servicing, and other payments. The shift in the pattern of asset-holding, on the other hand, indicated poor management of its finances by the government. Out of the expansion of Rs 1,436 million, the private sector accounted for Rs 1,002 million, against Rs 1,291 million during the same period the previous year. The private sector had shown an unusual expansion of Rs 1,365 million in July–December 1970, reportedly due to higher prices of cotton, a general increase in the cost of materials, etc., which increased the working capital requirements. A number of credit restrictions were imposed in January 1971 to cut back on the excessive expansion of bank credit. (The special team had recommended the exemption of East Pakistan from these restrictions.) Due to these measures, bank credit to the private sector had declined by Rs 361 million by the end of February. No such discipline was, however, enforced by the central government on its own largely unproductive operations. While business activities were curtailed, 79 per cent of the expansion in monetary assets was created by the government in order to meet its requirements.

In spite of this, up to February, a check was maintained on the overall level of expansion to contain inflation, and the government kept its deficit financing within that ceiling. After March, the control mechanisms became difficult to sustain. The Ministry of Finance warned in the meeting that the expansion in monetary assets by the end of June was likely to be in excess of Rs 2,500 million, of which the government sector would be appropriating as much as Rs 2,190–Rs 1,960 million to meet the budgetary deficit and Rs 230 million for state trading in wheat. In those days of prudent financial management, this was regarded as an unprecedented, expansion which, in a state of stagnant growth in the GDP and restricted imports, it was apprehended would exert severe pressure on prices. The deficit financing which was of the order of Rs 1,131 million up to February, compared to Rs 294 million in the same period the previous year, jumped to Rs 1,960 million in March when the East Pakistan crisis started. The civil servants, nurtured in conservative financial traditions, expressed shock at the unthinkable levels of monetary expansion and deficit financing. In frustration, seemingly unable to take any corrective action, they blamed the Ministry of Finance for not managing things properly and uttered platitudes about the dangers of deficit financing and the desirability of financing the development programme from real savings.

In the first week of June, however, the demonetization of currency notes provided a measure of relief to monetary management. On 8 June, a martial law regulation was issued whereby Pakistan currency notes of (i) all denominations marked with the expression 'Joy Bangla' or 'Bangla Desh' ceased to be legal tender with immediate effect; and (ii) 500 rupee and 100 rupee denomination currency notes also ceased to be legal tender, but could be surrendered for conversion according to the prescribed procedure. The reason for this extraordinary step given in the preamble of the regulation was that the large quantities of Pakistan currency looted from the government treasuries etc. in East Pakistan 'are likely to be used for activities prejudicial to the national economy and security of Pakistan'.[10] The immediate gain to the monetary system was the non-surrender of Rs 900 million of the high denomination notes. On the other hand, the deficit financing turned out to be only Rs 1,550 million by the end of June as against Rs 2,500 million expected earlier and Rs 600 million budgeted for the year.[11] Taking the non-surrendered amount into account, the monetary expansion due to deficit financing apparently came down to only Rs 650 million. However, the Economic Adviser's claim that demonetization 'has reduced the excess liquidity in the economy by about Rs 900 million due to non-surrender of notes' was debatable.[12] Of this amount at least Rs 600 million were the new notes from the currency chests and not from the currency in circulation.[13]

* * *

Two more high level meetings, of the National Economic Council and the Governors' Conference, were held in the middle of June, before the announcement of the budget and the annual development programme for 1971–2 in the third week of that month. The participants in the two forums were more or less the same but the items on the agenda reflected their different characters.

The agenda of the National Economic Council included the annual development programme for the next year and two other items: the industrial investment schedule for the fourth five-year plan and the report of the National Finance Committee. The latter two items, which had created so much controversy during the pre-March period, discussed in Chapter 3, had now ceased to be of any relevance in the absence of political representation from East Pakistan. The Council met on 16 June and, apart from the Cabinet Secretary, the PSO to the President, the Economic Adviser, and the Deputy Chairman Planning Commission, it was attended by sixteen secretaries, the five provincial governors (all generals), the three service chiefs, the provincial planning chiefs, and the staff of the Cabinet and Planning Divisions. Of the forty-one officials attending the meeting, including the President, the number of Bengalis did not exceed three or four, of whom A. Rab, Secretary Planning, was the only notable one.

Rab, presenting the summary, argued for a minimum of Rs 5,000 million for the coming year's development programme to meet the minimum requirements of ongoing and foreign-aided projects, the repair of the infrastructure, and the rehabilitation of the economy in East Pakistan. The Ministry of Finance, on the other hand, indicated a maximum resource availability of Rs 4,600 million: Rs 2,500 million external assistance and, after considerable persuasion by the Planning Commission, Rs 2,100 million domestic resources. The uncovered gap of Rs 400 million, the Planning Division suggested, should be met by deficit financing. Within the proposed development outlay, because of the provision for the Indus Basin Works in West Pakistan, which had been financed from outside the ADP in previous years, the Planning Division was obliged to suggest an allocation of less than 50 per cent to East Pakistan, as against 54 per cent of the ADP in 1970–1

A development programme lower than the previous years would have indicated an economic crisis, while the regime was insisting that everything was normal after the army operation in East Pakistan. Whereas earlier in June, the Ministry of Finance in technical meetings with the Planning Division was not agreeable even to a Rs 5,000 million programme, the Economic Adviser now announced an ADP of Rs 5,500 million for 1971–2 in his budget speech. The wizardry of the Finance Ministry in producing a public sector investment programme which was 11 per cent higher than the previous year, in spite of dwindling domestic resources, no foreign aid, and increasing non-developmental demands was impressive. It must have been a source of satisfaction to Yahya

Khan and the generals to find that their policies were having no adverse effects on the country's economic well-being. An analysis of the Rs 5,500 million programme reveals the cover-up of the disastrous consequences of these policies through spurious budgeting. Of the total amount, Rs 330 million was shown as 'operational shortfall', which purported to indicate that the agencies would not be able to utilize that amount, but actually meant that resources to this extent were not available, and that much of the programme would not be implemented. The device was one usually resorted to in planning documents to create an illusion of greater development than the actual. Of the net outlay of Rs 5,170 million (5,500 minus 330), external assistance was placed at Rs 2,560 million; the balance, Rs 2,610 million (5,170 minus 2,560), was to be raised from internal sources. The external aid represented the committed aid on ongoing projects, utilization of which required matching local currency; there were no prospects of new commodity or project aid. Of the internal resources of Rs 2,610 million, the provincial governments were expected to raise Rs 330 million from their revenue surpluses, a highly unrealistic assumption, particularly in respect of East Pakistan which was not in a position to meet even its revenue expenditure. The central government was thus responsible for finding only Rs 2,280 million (2,610 minus 330). On the basis of existing taxation, only Rs 1,335 million could be spared but, with new taxes and other administrative measures announced in the budget, the Economic Adviser hoped to raise an additional Rs 586 million, including the recovery of Rs 120 million from arrears; there was no reason to suppose that the tax collection agencies would suddenly be galvanized to realize these arrears. The final gap, thus reduced to only Rs 359 million (2,280 minus 1,335 plus 586), the Economic Adviser thought, could be appropriately covered by deficit financing.

On 17 June the Governors' Conference met. One of the subjects it discussed was the law and order situation in the country. It is not known who made the presentation on the subject, the Governors or the Ministry of Home Affairs. But the East Pakistan situation must have come up during discussion because the President complimented all the governors on 'curbing the anti-social elements' which action 'has improved the image of the administration', and exhorted them 'to instil a sense of discipline and control amongst all sections of people'.

The culmination of the extensive economic review was announcement of the budget for the year 1971–2 on 26 June by M. M. Ahmed. The budget speech referred to the problems arising from 'the economic consequences of the worst political crisis faced by the country in its history', resulting from the challenge of 'divisive forces' to the 'basic concept and ideology of Pakistan'. The nation was reminded that 'We owe a great debt of gratitude to the President and our Armed Forces for preserving the integrity and solidarity of the country.'[14]

* * *

The economic strains of the East Pakistan crisis manifested themselves at various points in national life. At the macro level, they were sought to be absorbed by adjustments in the import policy, the annual development programme, and the fiscal policies as discussed above. Specific problems were dealt with as best as they could be by improvised solutions.

One such issue, mentioned in passing in the last chapter, was the insurance claims arising out of the general upheaval in East Pakistan. A summary brought up by the Ministry of Commerce in the Weekly Meeting on 30 June reported heavy losses of stocks of raw materials and finished goods in the factories, godowns, and shops in East Pakistan; the damage to machinery and other fixed industrial assets was relatively light. Not all these properties were insured, but for those which were, claims could not be enforced against the insurance companies; the insurance policies did not cover risks like mutiny, rebellion, revolution, and similar uprisings. The Law Ministry confirmed the stand of the insurance companies that in the situation in East Pakistan they were not liable to compensate for damages from these excluded risks. In any case, even the preliminary estimate of insurance claims, of the order of Rs 80 to 100 million, was beyond the capacity of the insurance companies; it was equivalent to the profits of the entire insurance industry for the previous five years. The Ministry of Commerce considered it desirable to compensate the losses of insured properties, not only as a measure to revive trade and industry in East Pakistan, but also on moral grounds. Neither trade nor industry, it was maintained, were responsible for the losses, and the government had an obligation to compensate them for the consequences of its policies.

To indemnify the industrial and commercial establishments and the owners of vehicles used for public transport of goods and passengers for the losses on their insured properties, the Ministry of Commerce, therefore, recommended the setting up of a special fund. It was proposed to be created with an initial contribution by the insurance companies and an imposition of a surcharge of 10 per cent on the premiums of the ongoing general insurance business.

These proposals were severely criticized as socially unjust, favouring the big business establishments, and imposing a uniform rate of surcharge which was retrogressive in incidence. The President, who for the previous three months had been confronted with complex issues and a depressing state of affairs arising from East Pakistan, reacted strongly to the proposals and angrily observed that

> the principle of 100% compensation for all the insured properties did not appeal to him. The business houses could not absolve themselves completely of responsibility for the recent happenings in East Pakistan, firstly because it was this group which through exploitation and injustice had largely contributed to the social unrest which erupted in a violent form in the recent months, and secondly because it was their direct financial contribution to the political parties which enabled the latter to organize the large-scale disturbances that the country witnessed.

The matter was referred back to a working group for reconsideration. Eventually, in mid-July the Weekly Meeting approved the proposals, subject to exemption from surcharge where the total insured value of all the capital assets of a proprietor did not exceed Rs 0.1 million. It is not known whether the scheme was implemented but, if it was, the payments received by the West Pakistani business houses were not likely to have been ploughed back to the affected undertakings in East Pakistan.

Yet another example of the increasing burdens of the East Pakistan crisis was the substantial increase in the subsidy bill of inter-Wing flights. Before flights over India were banned, the government paid a subsidy of Rs 176 per economy-class passenger on these flights, out of the total fare of Rs 426. The cost of the fare, via Colombo, had gone up to Rs 940 and, on the basis of the pre-ban proportion of government support, the subsidy would now amount to Rs 390 per passenger. It was proposed that the fares should be increased, but the President wanted PIA to reduce the flights in such a manner that the operational expenditure due to the longer route remained the same as before. Some explaining had to done to the President that this was not possible. It was the wrong time to increase the fares, not so much because of any harm to the national integration which was the reason for the subsidy, but because it would have had an impact on the defence budget, as the army was being moved by air. However, the burden had to be borne, one way or another, by a subsidy from the budget or the profits of the national airline. But, like other difficult decisions, it was postponed for further consideration.

In the remaining months of united Pakistan, the economic strength built up during the previous two decades by hard work, sound planning, and foreign assistance, continued to be frittered away in the swamps of East Pakistan. All economic indicators showed a downward slide in the West Pakistan economy which, in the post-army operation period, was bearing the entire burden of internal security, relief, and rehabilitation in the eastern Wing, and the building up of a credible national posture against the Indian threat. According to one source, the defence expenditure, which was Rs 1,370 million in 1964–5, increased by 260 per cent to Rs 3,400 million in 1971–2, with another Rs 200 million hidden under other heads. During the period March–December 1971, the Ministry of Finance received 108 demands from the Defence Ministry involving a total annual cost of Rs 950 million, and approved each one of them within seven days. Roughly, after paying the provinces' share of about Rs 1,600 million from its total annual revenue of Rs 7,000 to 8,000 million, the central government was left with about Rs 5,500 million. Of this latter amount, defence was appropriating Rs 3,400–3,600 million, leaving very little for essential development. The 1971–2 budget had provided for the transfer of Rs 1,500 million from West to East Pakistan. But by October, the usually placid Ministry of Finance had lost its nerve under the burden of the endless demands of the East Pakistan administration.[15] In army circles, there was talk of open war against India, but not of a political settlement with the Awami League, as a better economic alternative.

The West Pakistan economy had reached a high growth rate of 8.2 per cent in real terms in 1964–5. In the following two years it was of the order of 4 to 5 per cent, bouncing back to 7.7 per cent in 1967–8 in spite of the disastrous war of 1965. In 1969–70, despite the political agitations, the growth momentum of previous years was still maintained at 6.9 per cent. The dismal performance of the subsequent two years of the Yahya regime was fully brought out much later in 1972, by Ghulam Ishaq Khan as the Governor State Bank of Pakistan. In 1970–1 the gross domestic product of West Pakistan rose by only 0.8 per cent (it was reported as 2.8 per cent in the Weekly Meeting of 2 June 1971) and increased marginally to 1.7 per cent in 1971–2. With a population increase of 2.7 per cent, the per capita income declined sharply in two successive years. The low growth was due to the poor performance of both the agricultural and industrial sectors. The output of the large-scale manufacturing sector, for the first time in the country's history, declined in absolute terms in 1971–2 which affected the tertiary sectors also. Public sector investment decelerated by 13 per cent in 1971–2; private sector investment recorded a much greater drop of 41 per cent. As a result, overall fixed investment dropped from 15 per cent of the gross domestic product of West Pakistan to 10 per cent in 1971–2.[16]

The downward slide in production, investment, and employment affected the budgetary position. The deficit financing resorted to by the government led to a sizeable expansion of monetary assets which, combined with the previous monetary overhang and the constraints on the supply side, exercised severe pressure on price levels. The wholesale price index registered an increase of about 12 per cent between July 1971 and April 1972 as against about 4 per cent in the same period the previous year. The clerical and industrial wage-earners' consumer price indices also registered sizeable increases. A major element affecting the price situation was the measures taken to protect the balance of payments. Severe restrictions were placed on imports, including essential ones, the landed costs of which rose sharply due to the shift of almost all of them on to the bonus list. This in turn raised the premium on bonus vouchers, leading to a substantial rise in industrial costs. As a result of these measures, imports fell by about 11 per cent. The only bright spot in an otherwise depressed economy was the remarkable initiative of West Pakistani entrepreneurs in finding export markets for goods which had hitherto been sold to East Pakistan. These efforts, combined with a large cotton crop, increased exports by about 41 per cent in 1971–2 compared to 1970–1. As a result, the trade deficit was sharply reduced from Rs 1,490 million in 1970–1 to Rs 400 million in 1971–2.[17]

The moratorium on certain debt service maturities imposed by the government of Pakistan in May 1971 was for six months. It was apprehended that any default beyond this period would cause serious legal and institutional difficulties for the donor countries. A special meeting of the consortium countries was held on 27 October in Paris to consider Pakistan's request for debt rescheduling and fresh aid for 1971–2. A powerful Indian delegation had also arrived in Paris a day earlier, to urge the consortium meeting to grant additional aid to India for the East Pakistan refugees and to stop all assistance to Pakistan. Mrs Gandhi was, at that very time, visiting European capitals, urging 'all sanctions short of war' against Pakistan in order to secure a political settlement of the East Pakistan crisis.[18] There was little hope of getting assistance of any kind in the hostile atmosphere prevalent in the donor countries.

By November, the gathering war clouds had led to the mobilization of all resources for the defence of the integrity of the country. The Planning Commission, which was struggling to adhere to some order of priorities, gave up all pretence of planning and admitted that the objects and targets of the annual development plan of 1971–2 were unrealistic, and under the special circumstances they would have to make room for other programmes which were not purely developmental. The conditions prevailing in East Pakistan, the Commission observed, were such that the prime consideration in 1971–2 would be rehabilitation and revitalization of the economy, rather than positive development.[19] Having gone bankrupt in more senses than one, the country was poised to go to war with India.

CHAPTER 8

The Politics of International Relief and Refugees

The legitimacy of the army operation in East Pakistan, as an internal police measure to prevent secession of a part of the country, was never accepted by public opinion or by the governments of the Western countries. In their media, the Pakistan army was projected as a mindless machine, playing havoc in East Pakistan and spilling human miseries into neighbouring India. The March operation, conceived as a one-time action to subdue the rebellious Bengali elements, very soon turned into a full-fledged civil war with no prospects of a victory for either side. In the build-up of world opinion against Pakistan, human sufferings were effectively exploited by India, the Bangladesh lobby, and other anti-Pakistan elements in the West to attain the political objective of an independent Bangladesh. The expanding dimension of the human tragedy in East Pakistan and beyond the borders could not be argued by the Pakistani diplomats, with any credibility, to be an internal affair of Pakistan. These humanitarian problems were regarded by the Americans and other Western countries as legitimate areas for intervention by the world community. They were (i) ensuring availability of sufficient food in East Pakistan, its distribution all over the province, and the ability of the people to buy it; (ii) to induct UN and foreign voluntary organizations into East Pakistan to oversee the implementation of (i); and (iii) the outflow of refugees from East Pakistan, their maintenance in India, and their return to their homes. These international concerns are discussed below.

Feeding the People

In early April, the provincial Food Department had carried out a detailed exercise for the special team about the availability of foodgrains in East Pakistan until September, on the basis of the existing stocks, likely off-take, and the import arrangements already firmed up. For 1970–1, the foodgrain deficit of East Pakistan was worked out at about 1.75 million tons of wheat and rice, of which 1.13 million tons (or 64 per cent) were being procured under grants or soft credits from Japan, the USA, and other Western countries. This aid financing covered 95 per cent of the wheat and 27 per cent of the rice included in the deficit quantity. West Pakistan provided 350,000 tons of rice or 20 per cent of the total foodgrain deficit and, including this quantity, Pakistan met only 35 per cent of the East Pakistan food gap from its own resources of cash foreign exchange and barter with Burma and China. This heavy dependence on foreign aid to meet foodgrain requirements put Pakistan, during the East Pakistan crisis, in a position highly vulnerable to foreign pressures for inducting the UN into the food management process of the province.

The import of the deficit quantity of wheat and rice from foreign countries and West Pakistan was fully programmed, and 0.93 million had been received by March 1971. Of the balance—0.82 million tons—shipping commitments for 0.31 million tons had already been made for arrival in April, May, and June. The government stocks of 0.62 million tons in the beginning of April, added to the expected arrivals, gave a total availability of 0.93 million tons which was somewhat higher than the stocks in the same period the previous year. The special team considered this quantity sufficient for four months; the provincial government thought that during the following three months the demand might be more than normal, and the available government stocks might last only three months. Accordingly, the import programme was revised to provide higher arrivals in May, June, and July. The shipping schedule envisaged a daily average unloading of about 4,500 tons at the two ports, Chittagong and Chalna, during the next six months. In normal times this would have been no problem, and the experts drawing up the import programme in early April assumed restoration of normalcy in the next one or two months. They allowed for the prevailing disturbed conditions by extending the shipments and arrivals over a longer period. In the event, the assumption about normalcy proved incorrect. The average daily arrivals of foodgrain at the two ports did not exceed 1,000 to 2,000 tons in June and July. But from September the imports picked up, and the daily unloading at the two ports reached about 6,000 tons in October and November.[1]

Imported foodgrain, however, accounted for only about 10 per cent of the total consumption in the province. The viability of the food situation essentially depended on the local rice production from the three crops—*aman, aus,* and *boro.*[2] In April, the *boro* crop was being harvested and it was satisfactory; *aus* sowing was in progress. Agriculture was one sector which the special team did not find adversely affected by the disturbed conditions. Fertilizer consumption up to February was 22 per cent more than for the same period the previous year, and sufficient stocks were available in the province. The stocks of pesticide were also enough, although ten out of the twelve aerial spray aircraft had been taken over by the army. The existing pumps and tubewells were in position, and new ones were being installed according to the programme, but their operation depended on the supply of about 500,000 to 700,000 gallons of fuel oil from May to September for the summer and winter crops. The problem, as in other sectors, was the transportation of these key inputs to the target areas.

In contrast to the somewhat optimistic picture presented by the special team, the United States Agency for International Development (USAID) in Pakistan considered the food situation most alarming in the short run, and heading towards widespread famine by the end of 1971. This was the conclusion of a draft paper titled 'Foodgrain Situation, East Pakistan' dated 19 April, prepared in its Office of Agriculture Policy.[3] It was accepted that foodgrain stocks in East Pakistan were near the highest level ever in late March and, in normal circumstances, could be expected to last three to four months without a continuing flow of imports. A crisis, argued the paper, was, however, likely to develop much sooner because (i) these stocks were not evenly located to meet the requirements of the people; and (ii) the quantity of domestic rice, 10 per cent of which normally moved through commercial channels to the deficit areas, coming to the market would be considerably less due to hoarding as a hedge against expectations of future shortages and higher prices, and the disruption in the transport system. Unless, therefore, the up-country movement of foodgrain from the ports was restored to a near normal rate in the immediate future, the food situation would become serious. Accordingly, the paper urged that all modes of transport should be activated, without specifying how, and concluded with a menacing rule of thumb that the probability of famine increased every day that less than 5,000 tons of imported grain was offloaded and dispatched up-country. The actual import of foodgrain in May, June, and July did not go beyond the daily average of 1,000 to 2,000 tons; it reached 4,500 tons only in the middle of September and exceeded 6,000 tons in October and November. The dispatches, however, remained much below the 'critical' figure; in July, August, and September the daily average was about 2,000 tons; it reached 4,000 tons in the middle of October, and then came down again.[4] With this level of dispatches, the USAID prediction assumed an increasing degree of probability and East Pakistan should have been in the grip of acute famine by September, if not earlier.

While in the short run the disruption in transportation and hoarding could be cushioned by abundant stocks, leading to local shortages only, the longer term prospects of rice production were, according to the USAID experts, positively leading towards famine. The production of the three rice crops in 1971–2 was projected at 10 per cent less than that of 1970–1, amounting to an absolute decline of 1.1 million tons. This was based on the assumption, explicitly stated in the paper, that the government's ability to organize procurement and distribution of key agricultural inputs and to implement local irrigation schemes was irretrievably lost after 25 March. The Pakistan government ceased to be responsible for East Pakistan after mid-December, and was spared the agony of living in fear of this doomsday prophecy which, given the dependence on foreign assistance, might well have been made to come true. It may, however, be mentioned that in East Pakistan the pre-*aman* harvest period of October–December was usually one of local or widespread food shortages, depending on available stocks. In 1971 there was no case of starvation; ample food was available everywhere as is shown by the records of price statistics and even during the war in the first half of December, the administration kept the food situation well under control.

That the problem of feeding the population of East Pakistan in the conditions of April–December was not easy cannot be denied. There is also no doubt that there was a real danger of some of these predictions of the foreign experts coming true; it is a tribute to the East Pakistan administration that they did not. But the point is that these assessments and studies, based on some hasty assumptions, were not always used for serious humanitarian responses in donor countries. They were widely disseminated to the members of the Congress and the media in the US and in other Western countries for causes other than purely humanitarian.

By June, the army operation was more or less over. The East Pakistan crisis was, however, kept alive in the Western media by the spectre of a famine of a magnitude similar to, if not greater than, the Bengal famine of 1942. The demand was being made to induct the UN, supported by international relief agencies, into the food administration of East Pakistan as a condition precedent to any kind of assistance to Pakistan. As part of a relief package and to mollify the US administration, M. M. Ahmed, during his visit to Washington in May invited Joseph A. Ryan, an official of the US Department of Agriculture to make an on-the-spot study of the food situation of East Pakistan.

The findings and recommendations of the Ryan mission were brought to the Economic Co-ordination Committee by the central Ministry of Food and Agriculture, with its comments, on 28 June. Ryan concluded that the existing stocks of 0.45 million tons would be quite sufficient for the next 3.75 months; he did not agree with the provincial Food Department which thought they would last only two months, up to August. In addition to these stocks, imported foodgrain was being unloaded at the ports. For the immediate period, Ryan made three recommendations: (i) to avoid local shortages, the stock position at various places should be kept under constant review (an obvious requirement of any food management system); (ii) to ensure sufficient purchasing power for the people, the rural works programme should be continued during the monsoon also; and (iii) to ensure good crops the procurement, movement and distribution of seeds, fertilizer, and pesticides should have the same priority as the foodgrain itself.

For 1971–2, Ryan estimated the foodgrain import requirements of East Pakistan at 1.59 million tons. The Ministry of Food and Agriculture and the provincial Food Department, however, pitched the estimated deficit at 3 million tons on the assumption of lower production and higher off-take from government stocks. This was in line with the tendency of the food and aid officials of the government of Pakistan to inflate the deficit figures; the former to cover themselves against any shortages, and the latter to make use of any opportunity to get maximum aid. The Economic Co-ordination Committee, however, had reduced this estimate to 2 million tons in an earlier meeting in the first week of June.

Ryan made a number of useful recommendations relating to the movement of foodgrain. They included maximization of Chittagong and Chalna ports operations, augmentation of road and railway capacities, improvement of the terminal capacity of Narayanganj, and an increase in the turn-round of riverine vessels. On the administrative side, he recommended that a senior officer be designated 'Food Czar', with full responsibility for co-ordinating the activities of various agencies involved in the procurement and distribution of food and relief, and rural works; the officer was to have direct access to the Governor of East Pakistan and the President of Pakistan to carry out his functions effectively.

More important and of immediate relevance were the Ryan recommendations about water transport. The Pakistan government had been highlighting this aspect in response to the concern of the international community about the widespread famine in East Pakistan. To meet the immediate problem of distributing food, the US expert recommended the purchase of additional coasters and other vessels on a priority basis.

All Ryan's recommendations were accepted by the central and provincial governments; some were implemented, and others, which were of the nature of guiding principles, were incorporated in the working procedures. Although the difficulties pointed out in the report were known and taken note of, Ryan's overall findings did not indicate imminent famine or widespread starvation as was being agitated in the US Congress and media. But the report emphasized the necessity for maintaining a regular flow of food imports, if necessary through commercial purchases by the government of Pakistan itself. Meanwhile, the government of East Pakistan was pressing the central government to ensure shipment of 0.650 million tons by September. Of this, 0.1 million was on its way, scheduled for arrival by 30 June, and shipping arrangements for 0.150 million were being finalized. For the remaining quantity of 0.4 million for arrival in August and September, the Pakistan government was depending on the resumption of PL 480 supplies.

On 5 June, the Assistant Secretary of State Joseph Sisco called the Pakistan Ambassador Agha Hilaly and, while 'highly praising' Yahya's statement of 24 May accepting international supervision of relief operations, expressed the 'great concern' of the US government on various matters pertaining to East Pakistan. On the food situation, Sisco made the following points: (i) civil administration for the distribution of relief had broken down; (ii) relief works for injecting purchasing power in the population had not yet started; (iii) there were reports of impending, even actual, starvation in cyclone-affected areas; (iii) there was relatively little movement of foodgrain from ports to the interior and no shipments as yet from Karachi; and (iv) stocks of foodgrain available in East Pakistan might have been seriously overestimated.

The concerns of the US government were, however, not very readily reflected in its responses to the requests of the Pakistan government on these matters. The Ryan report must have been submitted to the US government in the middle of June, but the Economic Minister of the Pakistan embassy in Washington was getting only the standard diplomatic reply that the 'matter was under review' from the Department of Agriculture about the resumption of PL 480 shipments. The stevedores at the US Gulf ports were likely to go on indefinite strike by 30 September. The Economic Minister asked the Foreign Office on 14 July to exert diplomatic pressure on the US embassy to finalize the purchase authorizations; he emphasized that it was 'imperative repeat imperative' that the maximum quantity should be shipped by 15 September.

Eventually, on 26 July Hilaly reported to the Economic and Food Advisers the agreement of the USAID (i) to the issue of purchase authorization by the Department of Agriculture for about 0.15 million tons of the PL 480 agreement of November 1970 which had been cancelled in April, after the formal extension of the agreement, instructions for which were being sent to the US embassy in Islamabad; and (ii) to the signing of a new agreement for a similar quantity for cyclone-affected areas, within two weeks. In the same message, Hilaly reported that Macdonald of the USAID had 'bitterly' complained that in spite of the repeated requests of the local AID officials the East Pakistan government had failed to supply a definite programme of up-country movement of foodgrain from the ports. The AID officials in Dhaka, Macdonald said, were consistently reporting the ineffectiveness of the government; according to them it was already too late to avert mass starvation which they predicted would be raging by the end of October. And even if foodgrain reached the target areas, the local American officials thought, people would not have enough money to buy them because the central government had failed to reactivate the rural infrastructure.

All these negotiations in July were in respect of the allocations of the previous fiscal year 1970–1 to cover the immediate foodgrain gap. In early August, Hilaly took up the question of a fresh PL 480 agreement for the current year 1971–2 with the USAID Administrator Dr Hannah, who was inclined to sign for at least a part of the amount required. But, significantly, his aide opposed it on the grounds that there were enough stocks in the pipeline up to November. The ambassador's request, in the same meeting, for release of at least a part of the previous year's commitment of $ 80 million commodity loan also did not evoke any response. As will be seen presently, in the case of coasters also, the time limit of absolutely essential humanitarian assistance set by the US Administration seemed to be November and anything which looked like support to the Yahya regime beyond this period was firmly rejected.

For the AID officials, their predictions of April were coming true. Yahya Khan was perturbed by the grim scenario depicted by the Americans and asked for a report on the 'food front' in East Pakistan. It was brought up in the Weekly Meeting of 14 July. Like the other fronts, the news was not good. The President started the meeting peevishly observing that

> he was not satisfied that all that was necessary had been or was being done and warned that unless the authorities concerned both at the Centre and in the province remained vigilant and acted with extreme care and dispatch, the forebodings of the country's ill wishers that East Pakistan would soon be taken over by famine might well prove true—a situation he would never allow to develop. [He also asked] what the response of the international community was which at one time was raising all manner of noises about humanitarian aid to East Pakistan.

A candid discussion followed the President's remarks and the following picture, as of mid-July, was presented. The existing stocks were sufficient for roughly three months; the import programme for the annual food gap of two million tons had been finalized. The problem was of transporting stocks and imports to deficit areas, a problem created by the dislocation of roads and railways and by the limited availability of river craft. The imbalance in distribution was reflected in prices; in some areas the price of rice was Rs 30 per maund, whereas in the deficit areas it was Rs 70 per maund. The private trade channels, which used to supplement government supplies in the deficit areas, had also dried up due to the general insecurity in the interior. But even if supplies had been made available everywhere, people would have been unable to buy; due to the stoppage of monetary transactions in trade and industry, they had very little purchasing power. This was borne out by the fact that the off-take from government stocks in June was only 80,000 tons, as against 150,000 tons in the same month in the previous year. The lack of transportation and purchasing power were likely to create famine conditions in certain areas in spite of there being plenty of stocks. The works programme had been initiated but its effect on the cash in the hands of the people would emerge only after some time. The availability of coasters, local, chartered, or purchased with foreign assistance, remained unsatisfactory and, on prevailing indications, was likely to remain so.

After the narration of these intractable facts of the situation, the debate ended with a whimper; the President directed that the Adviser for Food and Agriculture

> should forthwith look into the food situation in East Pakistan [as if he had not done so uptil now!] in all its aspects as discussed, and ensure adequate machinery was set up and other arrangements put in train for the proper supply and distribution of foodgrain all over the province down to Thana level.

Throughout the nine months of the East Pakistan crisis no problem engaged the attention of the civilian administrators in Islamabad and Dhaka more than the procurement and distribution of food to all parts of the eastern Wing. The key to the economic revival in general, and movement of foodgrain in particular, was the riverine transport. It was just possible that if enough of it had somehow been mobilized, the impact of the guerrilla activities would have been bypassed to a large extent and a degree of normalcy brought about in the province.[5]

The efforts to restructure the East Pakistan transportation system by permanent addition to the coaster fleet (briefly mentioned in Chapter 6) did not impress the foreign aid givers. But they were willing to finance the hiring of vessels, for short periods, under strict supervision, exclusively for the distribution of food and relief materials. Only the People's Republic of China promptly agreed to provide, on unconditional ownership basis, three vessels from the existing soft credit line to Pakistan; they were in operation by the end of July. In August, the Netherlands government, after persistent diplomatic representations and verbal and written guarantees by the government of Pakistan that they would not be used for military purposes, allowed the purchase of five coasters from its credit line; but these vessels would not be available before early October. In sheer desperation, the Pakistan government allocated $ 2 million for the purpose from its own depleted resources, and invited the private sector to purchase coasters against supplier credit on the government guarantee of repayment in foreign exchange; the utilization of both these modes got entangled in bureaucratic wranglings. Information was received from the UN representative in Dhaka that it might be possible to charter military vessels from certain countries with their own crews in civilian clothes with UN armbands; specific mention was made of the two British military units stationed at Singapore which had landing-craft. The USAID Director in Islamabad informally told Pakistani officials that the UN was willing to explore the possibility, provided a firm request was made by the government of Pakistan. The East Pakistan Chief Secretary was given a similar understanding by the UN chief in Dhaka. After a flurry of consultations in the Foreign Office and the CMLA secretariat, it was decided that, while there was no objection to obtaining the vessels with military crews under UN auspices, it would 'not be appropriate to confine such acquisition to only one country'. The Yahya regime, in view of the known attitude of the United Kingdom towards its East Pakistan policies, could not accept the British presence there.

The US government, up to the end of July, had provided $ 2 million against which seventeen vessels had been chartered. Instead of using this grant more economically for purchasing river vessels, the USAID insisted on only hiring them for three to four months. The price of a coaster of the specifications required in East Pakistan was in the range of $ 0.3 to $ 0.4 million; the time charter charges for similar vessels were $ 25,000 to $ 30,000 per month. The reason for keeping these craft outside the control of Pakistan, which purchase and transfer would have meant, was to prevent their use by the army. The US government had lodged protests from time to time against the continuous use by the army of the rivercraft donated by it for cyclone relief. Only three US-chartered vessels were expected to report in August, adding a mere 2,100 tons to the existing river transport capacity of East Pakistan. By the middle of August, only two had reported; the remaining fifteen were scheduled to reach East Pakistan at various times by 10 October. Meanwhile, a grant of another $ 2 million was given for more hiring which did not really mean any additional capacity. It was meant simply to maintain the short-period chartering cycle of the same number of vessels.

While the USAID itself showed no sense of urgency, it was continuously demanding from the Pakistan government voluminous documentation about the use to which these coasters would be put, even before complete information about their tonnage and arrival was made available.[6] Even after the arrival of the vessels, the East Pakistan administration was not free to deploy them to get optimum results; USAID restricted half of them for use in the cyclone-affected areas. They could not be used elsewhere, even if they were surplus to the requirements of these areas, without US approval. Although the humanitarian concern in many American forums was genuine, the reluctance of the US Administration to respond promptly to actual needs arose from an understandable annoyance that the problem was of Pakistan's own creation.

There was a deep distrust in the US bureaucracy that assistance like vessels would not only be misused for military purposes but, to the extent that it relieved human miseries, it would also bail out the military regime from the consequences of its policies. But it also reflected, particularly from August onwards, different perceptions about the East Pakistan crisis in the White House and the US bureaucracy. 'The new Nixon-Kissinger strategy [after the China trip of Kissinger]' says Christopher Van Hollen, 'was to separate the humanitarian aspects of the policy from the political'.

Senior US officials, however, believed that 'unless there was genuine progress on the political front, the refugees would not return to East Pakistan, India would not stop supporting the guerrillas, it would be impossible to administer humanitarian relief in East Pakistan, and the prospects of war would mount.'[7] Viewed in this perspective, all relief aid was futile and would only prolong the agony.

International Relief and Rehabilitation

The history of international relief started on 31 March when the International Committee of the Red Cross (ICRC) Geneva sent a team of four members with a plane-load of relief supplies to Karachi, without any request from the Pakistan Red Cross Society, as was necessary under its own rules. They were not allowed to proceed to East Pakistan and the plane returned with all the relief goods. The President of the International Red Cross (IRC) admitted to Pakistan's permanent representative in Geneva that the ICRC was 'over-zealous' in sending the relief plane without the consent of the government of Pakistan. The Swiss Foreign Secretary also told the Pakistan ambassador in Berne that the ICRC had committed a 'tremendous mistake'. However, the top officials of the IRC continued to insist that their assistance was required in East Pakistan, and that their representative should be allowed to go there. The IRC also sent a message to the President, and handed over an *aide-memoire* to Pakistan's permanent representative which, according to the Foreign Office, 'manifested its [IRC's] anxiety to acquire a *locus standi* in the situation in East Pakistan and to internationalize it'. Soon after this abortive attempt, on 10 April, the Foreign Office warned all the Pakistan missions abroad of the efforts of the ICRC and some other relief organizations and countries for internationalizing the East Pakistan situation through offers of humanitarian assistance, and of the need to resist such efforts.

On 22 April, the UN Secretary-General, U Thant, in a letter to Yahya Khan, while reaffirming that the events in East Pakistan fell within the domestic injurisdiction of Pakistan, suggested 'that the UN and its specialized agencies have a most useful role to play, with the consent of your government, in providing emergency assistance for the purpose of relieving widespread misery, hardships, and sufferings which have befallen the population in East Pakistan.'[8] As the pressures for foreign involvement in the crisis grew, the Foreign Office, on 24 April, reiterated to the Pakistan missions its policy on the subject. Explaining the rationale of Pakistan's stand, it was recalled that the IRC and other international humanitarian agencies had played a very controversial role in situations similar to East Pakistan. The Nigerian authorities had accused them of grave violations of their humanitarian charter, even of gunrunning to Biafra during the civil war in that country. The Foreign Secretary advised the missions that outside aid would be needed to restore the East Pakistan economy, and, at the appropriate time, the nature and extent of it would be indicated. But its utilization would be undertaken by the government of Pakistan itself and not by the foreign agencies. After the bitter experience of 'volunteers' in the cyclone relief operations of November 1970 in East Pakistan, the message added, foreigners would not be allowed to administer such assistance.[9] In the light of these considerations, the foreign missions were instructed to discourage all such initiatives for internationalizing the East Pakistan situation.

In line with this independent stance, the President rejected U Thant's offer of UN assistance, and on 29 April informed him that there was no shortage of daily necessities in East Pakistan for the time being, that the armed forces had restored law and order, and that an assessment of immediate and future possible assistance for relief and rehabilitation was being made. It was, however, made clear that the international assistance, if and when required, would be administered by Pakistani agencies.[10]

Four days after U Thant's offer, the US government requested that American voluntary agencies be allowed to operate in East Pakistan. On 26 April, the Pakistan embassy was informed by the State Department that a part of the PL 480 Title 2 supplies had been placed at the disposal of the American relief organizations operating in India. They would be distributed by them to the East Pakistan refugees in West Bengal without involving the Indian official and non-official agencies. On the same principle, the State Department requested facilities for the visit of the representatives of CARE and six other American voluntary relief organizations to East Pakistan to distribute relief goods such as clothes and foodstuff. The messy army operation was still going on, and it was an awkward time to allow foreigners to observe and report it to the outside world. The reply to the State Department, sent on 29 April through the Pakistan Ambassador, was on the same lines as the one sent the same day to the UN Secretary-General. Pakistan had no objection to the distribution of relief supplies by the American voluntary agencies in West Bengal, but the State Department was 'cautioned' about the highly exaggerated Indian figures of refugees. As for a similar operation in East Pakistan, the State Department was politely informed that because of the problems of logistics—transportation, lodging, security, etc.—it was not possible for foreign volunteers to undertake it there. To soften the impact of the rejection, the Foreign Office sought the intervention of US Ambassador Farland in Islamabad in support of its stand. The message to Hilaly ended with the optimistic observation that 'the US Ambassador fully understood and appreciated the situation and would be conveying it to the State Department'.

The lack of sensitivity of the Yahya regime to world opinion arose from the naivety of the generals in charge of the country, and the timidity of the Foreign Office. It was clear that economic and other realities could not sustain, for any length of time, the independence asserted by the government of Pakistan. The US request for the induction of voluntary agencies in East Pakistan was refused, but not without considerable anxiety about its consequences. The Foreign Secretary tried to limit them by backtracking on the closed-door policy on the very day the reply was sent to Washington. On 29 April, in a detailed letter to the heads of missions in major western countries and at the UN, Sultan Muhammad Khan gave three reasons why foreign volunteers were not being accepted in East Pakistan. Firstly, it was found, through the November 1970 cyclone experience, that the absence of the minimum of comforts and facilities expected by the foreigners, exposed the government to adverse publicity. Secondly, the security of foreign personnel could not be guaranteed as a large number of rebels were still at large. Thirdly—and this was the main reason—the government of Pakistan had no means to check the bona fides of these volunteers; they were likely to feed the world media with unfavourable accounts of the happenings in East Pakistan. The government would, therefore, distribute relief assistance through its own agencies and, for the information of the head of the mission only, it was intimated that the major responsibility for this purpose would be entrusted to the armed forces. In order not to cause avoidable offence to the donors, the heads of missions were asked to let it be known that, as and when the situation permitted, the government of Pakistan might also consider availing of the services of relief experts. Finally, the envoys were advised that this point of distribution of relief exclusively under government arrangements should not be emphasized too much. In less than a week these pretensions of keeping the foreigners away would be given up.

By early May, a consensus was emerging in Western forums for organizing relief under international supervision in East Pakistan, to avert famine and to help create conditions there to stop the exodus of refugees to India. In the face of irresistible pressures, the President, on 3 May, decided that the 'time had come' to accept official relief assistance from selected countries and international organizations; the emphasis was still to be on the means of distribution available in the country. In spite of this decision, the Foreign Office continued to repeat, for a while, its hard line for home consumption. Commenting on criticism of Pakistan for refusing to avail offers of relief assistance, the Foreign Office spokesman pompously remarked, on 6 May, that it would be accepted 'as and when the need arises. For the present we wish to concentrate on optimum utilization of our own resources to help ourselves.'[11]

The Washington visit of M. M. Ahmed has been mentioned in the previous chapter. This was the time when hostility to the Yahya regime was at its peak in the Congress, media, and the administration. The Press and television were flooded with accounts of atrocities in East Pakistan. The US Senate Foreign Relations Committee had voted for the suspension of arms sales until the civil war in East Pakistan was over. M. M. Ahmed met President Nixon and, apart from the heads of the World Bank and the IMF, all who mattered in the Congress and the Administration. He tried to explain Pakistan's case on the East Pakistan crisis, and to convince them that there was no danger of famine. The White House, under severe internal and external pressures, was urging Yahya Khan to accept international administration of relief operations in East Pakistan.[12] This was the message given to M. M. Ahmed by everyone he met in Washington.

Finally, Ahmed met the UN Secretary-General on 17 May and conveyed acceptance of the Pakistan government of humanitarian assistance under UN auspicces in East Pakistan. On 22 May, Agha Shahi, permanent representative at the UN, formally requested the Secretary-General for relief assistance with two provisos: (i) international assistance would be administered by Pakistan's relief agencies, though the UN agencies would be associated in the planning and organization of relief operations; and (ii) the government of Pakistan would be willing to receive the representative of the Secretary-General as a focal point, on the understanding that his role and activities would be within the framework of humanitarian assistance only.[13]

The UN promptly acted to move in on receipt of this letter. Ismet Kittani, Assistant Secretary-General, Office for Inter-Agency Affairs, reached Karachi on 3 June to discuss the modalities of relief assistance to East Pakistan from and through the UN.[14] He met the President on the following day. The Foreign Secretary, who was present at the meeting, recorded the following agreements: (i) relief materials would be distributed through Pakistan agencies and personnel but the nominee of the Secretary-General and the representatives of the UN agencies would be associated with the operations; (ii) Bahagat El-Tawil would be stationed as the co-ordinating representative of the Secretary-General in Dhaka; (iii) a Pakistani liaison officer with a nucleus organization exclusively looking after aid supplies would work with El-Tawil. The only issue on which there was no agreement was the coasters chartered for relief operations, on which the President wanted Pakistani crews to work alongside foreign crews under the overall control of the Pakistan Navy. Kittani, knowing that these conditions would not be acceptable to the donors, did not press the matter but otherwise he felt satisfied.

Kittani visited Dhaka on 7 June and on his return to New York announced that a UN co-ordination organization had been set up in East Pakistan to ensure maximum use of international aid. He said that the problem was not as urgent as it was originally thought to have been; there was enough food on the spot for two months, and more was in the pipeline.[15] The terms of reference of UN activities in East Pakistan formulated by the government of Pakistan tried to keep international involvement to the minimum. Firstly, only UN agencies were allowed to operate; foreign voluntary organizations were excluded. Secondly, the number of UN staff was kept limited. Thirdly, in spite of the fact that officers of the armed services were anathema to the donors, they were included in the cell created to liaise and co-ordinate with the UN agencies. The cell was a central government agency, though the actual relief operations would continue to be the responsibility of the provincial government. The status of the cell was carefully defined as a body created under the authority of the President under an officer appointed by the central government and supervised from Islamabad by Muzaffar Husain. This was because by June, the Western mass media and some other forums were referring to the government of Pakistan as the government of West Pakistan, implying its loss of authority in East Pakistan. The UN, with its involvement in the internal administration of the province, could be interpreted as having a *locus standi* in the internal affairs of Pakistan, independent of the central government or at least alongside it. For the actual relief operations, on 18 June the East Pakistan government announced a counterpart committee to the Inter-Agency Committee of the UN, with H. R. Malik, a Bengali CSP officer as the convenor.

On 17 June, after Kittani had tied up the system which took care of the susceptibilities of the donor countries in respect of the end use of their donations, the Secretary-General issued an appeal for assistance to East Pakistan, which opened up a number of blocked channels of food and related assistance, particularly from the US.

The counterpart committee headed by Malik formulated aid requirements of foodgrain, transport, and other relief needs in its first meeting held on 30 June, and conveyed them to El-Tawil on 4 July. The only item in the list which was properly quantified and was likely to produce an immediate and productive impact on the situation was riverine transport. The UN headquarters, to which these requirements were transmitted by El-Tawil on the day they were received, asked for confirmation in writing from the government of Pakistan that food movement would be given the highest priority. All donors were asking for this kind of assurance because of the suspicion that transport resources would be diverted for military purposes. The province being under military administration, and in a state of rebellion inside and under pressure on the borders, it was inherent in the situation that, on the ground, army needs would take precedence over any other. The writ of the government, administered through established administrative channels, was not acceptable to the harassed local commanders whose priorities were different and who did not hesitate to use force to enforce them. There were frequent clashes between the civil officers, engaged in food distribution, and the local army commanders on the use of available transport. In spite of government instructions, the local army formation would just seize the vehicles, river vessels, and even railway trains, and that would be that. By the time the matter was reported by the district officer to the chief secretary, who took it up with Major-General Farman Ali, who contacted Eastern Command, the movement programme had already been dislocated to the despair of hard-pressed civil officials. The problem was not merely at the local level. In the second week of July, the resident representative of the UNDP was complaining to the Secretary, EC&EA Division that the UN vehicles, launches, and equipment were still under requisition of the martial law authorities in East Pakistan. On 5 June, Sisco had complained to Hilaly about the public relations problems created for the administration by the reports of US boats donated for relief operations in East Pakistan being used for military purposes.

The UN headquarters, on receipt of the required assurances from the government of Pakistan, conveyed its reactions to the list of aid items; it accepted some, did not react favourably to a few, and sought clarifications in respect of others. The positive response was mainly on foodgrain. About riverine transport, the reply was rather evasive and referred to the grant of $ 2 million given by the US for the purpose. On 16 July, the UN office issued a press release entitled 'Secretary-General Receives Report for Relief Needs For East Pakistan; Initial Needs Estimated at $ 28.2 million'.[16] The assessments, according to this release, suggested that the problem was primarily one of distribution of food and other relief supplies. The aid amount, $ 28.2 million, endorsed by the UN in the press release was much less than the sum requested by Pakistan. It was recommended by the Secretary-General as the initial sum on the basis of 'United Nations estimate of food stocks and funding required, and as the first step in providing humanitarian assistance to the population of East Pakistan from and through the United

Nations'. In the transport sector, the request for landing craft of various types was not endorsed, presumably because in the earlier months the LCTs had become associated with military use. Malik in a letter to El-Tawil, on 2 August, mildly protested against the reduction in various relief items by the UN in the 'initial requests' incorporated in the press release of 16 July, and hoped that they would be restored to their original form 'in your future announcement for our immediate relief needs.'

On 2 August, Shahi reported that the Secretary-General believed that the time had come to strengthen the UN relief organization in East Pakistan. The proposals were (i) to expand the office of the Secretary-General's Representative at Dhaka by including a Deputy Representative, a voluntary agencies' liaison officer, and an information officer; (ii) to set up an advisory team consisting of six experts to assist the Representative; (iii) an operation unit with seventy-seven personnel; and (iv) a supporting administrative unit. The Secretary-General expected more funds if adequate UN staff was available on ground to handle the increased contribution.

On 13 August, the Secretary-General addressed a meeting of the permanent representatives of twenty-eight countries who had contributed to the relief assistance to Pakistan refugees in India, and for East Pakistan. He also gave them an *aide-mémoire,* giving an up-to-date account of the requirements of East Pakistan, the extent of contributions, and the shortfalls. The permanent representatives raised two questions. One was regarding the assurance that the relief goods would reach the target groups, and the other pertained to the security of the UN personnel. The Secretary-General said that while UN officials could not be present at each distribution point, by increasing the number of UN personnel, he would be able to assure the donors of proper utilization of their contribution. As regards security, it was appreciated that this consideration might militate against complete freedom of movement and the Secretary-General asked for full co-operation from the government of Pakistan to achieve the goal.

Agha Shahi in his report to the Foreign Office on this meeting, explained the thinking in the UN on the staffing of its organization in East Pakistan. The UN headquarters envisaged a three-phase expansion of its operations. In the first phase, it wanted additional staff in the office of the Representative in Dhaka and a number of area co-ordinators. Depending on the working of this phase, headquarters would launch phases two and three, which would in effect cover all the districts—each to be under the supervision of one UN official to watch over the handling and distribution of relief assistance by Pakistani officials. On 18 August, Shahi was informed by the Foreign Office that, since distribution would be handled entirely by Pakistani agencies, it might not be necessary to post a chief of operations, area co-ordinators, and radio operators. Subject to this, which left very little of the core proposals of the UN, Shahi was asked to convey the consent of the government of Pakistan to the staffing requirements of phase one, with no commitment about phases two and three.

In spite of the elaborate organization, and the increasing presence of underworked and highly paid UN officials in East Pakistan, the donor countries remained dissatisfied. The Secretary-General had this to say, in September, about their response to his appeal:

> The response to my appeal for the relief operation in East Pakistan . . . has been far from sufficient or adequate to the magnitude of the task. . . . In my dealings with the government of Pakistan, as well as in the organization of the relief effort in East Pakistan, I have been at pains to emphasize the necessity of being able to give to the donor countries appropriate assurances that their contribution will reach their intended destination—the people of East Pakistan.[17]

The only substantial assistance came from the US, which was negotiated directly by the government of Pakistan but only after the latter had accepted the *locus standi* of the UN in the humanitarian affairs of East Pakistan. The international presence through the UN, it appears in retrospect, was envisaged by the Western nations not only to administer such humanitarian aid as they would make available but also to act as a restraining influence on the military administration of East Pakistan.

* * *

One aspect of the international relief effort in East Pakistan, which caused considerable friction between the government of Pakistan and the UN and the Western governments, was the question of the participation of foreign volunteer agencies. In March 1971, the coastal areas of East Pakistan, which had been devastated by a cyclone in November 1970, were being served by international relief operations. The assistance had come from diverse sources and in various forms. The World Bank and the UNICEF had sponsored projects related to basic needs; the UK and other Western governments had offered bilateral project assistance; and a large number of non-governmental charitable organizations had come in a big way with men and materials, perhaps more of the former than the latter. In all, thirty-four charitable organizations had donated $ 20 million worth of relief supplies immediately after the cyclone. These were distributed by the government agencies in collaboration with the representatives of the donors or by the donor organizations themselves. Twelve organizations had undertaken projects in the coastal areas, for the implementation of which they had posted their own personnel. By May 1971, the priority given to the cyclone areas was submerged in the humanitarian concern for the whole province. The international charitable organizations, accordingly, wanted complete freedom to operate with their men and materials all over the province in the same manner as they had done in the coastal areas since November the previous year. These voluntary organizations exerted great influence, jointly, in the UN and other international forums, and individually in their respective countries. Their 'firsthand' accounts published in the Western media after the army action, had greatly influenced public opinion and the official policies of their countries.[18] This explained the deep suspicion with which any involvement of these organizations in East Pakistan was viewed by the government of Pakistan. The local heads of these organizations had returned to Dhaka by early June, when I had taken over as Member Planning Board and Programme Administrator of the cyclone-affected areas. They used to see me frequently in connection with various problems of their projects in the cyclone areas. It soon became clear to me that no work was immediately possible in the affected areas and that they knew this as well as I did. The overheads being incurred were quite out of proportion to the nature and size of the projects committed by the organizations. Apparently, they were maintaining their presence in anticipation of the larger relief programme in association with the UN.

The volunteer agencies were clamouring for permission to undertake relief operations in East Pakistan on their own, as well as in association with the UN efforts. They were, in fact, claiming a role equal to the UN itself, and exerting pressures on the UN in New York, with the backing of the Western media and governments, to this effect. As a result, on 18 June, the Secretary-General appointed Stephen R. Tripp as Co-ordinator for International Humanitarian Assistance to East Pakistan. From 1 July, this office started its operations from Geneva, the world centre for humanitarian relief activities. In New York the diplomats viewed the East Pakistan crisis in the wider political context of a secessionist movement, and not merely as a case of human rights violations. In Geneva, where the UN and other human rights bodies were located, it was projected on its humanitarian merits in order to condemn Pakistan.

On 19 June, the UN Under-Secretary for Political Affairs Guyear informed Shahi that Oxfam, the World Council of Churches, and other such groups were holding a convention on 28 June at the UN. They had approached the Secretary-General with a plea to ignore 'diplomatic niceties' and allow them to play a role in relief work in East Pakistan. Guyear, informing Shahi that the Secretary-General had rebuffed them, made a 'purely personal suggestion' that Pakistan should accept their services under the UN umbrella for the sake of public relations. Ismet Kittani extended the assurance that, if Pakistan accepted this suggestion, the UN would impose supervision on their activities. Oxfam had a powerful lobby in the UK, Kittani pointedly added, and the World Council commanded considerable influence in the US.

Consequent upon the visits of Kittani and Prince Sadruddin, the UN High Commissioner for Refugees (UNHCR), and the appointment of El-Tawil as the focal point of the UN, in the first half of June, Tripp formulated a system for the UN to administer international relief. On 28 June he informed the Pakistan mission that he intended to issue a statement, the main points of which were: (i) coasters would operate with international crews under the UN umbrella; (ii) LICROSS (League of Red Cross Societies) was to work under the UN umbrella to assist the Pakistan Red Cross Society in a survey of emergency relief requirements; (iii) UNHCR personnel would be stationed at reception centres set up for persons returning to Pakistan; (iv) the UN had been assured that the government of Pakistan would provide adequately for the resettlement of the displaced persons in accordance with UN principles; and (v) 'UN Personnel in East Pakistan with volunteers from LICROSS, CARE, CARITAS [three voluntary bodies] are prepared to work for us and with the Pakistan Government Counterpart Committee to establish an administrative framework for the co-ordination of international large-scale relief efforts.'

The UNHCR visit and the arrangements agreed to with him will be discussed in the next section. Here it may be noted that, in totality, the UN proposal blatantly envisaged handing over East Pakistan to the UN, its specialized agencies, and the foreign charitable organizations, under the guise of relief and rehabilitation. The government of Pakistan naturally reacted sharply to these proposals and, on 1 July, the Foreign Office asked Niaz Naik, permanent representative in Geneva, to inform Tripp that (i) there was no question of UNHCR personnel being stationed at the reception centres. The agreement with the UNHCR was to post two or three of its personnel at Dhaka who might visit different centres as and when required; (ii) Pakistan would provide adequately for the resettlement of displaced persons in terms of public assurances given by the President and 'not in accordance with certain undefined UN principles whatever they might be'; and (iii) charitable and voluntary organizations would co-ordinate their activities with the Secretary-General's Representative in Dhaka, and their aid would be administered and operated by Pakistan official agencies. It was emphasized to the Pakistan mission that any statement issued by the UN on its operations in East Pakistan must clearly reflect these points.

The UN Geneva informed El-Tawil of the Pakistan government policy as conveyed to them by Ambassador Naik, and left him to deal with the voluntary agencies as best he could. Representatives of a large number of these agencies were in Dhaka and they now besieged the local UN officials. The pressures were now direct and immediate on the ground, instead of in far-off Geneva. On 28 July, El-Tawil wrote an anxious letter to Malik which reflected his dilemma; he had to maintain good relations with the government of Pakistan, and the voluntary organizations belonged to the countries which were the major donors of the UN and everything it did. After giving 'ample thought to the import of that [Geneva] message and to the practical implications of its implementations . . . [and] Considering the obvious perils for the mission of the Representative of the Secretary-General of deep involvement in details of voluntary agencies activities', El-Tawil proposed a set of measures to his headquarters. They were : (i) the co-ordinating role of the UN mission should be limited at this time to a clearing-house function to avoid duplication of efforts in solving major problems; (ii) the appointment of an officer on the staff of the Secretary-General's Representative to deal with voluntary agencies; (iii) voluntary bodies to be encouraged to channelize their assistance through the projects undertaken by the UN agencies; and (iv) encouraging the voluntary organizations to simplify their set-up and procedures for the purpose of co-ordinating and communicating with the UN mission.

The proposed mode of co-ordination envisaged a minimum involvement of voluntary bodies in the UN operations, which El-Tawil was keen to keep free from any friction with the government. The matter, however, could not rest unilaterally with El-Tawil. Subsequent to the submission of his proposals to headquarters, he felt it necessary to call a meeting of voluntary agencies operating in East Pakistan 'to explore their thinking and views concerning the co-ordination function.' It was attended by twenty-two representatives of sixteen organizations.[19] They regarded the government policy irksome, and raised several questions 'concerning the purpose and scope of the new co-ordination requirement and procedures to be followed in its implementation'. El-Tawil transmitted these queries, in original, to Malik with a covering letter for clarifications by the government of Pakistan. On 2 August Malik sent a reply which, in essence, reiterated what had already been communicated to the UN.

Meanwhile, the role of foreign charitable organizations in East Pakistan was examined at length in the meetings held by the Economic Adviser and the Principal Staff Officer in the first week of July. The following policy decisions were conveyed by Muzaffar Husain to the secretaries, Foreign Affairs and EC&EA divisions: (i) aid for cyclone-affected areas already accepted by the government of East Pakistan should be scrutinized, and foreign personnel connected with its implementation should be replaced early; (ii) pending offers for the cyclone relief programme, unless absolutely essential, should not be accepted if tied to foreign personnel and volunteers; (iii) assistance in connection with recent events should be considered only after full details were made available through the UN, and, if accepted, should be channelized through the UN organization at Dhaka; and (iv) no foreign personnel and volunteers should be accepted with any offers of relief in connection with the recent disturbances in East Pakistan.

The voluntary organizations were themselves to blame for the restrictions placed on their activities in East Pakistan. After leading the anti-Pakistan campaign in the world media in the post-army operation period, they could not expect the government of Pakistan to take a benign view of their presence. An element of secretiveness in their activities, and the 'firsthand accounts' published by the representatives of some of them jeopardized their neutral and humanitarian status in the minds of Pakistan authorities. Although they had considerable resources and the will to do good in the unhappy situation in East Pakistan, they got themselves involved in controversial matters and lost sight of their basic charter of confining themselves to the alleviation of human miseries.

Refugees, Return and Rehabilitation

The most damaging aspect of the army operation which helped India to internationalize the East Pakistan crisis was the large-scale movement of local Bengalis to West Bengal. No attempt was made by the military administration to stop the outflow of these refugees to India. The Hindus as a community were more vulnerable to the excesses of the army than the Muslims. Their exodus after the army operation, resulting from a state of fear induced by numerous incidents of victimization, was understandable; it was welcomed as 'good riddance' by many West Pakistan civil and military officials. The West Pakistani establishment had always been obssessed with Bengali Hindus as instigators and mentors of the nationalist elements of East Pakistan. On 5 June Assistant Secretary of State Sisco had protested to Hilaly that 'there were numerous reports that the Pakistan Army had singled out Hindus for attacks', which explained their continuous influx into India, and that there were reports of repressive measures against those still left within East Pakistan.

There were differing estimates of the number of refugees that had entered India. According to the government of India, the daily influx from East Pakistan was 29,000 in April (mostly from the third week on), and jumped to 94,000 during May and June each; it came down to 19,000 in July, but again increased to 37,000 in August. The total influx up to the end of August, according to Indian officials, was about 8.2 million, of which about 7 million were Hindus, 0.54 million Muslims, and the rest others. Of these refugees, 5.7 million were in camps and the others living elsewhere. India had claimed to have spent $576 million up to the end of August on these refugees, of which it said that foreign assistance was only $147 million.[20] On 15 May, the *Guardian* reported that the number of people crossing the border from East Pakistan into India had risen from 50,000 a day in the previous week to roughly 100,000 a day that week.[21] Senator Edward Kennedy, in a statement on 11 May, estimated the total number at about 2 million, and the daily influx at about 50,000. The State Department had informed him that the influx would continue at a high level until the beginning of the monsoon.[22] The Pakistan government contested these figures as highly exaggerated. While the exact number may be debatable, there is no denying the fact that millions of people left their homes in East Pakistan for India, in search of security, during the period March–December 1971.

The Indian government sought and obtained relief assistance, on a local basis, from UN agencies like the FAO, WFP, and UNICEF, headquartered in Delhi, as soon as the refugee influx started in mid-April. Private agencies were similarly encouraged to come forward with whatever help they could extend. In addition, bilateral assistance from various countries, including the US, was also forthcoming on an emergency basis. The entire relief programme was being co-ordinated and controlled by the Ministry of Rehabilitation of the government of India. This was in contrast to Pakistan's resistance to the offers of such assistance, which it considered would internationalize its domestic crisis. India welcomed assistance from all official and non-official organizations or anyone who cared to give it, because it wanted to raise the issue beyond the level of regional conflict between two neighbours to one of global dimensions, both in political and humanitarian terms. In the prevailing situation, Pakistan had a lot to hide in East Pakistan from the world community; India's policy was the reverse, to open itself up completely, to expose the brutal suppression of the people of East Pakistan as a justification for their liberation struggle. The initiative in world forums and in international diplomacy was, thus, with India. Pakistan, in the nature of things, had to be on the defensive, more so because it had failed to control the insurgency. The continuous cycle of sabotage by the rebels and repressive measures by the army kept the issue of Bangladesh freedom in the limelight, creating intolerable political and diplomatic pressures on the government of Pakistan.

In the first week of May, the Indian government made a formal request to the UN Secretary-General 'to promote and encourage aid on behalf of the family of the United Nations' on a co-ordinated basis. Within three days, the matter had been discussed in the Administrative Committee on Co-ordination at Berne, in which all the UN agencies were represented, a three-man mission had left for India to make an assessment of requirements, and the UNHCR was designated as the focal point of all the relief assistance emanating through the UN system. On 19 May, the Secretary-General made an appeal for emergency help and, from the following day, flights were organized from Geneva to airlift medical supplies to India. The total assistance to India from the date of the Secretary-General's appeal up to 30 June amounted to $ 160 million.[23]

On 12 May, Ambassador S. Sen, permanent representative of India to the UN, raised the East Pakistan issue in the Social Committee of the Economic and Social Council (ECOSOC) during a debate on the agenda item 'Report of the Commission of Human Rights'. He referred to thirty-four UN instruments relating to human rights, and alleged violation of each one of them in 'East Bengal'. At the end of a long statement, he demanded that the Council ask Pakistan to agree to a co-ordinated relief programme under UN auspices to create suitable conditions in East Pakistan to stop the exodus.[24] Agha Shahi could not deny the fact of influx of refugees from East Pakistan, but rebutted the figures given by the Indian representative. He warned India against interfering in the East Pakistan crisis which, he said, was Pakistan's internal matter.[25] On 17 May, Ambassador Sen again spoke in the same forum and reiterated India's position, supported by extensive quotations from the international Press. Among other measures to contain the influx of refugees into India, he suggested that 'to tackle the problem at its roots, relief and rehabilitation measures require to be undertaken forthwith in East Bengal itself. The government of Pakistan must be asked to take these immediately and in close and effective co-operation with appropriate international agencies . . .'[26] This was at the time when the Pakistan government was still resisting international relief operations in East Pakistan.

The UNHCR, Prince Sadruddin Aga Khan, was faced with three problems as the focal point for co-ordinating all international relief assistance for East Pakistan refugees in India: one, to stop the inflow from East Pakistan; two, to repatriate those who had arrived in India; and three, to look after them while they were in India. The first two pertained to conditions in East Pakistan. In a press conference on 5 May, Sadruddin indicated that he was in contact with the Pakistan government in this regard. He wanted to induct his office 'to encourage conditions in East Pakistan to return to normal, possibly initiate some sort of arrangement where people who want to come home can do so and be received in such a way that they are given the necessary relief that they require, even in their homeland'.[27]

The long-awaited invitation by the government of Pakistan to Prince Sadruddin came through in the first week of June. The statement of President Yahya on 21 May inviting 'bona fide Pakistan citizens, who left their homes due to disturbed conditions and for other reasons . . . to return to their homes in East Pakistan' had brought about a situation which fell within the purview of the UNHCR.[28] Sadruddin arrived in Rawalpindi on 6 June, and the same evening Sultan Muhammad Khan and Umer called on him for preliminary discussions. Sadruddin first gave the background of his organization's association with the relief assistance in India. He asserted that the UNHCR, by assuming the role of focal point in India, had depoliticized the refugee question, and all governments were channelling their assistance through his Office, thus preventing political exploitation of bilateral dealings. If the UN Secretariat had taken charge of these operations, the issue could have been exploited for political purposes and the matter could also have been raised in the General Assembly by India. His representative, the High Commissioner informed his visitors, had successfully resisted attempts to inject political issues into purely humanitarian efforts by refusing to permit Bangladesh representatives to sit in on committee meetings. The President's statements urging the refugees to return, Sadruddin went on to say, could be substantiated and Pakistan's sincerity proved by allowing his (the UNHCR's) Office to establish its presence in

Dhaka, with facilities for visiting the reception centres on the borders. The observers from his organization would assure the refugees in the Indian camps, who were asking for guarantees, that they would not be prosecuted on return and that normal conditions had returned in the areas where they would be going. If this was agreeable to Pakistan, the High Commissioner would ask India to allow his representatives into the camps in West Bengal to give these assurances to their inmates.

Sultan Muhammad Khan expressed reservations about this plan. His argument ran like this: India could say that the return of the displaced persons depended upon political stability in East Pakistan and that this would emerge only if an understanding was reached with the Awami League leadership who were either in India or under detention in Pakistan. Therefore, the Indians might take the stand that if the UN wished the refugees to go back, it should involve itself in the process of this political understanding. In response to Sadruddin's query, the Foreign Secretary said that the legal aspects of such a stand, or procedural objections which Pakistan could raise, would not deter India from trying to internationalize the political situation in East Pakistan. The High Commissioner thereupon suggested an alternative of a one-time visit to the reception centres by his staff, and a statement on that basis that adequate facilities had been provided by Pakistan. For this, he added, it would be necessary to equip at least four or five centres promptly with shelter, food, medicines, and transport. A public announcement by the UNHCR of these arrangements would put the onus on India if the refugees were then not allowed to return. Pakistan authorities could also arrange visits by foreign journalists, British parliamentarians, and US Congressmen to these centres as an exercise in public relations.

Sadruddin knew he was treading on very soft ground and had to allay the suspicions of Pakistan. Unless the UNHCR Office got the co-operation of the Pakistan government and a footing in East Pakistan, it could not address itself to the task assigned to it. The apprehensions of the Foreign Secretary about India's attempt to link the return of refugees to a political settlement, though not of one through the UN, was real. In fact, this was already the line which India had started taking in its diplomatic offensive against Pakistan. A significant number of refugees returning to East Pakistan would have been a severe set-back to India's objective of bringing about the separation of East Pakistan. Apart from the moral and humanitarian considerations, it was in the interest of Pakistan to stop the outflow, arrange for the return of displaced persons, and, for this purpose, use the UNHCR. The Foreign Office, however, failed to realize that 'as the exodus of refugees continued, it [the Indian Government] was acquiring a powerful hold over Pakistan by becoming a necessary party to any [political] settlement . . . [and] the kind of settlement they [the Indians] thought appropriate could not be obtained [peacefully] through the United Nations.'[29] But Tikka Khan, who was personally directing the army operations during April and May, was oblivious of the dangerous implications of what he was doing. His conduct of affairs had resulted in the creation of a general state of fear among all classes in the province; he was, in fact, not unhappy at getting rid of the 'disloyal' Hindus and other elements.[30] The Foreign Office was either paralysed or too scared to force the issue and bring the matter to the notice of the President or his PSO.

On the following day, 7 June, when Sadruddin met Yahya, the latter himself took the initiative and asked for the UNHCR's help for the return of the refugees. The Prince was, of course, delighted and informed the President of the previous day's discussions with the Foreign Secretary. The President said that the Foreign Office would examine the plan for a permanent presence of the UNHCR, but the one-time exercise alternative could be implemented straight away.

Prince Sadruddin visited East Pakistan from 9 June to 12 June. He was accompanied by an officer of the central government, Akhtar Mahmood, who submitted a report on the visit to Muzaffar Husain after the departure of the Prince. The following description is drawn from this report.

Prince Sadruddin was received at the airport by the Chief Secretary; the Governor was represented by his Military Secretary. The programme given to the visitors at the airport included a visit to Muhammadpur and Mirpur refugee camps of non-Bengalis in Dhaka, and two jute mills at Khulna.

> This programme disappointed the Prince somewhat because his primary mission was to visit the Centres organized for the reception of displaced persons who had crossed over to India . . . He, therefore, asked me to request the Governor to enable him to see at least a few

> of the 21 Reception Centres established for the returnees from India. . The Governor readily agreed . . . [to the request of the High Commissioner] and he issued immediate instructions . . . [to revise the programme to include] two Reception Centres on the Western Border and two on the Eastern Tripura side of East Pakistan.

Tikka Khan, during discussions, gave Sadruddin a dramatic account of the movement of the Pakistan army from the narrow strips in Dhaka and Chittagong to the 6,500 square miles of East Pakistan, the role played by India in the disturbances, and the atrocities committed by the rebels. About the return of refugees, Tikka Khan informed the High Commissioner that twenty-one reception centres would be ready by 14 June to receive the displaced persons whose bona fides as Pakistani citizens would be checked; Pakistan would need substantial assistance from the UN to rehabilitate these persons. Prince Sadruddin patiently listened to the military exploits of Tikka Khan, politely 'admired' the way martial law authorities had tackled a difficult situation, but 'emphasized that it would be in the best interest of Pakistan to receive and rehabilitate its displaced citizens'.

The High Commissioner visited three reception centres. At one centre there were 191 persons, and another had been set up that very day and had no returnee. The Governor informed Sadruddin of a few thousands refugees living in the fourth centre but, he said, he could not send the Prince to it due to its dangerous proximity to the border. The centres were admittedly a hastily put up show, but the return of the refugees had nothing to do with them. The Pakistan government did not give a high priority to it nor was India willing to let go this lever before the achievement of its objectives. The Prince, a man of peace and goodwill, in private conversation with Akhtar Mahmood advised that the Pakistan government should

> examine the experience of Algeria and Viet Nam very closely and must avoid being caught in a vicious circle of terrorism by anti-state elements and massive reprisals by the military authorities. This process only alienates the local population and makes the complex task of the Authorities to restore confidence even more difficult.

This friendly warning was duly conveyed in the report submitted to the government by Akhtar Mahmood.

The state of security in the provincial capital was forcefully brought to the notice of Sadruddin in the afternoon of 10 June, when three explosions took place almost simultaneously in the Inter-Continental Hotel where he was staying, and in the *Jamaat Khana* (congregation hall) of the Ismaili community to which he belonged.[31] The Ismaili community also brought to the notice of the Prince cases of stabbing of members of the community and looting of their shops by the insurgents.

From Pakistan, Prince Sadruddin went to India at the invitation of the government of India. His visits to the reception centres, and exhortations to the government of Pakistan to facilitate the return of displaced persons had aroused deep suspicions in India. The Indian Press questioned his neutrality by referring to the large Ismaili community and its investments in Pakistan. He was also criticized by the vocal and well-financed Bangladesh lobby in the UK. On 23 June, clarifying his position in a press conference at the UN, he said he had received the full co-operation of Pakistan authorities to visit both the eastern and western borders in East Pakistan. He had travelled over a large area, including areas not originally in the programme, by diverting the course of the helicopter during flight. 'In these parts he could see that life was slowly returning to normal'; of course, he said, he 'could not vouch for all parts of Pakistan since he did not go to all parts.' He found the few reception centres he visited properly staffed and adequately stocked with food and medicines. The Prince, however, said that he could not 'claim to give any guarantee for the overall situation in East Pakistan.' In the face of the hostile array of questions about his guarded impressions of normalcy in East Pakistan, Sadruddin maintained his humanitarian and objective stand with great courage, although he conceded that 'In all cases of refugees . . . what brought people back was a political solution.' But then, he added, there were 'different interpretations of what was a political solution.'[32] With all his good intentions and genuine efforts to alleviate human sufferings, the Prince could not avoid becoming controversial. The Indian Press, the Bangladesh lobby in the West, and the obliging Western media all started a campaign against his neutral and non-political stand. Sadruddin called another press conference in London on 30 June, in which he explained to the Press and the voluntary agencies the purely humanitarian efforts of his Office in India and Pakistan. Apparently, referring to his statements reported in the Indian Press regarding his visit to East Pakistan, the representative of BBC TV said 'that you are alleged to have claimed that normal conditions have returned to Pakistan when other observers at about the same time spoke completely differently of the situation.' Sadruddin responded that he was 'not responsible for the Indian Press' in which 'I was misquoted or quoted out of context on a number of occasions'. He reiterated that he had given to the Indian Press his 'personal eye-witness assessment of what I had seen either flying low in a helicopter or travelling by car. . . . I also carefully pointed out that I had not visited the whole country. Nor could I speak for what happened before or after my visit.' He clarified that there were two distinct UN operations in Dhaka. One was under the Secretary-General's Office, responsible for international relief for rehabilitation of East Pakistanis and reported directly to the UN Headquarters in New York. The other was of the UNHCR, which was in the process of setting up an organization to deal exclusively with the returning refugees.[33]

During July, the refugee issue dominated the fifty-first session of the ECOSOC, which commenced at Geneva on 5 July. On 2 July, Niaz Naik in a frantic message informed the Foreign Secretary that Sadruddin and Rafeeudin (a Pakistani holding a senior UN position) had confirmed that India was lobbying hard to get the refugee issue included as a supplementary item on the agenda to get a resolution passed by the Council. Failing this, India intended to raise the matter in the annual report of the UNHCR, which was an agenda item of the ECOSOC. Prince Sadruddin was under pressure from most members to submit a written or oral report on the state of East Pakistan refugees in India. He, the message continued, intended to give a factual account of the assistance so far rendered through his organization, and the contributions received and disbursed through his organization, avoiding any reference to political and controversial aspects. The Pakistan delegation was advised by friendly sources to be prepared for a procedural or substantive discussion of the issue. The procedural debate was likely to take place on the opening day, 5 July, when the agenda for the session would be adopted.

Meanwhile, the Foreign Office was facing some problems in finalizing the composition of the Pakistan delegation for the stormy session. S. K. Dehlavi, Pakistan ambassador in Paris, who had earlier been nominated leader of the delegation, expressed his inability to undertake the assignment on the grounds of a lack of any background of ECOSOC items and its procedures, heavy engagements in Paris, and extremely short notice. Niaz Naik requested that he be excused from joining the delegation because of his preoccupations with the various UN committees. He urged that Agha Shahi be deputed from New York, because the delegations of most of the countries were composed of their permanent representatives and other officials based in New York, whom Shahi knew intimately. On 3 July, the Foreign Office replaced Dehlavi with Shahi, who was directed to proceed to Geneva immediately to lead the delegation; Naik was asked to leave all other work to his officers and place himself at the disposal of the ECOSOC delegation.

The East Pakistan refugees issue was brought up, as anticipated, at the inaugural meeting of the ECOSOC on 5 July, during discussions on the adoption of the agenda. Yugoslavia and New Zealand, supported by the Soviet Union, the UK, Hungary, Norway, and others, asked for a statement from the High Commissioner for Refugees, as a focal point, on the Pakistan refugees in India and for a debate on the subject. Pakistan raised the procedural point about the nature of the mandate of the High Commissioner for Refugees as a focal point in India, because there was no mention of it in his annual report before the Council. Prince Sadruddin explained that this particular function was not reported in the documents before the Council, firstly 'because that was not undertaken, strictly speaking, under the usual terms of reference of the High Commissioner for refugees but as the channel for all United Nations components channelling aid to India', and secondly 'because this particular crisis erupted . . . after the end of the particular period covered by the report.'[34] With millions of displaced East Pakistanis in India, it was no longer possible for Pakistan to obtain support for blocking the debate, as had been successfully done in May, on the grounds of it being an internal matter of Pakistan. The Council decided to invite the UNHCR to make a statement in his capacity as the focal point for assistance to the Pakistan refugees in India, and to devote a single sitting on 16 July to debating the issue.

The build-up to the formal debate had started from the inaugural day, 5 July, when the Secretary-General in his statement to the

Council referred to the heightened concern of the international community regarding 'the tragic and unprecedented situation stemming from the sizeable influx of refugees from East Pakistan into the adjacent states of India and from the need to alleviate the plight of the population in East Pakistan itself'.[35] On 9 July, Sadruddin in a press conference in Paris described the unhappy conditions of Pakistani refugees, who, according to Indian estimates, now numbered six million, and appealed for more aid.[36] India missed no opportunity of highlighting the refugee burden. Speaking on an unrelated agenda item the same day in the ECOSOC, the leader of the Indian delegation bemoaned the jolt to the tempo of social and economic development in India due to the 'tragic turn of events in East Bengal which has resulted in a massive influx of refugees'.[37]

On 16 July, the Council devoted the entire morning session to the East Pakistan refugee problem. Sadruddin gave a carefully-worded account of the emergence of the Office of the UNHCR as the focal point in India of multilateral assistance for the displaced persons of East Pakistan. The focal point had no operational responsibility and the government of India had made it clear that it had no intention of sharing it with any UN or foreign voluntary organization. In mid-May the government of India, the High Commissioner informed the session, had made her first global assessment of requirements amounting to $ 175 million, on the basis of an average refugee population of three million for a period of six months from end March. In the last week of June, the government of India revised the estimates to $ 400 million based on an average of six million refugees for the same period. Sadruddin called the situation 'one of stark tragedy, affecting an immense number of human beings', and offered his good offices for their repatriation to their homes. In this connection, he briefly referred to his recent visits to India and Pakistan, and informed the Council of the agreement of the government of Pakistan to the induction of a senior officer of the UNHCR in Dhaka, 'whose presence would be useful now, and more so later, when the process of voluntary repatriation gathered momentum.'

The Pakistani intervention in the debate, which followed the statement of Sadruddin, was mild and conciliatory compared to their tone in May.

In his opening remarks Shahi rather smoothly declared that the 'refugees who had moved into India were nationals of his country; hence, all those who were making donations or ministering to their needs were entitled to his country's gratitude.' He referred to the efforts being made by his government for the repatriation of refugees; the assistance of the UNHCR in the matter had been accepted and Dr A. M. Malik, a respected Bengali public leader, had been appointed Special Assistant for Displaced Persons, with the rank of Cabinet Minister and with direct access to the President of Pakistan. Shahi appealed for the co-operation of the government of India 'in its own interest and in that of Pakistan', to establish a climate of confidence in which the refugees could return to their homes. The Indian observer delegate, Krishnan, was, however, aggressive. Referring to the declarations of amnesty and appeals made by the President of Pakistan to the refugees to return, Krishnan said that 'The fact that over 3 million more refugees had crossed into India since then showed that those appeals must have caused even greater panic.' He declared that the 'only truly humanitarian and lasting solution of the problem lay in a viable political settlement', whereby 'military rule would give way to a truly representative and democratic rule'.[38]

Back in Pakistan, the government had announced its agreement to the appointment of John Kelly as the resident representative of the UNHCR at Dhaka. The Foreign Secretary, briefing the Governor on this appointment, explained that in accordance with the agreement with the UNHCR Kelly would act as a focal point for assistance from the UN system to the displaced persons returning to East Pakistan. His functions, it was clarified, would be quite distinct and separate from those of El-Tawil, the Secretary-General's Representative. Kelly would maintain contact with local authorities and also visit the twenty-one reception centres set up to receive the displaced persons.

The refugee problem was merely a manifestation of the political crisis in East Pakistan and could not be resolved by itself in a vacuum. By the autumn of 1971, the world was resigned to the inevitability of a war between India and Pakistan as the only solution of the East Pakistan problem.

CHAPTER 9

India, the World, and the Crisis

It would be naive to think that the Indian government was taken completely by surprise by the army action of 25 March in East Pakistan. It is possible, however, that the violent and widespread resistance to it, and the opportunities the turmoil afforded to India had not been exactly foreseen. The Indian intelligence agencies had always been active in East Pakistan, and would logically be more so in the turbulent post-election period, in order to keep their government informed of the rapidly deteriorating political situation during March.[1] In retrospect, it seems that the hijacking of the Indian Airlines aircraft to Lahore on 30 January by two Kashmiris was also linked with the East Pakistan crisis. Due to the inept handling of the incident by the Pakistan authorities, the plane was blown up on the tarmac by the hijackers. Subsequently, in mid-April, the judicial commission set up to inquire into the incident found them to be Indian intelligence agents.[2] The destruction of the plane gave an excuse to the Indian government to ban all flights between East and West Pakistan over its airspace. The isolation of the army in East Pakistan as a result of this ban had an important bearing on the strategy of the Awami League in its developing confrontation with West Pakistan.[3]

On 27 March, the Indian External Affairs Minister, Sardar Swaran Singh, in a brief statement in parliament expressed concern over the happenings in East Pakistan.[4] On the same day, in the lower house of parliament, Mrs Indira Gandhi, the Indian Prime Minister, said that 'something new had happened in East Pakistan' which was of 'historic importance' and to which 'we are fully alive'. She assured the agitated members that 'we shall keep constantly in touch with what is happening and what we need to do.'[5] A similar statement was made by her in the upper house on the same day.[6] Four days later, on 31 March, a resolution moved by Mrs Gandhi in the parliament, and unanimously passed by it, expressed 'deep anguish and grave concern at the recent developments in East Bengal', conveyed 'its profound sympathy for and solidarity with the people of East Bengal in their struggle for a democratic way of life' and recorded 'its profound conviction that the historic upsurge of the 75 million people of East Bengal will triumph.'[7] On 27 March, it was still East Pakistan in the official statements; thenceforth, for India it was East Bengal, and no longer part of Pakistan.

The 'historic importance' of the Awami League movement was translated into specific terms by K. Subrahmanyam, Director of the semi-official Indian Institute for Defence Studies and Analyses, in a symposium on 8 April. 'The breakup of Pakistan', he said, 'is in our interest and we have an opportunity the like of which will never come again.'[8] At this stage there was no refugee problem, which later was made out to be a security threat to India.[9] Subrahmanyam was not merely expressing his personal views. He was articulating the deep Indian hatred for the partition of the subcontinent leading to the creation of Pakistan. Even if it was not possible to undo the partition, the opportunity provided by the Awami League movement to break up Pakistan was not to be missed, irrespective of whether Pakistan had posed any threat to India or not. Later, of course, the influx of refugees would provide a credible excuse for India to do everything to achieve its objective.

While the objective of the breakup was clear, the timing of the various steps for achieving it had to be carefully orchestrated. The immense potential of the turmoil in East Pakistan was realized by the Indian government from the very beginning of the crisis. Immediately after the army action on 25–26 March, a wave of euphoria swept over India as highly exaggerated reports of the victories of the *mukti fouj* (liberation army) and set-backs for the Pakistan army were splashed in the Indian Press and over the government-controlled radio; an independent Bangladesh seemed about to come into existence. The responses of the Indian government, however, were controlled and co-ordinated. The earliest statements in the frenzied parliament on 27 March, referred to above, were mild; Mrs Gandhi paid lip-service to 'proper international norms', and Swaran Singh hoped 'that even at this late stage it would be possible to resume democratic processes' in East Pakistan. Four days later, on 31 March, however, the parliament committed India to the success of the secessionist movement; there was no mention of refugees or to a security threat in the resolution or in the earlier statements. The cause of India's concern was stated to be the violation of human rights, etc.

The security threat actually arose to Pakistan from the public commitment of India to supporting the secession of a part of its neighbouring country. India's East Pakistan policy was mainly based on the use of arms, directly by its own forces or through the rebels, to resolve the crisis in its favour. 'Even as early as the first week of April—when the armed forces were . . . hesistant to contribute to a policy of escalation that might lead to an all-out war, she [Mrs Gandhi] had taken action to assume a positive military posture. . . . She had alerted the Border Security Force (BSF) of the Home Ministry to handle the situation on the border. . . . It was the BSF who were the first to receive [rebel elements of EBR and EPR], accommodate, train, and equip the force that was eventually to burgeon out into the *mukti bahini* of Bangla Desh: and it was Mrs Gandhi who saw, more clearly than most of her advisers, that the security threat posed by Pakistan's rampage in Bangla Desh had to be met, from the very beginning, by a degree of military action.'[10] The problem, however, was not conceived as a purely military one by the Indian policymakers, though it was accepted as the predominant element for retaining the initiative in the developing situation, and as the ultimate instrument for achieving their goal.

The diplomatic and political aspects had also to be carefully manipulated. It could also be assumed that, given the rigidity of military regimes, the Indian policymakers did not ignore the high probability of Yahya Khan and his colleagues helping them by failing to take a timely political initiative to counter the Indian manoeuvres. To secure and justify the ultimate military solution, the Indian government initiatied a softening process through a sustained campaign on humanitarian issues in the Western media, the UN, and other international forums, and through bilateral pressures on major powers. The first step in this direction was taken as early as 30 March, when the Indian permanent representative at the UN submitted a *note verbale* to the Secretary-General on 'the question of the situation in East Pakistan'.[11] This was intended to turn the issue into one of concern to the world community, before Pakistan could complain of Indian interference in East Pakistan, relegating it to the level of a regional conflict. At the same time, the political dissidents, particularly the Awami League leaders who had come to India, had to be strictly controlled so that they did not reconsider their options and develop any tendencies to compromise with Pakistan. A Bangladesh government in exile of the elected East Pakistanis was established in Calcutta on 12 April. It acted as a focal point, under the guidance, and with the full material support of India, for the armed struggle within East Pakistan and for political legitimacy before the world at large. A clandestine transmitter operating from a ship, which was traced to the mouth of the River Hooghly in India, beamed to East Pakistan daily accounts of the achievements of the freedom fighters. The military preparations were to proceed simultaneously for the kill when the adversary was morally, militarily, and economically exhausted by external attrition and internal contradictions.

In the process of formulating responses to the East Pakistan crisis, Mrs Gandhi and her advisers were quite clear that it would be in the national interest to intervene in it. Mrs Gandhi and the Indian establishment were quite certain that it would be. But there was a difference of opinion about the diplomatic and military capability of India to bring about the breakup of Pakistan in the immediate future. It was asked whether it would not be cheaper and safer to let the Pakistan economy strangle itself by the civil war, eventually resulting in the disintegration of the country. Fears were also expressed in some quarters about the effects of the secession of East Pakistan on the disgruntled ethnic states of India. By the end of April, after intensive discussions and analyses of the military, diplomatic, and political aspects, key decisions had been taken to give practical shape to the policy implicit in the parliamentary resolution of 31 March.[12] The basic decision was to launch on all-out war in the last resort, if all other means failed, to bring about an independent Bangladesh. The Indian army wanted five or six months for a full-fledged war with Pakistan, (a) to complete its expansion and re-equipment programme; (b) to re-group and re-plan the deployment of troops on the eastern borders; and (c) to have dry weather. The army also wanted diplomatic measures to neutralize the Chinese threat, in case of India's attack on Pakistan.[13] This cautious approach was attributed to the timidity of the Indian army by the civilian establishment. Nevertheless, it was accepted and the timing of open war with

Pakistan was fixed for November, which was also thought at least to minimize the threat of Chinese intervention, due to adverse weather conditions on the northern borders, if diplomacy failed to eliminate it.

Having laid down a clear objective and a co-ordinated time-table for achieving it, the direction of its implementation was firmly retained in the hands of the Prime Minister and the political affairs committee of the Cabinet. The Chief of Army Staff, who was also the Chairman of the Chiefs of Staff committee, had direct access to the Prime Minister. The day-to-day management of the crisis, in all its aspects, was entrusted to a policy planning committee, set up in the Ministry of External Affairs very early in the crisis, under D. P. Dhar, a Kashmiri politician. On the military side, (a) a joint intelligence committee of the representatives of civil and military intelligence agencies was set up under the Vice-Chief of Army Staff; (b) a joint planning committee dealt with the inter-services co-ordination of operational plans; and (c) a combined services operational headquarters was set up soon after these policy decisions. On the civilian side, a secretaries' committee consisting of the secretaries of the Ministries of Defence, Home, Finance, and External Affairs, and the intelligence chief, was formed to co-ordinate government responses to the emerging aspects of the crisis. These processes of decision-making, planning, and execution sharply contrasted with the snap decision taken by a few generals in Pakistan to resort to army action without considering the political, economic, and diplomatic consequences; above all, without taking into account the Indian connection with the dissident elements. The same knee-jerk reactions characterized the management of national affairs during the post-army operation period.

* * *

While the Western media was in uproar over the army operation, the early official responses of the US and the UK were cautious. On 27 March, the British Prime Minister, Edward Heath, said that Britain would not involve itself in the East Pakistan crisis.[14] On 5 April, the British Foreign Secretary, Sir Alec Douglas-Home, reiterating the same position in the House of Commons, said that the British government had 'no intention of interfering in Pakistan's internal affairs.'[15] Sir Alec was criticized by the British Press for not supporting the Bangladesh cause and for not stopping economic aid to Pakistan. Although maintaining the public posture of non-interference, the British government was showing concern, at the diplomatic level, at the developing crisis in East Pakistan. During the course of negotiations between Yahya and Mujib in March, Heath had emphasized on the former the need for a peaceful settlement of political differences.[16] The Pakistan High Commissioner was called by Sir Alec, who asked to be 'informed of the Pakistan government's views on the situation in the eastern wing.'[17] Heath had also offered his good offices to Yahya as a mediator in the crisis.[18]

The first official reactions of the US government were somewhat similar to those of Britain. On 2 April, a State Department spokesman said that the US 'views what is going on in Pakistan as an internal matter'; on 5 April, he said that the US was 'naturally concerned at the reported loss of life, [and of] hardship, and damage. . . .' On 7 April, under pressure from public opinion and the Congress, the State Department issued a more positive statement; it believed that 'it is important that every feasible step be taken to end the conflict and achieve a peaceful accommodation.'[19]

The East Pakistan situation was kept under observation by the US government. Even before the army action, the State Department had prepared a 'contingency plan', involving aid of the order of $ 300 million to East Pakistan, in the event of its emergence as an independent state. The plan, deliberately or otherwise, was leaked out to the Press. To a query from the Foreign Office, the State Department clarified that every government, particularly one like the US with global responsibilities, had a duty to prepare contingency plans for all eventualities.

In the White House, Henry Kissinger, Assistant to the President for National Security Affairs, took note of the emerging trouble spot on 16 February, when he asked for an inter-agency study 'of the alternatives, should East Pakistan try to make a break.'[20] His own analysis, reported to President Nixon on 22 February, concluded that Mujib 'is now planning to stick with his demands for the virtual autonomy of East Pakistan and, if he does not get his way—which is very likely—to declare East Pakistan's independence.' In the Senior Review Group, which met on 6 March to discuss the inter-agency report, the 'consensus was that Pakistan would not be able to hold the East by force.' Kissinger informed the Group meeting that Nixon was not prepared to pressurize Yahya to desist from the use of force, though he would not object if other countries did so. It was agreed by all the US agencies that if there was a breakup of Pakistan, it should come through its internal stresses, and 'the United States should not get involved.' In early March, during and after the Indian general elections, which gave her an overwhelming vote, Mrs Gandhi had given no inkling of her subsequent reactions to the developments in East Pakistan. US policymakers, therefore, thought that East Pakistan could be left alone to sort itself out one way or the other. In the middle of March, the Indian Foreign Secretary assured the US ambassador in New Delhi that India wanted Pakistan to remain united. On 17 March, the Indian Ambassador in Washington 'spoke in the same sense' to Kissinger.

The army action on 25–26 March convinced US policymakers that the independence of East Pakistan was now inevitable, even without the help of India. The Washington Special Action Group (WSAG) which met on 26 March, and Nixon and Kissinger were all agreed that the US government should make no move to influence Yahya to any course of action, as it was likely to be interpreted as encouragement for the split-up of Pakistan. Kissinger was aware of West Pakistani suspicions of US encouragement of the secessionist movement.[21] The WSAG was informed that the British government (presumably for the same reasons) was also following the same line.

The policy of detachment from the humanitarian aspects of the East Pakistan crisis came under severe attack in the Congress and media, and from the US diplomats in Dhaka and New Delhi whose reports were deliberately leaked out to the Press. It was not only *realpolitik* which dictated US policy at that time. The disturbing events in East Pakistan had unfolded at a critical stage in a major US diplomatic initiative to establish relations with the People's Republic of China. Secret negotiations had been going on between the two countries through Yahya for quite some time. In December 1970 a message was sent to China for the visit of a US emissary to Beijing. There were strong indications that the response would be positive. Nixon had assigned a high priority to establishing relations with China, and Kissinger was handling the negotiations directly from the White House. The breakthrough would be the crowning achievement of their careers, and would achieve a desirable objective of US national policy in the wider global context. It was not to be risked at any cost. It was thought that pressurization of the Pakistan government might antagonize Yahya, and, given the Chinese diplomatic practices, it might take a long time to establish alternative channels.

The State Department, unaware of the China connection and 'heavily influenced by its traditional Indian bias', was doing precisely that, in early April, by placing restrictions on military and economic aid to Pakistan through procedural technicalities. It suspended issuance of new licences for the sale of ammunition and the renewal of expired licences, stopped deliveries from defence department stocks, and kept in abeyance the one-time exception package agreed to in 1970. Economic aid was being similarly restricted on the ground that ongoing programmes could not be implemented in the entire country because of civil war. The White House regarded these actions of the State Department as 'moving from a posture of detachment to one of dissociation from the Pakistan government', in violation of the spirit of the presidential policy.

The hostile domestic and world opinion against the army action, overt interference by India in East Pakistan, and the activism of the State Department all made it necessary to re-examine the East Pakistan policy. Kissinger's assessment of the ultimate shape of East Pakistan and India's involvement in its present situation, which he reported to Nixon on 29 April, was correct. But he was wrong in judging the thought-processes of Yahya, his colleagues, and the West Pakistani establishment throughout the crisis period. Kissinger thought that Yahya might realize the futility of the use of force, and 'move toward greater East Pakistan autonomy' which would lead to 'eventual independence.' At the same time, he opined that 'India's policy [of supporting the Bengali resistance force] was bound to work against such a settlement'. Yahya did not think at this time, or for that matter at any subsequent stage, of any meaningful compromise with the elected Bengali leadership. In fact, at least until the end of the monsoon period in July, he believed he had succeeded, through army action, in eliminating the Bengali nationalist leadership; and so did the army and the civilian establishment. Yahya, even if he were so inclined, could not convince the army to get out of the situation, which it had created, without strong external pressure. Kissinger never seriously tackled Yahya, nor did he tell him what he says in his memoirs he was forecasting about East Pakistan. Both he and Nixon, by cushioning Yahya from the pressures being exerted by other quarters for a political compromise, gave a false impression that the US government, in the last resort, would stand by him. On the other hand, they could not ensure even the existing military and economic aid to him, not to speak of special assistance, like riverine vessels, etc., to enable him to overcome the consequences of his policies.

Meanwhile, in the power game between the White House and the State Department, the latter had to be put in the strait-jacket of a formal policy framework, duly approved by the President. This would ensure that the specific military and economic issues arising out of the East Pakistan crisis were dealt with in accordance with the wishes of the White House, rather than the inclinations of the State Department. Accordingly, Kissinger asked the State Department to examine and recommend the policy options available to the US government in dealing with the crisis. Kissinger did not endorse the Department's views, and recommended to President Nixon: (a) a ratification of the unauthorized action of cutting off military aid supplies in the pipeline (it was not possible to do otherwise in view of Congressional and public opinion); and (b) to use the carrot of economic aid to help Yahya end the army action and establish an arrangement that could be transitional to East Pakistan autonomy. Nixon approved Kissinger's recommendations on 2 May, but with a warning: 'To all hands. Don't squeeze Yahya at this time.' Thus the policy of detachment considered eminently desirable in the last week of March was, by the end of April, transformed into one of softly influencing Yahya to reach a political settlement.

On 28 May, Nixon wrote letters to Yahya and Mrs Gandhi, urging restraint on both of them. The letter to Yahya 'was not exactly strong; it reflected our need for Yahya as a channel to Peking.' Nixon hoped that Yahya's declarations in the press conference on 24 May, about transfer of power to the elected representatives and the grant of general amnesty, would be translated into realities. As for Mrs Gandhi, he assured her that pressure was being exerted on Yahya, through quiet diplomacy, to seek political accommodation and to create conditions to stop the exodus and enable the refugees to return. These pressures, Nixon informed her, were succeeding, as will be seen by Yahya's announcements of 24 May. On 3 June, Kissinger briefed the US ambassador in India on the White House strategy of quiet diplomacy to nudge Yahya towards political accommodation with the dissident leadership and let realities assert themselves.

The claim that the major policy decisions of Yahya, like the acceptance of UN relief operations, amnesty, transfer of power plan (announced on 28 June), and later the replacement of Tikka Khan by a civilian governor, were taken at the behest of the US government is quite plausible. But all of them did not add up to any basic change in thinking. The US pressures were not strong enough to induce a credible change in policy; they were meant to be just sufficient to ward off the criticism of the Congress and media for the time being, without hurting the China connection.

Basically, there was no difference in the perceptions of the US and India about the inevitability of East Pakistan becoming independent. The divergence was with regard to its method and timings. India perceived its national interest to lie in bringing it about through its own efforts, and as soon as possible, before the issue lost its international focus. The world community might intervene to bring about some sort of compromise to keep Pakistan united, or Yahya Khan might make political concessions, as the Americans were pressing him to do. The Indian objective of the breakup of Pakistan would thus remain unfulfilled. Nixon and Kissinger, mainly because of the China factor, wanted to soften the process of the emergence of an independent East Pakistan by leaving it to the objective conditions. This might take longer, but the result would be the same as desired by India. Except the White House, no organ of the US Government or public opinion cared for this line of thought. The US establishment was agreed that the secession of East Pakistan was not against its national interests. The leadership of the new country would be in bourgeois hands, which fulfilled the American criterion of friendly regimes deserving support in the state of cold war. It was, therefore, safe for the Congress, media, and other power centres to indulge in a moral crusade, and give unstinted support to India to perform the operation.

* * *

In early April, a blunt official reaction came from the other super power of the times. In a letter to Yahya Khan, dated 2 April, the Soviet President, Nikolai Podgorny, expressed concern over 'the arrest and persecution of Mr Rehman and other political leaders' and appealed for 'most immediate measures so as to put an end to bloodshed and repressions against the population of East Pakistan and . . . [to bring about a] peaceful political settlement.'[22] The Soviet President did not stand on diplomatic niceties; it was a clear and preemptory demand, without any qualifications, to stop the use of force and seek a political solution of the problem in consultation with the elected leadership of East Pakistan.

The Soviet Union had been keenly watching the East Pakistan situation during the election campaign which lasted almost the whole year in 1970. The polarization between the rightist and leftist political forces involved China, Russia, and the US. The Russians supported Mujib because they saw in him a Pakistani leader who would seek reconciliation with India.[23] The subcontinent would thus be amenable to Soviet policies in respect of an Asian security system, discussed later. They made no secret of their keen interest in the outcome of the election results, and in the developments thereafter. At some time during Yahya's negotiations with Mujib, the Russian consul-general in Dhaka had called on the President, who had briefed him on his efforts to resolve the constitutional problem. On 28 March, the Soviet consul-general at Karachi had conveyed to the Pakistan government verbal message from Podgorny, seeking information on the events in East Pakistan. At the end of March, Yahya wrote to Premier Kosygin, explaining the background of the army action, and requested his help in finding a solution to the problem created by Indian interference.

The letter of 2 April was the first formal communication of Russian views. The Foreign Office interpreted the message as calculated to achieve certain political objectives by humiliating the regime and the President. It was rare in diplomatic practice to address a letter to a head of state, accusing his government of bloodshed, and demanding a specific solution to internal political problems. In the first week of April, the army was confident of controlling the situation; defeat in any form, or secession were both unthinkable. The Foreign Office, adapting its view of the world to the mood of the army, advised an equally sharp reply in tone and language, which, it thought, would be consistent with national dignity and self-respect. The reply sent on 5 April asked the Soviet President to use his 'undeniable influence with the Indian government' to prevent its interference in the internal affairs of Pakistan, which might lead 'to irretrievable consequences'. The reply reminded him that 'no country, including the Soviet Union, can allow—or has ever allowed—anti-national and unpatriotic elements to proceed to destroy it, or to countenance subversion.'[24] The correspondence was published by Pakistan unilaterally; the President's reply was widely applauded in West Pakistan.

The Soviet Union, as it was at that time, was a superpower with an arrogant attitude towards small countries. It never really forgave the Yahya regime for this sharp rebuff. For the time being, however, it softened its tone, but its basic position was reiterated from time to time. In a message on 17 April, Kosygin warned that 'the chance and time to gain a political settlement were not yet lost'. On 26 April, Kosygin in a meeting with the special envoy, Mian Arshad Hussain, stressed the necessity of a peaceful settlement in East Pakistan and peaceful co-existence with India. On 22 June, Kosygin advised the Pakistan ambassador that a process of consultation should be started with India and that the Soviet Union would be willing to play a role. On 24 June, Kosygin again sent a message to the Pakistan government, informing them that the refugee problem had taken the shape of an international issue; the Soviet Union was convinced that the solution of this and other problems arising from the developments in East Pakistan could be found if the martial law administration turned without delay to a political settlement. To be fair, the Russians, whatever their motives, were asking Pakistan to do what the rest of the world was asking, albeit crudely—seek a political solution instead of military action. Pakistan was determined to ignore it, as it did the advice from other sources.

* * *

On 30 March, Yahya wrote to Zhou Enlai, the Chinese Prime Minister, explaining the political developments up to 26 March and drawing his attention to the likelihood of physical intervention by India in East Pakistan. Referring to the common security concerns of the two countries, Yahya suggested the setting up of machinery for the co-ordination of policy between China and Pakistan. Meanwhile, Yahya requested a clear statement by China to the effect that the situation in East Pakistan was an internal affair of Pakistan. At about the same time, Yahya had also called the Chinese ambassador in Islamabad to explain the East Pakistan situation. The question of co-ordination of military planning between Pakistan and China had been discussed several times between the two sides since 1966. In May 1967, it was mentioned in the meeting of Premier Zhou Enlai with the Pakistani Defence Minister during the latter's visit to China. Pakistan also continued to lay emphasis on the supply of Chinese military equipment.

The first official reaction from China to the army operation in East Pakistan came in an indirect manner on 6 April. A mob of several hundred persons demonstrated in front of the Chinese embassy in New Delhi on 29 March against China's aid to the Pakistan government in the latter's 'war on the freedom-loving people of East Bengal.' In the Chinese protest note against the demonstration, the Indian government was accused of 'flagrantly interfering in the internal affairs of Pakistan'.[25]

On 9 April, Zhou Enlai sent a reply to Yahya's letter. He expressed the belief 'that through the *wise consultations* and efforts of Your Excellency and *leaders of various quarters in Pakistan* the situation in Pakistan will certainly be restored to normal' (emphasis added). The message criticized India's interference in the purely internal affair of Pakistan, and ended with an assurance that the Chinese government and people would 'firmly support the Pakistan government and people in their just struggle *to safeguard State sovereignty and national independence*' (emphasis added).[26]

In the diplomatic uneasiness created by the Soviet stance, the Chinese message, although belated and somewhat formally worded, was most welcome for the immediate purposes of gaining time until the army completed the operation. Diplomatic observers felt that the response was not as prompt, resolute, and unequivocal as Chinese support had been at the time of the September 1965 war with India. For one thing, the message came only in response to Yahya's letter and meeting with the Chinese ambassador in Pakistan. Then it was sent only after the Soviet Union's hostile message of 2 April. Moreover, the Chinese message had spoken of 'consultations' and 'leaders of various quarters in Pakistan' in order to restore normalcy; this was not an endorsement of the use of force, and indeed might be construed as emphasizing the desirability of negotiations with the elected leadership. Again, the support for 'State sovereignty and national independence' might be only for West Pakistan, though the unity of the people of East and West Pakistan was mentioned 'as the basic guarantee for Pakistan to attain prosperity and strength.'[27] In the light of subsequent developments, it would seem that the Chinese had conveyed, in the very first message to Pakistan, both the nature of their support, and a word of advice that the problem should be settled through negotiations.

The extremely cordial official relations and the emotional attachment of the people of West Pakistan to China since the Indo-Pakistan war of 1965 had led them to expect an immediate and unequivocal condemnation of Indian interference in East Pakistan. These expectations, like all others during the crisis, were naive. The issues and power alignments in 1971 were entirely different from those of 1965. In 1965 it was a clean war between two countries, against one of which China had also fought three years earlier on matters which were still unresolved. At that time, the Soviet Union was also neutral between the belligerents. It was thus possible for China to throw its full weight behind Pakistan against India without endangering its own security on the borders with Russia. In 1971, the situation had a moral aspect of resort to the use of force, in lieu of political compromise, against the East Pakistan leadership which had obtained an overwhelming mandate from their people. It was difficult to convince even the friends of Pakistan that India had created the constitutional crisis; it was merely taking advantage of one, the roots of which were within Pakistan. The prolonged use of a professional army against the civilian population posed a dilemma for Pakistan's friends, who found it increasingly difficult to defend the Pakistani position. Still, although the Chinese diplomatic support was somewhat limited (compared to 1965, but not compared to other powers in 1971), it did put a restraint on the Indian plans to break up Pakistan. It allowed Yahya time to resolve the crisis. The Chinese economic and military assistance, which was always liberal, was stepped up from April onwards.[28] The Chinese never wavered in giving what they promised. It was Pakistan which disappointed them by pursuing fatal policies.

The Chinese position was further elaborated during the visit of Sultan Muhammad Khan, Foreign Secretary, to Beijing on 10–11 April, when he met Zhou Enlai and held discussions with other leaders. He reported the following conclusions from his visit about the Chinese attitude. The initial silence of the Chinese was due to their method of working; China's open support (in the message of 9 April) had resulted in a set-back to the anticipated improvement in Sino-Indian relations, and meant that China looked upon the independence of East Pakistan against her national interest; China's help in raising two new divisions was a reaffirmation of its support to Pakistan; China was also willing to give Pakistan economic assistance; China expected political measures at the earliest to defuse the situation which, it thought, could not be resolved by military means only; in the meeting with the Foreign Secretary, Zhou Enlai hardly criticized India or Russia; most of the time he tried to understand the situation and emphasized its short and long-term implications. The significant parts of the discussions related to Zhou Enlai's worry about the effects of Pakistan's East Pakistan policy on the region and his emphasis on a political solution.

Zhou Enlai was more explicit two weeks later to the Pakistan ambassador, who met him on 26 April to deliver Yahya's letter. Responding to the ambassador's report of a gradual improvement in the situation, the Chinese Prime Minister observed that 'in resolving problems, political means were most important, military means could only be temporary'. He also advised that communal conflict in East Pakistan should be avoided. Zhou Enlai was a wise statesman, and a sincere friend of Pakistan. But his advice, like those of other friendly countries, was ignored by Yahya who could not see the non-military dimensions of the crisis.

Iran, a friend and neighbour of Pakistan, was worried about the situation in Pakistan for its own reasons. The Shah had expressed concern over the developing confrontation in East Pakistan to the visiting Pakistani Minister of Industries, at the end of January. The Shah feared that the separation of its two Wings would create problems not only for Pakistan, but for Iran and her friends also, by bringing West Pakistan still closer to China. On 28 March, the Iranian government in a statement said that it 'has strongly suggested to all nations of the world not to interfere in the internal affairs of Pakistan during the present crisis.'[29] During this period

Iran agreed to supply some helicopters and other military equipment to Pakistan. The Indian government lodged a protest with Iran, but the Iranian Foreign Office informed the Pakistan ambassador that it had told the Indians that in case of any external threat to Pakistan, Iran would stand by it. At the end of June, the Shah suggested to Mrs Gandhi that she meet Yahya at Persepolis during the celebrations of the 2500th anniversary of the Iranian monarchy. Mrs Gandhi refused, but the Shah succeeded in arranging Yahya's meeting with Soviet President Podgorny, which will be described later.

* * *

The reactions to the army operation in East Pakistan were not confined to bilateral exchanges or official statements of the individual governments. They reverberated in the UN when the Indian note on the crisis to the Secretary-General, mentioned above, was circulated as a press release on 31 March, and Agha Shahi rebutted it on 7 April. U Thant assured Pakistan that he regarded the East Pakistan crisis as a matter strictly within its domestic jurisdiction. Nevertheless, in a letter to Yahya Khan on 22 April, he said he was 'greatly concerned' at the humanitarian aspects of the situation in East Pakistan 'in the light of information I have received from various sources, including reports from UN personnel who have recently returned from there.'[30]

Agha Shahi gives the following account of the embarrassing position he found himself in at the UN, in the period immediately after the army operation.

> On 21–22 March, I was being congratulated by the ambassadors at the UN on successful completion of political negotiations at Dhaka. Four days later there were headlines in leading newspapers about military action and atrocities. I was being asked all sorts of questions by representatives of different countries at the UN. I asked for an official statement, brief, and instructions to rebut the adverse coverage in the media. But there was no response from the Foreign Office. I got a statement prepared in the mission on the basis of whatever material was available. But the newspapers wouldn't publish it. They said I was in New York and had not witnessed the situation which was being reported by eyewitnesses and their own correspondents. Around 6 April the provisional government of Bangladesh issued a paper on the

atrocities of the Pakistan army which was on the table of every delegation in the UN. Even the friendly ambassadors started saying that there must be some truth in the published reports. Later in April, the only instruction and brief I got from the government was to keep the UN out.[31]

In April and May, the regime deputed special envoys to the major powers to explain its position. In the last week of April, Mian Arshad Hussain, a former foreign minister in Ayub Khan's government, visited Moscow, London, and Paris to deliver Yahya's letters to the heads of government of these countries. On return from his odyssey, which found no mention in the Press of these countries, he observed that 'there was better appreciation in the Soviet Union, France, and Britain of Pakistan's action against the Indian-backed secessionist movement in East Pakistan', presumably after his presentation of Pakistan's case to Premier Kosygin, President Pompidou, and Premier Edward Heath.[32] The more meaningful visit, mentioned in previous chapters, was that of M. M. Ahmed in the second week of May to the US. Ahmed had met Yahya before he left, and fully briefed himself on the President's mind on the economic, political, and military aspects of the crisis. Yahya felt that he was being misunderstood abroad; he had never closed the doors of negotiations. In spite of provocations, he said, he did not crack down on Mujib in early March. Yahya desired M. M. Ahmed to meet President Nixon and those who mattered in the US establishment, and explain his position to them.

On his return, M. M. Ahmed reported to Yahya. He says:

On my return, I briefed the President on my impressions that Pakistan was totally isolated because of the atrocities reported in the Western Press and unless the refugees influx in India was controlled, India was likely to take some violent action. At this, the President called Sultan Muhammad Khan and asked me to repeat what I had told him. The President [then] said, 'I don't want war with India', and told Sultan Muhammad that the Foreign Office should keep it in mind.

It was a sign of the narrow political and diplomatic perceptions of the government that it never thought of inviting the eminent elected leaders of West Pakistan to visit the Western countries and explain the genesis of the crisis. They had participated in the

March negotiations with the Awami League and had, by and large, supported army action. Their presentation in the full glare of the world media, facing the critics on their own ground, would have led to a better appreciation of Pakistan's case by the world community. The issue had gone far beyond the confines of routine diplomacy of notes and letters to the heads of governments, or of hand-outs like the White Paper which was issued in August.[33]

The quality of political settlement being demanded by the Indian government, as a *sine qua non* of the solution of the East Pakistan crisis, was escalating in direct proportion to the influx of refugees, the inability of the army to restore an acceptable level of normalcy, and the growing hostility of world opinion. Starting from the position of just a 'political settlement' in April and May, India, by June, had also come to specify the kind of solution that would be acceptable to it. Mrs Gandhi told parliament on 15 June, with her usual double-talk, that 'Although a political settlement in East Pakistan is no concern of India', India would not accept a solution which might mean the death of Bangladesh.[34] The Awami League leadership in India would, thus, have little choice in negotiating a compromise with the Pakistan government, if indeed such a dialogue were allowed to take place by the Indians. A few days later, Mrs Gandhi further specified that a political settlement meant only an agreement with the Awami League led by Mujib.[35]

In June, the Indian Foreign Minister, Swaran Singh, visited the Soviet Union and the major Western countries to mobilize support against Pakistan. The timing was particularly chosen to influence the Pakistan consortium meeting of aid-giving countries on 22 June. The Indo-Soviet statement, issued on 8 June, called for immediate measures to 'ensure the stoppage of influx of refugees from East Pakistan.'[36] During his visit to Western Germany on 9–10 June, Swaran Singh in a press conference asked the 'big industrialized nations to cut off economic development aid to Pakistan'.[37] The foreign ministers of the two countries 'agreed that an early political solution of the problem was essential for the return of the refugees to their homes.'[38] In Paris, the French Foreign Minister, in the talks with Swaran Singh on 12 June, advised a political solution to the crisis 'which stops the flood of refugees and enables their return to their homes.'[39]

The British government was under intense pressure from the opposition and the media to stop economic aid to Pakistan. In early May, it was resisting the demand.[40] By June, however, it had veered round to the Indian view that an economic and political squeeze should be applied to Pakistan. Sir Alec, in statements made in the House of Commons on 8 and 9 June, recognized the 'great restraint' exercised by the government of India and emphasized the necessity of creating a political framework which would give confidence to the refugees to return.[41]

On 15 June, 120 Labour members, more than half the parliamentary Labour party, moved a motion in the House of Commons accusing the government of Pakistan of genocide, and demanding recognition of the provisional government of Bangladesh.[42] The strength of feelings led to the visit of two parliamentary delegations to Pakistan in the second and third weeks of June. The first one consisting of three members of Parliament, a Conservative Mrs Jill Knight, one Labour member, and one Ulster Unionist, visited Pakistan from 12 to 20 June. They met President Yahya on 12 June, and again after their visit to East Pakistan. 'The papers here in Britain' said Mrs Knight on her return, 'are still reporting atrocities and shocking evidence of violence but none of them is going on now. . . .' She paid a compliment to Yahya 'in trying his hardest, despite criticism from the rest of the world, to get the country back to normal.' The Labour member of the delegation also gave his impressions in a similar strain. There was an uproar in the British media against these statements. Mrs Knight, to save her political career, was forced to retract what she had earlier called 'a very good and accurate impression of what was going on' in East Pakistan. On 5 July, she wrote a letter to Yahya 'expressing grave concern at reports by fellow M.Ps [in the second delegation] of atrocities allegedly committed by the Pakistan army against civilians in East Pakistan.'[43]

The second parliamentary delegation, sponsored by the British government, consisted of four eminent members of the Parliament, two from the Labour party and two Conservatives. It was headed by Arthur Bottomley, former Secretary of State for Commonwealth and Other Relations. The purpose of the visit was 'to investigate conditions in East and West Bengal and the plight of refugees from East Pakistan.' The members of the delegation, after an extensive tour of East Pakistan, formed a very adverse opinion of the state of affairs there. One of the members, Toby Jessel, said in Dhaka on 28 June that after what he had seen and heard he could not tell the refugees to return. Later, on 1 July in New Delhi, Arthur Bottomley, on behalf of the delegation, said that they had been shocked by what they had seen in the refugee camps in West Bengal; in East Pakistan they found the atmosphere one of fear and 'continuing atrocities'. General Tikka Khan, Bottomley said, 'had no knowledge of or concern for the economic and social aspects of the situation.' But he found Yahya Khan 'an honourable man who did not seem to know what was happening in East Bengal.'[44] The solution, the delegation concluded, 'could only lie in a political settlement' with the elected representatives of East Pakistan led by Mujib.[45]

While the second parliamentary delegation was investigating the conditions in East Pakistan, Swaran Singh arrived in Britain. The agreed statement issued on 21 June, after Swaran Singh's meetings with Sir Alec and Heath, demanded that a political settlement 'acceptable to the people of East Pakistan' must be found to enable the refugees to return.[46] On 23 June, Sir Alec, speaking in the House of Commons, referred to discussions with Swaran Singh in which the latter had expressed his concern about 'the very great danger to the stability, created by the massive influx of refugees into India'. Sir Alec also mentioned the Pakistan Aid Consortium meeting on 21 June, which had refused to commit any new aid, and announced that the British government would not grant any further aid to Pakistan unless there was 'firm evidence that real progress is made towards a political solution.'[47]

As a result of the statements of the parliamentary delegation, the activities of the Bangladesh Action committee, the hostile attitude of the media, and the joint statement issued after the visit of Swaran Singh, Pakistan–UK relations became strained. During the week ending 5 July, three protest notes were sent by Pakistan to the British government.[48] On 15 July, an official spokesman disclosed that the government of Pakistan was seriously considering withdrawal from the Commonwealth.[49]

The Indian Foreign Minister, during his visits to Moscow and the Western capitals, had not made a secret of the ultimate step of military action that India might have to take.[50] The response of the Pakistan government to these rumblings and the diplomatic success of Swaran Singh in the major capitals was a message addressed by Yahya, on 18 June, to all heads of state or government of countries to which Pakistan missions were accredited. It drew the attention of these governments to the 'mounting threat to peace and security in the subcontinent as a result of India's policy and action'.[51]

The message had a general text for all countries, with specific paras added for Washington, Beijing, Moscow, etc., with reference to the special features of Pakistan's relationship with them. Thus, President Nixon was requested to use his influence on Mrs Gandhi 'not to compound our difficulties', and informed of the political plan Yahya proposed to announce on 28 June. China was requested to reiterate its traditional support for the territorial integrity of Pakistan, which 'will have a stabilizing effect'. The Soviet Union was reminded of the statement it had made to the Pakistan ambassador on 12 April that a political solution for Pakistan's problems could only be found by Pakistan's leaders; it was pleaded that 'at this juncture when I am committed to making an important announcement . . . threats and pressures to dictate a particular course on Pakistan would be most unfortunate.' The feedback from the missions indicated a lukewarm response from the governments. In many cases, the heads of missions could not get an appointment to deliver the message personally as required by protocol, and it was given to the foreign ministry of the country. In all cases, the replies were couched in bland diplomatic language, counselling a peaceful settlement of the problem.

In its follow-up to Yahya's message to President Sadaat, the Egyptian government hinted at an Islamic initiative in the crisis. In a meeting with Pakistan's ambassador on 24 June, the Egyptian Foreign Minister referred to the suggestion of the Minister of State, Hafiz Ismail, of a commission of Muslim countries to facilitate the return of refugees. But he himself hastened to brush it aside by saying that India would not accept such a proposal. The idea was not taken up by the Foreign Office, which was stuck in the rut of an inward-looking, barren policy. But in June U Thant requested the Secretary-General of the Organization of Islamic Countries, Tengku Abdul Rehman, to undertake mediation for a settlement between India and Pakistan. The Tengku, accompanied by a delegation of Iranian, Kuwaiti, and Saudi Arabian members of the Islamic Secretariat, arrived in Karachi on 18 July. Earlier, he had visited India, where the government had refused to allow the Kuwaiti and Iranian members to visit the refugee camps in West Bengal. On his return to Kuala Lampur in early August, the Tengku in an angry statement said that Mrs Gandhi had wanted him to secure the release of Mujib and condemn the killings in East Pakistan. He said that he did not want to get involved in the politics of the two countries; his only objective was to arrange the return of refugees under UN supervision. The Indian attitude, the Tengku concluded, made this impossible.[52]

The tentative initiative of Mrs Bandarnaike, the Sri Lankan Prime Minister, and the efforts of the Secretary-General of the Commonwealth Secretariat to build up a collective mediation by selected members of the Commonwealth on that, proved stillborn. India sternly warned Bandarnaike not to meddle, and Yahya asked her to dissuade India from interfering in the internal affairs of Pakistan; Britain was not enthusiastic about any third-party initiative.[53]

* * *

The decisive element in the diplomatic tangle of the East Pakistan crisis was the United States policy, which had become the victim of the tussle between the White House and State Department. The Nixon-Kissinger differences with the rest of the administration, Congress, and the media were mainly tactical in respect of responses to the current situation; otherwise, they were all agreed about its eventual outcome. Yahya failed to appreciate the dynamics of US policymaking. The White House support gave him the wrong impression that in the last resort, in any confrontation with India, the US would actively come to his aid. The Foreign Office did not educate him on the fact that in the absence of a consensus of dominant institutions, normally characterizing strategic foreign policy issues, the US President would not be able to help. In July, however, all eyes were turned to the visit of Kissinger to the subcontinent for a resolution of the crisis.

These high hopes were, however, soon to be dashed. Kissinger's tour of India and Pakistan, as part of a long itinerary, was a cover-up for his visit to Beijing as the US President's emissary, a visit which Yahya had helped to bring about. He was on the verge of making history on a grand strategic scale and deeply preoccupied in preparations for it. There was little time to attend to the concerns of his midway hosts. The mire of Indo-Pakistan politics offered no dramatic breakthrough for the talents of Kissinger. In fact, it involved the risk of tarnishing the image of a successful statesman.

In meetings with the Indian leaders in New Delhi, he purportedly 'followed the ritual of previous weeks' in respect of the East Pakistan crisis, i.e. the US wanted good relations with India, and was putting pressure on Yahya to grant autonomy to East Pakistan, etc. He also assured the Indians in vague diplomatic language, to the extent that this was possible without divulging forthcoming developments, that rapprochement with China would not mean any change in the friendly Indo-US relations.[54] At the end of the visit, Kissinger thought that he had prepared the Indians for the surprise that he was heading for, and felt quite smug about hiding from them the real purpose of his visit to the subcontinent.

Kissinger arrived in Islamabad on 8 July. He had left New Delhi with a definite impression that India was bent upon a military showdown to resolve the refugee problem. In between the cloak and dagger preoccupations with 'my impending journey to Peking', Kissinger held talks with Yahya and Sultan Muhammad Khan about subcontinental affairs. But he had neither the time nor the inclination for a straight talk conveying the impressions he had formed during the Indian visit. He was fascinated by the generals and mildly amused by their claim of the superiority of Muslim soldiers over the Hindus, their false confidence, and their complete unawareness of the isolation of Pakistan. With his international reputation, intellectual calibre, and barbed wit, Kissinger overawed Yahya and his colleagues. His diplomatic smoothness with them, without any hint of criticism of their policies or any warning about the dangerous course they were following, were taken by his hosts as broad endorsements of their positions. In a benign mood at Yahya's dinner, on the night before he left for Beijing, Kissinger affectionately chided Yahya Khan that 'for a dictator, you run a lousy election.'[55]

On 15 July President Nixon announced to the world that Kissinger had visited Beijing and that he (Nixon) had accepted the invitation of the People's Republic of China to visit their country before May 1972. The Sino-American detente caused a fundamental change in the international world order which would manifest itself in new diplomatic equations over time. Its impact on the brewing crisis in the subcontinent, however, was more immediate and tangible. Each of three parties involved in the crisis—Pakistan, the US, and India—reviewed its place and interests in the changed scheme of international relations.

The period immediately after the 15 July announcement was one of euphoria in Pakistan. The official circles, military and civil, and the West Pakistani public in general were jubilant. Although no one was very clear how the new development was going to help Pakistan to extricate itself from the mess, the army's faith in the omnipotence of US support was reinforced. The Foreign Office expected to be rewarded for services rendered, and started dreaming of a Washington–Islamabad–Beijing axis as a hedge against the evil designs of its neighbour.

Kissinger, however, had returned to Washington with a 'premonition of disaster' in the subcontinent. He was certain that India would attack Pakistan soon after the rainy season, and would not allow the US to complete the process of 'evolution that would lead to independence for East Pakistan'. Nixon considered the situation serious enough to call a meeting of the National Security Council on 16 July, in which Kissinger reported his impressions of his New Delhi visit. Secretary of State Rogers gave his opinion that India was doing everything to prevent the return of refugees. Nixon decided that Pakistan should be asked to do the maximum for the refugees, all efforts should be made to avoid war, and, if India used force, all American aid should be cut off.[56]

Kissinger says that there was no disagreement in the meeting with his analysis of the Indo-Pakistan situation. Christopher Van Hollen, who was Deputy Assistant Secretary of State for Near Eastern and South Asian Affairs at the time, however, denies that the meeting of 16 July deserved the label of an 'NSC meeting'; according to him, they were only high level *ad hoc* discussions. As against Kissinger's apprehensions, the State Department's assessment, Van Hollen says, was that 'there is no firm evidence that India by mid-summer had made a definite decision to go to war'. The policy that emerged on Kissinger's return from the Beijing visit, whether in the National Security Council meeting or in top level *ad hoc* discussions, was to extend liberal assistance for relief of the refugees, but otherwise to allow the situation to take its own course. Kissinger was convinced, Van Hollen says, after his discussions in Islamabad, 'that Yahya would accept advice on such questions as relief assistance for East Pakistan, but he would not be amenable to US suggestions for a political accommodation, especially, Yahya would not deal with members of the outlawed Awami League.' The State Department, however, was of the unanimous view that the separation of the humanitarian from the political aspects was not likely to resolve the East Pakistan crisis or to avert the danger of war.[57]

Kissinger's impression that Yahya would not be amenable to political pressure was not entirely correct, and in any case was not properly tested at any stage. Up to July, the reason was the China connection; thereafter, the impressions formed by Kissinger after 'tactful' soundings of Yahya Khan and the generals during his Islamabad visit remained the sole basis of the White House policy of watching a friendly country going to pieces. American diplomats are not known to be always tactful with small states on matters which they perceive to be of concern to them. Kissinger had informed Zhou Enlai that while the US 'would strongly oppose any Indian military action', its disapproval could not 'take the form of military aid or military measures on behalf of Pakistan.'[58] A statement of this kind to Yahya Khan would have had a salutary effect in two ways. Firstly, Yahya would have been compelled to review his options of either carrying on the barren policy of repression or of initiating some realistic political measures to resume the constitutional process. Secondly, the moderates in the army, though small in number, would have gained greater influence in the inner counsels of the regime for a more practical approach. True, a blunt statement of the US stand on a political settlement would have jeopardized Yahya's position, because he had closed his options by calling Mujib a traitor with whom it might have been difficult for him to deal. But the junta would have found some way to fall in line with American wishes. In the isolated situation of July onwards, Yahya and his generals were depending entirely on the US to see them through the crisis. It was not correct in the circumstances to assume, as Kissinger did, that the generals would have spurned political pressures of the friendly power which they regarded as their main strength.

Kissinger's memoirs do not indicate that he conveyed the 'premonition of disaster' and conviction of the inevitability of war to Yahya Khan in such an unequivocal manner as he did to Nixon on his return to Washington. In fact, the announcement of Mujib's trial in early August indicated a hardening of Yahya's attitude. Paradoxically, the view of the 'anti-Pakistan' State Department that Yahya should be made to face political realities would have served Pakistan interests better than the friendly drift of the White House.[59]

During his visit to New Delhi, Kissinger says that he had assured the Indians that the US 'would take a grave view of an unprovoked Chinese attack on India'.[60] But this was only to calm their suspicions which were bound to arise as soon as the Sino-American detente was announced. There were reports that Kissinger at other times and places had warned India that in case of a Chinese attack, in the context of the East Pakistan crisis, the US would not come forward to help India as it did in 1962. The warning was reported to have been repeated by Kissinger during his visit to New Delhi also.[61] While the Indian leadership was still reeling under the shock of the new power alignment in their neighbourhood, Kissinger summoned the Indian Ambassador, L. K. Jha, on 17 July to repeat similar warnings. Seymour M. Hersh, describing it as a 'reckless attempt to provoke the worst possible case', gives the following account:

> Kissinger gave the Indians a direct warning, as Jha reported in an urgent cable to New Delhi: If war broke out between India and Pakistan, and China became involved on Pakistan's side, 'we would be unable to help you against China.' Jha added in his summary of the meeting: 'He [Kissinger] could not but express the most serious anxiety and concern about an India-Pakistan conflict resulting from the present crisis. . . . While he did not know what the Chinese would do, it would be unsafe for us [India] to assume that they would not come to Pakistan's help'.[62]

Kissinger does not mention this meeting, which by itself could not have provoked the Indians to do something which they were not already doing. In their frantic state to achieve the breakup of Pakistan, the warning could at worst only have reinforced the Indian policymakers' search for insuring their adventure with the only superpower available at the time. In Beijing, the East Pakistan crisis had naturally come up in discussions, and Zhou Enlai without being specific, had made it clear to Kissinger that China would not be 'indifferent if India attacked Pakistan'.[63] The Chinese Premier was conveying a message not only to Washington; he apparently intended it to go to the Indians also. The Chinese position remained unchanged even when Kissinger responded that, though the US would oppose any Indian military action, it would not take any concrete measures on Pakistan's behalf. In the light of the historical experience of the 1965 Indo–Pakistan war, China not remaining indifferent in the event of hostilities in 1971 might have included some form of physical intervention against India. In which case, Kissinger thought, the Soviet Union might react. From this standpoint, Kissinger naturally felt concerned and warned India not to be reckless in forcing a military solution to the East Pakistan crisis.

Kissinger's attempts, before and after the Beijing visit, to manage India's responses to the Sino-American rapprochment proved a failure. His warning to the Indians about the Chinese military factor in the confrontation with Pakistan, of US support to Pakistan (of a limited kind), and the Western pressures on India to accept UN observers on the border, to be discussed presently, all were perceived by Indian policymakers as serious threats to their plans for the independence of East Pakistan. The Sino-American detente, though not directly related in timing or substance to the developing crisis of East Pakistan, was bound to have its reaction on South Asian politics. Coupled with these global developments were the domestic pressures on Mrs Gandhi to come up with some spectacular diplomatic initiative, comparable to Pakistan's role in bringing the US and China together. The Hindu nationalist party, Jan Sangh, was vociferous in demanding recognition of Bangladesh, and nine Indian states were going to the polls towards the end of the year to elect the state assemblies. Before discussing the equally dramatic Indian response to the so-called Beijing–Washington–Islamabad axis, mention may be made of the initiatives taken at this time by the UN Secretary-General to reduce the tension in the subcontinent.

* * *

By mid-July it was becoming increasingly clear that humanitarian measures, by themselves, were not enough to ease the confrontation between India and Pakistan. The transfer of power plan, announced by Yahya on 28 June, was rejected by the Indian government, and, therefore, by the Awami League leadership; it had also failed to have an impact on world opinion. In the third week of July, the UN Secretary-General took two steps to defuse the explosive situation. The first one was the proposal to station representatives of the UN High Commissioner for Refugees at selected crossing points on each side of the border between India and East Pakistan, to facilitate voluntary repatriation of refugees. The proposal was presented in an *aide-mémoire* to the governments of India and Pakistan on 19 July. It was pointed out that the UNHCR was already acting as the focal point in the two countries for UN efforts on behalf of the refugees. The proposal, it was explained in the *aide-mémoire,* would thus be merely an extension of the existing role of the UN accepted by both the countries in respect of the refugees.[64] The government of Pakistan immediately accepted the proposal on 21 July.[65] Indeed, it welcomed the posting of the UNHCR representatives on the borders, as they would have supervised not only the return of the refugees but, more importantly, also noticed the rebellious activities being conducted from the Indian side. For the same reason and with the same promptitude, the Indian government rejected the proposal on 22 July. The ostensible argument given by Swaran Singh was that the posting of UN observers 'would further aggravate the suffering of the people of Bangla Desh'; he informed the Security Council members that any kind of UN presence 'on her borders (either side) would be regarded as an unfriendly act' by India.[66]

The Secretary-General followed up the *aide-mémoire* to India and Pakistan by a memorandum to the president of the Security Council, on 20 July, on 'the possible consequences of the present situation . . . as a potential threat to peace and security.' The document, which was circulated by the president to the members of the Council and Indian and Pakistani delegates, highlighted the 'lack of substantial progress towards a political reconciliation and the consequent effect on law, order, and public administration in East Pakistan'. It stated that, without reconciliation and an improved political atmosphere, there was no possibility of the return of refugees. The Secretary-General considered the 'political aspects of [the situation] . . . of such far-reaching importance' that he asked the Council members to decide amongst themselves about measures 'to avert a further deterioration of the situation.'[67] The Secretary-General discussed the tension on the borders, in separate meetings, with the permanent representatives of India and Pakistan on 26 July.[68] The consultation of the president with the fifteen members of the Security Council could not produce any consensus on calling a meeting of the Security Council to discuss the threat to peace pointed out in the memorandum. India, determined not to let any third party interfere with its plans for the new regional map, warned the Council members that it would regard its meeting as an unfriendly act.[69] Although the Western governments supported the proposal for UN observers on the border, the Soviet Union was reported to be against it.[70] In the circumstances the permanent Council members thought that no useful purpose would be served by calling a meeting of the Security Council.

* * *

By mid-July the dominant elements of Indian opinion had reached a consensus, through the processes of mass hysteria created by leading public figures and sophisticated analyses by policymakers, that the independence of East Pakistan could be brought about only by military action against Pakistan. K. Subrahmanyam, head of the official think-tank, in mid-July produced and circulated to the Western Press a document with the descriptive title 'Bangladesh and India's National Security—the Option for India'.

The basic premise of the document, extensively reproduced in *The Times* of 13 July, was that having committed itself 'to rescue' the East Bengalis, the Indian government could not now resile from this position. The hopes that the world community would compel Yahya to reach a 'meaningful' political settlement, or that the *mukti bahini* would defeat the professional Pakistan army had been belied. The Pakistan economy had absorbed the cost of army operations in East Pakistan. It was necessary, Subrahmanyam argued, that now India itself should initiate armed intervention to internationalize the crisis. The object would be to wrest by military action a portion of East Pakistan. The location of the provisional government on the occupied ground would acquire all the attributes of *de facto* and *de jure* sovereignty. The Security Council would meet and ask for a cease-fire, which India might accept at its discretion, immediately or after some more fighting, provided the Bangladesh commander was recognized as a party to the cease-fire, and the Bangladesh government a party to the East Pakistan dispute.

Analysing the balance of power between the two countries, the document concluded that the Pakistan air force or navy would not be in a position to inflict much damage; rather, the hostilities 'will prevent East Bengal from being reinforced and will bottle up the forces there'. With regard to the likely reactions of Pakistan's military allies, Subrahmanyam ruled out intervention by the United States. The CENTO countries, Turkey and Iran, might give some assistance by way of supplies, but not on any significant scale. The danger of Chinese intervention which, in the words of Hazelhurst 'haunts the mind of every Indian hawk', was also excluded because of logistical and weather problems, coupled with the Indian capability now of using its air force on the northern borders, unlike 1962. The Soviet Union, of course, would be on the Indian side. Hazelhurst, commenting on the document in the same dispatch, considered it alarming, reflecting the 'growing mood of impatience in India', and demonstrating 'that war is seriously being considered in the most responsible circles in India.' There is no evidence that these warnings of disaster were seriously studied in the GHQ or the Foreign Office in Pakistan.

India was taken unawares by President Nixon's announcement of 15 July, and it was a few days before it realized the full implications of the Sino-American rapprochment for the subcontinent in general, and for the East Pakistan crisis in particular. Starting with the initial comment on the event as a 'significant, positive development', the Indian Foreign Minister by 20 July had come to regard the event as a means of the domination of the region by China and the US.[71] There was a xenophobic surge in the Indian Press and parliament against what was seen as a Sino–American–Pakistan axis to thwart Indian plans to bring about the independence of East Pakistan. Two factors were particularly galling to the Indian ego. One was the role of Pakistan in bringing the two superpowers together; this conferred a diplomatic glory not usually given to small countries. The second was the realization that Kissinger's discussions in New Delhi prior to his visit to Islamabad and Beijing were not meant to be a serious effort to attend to India's concerns. The Nixon announcement made India feel small, betrayed, and isolated.

The new relationship between Washington and Beijing, the Western and UN pressure for the acceptance of neutral observers, and the US suggestion on 4 August for the control of guerrilla activities on its side of the border required an urgent strengthening of the Indian diplomatic position to protect its plans. A flurry of diplomatic and political moves was observed in Moscow and New

Delhi in the first week of August. D. P. Dhar, former ambassador to the Soviet Union, paid a secret visit to Moscow. At about the same time, Tajuddin Ahmed, head of the provisional Bangladesh government, and his colleagues also secretly visited New Delhi to hold discussions with Mrs Gandhi and Indian officials. Earlier in the week, Dhar, the Foreign Secretary, and two senior military intelligence officers had a meeting with the Russian ambassador.[72] In the wake of all this hectic activity, there was all kinds of speculation in the Western Press.. The most striking was the report in *The Observer* of 8 August from its New Delhi correspondent that 'there is a feeling in the air that a chopping block is being prepared for Pakistan . . . it looks very much as if Pakistan is being goaded into drawing first'. On 8 August, Andrei Gromyko, the Soviet Foreign Minister, arrived in New Delhi with a twelve member team. On 9 August, the Indo-Soviet Treaty of Peace, Friendship, and Co-operation was signed by Gromyko and Swaran Singh.

* * *

On the geopolitical map of the time, Pakistan had occupied a strategic position in the Soviet Union's drive to contain China and bring South Asia under its influence. For some years preceding the Indo-Pakistan war of 1965, the Soviet Union had shifted from a position of unqualified support to India to one of neutrality in disputes between India and Pakistan. In terms of superpower rivalries, the Soviet Union saw in the 1965 war a threat to its position in the subcontinent; the consequences of the war would be exploited by the Western powers to compromise India's non-alignment and Pakistan's disengagement from military pacts. An area of conflict on its periphery was also considered a threat to its security by the Soviet Union. To safeguard its global and regional interests, it tried to bring about Indo-Pakistan reconciliation after the war, which effort resulted in the Tashkent Declaration.

In the post-Tashkent years, Pak–Soviet relations witnessed a radical improvement; trade increased, aid flowed, visits multiplied, and several agreements were signed. The peak was reached in the middle of 1968 when the Russians, rejecting India's objections, agreed to supply arms to Pakistan. In April 1968, during a visit to Pakistan, Premier Kosygin pledged close co-operation and promised to finance the Kalabagh steel mill and the Roopur atomic project (in East Pakistan). A few months later, the Commander-in-Chief of the Pakistan army visited Moscow and finalized an agreement for the supply of arms to Pakistan. In the second week of March 1969, Marshal Grechko, the Soviet Defence Minister, visited Pakistan. He proposed an annual exchange of Pakistani personnel to Soviet military academies, and the visit of Soviet naval ships to Pakistan ports for repairs and supplies. The political officers accompanying Grechko advocated a 'step by step' approach in solving Indo-Pakistan disputes and advised that, for tactical reasons, Kashmir should not be made the main item in Indo-Pakistan discussions. They expressed anxiety on the political and economic situation of India, and praised Pakistan's economic performance, though they were concerned about the political turmoil going on before their eyes. Their biggest worry, however, was China. They expressed the Russian belief that, despite the cultural revolution, the Chinese would find it opportune to provoke the Soviet Union while it was heavily committed in the Middle East.

The Russians were disappointed at the downfall of Ayub Khan, in whose continuance for a few more years they had made political and economic investments, even at the cost of Indian displeasure. Ayub had symbolized for them the political and economic stability of Pakistan, as against the prevailing political chaos and poor economic performance of India. The Russians, however, continued to be friendly with the Yahya government in the expectation of persuading it towards an Indo-Pakistan detente.

On 30 May 1969, barely two months after the takeover by Yahya, Kosygin visited Pakistan. He appreciated Yahya's political initiatives for the restoration of democracy and pleaded for the building up of genuine trust and confidence in Pak–Soviet relations. Kosygin told Yahya that both India and Afghanistan wanted Pakistan's friendship but Pakistan had not responded to their overtures. He suggested that intervention by a third party would not be very fruitful, as issues such as Kashmir and Pakhtunistan between Pakistan and its two neighbours were very complicated. This, he said, was proved by the short-lived spirit of Tashkent. Kosygin urged Yahya to hold bilateral talks with Zahir Shah and Mrs Gandhi. Kosygin was very critical of China's policies, and gave a veiled warning that the 'Soviet Union could not be indifferent to the question as to who supported China in the international field'.

More specifically, Kosygin put forward the proposal for a meeting between India, Pakistan, Afghanistan, and the Soviet Union to discuss a transit trade agreement between these countries. The meeting, which he said had been suggested by Afghanistan, did not contemplate any political discussions. Other countries, like Iran and Turkey, could come in later so that the transit trade could be extended to Europe. Yahya was not very diligent in mastering official briefs for negotiations; he prided himself on being a simple soldier and behaved like one in complicated affairs of state. Kosygin left Pakistan with the impression that the President had reacted favourably to the proposal.[73]

Soon after, on 7 June 1969, L. I. Brezhnev, addressing the World Communist Conference in Moscow, suggested 'the need to create a collective security system in Asia'.[74] The Soviet government gave an *aide-mémoire* on the subject to the Pakistan government and sought its comments. The proposition, it was stated, was not meant to create a military bloc, but to ensure security on the basis of peaceful co-existence of countries having different social systems. It envisaged a non-aggression agreement between Asian countries, renouncing the use of force, guaranteeing the territorial integrity of states and non-interference in each other's internal affairs. Pakistan could not possibly accept an arrangement which amounted to formally conceding Kashmir as an integral part of India. It was obvious to the Foreign Office that the Soviet proposal was aimed at isolating China. In its reply it, *inter alia,* pointed out that any Asian security system which did not include China could only aggravate tension and promote confrontation in Asia. Meanwhile, China had also cautioned Pakistan that the transit trade agreement was the thin end of the wedge, leading to joint economic ventures and an Asian security system. The move, they asserted, was aimed against China.

Mrs Gandhi's initial reaction to the Asian security system was somewhat guarded, but later, in March 1970, the Indian government described the plan as 'a new development of some significance' and 'a declaration of the fact that the Soviet Union was as much an Asian power as a European power'.[75] India also welcomed the proposal for a five-nation conference at Kabul to discuss a transit trade agreement.[76]

Pakistan rejected both the Brezhnev plan and the transit trade proposals. The Soviet Union reacted by suspending arms supplies in early 1970. In June 1970, Yahya Khan visited Moscow and raised the issue, but he received only vague replies. Podgorny urged Yahya to meet Mrs Gandhi alone as, he said, 'ministers and officials only complicated things'. Yahya showed willingness but asked that India should not make statements to the effect that Kashmir would be excluded from discussions. During the visit, the Soviet government pledged $ 200 million for the Karachi steel mill and expressed its willingness to increase economic collaboration. A system of periodic joint consultation was also agreed to, but the supply of arms was not resumed. In November 1970, the Soviet ambassador conveyed to the President that Mrs Gandhi did not consider the time opportune for a summit meeting, and had suggested a ministerial meeting to prepare for it at some future date.

The cut-off of Soviet arms supplies was a major set-back in Pak-Soviet relations, but inevitable in the power alignments of the times. The Soviet Union had gained nothing by the supply of arms to Pakistan. It had annoyed India, and Pakistan had not acceded to any of the Soviet concerns: Kashmir was not put on the back burner to normalize relations with India through a step by step approach; the Russian initiatives for an Asian security system and transit trade arrangements were rejected; and relations with China became closer still. In August 1970, the opening of the Karakoram highway had provided China access to the Indian Ocean. And while India had supported Russia in the Sino-Soviet border clashes, Pakistan had remained neutral.

Meanwhile, the Indian political scene was becoming clearer with Mrs Gandhi gaining ascendancy over her rivals. She needed unqualified Soviet support to ensure her victory, which she eventually scored by an overwhelming majority. At about the same time, Mujib swept the polls in East Pakistan, gaining an overall majority to form the government. With Mujib and Mrs Gandhi, both anti-Chinese, leading Pakistan and India respectively, the Soviet Union was satisfied with the course of subcontinental affairs. Given this background, the deep annoyance of the Soviet Union at the disruption of the political process by the army action on 25 March becomes quite understandable.

It was reported that in March 1971, soon after obtaining an

overwhelming mandate in the elections, Mrs Gandhi had initiated a reappraisal of India's foreign policy. The draft of the Indo-Soviet Treaty was reported to have been given by the Soviet Union in September 1967, as a follow-up of Brezhnev's call for Asian collective security.[77] India had for a long time been looking for some guarantees against China and, of late, there had been developments which were bringing it closer to the Soviet Union. Matters came to a head during the East Pakistan crisis at a stage when the issues were clarified; the US–China–Pakistan combination had to be met by a clear-cut Indo-Soviet alignment. Both the Soviet Union, which was trying to keep a balance in its relationship with India and Pakistan, and India, which was wary of any semblance of military alliance, had to give up their reservations.

The Indo-Soviet Treaty signed on 9 August was followed by a joint statement by Gromyko and Swaran Singh issued on 12 August. The preamble stated that the visit of the Soviet Foreign Minister was at the invitation of the government of India, which presumably was meant to convey that the immediate initiative for the treaty had come from India. Referring to the East Pakistan situation, the statement said both sides 'considered it necessary that urgent steps be taken in *East Pakistan* for the achievement of a political solution . . . which would answer the interests of the *entire people of Pakistan*' (emphasis added).[78] In the joint statement, a mild reference to the refugee problem, the mention of East Pakistan instead of East Bengal, and the necessity of a political solution for the good of Pakistan as a whole were obviously at the insistence of the Russians. This gave the impression that, in spite of the treaty, the Russians were perhaps still hoping to retain some influence over Pakistan.

The Western reactions to the Indo-Soviet Treaty, except for Kissinger's, were generally positive. Kissinger called it a bombshell which 'we learned first from the newspapers'. Hersh, however, says that the United States had received intelligence reports that the Soviet Union was going to sign the treaty to prevent India's recognition of Bangladesh.[79] Kissinger thought that the Soviet Union had seized a strategic opportunity. He called the Indian ambassador on the day the treaty was signed, and expressed concern that 'India might draw the conclusion that it now enjoyed freedom of action towards Pakistan'. He warned the ambassador of serious consequences to Indo-US relations in case of a war between India and Pakistan.[80] These warnings, however, were neutralized by other organs of the US government. Van Hollen says that the Indo-Soviet Treaty did not cause any concern to the State Department. In fact, it was seen, he implies on the basis of a CIA report, as an instrument with which the Soviet Union might exercise restraint on India. The State Department perception was that Mrs Gandhi, being driven into a corner by the Sino-American rapprochment and pro-Pakistan US policies, had no alternative but to seek security by collaborating with the Russians.[81]

The Western media considered the treaty merely a regrettable development in increasing the influence of the Soviet Union on subcontinental affairs, but one which was due to reasons beyond India's control. *The New York Times,* in an editorial on 10 August, justified the pact as being due to 'India's desperate sense of isolation', and held the United States responsible for handing over to the Soviet Union a major foreign policy coup. The British Press showed understanding of India's predicament, and gave some sensible advice to Mrs Gandhi on how best to go about achieving her objective of an independent East Pakistan.[82]

In the pluralist polity of India the reaction was mixed, though initially there was a general feeling of relief from the growing sense of isolation and inaction of the government. The ideologically anti-Soviet parties, considerable in number and influence, feared undue Soviet interference in India's policies. These quarters doubted whether the Russians would really come to the aid of India when it came to the crunch.[83] On second thoughts, the major disappointment to the generally hawkish public opinion was the joint statement which, by emphasizing a political solution of the crisis for the good of 'the entire people of Pakistan', seemed to rule out any military solution by India. This nullified the military provision of the treaty which, in any case, had only called for consultations in the event of 'either [India or the Soviet Union] being subjected to an attack or a threat thereof'.

The Awami League leadership in Calcutta was equally disappointed. They feared, Peter Hazelhurst reported in *The Times* of 20 August, that Mrs Gandhi had shifted her position under Soviet pressure. He opined that the political solution mentioned in the statement was open to interpretation; a settlement by Yahya with the West Pakistanis and some 'turncoats in East Bengal' might be claimed to have fulfilled the terms of the Indo-Soviet joint statement.

Another view of the treaty was that India had neither the desire nor the need to invoke the mutual defence clause in resolving the East Pakistan crisis. What the treaty had provided was a deterrent against any interference by Pakistan in India's training of guerrillas and providing of logistic support for the continuation of the civil war in East Pakistan. The repeated mention of the identity of views by the Indian and Soviet leaders implied the latter's support for this Indian policy, as long as it did not lead to war. This restraint suited India because, except for the Hindu extremist parties, Indian opinion in general favoured the least-cost method for bringing about the independence of Bangladesh through greater assistance to the *mukti bahini*.[84] Palit makes the same point slightly differently when he says that India signed the treaty 'more in the nature of surety than the forging of a coalition or bloc', and further 'neutralization of the Chinese threat'.[85] To these considerations may be added Kissinger's assessment that the treaty ensured for India a reliable source of arms supply in case of a war with Pakistan.[86]

The Indo-Soviet Treaty dampened the Pakistani euphoria which had been generated by the Sino-American detente. The immediate reaction of the Foreign Office to the treaty was rather mild. It conceded that 'recent developments in Sino-American relations may be one of the factors leading to the emergence of this new military pattern in Asia'.[87] But two days later, on 11 August, it reacted sharply to the Indo-Soviet joint communique which urged a political solution in East Pakistan, and called it 'unnecessary and gratuitious advice'.[88] On 12 August, it was reported that Sultan Muhammad Khan had been invited to visit Moscow in the first week of September.[89]

In a cynical defiance of the emerging combination of hostile forces and world opinion, it was officially announced on 9 August that the trial of Mujib, for waging war against Pakistan and for other offences, would be held before a special military tribunal, in camera, from 11 August. The decision exhausted whatever goodwill was still left for Pakistan in the world community. U Thant, in a statement on 10 August, informed the Pakistan government that the trial would 'inevitably have repercussions outside the borders of Pakistan'; the Foreign Office promptly lodged a sharp protest with the Secretary-General against his 'attempt to interfere in Pakistan's internal affairs'. Simultaneously, with a perverse sense of timing, Pakistan sought UN help 'to defuse the threatening situation', by proposing to the president of the Security Council the establishment of a good offices' committee of Council members to visit India and Pakistan.[90] Nothing, of course, came of this initiative.

Kissinger has called the trial a 'truculent move' of a desperate man. Eleven senators and fifty-eight representatives of the US Congress protested against it, and Secretary of State Rogers conveyed the American concern to the Pakistan ambassador. But Nixon would not agree to any serious pressure on Yahya to resolve political problems. It is surprising that a ruthless politician of Nixon's calibre could imagine Mrs Gandhi buckling under at the mere threat of aid cut-off and refraining from pursuing what she considered a matter of such vital national interest to India.[91]

On 17 August, Kosygin, through a verbal message delivered by the Soviet ambassador, expressed deep concern over reports of the trial of the 'pre-eminent political worker of Pakistan', Mujibur Rahman, and warned of serious consequences if a severe sentence was given to him. In the same message, Kosygin assured Pakistan that the Indo-Soviet Treaty was not directed against anybody, and that the Soviet Union was ready to continue developing relations with Pakistan to strengthen peace and security. In the context of this message, the Soviet ambassador had a series of meeting with the Foreign Office and the President; the meeting with the President on 17 August, according to knowledgeable circles in Islamabad, was not a very pleasant one.

The wilful military regime had eroded the independent advisory role of permanent services in the policymaking process. The silence or servility of the top civil servants, during the post-army operation period, was noted in the proceedings of the President's weekly meetings. In the same context, it will be instructive to describe here two meetings held by the Foreign Secretary and Major-General Umer and attended by Pakistani envoys; the first for fifteen envoys in Middle Eastern countries and North Africa at Tehran on 21–22 August; and the other, for those in Europe and America later at Geneva. One expected an in-depth discussion of the implications of the Indo-Soviet pact and some plain talking by professional diplomats, who were having a difficult time with an indefensible brief in their host countries; nothing like that happened. Quoted below are the impressions of the three participants of these meetings.[92]

Umer

> I came out with the idea of holding meetings of ambassadors. They did not know what was happening in Pakistan. There was all sorts of propaganda about atrocities. Pakistani officials did not have a clear understanding as to what was being thought abroad about Pakistan. I took Roedad Khan, Sultan Muhammad, and one or two others. But instead of telling us anything, they merely asked us to give them the line on which they should proceed. Only Agha Shahi was giving some sort of realistic diplomatic picture. But his dispatches were not finding their way to Yahya.

Roedad Khan

> Umer, I, and Sultan Muhammad addressed the meetings. We dwelt at length on the Bengali plans of secession, and how the army had saved Pakistan. We assured them that everything was under control and that the majority of Bengalis was with us. As evidence of Bengali plans, we referred to the television film which was prepared by Aslam Azhar. No one spoke or reacted, but they all requested us not to show the film.

Agha Shahi

> The ambassadors meeting in Geneva was a farce. General Umer and others briefed us that all was under control in Pakistan. No issues were raised or the desirability of political settlement discussed. We were told of impending political plans. But there was no discussion on them. The conference did not discuss any substantive issues. No one seemed to be interested in the ambassadors' views. The Foreign Office was playing no role. It was snubbing the ambassadors and to every new development was reacting with 'no intervention in our internal affairs'.

In the first week of September, Sultan Muhammad Khan visited Moscow, which had acquired a *locus standi* in subcontinental affairs now. But he had nothing positive to offer to form the basis of a dialogue between India and Pakistan, which the Soviet Union might be induced to promote. In the meeting with Sultan Muhammad on 6 September, Kosygin again urged Pakistan to stop repression and persecution, and to find a genuine political solution to the East Pakistan crisis. On 29 September, in the joint communique issued at the conclusion of Mrs Gandhi's visit to Moscow, India and the Soviet Union called for urgent measures to reach a political solution to enable the refugees to return.[93]

The Soviet Union continued to administer warnings through diplomatic channels, and press for a political solution in public pronouncements. On 7 October, Kosygin wrote to Yahya that the Soviet Union was convinced of the peaceful intentions of the Indian government and took exception to the bellicose statements of Pakistani leaders. He accused the 'Martial Law Administration of Pakistan' of shifting responsibility for its internal struggle to India, thereby creating grounds to launch armed action against its neighbour at any time. Kosygin warned Yahya, in no uncertain terms, that 'the initiative in unleashing military action against India, with which the USSR is bound by lasting friendship, will meet with the most resolute reaction in the Soviet Union.' At the same time, on 8 October, Kosygin joined the Algerian leaders in declaring 'respect for the national unity and territorial integrity of Pakistan', and appealing to both India and Pakistan to find a peaceful solution to their problems in the spirit of non-interference and mutual respect.[94] The Soviet public organizations and media, during the same period, mounted a campaign against 'irresponsible and adventurist' elements in Pakistan for creating a war psychosis in the subcontinent.[95] The Shah of Iran arranged a meeting between Yahya and Podgorny on 15 October at Persepolis, during the celebrations of the 2500th anniversary of the Iranian monarchy. Yahya explained the circumstances under which army action had had to be taken. Podgorny accepted the right of the government to suppress the rebellion, but questioned the objective of arresting Mujib, who was the representative of 70 million people. Podgorny assured Yahya that 'we stand for united one Pakistan. We oppose the separation of any part of Pakistan', but urged that Mujib should be released, in the interest of a political solution. Yahya said that was impossible; Mujib had committed treason.

At the end of October, the Soviet Deputy Foreign Minister, Nikolai Firyubin, visited India to hold 'mutual consultations' as provided in Article 9 of the Indo-Soviet Treaty, 'in the event that any of the parties is . . . threatened with attack'; India had invoked the provision because it had considered itself threatened with attack. The communique issued after the conclusion of consultations expressed the complete agreement of both parties in their assessment of the situation. The visit was accompanied by reports of large-scale supplies of Russian arms.[96]

With the rapidly deteriorating military situation and the isolation of Pakistan, the Soviet warnings, through diplomatic channels and the Russian media, of serious consequences, became more and more harsh and frequent. On 23 November, when war was imminent, the Soviet leaders sent another message to Yahya, blaming Pakistan for the tension in the subcontinent as the result of mass repression in East Pakistan and the removal of its well-known leaders. It warned that an armed attack by Pakistan on India, 'under whatever pretext', would lead to most resolute action by the Soviet Union 'with all its ensuing consequences'. Four days later, on 27 November, as the military confrontation continued to escalate, Kosygin sent another message to Yahya appealing to him 'to display courage and have a political settlement in East Pakistan on the basis of the elections of 1970'.

Perhaps the Russians genuinely wanted to avert a war in the subcontinent, and did not subscribe to the Indian commitment to the creation of independent Bangladesh. This was the dominant view of the Western media, which regarded the Soviet Union as the restraining hand on India. A united Pakistan under Mujib was certainly desirable from the Soviet Union's point of view. But even if East Pakistan ultimately seceded, Russian interests would still have required good relations with West Pakistan due to its geopolitical importance and the China factor. Viewed in this light, the repeated warnings of the Russian leaders could be interpreted as sincere attempts to prevent a war in which they would be obliged to take an open stand against Pakistan. Apart from the heavy-handed ways of conveying it, the position taken by the Soviet Union in respect of the East Pakistan crisis was, after all not different from that of the United States.

* * *

Mrs Gandhi, having firmed up Soviet obligations under the treaty during her September visit to Moscow, embarked on an extended tour of Western capitals on 25 October. This was intended to demolish whatever reservations that might still have been there in the Western world about the validity of an independent Bangladesh, to project India as the victim of a truculent and irresponsible neighbour, and to place on record a self-righteous India doing everything to avoid war with Pakistan.

The two countries which were crucial to the fulfillment of India's grand design were the UK and the USA. To the British Prime Minister, Edward Heath, Mrs Gandhi gave a warning that, unless Pakistan undertook immediate negotiations with Mujib, the Indian government would not be able to resist the domestic pressure to resolve the refugee problem through military means. On 7 November, immediately after the meeting, Heath wrote Yahya saying that 'We must take this very seriously. . . . Following my talks with the Indian Prime Minister, I remain deeply apprehensive.' He doubted the credibility of measures recently taken by Yahya to induct a representative government without the release of Mujib or the participation of the exiled Awami League leadership. Heath expressed his readiness to help in any way possible. Later, in response to Yahya's personal message of 23 November, Heath strongly repeated his advice of starting a dialogue 'with those who command the confidence of the people of East Pakistan' and offered his good offices 'in any way in which we can help'.

The US government was consistently advising Pakistan to find a political solution to avoid war with India. While the State Department wanted to push Yahya hard in this direction, the White House was saying the same thing in a much lower key, which gave the wrong message to Yahya. In the first week of October, M. A. Alvie, Additional Foreign Secretary, went to the US to deliver a personal letter from Yahya to Nixon seeking US assistance for urgent consideration of the situation by the Security Council. Agha Shahi recalls the relish and bravado with which Alvie and a lady member of the delegation talked about war with India. The ignorance of the advisers of the regime of the way the world was moving was quite depressing to the knowledgeable permanent representative. Yahya's message was delivered to Kissinger who, while promising to place the matter before President Nixon, gave his personal view that 'more could be done by talking to India and the Soviets'. In the Security Council, he remarked, the Soviet Union would exercise her right to veto, and the debates might also influence US public opinion and worsen Pakistan's image. This advice, which might have been correct at the time, was taken so literally by the Foreign Office that in the rapidly changing situation it was not reconsidered, in spite of the opinion of many friendly countries reported by Agha Shahi.

On 11 October, the US government, in a strongly-worded

message, expressed its deep concern over the East Pakistan situation, and urged the government of Pakistan to urgently find a political solution which would include direct participation of the elected East Pakistan leaders. On 30 October, in a personal letter to Yahya, President Nixon repeated the same advice.

On the eve of Mrs Gandhi's visit to Washington, Pakistan's Ambassador N. A. M. Raza had a lengthy meeting with Kissinger, who emphasized the need for a bold political initiative by Yahya. While assuring Raza that the US would advise the Indian Prime Minister to exercise restraint, Kissinger enquired about the proposals for a dialogue with the Awami League leaders which had been conveyed through Ambassador Farland. It was necessary for even the friendly White House to confront Mrs Gandhi with some plausible political initiative to persuade her to desist from escalating the crisis.

There are two interpretations of Mrs Gandhi's meeting with Nixon on 4 November—one that of the White House and the other that of the rest of the US establishment. During the conversation, Nixon says, he 'was disturbed by the fact that although Mrs Gandhi professed her devotion to peace, she would not make any concrete offers for de-escalating the tension.' Even as they were talking, Nixon complains, Mrs Gandhi knew that her advisers and generals were 'planning to intervene in East Pakistan and were considering contingency plans for attacking West Pakistan as well.'[97]

Seymour M. Hersh defends Mrs Gandhi who, he says, had come on a humanitarian mission to plead with the US President to ask Yahya to stop the killings. But she was treated shabbily by Nixon. On the first day, he referred in the welcoming speech to the devastating floods in India, instead of to the refugee problem, and on the second, he kept her waiting for forty-five minutes. 'At that point', Hersh says, 'only Nixon and Kissinger believed there was any chance of a negotiated settlement between Yahya Khan and the Bengalis.'[98] Van Hollen, giving an inside view of the State Department, also thinks that it was no longer possible for any negotiations to succeed, even with the participation of Mujib. A 'combination of factors', which included Soviet support and Chinese neutralization, he says, had made 'the military option increasingly attractive to India'.[99]

The fact of the matter is that, according to the Indian writers themselves, the Indian war machinery had been put in motion as early as April. In November, at the time of the visit of Mrs Gandhi to the USA, it was all set to go for a full-fledged war on both the eastern and western fronts. This is borne out by Van Hollen's own conclusion that no negotiations would have succeeded at that late stage. If it were so, and Mrs Gandhi knew it, then her visit could only be for the record to justify, later, the impending military action. It takes time to prepare and launch a war of the magnitude of the Indo-Pakistan one. It could not really have been the frustration arising from the attitude of Nixon and Kissinger that led Mrs Gandhi to plunge India into an attack on East Pakistan, barely three weeks after her return to India.

On 14 November, Farland informed the Foreign Office that the US ambassador in New Delhi had been told by the State Department to convey to the Indian government that 'the US would look with less than appreciation and understanding on Indian military involvement in East Pakistan'; and the US ambassador in Moscow had been asked to request the USSR to urge restraint on India. The US government also conveyed to Yahya their 'understanding of the pressures he is under and an appreciation of the restraint he has shown so far'. Towards the middle of November, Sultan Muhammad, during his visit to the US, was asked about the proposals for talks with Mujib and other Awami Leaguers in Calcutta, sent through Farland to Yahya. Sultan Muhammad knew nothing about them. On 25 November, in a last bid to prevent war, under Nixon's directive, Secretary of State Rogers informed the Soviet Union and India that Yahya was prepared to meet the representatives of the Awami League. These efforts, discussed in the next chapter, came to nothing, as Yahya disowned any understanding on the subject with Farland. In any case, it was too late. India had invested too much in political, diplomatic, and military preparations to miss the opportunity to break up Pakistan. On 23 November, Yahya wrote to Nixon, requesting his personal intervention to prevent war. Nixon replied on 27 November, 'assuring Yahya that the American government intended to continue as a concerned friend of Pakistan to act in ways that hopefully might help prevent war between India and Pakistan'. Up to the end of November, Nixon, in carefully-worded exchanges of communications, continued to assure Yahya of political, diplomatic, and moral support, without any mention of physical intervention. Yahya and the Foreign Office failed to read between the lines of Nixon's correspondence. The intimate relationship with the White House, strengthened by the visit of Kissinger and his personal involvement in the East Pakistan crisis, the personal rapport with Farland, and Nixon's messages all led Yahya to believe that, in the last resort, the American government would ensure the integrity of Pakistan in any military confrontation with India.

As Indo-Soviet consultations were going on, Russian arms were being rushed to India, and even the Chinese officials were privately suggesting that 'India and Pakistan must talk together', it was decided, in early November, to send a high-powered delegation to the People's Republic of China. It was intended not only to seek diplomatic and material support, but also to boost the nation's morale and send a message to India that Pakistan was not without powerful friends. At the end of September, China was informed by the Foreign Office of the Indian military concentration on Pakistan's borders. It was suggested that the military delegations of the two countries meet in secret to assess the threat to peace in the region and consider measures necessary to counter them. Later, it was proposed that these meetings should be well publicized.

Bhutto, who was on a private visit abroad, was recalled in great haste and asked to lead the delegation, which included the Chief of General Staff of the army, the C-in-C air force, and the Chief of Staff of the navy. The visit of the delegation, from 5 to 8 November, did not bring about any radical change in China's position. Chi Peng-fei, the acting Chinese Foreign Minister, publicly assured Pakistan of resolute support for the 'State sovereignty and national independence' of Pakistan.[100] But during private discussions it had become clear that the Chinese public expression for unity and integrity was going to be in a lower key. The Chinese did not think that the Soviet Union and the USA would be able to prevent India from going to war, and, while they were willing to meet the defence needs of Pakistan, they were not willing to go to the extent where this assistance itself might induce Pakistan to go to war. But, in case of war, further assistance was promised. Active intervention by the Chinese in the event of war was not discussed and, from the ambience of the meetings, it could not be inferred. The Chinese, under pressure on their Soviet borders, were, in fact, greatly concerned by the uncertainties created by the crisis in the subcontinent. The Pakistan government, however, domestically projected a more optimistic picture of the 1965 type.

* * *

The Shah of Iran was most worried about the implications of the Indo-Soviet treaty to Iran's security. He saw the treaty as one more Soviet military alliance, thwarting Iranian ambitions as a regional power by its encirclement by the Soviet grid of New Delhi–Baghdad–Cairo. At the same time, Iran was having problems with the Arabs due to its occupation of the Persian Gulf islands, Little and Big Thumbs. As a gesture of a peaceful and friendly neighbour, among the great powers the Soviet Union was the only one to send its head of state to attend the anniversary celebrations at Persepolis. In these circumstances, Iran feared that unreserved support to Pakistan, which was backed by China, against Soviet-aligned India would mean taking on Russia also. For Iran, it was vital to maintain friendly relations with its traditional enemy, Soviet Russia, to avert a threat to its security. It was not, therefore, as easy for Iran to extend moral and military assistance to Pakistan now, as it had been during the 1965 war when Russia had been neutral in the subcontinental conflict.

On 15 November, the Iranian Foreign Minister assured the Pakistan ambassador, rather vaguely, of full support, without committing any military assistance. On 23 November, Yahya sent a personal message to the Shah, on the same pattern as he was addressing to other heads of state. The Iranians were still not sure about how to respond to the Pakistani requests for military assistance. The Pakistan ambassador, who called on the court minister on 25 November to convey the contents of Yahya's message, was asked whether practical Chinese help was assured in the event of full-scale war. On receiving a reply in the affirmative, the court minister asked the information minister to arrange publicity of support to Pakistan, but on the vital question of military assistance the court minister was noncommittal. On 28 November, the ambassador was received in audience by the Shah who made it clear that, as a result of the Indo-Soviet treaty, it was impossible for him to extend open support to Pakistan in the Indo-Pakistan conflict in any manner which might invite Soviet hostility. Iran's security environment, the Shah added, had been aggravated by the Arab threat in the Persian Gulf. Consequently, Iran could not possibly supply Pakistan with major items of military hardware, although it would still try to help as much as possible. The Shah was disappointed that he could not arrange a dialogue between India and Pakistan, and felt aggrieved that Pakistan did not heed his advice regarding a political settlement in East Pakistan. 'Everybody believed' the Shah said, 'that I had a great deal of influence in Pakistan, but in actual fact I had very little influence indeed, and my sincerest words of advice were ignored'.

* * *

The UN Secretary-General had drawn the attention of the Security Council to the threat to peace in the subcontinent as early as July. At that time, Pakistan wanted a meeting of the Council but the members were not keen to be drawn into an acrimonious debate on Indo-Pakistan issues. After some initial reservations about internationalizing the East Pakistan crisis, Pakistan first suggested the posting of UN observers on both sides of the East Pakistan border, and, later, a Good Offices Committee of the Council members to visit India and Pakistan and defuse the situation. There was some sympathetic response to these suggestions from the UN members but India and the Soviet Union rejected them. On 20 October, the Secretary-General made an offer of personal good offices. Yahya not only accepted it immediately, on 21 October, and invited U Thant to visit India and Pakistan, but also suggested the withdrawal of the forces of both India and Pakistan to a mutually agreed safe distance.[101] India, however, rejected the proposals. During November, Agha Shahi at various times brought to the notice of the president of the Security Council the hostile activities of India in East Pakistan and the massing of troops on Pakistan's borders.[102] Yahya brought the situation to the notice of U Thant on 23 and 29 November and pressed him to intervene. The communications of both Yahya and Agha Shahi, however, carefully avoided any suggestion of a meeting of the Security Council. U Thant, in so many words, made it clear to Yahya on 26 November that, having brought the situation to the notice of the Security Council, he had gone as far as he could under the UN charter.

In appears intriguing that Pakistan was asking the Secretary-General to take a position which was not acceptable to India and the Soviet Union, but was not asking for a meeting of the Security Council, where friendly countries like the US and China would support its case. The military situation had been deteriorating from September onward; the Indian army and the *mukti bahini* had increased pressures on the borders as well as inside East Pakistan. The Western media was consistently reporting imminent war. U Thant had been constantly expressing concern over the situation since July. India and the Soviet Union had invoked the treaty provision of consultations under conditions of threat. By accepting the proposal for UN observers on the East Pakistan border, Pakistan had given up its reservations on internationalization of the crisis. Why was the one forum where, in November, the blatant intervention of India in East Pakistan could have been highlighted before the world community not invoked?

In early October, Kissinger preferred talks with India and the Soviet Union in the context of the forthcoming visit of Mrs Gandhi, whom he thought Nixon would be able to restrain on the basis of Kissinger's ongoing efforts to arrange negotiations between the Awami Leaguers and Yahya. But Mrs Gandhi was adamant, and war had become a certainty after her return from Washington. Agha Shahi informed the Foreign Office of anxious enquiries by friendly delegates about Pakistan's intentions regarding the Security Council meeting. But he was asked on 23 November to make no move for it without the express instructions of the government. Shahi, in desperation, resorted to a subterfuge to persuade the Foreign Office to reconsider:

> On 22 November came the news that India had attacked East Pakistan. Mrs Gandhi had said that if Indian troops were stopped it will be considered aggression. I thought this was the right time to go to the Security Council.
>
> I talked to the Turkish ambassador who said that now that India had entered East Pakistan the attitude of the countries was changing. He wondered why Pakistan did not want to go to the Security Council.
>
> I reported this view, quoting the words of the Turkish ambassador, to the Foreign Office to make the message more effective.
>
> I was specifically instructed not to do any thing by way of going to the Security Council.

On 24 November, the Americans also indicated that Pakistan should move for a Security Council meeting. But Yahya was not in a hurry even after the full-fledged war had started on 3 December. He was reported to have mentioned once or twice that, in the long run, Pakistan could not hold out militarily against India. Sooner or later, military resistance in East Pakistan would end, India would shift its forces from there to the western front, and Pakistan would lose whatever temporary advantage it had started with in the west. Apparently, he was confident of achieving some short-term gains on the western front, before the UN pressures for a cease-fire developed. This, he thought, would achieve three purposes: firstly, the conflict would focus the attention of the world on India's role, and compel it to do something; secondly, pressure on East Pakistan would be reduced by gains on the western borders; and thirdly, it would give Pakistan something to bargain with. Apart from these expectations, any discussion in the Security Council would bring up the question of a political settlement with the elected leadership of East Pakistan which remained a distasteful prospect for the regime. The mystical belief in the superiority of (Punjabi) Muslim soldiers over the Hindus was so persistently inculcated among the West Pakistani public and the army, that the higher command itself came to believe in it and overlooked the professional demands of a modern war. In this syndrome, a meeting of the Security Council was seen as restricting the army's freedom of action.

The failure to project Indian aggression immediately after 22 November severely weakened the credibility of the scale and intent of Indian military action alleged by Pakistan later in the Security Council. The overwhelming vote in the General Assembly on 9 December showed that the world community, whatever its reservations about Pakistan policies up to that point, was not willing to countenance an open armed attack on a member state. Pakistan was not without friends among the superpowers of the day. Yahya apparently regretted the decision, at a later stage, when in anguish he reminded the Americans of their October advice not to go to the Security Council.

CHAPTER 10

West Pakistan's Responses

The insensitivity of the influential classes of West Pakistan to the physical repression and political manipulation in the East Wing, after the army operation, exposed their pretensions as the guardians of the integrity of the Islamic Republic of Pakistan. There was no public protest at the outrageous policies, and no demand for national reconciliation. In view of the condemnation of Yahya and his generals ever since the separation of East Pakistan, it is necessary to put on record the complete endorsement, and the active participation in the execution of their policies by the dominant and vocal classes of West Pakistan.

The military and civil bureaucracies, big business, urban middle classes, elected representatives, and the independent Press welcomed the army operation. The decision-making elements in the establishment were predominantly from the Punjab; other segments located in Lahore and Karachi exercised considerable influence over national affairs. They all felt threatened by the Awami League challenge to the established economic and political order. Yahya could accommodate the Bengali demands only within the conventional state structure, which alone could protect and sustain these West Pakistani interests. For the same reasons, the newly-emerged Bengali middle class could not accept the traditional East–West relationships. Few, if any, in the West Pakistan establishment recognized the elemental nature of Bengali nationalist forces. They all expected the army to restore peace and the *status quo,* and continue with its rule. In the evening of 26 March, on his return from Dhaka, when Bhutto said that 'By the grace of God, Pakistan has at last been saved', he was giving public expression to the deep sense of relief in West Pakistan at the army action.[1] In fact, the words 'at last' depicted the general feeling that it should have been undertaken earlier. It was an ill-advised remark, but at the time it was widely endorsed. Bhutto himself, with his populist socialist slogans, however, did not inspire much confidence in the power centres; he posed a different kind of danger. Mujib was determined to extricate East Pakistan from the West Pakistan-dominated power structure; Bhutto was committed to reforming the privileged order of West Pakistan.

The army was given the open-ended objective of restoring the authority of the central government, by the President. No human parameters were laid down by the high command for the conduct of the operations. They were left to be subjectively determined by each field commander, according to his own sense of honour. The military virtues of fairness and protecting the unarmed, women, and children were soon eroded in the bitterness of civil war, under an inadequate professional leadership. The rebels were not bound by any code of conduct, but the army was. In April, I heard about the psychological breakdowns of a few officers under the strain of civilian casualties, and of fighting their erstwhile comrade-in-arms. One of the officers reported to have been court-martialled for refusing to take action under these circumstances was a highly decorated hero of the 1965 Indo–Pakistan war. Other than these isolated cases, the army, composed entirely of West Pakistani men and officers, as a class, did what it considered its duty. On the whole, the conduct of individual officers in East Pakistan and the corporate thinking of the army implied that the objective of the operation was the final solution of Bengali nationalism. Yahya's persistent refusal to address himself seriously to the political aspects of the East Pakistan crisis, and the irresponsible and vulgar utterances of the Commander Eastern Command, widely talked about in army and civilian circles at the time, brought ignominy to the nation.

In March, the West Pakistani civil servants in Islamabad and elsewhere, with few exceptions, agreed to the inevitability and even the desirability of armed action to restore order in East Pakistan. Their support, however, did not represent an irrevocable commitment which follows from participation in decision-making, as it did in the case of the army high command. Whatever their personal feelings about Bengali extremists, the civil servants were inclined towards a political compromise, after the army's failure to impose its will on East Pakistan. The senior civil servants, privately, took a dim view of the unsophisticated handling of civil affairs by the army, and were generally disillusioned with the regime in the later period of the crisis, and through informal channels pressed for a political compromise. M. M. Ahmed says:

> A fortnight after the army action, I had suggested to Yahya to hand over the political problems to the civilians. At that time I had got a paper prepared by Sartaj Aziz on the financial position of the two Wings. I sent it to the President pointing out that at this stage it was not in the interest of East Pakistan to secede because it was their opportunity now to get additional resources for East Pakistan development [in other words it was in the interest of West Pakistan to let East Pakistan go if it so wished. It was perhaps this paper mentioned by Karim]. Soon after the army action I asked Yahya's permission to publish a white paper on economic facts and the issues of the March negotiations. But the President and others didn't agree. They said, 'who would believe them?'.

The elected politicians of West Pakistan, representing all parties, supported the army action by words or silence, mostly by words and actions. They all condemned Indian interference for good reasons, but did not realize that the opportunity for it was provided by the failure to resolve the East-West political relationship. One elected leader said that 'He (Yahya) is no longer a soldier President but a popular President'.[2] Others urged Yahya to promulgate a Constitution of his own.[3] Maulana Syed Abul Ala Maudoodi, chief of the Jamaat-i-Islami, fully justified the army action.[4] They all gave the call for unity, not for national reconciliation and finding a way to live together, but to stand up against India. Bhutto was anxious to have power handed over to him in West Pakistan to resolve the national crisis.[5] The rightist and 'Islam-loving' leaders, elected and unelected, were equally determined not to let anything like that happen.[6] Instead of demanding resumption of the constitutional process to bring the Bengali leadership back into national politics, they took advantage of the East–West polarization. To snatch the maximum number of seats vacated by the disqualification of Awami league members, the politicians conspired with the military regime as will be described later.

The capitalist classes of Lahore and Karachi formed a powerful and vocal lobby. They protected their group interests through well-endowed trade bodies and chambers of commerce, the Press, and contacts with senior civil and military officers. The heavy financial stakes of the big business houses of West Pakistan in the East Wing have been described in Chapter 3. Their interests required full support to the regime's policy of maintaining the existing inter-Wing economic relationships.

The West Pakistan Press in 1971 included three major privately-owned independent dailies—Urdu *Nawa-i-Waqt* Lahore, Urdu *Jang*, Karachi and Rawalpindi, and English *Dawn* Karachi. Apart from these and some Urdu and English newspapers with a limited circulation, the Press, the domestic news agency (Associated Press of Pakistan), and the radio and television networks were wholly controlled by the government. Generally speaking, the privately-owned newspapers enjoyed a fair degree of freedom to take independent stands on issues; they were able to influence government policies even under the military regime.[7] Following the army action, they all lent their full support to it. They continued to toe the official line until the fall of Dhaka, in violation of their professional obligation to inform the people of the objective conditions in East Pakistan; in fact, at times they appeared more aggressive than the regime itself and seemed to be goading it to intensify defiance of world opinion. The martial law regime, with its regulations and informal pressures, no doubt, would not have allowed them to publish uninhibited accounts of the excesses of the army, which were being splashed in the world media. But there was no justification for banner headlines creating war hysteria, editorials praising the government for giving up the political process and urging it on in the same direction, and not questioning the aims and limits of army action. Under the precarious security circumstances in which the country was placed, this was not very responsible behaviour. The regulations may have prohibited publication of certain news items; they did not lay down the editorial contents or prescribe headlines.

A perusal of the issues of these papers, April–December 1971, makes depressing reading. The main features of their presentation of the East Pakistan crisis, which both reflected and moulded the perceptions of the West Pakistani intelligentsia, deserve to be noted. Firstly, the same issue of the newspaper would proclaim normalcy on the front page in one column, and the entry of the army into yet another town, after overcoming fierce resistance from the rebels, in the next one. The extracts of the dispatches of the foreign Press were reproduced in a mutilated form and out of context. Secondly, the editorials were chauvinistic and sycophantic; for example, the *Dawn* editorial of 4 April called President Yahya the soldier-statesman to whom, it said, the nation looked up 'with the same confidence . . . [to] meet this [Indian] challenge from without just as he firmly faced the threat of disintegration from within when Awami League's obduracy and adamant unreasonableness left no other course open . . .' *Nawa-i-Waqt,* true to form, in its editorial of 14 April invoked the usual West Pakistan bogies of Hindu influence, anti-Islamic forces, and the promotion of the Bengali language, and urged that they should all be strongly curbed. The purely internal political aspects of the crisis found no mention in the Press coverage; the entire focus was on Indian interference, which distorted the public perception of the Bengali grievances. The Indian interference, though it certainly aggravated the situation, was, in a way, a secondary issue. This gave rise to another contradiction; the crisis was attributed to external causes yet there was insistence, in April and May, that it was an internal affair of Pakistan. In the later months, the coverage was limited to favourable comments on the sincerity of Yahya and his tortuous political initiatives, and foreign conspiracies against Pakistan. Those of us who were serving in East Pakistan, on our visits to the West found its Press and people totally out of touch with the ground realities in the East Wing and apparently they could not have cared less. Thirdly, no one questioned the aims and objectives of the army action. The rightist Press urged war with India and postponement of any idea of reverting to a constitutional process. A number of editors and reporters occasionally visited East Pakistan, and they saw and were told what was happening there. Yet they, on return, were no wiser in that they did not temper their news analyses and editorial policies, even if they could not write what they had seen. To the Press, Hindu and Jewish conspiracies remained the main explanation of the crisis, and use of force the only viable instrument of policy to counter them. Lastly, the ban on political activities and censorship of these activities imposed by the regime was, in practice, applied by the West Pakistan Press only to East Pakistan politicians; the government political propaganda and the political statements of West Pakistan leaders were freely published. The Bengali case was deliberately blacked out, depriving the people of a balanced view of national affairs. Like all other institutions, in this grave national predicament, the Press failed to raise the voice of sanity.

It will be seen from the above that the interests or inclinations of the dominant classes of West Pakistan converged to support the Yahya regime and its policies in East Pakistan, which ultimately led to disaster. They all agreed that the army should continue to rule until such time as it could subdue the intransigent Bengali nationalism.

Yahya's broadcast of 26 March had given no indication of the political objectives of the army action. It was later reported that he had some sort of plan to set up an interim government in East Pakistan, headed by a right-wing politician, to be followed by fresh elections to the provincial assembly; a similar government was to be set up in West Pakistan under Bhutto or his nominee.[8] Any such plan was, for the time being, submerged in the bloody and drawn-out army operations. But, behind the scenes, political negotiations went on with West Pakistan leaders. After having heard Yahya's broadcast, Bhutto met Peerzada the same night and, while supporting limited military action, advised a solution of a political nature. On 14 April, Bhutto sent his aide, Ghulam Mustafa Khar, to Peerzada with a memorandum suggesting initiation of the democratic process at least in the West Wing, if it was not immediately possible in East Pakistan. He thought this would induce the Bengalis to fall in line. The domestic power struggle after the army action and the dispersal of the Awami League leadership in exile or in detention had gravitated to West Pakistan. Bhutto started a campaign for transfer of power in April. On 4 May he suggested that the formation of a representative government in West Pakistan, under an interim Constitution, would give a 'magnetic incentive' to the people of East Pakistan 'to bury the hatchet'.[9] He continued this pressure on the regime during May and June.[10]

* * *

The major political initiative of Yahya Khan was announced on 28 June. He had earlier given an indication of the lines on which he was formulating his political plan at a press conference on 24 May. Bhutto had his contacts in the army, and he had come to know of the regime's plan to renew its pre-election efforts to bring about a merger of various factions of the Muslim League, before implementing its constitutional arrangements. A day before the broadcast, 27 June, he wrote to Peerzada protesting against these manoeuvres which, he thought were directed against him. Nevertheless, Yahya went ahead with his broadcast, hinting that 'we must eschew this business of . . . sub-parties within a party.' The main features of the 28 June plan were: (i) the Awami League members of the National and East Pakistan Assemblies 'who have taken part in anti-State activities or have committed criminal acts or have indulged in anti-social activities will be disqualified from the membership'. The vacancies so caused, after investigations, would be filled through by-elections; (ii) meanwhile, an expert committee was preparing the Constitution which would be subject to amendment by the National Assembly according to the procedure provided in the Constitution itself; (iii) after the Constitution was ready and the by-elections had been completed, the President would summon the National and Provincial Assemblies, and governments would be formed both in the provinces and the Centre; but (iv) the plan in its entirety would be launched only after 'a reasonable amount of normalcy returns to the country'. In spite of persistent claims in the media, the President admitted that the country, that is East Pakistan, was not normal even after more than three months of the army operation. Yahya hoped to implement the complete plan in about four months.[11]

In fact, work on the plan had already started. In April, Yahya had called a meeting of M. M. Ahmed, Cornelius, Peerzada, and Hasan, and told them that he had decided to give the country a Constitution. He formed a committee, consisting of these four and G. W. Choudhury, to frame a Constitution, and asked them to make use of the draft prepared by Choudhury and incorporate in it such points of the Awami League as were acceptable. Initially, unsure of public reaction and perhaps as suggested by Bhutto, Yahya wanted to promulgate only an interim Constitution to induct selected political representation into the government. On 26 May, in a meeting, attended by all the committee members including Choudhury and presided over by the President, Cornelius presented the drafts of the proclamation and interim Constitution. By this time, Yahya had found that he had the full support of West Pakistani politicians who wanted him to impose a Constitution as the only way to counter the Bengali demands. Yahya informed the committee that he had now decided to give the country a permanent Constitution; the meeting 'appreciated that the political atmosphere now obtaining in the country was conducive to the acceptance of a Constitutional instrument to be given by the President to the Nation.' He gave the following directions to the committee.[12]

(i) The Islamic provisions should be kept intact; the President mentioned that Mujib did not want Pakistan to be called an Islamic Republic and had questioned why the head of state could only be a Muslim.

(ii) Provincial autonomy should not be to the extent acceded to under pressure of the Awami League in March.

(iii) The provinces, other than East Pakistan, could propose amendments to the Constitution on matters of common interest.

(iv) The senior most C-in-C of the three services would be responsible for preserving the Constitution; but the Turkish pattern should not be followed in this respect.

(v) The National Assembly might request the President and the CMLA to continue martial law till such time as he deemed fit.

(vi) In addition to the disqualifications prescribed in the LFO, the President could, after such inquiry as he might deem necessary, disqualify any member of the National or Provincial Assembly for a period of six years; such decision could not be questioned in any court of law.

(vii) There would not be more than three political parties in the country; a political party could not be subdivided into groups like the Muslim League, the majority of the members would retain the name and control of the party and the minority groups would stand liquidated; any party failing to secure the prescribed number of assembly seats would stand dissolved.

(viii) A special voting procedure was indicated for amendments in the Constitution moved by a member of one province which may prejudice the interests of another province.

(ix) There would be no general amnesty; the President would be the final judge to decide as to whom amnesty may or may not be granted to.

(x) Cornelius explained that it would be expedient to introduce the new Constitution through a proclamation of the CMLA; the Constitution would be deemed to have received the approval of the National Assembly after the members had taken the oath prescribed in it.

This was a complete departure from the LFO which was prepared by Choudhury in consultation with the Bengali leadership. He, the only Bengali on the committee, attended two meetings of the committee during brief visits to Pakistan from London, and stressed the prevailing East Pakistani point of view, which was more or less the same as that of the Awami League. Yahya's initiative was addressed mainly to the West Pakistani susceptibilities, and had ignored the concerns and consent of Bengalis. It led to regionalization of politics. In the absence of its bona fide leadership, East Pakistan's involvement in national affairs had become marginal, and the national political scene came to be dominated by the intra-West Pakistan power struggle. The conflict between the People's Party and rest of the political forces was based on personal and ideological elements. It also arose from the traditional as against the new populist type of politics. Bhutto presented a programme which appealed to the masses, and took it to the streets and huge public meetings; this was beyond the experience of his opponents who were used to indoor politics of negotiations, coalitions, and trade-offs. Both the religious parties, with their programmes of religious orthodoxies, and the old political parties, lacking a meaningful stand on important issues, inevitably looked to the regime for support against the formidable adversary. Bhutto's personality, style, and programme, and the obscurantism and personal rivalries of his opponents all made it difficult for any West Pakistani political consensus to be reached for resolving the national crisis.

A draft of the substantive provisions of the new Constitution was ready in July. Yahya had proposed to discuss it with the political leaders, including a visit to Dhaka to consult with the available Bengali leaders. The visit to East Pakistan never materialized; in any case, there was no bona fide leadership there to talk to. The People's Party was scheduled to consider the 28 June plan in its central committee meeting in mid-July. Meanwhile, its chairman, Bhutto, continued to call for transfer of power, and its general secretary, Kausar Niazi, announced that the party would participate in the by-elections, one of the main planks of Yahya's new system.[13] The heads of the two factions of the Muslim League, Qayyum Khan and Daultana, vehemently opposed transfer of power before complete normalcy had been restored in East Pakistan, and started preparations for contesting the by-elections;

Daultana called for strengthening the hands of the President, instead of transfer of power.[14] On the whole, except Bhutto, the West Pakistani politicians endorsed Yahya's political plan.

On 15 July, the central committee of the People's Party met for ten and a half hours to discuss the 28 June plan.[15] Bhutto, conveying the party's views in a letter to Yahya, expressed disappointment on the various undemocratic features of the President's plan. The underlying theme, however, was against the measures which threatened the dominant position of the People's Party in West Pakistan. Exception was taken to Yahya's intention to consult the 'defeated and discredited' West Pakistani leaders on the proposed Constitution. Similarly, the regime's efforts to amalgamate the three factions of the Muslim League were decried; 'one or three, they had all been rejected by the people' and did not deserve to be consulted or upgraded in any way. At this stage of political revival, the first priority of the People's Party was to occupy the high ground, as the sole representative of West Pakistan, in the framing of the Constitution, and for other national decisions. Given the reservations of a significant section of the regime, and of the rightist elements, the party's status was likely to be downgraded in the extra-constitutional process. In the National Assembly, on the other hand, it could assert its weight more effectively *vis-ā-vis* other parties of West Pakistan and the East Wing. Unless, therefore, the regime recognized the appropriate status of the People's Party in the drafting of its Constitution, Bhutto concluded his letter, 'we must seriously consider whether we should resign our seats; and then you may put forward yet another plan of action'.

Yahya could not afford yet another political confrontation, particularly with the majority party of West Pakistan. He met Bhutto on the following two days, 16–17 July, angrily told him that he did not like threats, but promised to hold talks at the end of the month in Karachi.[16]

On 29 July, a formal meeting was held in Karachi between Yahya and Bhutto and their aides; Yahya was assisted by Cornelius, Peerzada, and M. M. Ahmed, and Bhutto by nine party leaders. The People's Party delegation, composed of the party stalwarts of all the West Pakistan provinces, was obviously meant to impress upon the President the representative character of the party and its chairman. It was proposed by Bhutto that the draft Constitution be published by the President two or three weeks before the meeting of the National Assembly, which should meet as the Constituent Assembly. The Assembly could either accept the draft Constitution, as it was, within two weeks, by a simple majority vote or suggest amendments. In the latter case, if the amendments, were acceptable to the President, the Constitution would be finalized accordingly; but if not, the President would refer the matter back to the Assembly, which could pass them within 120 days, by a simple or specified majority, in which case the amendments would be incorporated in the Constitution. The People's Party delegation's understanding was that the President had accepted the 'Bhutto formula' in principle, and only the details had to be worked out by the aides.

The next round of talks between the People's Party delegation and the President's advisers was held from 25 to 27 August.[17] The meeting on 25 August was brief and acrimonious. Cornelius rejected the People's Party contention that the President had accepted the Bhutto formula. He maintained that the proposal was to be examined by him, and he had already given his considered views on it to the President, who was committed to consulting all the political parties before finalizing the Constitution. The present meeting, he said, was only to obtain the views of the People's Party on salient points that it was necessary to incorporate in the Constitution. This led to bitter exchanges, and the People's Party team left the meeting to seek further instructions from Bhutto. Later the same day, Bhutto and Yahya had a meeting without aides from 11.30 a.m. to 1 p.m. when Peerzada joined them and discussions continued up to 3 p.m.[18] They agreed that while the modalities of Constitution-making would be settled between them, the advisers could continue discussions on other matters to be incorporated in it.

On 26 August the two teams resumed talks. Rahim reiterated their stand on the National Assembly's role in Constitution-making. Cornelius declared that his brief, given by the Principal Staff Officer, was to discuss only the pros and cons of the proposal which had yet to be decided. Both sides maintained their respective stands, though M. M. Ahmed tried to ease the strained atmosphere by suggesting an open-minded discussion of the proposal by both sides. It was a dialogue of deaf-mutes, with shades of the mid-March negotiations with the Awami League.

Cornelius' approach was technical, that of a trained jurist: how could the President, occupying a plenary position, allow himself to be overruled by letting the Constitution be debated by the National Assembly, particularly when its members would be required to take oath to that very Constitution? For the other side, Constitution-making was a political exercise to be conducted in the National Assembly; as to the oath under the Constitution, they said, the history of Pakistan showed that it did not count for much. After heated discussion, Cornelius suggested a slight modification in his position: (i) a time-gap could be allowed between the promulgation of the Constitution and its coming into force, during which time, amendments could be made by the President under his own plenary powers, or on the suggestion of political parties; (ii) during a three-month period the President could amend the Constitution on the recommendations made by the National Assembly through a simple procedure; (iii) the President could, additionally have powers on the line of 'removal of difficulties' provision of the 1962 Constitution to amend or to add to the Constitution.

M. M. Ahmed pointed out that a debate on the Constitution could lead to a kind of pre-25 March crisis; for example, the majority party might walk out. It would be advisable, he said, that the President gave the Constitution with two methods of amendments; one, which enabled the National Assembly to propose amendments, by an easy procedure within a limited period; and the other, a regular procedure. The People's Party team suggested, as an alternative, a provisional Constitution given by the President which would recognize the right of the National Assembly to amend it. The President, if necessary, could be given the power of veto, subject to its being overridden by the National Assembly with a required majority. The discussion on the issue, however, remained inconclusive, and was left to be settled by Bhutto and the President.

The other constitutional matters of concern to the People's Party were joint electorates, registration of parties, the directive principles of state, and, particularly, in view of their socialist manifesto, fundamental rights. The party wanted the right of private property to be qualified; Cornelius thought it was contradictory to guarantee the right, and, at the same time, say that it should serve the common good. When pressed by the People's Party to accept their formulations, Cornelius reiterated that his team was only to hear and record the party views. At this the People's Party team said they could not be equated with other parties, and there was no point in continuing the meeting without any serious discussions. Cornelius, in the end, gave the participants a questionnaire and asked them to give their views on it the following day. On 27 August, the two sides met briefly. Rahim went over their proposal regarding the role of the National Assembly, refused to discuss the points raised in the questionnaire, and left the meeting.

Bhutto became more strident after the failure of these talks. He declared, with some truth as will be seen later, that the talks were being 'deliberately spun out to accommodate the reactionary forces opposed to the transfer of power.' On 2 September, he wrote to Peerzada demanding a representative government without delay and warning that if force continued to remain the main instrument of policy 'East Pakistan would be pushed beyond the pale'. On 7 September he again wrote to Yahya complaining about the attitude of Cornelius in refusing to accept the role of the National Assembly as a Constitution-making body. He called off his projected meeting with Yahya on 9 September, but met him on 13 September and pressed his demand. Eventually, in a broadcast on 18 September, Yahya revised his June plan, and accepted the National Assembly's role in giving final shape to the Constitution prepared by the committee.[19] Earlier in the day, Yahya had informed Bhutto that, although the June plan had been accepted by all the other parties, he had revised it to accommodate the People's Party. Under the circumstances, Yahya added, he could not go any further. Bhutto accepted the new Constitution-making modalities. He, however, kept up the pressure on Yahya, through harsh public statements and meetings, to secure his position against the regime's political manoeuvrings with his opponents.

* * *

While the discussions on the Constitution and other measures to implement the June plan were proceeding at a leisurely pace, some cosmetic changes in the East Pakistan administration were introduced to pacify foreign critics. On 1 September, Dr Abdul Motaleb Malik was appointed Governor in place of the controversial Tikka Khan; earlier, on 17 August, Muzaffar Husain had taken over as the Chief Secretary. Lieutenant-General Amir Abdullah Khan Niazi, Commander Eastern Command, became the Martial Law Administrator. The civilian team of top administrators was buttressed by a council of ten ministers who were sworn in on 17 September. Of the ten ministers, two were renegade elected members of the Awami League, one a Buddhist from the tribal area of the Chittagong Hill Tracts, and the remaining ones from political parties which had failed to win any seat in the elections.

The oath-taking ceremony for the new Governor was held in the Governor House with such pomp and guests as could be mustered under the siege conditions. This time, unlike in March when Tikka Khan could not find a judge to induct him into office, the Chief Justice was on hand to administer the oath. I do not remember what it was that Dr Malik solemnly swore to uphold under the circumstances, but the whole affair was very subdued. During refreshments after the brief ceremony, one of the generals running the civil administration remarked to a group of guests that the situation would soon return to normal; he was not anticipating this welcome development as a result of the induction of the civilian governor but rather pointedly attributing his appointment to the army's control of the Province.

The President's secretariat, while announcing the appointment of the civilian governor had given the assurance that the 'responsibility for running the civil administration of the province will vest fully in the Governor and his Council of Ministers . . . and [the army] will (only) provide such assistance to the civil administration as they may be called upon to undertake.'[20] The army never went back to what was called its 'primary functions'. The reality of its power was too pervasive and overwhelming to be removed without the withdrawal of martial law and the introduction of a representative government. On the Governor's staff there was only one junior civilian secretary, handling routine papers. The political and administrative policymaking remained in the hands of the same group of army officers sitting next door to Malik's office, and living in the annexes of the Governor House. Although Muzaffar Husain, unlike his Bengali predecessor, could handle more confidently the day-to-day interaction of the civil administration with the army at the provincial level, there was no way to control the excesses in the interior. The civil administration, largely manned by the Bengalis, was marginalized and too demoralized to act independently, and the few West Pakistani district officers also found it hazardous to assert themselves against the local army authorities.[21] Even the army officers, working in the martial law headquarters, who had acquired a working knowledge of the ethics of civil administration, found themselves helpless before local army commanders, of whatever rank, whose sway on the ground was absolute. The moral and professional inadequacies of Niazi, who was under some restraint of the senior general Tikka Khan, came to the fore as Martial Law Administrator. Malik was in no position to control him or the army on the ground.

Dr Malik was a decent, religious-minded politician of the old school. He had held important public offices, both in and outside Pakistan. But as Governor, he and his ministers were a pathetic lot. They were diffident in their offices, had little power to do any good, and devoid of any constituencies to draw political support. Farman Ali says that Malik had accepted the appointment on condition that he would be allowed to contact the exiles in India. If he had been given the authority, Farman thinks, he might have tried to bring about some sort of compromise. But Malik was not suited to cope with the rampant internal and external elements that were deepening the crisis. Nor did he enjoy the confidence of Yahya who, in any case, had no intention of reaching a compromise with those whom he had called traitors; above all, as asked by Bhutto, 'whom did Dr A. M. Malik represent ?'

* * *

Coming back to the process of the implementation of the June plan, measures were initiated to remove from amongst the elected members of the National and Provincial Assemblies all 'anti-social' and 'anti-state' elements. These two categories of activities, which would deprive a member of his seat, were never clearly defined at any stage, nor was a forum provided for the delinquent member to answer the charges against him. The 'thorough investigations' for disqualifications, promised by the President in his June broadcast, were entrusted to the intelligence agencies. They diligently applied themselves to ensuring that the legislature emerging from the exercise conformed to the pattern that had been envisaged by the regime earlier in the 1970 elections, but which it had failed to bring about. This time the intelligence operators had a free run, unhampered by laws, the Press, or the vigilance of political parties. Farman Ali recalls that:

> In July and August, meetings were held between N. A. Rizvi, director, Intelligence Bureau (IB), A. B. S. Safdar, deputy director, (a Bengali police officer posted at Dhaka and later suspected to be in league with the exiled Awami League), and Major-General Akbar, director-general, Inter-Services Intelligence (ISI) to discuss the filling up of seats. My suggestion was to call the National Assembly session and disqualify after some time those who did not attend. But I was overruled. They decided to disqualify all those who had gone to India and had committed atrocities. A team of the officers of IB and the ISI was set up to prepare lists of disqualified members and charges against them.

On 8 August, the list of 88 Awami League members-elect of the National Assembly allowed to retain their seats was published.[22] On 20 August, a similar list of 94 Awami Leaguers elected to the East Pakistan Provincial Assembly who would retain their seats was published.[23] It was announced that those not included in these lists would be given the opportunity to defend themselves against specific charges before their cases were finally decided. The procedure for defence was a public notice to the individual member-elect to present himself before the designated military authorities, without specifying the charges. By the third week of August, proceedings on these lines had been initiated against only 45 Bengali members of the National Assembly. On 4 September, 144 members of the Provincial Assembly were asked to appear before the sub-administrator martial law on 9 September, without indicating the reasons for doing so.[24] No one turned up to face the military courts.

The final number of vacancies announced for by-elections to the National Assembly was 78, which reduced the Awami League membership from 160 to 82 (total membership 300; East Pakistan 162). In the East Pakistan Assembly, 193 out of 288 Awami league members were deprived of their seats (total membership 300). On 20 September, the Election Commission posted notice of the election schedule for 78 National Assembly seats and 105 of the East Pakistan Assembly. It was to start from the filing of nomination papers by the contesting candidates on 29 and 30 September, leading through various stages to the final polling from 25 November to 9 December. On 21 September, by a revised notification, the nomination dates were advanced to 20–1 October, and polling to 12 to 23 December. On 3 October, the programme for the filling up of 87 more Provincial Assembly seats, vacated due to disqualification, and one due to death, was announced; the polling for these seats was fixed still later, from 18 December to 7 January 1972.[25]

As soon as the by-elections were announced, the political parties jumped into the arena to grab through the back door what they had failed to get in a democratic manner. On one side was the People's Party which had no constituency in East Pakistan; it joined the race not only to upgrade its image as more than a West Pakistani party, but also to retain at least its existing numerical dominance, relative to other parties in the National Assembly. On the other were the religious and rightist parties which had been roundly defeated in East Pakistan, getting only one seat in the National Assembly, and four in the Provincial Assembly; in West Pakistan, they had obtained only 42 out of the 138 National Assembly seats of West Pakistan. The rightists, dominated by the West Pakistani leadership and in collaboration with corresponding Bengali elements, now saw the chance to redeem themselves. In the sick political culture of the country no one questioned the morality and viability of a political system proposed to be built on the arbitrary removal of large number of freely-elected Bengali members. The only thing that mattered was obtaining a dominant position, however dubious the methods may be. The key to it was with the generals who would decide which party got what; to the President, therefore, they all converged with solemn assurances of their support to him, his plans, and the armed forces.[26]

Yahya apparently attached considerable importance to the support of the majority party of West Pakistan for his constitutional plans, even though they were uncritically endorsed by other parties. He was aware of Bhutto's influence in sections of the army, and his street power among the masses. During this period, according to both Peerzada and Umer, Bhutto had attained considerable influence in the corridors of the CMLA secretariat. Umer relates that he was even asked once during this period to sit with the People's Party team to draft Yahya's speech, which he did not do. At the same time, Yahya was quite wary of Bhutto. The generals did not want to botch things up this time and allow any one party or leader to achieve ascendancy like Mujib. At the operational level, therefore, the intelligence agencies and the troubleshooters of the regime worked for an electoral alliance of the marginal political elements to prevent the emergence of the People's Party as the sole spokesman of West Pakistan, or indeed of Pakistan, if it managed to get additional seats from East Pakistan.

On 12 October, Yahya announced the timetable for the transfer of power. The National Assembly would be summoned to meet on 27 December, after completion of by-elections by 23 December. The central government would be formed soon after the inaugural session of the Assembly. The provincial assemblies in West Pakistan could be summoned to meet at short notice after completing the few by-elections (arising from normal causes), and elections to the women's seats. The East Pakistan Assembly would meet later, after 7 January 1972, when by-elections for its 193 seats would have been completed.[27] On 14 October, a martial law regulation was issued allowing political activities within narrow limits. The announcement of the specific dates for the formation of elected governments galvanized all the political parties to seek maximum mileage out of the spoils of East Pakistan. Six rightist parties, the Pakistan Democratic Party, Jamaat-i-Islami, Nizam-i-Islam, and three factions of the Muslim Leagues came forward to appropriate all of them with a gusto which bore no relation to their earlier electoral performance. But it was not easy to make them agree to the sharing of the regime's bounty. The newspapers were full of their bickerings during September and October. The wranglings of the three factions of the Muslim League were particularly bitter. Each day there were reports, inspired by the intelligence agencies or the interested faction, that they were merging, and then not merging; each faction was denouncing the others, and the head of each was disowning one or the other of his lieutenants who themselves were on the lookout for defection to the more promising alignment. Ultimately, after intensive behind-the-scene efforts of the regime, it was announced on 20 October that the six parties had agreed to form an electoral alliance, distributing 78 National Assembly and 193 East Pakistan Assembly seats among themselves.[28] The Election Commission was tuned to the regime's political manipulations. Its first notification of 20 September had prescribed 29 September for the filing of nomination papers of the candidates, by which time the agreement could not be finalized. The date was accordingly advanced by the commission to 20–1 October, when the alliance parties were ready with their joint candidates. Nurul Amin of the Pakistan Democratic Party admitted that the postponement was made on advice from him and like-minded leaders.[29]

Bhutto saw the danger to his position in the National Assembly by the rightist alliance getting all the seats of disqualified members in East Pakistan. In the nature of the exercise, it was the regime, and not the actual polling that was going to decide which party got how many seats. Accordingly, the composition of the National Assembly was being manipulated to emerge roughly like this: Awami League (defunct) 82, People's Party 86, the rightists and religious parties 121, and independents 16, in a house of 300 members.[30] Neither of the major parties would thus be in a position to call the shots, and the regime would have enough margins to keep things under control. The position in the East Pakistan Assembly would be better still, with 193 seats out of 300 occupied by the alliance nominees.[31] The West Pakistan-dominated parties would thus enjoy majorities in both the forums, and, within that, the regime's supporters would hold the balance.

Bhutto made threatening statements against the regime's manipulations, but he could not afford to annoy it too much. On 10 October, a People's Party delegation, led by Mahmud Ali Kasuri, went to East Pakistan to prepare the ground for participation in the elections. They visited Chittagong, Khulna, Sylhet, and Rangpur. The party spokesman claimed that 52 persons had applied for party tickets, and 22 more were expected to apply. The delegation tried to form an alliance with a prominent leftist leader, Masihur Rahman, General Secretary of the National Awami Party (Bhashani group), who promised to visit Karachi to discuss with Bhutto participation in the by-elections by his party members. A few days later, however, he backed out.[32] Bhutto's problem was not just that he was being excluded from East Pakistan by the regime; in fact, such were the sentiments against him among the Bengalis that he was unable to find enough candidates willing to get a seat on the platter in his name.

In Dhaka the elections were being managed by Major-General Farman Ali. The cool and spacious lounge of the Governor House used to be overcrowded in those days with the hopefuls seeking his endorsement, which practically ensured the seat. Within the broad strategy (to the determination of which they had contributed), martial law authorities in Dhaka wielded complete power to select members for the vacated seats. Farman Ali recalls:

> The Governor House was asked to hold by-elections with Justice Abdus Sattar as the Chief Election Commissioner [he had held this position in 1970 elections also]. We came to the conclusion that if the pro-Pakistan parties did not form an alliance, they would lose even against independents. The Awami League had boycotted. The People's Party was promised some seats by the President. I was called and told to make arrangements to give 24 seats to the People's Party so that it enjoyed a majority in the first session of the National Assembly.

But the Dhaka authorities were not very sympathetic to the woes of the People's Party which seemed to be losing the race in the general scramble; the alliance seemed to be poised to grab all the 78 seats. Kasuri, still in Dhaka, alleged that the People's Party candidates were being prevented from filing nomination papers and its workers were being harassed by the rightist parties. He was, however, careful to compliment the army on achieving 'creditable success', which, he added, would not have been possible 'without the support of the people'. On 22 October, Bhutto went, in what was termed by the Press as a 'dramatic dash', to Rawalpindi to see Yahya amidst speculations that the People's Party was boycotting the by-elections. Bhutto himself confirmed this possibility on the following day.[33] The threat seems to have worked. The President called up Farman Ali,

> and asked me to do something for Bhutto. I persuaded Nurul Amin and other rightist leaders to give six seats to him. Hafeez Pirzada, Khurshid Hasan Mir, and Kamal Azfar etc. had come to Dhaka and opened an office which was blown up. They came to me and complained about seats. I told them, 'you can get a maximum of six seats and even for these you don't have candidates.' Kasuri said that Pirzada had flown with the list of their candidates to Karachi.

This time the authorities arranged to have five nominees of the People's Party declared elected unopposed by making the alliance candidates withdraw, much to the chagrin of Nurul Amin.[34] It was evident from the goings-on in the martial law offices in the Governor House that the electoral process would be completed before the actual polling, which, in any case, was not possible in the prevailing circumstances. Farman Ali, even after the sponsorship of alliances and the allocation of seats, however, believed that actual polling was desirable and that it was possible to hold it. He says he later learned that the idea was given up on the recommendation of Major-General Rahim Khan who could not spare the *Razakars* from operational requirements for polling purposes. By 30 October, 48 nominees of the regime had been declared elected unopposed to the National Assembly, either by getting the nomination papers of the other candidates rejected, or by making them withdraw.[35] To deal with the remaining 30 seats, where neither of the two methods had so far succeeded, the National and Provincial Assemblies (Election) Ordinance 1970 was amended on 11 November. By this amendment the last date for withdrawal of candidature, which was 28 October, was extended up to four days before polling day, enough time to apply the requisite pressure on unwanted candidates.

The alliance parties, having increased their combined strength from 37 to something like 116 seats in the National Assembly through this electoral farce, formed a new party called the United Coalition Party.[36] The regime had succeeded in fragmenting the elected structure. The Coalition Party claimed a share in power, under the leadership of Nurul Amin as prime minister, which was readily conceded by the Yahya regime. Bhutto could not contest the Bengali right to form the government, and demanded a president from West Pakistan (meaning a nominee of the People's Party), to which Nurul Amin quipped, 'let Mr Bhutto fight it out with President Yahya Khan.'[37]

The country was practically in a state of war on 26 November, when Yahya met Bhutto alone from 10.30 a.m. to 11.45 a.m. and thereafter up to 1.40 p.m. with aides. At the meeting, they discussed the salient features of the Constitution prepared by the committee. Yahya informed Bhutto that he proposed to remain President, Supreme Commander, C-in-C Army, and also to retain martial law powers.[38] There was also a provision by which the President would have 'special responsibilities for the preservation of the integrity and ideology of Pakistan and for the protection of fundamental rights'. Under the proposed Constitution, the President was to appoint the provincial governors, who would be responsible to him and would have the powers to dissolve the provincial assemblies. Bhutto met the President again on

28 November, and the same day sent to him in a letter his comments on the draft Constitution. He protested against too much concentration of power in the hands of the president, but agreed that, in the prevailing circumstances, it would be necessary for the C-in-C of the army to be president for quite some time. Yahya wanted this arrangement for at least two presidential terms, but on Bhutto's protest agreed that the Constitution would provide for him to continue as President for the first term; thereafter, he would seek election under the normal procedure prescribed in the Constitution. About the presidential responsibility to protect fundamental rights, Bhutto feared that the provision would prevent genuine reforms, but Yahya assured him that it could be amended by the Assembly, and the compensation determined by the legislature would not be subject to adjudication of the courts. A few other changes were also accepted without affecting the authoritative nature of the constitutional arrangements.

Too late in the day, and rather reluctantly, Yahya had realized the necessity of introducing some kind of representative government. On 30 November, he urgently called Bhutto to Rawalpindi and had two meetings with him, at one of which Nurul Amin was also present. They discussed the formation of a coalition government, but Yahya gave no hint of the impending war with India, which was declared three days later. On 3 December, Bhutto sent his party's acceptance of a coalition government on the following terms: (i) Nurul Amin would be the Prime Minister and Bhutto the Vice-Premier; (ii) there would be seven ministers from the East Wing and six from the West, with the same number of ministers of state; there would be no minister from the Jamaat-i-Islami; (iii) of the West Pakistani ministers, five from the Punjab and Sindh would be from the People's Party, and the sixth from the NWFP would be either an independent or from the Jamiat-i-Ulema (Mufti Mahmood and Hazarvi group), provided it did not join the United Coalition Party; (iv) Balochistan would be represented by a minister of state who would be either an independent or, with the same provision as in (iii), from the Jamiat-i-Ulema; (v) no minister from the NWFP or Balochistan would be from any component of the United Coalition Party; (vi) of the important portfolios, the People's Party would hold foreign affairs, establishment, and information and broadcasting; (vii) ministers of either Wing would not interfere in matters pertaining to the Wing other than their own.

No step was taken by Yahya to induct the civilian government until 7 December, when he asked Bhutto to go to New York to represent Pakistan at the UN. Bhutto pointed out that it would prejudice Pakistan's position if he went as a member of the military regime. Accordingly, it was announced on 8 December that a coalition ministry headed by Nurul Amin as prime minister and Bhutto as vice-prime minister would be formed shortly. Neither of them was formally inducted into office. Bhutto left for New York the same day as vice-prime minister and foreign minister-designate.

* * *

The political and constitutional processes that Yahya was leisurely putting in motion were rejected by the world community. They had no moral basis, and, in so far as East Pakistan was concerned, were totally irrelevant. The crux of the crisis was a compromise with its elected Bengali leadership. On 31 March, Mujib was brought to West Pakistan and lodged in Faisalabad jail, and then shifted to Mianwali jail when the war started. The question that arises is why Yahya did not reopen negotiations with him in the cooler atmosphere of West Pakistan, as the world was demanding.

G. W. Choudhury claims that Mujib's trial was not serious. Even at the time of its announcement, a dialogue with Mujib had been opened through his defence counsel, A. K. Brohi, with the knowledge of American officials. At the proper time and through appropriate face-saving devices, Choudhury says, Yahya was prepared to release Mujib.[39] Kissinger supports the assertion, and says that at this time (September) 'the release of Mujib was essentially a problem of face'.[40] Jackson calls the trial a 'trade off' to pacify the hawkish generals before introducing various political measures.[41]

Yahya had accommodated Mujib before the 1970 elections even against the advice of his generals. He had relied on his promises to negotiate with the West Pakistan leaders, and obtain a consensus of the regime and other parties on the Six Points after the elections. Mujib refused the Presidential invitation to come to Rawalpindi as the leader of the majority party, to discuss constitutional modalities. He was obdurate, and would not budge an inch from his rigid stand. All these snubbings deeply hurt Yahya's ego, and he felt betrayed and humiliated before those who were advising him not to trust Mujib. Yahya called him a traitor in his 26 March broadcast, and this finally closed any chance of communication between the two after the army operation. In Umer's opinion,

> as far as Mujib was concerned the President's mind was completely closed. Peerzada, who was dealing with the case, would not allow anybody to meet Mujib except Brohi (who was his defence counsel). The suggestion that Yahya wanted to negotiate with Mujib through Brohi is not correct. If they had ever thought at all of any understanding with Mujib to save the situation and wanted serious negotiations with him, the President would have turned to me. But once or twice when I put some questions regarding Mujib, Peerzada said, 'Don't interfere in this'.

There was nothing non-serious in the trial itself, which started on 11 August before a special military court, convened by the CMLA, with power and procedures as prescribed for a field general court martial under the Pakistan Army Act. It was presided over by a brigadier, and included two officers of the army, one naval officer, one air force officer, and a district and sessions judge from the Punjab. Of the twelve charges, the main one being that of waging war against Pakistan, three were under the Pakistan Penal Code, and the remaining ones under martial law regulations; most of them carried the punishment of death. Although Brohi had been appointed on his request, after hearing the tape of Yahya's 26 March broadcast in the court, Mujib refused to produce any defence and relieved Brohi. He said he now knew that his fate was sealed. Nevertheless, Brohi continued to represent him at the request of the court, without any instructions from the accused. The prosecution submitted a list of 105 witnesses, but actually produced only about half of them. The substantive evidence was the statements of the Bengali army officers who confessed to their involvement in the conspiracy, hatched under Awami League leadership, to rise in rebellion against the government. The confessions were obtained in police and army custody. Brohi wanted to call Cornelius, Peerzada, M. M. Ahmed, and Hasan as defence witnesses, but the court disallowed the request. On 1 December the case was closed, and on 4 December the court, except the civilian judge who was absent on that day because of the death of his father, unanimously found Mujib guilty of all the charges, and sentenced him to death, subject to confirmation by the Convening Authority, that is the CMLA. No judgment analysing evidence or reasons for the findings is required to be given by the military courts.

Roedad Khan remembers that the question of Mujib's fate was raised by General Gul Hassan at one of the regular meetings which used to be held by Yahya Khan in the GHQ during April. The issue was formulated as a question, and Yahya went round the table asking each one, liquidation 'with or without trial'. Some, including the two civilian participants, suggested he should be tried, but others, including the propounder, recommended 'without trial.' These were euphoric times; many responsible elements in the establishment regretted that the evil had not been eliminated in the first flush of army action. In August, the world community would not let the matter be treated so light-heartedly. The Americans demanded and obtained an assurance that the death sentence against Mujib would not be carried out. Yahya might have been compelled to spare Mujib's life against his wishes, but he was not prepared to give up his trial or release him, not to speak of negotiating with him. If the war had ended otherwise, and Yahya had survived in power, he might have still carried out the sentence.

Although the other top leaders of the Awami League were no less involved in what Mujib was charged with, Yahya was not averse to entering into negotiations with them. Karim, who had moved out as divisional commander in June, recalls the proceedings of a conference attended by him in mid-1971:

> In a divisional commanders conference he (Yahya) informed that negotiations were going on to get these people [Awami Leaguers] back. Major-General Gul Hassan, Chief of General Staff, said, 'Why don't you declare amnesty like Queen Victoria did? Let them come back and then sit down and sort out the thing.' There was strong opposition from the generals at the suggestion. They said, 'we must finish this thing'—sort of final solution.

Yahya was faced with a number of difficulties in resolving the political tangle with the elected leadership of East Pakistan. Mujib remained the key to the solution and he was available. But Yahya had deprived himself of the option by calling him a traitor. As the army operation had led to a serious external threat to the entire country, it may be asked whether the junta should not have replaced Yahya with some one who could make a fresh start, free from the bitterness and personal antipathy to Mujib. Umer remembers that the point did come up once or twice.

> But the army circles in West Pakistan, by and large, did not agree. I do not think the majority of them were aware of the gravity of the situation in which the country was placed. At no time was the Indian intervention taken seriously. Every one was taking things lightly. This partly explains why no one thought of a change at the top, which by itself might have made a difference. Yahya called Mujib a traitor, but then everyone in the army thought so. I do not think there was any one in the army at that time, not certainly any one of us, who would have been acceptable for negotiating with Mujib. In any case, the situation had deteriorated so much that even those who thought somewhat otherwise were not prepared to step in to take the place of Yahya.

Kissinger realized the desperateness of Pakistan's situation better than the Pakistani policymakers. Since Yahya was not prepared to talk with Mujib, the source near at hand, Kissinger initiated contacts with the exiled leadership of the Awami League to prepare the ground for negotiations. He gives the following account of these contacts.[42] In the last week of July, one Qaiyum approached the US consulate in Calcutta, on behalf of a faction of the Bangladesh leadership, with an offer of negotiations with the Pakistan government. The conditions were: the participation of Mujib in negotiations and acceptance of the Six Points in return for something less than independent East Pakistan. In mid-August, Ambassador Farland informed Yahya of these contacts, and he, to the surprise of Kissinger, not only welcomed the offer but also accepted Farland's good offices for arranging secret meetings with the exiles. In the first week of September, the US suggested contact with the foreign minister of Bangladesh to convey to him 'Yahya's willingness to engage in secret talks'. Kissinger admits 'it was an extraordinary proposal to make to the President of a friendly country' but adds that 'such was Yahya's quandary that he agreed'. In mid-September, when Qaiyum was asked to arrange the meeting, he pleaded his inability to do so due to the surveillance of the Indian intelligence. On 21 September, Yahya inquired of

Farland the progress made in the Calcutta contacts, whereupon the US ambassador suggested upgradation of the level of approach to the acting president of the Bangladesh government, 'if the foreign minister remained unavailable.' On 23 September, Qaiyum warned the US consul that the Indian government had formally asked the Bangladesh leadership to route all contacts through New Delhi. On 27 September, the State Department proposed to the Indian ambassador in Washington direct negotiations between Pakistan and the Bangladesh representatives without any conditions. The ambassador demanded the release of Mujib and the immediate independence of East Pakistan. However, on 28 September, the US consul had a meeting with Khondakar Mushtaque Ahmed, the Bangladesh foreign minister, who apparently was under watch and, therefore, for the record put all sorts of conditions, including the participation of the Soviet Union, on the negotiations. On 16 October, Qaiyum ruled out any meeting at the level of the acting president of Bangladesh due to Indian objections. By the end of October, according to Kissinger, all channels to the Bangladesh leadership had dried up, and the Indian Press was raising a hue and cry over stories of Bangladesh contacts with foreign representatives.

The US government, however, continued the search for a political initiative to boost up Pakistan's case before the world community.

Lawrence Lifschultz, in a study of the linkages of bloody coups in Bangladesh with its pre-independence factional politics, has given the following account of secret negotiations between the US and Mushtaque's group.[43] In June 1971, he says the US decided to explore the possibility of acting 'as a channel between elements of the Bengali leadership which Pakistan did not consider guilty of high treason and General Yahya Khan'. In all, eight secret contacts took place between the US officials and Bangladeshi representatives of the Mushtaque faction, mostly in Calcutta but some at other places also. According to a top official of the State Department, at some stage Kissinger talked directly with Mushtaque's representative. According to former officials of the Bangladesh provisional government

> the agreement between Mushtaque and the Americans . . . constituted the terms for a return to *status quo ante*. . . . Mushtaque and his Foreign

> Secretary, Mahbub Alam Chashi, had provisionally agreed to conditions for a separate peace: one which would maintain the unity of Pakistan, if the Pakistan Army would cease military operations, withdraw to barracks and allow new negotiations to begin, ending open warfare.

According to some sources, Lifschultz says, the time fixed for decisive action was October, when Mushtaque, as foreign minister, was expected to come to New York to present the Bangladesh case in the UN General Assembly. Lifschultz speculates:

> Had he [Mushtaque] suddenly, in New York, unilaterally and without warning, announced a compromise solution short of independence—a position that constituted a sell-out and a betrayal in the view of Tajuddin and the rest of the leadership—Mushtaque might at that stage have pulled off a full coup against the rest of the Awami League leadership back in Calcutta, and the history of Bangladesh might have been very different.

Umer gives a rather vague version of the connections. During August and September, he says, there was growing realization of the need for a political solution, and the President was holding a series of meetings with the political leaders;

> but there was nothing in them to tap and draw some line of rescue as far as the Awami League was concerned. Rumour would mention some contact with Bangladeshis and there will be some talk about release of Mujib and how to get the Awami League leadership out of the Indian clutches and so on and so forth. Just before the war, a message was received from our High Commission in London that some Bangladeshis had arrived there, and asked the President to send someone with authority to negotiate with them. Yahya asked me to be ready to leave for London. After fifteen minutes Peerzada asked me to stand down. This happened in the last week of November.

Peerzada, regarded as the most powerful man after Yahya, denies any direct knowledge of contacts with the Awami League leadership. He says:

> After the army operation my role was reduced to routine administrative files. Yahya had taken over as C-in-C in charge of military operations which were the main features of the March-November period. Umer was Yahya's political adviser, and all political initiatives were through

> him or with his knowledge. I knew about contacts with the Awami League only because of being on the precinct. Some vague rumours mentioning Mushtaque came to me. It was also being mentioned that Mujib will make an announcement on the radio. My impression was that Umer was dealing with these negotiations. The President never used me for this purpose.

Farman Ali recalls:

> We had received information in September–October through an Awami League member of the National Assembly from Khulna that the exiled leadership in Calcutta was frustrated. We made contacts with them through our agents although they were all under surveillance of the Indian intelligence. Our agents informed us that Mushtaque would say something in the UN General Assembly.

The secret contacts with the Awami Leaguers were also reported by the well-informed correspondent of *The Daily Telegraph* of London, Clare Hollingworth, on 4 August:

> the major group of Bangladeshi politicians now established in Calcutta under the leadership of Tajuddin Ahmed . . . would be willing to enter into secret talks with representatives of West Pakistan administration . . . were it not for the strong opposition of their military command under Col. Osmany who . . . has not unexpectedly gained ascendancy over the politicians.

On 19 August, Hollingworth again reported diplomatic initiatives by Iran, encouraged by the Americans and supported by Russia and China, to arrange secret contacts between Pakistan and the Bangladeshis. She was, however, not very optimistic 'about the outcome of any attempt at reconciliation, even if talks were to take place, which I think unlikely'.

Apart from secret approaches to bring the Bangladesh leadership and Pakistan to the negotiating table, the US government was working on some proposals of its own in a last bid to avert war between India and Pakistan. On 14 November, when Sultan Muhammad Khan reached Washington, the first thing Ambassador N. A. M. Raza asked him was about the proposal of talks with Mujib and his emissaries in Calcutta. Raza showed him a paper with three paragraphs, given to him by the State Department that day. The Ambassador was told that the Secretary of State,

Rogers, had spent lot of time on them, and that they had been conveyed to Yahya, who must have seen them perhaps on 13–14 November. Raza was also informed that Mrs Gandhi had also shown some interest in the third proposal. Later, when Sultan Muhammad met Kissinger, he spoke of the same proposals. Apparently, the US government was pinning a lot of hope on them to avert the war. But the Foreign Secretary knew nothing about the matter, and he sent a report by special courier to the President. On return, Sultan Muhammad was told by Yahya that he had received the proposals from Farland, but had made no firm commitment and had merely promised to consider them. Although there was little chance of any compromise at that late stage, the Americans saw it as an important tactical move in continuation of the earlier ones, sponsored by Pakistan under their promptings, of UN observers on the borders, unilateral withdrawal of forces from the Pakistan side, good offices of the Secretary-General, and others. Such tactical moves provided good arguments for one's case in the UN forums. The Americans knew that there was no time to lose, and, as war became imminent, Ambassador Raza informed the Foreign Office that Nixon had directed Secretary of State Rogers to convey to India and the Soviet Union that Yahya would be willing to meet the representatives of the Awami League. When this message was shown to Yahya, he denied having given any such undertaking or even understanding to Ambassador Farland, and asked Raza to clarify the position to the State Department.

Farman Ali thinks that Yahya was scared of the generals, and felt that if they came to know of his conciliatory gestures towards the Awami Leaguers he might be deposed. This may be the reason that even while the secret contacts were being established with his knowledge and blessings, Mujib's trial was started. But it is significant that the special military court, though not bound by the elaborate civil laws of evidence and procedure and subject to the directions of the commander convening it, was allowed more than three months to sentence Mujib. And this on the day following the start of war, which had eliminated any chance of a political compromise. Yahya could not afford to confide the secret to anyone on his side. He had to let Kissinger prepare the ground for negotiations. At the appropriate time, if the US had succeeded in weaning away the Mushtaque faction from the hardliners, the compromise formula could be presented to the junta with the full backing of the US. Until then, Yahya had to pursue the hawkish stance of punishing Mujib for treason. In view of the prevailing feelings in the army circles, Yahya could not possibly have approached Mujib for reconciliation during the trial. If negotiations with Mushtaque had succeeded, the secessionalist movement would have split up, and Mujib might have become irrelevant from the regime's point of view.

CHAPTER 11

War, Surrender, and Separation

Towards the end of October 1971, the *mukti bahini,* armed and trained in large numbers during the last six months in India, had intensified its operations inside East Pakistan and on its borders. The Indian army had taken over the border responsibilities in mid-summer from the Border Security Force, and the *mukti bahini* was operating under its command. Although Indian writers have minimized the role of the rebel force and guerrillas in the 'liberation' of East Pakistan, their contribution to the defeat of the Pakistan army was, in fact, very significant. Throughout the period March–November, the highly motivated rebel irregulars kept up the pressure on the Pakistan army with reckless courage, and prevented the resumption of transport, communication, trade, or any kind of economic activity in the province. They wore out and demoralized the Pakistan armed forces, and softened the ground for the Indian army which otherwise would not have found the so-called 'lightning campaign' in East Pakistan such a walk-over. By early November the guerrillas had occupied strips of territory on both the eastern and the western borders, and had intensified attacks to widen them. Given the nature of the border and the terrain and the rebels' line of communication with bases in India, the objective given to the Pakistan army to defend every inch of East Pakistan territory was an impossible one. There was bound to be technical transgression or artillery shelling into the Indian side while dislodging the infiltrators from Pakistan's territory. The border was mostly a notional line on flat land, without any identifiable marks; at places it ran through the middle of villages, many of which were situated at hailing distance on the two sides of the border.

'For tactical as well as emotional reasons, Jessore was a special target for the *mukti bahini*—it was here that they had suffered one of their major defeats in pitched battle during the early days of the insurgency. The *mukti bahini* had established a major base in Bangla Desh territory adjacent to Boyra [a village on the Indian side on the Jessore-Calcutta road].'[1] On 21 November, Pakistani troops, supported by tanks and artillery, launched an attack against the infiltrators around Boyra, which itself came under shelling. The Indian army was hoping for just such a response from Pakistan. It launched an attack against Jessore sector, on the night of 20 and 21 November, with one infantry brigade, supported by armour, artillery, and air force. The immediate aim was to capture Jessore. This was the first incident where the Indian army had openly attacked in the wake of *mukti bahini* infiltration. This main attack was accompanied by thrusts all along the international border, notably in the sectors of Rangpur, Sylhet, and the Chittagong Hill Tracts. Three Pakistan Air Force (PAF) planes were shot down over Indian territory and the pilots captured. On 24 November Mrs Gandhi told parliament that the Indian armed forces had been instructed to enter East Pakistan in 'self-defence'. 'This considerably raised the morale of the *mukti bahini*—particularly in the Jessore area—and it stepped up its guerrilla activities, even to the extent of mounting regular offensives. By this time, . . . [they] were equipped with light and heavy mortars and could operate in set-piece battles.'[2]

In early November, Ghulam Ishaq Khan, Cabinet Secretary, in view of the deteriorating military situation in East Pakistan and the growing Indo-Pakistan confrontation, set in motion certain preliminary measures to organize the civil machinery for any likely emergency. All major decisions were taken in the CMLA secretariat, and there was no institutional framework for co-ordination and consultation between it and the civil governmental machinery. To ascertain the regime's thinking on the current situation, the Cabinet Secretary submitted a note to the President on 6 November, informing him of the action taken up to that point by the Cabinet Division, and by implication seeking instructions for further measures, corresponding to what the President had in mind about the military course of action. The President, however, did not enlighten him, and returned the note after merely intialling it. The Cabinet Secretary took recourse to the book, and on 16 November in the Secretaries Co-ordination Committee on Defence Planning advised the secretaries to take all measures envisaged in the war book for precautionary stage. Roedad Khan, Information Secretary, complained that there was no forum where special problems relating to East Pakistan could be discussed to formulate a co-ordinated approach during the emergency. The Cabinet Secretary promised to bring the matter to the President's notice and seek his instructions.

In the government of Pakistan, the Cabinet Division, through its military wing manned by senior military officers, is responsible for keeping the civil plans up to date to mobilize the country in support of the armed forces in times of war, or threat of war. A comprehensive war book has been built up over the years, detailing the measures to be taken by each ministry of the central government, the provincial governments, and the agencies under them during the emergency. As soon as the government decision about a particular stage of emergency (the three stages being the standby, the precautionary, and the actual war) is communicated, each civil agency knows exactly what it has to do. The plans are under continuous review in peacetime through a series of subcommittees, in close consultation with the Ministry of Defence, under the supervision of the Secretaries Co-ordination Committee for Defence Planning which is headed by the cabinet secretary. The final authority for approval of the plans is the Defence Committee of the Cabinet which is presided over by the chief executive and is the highest body responsible for taking decisions relating to war and peace. In actual practice the various stages of emergency have tended to be merged, and the civil administration has usually found itself directly confronted with war. In 1971 there was no Defence Committee of the Cabinet; both war and peace decisions were exclusively taken by Yahya in consultation with the service chiefs and the senior generals close to him. But the functional organization and the emergency plans made under its aegis in peacetime stood the test as an efficient framework of total civilian mobilization for war efforts.

On 23 November the President being 'satisfied that a grave emergency exists in which Pakistan is threatened by external aggression' issued a Proclamation of Emergency.[3] Simultaneously, the Defence of Pakistan Ordinance, the legal enactment resorted to in time of war, was issued, which invested the government with sweeping powers. The same day, the President ordered the formation of an enlarged emergency committee (i) to deal on a day-to-day basis with all matters arising from the emergency; (ii) to co-ordinate defence efforts on the civil side; and (iii) to keep the internal situation, as it developed, under continuous review. The committee was headed by Ghiasuddin Ahmed, Adviser Defence, and included the Cabinet Secretary, Foreign Secretary, Information Secretary, Finance Secretary, Industries Secretary, Secretary National Security Division, and Director Intelligence Bureau. The committee was asked to co-opt some senior officers of the armed forces also as its members. The following day, 24 November, in the Weekly Meeting the President mentioned the Indian attack on East Pakistan, which had necessitated the declaration of the state of emergency. The armed forces had been placed on full alert, he said, and 'God willing they will give a befitting reply to the enemy at the opportune time'. The emergency committee started meeting forthwith almost every day, and often twice a day. The minutes of the meetings were issued by the Cabinet Division, with copies to the Principal Staff Officer to the President; but no record was kept of the discussions and decisions on 'sensitive' issues. From its inception on 24 November until 30 December, it held thirty-one meetings.

In the first few days, the committee went over the provisions of the war book, identified the areas which needed to be activated immediately and attended to the pressing problems brought up by the different ministries. Thereafter, at the top of the agenda of its daily meetings held in the Ministry of Defence were three briefings: (a) on the military situation, by Major-General Ghulam Jilani, Director-General, Inter-Services Intelligence (ISI); (b) on political and diplomatic aspects, by Sultan Muhammad Khan or the Additional Foreign Secretary, Alvie; and (c) on Press and publicity by Roedad Khan. The decisions on individual problems brought up by the various agencies, or taken note of by the committee itself, were taken in the light of these briefings.

In the meeting of 29 November, Alvie presented to the committee a highly optimistic picture of the world's view of Pakistan affairs. A similar assessment, which suggested all-out war as a viable option to resolve the East Pakistan crisis, must have been one of the important factors in Yahya's decision to open the second front in West Pakistan. Alvie informed the committee that (a) world opinion had turned to Pakistan's favour and the East Pakistan situation was now much better understood than before;

(b) India's belligerence was being criticized more and more by the world Press; (c) the Chinese Prime Minister had sent a positive reply to the message of the President and had asked to be kept informed of developments; (d) Pakistan would refer the matter to the Security Council when it felt confident of a suitable resolution from it, consultations in the matter were being held with the US and China; (e) a proposal had been made to the UN Secretary-General for posting UN observers on the Pakistan side of the border. Ghulam Ishaq Khan made the point that if Pakistan had to go to the Security Council it should go before any sizeable territory was lost in East Pakistan, as seemed likely, and India recognized Bangladesh. The Foreign Office was asked to consider these eventualities, and whether mere bilateral diplomatic overtures would be enough to meet the serious situation. Ghiasuddin asked Alvie to bring these points to the notice of the President during Foreign Office briefings to him.

In the emergency committee meeting of 1 December when the military briefing depicted the situation in East Pakistan as being well under control, some members were sceptical of the claim and referred to Press accounts of loss of territories there. The two senior army officers present reassured the members that the fighting was confined to the borders and there was no reason for despondency or alarm. By about this time the following territory along the borders, including some well-known places, had fallen to the enemy: areas including Chuagacha and other villages in Jessore sector; areas north and north-west of Thakurgaon (subdivisional headquarters), and other places of Dinajpur district, the railway line passing through Hilli had been cut; areas in Kurigram subdivision of Rangpur district; areas, including the town of Shamshernagar, in Sylhet district; the eastern border belt and other areas in the Chittagong Hill Tracts.

In the middle of November, I had come to Islamabad during the Eid holidays, and arranged some meetings to extend the stay on official business. In spite of the fact that the situation in all respects was the worst that the country had ever been placed in, the regime was exuding confidence. The line in the official media was the same that was being repeated for the last seven months: the overwhelming majority of Bengalis were for united Pakistan, stories of atrocities were fabrications of India and the foreign correspondents, and that any attack on East Pakistan would mean an all out Indo-Pakistan war. The independent Press was still more hawkish and it even accused the television and radio of not projecting the ideological-cum-patriotic theme enough to boost the morale of the people. As I moved round the military and civilian circles of Rawalpindi and Islamabad, I became certain that war with India was imminent. There was a consensus among the vocal and influential classes that this was the only solution to the crisis. Everyone was expecting substantial gains on the western front which would counterbalance the Indian military moves in the east; East Pakistan would be defended on the plains of the Punjab. This was the doctrine on which the entire defence structure of Pakistan was built and which the people had been led to believe for the last twenty-five years. But in the general enthusiasm for victories in the west, although no one was thinking specifically of its separation, East Pakistan vaguely figured as a side issue; the psyche was to retrieve the fruits of victory of which the nation was deprived by Ayub's cease-fire in the 1965 war. Private cars and public vehicles and places were plastered with 'Crush India' stickers. The radio was blaring martial music exhorting people to be ready for *'jehad',* interspersed with vulgar parodies of Indian film songs about the person of Mrs Gandhi. The people—and they included the well-educated classes—had been carried away by the 'one Muslim equal to ten Hindus' syndrome which had caught the imagination of even the professional soldier, who ought to have known better.

On 29 November, the emergency committee discussed the intelligence reports of the public criticism of the army as having neither the will nor the capacity to take action in the west. It was decided to ask the C-in-C Navy and the Chief of Staff Army to inform the nation that the armed forces were fully prepared to meet the Indian aggression, on the occasion of the passing out parade of the Naval Academy on 5 December. The President, when informed of this decision in the last Weekly Meeting on 1 December, gave a meaningful smile and asked a rhetorical question 'Will the COS be able to go?' From the President's remark and gestures the secretaries deduced that some military event was in the offing in the next few days.

This exuberant sabre-rattling was in stark contrast to the bleak life in East Pakistan. The army there had moved out to the borders, and the guerrillas had a free run of Dhaka except during the few daylight hours. Those of us who had been witnessing the gradual demoralization and fatigue of the army, and the increasing boldness of the insurgents over the last seven months had no illusions about the capabilities of the armed forces to hold East Pakistan. In private conversation, the army officers serving there agreed with this assessment. In West Pakistan, few in the higher civil service, or for that matter in the army high command, had an idea of the ground conditions in the East; few of them cared to visit it after March, from the President downward, and those who did, believed war a desirable solution. My colleagues were imbued with the spirit of the times. They showed concern about our plight and safety in Dhaka, were extra polite, and invited me to dinners, but for all their light-heartedness I might have been an alien from a distant land.

Sheikh Rauf, Additional Secretary Planning, who had held a meeting for my benefit on 28 November, offered to continue discussions over the next two or three days to give me an official reason to prolong the stay. There was not much to discuss under the circumstances about economic planning. The same evening I left for Karachi, and by pulling a few strings, managed to get a seat for Dhaka on the night of 30 November and 1 December. These were grave times. East Pakistan was far off, surrounded by the sea or the enemy, and it was not easy to get out from it. The fragile air link could snap at any time. The final moment of farewell to my wife and daughter was not easy. I kissed them and hurried into the darkness towards the plane. It would be more than two years before we met again. Many others went through the same agonies of pointless calls of duty 'to serve' the people who did not want 'outsiders' in their country.

Governor Malik and Muzaffar Husain were also in Islamabad in the last week of November. They had meetings with the officials concerning the requirements of the province, but no military briefing was given to them. Malik met the President who gave no inkling to him of the war which he had decided to declare a few days later and of which the main brunt would be borne by East Pakistan.

The logic of the regime's policies in East Pakistan, and the buildup of 'patriotic' fervour against India through the media in West Pakistan had brought the inevitable moment of truth. Yahya knew that East Pakistan was indefensible, and soon military resistance there would collapse. He had to decide whether to let it happen, or invoke the conventional strategy of defending it by opening the western front where, for the time being, Pakistan had some superiority. There is no evidence that the Indians were at the time planning to attack West Pakistan, and the hostilities would have ended with the fall of East Pakistan. But, as Yahya confessed later when confronted with defeat, the army could not have lived down the ignominy of losing East Pakistan without an all-out war with India. The senior command was seething under the increasing public criticism. Roedad Khan recalls General Gul Hassan giving vent to the army's anger on the day war was declared: 'we had to take this action, otherwise we will not be able to wear our uniforms. We are being exposed to the charge that we are sitting and doing nothing. I told the COS to explain it to the President and offered to go with him if he was not willing or able to do so'. Yahya, in spite of all the adverse factors, could not in the circumstances avoid a total war, even assuming that he realized its perils. And this option had to be exercised as early as possible while the Indians were still involved in East Pakistan and before they bore down on West Pakistan with the full might of their formidable war machine. That Pakistan was in no position to fight on two fronts was borne out by its urgent requests to friendly countries for physical intervention and material assistance simultaneously with the declaration of war. In East Pakistan the Commander was inquiring about foreign intervention and waiting for the army offensive in the west from the third day of hostilities. The decision to go for an all-out war was clearly not taken on purely military considerations. It was based on a mixture of fear of public wrath, false assumptions of intervention by friendly countries, and hurt egos from the failures of the previous eight months.

The decision to open the western front was taken on 29 November by Yahya in consultation with the Chief of Staff Army and the C-in-C Air Force; the C-in-C Navy was later summoned and informed of the decision. Originally the date was 2 December, but later it was advanced to 3 December.

The Pakistan defence plans envisaged immediate retaliation on the western front in case of an Indian attack on East Pakistan. In East Pakistan the operational plan was based on a forward defensive posture. 'The border outposts were to be backed by strong points and defences as far forward as was tactically sound on all major land approaches from India into East Pakistan. These defences were to be stocked with supplies and ammunitions varying from 7 to 15 days with 15 to 30 days reserves held in the rear areas. If and when the forward defences became untenable, units and sub-units were to withdraw to communication centres like the towns of Jessore, Khulna, Jhenida, Bogra, Comilla, Luksham and Chittagong and convert them into strong points.' The objective was to seal the borders and deny any territory to the enemy to achieve its political objective of setting up an independent government. It was assumed that (i) by the time the Indian threat materialized, normalcy would prevail in the province and the population would be pacified; (ii) the Indian offensive would be launched with only five or six divisions (actually the Indian attack was by three army corps, a communication zone headquarters which acted as a mobile operational formation, and the *mukti bahini* estimated to be about 100,000 strong); and (iii) India would not directly attack East Pakistan but would give all support to the *mukti bahini* to capture some territory as a base for declaring independent Bangaldesh which would be recognized by India. All these assumptions had become invalid by November, but the plans prepared and approved by the COS in August 1971 were not changed. In West Pakistan and Azad Kashmir the operational plans envisaged maintaining an aggressive defensive posture, and an offensive to seize maximum territory of political and strategic significance. This offensive was to be launched by a corps with an armoured division and two infantry divisions to be reinforced after the initial attack by more troops and armour. The role of the remaining portion of the army was to fix the enemy all along the western border to prevent it from organizing an offensive capability, and to undertake planned actions to divert the enemy reserves and forces from the general area of the target of the main offensive. The timing of the offensive was set for some time after preliminary operations by the holding formations to fix the enemy and divert its attention had been completed.[4]

On 2 December Yahya, in a letter to Nixon, formally invoked Article 1 of the Pakistan–US Bilateral Agreement of 5 March 1959 for direct military assistance from the US against Indian aggression.[5] He also requested for (a) a strong statement condemning Indian aggression, calling an immediate end to hostilities, and withdrawal of forces from the borders; and (b) another statement urging the Soviet Union to stop military support to India.

3 December

West Pakistan: Rawalpindi

At 1.20 p.m. the COS informed the Commander Eastern Command: 'Total war imminent. Redeploy forces in accordance operational tasks. Consider areas of tactical strategic and political importance'. The vagueness of these instructions gives the impression that GHQ was attempting to distance itself from the East Pakistan operations.

Roedad Khan was asked to be at GHQ at 4.25 p.m. At 5 p.m. he was taken by the CGS to the air force operation room. The President dictated a brief statement and directed it to be broadcast immediately. It was done by interrupting the regular programme on Radio Pakistan at 5.40 p.m.

The Defence Adviser and the Foreign Secretary heard the news on the radio, and frantically tried to confirm it from each other. Ghiasuddin first went to the GHQ, where the Vice Chief of General Staff confirmed the news of the attack, and then proceeded to his office and called a meeting of the emergency committee. He also obtained the orders of the President to enforce the war stage plans. It was decided to enforce a blackout throughout West Pakistan. Yahya later asked the Foreign Secretary to bring the Chinese and US ambassadors separately to the President House, the same evening, for a briefing by him.

The Pakistan air force commenced attacks on Indian bases at 5.20 p.m. According to Palit, the pre-emptive strike which assumed that the Indian squadrons had been placed on the forward bases and that they would be parked in the open indicated 'a drastic breakdown of Pak intelligence'. He claims that 'these attempts were so clumsy that not one Indian plane was lost on the ground'.[6] The PAF did not make any claims and the strike was later called 'simply a defensive move and aimed at preventing the IAF using forward bases.'[7] The course of the war showed that it did not achieve even this modest aim.

During the night between 3 and 4 December, the Pakistan army formations launched limited offensive operations as planned; some ground was gained and the defensive positions of the holding formations were improved. The primary aim of these formations was to draw the Indian reserves into the open.

Yahya sent an urgent message to the Shah of Iran requesting the Iranian government for immediate implementation of the mutually agreed contingency plans. He also submitted for 'Your Imperial Majesty's gracious consideration' the urgent need for gunboats, in view of the Indian naval threat, and the equally pressing need for missile-carrying helicopters.

East Pakistan: Dhaka

The direct result of the opening of the western front was to give India a free hand to carry out its plans to invade East Pakistan without any cover of the *mukti bahini*. They launched full-scale air attacks on Tejgaon and Kurmitola airfields during the night, and caused major damage. They were met by anti-aircraft fire; the PAF, consisting of 14 Sabre planes, had no capability for night operations.

4 December

East Pakistan: Dhaka

Early in the morning Muzaffar Husain saw the Governor who was very bitter at not being taken into confidence about the war. 'Yahya has bluffed us,' the Governor said and he asked the Chief Secretary to see Niazi and let him know the situation. The Indian air attacks continued throughout the morning and later in the day. The Pakistani planes were also seen going on sorties. The road to the cantonment running along the airport was under constant attack. Muzaffar Husain met Niazi at the tactical headquarters, which was located underground in a grove in a secluded part of the cantonment. Major-Generals Farman and Jamshed, Brigadier Baqar Siddiqui, Chief of Staff to the Commander Eastern Command, Rear-Admiral Shariff, and the Naval Captain Zamir were also present and having coffee. Some one from the air base informed them that Amritsar had fallen. At this, caps were thrown in the air, hurrahs were shouted, and they embraced each other without bothering to confirm the news.

It was agreed that Niazi would brief Muzaffar Husain on the military situation every day, and he in turn would keep the

Governor informed. Muzaffar Husain found Niazi unsure of himself, and looking more towards the western front than his own precarious defence lines. He complained of lack of sufficient firepower and the disruption of communications with sector commanders, and was apprehensive of the full-scale Indian armour attack which, in fact, had already started. Niazi was not sure he would be able to withstand the onslaught.

It took Muzaffar Husain two hours to return to the Governor House due to heavy air raids. He gave his assessment to the Governor that the army would not be able to hold out for more than a week. There was already talk of a cease-fire and of Chinese help. Farman was also was not very optimistic. The Governor was bewildered; first, they went to war without so much as even informing him, and the next day they were saying that there was little hope. During the day, the Governor, in meetings with the Chief Secretary and Farman, decided to bring the real situation to the notice of the President. A message was drafted. But Farman Ali was reluctant to pursue it because he thought Niazi would oppose it.

The Bengali ministers were jittery and demanding to know why help from abroad was not coming. They were in hourly contact with Nurul Amin in Rawalpindi and getting disinformation of help on the way. News was received that the *mukti bahini* was collecting in very large numbers at Demra on the outskirts of Dhaka for an attack on the city. This further unnerved the council of ministers.

West Pakistan: Rawalpindi

Pakistan again approached the US government under Article 1 of the Bilateral Agreement. As an alternative, however, it was suggested that, should the circumstances within the US preclude it from giving direct or indirect military assistance, the embargo on friendly countries be lifted for the specific purpose of supplying arms and spares to Pakistan.

Washington and the United Nations

Kissinger, in response to Pakistan's request for military assistance, told the Pakistan ambassador that US military involvement was out of the question. But he agreed to Iran and Turkey giving

Pakistan American arms. He also offered, perhaps facetiously, American arms from Israel.

As early as 24 November, the Americans had given clearance to Pakistan to move the Security Council. At the time of the Indian attack on East Pakistan on 22 November, the Third Committee of the General Assembly was debating the question of East Pakistan refugees. The Soviet Union and Western European countries fully supported the Indian stand that political conditions conducive to the return of refugees should be created in East Pakistan. The Afro-Asian and Muslim countries' delegations, reacting to the aggressive Indian stance and its support by West Europeans and influenced by the strong opposition by China, spoke against politicization of the refugee issue. Accordingly, the General Assembly, on the recommendations of the Third Committee, adopted two resolutions which, without specifically mentioning political settlement, called for the creation of a favourable climate for the return of refugees by working in the spirit of the principles of the UN Charter. The anxious inquiries of some of the friendly delegations regarding Pakistan's intentions about the meeting of the Security Council to discuss the Indian invasion were conveyed to the Foreign Office, which forbade the mission to make any move for it without the express instructions of the government. Apparently, Yahya's anxiety between 21 November and 3 December was to avoid any pressure by the world community for political accommodation with the Awami League, which a debate in the Security Council was bound to generate. In the UN, the impression spread that either the government of Pakistan had lost touch with realities or perhaps it was confident of substantial gains on the western front, and did not want its freedom of action to be circumscribed by UN resolutions.

After the outbreak of hostilities, the Foreign Secretary requested approval for nominating the leader of the delegation in preparation for going to the UN, but the President said there was no hurry. At the start of the war, apart from fearing pressure for a political settlement, Yahya was presumably expecting some gains on the western front to reduce the pressure on East Pakistan, and of going to the UN with something to bargain with. The Foreign Office, however, had started working on a draft resolution of its own a few days earlier. It had also initiated discussions with friendly powers but no understanding had been reached by

4 December, when the Americans informed Pakistan that they were requesting an emergency meeting of the Security Council on their own, whether the government of Pakistan agreed or not. The American initiative seemed to have emanated more from the running differences between the State Department and the White House on South Asia policy than objective considerations. As Kissinger says, it was to avoid taking sides in the Indo-Pakistan conflict, which the White House was pressurizing the State Department to do: 'Having opposed recourse to the Security Council earlier, State (Department) now favored it . . . to delay our [US] having to take any position at all . . . [and] slide off the condemnation of India that Nixon had ordered.'[8]

Although the US insisted on taking the issue to the Security Council, it accommodated Pakistan's sensitivities by agreeing to delete the word 'political' from the operative paragraph 4 of its draft resolution (S/10416) which originally had called for the creation of 'a political climate conducive to the voluntary return of refugees to East Pakistan.' The Security Council met on 4 December at 5 p.m. (1606th meeting) at the request of the US and eight other countries. The Soviet Union proposed an invitation to the representative of Bangladesh along with those of India and Pakistan. China and Argentina strongly opposed this and the matter was deferred. The US representative, George Bush, then introduced draft resolution S/10416 in which specific changes desired by Pakistan had been incorporated. It called for an immediate cease-fire and withdrawal of forces, which, Bush said, were necessary for a political settlement in East Pakistan. Except the Soviet Union and Poland, all the members stressed immediate cessation of hostilities and subsequent consideration of the causes which had led to war. China and one or two other countries also emphasized the need for withdrawal of forces of both the sides within their own territories. France and the UK made it clear that they would not vote for any resolution which did not command the unanimous approval of the Council. The strongest statement was that of China which condemned India, and pledged full support to Pakistan. The Soviet Union equally condemned Pakistan and praised India. Out of fifteen, the resolution received eleven votes in favour, two abstained (the UK and France), and two opposed (the Soviet Union and Poland); the negative vote of the Soviet Union vetoed the resolution.

The American resolution introduced in the Security Council *ab initio* a controversy in the global order of superpower politics. Perhaps it was inevitable, but one view was that the position might have been different if Pakistan had requested for the meeting of the Council, and, in case of Soviet opposition, mustered the support of the US, China, and other friendly countries. To counter the American initiative, the Soviet Union, on the same day, 4 December, moved its own draft resolution (S/10418) which called for a political settlement in East Pakistan and asked the government of Pakistan to cease all acts of violence by the Pakistan forces there. Discussions on this and two other resolutions, S/10417 (Belgium, Italy, and Japan) and S/10419 (Argentina, Burundi, Nicaragua, Sierra Leone, and Somalia) moved on the same day, were postponed until the next meeting which was fixed for 2.30 p.m. on 5 December.[9]

5 December

East Pakistan: Dhaka

There had been substantial losses in East Pakistan in the foregoing two days. Darsana, Thakurgaon, Kamalpur, and Akhura fell, and the Indian air force continued massive, almost round the clock attacks on Dhaka. Baqar, in briefing Muzaffar Husain, merely informed him that the army was holding out in some sectors, while in others the position was not so good; none of these losses of important towns was mentioned. The tactical headquarters was in gloom. Niazi was grieving, 'I have never harmed anyone. Why should this happen to me?' Shariff agreed with Muzaffar Husain that the army could not hold out for more than a week. The Chief Secretary informed the Governor that the situation was getting out of hand, and while the Eastern Command itself was not willing to inform Rawalpindi about it, it would not be averse to the Governor doing so. The Governor instructed that a message to Yahya should be drafted.

West Pakistan: Rawalpindi

The COS Army, consequent upon the rapid advances of the Indians, and sensing the declining morale of Niazi's command, for the first time explained the role of the eastern theatre in the war. In a message sent at 11.15 a.m. on this date, he said that the enemy's intention was to capture East Pakistan swiftly and then shift forces to West Pakistan, and asked the Eastern Commander not to let it happen and to continue fighting, irrespective of the loss of territory, by concentrating on vital areas. Not perhaps quite sure that an order would be enough to sustain the garrison's will to fight, he concluded the message with the hope 'of early activities by the Chinese'. In other words, the strategy on the second day of the war had gone in reverse; East Pakistan was to go on fighting to the last soldier in its garrison to save West Pakistan until foreign help came (for which no firm commitment had been obtained beforehand) or until a cease-fire was arranged. For the preceding twenty-five years, all pleas of the East Pakistanis to make them self-reliant in defence had been rejected. They were told that they were indefensible, and their security lay in the plains of the Punjab, where immense resources of both the East and West Wings had been spent to launch a blitzkrieg into India. Niazi's position was untenable; it was neither in the plans nor was he given the resources for the role he was now asked to play to save the country. He was holding out under the most adverse circumstances, fighting the local population as well as the vastly superior enemy.

Meanwhile, nothing was happening on the western front, and the whole purpose of opening the second front was being lost. The people were getting impatient at the lack of any action, which they had been led to expect; one newspaper openly criticized the government-controlled media for suppressing the achievements of the armed forces. When this was brought to the notice of Yahya, he compared the western situation, to some members of the emergency committee, 'like two boxers or wrestlers having taken up positions and looking at each other with their hands stretched to grapple.' 'We are,' he said, 'at the moment awaiting the response of the Indian armed forces to the threat we have posed to their positions at four or five places. After that we will make a massive breakthrough at another salient.' Yahya then angrily told the civilians that these were military matters for the military commander to decide, and that 'he would not throw away military manpower in a gamble to satisfy the demands of the uninformed public opinion'. The President also observed that it would be a hard and long conflict with India.

The United Nations

The majority of the members of the Security Council felt dissatisfied with the US and Soviet resolutions which they thought did not meet the requirements of the situation. They held that a resolution, to escape a veto and be effective and balanced, had to contain three elements: cease-fire, withdrawal of forces, and an early political solution in East Pakistan. The eight non-permanent members, accordingly, started drafting a new resolution. In its original version the draft produced by them called for a cease-fire, withdrawal of forces, and simultaneous creation of conditions necessary for the return of refugees. To please the Soviet Union, the draft also included a clause about Pakistan ending the state of emergency and military operations in East Pakistan; this was deleted at Pakistan's objection. Pakistan also succeeded in getting the word 'simultaneous' removed to make the cessation of hostilities and withdrawal of forces immediate, as the creation of conditions for the return of refugees was bound to take time. The eight-power draft that finally emerged represented an attempt to modify the original US draft resolution by incorporating the element of political settlement in the preambulatory paragraphs. The operative part was confined to the cease-fire and withdrawal of forces, and on the return of refugees the formulation of the resolution of the Third Committee of the General Assembly was adopted. Since the sponsors of the two earlier resolutions had now agreed to co-sponsor a new draft, documents S/10417 and S/10419 were withdrawn and draft resolution S/10423 was jointly moved by them in the Security Council. China also agreed with the final draft of this resolution. On the morning of 5 December the contents of the draft were communicated over the telephone to the Foreign Secretary who asked the mission to prolong discussions for two days. But news of fierce fighting on all fronts in Pakistan had created a sense of urgency in the UN forum, and it was not possible to persuade the sponsoring countries to delay their resolution.

There were now two resolutions, the Soviet one, and the eight-power one, before the Security Council which met as scheduled on 5 December (1607th meeting). The Soviet Union again raised the question of inviting the representative of Bangladesh, but did not press it in the face of opposition from China and some other countries. After a somewhat acrimonious debate, the two resolutions were put to vote. The Soviet resolution, S/10418, received two votes (the USSR and Poland) in favour, one (China) against, and twelve abstentions. The eight-power resolution, S/10423, received eleven votes in favour, two (the USSR and Poland) against, and two (the UK and France) abstentions; it was vetoed by the Soviet Union.

In the ensuing stalemate, the representative of France suggested further consultations on the basis of what appeared to be the common elements in the stands of all parties: immediate cessation of hostilities and promoting a political solution to enable the refugees to return. The representative of Italy then moved a short resolution (S/10425) which provided for an immediate cease-fire, and thereafter consideration by the Security Council of measures to restore peace in the region. The co-sponsors of this draft were Belgium, Japan, Nicaragua, Sierra Leone, and Tunisia. Yet another resolution, S/10421, sponsored on this date was by the People's Republic of China which condemned India, called for a cease-fire and withdrawal of forces by the warring parties, and asked 'all States to support the Pakistan people in their just struggle to resist Indian aggression.'

The debate was marked by recriminations and vituperative speeches by China and the Soviet Union. In a highly charged and polarized atmosphere, consideration of the Chinese and Italian resolutions was postponed until further consultations could take place.

By now, three distinct positions had emerged in the Security Council. The first was that of the majority, articulated in the US resolution (S/10416), for an immediate cease-fire and withdrawal of forces, and thereafter consideration of the issues which had caused the conflict. The second position was represented by the Soviet draft (S/10418) which made a cease-fire conditional on political settlement and cessation of acts of violence in East Pakistan. The third was that of Britain and France which would accept only a draft which would not attract the Russian veto.

6 December

East Pakistan: Dhaka

All sectors in the north, east, and west were under great pressure. There was a complete blockade by sea and air. Dhaka and

Kurmitola runways were effectively bombed, and the IAF ensured by repeated attacks that they remained out of service. The PAF was completely grounded with effect from the evening of this date. The Indians were trying to achieve a quick breakthrough wherever possible.

At 10.05 a.m., the Commander Eastern Command sent the following special message (G-1233) to the COS at Rawalpindi:

> Enemy offensive intensified. IAF causing maximum damage. Rebels highly active. Local population also hostile. Main border towns and cities under pressure. Absence adequate firepower support aggravating situation which is becoming critical. Own forces now reaching pre-planned lines of defence [i.e. retreating]. Restoring to fortress/strong point basis. Will fight to last man last round. Request expedite action on G-0235 of 5 Dec [which had hoped for activities by the Chinese].

About twelve hours later the same day, at 11.15 p.m. Niazi sent another message to General Hamid asking him the likely date and nature of Chinese activities to plan his further action.

The movement of foodstuffs, which had been the nightmare of civil administration during the last nine months, had come to a halt. Stocks of petrol and kerosene oil were running low. The emergency plans envisaged rationing, but there was no one to administer it. Attendance in the Secretariat had come down to less than 50 per cent; the corridors and rooms were deserted. Rumours of a *mukti bahini* attack on Dhaka and a massacre in the city were rife. The locals were moving out to the safety and anonymity of villages. Frequently one would come across wheelbarrows piled high with pots and pans, with families trailing behind on their way out of the city. A number of shops were open and those selling provisions and medicines were doing brisk business. On the whole, now that air attacks had ceased, traffic had reappeared and the city wore a bustling look, with an expectant air, during the short winter daylight hours before the curfew.

At about this time it was reported that the Central Circuit house, where all the senior West Pakistani officers were living, guarded by a small detachment of West Pakistani police, was under grave threat of attack by the guerrillas. With the persistent reports of the *muktis* collecting at Demra, the danger of their storming the city seemed, under the prevailing uncertain circumstances, a real one. The Chief Secretary in a meeting with the Inspector-General Police, the Commissioner of Dhaka, and other senior West Pakistani officers tentatively decided to shift to the President House in the same Ramna area. With walls seven feet high, it was thought to be a more defensible place. Earlier, when Niazi was requested to take the West Pakistani civil officers to the cantonment, he offered a school building which had only one latrine and bare halls, although a number of houses and messes were lying vacant. Even the school building was eventually not available. For the time being, however, we decided not to move as it might have created panic in the city.

Rawalpindi

The Press briefings by the military spokesman continued to be highly optimistic and the domestic media kept faithfully reproducing this picture. The foreign media, however, were depicting a totally different position. The emergency committee in its meeting of date took note of the dangers arising from the public euphoria built up by exaggerated stories of successes. It emphasized the necessity of objective and correct news reporting 'so that later the public does not become a victim of despondency.' The committee thought that the struggle would continue for at least another three months and all planning had to be done on that basis. It was decided to set up a National War Front under the leadership of the Information Secretary, to prepare the nation for a long-drawn-out struggle, privations, shortages, and other difficulties.

Ambassador Raza in Washington was asked to press the White House to decide quickly in what manner the US would extend material assistance to Pakistan. A similar message was handed over to Farland on the following day, 7 December.

The United Nations

The Security Council, convened on 6 December (1608th meeting), had before it two draft resolutions—China's S/10421 and the 5-power S/10425, sponsored by Italy. The latter did not provide for withdrawal of forces and Pakistan threatened to have it vetoed by China, if passed by the Security Council.

The Soviet Union was totally unaffected by its isolation, but slightly modified its stand. Its representative now said that he would accept an immediate cease-fire provided an addition was made in the 5-power draft calling upon the government of Pakistan simultaneously to give effect to the will of the people as expressed in the elections of December 1970. He insisted that the cease-fire and the political settlement were 'organically and inseparably bound together'. At this, Italy withdrew resolution S/10425.

The representative of India then read out a long statement made by Mrs Gandhi in the Indian Parliament on 5 December, announcing the recognition of Bangladesh as an independent and sovereign state. He also quoted excerpts from western newspapers about atrocities in East Pakistan. The representative of China strongly attacked the Soviet Union.

After the withdrawal of the 5-power resolution, the amendment, by way of addition, proposed in it by the Soviet Union also lapsed. The Soviet Union then immediately circulated its own draft resolution, S/10428, which was an improvement over its previous resolution S/10418. It recognized the hostilities as a threat to international peace and security, called upon the parties for an immediate cease-fire as a first step, and asked the government of Pakistan to give simultaneous effect to the will of the people of East Pakistan as expressed in the elections of December 1970. The representative of the Soviet Union, in replying to Chinese criticism, was vitriolic and almost abusive. Pakistan opposed the Soviet resolution which, in the highly polarized atmosphere, was not pressed for voting by the sponsor.

We will revert to the second Soviet resolution, S/10428, later while discussing the controversy about the Polish resolution. At this point it may be noted that its acceptance would have avoided the surrender in Dhaka, though the withdrawal of the army from East Pakistan required by it would have been just as humiliating within and outside Pakistan. Moreover, it would not have been easy to persuade China and US, which for their own reasons were not prepared for any compromise with the Soviet Union on the issue of Indian aggression. The military situation, however, was deteriorating so rapidly that after forty-eight hours even this offer of a cease-fire was not available.

There were a number of other drafts going round amongst the delegates at this time. But the non-permanent members of the Security Council led by Somalia and Argentina, and backed by the US and China, decided to move for referring the matter to the General Assembly under 'The Uniting for Peace Procedure'. The

Security Council adopted a six-power resolution 303 (1971) to this effect by eleven votes in favour with four abstentions (the Soviet Union, Poland, Britain, and France).

7 December

Washington and the United Nations

'On December 7 Yahya informed us that East Pakistan was disintegrating.'[10] Kissinger, as always, tried to help. These emergency requests for military help came under discussion in the WSAG which had been meeting regularly in the Situation Room of the White House since the start of the war. In the 6 December meeting, Kissinger asked whether 'we have the right to authorize Jordan or Saudi Arabia to transfer military equipment to Pakistan.' The State Department representative opined that, in view of the Congressional ban imposed in January the previous year, 'the United States cannot permit a third country to transfer arms which we have provided them when we, ourselves, do not authorize sale direct' to Pakistan. Kissinger said that 'the President may want to honour those requests [from Pakistan]', and pressed for some action. Joseph Sisco, Assistant Secretary of State Near Eastern and South Asian Affairs agreed, but said that 'it should be done very quietly.'[11]

In subsequent WSAG meetings, the question of military assistance to Pakistan remained under discussion, and the formal position as stated above was reiterated. On the specific request of Jordan to allow the transfer of F-104s to Pakistan, Kissinger desired 'to keep Hussein in a "holding pattern" . . . and that he should not be turned off.' President Nixon wanted time to consider the issue.[12] In spite of strong opposition to any help to Pakistan by the State Department and other organs, the White House had given hints to Iran, Turkey, and Jordan that they might extend arms support to Pakistan. The problem with the planes was not only the embargo, but the friendly countries' worry about their own security. Jordan's position was likely to be weakened by the transfer without a promise of replacement for which 'we do not have any more M.A.P. [military assistance programme] left.'[13] In the absence of an open commitment by the US matching that of the Soviet Union to India, the Shah of Iran said, Iran could not possibly incur the risk of Soviet retaliation by its open intervention in the Indo-Pakistan conflict.

At about this time, Kissinger says, 'A report reached us from a source whose reliability we had never any reason to doubt . . . that India would not accept any General Assembly call for a cease-fire' until East Pakistan was liberated. Thereafter, the Indian forces would concentrate on the southern part of Azad Kashmir 'and continue fighting until the Pakistan army and air force were wiped out.' Mrs Gandhi also told colleagues that in case China intervened, 'the Soviets had promised to take appropriate counteraction.'[14] Henceforth, Kissinger's worry was the existence of what remained of Pakistan.

The General Assembly met on 7 December with a due sense of urgency. In an unprecedented move, it imposed a time limit on speeches and allowed no interruptions until the end of two sessions (2002nd and 2003rd) on the same day. Two draft resolutions were moved. One, A/L 647 Revision 1, was practically the same as the draft submitted to the Security Council by the eight non-permanent members (S/10423), and vetoed by the Soviet Union on 5 December. Besides these eight powers, four other countries became co-sponsors when this draft resolution was introduced in the Assembly; by the time of voting, the number of sponsors had increased to 34. The other draft resolution, A/L 648, was moved by the Soviet Union, and was identical to its second draft, S/10428, which it had moved in the Security Council the previous day but had not pressed for voting.

Nearly 60 delegations participated in the debate and expressed serious concern over the inability of the Security Council to bring about the end of the full-scale war between the two largest nations in Asia. The Indian representative stated that India would not accept the provisions of A/L 647 Revision 1, and said:

> The representative of Pakistan was moved about the break up of his country . . . but we have to face the fact that it has broken up; nothing on earth can stop it; it has happened . . .

The draft A/L 647 Revision 1, renumbered 2793 (XXVI), was put to vote and adopted by 104 votes in favour, 11 against, and 10 abstentions. It called for an immediate cease-fire and withdrawal of forces, and thereafter for dealing with the issues which had caused the hostilities. The Assembly decided not to vote on the Soviet draft.

After the adoption of document 2793 (XXVI), Pakistan intervened in the General Assembly to make it clear that the provisions of the resolution about 'an early political solution' and 'the need to deal appropriately at a subsequent stage' with the issues that had caused the hostilities and to restore conditions necessary for the return of refugees must all be construed within the UN Charter, that is within the principle of the territorial integrity and national unity of Pakistan.

The text of the Assembly resolution with the mission's comments on its main provisions was conveyed the same evening by telephone to Islamabad via Stockholm, the only link available. (Due to the time difference and transmission time it was received in Pakistan on 8 December).

West Pakistan: Rawalpindi

On the western front by 7 December the 'Indian divisions had been fixed in their areas by various operations of Pakistani divisions.' The planned attack on Poonch had failed. In the Sialkot–Shakargarh area, 1 Corps was putting up a passive defence, but had lost the Pukhlian salient. 4 Corps, Lahore–Bahawalpur sector, 'was given the task of limited offensive action—to seize features of tactical importance to improve its defensive posture.' It had captured its limited objectives. In Rajasthan, 18 Division 'had suffered a debacle and was withdrawing to its prepared positions.' The Indian 1 Armoured Division was located, still uncommitted, in addition to one armoured brigade, at Ajnala. All other Indian troops had been committed; the local reserves of the divisions and corps could have been mobilized in case of a Pakistani offensive but only over time and 'might not have influenced the initial breakthrough.' Lieutenant-General Tikka Khan, commanding the Reserve Corps, had a meeting in GHQ on 7 December, but did not get the green signal.[15] The Pakistan high command, at the time, was apparently not certain that the enemy reserves had been sufficiently involved and were not in a position to interfere with the offensive. The other view was that opportunities for launching the main offensive by army reserves existed, though the IAF raids on the railway system were a cause for concern.

East Pakistan: Dhaka

In reply to the previous day's message (G-1233) of the Commander Eastern Command, the Chief of General Staff, Lieutenant-General Gul Hassan, informed Niazi (vide No. G-0907)

> Position appreciated. Eastern Command's tactical concept approved. Hold position in strength without territorial considerations including Chittagong. Maintain entity of force intact and inflict maximum attrition on enemy.

In another message (G-0908) the same day, the CGS assured Niazi about the Chinese: 'Matter receiving urgent attention at other end.'

This was precisely the time when East Pakistan badly needed relief from the intense Indian pressure on all its borders. An offensive on the western front might have given some hope to the eastern garrison. Jessore had fallen and the Indians were advancing towards Khulna and Faridpur in pursuit of retreating Pakistan forces. The Indian navy had effectively blocked all the sea routes. The IAF was concentrating on river communications to immobilize the Pakistani forces on the ground.

On 7 December at 11 a.m., Lieutenant-General Niazi was called by the Governor for a briefing on the military situation. After the briefing, at which Muzaffar Husain and Farman Ali were also present, the following message (A-6905) was drafted then and there, and sent to the President at 12 a.m:

> From Governor East Pakistan
> For President of Pakistan (.) It is imperative that correct situation in East Pakistan is brought to your notice (.) I discussed with Gen. Niazi who tells me that troops are fighting heroically but against heavy odds without adequate artillery and air support (.) Rebels continue cutting their rear and losses in equipment and men are heavy and cannot be replaced (.) The front in EASTERN and WESTERN sectors has collapsed (.) Loss of whole corridor EAST of MEGHNA river cannot be avoided (.) Jessore has already fallen which will be a terrible blow to the morale of pro-PAKISTAN elements (.) Civil administration ineffective as they cannot do much without communications (.) Food and other supplies running short as cannot move from CHITTAGONG or within the PROVINCE (.) Even DACCA city will be without food after 7 days (.) Without fuel and oil there will be complete paralysis of life (.) Law

> and order situation in areas vacated by army pathetic as thousands of pro-PAKISTAN elements being butchered by rebels (.) Millions of non-Bengalis and loyal elements are awaiting death (.) No amount of lip sympathy or even material help from world powers except direct physical intervention will help (.) If any of our friends is expected to help that should have an impact within the next 48 rpt 48 hours (.) If no help is expected I beseech you to negotiate so that a civilized and peaceful transfer takes place and millions of lives are saved and untold misery avoided (.) Is it worth sacrificing so much when the end seems inevitable (.) If help is coming we will fight on whatever the consequences there may be (.) Request be kept informed.

The President replied (vide A-4555) the same evening at 7.25. He exhorted the Governor and the military Commander to fight to the last and entrusted them to God with his prayers. The message read as follows:

> From President for Governor (.) . . . (.) All possible steps are in hand (.) Full scale and bitter war is going on in the West Wing (.) World powers are very seriously attempting to bring about cease-fire (.) Subject is being referred to the General Assembly after persistent vetoes in the Security Council by the RUSSIANS (.) A very high powered delegation is being rushed to NEW YORK (.) Please rest assured that I am fully alive to the terrible situation that you are facing (.) Chief of Staff is being directed by me to instruct Gen. Niazi regarding the military strategy to be adopted (.) You on your part and your Government should adopt strongest measures in the field of food rationing and curtailing supply of all essential items as on war footing to be able to last for a maximum period of time and preventing a collapse (.) God be with you (.) We are all praying.

The helplessness of the message further eroded the morale of the Eastern Command. The same evening I met Muzaffar Husain for the first time since the start of the war. In his elegantly-furnished room in the Circuit House things did not seem so desperate. But apart from the atmosphere of the room, such was our self-deception fed by the media that when Muzaffar Husain told me that Jessore had fallen and, in his opinion, it was all over so far as East Pakistan was concerned, many of the West Pakistani officers did not believe him. Some were also angry with him for such inauspicious thoughts. That evening it was decided to avail the invitation of the considerate Governor to shift to the Governor House on the following day.

8 December

West Pakistan: Rawalpindi

'Hold defensible position where possible regardless of loss of territory. Discuss matter with Governor. All efforts being exerted at political level.' This was the message (G-0910) sent by the C-in-C, Yahya Khan, to the Commander Eastern Command at 00.15 a.m. on 8 December. This was the strategy promised in the message sent to the Governor earlier in the evening, and it was a measure of desperation that the Army Commander was being asked to discuss the matter with the Governor. Later the same day at 1 p.m. the CGS informed Niazi (vide G-0912): 'Reference G-0908 [which was about the Chinese]. Activities begun.'[16]

There was little change on the western front. But on this date the Director Military Operations and his deputy warned the COS that the time for an offensive 'was slipping by and gradually the initiative was being snatched away by India.' The COS promised to give a decision the next day.[17]

East Pakistan: Dhaka

Brahmanbaria had fallen, Comilla was encircled, and the Indians were advancing towards Chandpur. The whole of the sector opposite Tripura came under Indian control; an Indian column was racing down in the south to Chittagong. Dhaka continued to be subjected to intensive unhindered air strikes by the IAF.

In the afternoon we packed up whatever we could and loaded our cars. It was a sorry sight: the top administration moving in a procession of self-driven cars (the Bengali drivers had disappeared) under West Pakistani police guard on the deserted roads towards the safety of the Governor House. The Military Secretary, seeing the lot of us, was very unhappy. He thought the place would now come under attack by the *muktis* or the IAF. We, however, could not be turned back. Grudgingly, he directed us to some annexes which had been occupied by the martial law officers but were lying vacant now. We apportioned them amongst ourselves. Muzaffar Husain and some others occupied the VIP suites on the top floor of the main building.

The United Nations and Washington

On 9 December the Foreign Secretary informed the mission at New York that the government of Pakistan had accepted the General Assembly resolution. Agha Shahi, however, was instructed that in conveying this to the Secretary-General, the references in the resolution to Article 2 of the UN Charter and paragraphs 4,5, and 6 of the Declaration on the Strengthening of International Security which enjoin respect for the territorial integrity of the member states, should be emphasized. The instructions further asked the mission to request for concrete action by the UN for cessation of hostilities with immediate effect, withdrawal of forces, and posting of UN observers on both sides of the borders to oversee these measures. The mission was informed that Bhutto was on his way to New York and transmission of formal acceptance to the Secretary-General might await his arrival. However, the permanent representative was authorized to convey it immediately, in case he thought that the delay would not be desirable.

The General Assembly resolution was a moral victory for Pakistan, but it was at a time when the world perception was that Pakistan was putting up a determined resistance to Indian aggression. But the very next day news came of the fall of Jessore and of the rapid Indian advance towards Dhaka. The anxiety of the government of Pakistan, at that stage, to settle for a cease-fire and withdrawal of forces indicated that there was no hope of compensating gains on the western front. The mission, accordingly, thought it prudent to convey the acceptance of the resolution to the Secretary-General on the morning of 9 December in terms of instructions. Bhutto later protested to Yahya for having taken this action without consulting him.

Ambassador Raza again met Assistant Secretary Sisco and pressed for military assistance. Sisco explained the Administration's difficulties with the Congress and public opinion which strongly opposed any US involvement.

9 December

West Pakistan: Rawalpindi

Karachi harbour area was hit by Indian missile boats, setting on fire the oil storage tanks nearby. Malir ammunition depot was strafed and rocketed by the IAF.

Most of the Indian reserves had been identified and partially drawn into the Sialkot sector. In the process, the Indians had gained substantial area in the Shakargarh–Zafarwal sector and also in lower Sindh. The Pakistan high command, however, still believed that the Indians had retained some counter-offensive capability. The IAF was concentrating its main effort on disrupting the communication system in the southern areas of West Pakistan.

East Pakistan: Dhaka

The Indian government was under international pressure for a cease-fire and Dhaka had to be captured before that. On 9 December the Indian thrust from Akhura had reached the River Meghna at Ashuganj where the rail bridge had been damaged by the retreating Pakistan army. The local population came forward with a large number of boats and rafts to help the Indians to cross the river.[18]

Niazi sent the following message (G-1255) to the CGS on this date at 9.30 a.m.:

> Regrouping and readjustment not possible due enemy being 'Master of Skies'. No air support mission possible during last three days and in future. All jetties, ferries, river crafts destroyed by enemy air. Bridges demolished by rebels. Stress and strain telling upon own troops. Not slept for twenty days. Situation extremely critical. Request strike at enemy air bases. Reinforce Dacca by air borne troops.

The Governor summarized the military situation more succinctly the same day at 6 p.m., in the following message (A-4660) to the President. This was drafted by Muzaffar Husain and Farman and cleared by Niazi.

> From Governor East Pakistan
> for the President (.) Military Situation Desperate (.) Enemy is approaching FARIDPUR in the WEST and has closed up to the river MEGHNA in the EAST bypassing our troops in COMILLA and LAKSHAM (.) CHANDPUR has fallen to the enemy thereby closing all river routes (.) Enemy likely to be at the outskirts any day if no outside help forthcoming (.) Secretary General UN's representative in Dacca has proposed that DACCA CITY may be declared as an open city to save lives of civilians especially non-Bengalis (.) Am favourably inclined to

> accept the offer (.) Strongly recommend this be approved (.) Gen. NIAZI does not agree as he considers that his orders are to fight to the last and it would amount to giving up DACCA (.) This action may result in massacre of the whole army cmm WP Police and all non-locals and loyal locals (.) There are no regular troops in reserve and once the enemy has crossed the GANGES or MEGHNA further resistance will be futile unless CHINA or USA intervenes today with massive air and ground support (.) Once again urge you to consider immediate cease-fire and political settlement otherwise once Indian troops are free from East Wing in a few days even West Wing will be in jeopardy (.) Understand local population has welcomed Indian army in captured areas and are providing maximum help to them (.) Our troops are finding it impossible to withdraw and manoeuvre due to rebel activity (.) With this clear alignment sacrifice of West Pakistan is meaningless.

At 11 p.m. the same evening, the President sent the following reply (G-0001) to the Governor, repeated to the Commander Eastern Command.

> Your flash message A 4660 of 9 December received and thoroughly understood (.) You have my permission to take decisions on your proposals to me (.) I have and am continuing to take all measures internationally but in view of our complete isolation from each other decision about East Pakistan I leave entirely to your good sense and judgement (.) I will approve of any decision you take and I am instructing Gen. NIAZI simultaneously to accept your decision and arrange things accordingly (.) Whatever efforts you make in your decisions to save senseless destruction of the kind of civ that you have mentioned in particular the safety of our armed forces cmm you may go ahead and ensure safety of our armed forces by all political means that you will have to adopt with our opponent.

Washington

On 9 December Brezhnev replied to Nixon's message of 6 December which had emphasized restraint and the territorial integrity of the subcontinent. It proposed a cease-fire and resumption of negotiations with Mujib at the point they were broken off on 25 March. While the negotiations, under the circumstances, would inevitably result in practical independence of East Pakistan, Kissinger thought it was a good face-saving formula to ensure the integrity of West Pakistan. The only thing which worried Kissinger was that while the dialogue was being arranged, the Indians might try to overrun West Pakistan. The Indian ambassador assured the US about the territorial integrity of West Pakistan but did not commit anything in respect of Azad Kashmir.[19]

10 December

East Pakistan: Dhaka

Bitter fighting was raging in the north in Hilli sector. 'Some of the strongest resistance by Pakistani garrisons was met in this sector . . . the enemy in this sector resisted to the last.'[20] In the east, the Indians did not bother to reduce the so-called fortress of Comilla cantonment, which had shut itself in with two brigadiers, two infantry battalions, and two tanks.[21] They were rescued by the Indians, after the surrender, as prisoners of war. Since the Ashuganj bridge had been damaged and artillery, ammunition, and other heavy equipment could not be taken across to the western bank by country boats, which were volunteered in large numbers, the Indians started ferrying troops by helicopter on 10 December. 'The strong enemy garrison at Bhairab Bazar made no move to oppose the crossing, though they could not have helped observing the helicopters in action' says Palit; by the following day there was a sufficient Indian force to resume the advance towards Dhaka.[22] Salik gives this account of the same events: '27 Brigade . . . crossed over to Bhairab Bazar on the night of 10/11 December. The new defences of the Bhairab Bazar fortress were organized the following day. . . . While the 27 Brigade waited . . . the enemy helicopters ferried troops across the Meghna . . . in the Raipura–Narsindgi area, about fifteen kilometers south of Bhairab Bazar.' The tactical headquarters of 14 Division had also shifted a little earlier to Bhairab Bazar on the western bank. 'The heliborne force threatening Dacca was not disturbed by 14 Division or 27 Brigade, as it lay technically outside their jurisdiction.'[23]

The most important event of the thirteen-day war took place on this date. After a briefing on the military situation by Niazi, a message to the President and a note to the UN were drafted in the Governor's office by Farman and Muzaffar Husain and approved by all the four. The message (A-7107) was as follows:

> For President of Pakistan (.) Your G 0001 of 092300 Dec. [9 December 11 p.m.] (.) As the responsibility of taking final and fateful decision has been given to me I am handing over the following note to Assistant Secretary General Mr Paul Mark Henry after your approval (.) Note begins (.) It was never the intention of the armed forces of Pakistan to involve themselves in the all out war on the soil of East Pakistan (.) However cmm a situation arose which compelled the armed forces to take defensive action (.) The intention of the Government of Pakistan was always to decide the issues in East Pakistan by means of a political solution for which negotiations were afoot (.) The armed forces have fought heroically against heavy odds and can still continue to do so but in order to avoid further bloodshed and loss of innocent lives I am making the following proposals (.) As the conflict arose as a result of political causes cmm it must end with a political solution (.) I therefore have been authorised by the President of Pakistan to hereby call upon the elected representatives of East Pakistan to arrange for the peaceful formation of the Government in Dacca (.) In making this offer I feel duty bound to say that the will of the people of East Pakistan would demand immediate vacation of their land by the Indian forces as well (.) I therefore call upon the United Nations to arrange for a peaceful transfer of power and request:- ONE (.) An immediate cease-fire (.) TWO (.) Repatriation with honour of the Armed Forces of Pakistan to West Pakistan (.) THREE (.) Repatriation of all West Pakistani personnel desirous [sic] of returning to West Pakistan (.) FOUR (.) Safety of all persons settled in East Pakistan since 1947 (.) FIVE (.) Guarantee of no reprisals against any person in East Pakistan (.) In making this offer cmm I want to make it clear that this is a definite proposal for peaceful transfer of power (.) The question of surrender of the armed forces would not be considered and does not arise and if this proposal is not accepted the armed forces will continue to fight to the last man (.) Note ends (.) Gen. NIAZI has been consulted and submits himself to your command (.) Request your immediate approval.

I remember it was nearing lunch-time when Muzaffar Husain came to his suite with some papers from which he typed on his own typewriter. He briefly told some of us who were sitting in the adjoining rooms about a message being sent to the UN with the approval of the President about the cessation of hostilities. We were all extremely happy. Soon after typing a few pages, he went down to the Governor's office.

The President did not agree with the proposed note to the UN, and conveyed a revised draft in the following message (G-0002) to the Governor:

> The proposed draft of your message has gone much beyond what you had suggested and I had approved (.) It gives the impression that you are talking on behalf of Pakistan when you have mentioned the subject of transfer of power cmm political solution and repatriation of troops from East to West Pakistan etc. (.) This virtually means the acceptance of an independent East Pakistan (.) The existing situation in your area requires a limited action by you to end hostilities in East Pakistan (.) Therefore suggest a draft which you are authorised to issue (.) Quote (.) In view of complete blockade of East Pakistan by air and sea by overwhelming Indian Armed Forces and the resultant indiscriminate and senseless bloodshed of civil population have introduced new dimensions to the situation in East Pakistan (.) The President of Pakistan has authorised me to take whatever measures I may decide (.) I have therefore decided that although Pakistan Armed Forces have fought heroically against heavy odds and can still continue to do so yet cmm in order to avoid further bloodshed and loss of innocent lives I am making the following proposals (.) ONE (.) An immediate cease-fire in East Pakistan to end hostility (.) TWO (.) Guarantee of the personnel settled in East Pakistan since 1947 (.) THREE (.) Guarantee of no reprisals against any person in East Pakistan (.) Safety of all Armed Forces personnel in East Pakistan (.) I want to make it clear that this a definite proposal of ending all hostilities and the question of surrender of armed forces would not be considered and does not arise (.) Unquote (.) Within this framework you make additions or changes as you desire (.) The question of transfer of power and political solution will be tackled at National level which is being done.

The note to the UN reproduced in message no. A-7107 had already been handed over to Paul-Marc Henry and communicated to New York by the time the President's rejection of it was received.

This note to the UN has ever since been considered one of the controversial events of the East Pakistan crisis. Externally, it ended whatever remote chance there was of obtaining some sort of face-saving resolution from the Security Council. Internally, it shattered the self-deceptions of the establishment and intelligentsia, which had been moulded and encouraged by the Inter-Services Public Relations (ISPR) throughout the last nine months. Even the emergency committee, rather belatedly on 6 December when the military situation showed no improvement, had taken note of the unwarranted public euphoria and emphasized that it should be checked by correct reporting of the news. Ever since the fall of Dhaka, the vocal classes of Pakistan have sought scapegoats to cover their own guilt of collaboration with the misguided policies of Yahya. In this event it is Farman Ali, who had handed over the note to the UN Secretary-General's representative, Paul-Marc Henry, in Dhaka.

There is some confusion about how the note was delivered. Salik says it was given to Henry in the Governor's office in the presence of Malik, Muzaffar Husain, and Farman Ali.[24] Muzaffar Husain does not recall that, but thinks that perhaps Farman Ali had given the said note informally to Henry to enable him to be ready to initiate action but only when he was formally approached.[25] The way it was handled by the Secretary-General in New York, as we will presently see, does not suggest that the document was meant to be unofficial. But if this was so, then the procedure adopted was very naive; an internal document, which, on this assumption the note was, proposing a particular course of action in a state of war cannot be handed over to an international body which is not bound by diplomatic secrecy of the kind practised in bilateral relations among countries. The language of the message (A-7107) itself can be variously interpreted. It reproduces the note which, it says, was being handed over to Paul-Marc Henry 'after your approval', apparently referring to the authority given to the Governor by the President in message no. G-0001. At the end, however, it sought immediate approval of the President without making it clear whether it was for the note or for its being handed over. The President's message G-0001 was equally vague and apparently gave blanket authority to the Governor in matters of war and peace. Advice to the President about instructions of this nature would require very careful thought and consultations in some high-level body which would submit the final draft for his approval. But it was typical of Yahya's style of governance that nobody in the government seemed to know about the President's exchanges with the Governor. Nobody knows who drafted these messages. There was no application of the institutional wisdom of government machinery in the content and formulation of these important documents, dealing with life and death issues for the nation. It was irresponsible personal rule which led to confusion and despair among the functionaries and humiliation of the nation in disowning its own representatives in

East Pakistan before the international forum. But the East Pakistan administration was more structured and was manned by seasoned administrators. The subject matter of the note given to the UN pertained to the whole of Pakistan, and, although President had given authority to the Governor, prudence and official practice required that they should have waited for the approval of the exact formulation of the proposals by the government of Pakistan before transmitting them to the UN.

From the point of view of the authors of the note, the proposals contained in it could be justified by the circumstances in which they were formulated. Firstly, the note was drafted immediately after the hopeless military appreciation given by Niazi. It was a consensus document of the civil and military administration of East Pakistan, subscribed by the Governor, Chief Secretary, Farman Ali, Niazi, and other senior officers of the armed forces. It was transmitted in the name of Farman Ali because as Adviser to the Governor and Major-General Civil Affairs in the martial law administration he was the kingpin of the civil and military administration in East Pakistan. Secondly, the President, in message G-0001, had approved the Governor's proposals (of message A-4660) for an immediate cease-fire and political settlement, and had given him the authority 'to go ahead and ensure safety of our armed forces by all *political means that you will have to adopt with our opponent*' (emphasis added). What did it mean ? It certainly did not imply a mere cease-fire which was a purely military matter; if that was the intention, the President should have addressed himself to Niazi. The Governor had suggested a political settlement along with a cease-fire. What could the political settlement be but a political government, and who could the politicians be, under the circumstances, but the elected ones? The starkness of the message showed that the President himself was in no position to help East Pakistan in any way. Thirdly, from the beginning of the war, the Eastern Command and the Governor were being given to understand that the western front would reduce the pressure on East Pakistan. Then, from 5 December, hopes of Chinese intervention were being given in official messages. Similar assurances of foreign help were being given to the Prime Minister-designate Nurul Amin and the Bengalis in Rawalpindi who were passing them on to their friends in Dhaka. Meanwhile, the army was in full retreat, and the Indians were racing towards Dhaka. But no relief of any kind was in sight. Fourthly, the siege conditions of Dhaka at the time when this message was drafted should be appreciated. The Governor's message of 9 December to the President had summarized the desperate situation. On the following day it had worsened when the Indians crossed the Meghna, and there was nothing between them and Dhaka. With the enemy rapidly closing in on Dhaka, the *mukti bahini* hordes expected to be on the rampage any time, the city under continuous curfew and heavy bombardment, all civic services suspended, and no hope of any assistance from any quarter, the proposal to the UN was certainly a desirable alternative to what eventually happened. Fifthly, there is no doubt that the Dhaka message to the UN was a great diplomatic setback and disappointed Pakistan's friends. But the East Pakistan administration was never taken into confidence about the state of diplomatic efforts in the UN. After the General Assembly resolution, no further meeting of the Security Council was in sight. If the framers of the UN note had been given the correct picture, and informed how important it was to hold out for two or three days more, particularly in response to the Governor's message A-4660, the Dhaka administration would have certainly refrained from taking the UN initiative. After all, they lived with a far worse situation for another six days. Yahya had objected to the contents of the note but not to the approach to the UN. In the event, the revised draft of Yahya would have had the same effect on diplomatic proceedings in New York as Farman's note did. Although the two notes were materially different, each clearly indicated that Pakistan was in no position to sustain the war and India had achieved the objective of 'liberating' East Pakistan.

The United Nations and Washington

Agha Shahi describes the diplomatic agitation which East Pakistan's proposals caused in New York:

> At 5 a.m. on 10 December I was woken up by Brian Urquhart of the UN Secretariat, to convey the cease-fire proposals given to Paul-Marc Henry by Farman Ali and Dr Malik. At 8 a.m. he informed me that U Thant had decided to inform the president of the Security Council. Under Secretary-General Guyear sent a copy to the leader of the Chinese delegation who later told Bhutto that he had declined to accept

it. Farman Ali was also reported to have requested the Russian, British, French, and US representatives to take over Dhaka and East Pakistan and had desired that the Chinese delegation in New York be informed of the offer.

I said I would accept it only if it comes from the President of Pakistan. I also insisted that it should not be circulated before I talk to Pakistan as it would prejudice our case. It was not easy to get in touch with Pakistan. I could contact Stockholm through which I sought clarification. At 10.30 a.m a garbled message came via Stockholm from the foreign secretary informing me that Farman Ali's note was unauthorized. In supersession of it the President had authorized Governor Malik to make a definite proposal of cease-fire only and that the question of surrender of the armed forces did not arise. I was asked to inform the Secretary-General that this was the authorized proposal. I decided to wait for Bhutto's arrival. At 5.30 p.m. telephonic instructions were received from the foreign secretary to withhold the authorized version and ask the Secretary-General to disregard Farman Ali's note. U Thant nevertheless circulated the Dhaka message to the permanent members of the Security Council.

Bhutto had left Pakistan on 8 December and had to take a circuitous route to reach New York, which he did on 10 December. Agha Shahi spoke to him in Bonn :

> I told Bhutto that India had advanced into Pakistan [Jessore had fallen]. The Soviets would go on vetoeing every resolution asking for withdrawal or unconditional cease-fire. I said, 'If you are coming only to announce a cease-fire, it might affect your image.' Bhutto replied, 'I understand but as a political leader I must come.'

Bhutto reached New York in the afternoon of 10 December at 3 p.m. Shahi describes the arrival:

> I went into the plane as it landed and in the general bustle of getting down told him about Farman Ali's message. When we were in the car along with an army officer of the ISI Bhutto said, 'Shahi what were you saying about Farman's message in the plane? You were not very coherent.' When I repeated the contents, addressing the army officer he said, 'Look Colonel, we have been betrayed.'

The same evening Bhutto asked Yahya to rescind the authority given to Governor Malik to approach the UN, and informed him that he had already asked Shahi to inform the Secretary-General to disregard Farman's message. Bhutto threatened that unless his advice was accepted he would return to Pakistan immediately.

Earlier in the day, Yahya had agreed with Kissinger on a proposal for the United Nations on the lines suggested by Brezhnev. It envisaged a cease-fire in place, without withdrawal of forces, and resumption of negotiations with the Awami League at the point at which they had been interrupted in March : 'In short, Pakistan, in return for an end to Indian military operations in the West, was prepared to settle for the military *status quo* in the East . . . and to enter [into] negotiations . . . whose only possible outcome could be the emergence of an independent Bangladesh.'[26]

Kissinger was upset on hearing about East Pakistan's offer of a cease-fire to the United Nations. He called in Ambassador Raza and 'urged him to make the cease-fire proposal consistent with what had been agreed to with Yahya', that is, it should cover both East and West Pakistan, 'otherwise the danger to the West would mount as operations in Bengal concluded.'[27] Kissinger emphasized the danger facing West Pakistan which, according to American appreciation, would not be able to offer resistance for more than two or three weeks, once Indian forces were released from East Pakistan. Kissinger also informed Ambassador Raza that an aircraft-carrier task force was on its way to the Bay of Bengal, but would not be seen for another 48 hours. Military assistance from friendly countries, Kissinger said, should also be on its way to Pakistan.

Consequently, in the early hours of 11 December, the President's message (G-0002) authorizing the Governor to hand over the revised note to the UN was cancelled. The President instructed the Governor:

> Do not repeat do not take any action on my last message to you (.) Important diplomatic and military moves are taking place by our friends (.) It is essential that we hold for another 36 hours at att costs (.) Please also pass this message to Gen. Niazi and Gen. Farman (.)

The task force was kept east of the Strait of Malacca before steaming into the Bay of Bengal, because Kissinger wanted to consult the Chinese before making further moves. On the evening of 10 December he met Huang Hua, the Permanent Representative of the People's Republic of China to the United Nations, in New York. Huang Hua insisted on the principle of withdrawal of forces before negotiations; he showed concern 'that a precedent was being set by which other countries might be dismembered by Indian–Soviet collusion.' Kissinger warned that the insistence on such a position 'would play right into the hands of Indian and Soviet strategy to dismember' West Pakistan also.[28]

Rawalpindi

The emergency committee was confused. The army briefings to it were still belittling the Indian advances and painting a reassuring picture. The members were no longer prepared to accept these claims; the realities on the ground and in the air, and the news from foreign media could no longer be ignored. Rumours were also circulating in higher circles of some initiatives for a cease-fire taken by the East Pakistan administration. The Cabinet Secretary in the meeting on 10 December stated that it was evident that, unless some means were found to relieve the pressure, the collapse of East Pakistan was now only a matter of days. The entire might of India, he apprehended, would then be turned on West Pakistan and it would be impossible to get the aggression vacated through a cease-fire arranged by the UN. It was not only the East Pakistan garrison but the very existence of Pakistan that was now at stake. This appreciation coincided with Kissinger's worry about the West. Ghulam Ishaq Khan suggested that the committee should consider this grave situation and submit its recommendations to the President. It was decided that a subcommittee consisting of Ghulam Ishaq Khan, Roedad Khan, Qamarul Islam, and Alvie should draw up specific recommendations and, along with Ghiasuddin, the Defence Adviser, wait upon the President. A note was drafted by Alvie, and an interview was sought with the President who called them immediately. Ghulam Ishaq Khan read out the note to the President. The note was confined to diplomatic appreciation, and concluded with the recommendation that the President should call the US and Chinese ambassadors and urge immediate physical intervention. Alvie, whose note it was, with which other members had gone along, was aware that the two countries were fully briefed about the grave military situation and repeated requests had already been made to them for assistance. There was no commitment by either of them to intervene physically. Having chosen the course of all-out war, Pakistan could not expect a diplomatic solution more favourable than the military situation on the ground.

After the Cabinet Secretary had read out the memorandum, the President informed the subcommittee of the latest American proposal mentioned above. Yahya said that the Americans had assured him that, after the cease-fire, the Russians would ensure withdrawal of forces as soon as a political settlement had been arrived at, through formal negotiations between the governments of Pakistan and India, and the representatives of Bangladesh in Calcutta. The Russians had offered the assurance that the settlement would be within the framework of united Pakistan. The President said that he had conveyed his favourable reactions to the proposal to Nixon. Apparently, the Foreign Office did not know about this because when the Foreign Secretary asked whether he could ask the American ambassador for a copy of the message sent by him to Washington, the President replied that such a request would not be proper at this stage.

While the meeting was in progress, an air raid siren sounded, and the President and the subcommittee moved to the bunker. Ghulam Isḥaq Khan and Roedad Khan, while waiting for the all-clear happened to be in the same bunker as the President. Ghulam Ishaq Khan recalls:

> I was next to him [Yahya] in the bunker, and the Information Secretary was on my right. The President offered me a cigarette and said jovially, 'Let us have a cheroot.' He was in a relaxed mood. Taking advantage [of this], I told him nothing was happening on the Western front and the people were anxious for quick results. I reminded him of our strategy of defending East Pakistan in the West. Yahya said: 'What do you do in wrestling or boxing? You get hold of your opponent with one hand and then give him a punch with the other. That is exactly what we are doing at present. We will give him a punch and we are drawing him out, but he is not biting for the time being. We have to wait for the right opportunity. . . .' In any case, the President said, he could not allow the crowds to dictate his strategy.[29]

The implications of the American proposals worried the Cabinet and Information Secretaries who drafted a memorandum on them for the President's consideration. It was pointed out that our principled stand of a cease-fire to be accompanied by withdrawal of forces had been accepted by the General Assembly by an overwhelming majority. The earlier Russian resolution for the end of hostilities without withdrawal of forces was not accepted in the

Security Council; acceptance of the American proposals now would annoy the Chinese, and Pakistan would be further isolated. The political settlement after the cease-fire may, at best, have to be a confederation which was proposed by the Awami League in March. This, they said, the other political parties would not accept. It was extremely unlikely that India, in the euphoria of its military occupation of a major portion of East Pakistan, would accept anything less than an independent sovereign state of Bangladesh. The Soviet Union would be in no position to force India to accept East Pakistan as part of Pakistan, and de-recognize independent Bangladesh. The memorandum concluded that, in case effective Chinese intervention was not forthcoming as requested and the response was not found satisfactory, the President should, in consultation with the elected leaders, take a final decision which may well be the acceptance of the American proposals.

Later, in the evening, the handwritten memorandum, signed by Ghulam Ishaq Khan and Roedad Khan, was formally submitted to the President.

11 December

East Pakistan: Dhaka

By 11 December, the bulk of the Pakistani forces west and south of the Ganges or Padma River, and east of the Meghna had been encircled and their retreat for the defence of Dhaka was cut off; in the Dhaka bowl there was only 93 Brigade in the Jamalpur–Mymensingh sector commanded by Brigadier Qadir. All appeals for help by the Eastern Command to the fortress commanders of Comilla and Bhairab Bazar to break out and try to reach Dhaka had failed to move them; Nazar Hussain Shah was asked to send 57 Brigade, but he sent a battalion which failed to cross the Jamuna River. Brigadier Qadir received withdrawal orders on 10 December for redeployment on the northern perimeter of Dhaka. His telephone calls to his GOC to plead for cancellation of movement orders would not be received in Dhaka; instead, a staff officer would check up at frequent intervals to verify whether the brigade had started moving.[30]

To the Indians, 93 Brigade together with the retreating forces from Ashuganj and other places seemed considerable re-inforcement for the Dhaka garrison, which had some 5,000 assorted troops, although not of regular infantry formations. On the Mymensingh front, an Indian brigade was investing Jamalpur, which was cut off from all sides. Another brigade was proceeding towards Mymensingh. The Indians, however, were not sure that Qadir's brigade would not break out to reach Dhaka via Tangail. To prevent such an eventuality, a battalion of an Indian Parachute Brigade, together with its supporting arms, was para-dropped in the Tangail area in the afternoon of 11 December.[31] The countryside in this area was under the control of a powerful group of *mukti bahini*. 93 Brigade was practically annihilated in its efforts to reach Dhaka, and Qadir was the first senior Pakistani officer to surrender.

In the early hours of 11 December, Niazi sent the following report (message no. G-1265) to the Chief of General Staff:

> Our forces all sectors under extreme pressure. Isolated in fortresses and invested by enemy. Enemy possess mastery of air. Local population and rebels out to destroy own troops. All communications cut off. Order issued 'last man last round'. But will be difficult to hold positions when weapons and ammunitions exhaust in few days. Advice solicited.

Later, in the afternoon, the developments of the day which sealed the fate of Dhaka were reported (message no. G-1272) as follows:

> Enemy heli-dropped approx one brigade south of Narsingdi and landed one para-brigade in Tangail area. Request friends arrive Dacca by air first flight 12 December.

West Pakistan: Rawalpindi

A fierce battle was raging in 1 Corps area which was strengthened by a brigade of one of the army reserve formations, 33 Division. Another brigade of the same formation was sent to the Rajasthan sector to fortify the defences of the badly-mauled 18 Division. The splitting-up of the reserve formations considerably reduced the striking power of the Pakistan army for the proposed offensive; 'somewhere along the line the C-in-C and the COS had forgotten that the main aim [of opening the second front] was a counter-offensive' to the Indian attack on East Pakistan.[32] Four reserve formations, 1 Armoured Division and 7 Division under 2 Corps, and 6 Armoured Division and 17 Division were, however, still available for the offensive.

Ghulam Ishaq Khan informed the emergency committee of the contents of the note submitted by him and Roedad Khan to the President on the import of the American cease-fire proposal. All other members agreed to it and offered to add their signatures to it. The Farman Ali message had created a stir, but the committee's knowledge of it was based only on the bits and pieces of it appearing in the foreign media. They were not taken into confidence about the exact contents of the messages exchanged between the President and the Governor, leading to the approach to the UN. It was typical of Yahya's fragmented handling of national affairs to avoid consultations, particularly with the civilians, and to evolve a co-ordinated reaction to critical events.

The President was angry. He is reported to have said, 'the Governor and General Farman had no business to send messages direct to the UN. They had submitted a draft to me for approval but without waiting for it they had simultaneously handed over a copy of it to the UN representative. It was totally unauthorized and utterly irresponsible. I know how and why it had been done and I am going to see that those responsible get it in the neck for it.'

But he was in raptures over Niazi's statement that the enemy would enter Dhaka over his (Niazi's) dead body. This statement was given in a roadside press conference with foreign correspondents at the gate of the Hotel Inter-Continental, at about the time Farman Ali's note—to which Niazi had fully subscribed—was disowned by Yahya. (The foreign residents of the hotel had objected to Niazi's entry which, they thought, would jeopardize the neutral status of the premises.) On hearing Niazi's statement, Yahya effusively remarked, 'Now that is the spirit of the army. What a brave man, fighting and willing to die to stop the enemy! We cannot afford to lose him. He must live to fight another day.'

The United Nations

Bhutto met Kissinger in the morning of 11 December at breakfast. Agha Shahi describes the meeting:

> I, Ambassador Raza, George Bush, and a State Department official were present in the breakfast meeting. Kissinger gave an analysis of

> the situation; he was very fond of giving such analyses. He told Bhutto, 'We have received information that after overrunning East Pakistan Indian troops will be transferred to West Pakistan. We should get a cease-fire before that. You are going for withdrawal of forces which is being vetoed by the Russians. But I am going for a cease-fire from the Security Council. However, you should not seem desperate. The best thing would be to go to the Security Council with the resolution of the General Assembly which will be vetoed. Then you should go for a cease-fire. The time-frame for this strategy would be determined by you which would depend on Pakistan forces' ability to hold on.' Kissinger then turned round to Raza who said, 'we will fight to the last.'

Kissinger's own version of this meeting is tougher. He warned that 'Pakistan would not be saved by mock-tough rhetoric; we had to develop a course of action that could be sustained.' He told Bhutto 'to work out a common position with the Chinese; we would not be buffeted by those we were trying to help. If it kept up [insistence on withdrawal of forces] we would help pass formalistic UN resolutions but we would lose the ability to be effective. The next forty-eight hours would be decisive.' It was finally agreed that if nothing was heard from Moscow (about the American proposals for an immediate cease-fire on both the fronts, which had been conveyed by Nixon in a letter to Brezhnev the previous day) by noon on 12 December, the issue would be taken up in the Security Council. To begin with, a cease-fire along with withdrawal of forces would be demanded but 'we would settle for a simple cease-fire in place, in effect accepting the Indian *fait accompli* in Bengal. I had to count on Bhutto to make sure the Chinese understood our position.'[33]

Bhutto had met the Chinese Deputy Foreign Minister soon after his arrival the previous evening. In a message to Yahya on 11 December he referred to the differences between the Americans and the Chinese, the efforts he was making to reconcile them, and suggested waiting seventy-two hours before going to the Security Council again. In the present situation, he said, acceptance of a cease-fire resolution without withdrawal would only be a piece of paper and enable India to turn her full attention to West Pakistan. Meanwhile, Bhutto informed Yahya, he had strongly urged the Americans and the Chinese for effective intervention. He reminded Yahya that he had been in New York only for twenty-four hours during which he had had to re-establish credibility, which had been completely eroded by Farman Ali's message. He also indicated that if the ground situation could be held and possibly improved upon for a week, the diplomatic position in the UN could take a turn for the better. In an earlier message, Bhutto had blamed Yahya for putting him (Bhutto) in an embarrassing position by authorizing Farman Ali's proposals to the UN.

12 December

East Pakistan

The situation was getting worse. Pakistani troops had begun surrendering in various sectors. The Indian para-brigades had started moving towards Dhaka from Tangail in the north and Narsingdi in the east. The Indian troops were pressing hard to capture Bhairab bridge and to close up to Chandpur and Daudkandi on the Meghna. Chittagong was bombarded from the sea and the pressure on Sylhet was increasing. The crucial operation was the capture of Dhaka for which para-brigades were landed to short-circuit the fortresses.

Meanwhile, All India Radio broadcast the first message of the Indian army chief, General Manekshaw, to the Commander Eastern Command and his troops to lay down arms, as they were encircled from all sides, and assuring them of safety and proper treatment under the Geneva Convention. The message did reflect the situation on the ground, but its main purpose was to demoralize the Pakistani troops. It had a great psychological impact on the fighting will of the Pakistani troops who, in any case, had lost much of it by now. It was part of the warfare which the Indians were desperately trying to bring to an end by the capitulation of the Pakistan army in East Pakistan, before the Security Council could order a cease-fire in both the Wings. Three such messages were broadcast, each successive one being more effective, corresponding to the deterioration in the military situation.

West Pakistan: Rawalpindi

The reserve formations, except 33 Division, were still intact, whereas the bulk of the enemy reserves was gradually getting involved in the battle of Zafarwal–Shakargah. A suggestion by 4

Corps to launch an army offensive through Khemkaran was briefly discussed in the GHQ and it was decided to examine it further at the HQ of 4 Corps the next day. The original offensive plan was through Bhawalnagar–Haroonabad–Fort Abbas area, and consideration of an alternative plan at this late stage indicated doubts in the higher command about the feasibility of an army offensive. This was attributed to the adverse air situation in the southern sector where the Indians were pounding the railway system and also due to growing apprehensions about the ability of the Pakistan air force to support the offensive.

Yahya had apparently pinned all hopes now on a cease-fire arranged by the UN. In response to Bhutto's messages of the previous day, he sent the following instructions:

> Your thinking about delaying reference to Security Council and holding out military for at least one week will be fatal to our position and multiply difficulties. The fall of East Pakistan will permit [India] . . . to switch over to West Pakistan and this will weaken our negotiating position. The situation demands fastest action especially now when Chinese Russian and American thinking alike on question of cease-fire negotiations and withdrawals [in that order].
>
> You have stressed need for a big push in West. This consideration is actively borne in mind but it is a military situation and has to be left to military commanders. We cannot blunder into a situation to our . . .
>
> Please consult with all interested parties urgent for moving a resolution in Security Council immediately.

In another message to Bhutto the same day, Yahya defended himself against Bhutto's protest about Farman Ali's proposals to the UN:

> I am amazed at some of the observations in your telegram . . . You should not have concluded without verification that Farman's message had my approval because he said so. The slip made by Farman was nipped in the bud before you reached New York. My instructions to this effect were dictated on telephone. . . . My own message confined itself only to cease-fire and was therefore a major modification of what Farman had communicated. On subsequent developments even this has been withheld.
>
> There is no question of surrender but the situation in East Pakistan is such that operations cannot be continued for long . . .

> I am continuously in touch with the Chinese. . . . I am also doing everything possible to get United States material assistance and political support . . .

The United Nations and Washington

Kissinger, after meeting Bhutto, returned to Washington and conveyed to Vorontsov of the Soviet embassy in Washington that unless the Russians responded to the 10 December proposals by noon of 12 December, the US would take whatever action it thought fit. Vorontsov informed him that the Russian deputy foreign minister had been sent to New Delhi to urge restraint. But Kissinger was not sure of the advice the Soviet Union was giving to India. While the Indian government was assuring the UN that they had no territorial ambitions in West Pakistan, they avoided specific mention of Azad Kashmir which was not recognized by them as part of Pakistan. Kissinger feared that 'they deliberately kept open the possibility of the kind of annexation [of Azad Kashmir] achievable only by the total destruction of the Pakistan army and the consequent disintegration of Pakistan.'[34]

On 12 December at 11.30 a.m. Nixon sent a message on the hot line to Moscow informing them 'that the Indian assurances [about West Pakistan] still lack any concreteness', and while the US, after vainly waiting for a Russian response, had initiated certain moves in the Security Council, they were still prepared for a cease-fire in place and immediate negotiations. Giving a veiled warning, Nixon told Moscow that 'time is of the essence to avoid consequences neither of us want.' The Seventh Fleet movement was held up for twenty-four hours to wait for the Russian response. In the early hours of 13 December the Soviet Union sent a vague reply that they were discussing the matter in India and would inform the US of the results as soon as possible.[35]

Meanwhile, the Chinese conveyed to Kissinger their agreement to the American proposals of demanding, through the Security Council, a cease-fire with withdrawal, but eventually accepting a cease-fire in place. China understood Pakistan's desperation for a cease-fire and the danger to West Pakistan and eschewed its principled stand.

On 12 December the Indian government formally conveyed its views on the General Assembly resolution to the Secretary-General, *inter alia,* as follows:

> So far as the armed forces of India are concerned there can be a cease-fire and withdrawal of Indian forces to its own territory if the rulers of West Pakistan would withdraw their own forces from Bangla Desh and reach a peaceful settlement with those who were until recently their fellow citizens but now owe allegiance to the Government of Bangla Desh which has been duly constituted by the representatives chosen freely in the elections held in December 1970.

The Security Council was reconvened on 12 December (1611th meeting) at the request of the United States. The Indian foreign minister stated that the presence of the representative of Bangladesh in the meeting was necessary for the success of any cease-fire proposal. The US permanent representative, after reading a long statement blaming India for the war, moved a draft resolution (S/10446. Rev. 1).[36] This resolution, which was identical to the General Assembly resolution, provided for a cease-fire and withdrawal of forces. The Soviet representative, determined to delay the passage of any resolution, raised a point of order, claiming an understanding that the meeting was to be confined to the statements of the parties and the US representative. After the Indian and US speeches, Bhutto addressed the Council. The Council president thereafter suggested an adjournment of the meeting to enable the delegates to obtain instructions from their governments. The United States pressed for immediate voting. The Soviet Union opposed it, accusing the US of forcing it to veto the resolution. The meeting was adjourned to the following day.

Kissinger has given an account of various pressures that he was exerting on the Russians, in the meanwhile, to persuade India to accept a cease-fire. The most visible and publicized step was the deployment of the American task force in the Bay of Bengal. Kissinger has justified it as a bluff, committing 'us to no final act, but . . . [creating] precisely the margin of uncertainty needed to force a decision by New Delhi and Moscow.'[37] Kissinger's detractors have criticized him for creating a superpower confrontation for which there was no occasion. Van Hollen says that Task Force 74 which did not arrive in the Bay of Bengal until 15 December had no 'immediate political or military impact on events in South Asia.'[38]

13 December

East Pakistan: Dhaka

Indian helicopters had set up shuttle services to strengthen the forces landed north-west and north-east of Dhaka. Indian troops were exerting severe pressures against the Pakistani fortresses on the borders. On 12 December the Indian brigade coming down the Jamalpur road linked up with the paratroopers in the Tangail area; soon after, the GOC General Nagra also reached Tangail with his tactical headquarters. The leading brigade was sent onwards to Joydebpur, a suburb of Dhaka, another brigade was dispatched in the same direction a few hours later. When the leading brigade met some resistance at Joydebpur, the second brigade passed through and continued the advance towards Dhaka. After overcoming a river obstacle, it pushed forward to Tangi, which adjoined the cantonment.[39]

Niazi reported the situation to GHQ in the evening of 13 December as follows (vide message G-1286):

> All fortresses under heavy pressure. No replenishment even of ammunition. Dacca under heavy pressure. Rebels have already surrounded the city. Indians also advancing. Situation serious. Promised assistance [Chinese] must take practical shape by 14 December. Will be effective in Silliguri not NEFA and by engaging enemy air bases.

In the Governor House the boom of artillery, heard for the first time on 12 December, seemed to be coming nearer. The air attacks in daylight on strong points of the city such as Peelkhana, the headquarters of the police and paramilitary forces, became more frequent. The city had been under a 24-hour curfew since 11 December, with a short break of an hour or so in the morning. Electricity and water supplies were intermittent. Fresh food supplies were becoming scarce.

We, the West Pakistani civil officers, were now on our own, marooned in the city. Two days earlier, Farman Ali had suggested that we should go to Akyab in Burma, and stay there until the cease-fire. He also talked to someone in the cantonment for one or two planes which were available. These were the Beavers used for aerial spraying. Muzaffar Husain got hold of large-scale maps of the province, and with Yousuf, the Governor's pilot, we went over the flight paths to Akyab and timings to avoid the Indian radar. The air force chief, Inamul Haq, however, refused to authorize any flight for us, reportedly saying 'They should suffer the same way as we would'. The evacuation of certain army personnel, however, continued until the morning of 16 December.

On the evening of 13 December, Muzaffar Husain talked to Ghiasuddin, Sultan Muhammad Khan, and M. Qayyum, apprised them of the situation, and sought some guidance. They had nothing to say. Qayyum assured him that everything was being done and there was nothing to worry about: Niazi would protect us. Ghiasuddin sympathized, and said he and others had called on the President a few hours earlier, and he would again bring the matter to his notice. Sultan Muhammad said Bhutto in New York had been briefed about the situation, but he was more concerned about his image. Sitting in the dark with two small candles in Muzaffar Husain's once cheerful suite with the din of artillery coming from afar and machine-gun chatter seemingly from next door, and intermittent air raids, we discussed the possibilities of breaking out to Nepal. A little later, Farman Ali also joined us and we had dinner together. Farman reminisced about the events of the past year, and the advice he had been giving to Yahya. The agony was deep and nerves were frayed but mutual recriminations did not help to relieve our plight. There would be time enough later to apportion blame. Farman suggested that all of us should now move to the neutral zone of Hotel Inter-Continental, and said that he would make arrangements the next morning. Such was the ignorance of the central secretaries managing the emergency that the Communication Secretary sent telegraphic orders on 12/13 December to the Chief Secretary to seize, from all over the province, rivercraft belonging to enemy nationals. On the following day, the Industries Secretary sent orders for arranging the movement of jute for export.

West Pakistan: Rawalpindi

At Headquarters 4 Corps a high level meeting was held to discuss the revised plan to launch the army offensive. The proposal was, however, dropped due to non-availability of additional troops, and it was decided to revert to the original plan which had to be revised due to the split of 33 Division. On 13 December at 9 a.m. the Chief of Staff, General Abdul Hamid, gave his approval for launching the offensive. The attack was to start on 16 December; later it was postponed for twenty-four hours. The revised operational instructions were flown by special couriers to all concerned.[40] Valuable time was lost in examination of the alternate plan.

The United Nations

The Security Council met, as scheduled, in the afternoon of 13 December (1613th meeting). The newspapers of the day had carried the Indian claim that fighting in East Pakistan had entered the final and decisive stage, and this was generally believed by the delegates. It was clear that the Soviet Union was going to veto every resolution which did not link a cease-fire with transfer of power to the Awami League (diplomatically termed as a 'political settlement') in East Pakistan. This would continue until such time that the imminent Indian occupation of East Pakistan materialized. The American proposals of a standstill cease-fire, negotiations, and withdrawal of forces, formulated on the lines indicated by Brezhnev on 9 December were overtaken by the military situation in East Pakistan. The Indians and the Soviet Union now practically demanded that Pakistan should hand over East Pakistan to the Awami League and get out. And if it did not do that, the Indian armed forces would accomplish the task. It should also be remembered, in the context of later controversies, that, even at this very late stage, although Yahya had agreed to the American proposals, the senior civil servants, largely due to their ignorance of the actual military situation, were as unhappy about them as Bhutto was.

In fact at this stage the Indians were not interested in any resolution at all. They only wanted about twenty-four hours or so to conclude the military operation in the east. Accordingly, the Soviet Union resorted to filibustering. It again demanded an invitation to the representative of Bangladesh. After the procedural debate, the US representative moved a revised version, S/10446, Rev. 1, of its draft resolution. The Soviet representative made a long statement, condemning Pakistan more strongly than ever before. The Indian Foreign Minister made a lengthy acrimonious speech. The resolution when put to vote, received 11 votes in favour, two (Poland and the USSR) against, and there were two abstentions (France and the UK).

After the third Soviet veto, the delegates of the UK and France announced that they would work for a formula acceptable to all, on the basis of three elements: cessation of hostilities, disengagement of forces, and ensuring justice—meaning a political settlement. But the representative of Italy immediately moved a new draft resolution, S/10451, in the name of Japan and his own delegation. The Pakistan delegation later complained to the Italians for not having been taken into confidence about the new draft. The Italians explained that they moved it only to keep the issue alive in the Security Council. If they had not put in a draft resolution, the Council would have had nothing pending before it and there was a danger of the debate dying out. After a procedural debate, it was decided that consultations should be held on the following day from 9 a.m. to 1 p.m., and that the Council should meet at 3 p.m.

The French and UK delegations privately criticized the US for pressing a resolution which was certain to be vetoed. It became apparent that they were waiting for the fall of Dhaka to induce Pakistan to accept a call for a political settlement and to present their own draft resolution which would be acceptable to the Soviet Union and India.

14–15 December

East Pakistan: Dhaka

At midnight of 13–14 December, the COS, in response to Niazi's message, assured him:

> Reference G-1286 UN Security Council in session. Most likely will order cease-fire. Matter of hours. Hold out till UN resolution passed. Fully realise most critical situation [of] Eastern Command.

The Governor on the morning of 14 December directed in writing that the group of West Pakistan civil servants should seek refuge in the neutral zone. Farman Ali called the representatives of the International Committee of the Red Cross and asked them to allow us to shift to the hotel. They went back and an hour later, presumably after checking up with the *mukti bahini* or the Indians, rang back to invite us to the neutral zone. So we packed up and once more moved out in a small procession and reached the Inter-

Continental at about 12 noon. We left our cars in the nearby deserted bungalows and lugged our suitcases to the hotel. At the entrance, there was a jostling crowd of foreign correspondents. Our arrival was big news. Inside, the lobby was full of foreigners, mostly media people. Clare Hollingworth was describing the historic fall of cities during the Second World War, and their expectations of last-minute help which never came. She was speaking with reference to the Dhaka rumours about the US or Chinese intervention to relieve the Pakistan army.

At 1.32 p.m. on 14 December the following unclassified message (G-0013) was sent by the President to the Governor and the Commander Eastern Command. It arrived in Dhaka at 3.30 p.m.

> For Governor and General Niazi from President (.) Governor's flash message refers (.) You have fought a heroic battle against overwhelming odds (.) The nation is proud of you and the world full of admiration (.) I have done all that is humanly possible to find an acceptable solution to the problem (.) You have now reached a stage when further resistance is no longer humanly possible nor will it serve any useful purpose (.) It will only lead to further loss of life and destruction (.) You should now take all necessary measures to stop the fighting and preserve the lives of all armed forces personnel all those from West Pakistan and all loyal elements (.) Meanwhile I have moved UN to urge India to stop hostilities in East Pakistan forthwith and to guarantee the safety of the Armed Forces and all other people who may be the likely target of miscreants.

Soon after we left the Governor House, it was strafed by the IAF while a cabinet meeting was going on. There was nothing left of the government, the administration, or the army now in Dhaka. The Governor had been trying to talk to Yahya who did not take the call. During all the days since the start of the war, the President had never once spoken to his representative in Dhaka. In the afternoon the Governor resigned, and he and the Chief Secretary also shifted to the hotel. Farman Ali, we were told, had moved to the cantonment. This was the end of the 24-year old East Pakistan government.

Lieutenant-General Niazi went to the US Consul-General in Dhaka on the evening of 14 December to send a message to General Sam Manekshaw, the Indian army chief, for a cease-fire. On his return from the American consulate, the following message

(G-1305) was sent by him to the GHQ Rawalpindi at 12.30 a.m. on 15 December.

> Reference No. G-0013. Met American Consul General. Handed over following note. 'To save innocent lives request arrange immediate cease-fire under following conditions: (1) Regrouping Pakistan Armed Forces in designated areas by mutual agreement between opposing forces (2) Safety all military and para-military forces (3) Safety all those settled in East Pakistan since 1947 (4) No reprisals against those who helped administration since March 1971. Will abide by UN resolutions'.

The Consul-General, instead of passing the message to the Indians, sent it to Washington. At about the same time the following note was given to the UN Representative at Dhaka by the Commander Eastern Command:

> To bring to an end loss of further human lives and destruction we are willing to under honourable conditions:
>
> A. Cease fire and stop all hostilities immediately in East Pakistan.
>
> B. Hand over peacefully the administration of East Pakistan as arranged by the UN.
>
> C. The UN should ensure:-
>
> (1) Safety and security of all Armed Forces personnel of both military and para-military forces of Pakistan pending their return to West Pakistan.
>
> (2) Safety of all West Pakistan . . . civilians and civil servants, pending their return to West Pakistan.
>
> (3) Safety of non-locals settled in East Pakistan since 1947.
>
> (4) Guarantee of no reprisal against those who helped and served the Government and cause of Pakistan since March 1971.

A copy of this note was delivered to the Governor by Farman Ali in the Hotel Inter-Continental, perhaps in response to the following letter written by the former to Niazi from the hotel on 15 December.

> 15 - 12 - 1971
>
> My dear General Niazi,
>
> May I know if any action has been taken from your side, on PAK ARMY Signal no. G-0013 dated 14-12-1971 from the President to you and to me as the Governor? This message clearly said 'you should take all necessary measures to stop the fighting and preserve the lives of all armed forces personnel, all those from West Pakistan and all loyal

elements'. The signal also says 'you have now reached a stage where further resistance is no longer humanly possible, nor will it serve any useful purpose'. Hostility is still continuing and loss of life and disaster continue. I request you to do the needful.

With regards,

Yours sincerely,

A. M. Malik
Phone: 252911 - 12

The telephone number was that of the hotel; only the Governor was allowed outside contacts by the ICRC.

On 15 December at 10.30 p.m. Niazi requested the COS (vide G-1310) for 'advice if any on my signal no. G-1305 to President'. The UN people told us in the hotel that they had been trying to establish contacts with the Indian army through their communication system. Manekshaw replied to Niazi's offer on 15 December; he guaranteed protection as demanded, provided the Pakistan army surrendered to the advancing Indian troops. General Abdul Hamid, the COS, sent the following reply to Niazi (vide G-0015) at 11.50 p.m. on 15 December.

> Reference G-1310. Saw your reply to President and heard Indian COAS reply on AIR. Suggest accept terms by COAS [India] as they appear to meet your requirements. Will however be local military decision with no bearing on political outcome.

Earlier in the day, GHQ had directed Eastern Command, in continuation of its previous day's orders for the destruction of currency notes, to destroy travellers' cheques, National Bank treasury cheques, and signal and code books. The State Bank was opened on the night of 15–16 December and notes were burnt. This action, severely criticized in Bangladesh after the surrender, was part of the standard operating procedure of denial in the face of imminent occupation by the enemy.

West Pakistan: Rawalpindi

The emergency committee, the top crisis management body, was totally confused. It did not know with any certainty what the

President was telling the East Pakistan Governor and the military commander. News agencies were reporting the virtual rout of the garrison in East Pakistan and the imminent fall of Dhaka. But no authentic briefing was forthcoming from the representative of the military. The committee concluded that, due to its ignorance of the factual position, it was in no position to function effectively as a co-ordinating body. It was not even told about the unclassified 14 December message to Dhaka to stop the fighting. When the news of the Governor's resignation came over the wire services, the committee in its meeting on 15 December innocently asked the representative of the CMLA to obtain the orders of the President about alternate arrangements and communicate them to the Cabinet Division—about the appointment of a new governor.

The Information Secretary as the government spokesman was harassed by the home and foreign media for a confirmation of developments in East Pakistan. He met Yahya on 14 December at 11 a.m. to seek guidance on the cease-fire, the surrender, the situation in East Pakistan, the contents of Farman's message and its contradiction, etc. Yahya had lost all touch with reality and was still smarting at Farman's message, which was no longer relevant. To the long list of the Information Secretary's woes, formulated in the form of questions, he complained 'they sent me a draft [from Dhaka] and without getting my approval they delivered a copy to Paul-Marc Henry. This was intentionally done by Malik, Farman Ali, and Muzaffar. They had no business to do this and they will have to pay for it.' When the Information Secretary tried to bring him back to the specific questions of the day he said, 'Well, how can I tell you? I don't know myself,' and turning round continued, 'I understand some of you have been talking out of turn in the emergency committee on matters which are none of your business. You are bureaucrats. You have to carry out orders. You are there only to provide civil backing for the armed forces in the promotion of the war. Convey my displeasure to them.' The Information Secretary tried to explain that they were all worried not only as civil servants but also as patriotic Pakistanis about the difficult times the country was passing through. Their suggestions, he said, should be taken in that spirit. At this Yahya calmed down and said, 'I am not suggesting that you should not discuss these matters but discuss them in a smaller group.'

The committee was told that the Americans had asked for

Farman's message of 10 December to be withdrawn, and fighting to be continued for another 36 to 48 hours, by which time the American Task Force would arrive in the Bay of Bengal. It had still not appeared after 72 hours. In the afternoon of 14 December, Ghiasuddin, Ghulam Ishaq Khan, Qamarul Islam, Roedad Khan, and Sultan Muhammad Khan informally met M. M. Ahmed at his residence. Unaware that the President had already ordered stoppage of fighting in East Pakistan, and that Niazi had offered terms for a cease-fire to Manekshaw, the group discussed the situation. On 15 December they called on the President. A. G. N. Kazi also joined them. Peerzada was also present during the meeting. M. M. Ahmed, as spokesman of the group, explained the gravity of the situation at some length and made the following submissions: It was generally felt in the country that maximum efforts of which the army was capable had not been made on the western front to relieve pressure on East Pakistan. It had always been maintained that the defence of East Pakistan lay in West Pakistan and now we were losing ground in the west also. It was difficult to explain this situation to the people. To boost the nation's morale and to demonstrate that all efforts had been made to save East Pakistan, it was necessary to make substantial gains on the western front which would eventually also be helpful in negotiating a favourable cease-fire. The war must continue in West Pakistan, even if East Pakistan had collapsed, as a tangible proof of the resolve to maintain the integrity of the country. Otherwise the people would not forgive the regime. Yahya accepted that territorial gains in the west were important but stated that the enemy was clever and was not falling into the trap set for him. In any case, the President did not think it was for the people to decide military strategy. In an anguished tone he then laid bare the basis of his obdurate policies of the last nine months. 'There was always the possibility,' he said, 'that events in East Pakistan might take the course that they have taken but I had no alternative. People would not have excused me if I had allowed East Pakistan to secede, as the Awami League was determined on doing, without a fight.' Recapitulating the events since the postponement of the National Assembly in March, Yahya said that at each stage he had enjoyed the support of those interested in the unity and integrity of the country. 'If the outcome of these actions' he added, 'now is different than expected for reasons beyond control, no one man can be blamed for it.' Yahya had a point. Any step other than those taken since March would have been unacceptable to the army, the Punjab, and to West Pakistan in general.

Yahya agreed that fighting should continue in the west even after the collapse in East Pakistan, which should be taken as 'a reverse in one theatre of war'. Ghulam Ishaq Khan emphasized the necessity for the support of all political parties for successful prosecution of the war in the west. It was also agreed that the programme for the introduction of the Constitution and transfer of power, as already announced, should be adhered to. A subcommittee consisting of M. M. Ahmed, Peerzada, Ghulam Ishaq Khan, and Roedad Khan was formed to draft a speech to the nation by the President on the East Pakistan situation. By early afternoon, the draft prepared by Roedad Khan was finalized by the subcommittee with some modifications. It was read out over the telephone to the Foreign Secretary who suggested inclusion of some points and moderation of its tone. The points were incorporated, but the rhetoric of the speech was not changed. Roedad Khan took it to the President at 7 p.m. and he approved the speech, saying that he had expected it to be much tougher. The President agreed that the draft be shown to Nurul Amin, but did not think it feasible to consult Bhutto, in view of bad communications with New York.

At 8.30 p.m. Roedad Khan went to the East Pakistan House, and showed the draft speech to Nurul Amin, who was sitting with Mahmud Ali. Amin was shocked and wanted to see the President immediately. A meeting was fixed for 9 p.m. and he, along with Roedad and Mahmud Ali, went to the President House. Before sitting down Nurul Amin asked, 'Mr President am I living to see this day that East Pakistan has been so cheaply written off?' Yahya queried, 'Have I said so anywhere in my speech?' Nurul Amin replied, 'There is no need of any argument. Anyone having an ounce of brain in him would know what has happened.' Yahya asked Nurul Amin whether he had not agreed with his (Yahya's) policies, and whether the 25 March army action was not justified. Yahya tried to explain the compulsions of the situation, and repeatedly assured Nurul Amin that 'we will keep fighting the battle for Pakistan in West Pakistan.' Nurul Amin wanted an immediate announcement regarding the grant of autonomy to East

Pakistan which Yahya promised to make the next day. Eventually, Nurul Amin seemed to be reconciled to the speech.

During the night of 15–6 December, the final draft of the broadcast speech was translated into Urdu, and both the English and Urdu versions were delivered to the President House on the morning of 16 December.

The United Nations

In the morning of 14 December there were consultations among the members of the Security Council about the resolutions coming up before it. The newspapers had carried a report of the call of the Indian Army Chief of Staff to the Pakistan garrison in East Pakistan to surrender. The Indian spokesman had announced that Indian forces would encircle Dhaka in 24 to 48 hours. There were rumours of Chinese intervention, confirmed in a general way by the Indian government. The Tass agency, referring to the movement of the American Task Force, accused the US of 'gunboat diplomacy'. For the first time, since 4 December, the French and UK delegations were taking an active part in consultations. A few hours before the meeting of the Security Council, they handed over a copy of their draft resolution to the Pakistani delegation. It provided for (i) an immediate cease-fire on the West Pakistan border and on the 1965 Cease-fire Line in Kashmir; (ii) negotiations between the military commanders of both sides in East Pakistan for an immediate cease-fire by all forces under their command; (iii) an immediate and durable cease-fire and cessation of all hostilities in all areas to remain in effect until operations of disengagement leading to withdrawal of forces had taken place in both the theatres; (iv) the urgent conclusion of a comprehensive political settlement in accordance with the wishes of the people as expressed through their elected representatives; and (v) an affirmative response by the two governments to the proposal of the Secretary-General offering his good offices.

The Anglo–French resolution, S/10455, which pushed the Italy-Japan resolution to the background, did not call for withdrawal of forces, not even an immediate cease-fire in East Pakistan, but merely negotiations for it. It, in fact, sought to give juridical sanction to the situation on the ground there, and asked Pakistan to negotiate surrender. At this time it was the only proposal seriously under discussion among the Security Council members.

Pakistan's negotiating position had become extremely weak after Niazi's approach to the Indians for a cease-fire, and the resignation of Governor Malik. The only option available to it was to get the Anglo-French resolution vetoed by China, but this would leave no resolution before the Security Council, and the issue would die out. This did not bother the Indians or the Soviet Union, but for Pakistan the only hope, however remote, for survival was now in the UN. The text of the Anglo-French resolution was telexed to the Foreign Office informing it that the mission was trying for certain modifications in the draft.

In the background of the complete military collapse in East Pakistan, and its diminishing diplomatic stature, the Pakistan delegation faced the 1614th Security Council meeting held in the afternoon of 14 December. There was no substantive discussion on the resolution. The UK representative proposed an adjournment for consultations which was opposed by the US, China, and Somalia, but supported by the Soviet Union and Poland. At this stage, the Americans informed the Pakistan delegation that they had not been able to persuade the Soviet Union to accept a simple cease-fire resolution. It would be recalled that this was part of the diplomatic strategy, agreed between Bhutto and Kissinger, which envisaged first proposing a draft in the Security Council on the lines of the General Assembly resolution, and, after its veto by the Soviet Union, settling for a simple cease-fire resolution which Kissinger had thought would be acceptable to the Russians. China had also reluctantly agreed, under US and Pakistan pressure, to abandon the principle of withdrawal of forces.

On the morning of 15 December it was reported that, in response to Niazi's proposal for a cease-fire in East Pakistan, the Indian Army Chief of Staff had demanded full surrender. The UN Secretariat had also received a message from their office in Dhaka that Governor Malik and Farman Ali had intimated the desire of the government of Pakistan to end hostilities in East Pakistan and that they had requested a cease-fire of a few hours to discuss the terms. These developments left open no possibility of obtaining a resolution from the Security Council which would safeguard the integrity of Pakistan and which would not be vetoed by the Soviet Union.

In another diplomatic bid to salvage its integrity, Pakistan on the same day, 14 December, requested an immediate meeting of the Security Council which was convened (1614th and Adl. 1 meeting) at less than an hour's notice. Nothing came of it. Bhutto made an emotional speech and walked out from the meeting.

The next day, 15 December, the meeting of the Security Council (1615th meeting) scheduled for the afternoon actually met at 7 p.m. Four resolutions were moved. First, S/10456 was introduced by the Syrians followed by the Anglo-French draft, S/10455. Both of them were opposed by the Soviet Union which moved its own resolution S/10457. The representative of China strongly attacked the Soviet Union which replied in the same tone. Next, the representative of Poland introduced a revised version, S/10453 Rev. 1, of his original draft S/10453. All these resolutions, in varying degrees, emphasized a political settlement in East Pakistan. In the Soviet draft the political settlement was to be simultaneous with a cease-fire. In the Syrian and Anglo-French drafts it was to follow the cease-fire, and was to be in accordance with the principles of the UN charter, which ensured the integrity of Pakistan. The Soviet draft made no mention of withdrawal of forces, the Syrian resolution called for it but not forthwith, the Anglo-French text merely provided for 'operations of disengagement leading to withdrawal' after an immediate cease-fire in both the theatres of conflict. This formulation kept the withdrawal open-ended, and India had no serious objections to it. In the context of the Indian occupation of East Pakistan, it was basically the same as the Soviet draft resolution S/10457, which in turn was identical to its 6 December draft S/10428.

During negotiations on the Anglo-French text with its sponsors, when the news of Niazi's offer of cease-fire reached the UN, the British delegation told the Pakistanis that they were no longer in a position to incorporate the principle of withdrawal of forces in their draft. It was unlikely now that the Indians would agree to the modifications suggested by Pakistan, and the French and British would not move the resolution unless it was acceptable to all parties. The mission in a telex message sent in the evening of 15 December informed the Foreign Office of this development, and said that efforts would now be made for a simple cease-fire resolution with a call for adherence to the Geneva Convention. The message also conveyed Bhutto's advice that, after the Indian occupation of East Pakistan, inclusion of a political settlement in any resolution would mean juridical sanction of it. Islamabad was also informed that the Soviet representative had instructions to veto even a simple cease-fire resolution. The most that the Indians would agree to, the message added, was a loose formulation calling upon the parties to take steps to bring about a cessation of all hostilities, leading to lasting peace. This obviously meant that the Indians would determine the timing and terms for the cessation of hostilities.

Of the four resolutions tabled on 15 December, the Polish draft resolution, S/10453 Rev. 1, has somehow come to be regarded in Pakistan, ever since, as the best deal which, the opponents of Bhutto maintain, should have been immediately clinched by him. In UN circles the draft was never taken very seriously at the time, as it represented the Indo-Soviet stand and was too one-sided to be acceptable; Poland had voted with the Soviet Union on all the resolutions. In view of the controversy, let us examine the operative clauses of the Polish resolution. These were (i) the immediate release of Mujibur Rahman (this was deleted in the revised version) and transfer of power to the elected representatives in East Pakistan; (ii) an initial cease-fire in all areas of Pakistan for a period of 72 hours immediately *after* the beginning of the process of power transfer; (iii) regrouping of Pakistani armed forces in East Pakistan to pre-set locations for evacuation from there; (iv) all West Pakistani civilian personnel and other persons willing to return to West Pakistan, and East Pakistani civilian personnel and other persons in West Pakistan willing to return to East Pakistan to be given an opportunity to do so under the supervision of the United Nations; (v) the cease-fire to become permanent soon *after* the withdrawal of Pakistani troops and their concentration for that purpose had started during the period of 72 hours; (vi) withdrawal of Indian armed forces from East Pakistan to start soon *after* the evacuation of nationals from both the Wings and the Pakistan armed forces from East Pakistan had started; and (vii) the withdrawal of Indian troops to actually start in consultation with the newly-established authority in East Pakistan.

It will be seen that the conditions which the Polish resolution had prescribed for Pakistan to fulfil before cease-fire were the most stringent and specific of any of the drafts that had come up so far before the Security Council. It asked Pakistan to transfer power in East Pakistan immediately before the interim cease-fire, and evacuate its armed forces from there before a durable cease-fire. But the Indian forces could stay there without any condition. The argument given in favour of the resolution is that it would have saved the Pakistan army from the humiliation of surrender. It can equally be argued that the Polish terms were no less humiliating. In any case, it was no longer possible to avoid the surrender. By 15 December the Indians had encircled Dhaka and reached its suburbs, and could have walked in without much loss. They had accepted Niazi's offer of a cease-fire, subject to the surrender of Pakistan forces, and the Pakistan Army Chief of Staff had permitted Niazi to accept the Indian conditions. There was no question of the Indians at this stage heeding any UN resolution on East Pakistan, or indeed of the Soviet Union allowing any such document to be passed by the Security Council. An acceptance of the Polish resolution would only have given legal sanction to the Indian occupation without any relief to the armed forces or West Pakistani civilians in East Pakistan. Compared to this, the second Soviet resolution of 6 December, S/10428, was much better.

It should also be remembered that in all matters, particularly those of vital national concern in a situation like that of December 1971, the Pakistani delegation to the UN, however high-powered it might be, acts entirely on the instructions of the home government. The Pakistan mission feeds the Foreign Office, at all hours, all UN documents by telex or otherwise, and demands instructions about the stand to be taken on the issues arising from them. The delegation's approach on important matters before the international forum is determined in terms of the brief given to it by the government. The UN mission or the delegation may advise the government on a particular approach, but the system admits no discretion to either of them to act on their own.

The position of the government of Pakistan in the UN since 4 December had been to exclude the mention of a political settlement, but to insist on the inclusion of withdrawal of forces in any cease-fire resolution. The Pakistan mission in New York was given strict instructions to work on this brief in complete disregard of the state of world opinion. The Foreign Office forsook its role of giving independent advice, and reduced itself to just carrying out uncritically the half-baked and fragmented instructions of Yahya. It ignored the advice of its representative in New York, for example, on going to the Security Council in the last week of

November. Even the friendly countries had long come round to the view that the East Pakistan crisis could be resolved only through a political settlement with the elected leadership of the region. The rigid posture could have been sustained only by dominating the military situation, which leverage Yahya, as C-in-C, should have known was not available to him at any stage during the war while the UN was deliberating. He remained oblivious of the rule that what was lost on the ground cannot be retrieved on the table. In desperation, one of the two stands, withdrawal of forces, was abandoned, but by then the military situation had deteriorated to such an extent that even pleadings for a simple standstill cease-fire went unheeded by the world community.

Of the four resolutions tabled on 15 December, government instructions were given only in respect of the Anglo-French resolution as will be presently seen. The Polish resolution was so much at variance with the Pakistani position that apparently no notice of it was taken by the Foreign Office. The question of Bhutto accepting or rejecting it, therefore, did not arise. There was no way to save the honour of the country through the United Nations. But, ironically, the humiliation of surrender could have been avoided if Farman Ali's proposals of 10 December to the UN had been allowed to be acted upon. These proposals were more dignified than the Polish resolution. They were acceptable to the Soviet Union, whose delegate had appreciatively referred to them on 13 December in the 1613th meeting of the Security Council. Such are the vagaries of the vocal classes of Pakistan that, to this day, what Farman Ali is severely criticised for, Poland is applauded for.

16–17 December

In the few remaining hours of united Pakistan, the emergency committee on the morning of 16 December again discussed the theme of the President's speech due to be recorded at 12 noon. The meeting, joined by M. M. Ahmed, asked the Information Secretary to bring the following points to the notice of the President for incorporation in the broadcast: (i) specific mention of the transfer of power to the elected representatives according to the time-table already announced; (ii) the Foreign Office point of view; and (iii) a realistic presentation of the military situation and the capability of continuing the fighting in the west, of which the defence authorities alone were the best judge. The President approved the transfer of power theme which Roedad Khan added in pencil to the speech before the recording, but did not agree to the Foreign Office suggestion to tone it down. In fact, the President considered the draft, as it was, quite mild and not strident enough.

Yahya's speech declaring his firm resolve to continue the war in West Pakistan was broadcast at 8.30 p.m. on 16 December; 'a temporary setback in one theatre of war does not by any means signify the end of the struggle' the President declared. Later, the same evening, Mrs Gandhi in a broadcast announced a unilateral cease-fire on the western front to begin at 8 p.m. on 17 December.

Meanwhile, the director-general Radio Pakistan and senior officials in the Ministry of Information and the Inter-Services Public Relations were engaged in hectic discussions to find suitable wording for broadcasting the act of surrender in Dhaka on Pakistan radio and television; the word 'surrender' had to be avoided. The ingenious formulation that eventually was given out in the press release of the ISPR dated 16 December 1971 was: 'Latest reports indicate that following an arrangement between the local commanders of India and Pakistan in the Eastern theatre, fighting has ceased in East Pakistan, and Indian troops have entered Dacca.'[41]

* * *

Consequent upon the go-ahead signal by the COS for the army offensive, the formations started moving to forward concentration areas during the night of 14–15 December. At that very time, fierce fighting was raging in the 1 Corps area. The Indians had launched an attack to capture Shakargarh town, and had broken through the defences. The attack was repulsed. 'On December 15/16 another Indian attack was launched across the minefields in area Lagwal–Zafarwal sub-sector . . . [the enemy] succeeded in throwing back the holding troops. By the night of 15 December, the Indians had pushed two tank regiments and two infantry battalions into this gap. . . . The Indian aim in this area was to cut the Zafarwal–Shakargarh road.'[42] On 15 December, Lahore city and railway station, Sahiwal and Samasatta railway stations, and gas installations at Sui were hit by the Indian air force. During the night of 15–16 December, troop movements were disrupted by a number of railway accidents and derailments. On the evening of 16 December, 'during a normal briefing the COS abruptly said: "Freeze Tikka".'[43] This was the end of the army offensive in the west.

The question arises whether Yahya had ever intended to launch an offensive in the west. The evidence is mixed. In the middle of November the Americans had informed Mrs Gandhi that Yahya was willing to meet the Bengali leaders in India, or even a representative designated by Mujib; Yahya's only reservation was talking directly with Mujib.[44] As late as 27 November, according to Kissinger, Yahya was desperately seeking negotiations with Bangladesh representatives.[45] This may explain why he did not go to the Security Council soon after the Indian attack in East Pakistan on 22 November. He perhaps thought that direct negotiations had a better chance of securing an acceptable political settlement than the Security Council where the Indo-Soviet pressures would be of an extreme kind. Once war was declared, perhaps, for a day or two, Yahya entertained hopes of substantial gains in the west. But he seemed to have lost his nerve at an early stage, and started looking to the UN for a cease-fire from 4 December onward. Perhaps he never intended to jeopardize West Pakistan by throwing everything into the army offensive. He started the war with the certainty that, in the last resort, Nixon and Kissinger would bail him out, by direct military intervention, getting a favourable resolution from the Security Council, or by using any other lever of superpower politics. He was encouraged in this assumption by his personal rapport with them, and by the fact that throughout the crisis period he was never once seriously told the limits of American support to him.

In the event, an army offensive, given the morale of Pakistani men and officers and the material superiority of the Indians, would have been a very dangerous gamble. As it was, Pakistan lost about 5,795 square miles of which about 5,000 were in the Rajasthan sector, 364 in the Northern Areas, and 386 in the Sialkot–Shakargarh sector. The eastern garrison held on for sixteen days against all odds, giving enough time to the high command to prove that the defence of East Pakistan lay in the west. In East Pakistan the number of those killed was 115 officers, 40 junior commissioned officers, and 1,182 other ranks; in West Pakistan the corresponding number was 70, 59, and 1,482 respectively. Proportionate to the size of the army in the two Wings, the casualties in the east were higher than in the west.

The instrument of surrender was signed in Dhaka at 4.31 p.m. on 16 December (about 6 a.m. New York time). At 4.30 a.m. Yahya instructed Bhutto (vide telegram no. 9648) to accept the Anglo-French draft preferably with modifications, but failing that, as it was. But, the telegram continued, if the

> Anglo-French draft fails to secure acceptance we would have to revert to a simple cease-fire resolution. Before we do that please seek a meeting with President Nixon soonest possible in the light of my letter to him dated December 14. . . . Following is also relevant. On December 11 we received advice and implied assurance from Dr Kissinger on behalf of White House. He strongly advised against going to the Security Council with any amended proposal of what Farman Ali had relayed to UN (as communicated in message no G-0002 of 10 December to Malik) on the ground that it would weaken our bargaining position. He urged that we hold out for 24 to 36 hours in East Pakistan. He also stated that strongest possible *démarches* had been made in Moscow and they had been threatened that should there be no immediate cease-fire in both wings of Pakistan US would not remain a mere onlooker because of treaty arrangements with Pakistan. The Indians were also to be warned in strongest terms and asked to accept cease-fire in both wings. In the same context Dr Kissinger stated that Seventh Fleet had been ordered to move.
>
> We would now plainly tell Americans that we find ourselves in present position as a direct result of their assurances given above otherwise my proposal (of message G-0002) would have given us a cease-fire while we still retained some territory in East Pakistan and our armed forces would also have remained intact.
>
> We should then ask Americans if they are prepared to militarily fulfil their obligations. In this connection the least they can do is to move adequate naval units into Karachi open up the sea lanes and resume military supplies needed by us.
>
> If American response is positive and immediate assistance is forthcoming then we would not (repeat not) pursue a simple cease-fire idea. However if American reaction is evasive then we should try for a simple cease-fire resolution on best terms you can secure.

The brief shows the very poor judgement of the Foreign Office about the trends in the UN and the limitations of the White House. The day-to-day developments in the Security Council, recorded above, clearly show that the Soviet Union, speaking for India, was not prepared to let Pakistan off the hook at any stage without a transfer of power to the Awami League in East Pakistan. The revised proposal of a simple cease-fire, which Yahya authorized Malik to negotiate vide message G-0002 of 10 December, was not tested as it was withheld. But there was no chance of its being accepted by the Soviet Union when the Indian victory was in sight. Kissinger could not persuade Moscow to accept even his proposals formulated on the lines indicated by Brezhnev, cease-fire–negotiations–withdrawal. It was only Farman Ali's proposals that had a chance of becoming the basis of a resolution acceptable to the Soviet Union. As regards expecting the White House to come up with military intervention and assistance to enable Pakistan to hold on to its East Wing against the opposition of the Congress, the Administration, and public opinion, one can only feel depressed at the undignified persistence of the Foreign Office which was repeatedly told that American military involvement was out of the question.

The next meeting of the Security Council (1616th meeting) was held at 12.05 p.m. on 16 December. The Pakistan delegation did not attend the meeting. The instructions of the Foreign Office could be not be acted upon because the UK and France no longer pursued their resolution after the news of the surrender. The Indian Foreign Minister read out the Indian Prime Minister's statement containing a unilateral declaration of cease-fire. Another meeting of the Council (1617th meeting) was held on the same day at 5.15 p.m. The representative of the Soviet Union moved its draft resolution (S/10458) welcoming cessation of hostilities in East Pakistan, and seeking the continuation of the cease-fire there to ensure 'unimpeded transfer of power to the lawful representatives of the people elected in December 1970'. It also called for a cease-fire along the India–West Pakistan border and along the cease-fire line of 1965 in Jammu and Kashmir and asked Pakistan to accept the Indian offer for this. The resolution was not voted upon. This was the end of the UN involvement in the Indo-Pakistan war.

Immediately after the Foreign Secretary heard the news of the Indian offer of a cease-fire on the radio, he telephoned the

President, who asked him to meet him the next morning. On 17 December at 9 a.m. Yahya, after a brief discussion with Sultan Muhammad, agreed that the cease-fire offer should be accepted, but within the framework of the General Assembly resolution. Barely twelve hours earlier, he had been complaining that his speech promising to continue war on the western front was not tough enough. Soon after, Ambassador Farland was announced. He had brought a message from Kissinger which said that Kissinger had learnt from the British that the Indians would keep the offer open only for twenty-four hours, and the Soviet Union would move a resolution in the Security Council that night in line with its previous drafts. Kissinger advised Yahya to publicly accept the Indian offer before the expiry of the deadline on a purely bilateral basis. This would deprive India of an excuse to justify the continuation of hostilities in the west, and would also allow sufficient time to work out an acceptable UN resolution in terms of a bilateral agreement between the two countries.

Farland strongly urged Yahya to accept Kissinger's advice, as he must have been instructed to do. He said that Pakistan faced great danger as India could turn her entire air force against West Pakistan. He gave the doomsday expert opinion of his Air Attache that India could muster a hundred planes for one attack. The entire Pakistan air force would then have to scramble up and, while such of them as survived the air combat landed on such air strips as were still operational to refuel, a second Indian attack would destroy them on the ground. The President peevishly responded that wars were not won in the air; a lot depended on the attitude of the US and that he was still awaiting a reply to his letter of 14 December to President Nixon. It was not clear, the President continued, whether the Indian announcement of a cease-fire was an offer or an ultimatum. Yahya then bluntly asked Farland, 'Are you going to help or am I going to be left in the lurch?' and added in the same tone, 'I do not want to be led up the garden path. Several promises and hopes have been held out but until now I do not see any sign of practical help.' Farland explained Nixon's difficulties; the Press had severely criticized him for helping Yahya, it was election time, the Democrats were making it an election issue, etc. Nixon would give whatever assistance was possible as soon as he could, he added.

Farland tried to console Yahya by pointing out the positive aspects of the separation of East Pakistan. Pakistan, he said, relieved of the burden of East Pakistan would be a prosperous and powerful country with the economic and political support of the US. But before leaving, he left Yahya in no doubt, by the following exchange, of the American reaction to the rejection of the Indian offer.

> Farland: I have a request. If you are not accepting the cease-fire, please let me know. I want to evacuate the Americans.
>
> Yahya: Why?
>
> Farland: Pakistan is not going to be a fit place to live in if India really starts this offensive.
>
> Yahya: Don't lose your bloody nerve like that.
>
> Farland: Not as a friend but I am asking you as ambassador of my country that if you are not accepting, please let me know in time so that I evacuate Americans. Pakistan will not be a healthy place for any human being.

Farland also conveyed the American opinion that the Indians were hoping that Pakistan would refuse, so that they could come with their full might to West Pakistan.

After the US Ambassador left, Yahya asked Sultan Muhammad to draft a statement accepting the Indian offer of a cease-fire, and summoned General Hamid, Chief of Staff, Lieutenant-General Gul Hassan, Chief of General Staff, and Air Marshal Rahim Khan, C-in-C Air Force. He briefed them about his meeting with the US Ambassador and gave his opinion that this was no empty American threat. All the three agreed with the President.

Meanwhile, Sultan Muhammad produced a draft which included the following paragraph.

> The cessation of hostilities should be followed by withdrawals of her armed forces by India from all territories of Pakistan. Further so far as East Pakistan is concerned it is an integral part of Pakistan and India should end her military aggression there allowing the people of East Pakistan freely to determine their relationship within the framework of unity of Pakistan without fear of coercion and threat of force by India.

Yahya, Hamid, and Gul Hassan thought that this para might be used as a pretext by India to go back on its cease-fire offer; she might say that Pakistan, by putting conditions, had not really accepted it. The Foreign Secretary argued that in a formal announcement of this nature the principle of the unity of the country should be asserted to avoid misunderstandings at home and abroad. The President, however, showed a greater realism, which had dawned on him after the White House had finally told him that he should not expect any help from them, and he ordered the deletion of the para from the draft statement accepting the cease-fire. This was done and it was agreed that the announcement by Pakistan should be made over the radio at 3 p.m. the same day.

At about the same time, unaware that a decision had already been taken in the President House on the cease-fire, the emergency committee was discussing it less than a mile away in the Defence Adviser's office in Secretariat II. M. M. Ahmed, who had also joined the meeting, was in favour of accepting the cease-fire. He argued that the world community, which was trying to bring about cessation of hostilities through the UN, would not support Pakistan in continuing the strife. He apprehended that an outright rejection of the cease-fire offer would give an excuse to India, backed by the Soviet Union, to launch an all-out attack on West Pakistan. After some discussion, the committee decided to advise the President that (a) the cease-fire may be accepted only within the framework of the General Assembly resolution of 7 December; and (b) in the alternative, troops of both the countries in the eastern and western theatres of conflict should be withdrawn; the vacuum in East Pakistan created by the withdrawal of Indian and Pakistani troops should be filled by a UN peace force, pending a political settlement there. While the meeting was in progress, the President summoned M. M. Ahmed; a little later the members of the emergency committee were also called. On reaching the President House at the appointed time, 12 noon, the members found Ahmed and Sultan Muhammad Khan waiting in the ante room. Yahya met them in the verandah of the President House, where he was sitting with Hamid, Rahim Khan, Gul Hassan, and Peerzada.

Yahya gave a review of the situation since the beginning of the crisis, and attributed the loss of East Pakistan to the lack of air cover and inadequate logistic support due to the naval blockade.

In West Pakistan except some oil, ammunition, and a couple of planes, the expected foreign assistance did not materialize. The Chinese were not in a position to provide any support due to the weather conditions. India, on the other hand, was receiving massive assistance from the Soviet Union. President Nixon, Yahya stated, had informed him that according to their computerized estimates, oil supplies in Pakistan would not last for more than 10 to 12 days. Qamarul Islam intervened, saying that stocks for a month were available. The President asserted that the Indians would be able to mobilize twelve squadrons. Air Marshal Rahim Khan corrected the number to eight. Yahya, however, continued with the scenario of the vulnerability of the Pakistan air force given by Farland. Pakistan was in no position to face India economically or militarily. President Nixon, he said, had advised him to accept the cease-fire offer, otherwise India assisted by the Soviet Union had the capability to destroy West Pakistan. Continuing in the same strain and emphasizing the need to survive and build up a militarily strong Pakistan to fight another day, he informed the members that he had decided to accept the American advice and order a cease-fire. M. M. Ahmed as the spokesman of the committee said that the committee, after discussions that morning, had also concluded that the Indian offer should not be rejected, but it should be accepted within the framework of the General Assembly resolution. Yahya said that any mention of that resolution or of a UN peace force would be regarded as conditions and would provide India with the excuse it was seeking to go back on its offer; whereas, Yahya said, he wanted to save West Pakistan at least.

At this stage, the President asked the Foreign Secretary to distribute typed copies of the statement proposed to be issued, and commented that since the cease-fire in the General Assembly resolution had been accepted, there was nothing new in accepting the Indian offer. Roedad Khan referred to the President's broadcast of the previous evening, and pointed out that since withdrawal of troops was not envisaged, the acceptance of the cease-fire would be in terms of the Indian offer, and not in the context of the General Assembly resolution. Yahya ended the discussion by saying that 'The responsibility is mine and I am not going to shift it to anybody else. Whether it is popular or not, I will do it.' To the apprehensions of the Information Secretary about the adverse public reaction, particularly in the context of the previous evening's speech which had promised to continue the fight, Yahya in his typical style said, 'The people should have been prepared. If they are not, it is your problem.' After some changes had been made in the wording, the members finally agreed with the formulation of the draft announcement. The acceptance of the cease-fire was announced at 3 p.m.

Epilogue

For two or three days following the acceptance of the cease-fire on 17 December, *de facto* Pakistan, consisting now of the West Wing only, was in turmoil. Yahya was no longer the centre of power. The people were bewildered and there was no one to explain to them what had happened. The national frustration found its expression in spontaneous demonstrations and processions against the regime and the army in major cities.

On 18 December a meeting was held in the President House attended by the COS, Air C-in-C, the PSO, and the members of the emergency committee. The Information Secretary, who was besieged by the media, suggested that the 'military debacle' and the acceptance of the cease-fire should be explained to the Pakistani editors and Press correspondents by a senior army officer. Yahya took strong exception to the expression, and said that what happened could be called a 'setback' but not a 'debacle', and what the Information Secretary was suggesting should have been done earlier. Now, he said, 'talk only about the cease-fire and why it had to be accepted.' There was no need, the President went on to say, to explain the military collapse and the public should only be told that 'We had already accepted a cease-fire and we are committed to it. India was not willing to accept it. Now that Indian has agreed to it, how can we say no to it? The whole world will turn against us.' The President further directed that the Information Secretary, and all other secretaries, as well as commissioners and deputy commissioners, should use their influence to make the cease-fire acceptable.

It was also suggested in the meeting, among others by Ghulam Ishaq Khan, that Bhutto should be sent for. Yahya sent a message to New York telling Bhutto 'it is imperative that you should return home immediately. If you have not met Nixon so far please do not wait for it. Kindly proceed to Tehran from where one of our Boeings will be flying you direct to Rawalpindi.' Later, Farland informed Yahya that Bhutto was meeting Nixon the same day, and Yahya sent another message asking him to leave for Pakistan immediately after meeting the US President.

Originally, the idea was that President Yahya would explain the outline of the Constitution in his broadcast of 16 December. On the morning of that day, however, Peerzada told Roedad Khan that the Constitution would be announced separately on the following day, and not in the President's speech. The last meeting of the Constitution committee with the President was held on 15 December when a bound copy of the Constitution was presented to him. The committee had discussed the date of enforcement of the Constitution, whether this should be with effect from the date the prime minister was sworn in or from the date on which the National Assembly first met. The President had decided it should be the former date. Such was Yahya's detachment from reality that during the meeting of the committee he was tuning in to the radio on the hour for the news, and when he heard of paratroops landing near Dhaka he exclaimed, 'this is going to be an epic battle—there will be hand-to-hand fighting'.

The announcement regarding 'Salient Points of the Constitution' was scheduled to be made at 7.15 p.m. on 17 December, but it was postponed, at the last moment, for the following day at the same time.[1] On 18 December, in the emergency committee meeting held at 6 p.m. in the Defence Adviser's office, as the time for the announcement was drawing near, a member suggested again postponing it to the next day. Roedad Khan checked up with Peerzada who confirmed that it should be done the same evening. The members, however, felt that the announcement of the Constitution in the prevailing uncertain atmosphere would create still more confusion in public minds. Lieutenant-General Gul Hassan was consulted and he also advised against any broadcast of the 'Salient Points'. This was then brought to the notice of the President who agreed with Gul Hassan and the statement was withdrawn just a few minutes before it was scheduled to go on the air at 7.15 p.m. Earlier, at 6.45 p.m. when the Information Secretary had advised him on the same lines, the President had angrily remarked, 'If you people want me to resign, please say so.' Peerzada later rang up to find out what had happened to the broadcast, and who in the GHQ had stopped it, and whether the President had agreed. He was surprised at the cancellation of the announcement because, he said, 'he had cleared it with the President in the afternoon.'

Yahya was oblivious of the nation's trauma and the deep and widespread humilitation felt in the army by its defeat and surrender. He thought he could continue to be the president under the new Constitution which was ready for promulgation. He had asked Bhutto to return immediately, most probably to take over as prime minister under him.

Still hoping to remain in power, Yahya instructed the Information Secretary on 19 December, as a damage control measure, to use all powers to prevent the publication of the news of processions and disturbances, which had followed the cease-fire, from appearing in the Press. When the Information Secretary reported these orders to the emergency committee in the evening, it was decided to request the President to reconsider the matter. The Chief of General Staff was consulted by the Defence Adviser who said, 'Explain all this to the President. It is too technical.' Ghiasuddin then spoke to the President who agreed to withdraw the pre-censorship order. It is significant that during these few days instructions were being sought by the emergency committee from Gul Hassan and not Peerzada.

* * *

At that very time Gul Hassan was engaged in containing a revolt in the army. The discontent in the army had taken concrete shape on 19 December in demanding the removal of Yahya and his colleagues. Two reserve formations, 6 Armoured Division, commanded by Major-General M. I. Karim (who as brigadier had served in the CMLA Secretariat) and 17 Infantry Division, commanded by Major-General R. D. Shamim formed Strike Force North under the *ad hoc* command of Major-General Bashir. These formations located at Gujranwala had remained inactive while the Indians were gaining territory in the Sialkot–Shakargarh sector. Whatever the strategic reasons for keeping these formations in reserve, to the local people their non-participation in the battle was inexplicable. After the cease-fire, at places there were humiliating slogans raised in public demonstrations against the army, and army vehicles and personnel were stoned. This was an unusual phenomenon in the heartland of the Punjab where the army had always enjoyed respect and affection.

In this state of affairs, some officers decided to convey formally to GHQ that they no longer had any confidence in the government and military leadership. On 19 December a conference was held in the headquarters of 6 Armoured Division by Major-General Karim. It was attended by his brigadiers and Colonel-Staff and two other generals, Bashir and R. D. Shamim. Brigadier Farrukh Bakht Ali and Brigadier Iqbal Mehdi Shah took the stand that the army would not obey any order to use force against the people, and a new government acceptable to the people should be inducted. The officers generally supported them, but the views of the generals differed. Major-General Bashir was opposed to taking any formal stand. Major-General Karim was sympathetic and first offered to convey the officers' feelings unofficially, but seeing how strongly his subordinates felt about the situation he agreed to take up the issue formally also. Major-General Shamim committed himself and his 17 Division to supporting the officers. Bashir informed Gul Hassan about the agitation among the officers in his command and asked him to come down and pacify them. Gul Hassan invited him to come to Rawalpindi but Bashir deputed two staff officers, Colonel Aleem Afridi and Colonel Javed Iqbal. They brought two letters from Karim and Shamim expressing the feelings of the officers of their formations that they wanted Yahya and his colleagues to hand over power to the elected representatives. The staff officers met Gul Hassan at 4 p.m. on 19 December and found him dejected, complaining that no one listened to him, the President would not see him, and that he was being blamed for everything. He called Rahim Khan, C-in-C Air Force, who tried to pacify the staff officers but they were adamant and threatened to bring a unit to Rawalpindi to remove Yahya and his junta to pave the way for the elected representatives to take over power. At 5 p.m. Gul Hassan and Rahim Khan went to General Hamid and told him of the officers' demands. Hamid rang up Bashir and arranged with him for the Director Military Intelligence (DMI), Brigadier M. Iqbal, to visit the headquarters of 6 Armoured Division.

Gul Hassan, Rahim Khan, and Abdul Hamid met Yahya at 7 p.m. and conveyed to him what the staff officers had told them. Yahya rang up Bashir who did not want to take the call and, while Karim and Ali were persuading him to explain the position to the President, after waiting for some time, Yahya went off the line. Gul Hassan persuaded Yahya to resign and read out a short message to this effect, which Yahya approved. Gul Hassan rang up Roedad Khan, who was in the emergency committee meeting, from the President House and dictated to him the text of the announcement which he directed should be made immediately. It was now 7.30 p.m. The emergency committee, unaware of the mutinies in the army, felt that the announcement would create a constitutional vacuum and Roedad Khan rang back Gul Hassan to convey these views of the committee. Gul Hassan, however, insisted that the announcement be made and said there would be no problems. Yahya's resignation was accordingly broadcast in the 8 p.m. news bulletin of Radio Pakistan.

Back at the 6 Armoured Division HQ, Major-General Jillani, Director General Inter-Services Intelligence, and Brigadier Iqbal of Military Intelligence arrived at 10 p.m. and spent three hours talking to the three generals, Bashir, Karim, and Shamim in the presence of Brigadier Iqbal Mehdi Shah and Brigadier Farrukh Bakht Ali. The DMI thereafter talked separately with the two brigadiers and tried to persuade them that the army should remain united behind the regime against the politicians. After he failed to convince the brigadiers of the armoured division, Brigadier Iqbal went to the commanding officer of a battalion of 17 Division to ascertain whether he would be prepared to surround the armoured division headquarters and arrest the recalcitrant officers. The commanding officer said he would not do it. Iqbal and Jillani returned to Rawalpindi at 1 a.m. There was also some talk of using the commandos of the Special Service Group, in support of the regime, to arrest the mutinous officers.

Consequent upon the resignation of Yahya, General Abdul Hamid perhaps thought of taking over. He, however, wanted to be sure of the army's support before doing so. A meeting of the senior army officers, lieutenant-colonels and above, was called on 20 December by General Hamid Khan in the GHQ auditorium. Later, all officers of the GHQ were invited and, still later, all officers of the Rawalpindi garrison were directed to attend the meeting. The expansion of the audience at the meeting was significant, and it 'may have been Gul Hassan who, as Chief of General Staff, had these orders issued through the Staff Duties Directorate. It is believed that Gul Hassan advised some officers . . . not to withhold their opinions or mince their words.' The young officers did precisely that in the meeting which ended in pandemonium, leaving no doubt in the mind of senior command that the old order would not be allowed to continue.[2]

From 18 to 20 December there was intense jockeying for power in the senior command in the GHQ , which was reluctant to allow transfer of power to the civilians. *De facto* power was in the hands of Gul Hassan who at one time was in the run for the presidency with Hamid as C-in-C army. Then there was a lobby for Asghar Khan to be made the president; he was staying with Brigadier Afridi who was his relative. Cornelius was informed by Lieutenant-Colonel Hasan at 9 p.m. on 19 December that Yahya had decided not to promulgate the new Constitution and to hand over power to Bhutto. Cornelius suggested that Yahya could transfer power under his Constitution, by nominating Nurul Amin as president who then could swear in Bhutto as the leader of the majority party. Peerzada demurred, and suggested that Cornelius himself might put the proposal to the President, at the same time saying that probably he had retired for the night and might not be in a good mood.

The struggle, however, was decided by the middle cadre of the army in favour of the majority party leader of West Pakistan, which was the only viable and realistic course of action. This was also the consensus view of the civil service leadership, and so Bhutto arrived in Rawalpindi on 20 December. He was received at the airport by Gul Hassan and Rahim Khan and taken straight to the President House where he was sworn in as the President.

* * *

In Bangladesh there was no authority to replace the former government of East Pakistan after the surrender except the Indian army. Dhaka city was in the hands of guerrillas and the *mukti bahini*. They were on a revenge-taking spree, seeking out real or imaginary collaborationalists and non-Bengalis. There were large-scale killings and arrests by these heavily-armed militants and the Indian army, the only *de facto* organized authority, was careful to avoid any confrontation with them. It was not until 22 December that the provisional government of Bangladesh arrived in Dhaka.

Its arrival, however, made no difference. This faction-ridden body, without the strong hand of Mujib, was as insubstantial as Mujibnagar from where it was purported to have come. The big event for which everyone was waiting was the arrival of Mujib. Every day there were large public meetings and processions demanding the return of Mujib, hurling abuse at Pakistan and Bhutto, and dire threats to the West Pakistanis in Dhaka.

On the night of 19–20 December the group of West Pakistani civilians and Governor Malik and his family were shifted in great secrecy and under heavy escort of the Indian army to the relative safety of the cantonment. Niazi, Farman Ali, and other senior Pakistan army officers were flown to Calcutta soon after the surrender, even before they had been registered by the ICRC as prisoners of war. The Indians had kept ready a large number of POW camps in various parts of India. The movement of the Pakistani prisoners of war started from early January 1972 by special trains directly from Khulna and other stations to the assigned camps. It was an extremely well-organized movement of about 90,000 POWs and civilian internees.

Meanwhile, there was great anxiety amongst us about Mujib. Eventually he arrived in Dhaka on 10 January.[3] On 12 January he was sworn in as the Prime Minister of the People's Republic of Bangladesh, which had been recognized as an independent sovereign state by most of countries of the world within about a month or so of its *de facto* emergence. A few days later he called us to the Eastern Command auditorium and addressed us. He was very calm, but bitter about his imprisonment. He invited us to stay in Bangladesh where, he assured us, we would be well looked after. Being aware of the bloodthirsty atmosphere of the city we were not prepared to accept the offer. We trusted the Indians more, because under the Geneva Conventions they were responsible for our safety.

Our group of civil and police officers was moved out from Dhaka by steamer to Khulna and from there by train directly to the Bareilley camp. The journey and the camp reminded us of films we had seen of the Second World War. We would stay in this camp for more than two years, while the debris of the breakup of Pakistan was being cleared.

Mujib was assassinated on 15 August 1975, after a military coup. Bhutto was executed on 4 July 1979, after a military coup. Indira Gandhi was assassinated on 31 October 1984. Yahya died of natural causes on 8 August 1980.

Appendices

Appendix 1

R. G. Casey to Viscount Wavell

Government House,
Calcutta,
17th December 1944.

My dear Lord Wavell

I write in extension of my letter to you of the 6th November on All-India politics.

2. I have not got any major matters of information or suggestion to put up to you–but a number of points have occurred to me in the last month or two that I think justify being put down on paper for what they are worth.

3. A considerable number of Indians (some Muslims but mainly Hindus) bring up, in conversation with me, the subject of the political future of India. On looking up my diary notes of these talks I am struck by the remarkable paucity of constructive ideas or proposals. Two well-known and responsible Hindus have suggested to me that the solution lies in the abolition of communal electorates; two others have suggested that the next move of consequence must be the release of the members of the Congress Working Committee. Another has suggested that this is the psychological moment for the release of Maulana Abul Kalam Azad (the Muslim President of the Congress)–but not necessarily the other members of the Working Committee.

4. It is quite remarkable that, in the course of a dozen or so interviews over the last two months, no more fruitful suggestions have emerged than the above. One cannot escape the conclusion that there is almost complete bankruptcy of political resource amongst Indians at present.

5. In these circumstances, I think that it is fair to say that we (the British) will have to find a way to enable them (the Indians) to get rid of us (the British)–if post-war Anglo-Indian relations are to remain reasonably good, and India remain within the British Commonwealth.

6. I may say that in these many conversations, I never take the initiative–although I make it quite easy for them to raise the subject of All-India politics and to express themselves freely and confidentially to me on the subject. I do not hide the fact that I am very much interested in the subject–but I confine my comment very largely to questions.

7. In conversation with Muslims, I find no dearth of questions to ask about "Pakistan". I often say that I would feel much happier in my mind on their account if I could be assured that they had taken into account the essential economic and financial problems of "Pakistan". Usually they become rather embarrassed when one asks if a number of very practical economic and financial matters have been worked out satisfactorily. Actually, I suspect that they have done practically no work on this aspect of things at all. I have no reason to believe that the conception of "Pakistan" has advanced beyond the stage of political wishful thinking. I realise that it has proved a very valuable bargaining counter–but I hope that Mr. Jinnah will compromise before Pakistan turns into a tiger that he is riding.

8. Some adequately equipped persons might, with advantage, write a book on the "Economic consequences of Mr. Jinnah" on a famous parallel.

9. My present belief is that the problem of "Pakistan" represents the biggest (and, indeed, practically the only) hurdle standing in the way of the constitutional settlement of the Indian problem.

I realise that the Congress is basically responsible for the growth of the Pakistan idea, by the way they have treated the Muslims–but equally do I believe that, unless the Pakistan idea is squashed (and some other means of satisfying the Muslims substituted for it), it is likely so to delay the implementing of independence for India that Anglo-Indian relations will suffer grievously.

I believe that a considerable amount of work will have to be done on the Muslims if they are to be weaned away from the Pakistan idea.

If it were your wish that I should pursue the matter here in Bengal, I believe that I might be able to influence a certain section of the Muslims here away from the Pakistan idea by discreet conversations in the course of the next six months or so–and I believe that I could do so without raising any ill feeling or running the risk of being accused of taking sides. I fully realise the risk of any of us being able to be accused of being partisan. Indeed, I stressed this in paragraph 18 of my letter of November 6th.

10. In particular–I believe that the idea of the possibility of a plebiscite amongst the Muslims of Bengal only (i.e. to the exclusion of the rest of the population of Bengal) should be debunked as quickly as possible. It cannot be defended on any democratic or other grounds that I can think of.

11. Also–I believe that if the Muslims could be got to realise that the inclusion of Greater Calcutta in "Pakistan" is a complete impossibility–then the idea of "East Pakistan" would receive a great blow. The Muslims do not want a sylvan retreat. They must be made to realise that Calcutta is more than the capital city of a province–that it is an All-India city that happens to be in Bengal.

12. I don't think that I have made it clear in earlier letters that the conception of "Eastern Pakistan" held by Nazimuddin (and so, I imagine, by the Muslim League in Bengal) is not the standard idea of a Muslim State. He paints the picture of a wholly autonomous sovereign state with a bare Muslim majority of population, in which Muslims and Hindus would live in amity and share the responsibility for the business of Government (and all else) in approximate proportion to their numbers. He would expect the benefits to be derived from such a state to become so clear to the Hindus, after a relatively short time, that they would become as keen about its continuance as the Muslims–and, indeed, that contiguous areas (even with a Hindu majority) would knock at the door of "Eastern Pakistan" and ask to be allowed to throw in their lot with them.

13. As I have said, I believe that this fanciful conception has been arrived at without any real investigation of the prospective economic position of "Eastern Pakistan". Close objective examination of a problem is not a notable feature of Muslim thought in this Province.

14. Nazimuddin's conception of "Eastern Pakistan" would seem to me to have all the disadvantages of a small State that would not be an economic unit–and to have none of the advantages of a National Home for the Muslims that seems to me to be the only tangible reason advanced publicly for its creation.

15. However, this conception is interesting because it seems to show that they are groping after a state in which Hindus and Muslims would live together in amity, rather than upon any belief that the interests of the two communities are irreconcilable. The basis of that community of interests can only be the general feeling in Bengal, shared by both Hindus and Muslims–(1) that Bengal is and always has been a region apart;– (2) that it has never had a 'fair deal' from India;–(3) that All-India politics and

administration are increasingly dominated by Bombay and Madras, and by the provinces nearer Delhi.

16. One can sum all this up, not unfairly I think, by saying that the Bengalis are suffering from "Centrophobia".

17. The point here is that, although Nazimuddin may continue to shout for Pakistan, his belief that he may get the Hindus to agree to the idea of an independent Eastern Indian State (in which the Muslims will have scarcely any effective majority) suggests that his support for Pakistan is a bargaining counter, and that what he is really after is a guarantee that a Hindu-ridden Centre shall not have any effective control over the welfare of the people of Bengal.

18. All this has relevance to the question whether there is either advantage to be gained or prospect of success in a definite attempt to argue the Muslims out of their demand for Pakistan and to provide them, as an alternative, with 'safeguards' for what they really want. I would be grateful to have your views on this.

19. As you agreed to my discussing my letter to you of November 6th with the other Governors here recently, I am sending copies of this letter to the Governors of the U.P., Bihar, Orissa and Assam.

I am Yours sincerely

R.G. CASEY

His Excellency Field-Marshall
The Rt. Hon. Viscount Wavell,
GCB, GMSI, GMIE, CMG, MC., Viceroy & Gov-Gen. of India.

Appendix 2

H. S. Suhrawardy to Liaquat Ali Khan

Bengal Secretariat,
Calcutta,
21 May 1947

My dear Liaquat Ali Sahib,

I have had a talk with Maulana Akram Khan. I feel that I must once more impress upon the Quaid-i-Azam through you the disaster that will overtake us if Bengal is partitioned or if the partition of Bengal is announced on the 2nd of June, that is to say, if we cannot come to an agreement before the 2nd of June. He seems to think that the Quaid-i-Azam feels that any settlement with the Hindus here or the local Congress, which will of course have to be ratified by the High Commands, will mean that we are giving up our principles - referring probably to the two-nation theory or to Bengal being declared a Muslim zone or to Bengal from the beginning forming part and parcel of a Pakistan Federation. Now my submission is this, that we are not compromising our principles in any way by coming to an agreement for Bengal, and even if we do, the compromise will be of such a minor nature that it will be expedient to make that compromise in view of the terribe disaster that will overwhelm Bengal, and particularly the Muslims of Bengal, if Bengal is partitioned. I wish to expand this. The Lahore Resolution visualised Independent Sovereign States of those areas where the Muslims are in a majority with such readjustments, etc., etc. This in practice came down to provincial boundaries to start with. Hence a Free State of Bengal subscribes to this criterion. Nowhere do I find it stated that there must be a declaration from the beginning that it will be Pakistan or that it should form part of a Federation of Pakistan States. So, what principles after all are we compromising? As regards joint electorate within the agreement, the present formula is equivalent practically to separate electorate, and it may surprise you to know that our formula of joint electorate with adult franchise unadulterated has alarmed the Hindu leaders who are demanding reservation of seats in proportion to the population, giving us therefore a statutory majority. Also the formula which has been accepted means practically separate electorate. It keeps their face, viz. their demand for joint electorate, and at the same time it gives us what we want, viz.

separate electorate. Joint Ministries have, as I have said over and over again, been treated as an all-India issue. But when India is definitely going to be partitioned into Zone A and Zone B and we are pulling out, each one framing its own constitution, then we may be left to frame ours, and the manner in which we settle our affairs will not affect the Ministries either of Zone A or of Zone B. And what after all is the alternative unless we come to an agreement now? It would appear that the Quaid-i-Azam intends to fight against the partition inch by inch even after the declaration, that is to say that he will fight in the Legislative Assembly, in the Notional Assemblies and even at the time of a referendum which he hopes will be granted but which the Viceroy has reiterated over and over again cannot be conceded. Now may I say with great respect that there is no hope whatsoever of retrievement if partition is declared on the 2nd of June. We may force a non-partition resolution in the Assembly, but this is valueless as there will be Notional Assemblies. In the Notional Assembly of the Hindu majority areas composed of the present Members of the Legislature on the basis of one for a million or one for two millions, there is absolutely no hope of getting a single Hindu vote in our favour. Even if we today arouse a volume of opinion amongst the Scheduled Castes - and I can tell you that the task is extremely uphill and except two meetings in the Burdwan Division it has not been possible to hold more, and the Scheduled Caste workers are even afraid to go amongst the Scheduled Castes in the Burdwan Division, and they want protection and they want officers to support them - even if we were able to arouse Scheduled Castes public opinion in any degree or form, the present representatives of the Scheduled Castes or those that will be elected by the present representatives will all vote in favour of partition. Further, once partition is announced, there will be no hope of trying to get Hindu opinion in our favour, Scheduled Caste or Caste. The propaganda of the Scheduled Castes in our favour will be that they will be divided, hence there should not be a partition. This is weak against the propaganda of the Hindus, viz. that 'we Hindus of these areas, both Caste and Scheduled Caste, will govern together and have a great Hindu province which will be linked to the Hindu provinces of the rest of India and which will dominate over the Muslims, a province which will be rich in resources and which we shall not surrender'. Please realise that this partition will give to the Western Bengal Hindus such a great victory that they will not give up an inch of ground once the partition is announced. So, neither shall we win in the Notional Assemblies nor is there any hope of winning even if a referendum is given at a subsequent stage. And what I am telling you is an absolute fact which everyone here knows, and let there be no misconception regarding this. I repeat, once the partition is announced there is not the slightest hope of getting Hindu opinion from any section against that partition. West Bengal, which will be Hindu-dominated, will be rich in resources, and why should they agree to link themselves up with a large rural population with the prospect of utilising their resources for the benefit of the rural population and with the further prospect of being dominated by Muslims, whereas they can utilise all those resources for their own wealth and development and at the same time save themselves from Muslim domination. I use the word 'domination' because if all these things are not being done by agreement but are based upon a struggle, that will be the result in spite of all that we may say about treating the Hindu minorities fairly and squarely and everybody having a share in the administration. And what will be the disaster? If there is a struggle, nothing can save the Muslims of West Bengal from being wiped out, and nothing can save the Hindus of East Bengal, even the Scheduled Caste Hindus, from being wiped out. I am including the Scheduled Castes also because however much we may try and differentiate between Caste and Scheduled Caste Hindus, there is no differentiation made where there is a communal struggle as is evidenced by the fact that the Muslims attacked the Scheduled Caste Hindus in Tippera and Noakhali, and the Hindus attacked the Congress Muslims and killed them in Calcutta and Bihar. Now no government is powerful enough to be able to save this province however much we may try. Before Government's resources can be mobilised - and these resources are really peace-time resources–the mischief will have been done and the massacre already enacted. If we use the army, what is the army we are getting here? It is all a Hindu army. It would seem as if there are no Muslims in the army, and while they talk about the army being free from communalism, they will not send Muslim troops to Bengal. So, the army will not come to our help but will actually work against us.

So much for life and death. Then comes the condition of East Bengal. I have in a previous letter told you how absolutely unprepared East Bengal is for a struggle for existence. I will not repeat it here. Please once more refer to the previous letter. If North Bengal also goes to the Hindus, viz. the areas of Jalpaiguri and Darjeeling and the top portion of Dinajpur (which may go to them when a Boundary Commission is set up), then one more commodity, viz. tea also goes to them. What will be left of East Bengal will be an area absolutely deficit in foodgrains, and by the time other Muslim areas or surplus areas send foodgrains to us the Muslims of East Bengal will be dead; they will have to pass not through one famine but through several famines, and I can quite visualise that within six months of the partition the Muslims of East Bengal will be kneeling before West Bengal or before Group A or before the Congress to be taken in into their fold. What else after all is the alternative? So, will you please give some thought to the problem of Bengal and discuss this matter with the Quaid-i-Azam? Pakistan having been gained, is it not worthwhile that we should consolidate our gains? Will you also realise that with the partition cry having been raised, how difficult indeed is it to induce the Hindus to co-operate with us on the basis of a Free State of Bengal? But some who have vision and some who do not wish to hold themselves responsible for the murder of Hindus and Muslims that will surely follow if Bengal is partitioned, are prepared to come to an agreement with us. For Heaven's sake let us take advantage of this. And now there will be only one snag, it may be a very big snag but it will be a snag for which we shall not be responsible either before God or before Man or before our own conscience, and that is the Congress High Command in its dream of giving a blow to Pakistan Bengal and in its dream of dominating the Muslims in one section of Bengal may not agree to the agreement arrived at between ourselves. If so, all that can be said is that we have done our best, and we or the Muslim League will not be held responsible for the horrors that will follow. Secondly, if we had agreed and if the Quaid-i-Azam also says that he is prepared to agree on these terms and if the Congress stands out, then it may well be that the Viceroy may not announce the partition of Bengal in view of the unreasonableness of the Congress attitude; it may well be too that the Viceroy may force the Congress to yield. But let us not, for fear that the Congress High Command may not accept, also fail to do our bit. The Quaid-i-Azam has always been brave and courageous to do the right thing, and although the Congress High Command has not accepted, he has come out in shining glory because he has done the right thing and without considering whether the Congress will accept or not.

Please may I have an answer?

Yours sincerely,

H. S. SUHRAWARDY

The Hon'ble Mr. Liaquat Ali Khan,
8, Hardinge Avenue,
New Delhi.

Appendix 3

H. S. Suhrawardy to Liaquat Ali Khan

Bengal Secretariat,
Calcutta,
21 May 1947

My dear Liaquat Ali Sahib,

I am sending you the final draft of the agreement which has been arrived at between us. This agreement appears to our limited intelligence to be eminently reasonable. Mr. K. S. Roy is going to Mussoorie tomorrow to see his High Command and ascertain their reactions and try and induce them to accept, if the local Congress Committee accepts it. Mr. Sarat Chandra Bose and Mr. K. S. Roy either individually or together would like to see the Quaid-i-Azam to ascertain his reactions and to get his consent. Will you please do me the favour of letting me know what you think about these terms. Members of the Working Committee here will probably consider them reasonable.

2. There is another avenue open and that is to form a Coalition Ministry without conditions but only on one condition that if a Coalition Ministry is formed Bengal will not be partitioned. As I have said in an earlier letter, I can quite see that Coalition Ministries have an all-India background as long as the contest is on but once it is settled that India will be partitioned, Bengal may be permitted to have a Coalition Ministry in order to somehow or other avoid the evil day. A letter or a telegram or a telephone call will greatly oblige.

Your sincerely,

(H. S. Suhrawardy)

The Hon'ble Mr. Liaquat Ali Khan,
8, Hardinge Avenue, New Delhi.

APPENDIX 4

The Civil & Military Gazette

Saturday 24 May 1947

Hindu–Muslim Pact for Bengal

CALCUTTA, May 23. — It is learned from authoritative sources that concrete terms have emerged out of the discussions that have taken place between Mr. Sarat Chandra Bose and certain prominent Congress and Muslim League leaders regarding the future constitution of Bengal and the formation of a new Cabinet.

The terms are as follows:

1. Bengal will be a free State. The free State of Bengal will decide its relations with the rest of India.

2. The constitution of the free State of Bengal will provide for election to the Bengal legislature on the basis of joint electorate and adult franchise, with reservation of seats proportionate to the population amongst Hindus and Muslims. The seats as between Hindus and Scheduled Caste Hindus will be distributed amongst them in proportion to their respective population or in such manner as may be agreed among them. The constituencies will be multiple constituencies and the votes will be distributive and not cumulative. A candidate who gets the majority of the votes of his own community cast during the elections and 25 per cent of the votes of the other communities so cast will be declared elected. If no candidate satisfies these conditions, that candidate who gets the largest number of votes of his own community will be elected.

3. On the announcement by His Majesty's Government that the proposal of the free State of Bengal has been accepted and that Bengal will not be partitioned, the present Bengal Ministry will be dissolved and a new interim Ministry brought into being consisting of an equal number of Muslims and Hindus (including Scheduled Caste Hindus) but excluding the Chief Minister. In this Ministry the Chief Minister will be a Muslim and the Home Minister a Hindu.

4. Pending the final emergence of a legislature and a Ministry under the new constitution the Hindus (including Scheduled Caste Hindus) and the Muslims will have an equal share in the services including military and police. The services will be manned by Bengalese.

5. A Constituent Assembly composed of 30 persons, 16 Muslims and 14 non-Muslims, will be elected by the Muslim and non-Muslims of the legislature respectively, excluding the Europeans.

The terms emerged in this form at a conference which was held at Mr. Bose's residence last Tuesday evening which was attended by several leaders.

It will be remembered that the discussions were initiated by Mr. Bose in January last. The terms will be placed before the Congress and Muslim League organizations for discussion.

APPENDIX 5

H. S. Suhrawardy to Liaquat Ali Khan

40, Theatre Road,
Calcutta.
11th June, 1948.

Mr dear Liaquat Ali Sahib,

I am making a fervent appeal to you to do justice and to undo the great wrong which has been done to me by the East Bengal Government. I can only hope that you do not support it.

You will pardon me if I protest against what I consider to be a deliberate policy to malign me and to exclude me from Pakistan Constituent Assembly, but there was no justification for stopping me from carrying on my Communal Harmony Movement in East Bengal which I had hoped to extend to other parts of the Indian Union and Pakistan. I assure you that I would never have undertaken this task if the Ministers themselves had toured within the province, reassured the minorities, made it clear to their officers on the spot that they had to do justice to the minorities, and had rectified local grievances. I had suggested this in one of my statements but no Minister moved out. Mr. Nazimuddin's first point is that my touring in East Bengal directs the attention of the people and of the world outside to East Bengal and gives them a wrong impression that something is wrong in East Bengal and that the minorities are oppressed there and that I should work in West Bengal. I think this is very unfair. A person moves in the area in which he thinks he can do some good work and where he can be useful. I, as a Muslim and as one who has moved in East Bengal could render more service to the minorities by working in East Bengal among Muslims, than by working in West Bengal among Hindus. For my work essentially consists of appealing to the majority community for consideration and co-operation with the minorities for the welfare of the State. Far from lowering the prestige of East Bengal, I have stabilized it. Before I went, the Hindus were fleeing from East Bengal; exaggerated reports of incidents of oppression and communal lawlessness were being published and believed, and the explanation and denials of the East Bengal Government were discounted as emanating from an accused party; the refugees that came from East Bengal - and that they do not number 2 lakhs but 12 lakhs - were exciting Hindu opinion against the Muslims and a very serious situation from the Muslims was developing in Calcutta and in the border districts. The Government of East Bengal was taking no steps to stop the Hindus from going out other than the issue of weak statements that there was no reason for the exodus, I could see that if the Hindus continued to leave, the Muslims of Calcutta and of West Bengal, and of all the adjacent provinces upto U.P. and thereafter, once mass exodus of Muslims began, all the four crores Muslims of the Indian Union would be doomed - they were doomed to annihilation, subservience, conversion or total migration, in the process of which, they would become sub-human.

My propaganda in East Bengal reassured the Hindus. I pointed out that there was really nothing seriously wrong in East Bengal; that Government have given them security and the majority population were well inclined towards them. I pointed out to them that if they wanted communal harmony, and the goodwill of the Muslims, they must accept the division of India and the partition of Bengal; and proceed to mould their policy on that basis, and that they must be loyal to Pakistan. This was prominently brought out in my Blue Print scheme of the communal harmony movement, which is the foundation and basis of the work I am doing. I do not know whether you, or the Ministers of the East Bengal Government even read it, although it was given publicity in the Press. In order that the Government of East Bengal should know my policy, I even personally presented a copy to Khwaja Nazimuddin who had not read my statement. I doubt very much whether he read it thereafter. I really put the Government of East Bengal on the map and discounted all propaganda against it and this is what I get in return. Moreover, I feel that I can best serve the Muslims of the Indian Union not by carrying on propaganda in West Bengal and in the Indian Union, but by looking after the interests of the Hindu minority in Pakistan, which would have its repercussions on this side and which would lead to better consideration for the Muslims of the Indian Union both by the Government here and by the majority population. I know that I am right in this, as many events have proved. I feel that the problem is to get the majority population educated. It can be done by the Muslims and not by Hindus in Pakistan; in the Indian Union it can be done by Hindus and not by Muslims. A voice raised by the minorities will cut no ice with the majority population. Inspite of this, however, I had arranged after the first portion of my tour in East Bengal, and after fortifying myself with the right to appeal to Hindus to go out in West Bengal with Dr. P. C. Ghosh and other Hindu leaders. I had also arranged with them that while I was touring in East Bengal they would tour in West Bengal and they have actually visited some areas, So, I was not unmindful of this side of the work as well. The Inter Dominion Board, which I hope will be useful still remains to function; it has been heralded with great optimism and we can only trust it will not disappoint the minorities (of Pakistan and the Indian Union) who will be compelled to lodge their grievances with their Government sometimes against the majority population, sometimes against the officials, high and low, and sometimes against the Ministry or the Government itself. It cannot adequately deal with the creation of active goodwill and co-operation which is the purpose of my movement.

After giving me this advice, which I sincerely believe is based on an incomplete understanding of the problems, Nazimuddin proceeds to make charge against me of being the centre of a secret conspiracy with the enemies of the State - of all kinds of horrible, treacherous conduct which repel me not only by their repetition, but by the magnitude of the lies and of the riotousness of the imagination. He appears to think that by laying it on thick and repeating lie after lie, a falsehood can become truth and will be accepted as such by at least some people prepared to believe anything appearing in the name of Pakistan. I appeal to you who know me. Do you think it is possible that I can carry on secret conspiracies with anyone to upset Pakistan, or for the matter of that conspire secretly with anybody for any nefarious purpose? Let us examine the position a little.

I consider the pursuit of communal harmony and promotion of goodwill to be a holy duty. I feel that people have suffered too much and everyone should do what he can to ease the burden of that suffering. I have refused all these tempting offers which you have been kind enough to bestow upon me - why? That I should wander about leaving all the comforts of home for the purpose of conspiring secretly with a mere handful of people. Can anything be more ridiculous? I made it clear in statement after statement issued by me from the time I started the peace movement on 12th August '47, that there can be no communal harmony, no peace and goodwill in Pakistan, unless the division is accepted. I had called upon the Hindus to be loyal to Pakistan as a fundamental of their own security and safety. This was uttered in the presence of lakhs upon lakhs of people and here I am accused of talking secretly with a few people to bring about a United Bengal. In his letter written on the 2nd June he charged me with encouraging those who wanted United Bengal; in the communique of the Govt of East Bengal issued on the 3rd June, I am charged with conspiring secretly to unite the two Bengals with the intention of including Bengal in the Indian Union. That this has been done with a foul purpose and crooked intent is clear to everybody. Can anything be more preposterous than this and thank God, that no one who knows me believes it. But it provides a handle to Government to hound me; and undoubtedly has been manufactured to provide the Government with some excuse. When I first went to Jessore, where certain incidents had occurred and from where the Hindus were fleeing in large numbers and creating a serious situation in Calcutta and other border areas, the police officers of the intelligence Branch took the cue from somebody high up that the East Bengal Government wanted reports of such propaganda. I have never had secret meetings with anyone wherever I have been - there can be no question of secrecy with me, because at all my meetings and talks whether with Muslims or Hindus, anybody could come in if they wanted to. I have been meeting Hindus in order to find out what their grievances were, then with the Muslim to discuss these grievances, then with both to bring about a settlement. I have spoken to people who like to call themselves 'workers' that they should work themselves for communal harmony. Have I not intelligence enough to know that if I work for United Bengal, I shall not be able to carry on any kind of work in East Bengal, communal harmony or otherwise? Why should Muslims consider such a proposition after having obtained Pakistan where they are reaping the fruits of an overwhelming majority? There are three alternatives; (i) to unite, and then become a part of the Indian Union. Pakistan can never agree, (ii) To unite, and then become a part of Pakistan. The Indian Union can never agree, (iii) To unite and become Sovereign. Neither will agree.

I suppose the Nazimuddin Government has had to invent these lies and accept these inspired police reports with alacrity, supposed to be from independent sources, as he has no other weapon with which he can malign me or blacken my face, or justify the action of exclusion. Even you asked we whether I had carried on such propaganda - such is the effect of slander. I was thunder-struck when you asked me that question, that anyone in his senses could possibly believe that I was a secret conspirator. But still I suppose you had to go by the reports supplied by the underlings, who know what kind of reports their overlords want. I am afraid that all this is due to the perverted imagination of some of the Ministers of East Bengal Govt who think that every calumny or slander is justified to achieve their purposes and some of whom have a personal vendetta against me. I appeal to your sense of justice and honesty and decency in the name of the high office that you occupy and your responsibility to God and man to see that so much wrong is not done to me in your State.

Then comes the passage of loyalty to the State etc., etc., and how a citizen of the Indian Union should not interfere in the internal politics of Pakistan. I still maintain that the question of citizenship has not yet been concluded or decided, and I still maintain that it should not be decided unless and until the minorities in both the Dominions have become sufficiently stabilized; that is to say, that they know for certain what their future is going to be, and migrations backwards and forwards after the position has crystallised cease. But even if I was a citizen of the Indian Union exclusively, has the Muslim of the Indian Union no right to appeal to the Muslims in Pakistan in much a way and in such a manner that it will have a salutary repercussion on the future of the Muslims of the Indian Union?

Pakistan was formed to save not only the Muslims of the majority areas but also of the minority areas. On this basis, Muslims of the minority areas contended for Pakistan. Please do not break their hearts by such statements that they can have no voice or should not be heard even within Pakistan; that they cannot address meetings of their own brethren within Pakistan.

As regards internal politics; if by that is meant the Ministry you must know that I have deliberately refrained from even entering East Bengal, lest there should be any idea anywhere that I was seeking to come in. Even when the majority of the members were against Nazimuddin, I refused even to set foot in Dacca, although I was begged to do so; and I only went there after the Quaid-e-Azam had fixed the Ministry firm in the saddle, and the party that was supporting me had accepted my advice to support that Nazimuddin Ministry and even to join it, if offered.

There is so much more that I could write, but my heart is overburdened with sorrow. I never expected so much vindictiveness and falsehood and deliberate oppression. Are these the fruits of independence. Does independence give rights to governments to ride roughshod over the liberty of the individual, and to heap such serious charges and insults on his head, in the plenitude of its power. I am sure that in the time of the British Government, such an action could never have been taken on such flimsy grounds, and for the personal aggrandisement of the Ministry; and if taken would never have been tolerated; and public opinion would never have been suppressed.

If you will allow me, I would like to see you personally in this connection. You are, I believe going to Delhi on the 15th. I shall be glad to come up to Delhi to meet you even in this heat if you will give me an opportunity to place my case before you. Otherwise, I hope you will give me an interview at Karachi.

Yours sincerely,

H. S. SUHRAWARDY

APPENDIX 6

H. S. Suhrawardy to Liaquat Ali Khan

13-A, Kutchery Road,
Karachi.
8th July, 1948.

My dear Liaquat Ali Sahib,

I thank you for promising to look into my matter and to call for the paper. I had hoped that you would have called for the papers on receipt of my letter but apparently you have not had time to go through its contents. I shall be grateful if you will peruse it as it substantially sets out my view of the case. Any points left out in the letter are covered by my press statement.

I would like to reiterate that the best service that I can render to the minorities in the Indian Union is by helping the minorities in Pakistan and educating the majority here. Nazimuddin's point of view that I should carry out my work in the Indian Union is meaningless as I can cut no ice in the Indian Union and I am still regarded with distrust by the militant Hindu section. Moreover it is only a Muslim who can appeal to the majority in Pakistan, and a Hindu who can appeal to the majority in the Indian Union. I would like to direct your attention pointedly to the manner in which the charges have been strengthened in the communique of the 3rd June as compared to the charges in the letter of Nazimuddin of the 2nd June. It is obvious that evidence to which he paid little credence on the 2nd had become sacrosanct on the 3rd. The charges against me are so obviously false and stupid that I would earnestly press you to scrutinize the papers and come to a decision at an early date. I think it is entirely wrong on the part of Nazimuddin to be complacent about the position of the Hindu minorities in Eastern Pakistan. Such action as he has taken will be construed by the Hindus that he does not want communal harmony and is prepared to make the baseless and most stupid charges against a person who has dedicated himself to that cause, and it will be construed by the Muslims of the Indian Union that Pakistan is in no way concerned with their fate.

An early decision will oblige. If you like I can send copies of (i) Nazimuddin's letter to me dated the 2nd June 1948; (ii) communique of the Government of East Bengal dated the 3rd June; (iii) my statements to the press and (iv) my letter to you dated 11 June in case you have mislaid the letter.

It may interest you to know that the East Bengal Government actually passed an Ordinance overnight in order to serve the order upon me.

Yours sincerely

Shaheed Suhrawardy

H. S. Suhrawardy
40, Theatre Road,
Calcutta.

Appendix 7

Liaquat Ali Khan to H. S. Suhrawardy

No. 2047-Ps/48.
Karachi,
July 13, 1948

I am in receipt of your letter of the 8th July. When you met me the other day you told me that there was no truth in the allegations made by the East Bengal Government against you and that a great injustice had been done to you. You requested me to intervene in the matter. I told you that I was not in possession of the material on which action had been taken against you and therefore I could express no opinion. I further explained that it was a matter entirely for the Provincial government and I could not interfere in their administration. I however told you that I shall convey to the Premier of East Bengal all that you had told me.

I am afraid I can not agree with you that Khawaja Nazimuddin is complacent about the position of the Hindu minority in East Bengal. His Government has been doing everything possible to give protection to and safeguard the legitimate rights of the Hindu minority in East Bengal. If the Muslims in the Indian Union received the same treatment as the Hindus are receiving in East Bengal there would be no cause for complaint.

Sd/-

(Liaquat Ali Khan)

H. S. Suhrawardy Esq.
40, Theatre Road,
Calcutta.

APPENDIX 8

H. S. Suhrawardy to Ataur Rahman Khan

TOP SECRET

Karachi, April 17, 1957.

My dear Chief Minister,

Please refer to your semi-official letter No. 196/56-CM dated 27th December 1956.

2. Let me at the outset say that it is not correct that General Mohd Ayub Khan made a statement that East Pakistan cannot be adequately defended. What he said was that the strategic defence of East Pakistan rests on Lahore front. If that holds, East Pakistan is safe as it has remained so far. The Commander-in-Chief is of the opinion that we have enough strength in East Pakistan to hold up to three or four Divisions and it is not expected that our enemy can spare more than that so long as the Lahore front is held.

3. The physical features of East Pakistan have certainly been taken into consideration in drawing up its defence. There is no doubt that small river crafts would be useful in dealing with hostile crafts. A scheme for provision of fast patrol boats is at the moment under examination of the Ministry of Defence.

4. It is necessary that the Headquarters of Pakistan Navy should be located in the same place as the Ministry of Defence. If the General Headquarters is at Rawalpindi, it is only due to shortage of accommodation in Karachi. While for administrative reasons it is not possible to establish Naval Headquarters in East Pakistan, action is being taken to establish a Naval Base at Chittagong. The slow progress so far has been due to lack of funds. A re-phased programme which is expected to accelerate the construction of the Naval Base is at present under active consideration. Action is also being taken to expedite the construction of the Recruiting Centre on the land given by East Pakistan Government, in Dacca.

5. I am fully aware of the necessity of strengthening the defences in East Pakistan and this matter has constantly been engaging my attention since my assumption of the office of Defence Minister. You may rest assured that I would do what I can to ensure that adequate opportunities for Military training are afforded to the youth of Bengal to enable them to play their proper role in the defence of the country.

Yours sincerely,

(H. S. Suhrawardy)

Ataur Rahman Khan, Esq.,
Chief Minister
East Pakistan,
Camp Karachi.

Appendix 9

Notification of the Special Team of Central Government Officers Deputed to East Pakistan

HQ CHIEF MARTIAL LAW ADMINISTRATOR
PRESIDENT'S SECRETARIAT
PRESIDENT'S HOUSE, RAWALPINDI

The Chief Martial Law Administrator has directed that a team composed of the following will proceed to Dacca on Monday, April 5th, in order to assist and advise the Martial Law Administrator Zone 'B' and facilitate coord with the Central Government. The team will initially be required to remain in Dacca for a period of one month:-

a. Mr Muzaffar Hussain
   Secretary National Assembly – Leader of the Team
b. Mr Ayub) Ministry of Food &
c. Mr Kazim) Agriculture
d. Mr Sartaj Aziz) Planning Division
e. Dr Baqai)
f. Mr S B Chaudhry CCIE – Ministry of Commerce
g. Mr Javed Mirza – Ministry of Industries
h. Mr Abid Hussain – CBR
J. Mr Saeeduzzaman – Ministry of Finance
k. Mr Waris Ali – Establishment Division
l. Mr Mustafa – (Chairman EPSIC) who will be coopted by the Leader for coordination work.

Brig
for PSO to the President & CMLA
(M. I. Karim)

No 201/1/CMLA, dated 02 April 1971

To: All Ministries concerned
Establishment Division

Info: CGS, GHQ, Rawalpindi
Secretary to the President
Maj Gen Civil Affairs, Dacca

CONFIDENTIAL

Appendix 10

Port Operations, April–November 1971

The most critical factor in the rehabilitation of East Pakistan's economy and management of the food situation in the post-25 March period was the restoration of loading and unloading capacities of Chittagong and Chalna ports. The level of port operations was the index of the degree of normalcy achieved in the province. It was also important from the political point of view because of the widespread campaign in the Western Press about the impending food crisis in East Pakistan. Accordingly the port's performance and movement of imported foodgrain were intensively monitored both by the provincial administration and the central government.

The central government was obtaining periodical reports from the Director-General Ports and Shipping Karachi which used to be addressed to the Ministry of Defence (which was the administrative ministry in respect of ports and shipping—both central subjects) and copies endorsed to the Economic Adviser, Deputy Chairman Planning Commission, Secretaries Planning, Industries, Commerce, Agriculture, and the National Assembly (as Chief of the East Pakistan Cell in the Centre), Chief of Naval Staff, and Director General Public Relations, Ministry of Information. Tables I and II have been compiled from these reports. The reporting started from the last week of April and continued throughout May and early June on a daily basis. From the second half of June the daily reports were replaced by weekly reports from which the daily averages have been worked out. No uniform format seems to have been prescribed or followed, which explains the periodical gaps under various heads of activities in the tables. It may be noted that the combined daily average of cargo handled at the two ports in October had almost reached the average of July–December 1970.

Table 1: Chittagong Port Operations

(Figures in brackets are of foodgrain)
(Columns 4-7 in tons)

	Number of Port Employees	Number of Dock Labour	Import	Export	Total cargo handled	Dispatches up-country or for storage elsewhere
29 April	2806	1300	3286	–	3286	2707
Daily average for the month of May	2806	1567	3286	1220	4506	2856
Week ending 25 June	3067	1807	1668 (336)	400	2068	2963
Week ending 8 July	3152	2000	3438 (1666)	1520	4958	3027
Week ending 15 July	3142	2100	3020	1815	4835	3350
Week ending 21 July	3112	2150	1468	1073	2541	N.A.
Week ending 28 July	3140	2156	3083 (750)	1073	4156	2481 (587)
Week ending 5 August	3140	2150	4285 (771)	1612	5897	1821 (294)
Week ending 11 August	3140	2150	3072 (590)	–	3072	–
Week ending 25 August	3145	2160	5025 (2908)	1088	6113	3955 (1079)
Week ending 15 September	3385	2560	7471 (3873)	911	8382	7879 (1390)
Week ending 22 September	3385	2565	3808 (2442)	1372	5180	3967 (1369)
Week ending 13 October	3677	3000	8686 (4447)	1077	9763	7000 (2169)
Week ending 20 October	3690	3000	7628 (4190)	1500	9128	7555 (1985)
Week ending 10 November	3721	3250	6381 (3827)	1127	7508	7183 (752)

Notes:

a) Columns (2)&(3): The pre-disturbance strength of port employees was 5,500 to 6,000 and of dock labour 5,000. Considering that the normal strength included the usual over-staffing and that the cargo offered during the post-25 March period was much less than the normal, the reduced number of staff and labour were considered sufficient. The daily average unloading at Chittagong during 1969–70 was roughly 11,500 tons; the daily average loading of exports was roughly 1,644 tons. It was also claimed that labour productivity during the period increased due to more energetic management. Labour was never regarded as a constraint on Chittagong Port operations.

b) Columns(4)&(7): Foodgrain figures given in brackets were not regularly reported separately. Perhaps the import of foodgrain and dispatches up-country were more than those recorded in the Table and included in the total figures.

c) The grain silos at Chittagong Port were reported to be in operation from the first week of May. The unloading seems to have gained momentum from the third week of August only. In mid-October, foodgrain unloading reached a peak when 1,400-1,700 tons per day were being unloaded in the silos and foodgrain stocks in silos were about 12,000-14,000 tons.

Table 1A: Daily Average Tonnage Cleard by Different Means of Transportation From Chittagong Port Up-Country

(Figures in brackets are of foodgrain)

	RAIL	ROAD	RIVER
Month of May	489	1,139	908
Week ending 25 June	285	1,898	708
Week ending 8 July	707	1,708	612
Week ending 21 July	392	–	–
Week ending 28 July	621 (150)	1,117	683
Week ending 5 August	352 (13)	1,121 (24)	348 (256)
Week ending 25 August	1,036 (660)	2,183 (36)	736 (383)
Week ending 15 September	1,193 (529)	4,055 (37)	2,631 (824)
Week ending 22 September	870 (525)	2,430 (92)	(666)
Week ending 13 October	763 (297)	4,094	2,142 (1,873)
Week ending 20 October	1,104 (79)	4,454	1,997 (1,906)
Week ending 10 November	765 (50)	2,388	876 (676)

Notes:

a) In the earlier part of the period, the breakdown of the cargo cleared by various means of transportation was not indicated in the periodical reports; nor were separate figures for foodgrain always shown.

b) The daily average for the month of May has been worked out on the basis of the breakdown available for nine days only. These dates are 6-9, 11, 14, 16, 20, and 21 May.

c) Rail movement resumed from Chittagong up to Chandpur and Comilla from 4 August. From mid-August there was an increase in rail movement for a month or so before train operation was disrupted again.

Table 1B: Ground Balances of Dry Cargo at Chittagong Port

(Tons)

	Foodgrain	Cement	Fertilizers	Coal	General/Other Cargo	Total
6 May	78,020	12,242	12,625	92,445	99,935	295,267
14 May	74,936	11,973	8,836	92,085	104,244	292,074
21 May	69,824	16,725	8,145	90,720	109,101	294,515
28 May	66,909	19,474	–	89,219	35,427	211,179
4 June	58,442	19,149	3,733	68,184	108,922	258,430
11 June	52,765	17,423	2,539	67,909	119,217	259,853
18 June	85,678	7,981	14,027	101,295	78,765	287,746
25 June	43,759	6,873	57	67,646	116,082	234,417
2 July	42,343	6,873	51	68,234	112,765	230,266
9 July	52,163	3,857	–	67,345	123,961	247,326
16 July	50,274	2,943	–	67,321	123,404	243,942
21 July	56,680	2,624	653	67,595	85,254	212,806
29 July	55,657	N.A.	N.A.	N.A.	202,991	258,648
4 August	58,337	N.A.	N.A.	N.A.	217,879	276,216
11 August	60,372	N.A.	N.A.	N.A.	210,422	270,794
26 August	70,662	N.A.	N.A.	N.A.	216,651	287,313
22 September	75,555	N.A.	N.A.	N.A.	206,564	282,119
13 October	89,348	N.A.	N.A.	N.A.	207,572	296,920
21 October	87,932	N.A.	N.A.	N.A.	221,495	309,427
10 November	112,351	N.A.	N.A.	N.A.	243,203	355,554

Table 2: Chalna Port Operations

(Figures in brackets are of foodgrain)
(Port labour actual numbers. All other figures in tons.)

Daily Average for the	Port Labour	Import from		Export to		Total cargo handled	Dispatches
		Foreign	Karachi	Foreign	Karachi		
Month of June	1,100	945 (669)	–	1,924	132	3,001 (669)	(1,065)
Week ending 9 July	1,100	994 (938)	557 (550)	1,555	1,183	4,289 (1,488)	(2,221)
Week ending 16 July	1,100	1,073 (1,045)	744	1,732	12	3,561 (1,706)	–
Week ending 21 July	1,100	–	508 (571)	1,143	213	1,944 (571)	–
Week ending 30 July	N.A.	1,173 (992)	–	1,704	544	3,421 (992)	(2,125)
Week ending 4 August	1,150	1,000	–	2,957	429	4,336	–
Week ending 11 August	1,500	1,957	706	2,537	788	5,988	–
Week ending 27 August	N.A.	2,555 (1,516)	1,140 (1,090)	1,468	255	5,418 (2,606)	(1,244)
Week ending 17 September	3,000	1,663 (375)	(245)	1,934	17	3,859 (620)	(619)
Week ending 24 September	3,100	(506)	2,195 (1,846)	807	199	3,707 (2,352)	(1,438)
Week ending 14 October	3,000	1,080 (434)	2,907 (1,695)	524	238	4,749 (2,129)	(1,839)
Week ending 21 October	3,000	1,331 (1,171)	1,876 (1,223)	1,423	483	5,113 (2,394)	(1,857)
Week ending 11 November	3,000	2,424 (2,150)	1,067 (382)	1,106	139	4,736 (2,540)	(2,456)

Note: The daily average loading and unloading at Chalna during 1969–70 was roughly 2,740 tons each.

APPENDIX 11

Operation of the Branches of Commercial Banks in East Pakistan As Reported to the Additional Finance Secretary, K. Mahmood (Position as on 7-5-1971)

S. No.	Name of the Bank	Total No. of offices in East Pakistan	No. of offices with whom contacts have been established		No. of offices which could not yet be contacted
			Functioning	Not Functioning	
1.	Eastern Mercantile Bank Limited	98	36	4	58
2.	Eastern Banking Corporation Ltd.	56	33	7	16
3.	Union Bank Ltd.	23	21	–	2
4.	National Bank of Pakistan	263	115	28	120
5.	Habib Bank Ltd.	209	84	17	108
6.	United Bank Ltd.	225	106	58	61
7.	Muslim Commercial Bank Ltd.	87	52	–	35
8.	Standard Bank Ltd.	33	21	1	11
9.	Commerce Bank Ltd.	36	21	4	11
10.	Australasia Bank Ltd.	42	23	4	15
11.	Bank of Bahawalpur Ltd.	2	2	–	–
12.	Premier Bank Ltd.	1	1	–	–
13.	Agricultural Development Bank of Pakistan.	75	20	–	55
	Total	1150	535	123	492

All the Offices of the Exchange Banks in East Pakistan are functioning normally.

APPENDIX 12

List of Chests which have been looted as per verbal information from Martial Law Authority and written information from N.B.P. as given the Additional Finance Secretary, K. Mahmood

Name of Chest		Chest balance	Small Coin Depot Balance	Total	Remarks
1. Bhola	S.T.O.	8,488,000	—	84,88,000	—
2. Pirojpur	S.T.O.	9,211,000	—	92,11,000	Rs. 23,52,50/00 is reported to be recovered.
3. Brahmanbaria	N.B.P.	13,895,000	25,700	1,39,20,700	Actual loss Rs. 2,64,430/00
4. Magura	N.B.P.	25,964,000	32,730	2,59,96,730	—
5. Jhenidah	N.B.P.	22,883,000	38,500	2,29,21,500	Partly looted
6. Satkhira	N.B.P.	20,026,000	91,955	2,10,17,955	—
7. Chaudanga	N.B.P.	15,488,000	—	1,54,88,000	—
8. Meherpur	S.T.O.	82,70,000	—	82,70,000	—
9. Bhairab	N.B.P.	4,35,37,000	17,900	4,35,54,900	Actual loss Rs. 2,27,20,000/00
10. Kishoreganj	N.B.P.	1,88,58,000	2,63,950	1,91,21,950	Actual loss Rs. 1,04,00,000/00
11. Ketrokona	N.B.P.	2,43,18,000	46,350	2,43,64,350	Actual loss Rs. 46,32,755/00
12. Bogra	S.B.P.	8,74,03,261	12,23,956	8,86,27,217	Actual loss about Rs. 7 crores
	TOTAL	29,92,41,261	17,41,041	30,09,82,302	
13. Gopalganj	N.B.P.	2,25,36,000	25,980	2,25,61,980	Not yet confirmed
14. Feni	N.B.P.	3,02,09,000	64,810	3,02,73,810	Not yet confirmed
	TOTAL	5,27,45,000	90,790	5,28,35,790	
GRAND TOTAL		35,19,86,261	18,31,831	35,38,18,092	

STO = Sub Treasury Office at Subdivisional headquarters
NBP = National Bank of Pakistan.
SBP = State Bank of Pakistan.

APPENDIX 13

Statement Showing the Damage to Major Bridges on P.E. Railway as submitted to the Transport Department by the Railway Authorities (Position as on 26–5–1971).

S. No.	Section	Bridge No.	Span	Remarks
1.	Chittagong–Laksam Section.	76 No. 20/1-2	1 x 40'	Both Up and Down Line—40' girders were damaged. These have been replaced.
2.	— do —	81 M. 44/20-45/0 Feni Bridge at Dhoom Ghat.	1 x 150' 7 x 80'	One 150' and 1 x 80' girders have fallen down as pier No. 1 has been blasted. Repair work is in progress.
3.	— do —	Bridge No. 185 (Muhuri Bridge)	7 x 60'	One girder from Chittagong end has been blasted. Repair work is in progress.
4.	— do —	207 M. 65/14-15	6 x 60'	3rd pier has been blasted and 2 girders have fallen down. Repair work is in progress.
5.	— do —	209 M. 68/2-3	2 x 20'	One girder has fallen down. Repair work is in progress.
6.		Between Gunabati–Hasanpur 276 M. 122/6-7	3 X 60' 2 x 40'	No details were available.
7.	Tangi–Bhairab Bazar	Between Gangasagar–Akhaura 45 M. 151/10-11	4 x 40'	The abutment of the *BCI end was damaged. Traffic has been restored by resting the girder on sleeper crib.
8.	— do —	48 M. 154-10/11	1 x 20'	Ballast wall of embankment of Bhairab Bazar end was damaged up to bed block level. Diaphragm of girder was also damaged. Temporary repairs were done and traffic has been restored.
9.	— do —	54 M.146/8-10	1x100', 2x100' 5x60'-0"	The 60' span at Bhairab Bazar end was damaged. The abutment and part of the girder was damaged. The bridge has been temporarily repaired and traffic restored.

S. No.	Section	Bridge No.	Span	Remarks
10.	Bhairab Bazar–Akhaura Section.	1 M. 25/18-25	2x100-4x60' 1x95'-6" 1x67'-6" 1x53'-4"	The Akhaura end of the 60 ft. span was badly damaged affecting the abutment and part of the girder. It has been repaired temporarily and the traffic has been resumed.
11.	Bhairab Bazar Gauripur–Mymensingh Section.	44 M. 185/5-4 (Bridge near Nilganj)	4 x 60'	One 60 ft. girder has been damaged making the girder unserviceable. Work is in progress.
12.	Tangi–Mymensingh Section.	119 M. 2105-16	5x40', 1x60'	Ballast wall on Tangi approach was damaged. Repair work is in progress.
13.	Mymensingh–Jamalpur Section.	230 14223/20-21	3 x 40'	Ballast wall of embankment of Bhairab Bazar end was damaged up to block level. Diaphragm of girder was also damaged. Temporary repairs were done and traffic restored.
14.	Akhaura–Comilla Section.	(Gangasagar) Bridge		One 60 ft. semi through girder damaged badly making the girder completely unserviceable. Both the piers supporting this girder are also partly damaged. Repair work is in progress.
15.	Akhaura–Chhatak	8 M 127/11-12	1 x 40'	Akhaura end of the girder is damaged badly making it unserviceable, and replaced by a new one which was available locally. Abutment is also party damaged and was being repaired. Work was in progress.
16.	— do —	43 M 221/13-14	8 x 40'	One pier has been damaged and consequently 2 adjacent 40 ft. girders are hanging partly submerged under water. Communication in the section had been restored with temporary transshipment of the passengers by country-boat. Repair work was in iprogress.

Notes:

(1) The position of the bridges between Singerbeel station and Shahji Bazar station on the Akhaura–Chhattak Bazar Section could not be ascertained as clearance had not been received by the Army Authorities.

(2) Divisional Superintendent, Paksey and Deputy Chief Engineer (West), who were available in the Secretariat Office at Dacca stated that the extent of damage to bridges on Lalmunirhat and Paksey District was not much. At a few places, the miscreants had removed the timber from bridges and had cut the railway banks on either side of the bridges which damage had already been repaired and the sections declared fit for traffic.

APPENDIX 14

Damage to Major Road Bridges in East Pakistan in May 1971 as Reported by the Additional Chief Engineer to the Transport Department

S. No.	Location	Total length	Length damaged	Description of dmage	Remarks
1.	Suvapur bridge 16th mile from Feni towards Chittagong on Dacca–Chittagong Trunk Road.	1200'-0"	4 spans of 80'=320'-0"	2 R.C. piers failed, 4 spans steel truss on bridge deck failed.	One temporary diversion bridge with Baileys since made.
2.	Bridges on Dhoom–Ramgarh Road. (2 nos.)	80'-0" each	2 bridges of 80'=160'-0"	Complete collapse.	Temporary diversion made
3.	Titas bridge on Brahmanbaria–Companyganj Road.	500'-0"	200'-0"	Pier failed, R.C.C. girders sagged.	Temporary supports given.
4.	Titas bridge on Brahmanbaria–Madhabpur Road	700'-0"	300'-0"	Piers failed, girders collapsed.	Ferry maintained.
5.	Madhupur bridge on 30th mile of Mymensingh–Tangil Road.	100'-0"	100'-0"	Abutment & piers failed. Temporary support given.	Action being taken for construction of temporary bridge.
6.	Eliotganj bridge on Daudkandi–Comilla Road.	120'-0"	120'-0"	Piers blasted, bridge collapsed.	Traffic maintained on, old District Board bridge. Action being taken for construction of temporary bridge.
7.	Katakhali bridge on Rangpur–Bogra Road—40 miles.	500'-0"	200'-0"	Piers failed, girder sagged.	Temporary arrangements being made.
8.	Moosuli bridge on Mymensingh–Kishoreganj Road.	200'-0"	200'-0"	Complete failure	Ferry maintained.
9.	Madhapur bridge on Brahman-baria–Sylhet Road.	230'-0"	230'-0"	"	—
10.	Shaistaganj bridge on Sylhet–Teliapara Road.	320'-0"	320'-0"	"	—

APPENDIX 15

Minute

AJAG

Subject: Minutes of the meeting (Cornelius Committee) held on 26th May, 1971 at 1800 hours at the President's House.

The President was pleased to preside over the meeting.

The following participated:

(a) The PSO.
(b) The Law Adviser.
(c) The Economic Adviser.
(d) Dr. G. W. Choudhury.
(e) Lt. Col. M. A. Hasan.

2. The Law Adviser presented the draft of the Proclamation and that of the Interim Constitution, to the President.

3. The President was pleased to observe that in compliance with the desire of the people of Pakistan, he has now decided to give the country a complete Constitution and not an Interim Constitution. It was appreciated that the political atmosphere now obtaining in the country was conducive to the acceptance of a Constitutional instrument to be given by the President to the Nation. The President directed the Committee to provide for the following in the new draft Constitution:-

(a) The Constitution shall ensure the preservation of the Islamic ideology and shall contain necessary provisions to this effect (the President was pleased to mention that at one time Mr. Mujib had said, "Why call the country, the Islamic Republic of Pakistan" and why should the President of Pakistan be a Muslim).

(b) The political stability and the revival of the economy, which are interlinked, shall be ensured.

(c) The National Assembly shall cease to be the Constituent Assembly as provided for earlier in the L.F.O. When summoned, the National and the Provincial Assemblies shall function as legislative bodies. The Provinces shall be granted maximum autonomy, without prejudicing the integrity and security of Pakistan.

(d) The Centre shall be strong enough to discharge its responsibility unhampered.

(e) Keeping in view the geographical and economic position of the Province of East Pakistan, maximum autonomy shall be granted to that Province but not to the extent to which was acceded to under pressure during the parleys. The wishes of the people of the Provinces of Pakistan shall be reflected in the Constitution, without diluting the provisions too much.

(f) The Provinces other than the Province of East Pakistan, shall have the right to propose amendments in the Constitution on matters of common interests.

(g) Members-elect of the National and the Provincial Assemblies shall hold office for a period of 5 years from the date of commencement of the Constitution, unless dissolved earlier by the President, whereafter fresh elections shall be held on the basis of separate electorate. (Pakistan itself was made on the basis of separate electorate).

(h) The Constitution shall define the minority communities in Pakistan i.e. Schedule Caste, Hindus, Buddhists, Christians, etc.

(i) The Constitution shall reflect the aspirations of the people of Pakistan. It shall be so drafted as to resolve the existing economic, social and other problems of the country. For this purpose, the Committee shall carry out a scientific study of the Constitutions of various countries in the back-ground of the problems of Pakistan. A mention of such study shall be made in the Constitution.

(j) The senior most C-in-C of the Armed Forces, shall be responsible for preserving and defending the Constitution in order to exclude the possibility of its abrogation. However, the provisions to this effect to be incorporated in the Constitution shall not follow the pattern of the Turkish Constitution.

(k) At such time as the President may deem fit the Chief Election Commissioner shall be directed to hold by-elections simultaneously with respect to the vacancies caused in the National and the Provincial Assemblies. The electioneering compaign for these elections shall be in keeping with the 5 fundamental principles, as laid down in Art. 20 of the L.F.O. Such campaigns shall not last for a period exceeding 10 days, whereafter, the by-election shall be held and completed within two to three days.

(l) The President shall appoint Governors, keeping in view the public and the world opinions, who shall hold their offices during the pleasure of the President.

(m) The President, at such time as he deems fit, shall summon the National Assembly and direct the Governors to summon the Provincial Assemblies simultaneously. In deciding the date and time for summoning the National Assembly the President may keep in view the economic, law and order situation obtaining in the country.

(n) After the members of the National Assembly and the Provincial Assemblies have been administered oath, the President or the Governors, as the case may be, shall call upon the leaders of the majority party to form the Cabinet. In order to ascertain whether or not such leaders actually command the majority, necessary steps shall be taken. In case, none of the leaders of the political parties is found to command majority in an Assembly, a coalition Government shall be formed. However, if it appears to the President or a Governor, as the case may be, that a coalition Government cannot prolong, the President may dissolve the Assembly and order for fresh elections.

(o) Soon after the commencement of the Constitution, all Martial Law Administrators, Military Courts etc. shall cease to function. Martial Law, however, shall remain in force in vestigial form It shall be abrogated only when the C.M.L.A. is satisfied that the civil Governments formed under the new Constitution have restored law and order and revived the economy.

(p) The National Assembly might itself request the President and the C.M.L.A. for the continuance of the Martial Law till such time as the CMLA deems fit.

(q) A member of the National or a Provincial Assembly shall be deemed disqualified, for a period of 6 years, from being a member of an assembly if he suffers from any of the disqualifications given in Art. 9(2) of the L.F.O. or the President, after such inquiry as he may deem necessary, declares him to be so disqualified. The decision of the President in this respect shall not be questioned in any court including a High Court and the Supreme Court.

(r) The Constitution shall provide for strict party discipline —
 (i) there shall be not more than three parties in Pakistan;
 (ii) no political party shall be permitted to be sub-divided into groups (like Muslim League). If the majority of the members of a political party disagree with the minority, the majority shall have the right to control that political party and retain its name. The minority shall not be allowed to form a separate group within that party. Such groups shall stand liquidated;
 (iii) if a political party fails to secure minimum (to be specified) number of seats in the National or a Provincial Assembly, it shall stand dissolved;
 (iv) members elect of an Assembly belonging to the outlawed Awami League, and not otherwise disqualified shall be entitled to join any other political party or to form a new political party but once they have done so, they shall stand disqualified, if they withdraw from such a political party. (Political Parties Act, 1962). Same shall apply to the members elected in by-elections.

(s) In order to ensure that the members of the National Assembly belonging to one Province may [not] prejudice the interest of another Province, the following procedure shall be adopted for amending the Constitution:-

 (i) a bill to amend this Constitution shall not be presented to the President for his assent unless—
  (1) it has been passed by the votes of a majority of the members of the National Assembly from each Province and the votes in favour represent not less than 2/3rd of the total number of the members of the National Assembly;

  (2) where the amendment affects only the Province it has also been approved by a resolution passed by a majority of not less than 2/3rd of the total membership of the provincial assembly of that Province;

  (3) where the amendment affects more than one Province, it has also been approved by resolution passed by majority

of not less than 2/3rd of the total membership of the Provincial Assembly of each Province in Pakistan.

(t) The amnesty shall be granted to the people of the Province of East Pakistan in due course of time, but not in the form of general amnesty. The President shall be the final judge to decide as to whom amnesty may or may not be granted.

(3) The Law Adviser explained that it would be expedient to introduce the new Constitution by means of Proclamation from the C.M.L.A. After the members of the National Assembly have taken the oath provided for in the Constitution, the Constitution shall be deemed to have received the assent of the National Assembly.

Lt Col
(M. A. HASAN)
AJAG
4th June, 71

Notes and References

Chapter 1

1. Z. H. Zaidi, ed., *M. A. Jinnah – Ispahani Correspondence 1936-48* (Karachi: Forward Publication Trust, 1976) 8-9. The *Introduction* analyses the politics of Muslim Bengal during the period 1936-46.
2. Ibid., 21-2.
3. Kamruddin Ahmad, *The Social History of East Pakistan* (Dhaka: Mrs Amina Khatun, 1967) 34. It is a personal account of pre-1947 political developments and of the East-West Pakistan relationships from a Bengali nationalist point of view, which greatly influenced Bengali middle-class thinking in the late 1960s.
4. Ibid., 37.
5. Syed Sharifuddin Pirzada, ed., *Foundations of Pakistan* (Karachi: National Publishing House, 1970) vol. II, 261.
6. Ibid., 321.
7. Ibid., Introduction, xxi.
8. Khalid bin Sayeed, *Pakistan: The Formative Phase 1857-1948* (London: Oxford University Press, 1968) 110-12. Sayeed describes the various schemes propounded in the post-Government of India Act of 1935 period, leading up to the passing of the Lahore Resolution in 1940, 106-13. Pirzada in the Introduction to *Foundations,* vol. II, gives a panoramic account of the genesis of the idea of Pakistan.
9. Pirzada, ed., *Foundations,* vol. II, xx–xxi. I have not been able to find the decision to move a resolution for a separate homeland in the minutes of the Working Committee meeting of 4 February, or those of the Council meeting of 25 February 1940 as available in the Archives of the Freedom Movement, Karachi University. Resolution No. 2 of the Council only confirms the dates of the 27th Annual Session of the All-India Muslim League at Lahore on 22-24 March 1940.
10. Kamruddin, *Social History,* 45-6.
11. Pirzada, ed., *Foundations,* vol. II, 340.
12. For text of the Lahore Resolution see ibid., 341.
13. Ibid., 372.
14. Kamruddin, *Social History,* 44-5.
15. Zaidi, ed., *Correspondence,* Appendix III reproduces the letter of resignation dated 8 September 1941 of Fazlul Huq addressed to Liaquat Ali Khan, General Secretary of the All-India Muslim League.
16. Ibid., 63-4.
17. Kamruddin, *Social History,* 68. Also see Ispahani's letter dated 1 October 1945 to Jinnah in Zaidi, ed., *Correspondence* 456–60.

18. *Pirzada*,ed., *Foundations,* vol. II, xxxii. According to Zaidi, ed., *Correspondence,* 72, however, the Muslim League won 'every single seat in the Constituent Assembly and the Bengal Legislative Assembly except one in each of the Assemblies – that of Fazlul Huq.'
19. Zaidi, ed., *Correspondence,* 72.
20. Sayeed, *Formative Phase,* 188-9.
21. Pirzada, ed., *Foundations,* vol. II, xxxiii.
22. Ibid., xxxiii. Also see Kamruddin, *Social History,* 73, and Sayeed, *Formative Phase,* 116.
23. Pirzada, ed., *Foundations,* vol. II, xxxiii.
24. Kamruddin, *Social History,* 74-5.
25. See *Quaid-i-Azam Papers,* (National Archives of Pakistan) F. 568/173-4, Application form for primary membership of city ward no. 1 Bombay, signed by the Quaid-i-Azam on 2 March 1947.
26. Pirzada, *Foundations,* vol. II, 566-8.
27. See Appendix 1.
28. Raghib Ahsan to Jinnah with a copy of the joint memorandum of the Calcutta District Muslim League and Indian National Maritime Union pleading for the inclusion of Calcutta in East Bengal, F.10/24-35, *Quaid-i-Azam Papers,* Also see Hamidul Haq Choudhry's article arguing for the partition of Bengal, F. 722/15-19, ibid.
29. *Pakistan Times,* 29 April 1947.
30. Ibid., 9 May 1947. Casey had predicted that the inclusion of Greater Calcutta in 'Eastern Pakistan' is a complete impossibility . . . Calcutta is more than the capital city of a province . . . it is an All-India city that happens to be in Bengal'. See Appendix 1.
31. *Pakistan Times,* 1 May 1947.
32. *Transfer of Power,* vol X, 448-9.
33. *Civil and Military Gazette,* 24, 25, 27 May 1947. Also see Kamruddin, *Social History,* 87.
34. Suhrawardy to Liaquat Ali Khan dated 21 May 1947, F. 458/74. *Quaid-i-Azam Papers*. See Appendix 2.
35. Suhrawardy to Liaquat Ali Khan, 21 May 1947, F. 458/74-9. Appendix IV.
36. Sardar Shaukat Hayat told me that on 10 June 1947 there was a dinner on the lawn of the Imperial Hotel after the All-India Muslim League Council had approved the 3 June Plan earlier in the day. Suhrawardy approached the Quaid-i-Azam, who was sitting on a sofa, and sought his blessings for United Independent Bengal. The Quaid said 'Go ahead, but the Hindus and Congress will not agree.'

Chapter 2

1. The Government of India Act, 1935; neither the original nor the one adopted as the interim Constitution of Pakistan, mentioned the offices of Prime Minister or Chief Minister. The Official Report of the East Bengal Legislative Assembly Proceedings recorded the designation of the provincial chief executive as Prime Minister until the introduction of the 1956 Constitution which provided

for the office of provincial chief minister. For the provincial chief executive the term 'chief minister' has been used throughout for the sake of uniformity.

2. The Province of East Bengal was redesignated as the Province of East Pakistan according to Article 1 of the Constitution of 1956. For the sake of uniformity the eastern wing has been referred to as East Pakistan throughout, except where the argument requires otherwise.
3. Kamruddin, *Social History*, 83. After the assumption of power by Suhrawardy in Bengal in 1946, the usual tussles between the Provincial League and the Parliamentary Party developed, and the two drifted apart.
4. Kamruddin, *Social History,* 83-4.
5. Ibid., 106-7.
6. M. Rafique Afzal, *Political Parties in Pakistan 1947–1958* (Islamabad: National Institute of Historical and Cultural Research, 1986) vol. I, 98–9.
7. The East Bengal State Acquisition and Tenancy Bill was introduced in the first session of the Provincial Assembly, in April 1948. It involved repeal of 40 Acts and Regulations, going back to the Permanent Settlement Regulation introduced by the East India Company in 1793. A special committee of 45 members of the House examined the Bill in 54 sittings from June 1948 to January 1949. In the Assembly 600 amendments were moved in 34 sittings before the Bill was finally passed into Act on 16 February 1950. See *East Bengal Legislative Assembly Proceedings (EBLAP),* vol IV, No. 6 (February 1950) 135-6. The measure was bitterly opposed at all stages by the Hindu members *en bloc* through filibustering.
8. The East Bengal Transfer of Agricultural Land Act was passed some time after the State Acquisition and Tenancy Act. During this period, Hindu landlords sold their lands at whatever price they could get and transferred capital to India. The Hindu members attributed communal motives to these legislative measures. During the debate on the bill, one Hindu member said 'landholders belong to a particular class of people . . . economic classes are divided community-wise . . . the situation is more accentuated by the fact that the national State of Pakistan is being ruled by an organization which is not national and by a Government in which the representatives of the class of people who own most of the lands are not represented.' *EBLAP,* vol. VI, No. 1 (October 1951) 147.
9. *EBLAP,* vol. IV, No. 1 (November 1949) 63. Remark made during the bitter debate on the State Acquisition and Tenancy Bill.
10. Ramkrishan Mukherjee, 'The Social Background of Bangladesh' in Kathleen Gough and Hari P. Sharma eds., *Imperialism and Revolution in South Asia,* (Lahore: Peoples Publishing House, 1973) 404.
11. Geographically and economically, east and west Bengal were so inextricably linked that Suhrawardy had serious doubts about the permanence of Partition. In his letter to Liaquat Ali Khan, arguing for United Independent Bengal, he said that East Bengal was 'absolutely unprepared to stand on its own legs . . . East Bengal will be an area absolutely deficit in foodgrains, . . . they will have to pass not through one famine but through several famines, and I can quite visualize that within six months of the partition the Muslims of East Bengal will be kneeling before West Bengal or before Group A or before the Congress to be taken into their fold.' Suhrawardy to Liaquat Ali Khan, 21 May 1947, Appendix 3.

12. Mukherjee, 'Social Background', 407.
13. Afzal, *Political Parties,* vol. I, 115.
14. The Calcutta Bengali daily *Swadhinata,* mouthpiece of the Communist Party, published two articles on the background of the language movement in its issues of 10 and 11 March 1952, listing the activities of the Party in East Pakistan during the period 1950–1. The second article concluded with the claim that the Party 'rendered assistance in conducting the language movement towards the right direction; the Communist Party endeavoured to form an All-Party Language Committee and to make the Language Movement an extensive one in every district'. The Chief Minister produced copies of these articles in the East Pakistan Assembly during the debate on the 1952 language riots firing (*EBLAP,* vol. VIII, 11). These activities of the communists used to be well covered by the intelligence reports to which I had access during my service in the government of East Pakistan.
15. Nazimuddin was elected leader of the Parliamentary Party because of the support of Liaquat Ali Khan; he and his group occupied ministerial positions both in the Province and the Centre. When Nazimuddin became Governor-General, the Centre authorized him to nominate his successor and the Parliamentary Party was not given an opportunity to freely elect its leader. Afzal, *Political Parties,* vol. I, 73.
16. *Constituent Assembly (Legislature) of Pakistan Debates (CALD),* vol. I, No. 18 (5 April 1952) 1063-4.
17. Lawrence Ziring, *Pakistan: the Enigma of Political Development,* (Kent, England: Dawson, 1980) 111-17 discusses the inability of the dominant leadership of the Muslim League to appreciate the contradictions resulting from retaining the communal character of the party, equating it with Pakistan, and its failure to transform itself to meet the new challenges.
18. Pirzada, *Foundations,* vol. II, 572.
19. See Appendix 5. Suhrawardy was referring to the visit of the Quaid-i-Azam to Dhaka in the third week of March 1948, immediately after the language riots. There is some substance in Suhrawardy's claim that he could have obtained a majority in the Provincial Assembly; 42 Hindu members would have certainly preferred the secular-minded Suhrawardy and many Muslim members would have perhaps joined him after the language riots.
20. *Constituent Assembly of Pakistan Debates (CAD)* vol. III, No. 2 (18 May 1948) 43. The Constituent Assembly amended its Rules of Procedure whereby a person not resident in Pakistan ceased to be a member of the Assembly. Suhrawardy was hit by this amendment.
21. Afzal, *Political Parties,* vol. I, 91.
22. *Dawn,* 26 January 1951. Statement of some Awami League workers.
23. K. K. Aziz, *Party Politics in Pakistan 1947 –1958* (Islamabad: National Commission on Historical and Cultural Research, 1976) 95–6.
24. Mushtaq Ahmad, *Government and Politics in Pakistan* (Karachi: Space Publishers, 1970) 137–8.
25. *Dawn,* 5,10 July 1953.
26. Ibid., 10 July 1953.
27. *CAD,* vol. II (25 February 1948) 15; motion moved by D. N. Dutta, quoted by Keith Callard, *Pakistan* (Karachi: Oxford University Press, 1958).

28. Kamruddin, *Social History,* 110.
29. *EBLAP,* VII (21 February 1952), 109; statement of the Chief Minister Nurul Amin. Also see *EBLAP,* vol. VIII (25 March 1952) 67–70 for the speech of Shamsuddin Ahmed who referred to it during budget discussions.
30. Keith Callard, *Pakistan,* 182.
31. *Quaid-i-Azam Papers,* Notebook, F. 42.
32. Conversation with M. Azfar, an Indian Civil Service officer who was serving in East Pakistan at the time. He says that the Quaid sought to shore up the Nazimuddin ministry by the offer of jobs to Suhrawardy supporters. According to him, some of the senior civil servants in East Pakistan who had served under Suhrawardy in pre-Independence Bengal were his supporters.
33. Pirzada, *Foundations,* vol. II, 279. Also see Sayeed, *Formative Phase,* 210.
34. *EBLAP,* vol. V, No. 1 (28 February 1951) 461; a Hindu member complained: 'if you refer to the [text] books you will find that the language now introduced is not strictly Bengali . . . It is impossible to understand the language . . . is it treason to read the life of Mahatma Gandhi, is it treason to read the life of Iswar Chandra Vidyasagar, or is it treason to read the life of Raja Mohan Roy?' The Education Minister, replying to the points raised by Hindu members during discussion on the Compulsory Primary Education (Sylhet) Bill, said 'if Muslim boys for centuries could be taught "Jagadishshar" or "Parameswar" [Hindu names of God], I do not think it would be sane to make a complaint about Hindu boys being taught the word Allah . . .' *EBLAP,* vol. VI, No. 2 (10 November 1951) 350.
35. E. H. Slade, *Census of Pakistan, 1951,* Volume 1. Pakistan Report & Tables, (Karachi: Manager Publications, Government of Pakistan) Part I, 70, 76-7; Part II, 8-3.
36. Mukherjee, *'Social Background',* 414.
37. Conversation with M. Azfar.
38. *EBLAP,* vol. VIII (March 1952) 70; speech of Shamsuddin Ahmed during budget discussion.
39. The general view in the East Pakistan administration of the time was that the police firing could have been avoided. The District Magistrate Dhaka, S. M. H. Qureishi, had taken charge only a few days before the incident. The Additional Superintendent police, Masood Mahmud, was not a very stable and tactful officer. He was unpopular among the students because of his intemperate behaviour. He was widely believed to have signalled the police to shoot without obtaining the orders of the magistrate as required under the law. Altaf Gauhar, who was serving in East Pakistan at the time, says that Aziz Ahmed, Chief Secretary, fully supported Masood Mahmud and the police action; the administration had decided to adopt a tought line.
40. *EBLAP,* vol. VII (February 1952) 89–90.
41. Ibid., 90, 108. Nurul Amin derisively alleged that the 'newly elected leader of this party, the name of which I do not know yet, is taking orders from the first day from Mr Data . . .' Although the East Pakistan Awami League had the appellation 'Muslim' until the end of 1953, it has throughout been referred to without it, as in popular parlance.
42. I have seen these reports of Firoz Khan Noon.
43. *CAD,* vol. V, No. 1 (7 March 1949) 1.

44. Ibid., vol. V, No. 5 (12 March 1949) 89-90. Speech by Sris Chandra Chattopadhyaya.
45. Ibid., 91.
46. Ibid., 95.
47. Ibid., vol. V, No. 3 (9 March 1949) 45.
48. Report of the Court of Inquiry Constituted Under Punjab Act II of 1954 to Enquire into the Punjab Disturbances of 1953 (Lahore: 1954) 286. The Report is commonly known as the Munir report.
49. *CAD,* vol. V, No. 5 (12 March 1949) 101.
50. Ibid., vol. VIII, No. 1 (28 September 1950) 2. Annexure I contains the full Report.
51. Ibid., vol. VIII, No. 6 (21 November 1950) 183, speech by Nur Ahmed.
52. Kamruddin, *Social History,* 114. Appendix C reproduces the outline Constitution proposed by the convention. Also see G. W. Choudhury, *Constitutional Development in Pakistan* (London: Longman, n.d.) 72. Choudhury gives a somewhat different version of the convention's proposals; according to him, the alternative Constitution provided for a central parliament on population basis with powers to deal with defence, foreign affairs, as well as currency.
53. Choudhury, *Constitutional Development,* 72–3.
54. *CAD,* vol. VIII, No. 6 (21 November 1950) 181.
55. *Dawn,* 4 December 1953. Statement made by Nazimuddin during cross-examination before the Court of Inquiry into the Punjabi disturbances of 1953.
56. Keith Callard, *Pakistan,* 98.
57. *CAD,* vol. XII, No. 2 (22 December 1952) 57-63.
58. *Dawn,* 11 January 1953.
59. Ibid., 22 January 1953.
60. *Index* to the *Constituent Assembly of Pakistan Debates,* vol. XV, (1953) (22 September 1953 to 14 November 1953) 792, 874.
61. *CAD,* vol. XII, No. 3 (1 January 1953) 169.
62. Ibid., 172. The Report of the Basic Principles Committee is given as Appendix I of Vol. XII, No. 2. Its covering note, according to the Report, has purportedly been signed by the three Punjabi members.
63. Afzal, *Political Parties* , vol. I, 116.
64. Twenty-one Point Programme of the United Front is given in Ibid., Appendix I
65. *Dawn,* 29 June 1954. Speech of Prime Minister Muhammad Ali in Parliament.
66. Ibid., 31 May 1954.
67. *Index* to the Constituent Assembly of Pakistan Debates, vol. XVI, 1954 (14 March 1954 to 21 September 1954).
68. *CAD,* vol. XVI, No. 27 (15 September 1954) 375. Speech of Dhirendra Nath Datta, moving amendment to Schedule I of the Report.
69. Ibid., 364. Speech of Syed Shamsur Rahman.
70. *CAD,* vol. XVI, No. 30. (20 September 1954); *CAD,* vol. XVI, No. 31 (21 September 1954).
71. *Basic Constitutional Documents* (Islamabad: National Assembly Secretariat) vol. I, 279.

72. *All Pakistan Legal Decisions (PLD)* 1955, vol. VII, Opinion of the Chief Justice of Federal Court on the Reference by H.E. the Governor-General, 447–8.
73. Afzal, *Political Parties,* vol. I, 147.
74. The Speaker of the dismissed Assembly had gone in a writ petition to the Sindh Chief Court which issued a writ against the Governor-General. In appeal, the Federal Court did not go into the merits of the Governor-General's action of dismissing the Assembly. It took recourse to the technical argument that amendment in the Government of India Act 1935 (which was the interim Constitution of the country), conferring jurisdiction on the courts to issue writs, was not valid as it had not received the assent of the Governor-General. *PLD,* 241. Subsequent on the reference by the Governor-General, the court in its judgment on 10 May 1955 held the Governor-General competent to dissolve the Assembly.
75. Afzal, *Political Parties,* vol. I, 150.
76. Ibid., 165. Also see Kamruddin, *Social History,* 133–5.
77. *Dawn,* 25 April 1955. Resolution of the United Front Parliamentary Party.
78. Mohammad Ayub Khan, *Friends Not Masters* (Karachi: Oxford University Press, 1967) 192.
79. Sir Archibald Rowlands' report on the economic prospects of Pakistan. See Rowlands to Quaid-i-Azam, No. 229/AGG, 4 December 1947, *Rizwan Colletion* (Hamdard Library, Karachi).
80. Choudhury, *Constitutional Development,* 93.
81. *Dawn,* 23 February 1955.
82. I have a copy of record proceedings of the subcommittee. The main discussion was on the list of central and provincial subjects.
83. Choudhury, *Constitutional Developments,* 98–9.
84. Afzal, *Political Parties,* vol. I, 174.
85. *National Assembly of Pakistan Debates* (new designation of the Constituent Assembly under the 1956 Constitution; hereafter referred to as *NAD)* vol. II, No. 3 (10 October 1956) 163.
86. I was posted to a remote subdivision soon after the Awami League had taken power in East Pakistan. It was a reasonably effective government and enjoyed the support of the people. The ministers were considerably mellowed by the heavy responsibilities placed on them. But the government was faced with serious food shortages and very soon there were rumours of corruption, particularly about Mujibur Rahman, who was Minister of Commerce and Industries.
87. *East Pakistan Assembly Proceedings* (new designation of the Provincial Assembly under the 1956 Constitution, hereafter referred to as *EPAP*) vol. XV, No. 3 (Third Session 1956).
88. *NAD,* vol. II, No. 4 (11 October 1956) 346–7.
89. *Dawn,* 9 February 1957.
90. *Dawn,* 8 February 1957.
91. *EPAP,* vol. XVI, No. 6 (3 April 1957). 144 Quotation from the speech of Syed Quamarul Ahsan on the resolution.
92. *Dawn,* 5 April 1957.
93. *Dawn,* 14 June 1957.
94. *NAD,* vol. I, No. 14 (22, 23, 25 February 1957).

95. Aziz, *Party Politics,* 113–4.
96. *Jang,* 18 September 1957.
97. See *Memoirs of Huseyn Shaheed Suhrawardy,* Mohammad H.R. Talukdar, ed. (Dhaka: University Press Limited, 1987) 53–4 for economic policies of the Suhrawardy Government.
98. In 1963, the Nawab of Kalabagh, Governor West Pakistan, during a meeting with me as Deputy Commissioner Faisalabad, severely criticized Iskandar Mirza for allowing Suhrawardy to become Prime Minister in spite of 'their' [perhaps the Punjabi landlord class] strong opposition. The civil service generally respected Suhrawardy for his competence and dynamism but the various power centres distrusted the party he represented because of its leaders' extremist utterances.
99. Ayub Khan, *Friends,* 37.
100. See Khalid bin Sayeed, *The Political System of Pakistan* (Boston: Houghton Mifflin, 1967) 86-92 for an account of political fragmentation during this period.
101. Aziz, *Party Politics,* Appendices II, VII, and VIII.
102. Rowlands, Report.
103. *CALD,* vol. I, No. 2 (21 March 1951) 53.
104. Ibid., vol. I, No. 4 (24 March 1951) 271–2.
105. Ibid., 275.
106. Ibid., 278.
107. Ibid., 279.
108. *EBLAP,* vol. V, No. 1 (26 February 1951), 382.
109. *CALD,* vol. I, No. 5 (25 March 1951), 311-12. Speech by Nurul Hossain Khan.
110. Ibid., vol. I, No. 4 (24 March 1951) 272. Ghulam Muhammad wanted the question of allocation of revenues between the Centre and provinces to be resolved in the new Constitution.
111. *EBLAP,* vol. VII, (20 February 1952),16.
112. Ibid., 16-17. For recommendations of Raisman Award also see Budget Speech of the Finance Minister in *CALD,* vol. I, No 2 (15 March 1952) 8,9.
113. Ibid., 44.
114. Rowlands, Report.
115. *Report of the Economic Appraisal Committee,* Ministry of Economic Affairs (Karachi: Government of Pakistan, 1953) 8.
116. *Pakistan Jute Survey 1949-50* quoted in the debate on Jute Policy, *CALD,* vol. II, No. 9 (6 October 1953) 1040.
117. *CALD,* vol. I, No. 1 (13 March 1950) 4. Budget Speech.
118. Ibid., 4.
119. Ibid., vol. I, No. 3 (16 March 1950) 52. Information given in reply to a question.
120. *Economic Development in East Pakistan* (Karachi: Government of Pakistan, 1971) 50.
121. *CALD,* vol. I, No. 4 (19 March 1956) 237–8.
122. Ibid., 237.
123. Ibid.
124. Albert Waterston, *Planning Pakistan* (Baltimore: The Johns Hopkins Press, 1963) 13.
125. *Six Year Development Programme of Pakistan July 1951 to June 1957* (Karachi: Ministry of Economic Affairs, n.d.) 3.

126. *Appraisal Report,* 135, 138.
127. Ibid., 139.
128. *The First Five Year Plan 1955-60* (Karachi Government of Pakistan, 1957) 13.
129. *The Economists' Report on the First Five Year Plan 1955-60 (Draft)* (Karachi: Planning Board, 1956) 22–4.
130. 'National Economic Council Statement on the Five Year Plan 1955-60.' *Report to the National Economic Council for the Year 1957-58,* 25.
131. *The First Five Year Plan,* 26.
132. 'National Economic Council Statement.'
133. *EBLAP,* vol. IV, No. 7 (1 March 1950) 131. Speech by Shamsuddin Ahmad.
134. Ibid., vol. V, No. 1 (21 February 1951) 197.
135. Ibid., 354. Speech by Gobindalal Banerjee.
136. *CALD,* vol. I, No. 4 (24 March 1951) 275.
137. *Basic Constitutional Documents,* vol. I, 401. Second Schedule of the 1956 Constitution prescribed the oath of the President.
138. Ibid., 420–2.
139. Based on documents and conversations with persons involved in the prosecution and defence of the accused before the Special Tribunal set up to try the case. The conspiracy was corroborated in details by oral and documentary evidence. It was not a 'put-up show' as alleged by some writers.
140. Afzal, *Political Parties* , vol. I, 115.
141. *CALD,* vol. I, No. 2 (21 March 1951) 34.
142. Ayub, *Friends,* 35.
143. Francis Ingall, *The Last of the Bengal Lancers* (London: Leo Cooper, 1988) 142–3.
144. Ayub, *Friends,* 38.
145. Ibid., 39.
146. Based on documents and conversations, long after the event, with senior officers who dealt with the situation.
147. See Ayub, *Friends,* 30. He chided Tamizuddin Khan, Speaker of the National Assembly, for changing the Constitution through 'subterfuge', and 'destroying the focal point of authority'.
148. Ayub, *Friends,* 186–91.
149. Ibid., 72.
150. I was in charge of a border subdivision in East Pakistan at that time and experienced the tensions created by the overlapping jurisdictions between the civil and military officers who reported to the provincial government and the General Officer Commanding respectively at Dhaka.
151. *Fiscal Policy in Pakistan* (Government of Pakistan, Ministry of Finance) vol. I, 24.
152. *Pakistan Economic Survey* 1970–71 (Ministry of Finance) Table 44 of the Statistical Section, 97.
153. Brief of the Ministry of Defence for the reply to the statement made by an Awami League member in the National Assembly.
154. *Foreign Relations of the United States, 1955-1957,* vol. VIII, South Asia (Washington: United States Government Printing Office, 1987) Meeting of the National Security Council, 3 January 1957, 25–6.

155. Ibid., Langley to the Assistant Secretary of State for Near Eastern, South Asian, and African Affairs, 488–9.
156. When President Iskandar Mirza appointed Suhrawardy Prime Minister, he arranged for him to meet Ayub Khan; the latter bluntly told the Prime Minister who held the defence portfolio also, in the presence of Iskandar Mirza, 'I would expect that there would be no interference in the internal affairs of the army.' Ayub, *Friends,* 37.
157. *Jang,* 21 July 1958. The preparations were complete for polling in November 1958 when in late 1957 the central government asked the views of the district officers whether November would be a suitable month for elections. I was serving in East Pakistan at that time and as subdivisional officer was in charge of election arrangements within my jurisdiction. Doubts arose at the time about the prospects of elections. In February 1958, F. M. Khan, the Chief Election Commissioner, a friend of Mirza, during a conversation at a private function denigrated the elections as 'this farce of counting sheep and goats'. The remark was reported by the Intelligence Bureau but such was the helplessness of the Prime Minister that, instead of taking action he requested the President to find out from Khan whether the statement attributed to him was true.
158. Afzal, *Political Parties,* vol. I, 218.
159. Herbert Feldman, *Revolution in Pakistan* (London: Oxford University Press, 1967) 29.
160. Officers who had served in Kalat told me that the Ruler's followers openly claimed that the Khan's policies had the blessings of Iskandar Mirza. These rumours were mentioned in the reports to the Government as well. Also see Ayub Khan, *Friends,* 57.
161. *CALD,* vol. I, No. 3 (18 March 1956) 117–18. Speech by Mosleim Ali Molla.
162. Ibid., 120. Speech by Farid Ahmed, Nizam-i-Islam Party.
163. Ibid., No. 4 (19 March 1956) 214-15, 218-19. Speech by Ataur Rahman, Awami Leaguer.
164. Ibid., No. 5 (20 March 1956) 273-4. Speech by Zahiruddin, Awami Leaguer.
165. Ibid., No. 6 (21 March 1956) 310-13. Speech by Mujibur Rahman, Awami Leaguer.
166. Ibid., 307. Speech by Zahiruddin, Awami Leaguer.
167. Hildreth to Department of State (12 August 1955), *Foreign Relations,* 434.
168. Memorandum on the Substance of Discussion at a Department of State–Joint Chiefs of Staff Meeting on 14 January 1955, ibid., 412.
169. National Intelligence Estimate on Probable Developments in Pakistan, 15 March 1955, ibid., 423.
170. Hildreth to Department of State, 30 June 1955, ibid., 432.
171. Hildreth to Department of State, 12 August 1955, ibid., 434–5.
172. Hildreth to Department of State, 24 September 1956, ibid., 470-1.
173. National Intelligence Estimates, 13 November 1956, ibid., 473.
174. Gardiner to Department of State, 9 May 1957, ibid., 479-80. One can assume that at this stage, planning for the *coup d' état* was underway. The usual instrument of US policy in such matters was the Central Intelligence Agency (CIA) and not the formal diplomatic channels. Given the deep US involvement in Pakistan affairs, evident from the published records quoted here, it can be

assumed that Mirza's abrogation of the Constitution was in the knowledge of, and with the blessings of the CIA and the US government.

175. Ayub's Broadcast Statement, 8 October 1958.
176. M. Azfar told me about this meeting and Mirza's plans. He said it was related to him by the Raja Sahib of Mahmudabad who was a friend of Mirza.
177. Afzal, *Political Parties,* vol. II, 14-16.
178. Feldman, *Revolution,* 81.
179. Afzal, *Political Parties,* vol. II, Appendix I.
180. Ibid., 14.
181. Ayub, *Friends,* 210.
182. *Basic Constitutional Documents,* vol. II, 7. The Presidential (Election and Constitution) Order, 1960.
183. Feldman, *Revolution,* 108–9.
184. *Report of the Constitution Commission* (Pakistan, 1961) 1, hereafter referred to as *Report.*
185. *Jang,* 18, 21 December 1959.
186. Quotations in the para are from the *Report,* 2-3.
187. *Report,* 2.
188. According to the 1961 Census, in East Pakistan the proportion of the age group of 20 years and above was 54 per cent, and in West Pakistan 51 per cent; *20 Years of Pakistan in Statistics 1947–1967* (Central Statistical Office, Government of Pakistan) 22.
189. *Report,* 40.
190. Ibid., 19.
191. Ibid., 86.
192. Ibid., 37.
193. Ayub, *Friends,* 213.
194. Muhammad Ibrahim remained away from Rawalpindi and there were rumours in those days that he was under house arrest in Dhaka.
195. Ayub, *Friend,* 225.
196. See Talukdar, *Memoirs,* 167, for the reasons for the arrest; the famous letter of Suhrawardy to Ayub has been reproduced in it as Appendix I.
197. Feldman, *Revolution,* 161.
198. *Dawn,* 30 June, 15 July 1962.
199. The nine Bengali leaders representing mainstream politics were: (i) Nurul Amin, Muslim League (ii) Abul Hossain Sarkar, KSP (iii) Hamidul Huq Choudhury, KSP (iv) Syed Azizul Haq, KSP (v) S. M. Solaiman, KSP (vi) Ataur Rahman, Awami League (vii) Mujibur Rahman, Awami League (viii) Pir Mohsenuddin, Nizam-i-Islam Party (ix) Mahmud Ali, National Awami Party; Talukdar, *Memoirs,* 176–7.
200. Talukdar, *Memoirs,* 69–70.
201. Ibid., 211. Afzal in *Political Parties,* vol. II, 40, mentions Suhrawardy as one of those who applied for pardon.
202. *Dawn,* 10 May 1963.
203. I served in various capacities in the Government of West Pakistan during the governorship of Nawab of Kalabagh and have personal knowledge of his feudal style of administration.

204. See Talukdar, *Memoirs,* for Suhrawardy's arguments against the formation of the National Democratic Party, 208–9.
205. Ibid., 207.
206. *Dawn,* 28 January 1964.
207. Ibid., 6 June 1964.
208. Afzal, *Political Parties,* vol. II, 110.
209. Based on personal experience as district officer in two districts of the Punjab during the period. Ayub Khan paid more attention to the views of the district officers than to the local leaders of his party who took good care to stay on the right side of Kalabagh.
210. Full text of the manifesto of the COP is given in Appendix III in Afzal, *Political Parties,* vol. II.
211. Miss Fatima Jinnah came to Lahore on her election campaign in the last week of December 1964. Her procession from the airport, passing in front of the Governor House, was reported to be the longest in the living memory of Lahore. Kalabagh was worried that Ayub Khan, who happened to be staying there that day, might hear the opposition slogans. To Kalabagh this would have meant losing face with the President. The district administration came up with the neat solution of advancing the time of the function which Ayub was to attend at the University Campus. I was told that, later in the day, when Ayub asked the size of the procession, one of the ministers promptly came forward with a figure of a few thousand people only.
212. Ayub, *Friends,* Appendix VII.
213. 'The nation had given a clear and final verdict on the Constitution.' Ibid., 240.
214. I have copies of this evaluation and the minutes of the meeting.
215. In West Pakistan, Kalabagh ensured that the ruling party candidates not liked by him and nominated by the central leadership were not elected.
216. *Report of the Panel of Economists on the Second Five Year Plan (1960–65),* 14. It was submitted to the Planning Commission in August 1959. Hereafter referred to as *Second Plan Panel.*
217. Mahbubul Haq, *The Strategy of Economic Planning* (Oxford University Press, 1963) 92–4.
218. *Economic Relations Between East and West Pakistan* (Ministry of Finance, 1961) 57. [Hereafter referred to as *Economic Relations.*]
219. *Report of the Finance Commission* (Ministry of Finance, 1962) 66. Hereafter referred to as *Finance Commission,* 1962.
220. Haq, *Strategy,* 100.
221. *Economic Relations,* 50.
222. Haq, *Strategy,* 102.
223. *Economic Relations,* 44.
224. Ibid., Annexure 2.
225. Ibid., Annexure 3.
226. Haq, who was member/secretary of the Panel, subsequently rejected this West Pakistani position in *Strategy.* Anisur Rahman, a noted Bengali economist, wondered whether the services claimed by West Pakistan were not 'disservices' in 'East and West Pakistan: A Problem in the Political Economy of Planning', mimeo (The Center for International Affairs, Harvard University, n.d.) The contents show that it was written round about 1965.

227. *Second Plan Panel,* 16.
228. Ibid., 16, 19.
229. *The Economists' Report on the First Five Year Plan,* 24.
230. *The Second Five Year Plan (1960-65),* (Planning Commission June 1960) 397-8.
231. There is no indication in the Report of its author, or the authority under which it was undertaken. V. A. Jaffery, who was serving in the Ministry of Finance in the early 1960s, told me that after an acrimonious discussion in the Cabinet on the East-West economic imbalance, Ayub directed a study of the subject and that he was entrusted with it. It was for official use only.
232. *Finance Commission,* 1962, 38.
233. Ibid. The Chairman's Report and the West Pakistan Report agreed on all matters relating to East-West relations. The regional polarization was as follows:
(1) Chairman's Report signed by (i) H. A. Majid, Secretary, Ministry of Finance (Economic Affairs Division), Chairman of the Commission (Punjabi), ICS officer of 1931; (ii) Zahiruddin Ahmed, Joint Secretary, Ministry of Finance (Punjabi); (iii) S. A. Meenai, Economic Adviser, State Bank of Pakistan (Mohajir).
(2) West Pakistan Report signed by (i) M. M. Ahmed, Additional Chief Secretary, Government of West Pakistan (Punjabi), ICS officer of 1938; (ii) A.G.N. Kazi, Finance Secretary, Government of West Pakistan (Sindhi), ICS officer of 1944.
(3) Bengali Report signed by (i) D. K. Power, Additional Chief Secretary, Government of East Pakistan (British married to a Bengali), ICS officer of 1941; (ii) S. A. F. M. A. Sobhan, Joint Secretary, Ministry of Industries, Government of Pakistan (Bengali); (iii) M. Raschid, Managing Director, Industrial Development Bank (Bengali); (iv) Abdul Khair, Finance Secretary, Government of East Pakistan (Bengali), CSP officer of 1950; (v) Dr Nurul Islam, Professor of Economics, Dhaka University (Bengali).
The years noted against the ICS/CSP officers are of entry into the service and denote seniority as given in the Gradation List of the Civil Service of Pakistan of 1957, issued by the Establishment Division of the Government of Pakistan.
234. One of the Bengali CSP officers was in serious trouble in the early 1960s for arguing two economies in the context of East-West Pakistan relations in an internal working paper. The displeasure of the government was conveyed to him for such subversive ideas.
235. *Budget Speeches,* Finance Division, vol. II, 56. Finance Minister's speech on the Budget of 1962–3.
236. *The Third Five Year Plan (1965-70)* (Planning Commission, 1965) 13. Hereafter referred to as *Third Plan.*
237. *Budget Speeches,* vol. II, 101. Finance Minister's speech on the Budget of 1965–6.
238. *Third Plan,* 142–3.
239. Ibid., 12.
240. Report on Inter-Regional and Intra-Regional Disparities (Planning Division, May 1966). Similar Reports were produced by the Cabinet Division in December 1967 and December 1968. These Reports were required to be submitted to the National Assembly under Article 145(8) of the Constitution of 1962.
241. Anisur Rahman, *East and West.*

242. *Third Plan,* 143–4.
243. The quotations and statistics in this para are from *Preliminary Evalution of The Third Five Year Plan (1965—70)* (Planning Commission, August 1970) chapters 1–6.
244. *CALD,* vol. I, No. 5 (20 March 1956) 271–84.
245. Appendix 8.
246. *Pakistan Chronology 1966* (Ministry of Information and Broadcasting, Government of Pakistan) 10.
247. Afzal, *Political Parties,* vol. II, 113–4.
248. *Pakistan Chronology 1966,* 20.
249. Afzal, *Political Parties,* vol. II, 171.
250. Ibid.
251. *Pakistan Chronology 1969,* 3.
252. Afzal, *Political Parties,* vol. II, 172; *Pakistan Chronology 1969,* 4.
253. Tariq Ali, *Can Pakistan Survive?* (Penguin Books, 1983) 81.
254. *Pakistan Chronology 1969,* 24.
255. Ibid., 29.
256. Afzal, *Political Parties,* vol. II, 179-80. Also see Mujib's address to the Round Table Conference in *Bangladesh Documents* (Ministry of External Affairs, New Delhi) 33-8.
257. Bengali civil servants in Islamabad generally held this view in those days.
258. Conversation with Altaf Gauhar, Secretary Information at the time, and a close adviser of Ayub.
259. Interview with General M.I. Karim. Statements attributed to him are throughout from it.
260. Herbert Feldman, *The End and the Beginning, Pakistan 1969–1971* (Karachi: Oxford University Press, 1975) 16–22.

Chapter 3

1. *Pakistan Chronology 1969,* 35
2. The Provisional Constitution Order is included in the *Basic Constitutional Documents,* vol.II (Islamabad: National Assembly Secretariat) 315–16.
3. See Feldman, *End and Beginning,* Chapter II for an analysis of some of the more draconian Martial Law Regulations.
4. Interviews with Karim and M. Qayyum, Secretary to the President.
5. Conversation with M. M. Ahmed. Statements attributed to him are throughout from it.
6. Interview with Lieutenant-General Peerzada. Statements attributed to him are throughout from the interview.
7. Interview with Colonel M. A. Hasan, who was the legal expert of the CMLA Secretariat and remained associated with all the constitutional affairs and negotiations of the regime with politicians. Statements attributed to him are throughout from the interview.
8. Interview with M. Qayyum.
9. Interview with Major-General Ghulam Umer. Statements attributed to him are throughout from it.

10. Major-General Fazal Muqeem Khan, *Pakistan's Crisis in Leadership* (Islamabad: National Book Foundation, 1973) 40.
11. Yahya's press conference, 10 April 1969; *Pakistan Chronology 1969,* 41.
12. I remember seeing a note from the CMLA Secretariat setting up a committee on prices, and directing it not to confuse its recommendations by the usual analysis of supply and demand. Curiously, Hamza Alvi, the noted leftist academic was also working as an expert in the CMLA HQ. Karim says he tried to get some Bengali economists to work in the central government but failed to get anyone on a regular basis. The labours of these expert groups remained unknown and unrecognized in the ministries.
13. This working of the Yahya regime is based on personal experience. Fazal Muqeem in Chap II of *Leadership* has also given a similar description.
14. *Pakistan Chronology* 1969, 59, 60, 63
15. Ibid., 80,82.
16. Ibid., 60,63,79–80.
17. *White Paper on The Crisis of East Pakistan,* (Government of Pakistan, August 1971) 28 November broadcast of Yahya, given in Appendix A.
18. Ibid., Appendix B, Legal Framework Order.
19. G. W. Choudhry, *Last Days of United Pakistan* (Bloomington: Indiana University Press, 1974) 81.
20. Ibid., 86–87
21. Ibid., 87
22. Ibid., 98
23. Ibid., 93
24. Feldman, *End and Beginning,* 80–1.
25. Case FIR (First Information Report) No.97 dated 18 April 1972 under Section 419/420/409/467 Pakistan Panel Code and 5 (II) 1947 Prevention of Corruption Act registered at Police Station New Town, District Rawalpindi against N. A. Rizvi, ex-Director Intelligence Bureau, and the Assistant Director Intelligence Bureau. Apparently there was sufficient documentary evidence, but the prosecution was not followed up and brought before the court.
26. Lawrence Lifschultz, *Bangladesh: The Unfinished Revolution* (London: Zed Press, 1979) 27–9.
27. *Bangladesh Documents* (New Delhi: Ministry of External Affairs, n.d.) 99-100.
28. Ibid., 101.
29. Choudhry, *Last Days,* 119–20
30. S. M. Ali, 'Children of Storm', *Far Eastern Economic Review,* 16 January 1971.
31. Kathleen Gough, 'Imperialism and Revolutionary Potential' in KathleenGough and Hari P. Sharma, eds., *Imperialism and Revolution in South Asia* (Lahore: People's Publishing House, 1975) 18.
32. Lifschultz, U*nfinished Revolution,* 21.
33. Ali, *'Storm'.*
34. *Report of the Panel of Economists on the Fourth Five Year Plan (1970–75)* (Planning Commission, 1970) 94.
35. Ibid., p. iii-v.
36. *Bangladesh Documents,* 137–8. The text of the oath is given in A. H. Kardar, *Pakistan's Soldiers of Fortune* (Lahore: Ferozsons, 1988) 65. It did not mention the six points, but only allegiance to the 'principles, ideology, objectives and

programme of Awami League.' In 1988, Kamal Hossain told me that the public oath was taken to prevent any defection of the Awami League Assembly members to the West Pakistani side, as had been happening in the past.

37. *Bangladesh Documents,* 140.
38. T. J. S. George, 'Jai Banglar, Jai', *Far Eastern Economic Review,* 16 January 1971.
39. Ali, 'Storm', *Far Eastern Economic Review,* 16 January 1971.
40. Ibid.
41. Ibid.
42. *Pakistan Times,* 22 December 1970.
43. *Dawn,* 12 January 1971.
44. Choudhury, *Last Days,* 141–3, says that as directed by Yahya, in early December, he had drafted proposals on centre–provinces relations in anticipation of controversies after the elections. If so, Yahya did not put forward these proposals to counter the six points in the January meeting with Mujib.
45. *Dawn,* 17 December 1972.
46. *Bangladesh Documents,* 144–5.
47. Choudhury, *Last Days,* 128–9.
48. Z.A. Bhutto, *The Great Tragedy* (Pakistan People's Party Publication, 1971) 24–5.
49. Ibid., 22, 24.
50. *Dawn,* 16 February 1971.
51. Statement of Mufti Mahmud of Jamiat-i-Ulema-i-Islam (JUI); *Jang,* 26 February 1971.
52. Ibid., 20 February 1971.
53. Conversation with Sahibzada Yakub Khan, who showed me his letter of resignation and the messages exchanged with the CMLA Secretariat from 22 February to 1 March. Ahsan later said, 'Throughout the meeting the President never once looked into my eyes. I could no longer consider his intentions devoid of guile or devoid of guilt.'
54. Rashid Amjad, 'Industrial Concentration and Economic Power' in Hasan Gardezi and Jamil Rashid, eds., *Pakistan: The Unstable State* (Lahore: Vanguard Books Ltd., 1983) 178–9.
55. The six-point formulation had undergone some semantic changes since first presented in 1966. This discussion is based on the Awami League manifesto version given in Appendix C of the *White Paper,* op.cit.
56. See, for example, the lengthy statement 'Six Point Formula—Our Right to Live', issued by Mujib on 23 March 1966; *Bangladesh Documents,* 23–33.
57. Bhutto threatened the West Pakistani members in general of dire consequences if they attended the Assembly session; the recalcitrant People's Party members were threatened with broken legs which may have been a figure of speech, and not necessarily intended to inflict physical violence.
58. Yahya met Bhutto at Karachi before announcing the all-party conference; *Jang* 3 March. Yahya invited Bhutto to Rawalpindi and had a five and a half hour meeting before his broadcast fixing 25 March as the next date of Assembly session; *Jang,* 6 March. On 14 March on his way to Dhaka, Yahya again met Bhutto at Karachi; Bhutto agreed with the four demands of Mujib, but insisted that the settlement should only be with the consent of the People's Party. On

the night of 16 March after meetings with Mujib, Yahya sent a message to Bhutto to reach Dhaka on 19 March.

59. See *Bangladesh Documents,* 216–18 for the 7 March public meeting of Mujib. I was told in Dhaka in 1971 that on the night of 6-7 March at about 2.30 a.m., two close associates of Mujib came to Major-General Khadim Hussain Raja, GOC Dhaka and DMLA Zone B, with a message from Mujib that he was under great pressure from the extremist elements to declare independence at the public meeting. Mujib did not want to do that and wanted the army to arrest him. The General's appreciation was that the message was intended to gauge his reactions, in case such a declaration was made. He told the emissaries that he did not believe that Mujib was helpless and if he declared independence or something of that nature, he would 'come out with guns blazing and tanks rumbling' against him, and would ensure that Mujib and his associates were no longer there to rule East Pakistan in that event.
60. *Jang,* 15,16 March 1971.
61. This account of the dialogue with the Awami League from 15 March to 24 March has been reconstructed from interviews and conversations, over a long period extending from April 1971 onwards, with the participants and others who, in their official capacity, observed the events in the President House, and on published and unpublished material.
62. According to Hasan and Peerzada, the first Yahya-Mujib meeting took place on 15 March. According to the White Paper and an unsigned paper recapitulating the events of the period given to me by Karim, the first meeting was held on 16 March.
63. Bhutto, *Tragedy,* 41-6, for Bhutto's version of his meetings.
64. *White Paper,* op.cit., 21–2.
65. See ibid., 19–20, for the main features of the draft Proclamation of the President's Team and its Appendix E for the Awami League's draft.
66. *Bangladesh Documents,* 291-8. Tajuddin's statement of 17 April 1971.
67. Conversation with Kamal Hossain in 1988.
68. Bhutto, *Tragedy,* 49.
69. Siddiq Salik, *Witness to Surrender* (Karachi: Oxford University Press, 1977). The text of the plan 'Operation Searchlight' is given in Appendix III and the process of its formulation in supersession of 'Operation Blitz' on 63.
70. Interview with Major-General Rao Farman Ali. All statements attributed to him are throughout from this interview.

Chapter 4

1. Yahya Khan's broadcast of 26 March 1971.
2. Statement of Tajuddin Ahmed, 17 April. *Bangladesh Documents,* 291-8.
3. Based on interviews, conversations, and documents.
4. See Dr Safdar Mahmood, *The Deliberate Debacle* (Lahore: Sh. Muhammad Ashraf, 1976) 128–9.
5. *The Events in East Pakistan, 1971,* A Legal Study by the Secretariat of the International Commission of Jurists (Geneva, 1972) 23.
6. In May, my Bengali driver took me to see one of the hostels attacked by the

army, Jaganath Hall, and pointed out the mass grave of the students, in a corner of the lawn, killed during the action. The interior, although whitewashed, looked grisly.

7. Salik, *Surrender,* 'Operation Searchlight' includes the list of 16 Awami Leaguers, student activists, and pro-Moscow communists who were to be arrested. Curiously, Bhashani and other pro-Peking leftist leaders were not named in the list.
8. Conversation with Roedad Khan.
9. Sydney H. Schanberg's account of the army operation in Dhaka was published in the *New York Times* of 28 March 1971; the *New York Times Index,* 1991, 1288–9.
10. UPI report, Hong Kong 29 March; *Bangladesh Documents,* 382–5.
11. The account of the revolt of the Bengali armed forces and of the ensuing battles is based on interviews and conversations. The army's claim of extending control over the province by early May was generally accepted; see Werner Adam 'Words After Warfare', *Far Eastern Economic Review,* 8 May 1971, 6–7. Also Fazal Muqeem, *Leadership,* 115.
12. The incident narrated to me in the Secretariat on that day and later confirmed by Shafiul Azam when I met him was this: Mrs Azam's brother, a young CSP officer, was subdivisional officer Sirajgunj. In the general confusion of the army operation he crossed over to India but soon came back and on the advice of Azam reported for duty in Dhaka. He was arrested by the army authorities and taken to the cantonment. After a few days a message was sent to his parents that their son had died of heart failure and they could take away the body, provided they gave a written undertaking that they would not insist on a post-mortem. When the relatives went to take the body, a fresh grave was pointed out where they were told the young officer had been buried. About a month later I happened to meet the Brigadier in charge of the detention camp of the Bengali civil servants at a party. He used to investigate and grade them into various hues—jet black (completely disloyal), black, grey, and white. The Brigadier said he was determined to ensure that 'this does not happen next time'. To my remarks on the need for healing the wounds and national reconciliation, and that there might not be a next time, he was enraged and questioned my patriotism. In the December war he was responsible for the maximum casualties of his men and was the first senior officer to surrender. The 'cleansing' process was going on in the field also. Major-General A.O. Mitha was rumoured, in whispers even in cantonment circles, to be conducting pre-dawn helicopter operations in the districts against disloyal officials through the Special Services Group (SSG).
13. Kessing's *Contemporary Archives,* 4–11, September 1971, 24802; report of The *Times* correspondent on 9 July.
14. Clare Hollingworth, 'If India Decides to March in', *The Daily Telegraph,* 4 August 1971.
15. Ibid.
16. Kessing, *Archives;* dispatch of *The Daily Telegraph* correspondent on 22 August.
17. *Jang,* 5 November 1971.

Chapter 5

1. Anthony Mascarenhas, *Bangladesh: A Legacy of Blood* (London: Hodder and Stoughton, 1986) 118; the word 'revolutionary' was dropped two days later.
2. Ibid., 119. The radio announcement of 26 March was reported in *The Statesman* of 27 March; *Bangladesh Documents,* 280–1.
3. Ibid., 120.
4. *Bangladesh Observer,* Dhaka, 19 January 1974, quoted in Mahmood, *Deliberate Debacle,* 127.
5. Text of Proclamation of Independence Order dated 18 April 1971 is given in *Bangladesh Documents,* 281–2.
6. Broadcast by Tajuddin Ahmed on 11 April *The Statesman* 14 April; ibid., 286–8.
7. *The Times of India,* 3 April; *In Statesman,* 14 April; ibid., 286-8.
8. *The Sunday Statesman,* 18 April; Ibid., 289–91.
9. Kathleen Gough, 'Imperialism and Revolutionary Potential', 23–4 analyses the nature of resistance forces in East Pakistan from a leftist's point of view.
10. Henry S. Bradsher, 'Despatch from Calcutta', *The Evening Star,* Washington D.C., 27 July 1971.
11. Gough, 'Imperialism', 24.
12. Lifschultz, *Unfinished Revolution,* 22.
13. Mohammad Ayoob and K. Subrahmanyam, *The Liberation War,* (New Delhi: S. Chand & Co, 1972) Chapter 8. It was fortunate for the Pakistan army that 20,000 Bengali ranks and 1,000 officers in the armed forces were stationed in West Pakistan at the time.
14. Ibid, 152.
15. Lifschultz, *Unfinished Revolution,* 32–3.
16. Ibid., 33.
17. Bradsher, 'Despatch'.
18. Clare Hollingworth, 'If India Decides to March In', *The Daily Telegraph,* 4 August.
19. Kathleen Gough, 'Imperialism', 25.

Chapter 6

1. See Appendix 9.
2. There was a well-furnished guest house of the central government in the exclusive residential locality of Ramna for its officers visiting Dhaka. The financial rules provided for boarding and lodging in it and not in the five-star hotels. These rules had to be amended, on security grounds, for the members of the team and subsequently for all the senior officers of the Centre.
3. I have a copy of the Report
4. During interviews of military officers holding key positions in the Yahya regime, as the various issues and events came up I asked whether any record was kept by them of what they were stating now, or whether the CMLA Secretariat maintained minutes of the meetings, etc. They all replied in the negative. Sahibzada Yakub Khan very graciously showed me some of his personal papers. Kazim and some others officers gave me copies of certain documents.

5. Note dated 4 June 1971, recorded by Khaqan Mahmood after his visit to Dhaka. See Appendices 11 and 12.
6. *Dawn* 25 May 1971.
7. Note dated 21 May, 1971 recorded by Qamarul Islam, Central Industries Secretary, after his visit to Dhaka.
8. The text of the statement issued at the end of the informal meeting of the Aid-to-Pakistan Consortium is given in *Pakistan Horizon,* vol. xxiv, No. 3, 142-3.
9. *The Times,* 12 July 1971.
10. *Pakistan Horizon,* op.cit., 79-82.
11. 'The Situation in East Pakistan: A Report by an IBRD / IMF Mission', 8 July 1971. I received a copy on request from the World Bank in 1985.
12. *Economic Survey* 1970-71 (Ministry of Finance, Government of Pakistan) Statistical Section, Table 58, 133.
13. Ibid.
14. Note dated 14 June 1971, on 'Emergency Transportation Requirements of East Pakistan' by Zafar Iqbal Joint Secretary, EC&EA Division; also see Appendix 10 on Port Operations.
15. Appendix 13 and the map give details of damaged major railway bridges.
16. Appendix 14 and the map give details of damaged major road bridges.

Chapter 7

1. Except where otherwise indicated the figures quoted in the chapter are from these papers.
2. *Pakistan Economic Survey,* 1970-71, Statistical Section, Table No. 37, 74.
3. An Associated Press of America report datelined 5 May 1971 Karachi had this to say about the foreign exchange reserve position:

   'According to reliable sources, the government [of Pakistan] had foreign assets of 163 million dollars at the end of March, including assets held by scheduled banks. Foreign assets of the State Bank amounted to 129 million dollars of this total. Economists said this figure represented a decline of 120 million dollars since June 1970.

   'But the economic sources said the "freely available resources" which the State Bank could spend without special government decision had dipped into the negative side in December (1970) and as a result Pakistan was drawing on capital assets to finance imports.'
4. *Economic Survey,* op. cit., 120.
5. Ibid.
6. Ibid., 103.
7. Background Document on Pakistan's Debt Problem for the Aid-to-Pakistan Consortium Meeting on 15–16 May 1974 (Economic Affairs Division) 9.
8. *Dawn,* 5 May 1971.
9. Ibid.
10. *Dawn,* 8 June 1971. The apprehensions of the regime that the looted amount might be used for activities prejudicial to the security of Pakistan was not entirely justified. A substantial part of the loot, according to talk in responsible official circles, was shared by 'patriotic' West Pakistanis.

11. *Fiscal Policy in Pakistan, A Historical Perspective* (Ministry of Finance) vol 2, 764; 1971-2 Budget Speech of the Economic Adviser.
12. Ibid., 765.
13. This minimum figure of the looted amount was announced by the President; *Dawn,* 25 May 1971.
14. *Budget Speeches,* (Finance Division, November 1984) vol. III, 31.
15. The government of East Pakistan during this period was most of the time busy in updating the requirements for buses, trucks, coasters, and relief and rehabilitation materials, to make up the sabotage losses, and was demanding funds from the central government. In addition, the provincial government also required funds for its normal expenditure. All those dealing with the crisis, in the East Pakistan and central governments, were working under great pressures without any respite. In October, Muzaffar Husain, who was Chief Secretary in East Pakistan now, and myself from the provincial planning board had a meeting with Kazi in Islamabad about some rehabilitation and repair proposals involving Rs 200 million. Kazi, a very peaceable man by nature but whose position as finance secretary was becoming more and more unenviable, flared up in a rare show of impatience at the unending demands of East Pakistan. He called East Pakistan a bottomless pit and blamed the East Pakistan government for wasting national resources and diverting allocations to unapproved purposes. Tempers rose, voices were raised, and the arguments went back and forth. Finally, Muzaffar Husain invited Kazi to Dhaka to see conditions for himself, and how the central grants were being spent. Kazi was not unaware of the conditions and did not relish the idea of visiting the beleaguered region. Eventually he admitted that 'we are facing a war situation', and agreed to give us some fraction of our demand.
16. Figures quoted in this para are from the address of Ghulam Ishaq Khan, Governor State Bank (Cabinet Secretary in the Yahya regime) at the 24th Annual General Meeting of the shareholders.
17. *Pakistan Economic Survey,* 1971-72, xiii-xiv.
18. *Pakistan Horizon,* vol. xxiv, No. 4, 109.
19. *Dawn,* 18 November 1971.

Chapter 8

1. See Appendix 10.
2. The relative importance of the three rice crops in the production estimates of 1970-71 was as follows:
   (i) *Aus* planted in April, harvested in August — 2.9 million tons
   (ii) *Aman* planted in September, harvested in January — 6.9 million tons
   (iii) *Boro* planted in January, harvested in March/April — 1.8 million tons
3. I have a copy of this paper.
4. See Appendix 10.
5. Report of the IBRD/IMF Mission, op. cit., did not regard a breakthrough in one of the key areas having a 'snowball' effect inconceivable: 'Thus, it is possible that the railway will function better . . . [and if the] the carrying capacity of the coastal fleet is increased considerably . . . the physical constraints to recovery

could be reduced considerably, and thus incentives for renewed economic activity be strengthened to the point where the psychological constraints lose some of their power.'

6. Thus, the utilization plan submitted by the Transport Department of the government of East Pakistan to meet the conditions of the $ 2 million grant for 17 vessels, was based on complete information regarding tonnage etc. in respect of nine vessels only; of these, the expected date of arrival was intimated for six only. The plan was based on the assumption that all the 17 vessels would be available by mid-September. In the second week of August it was intimated that the delivery would not be completed before 10 October.
7. Christopher Van Hollen, 'The Tilt Policy Revisited: Nixon–Kissinger Geopolitics and South Asia', *Asian Survey,* vol. XX, No. 4, April 1980.
8. Text of the letter in *Pakistan Horizon,* vol. XXIV, No. 2, 140.
9. It was widely believed in West Pakistan that arms were smuggled for secessionist elements in the foreign relief consignments and sea vessels which came to the affected coastal areas after the November 1970 cyclone. The foreign volunteer workers were especially considered to have played some inexplicit subversive role in fomenting trouble in East Pakistan. No hard evidence was produced officially or otherwise to support the charge.
10. Text of the President's reply in *Pakistan Horizon,* vol. XXIV, No. 2, 141.
11. *Dawn,* 7 May 1971.
12. Henry Kissinger, *The White House Years* (London: Weidenfeld and Nicolson and Michael Joseph, 1979) 857.
13. *Pakistan Horizon,* vol. XXIV, No. 2, 79.
14. Foreign Office brief to the Economic Adviser said 'Mr Ismet Kittani is an Iraqi (Kurd) National. His rise to the high position was generally attributed to his personal qualities and ability and he was reported to be a great favourite of U Thant. His recommendations were likely to carry considerable weight with U Thant.'
15. *Dawn,* 13 June 1971.
16. Press Release 1 HA/2, 16 July 1971, issued by the Information Service United Nations Office Geneva.
17. Extract relating to East Pakistan from the 'Introduction to the Report of the Secretary-General on the Work of the Organisation', September 1971, received by the Foreign Office from its UN mission.
18. See *Bangla Desh Documents,* for a selective compilation (projecting anti-Pakistan angle) of articles, broadcasts, and reports from the representatives of voluntary agencies, particularly 447, 453, 575, 606, 611. These 'first-hand accounts' were provided as briefs to the parliamentarians and government officials or directly published or broadcast by the executives of the volunteer organizations, greatly influencing public opinion and the government policies of their countries.
19. The Organizations were:
    1. Catholic Relief Services
    2. Norwegian Church Relief
    3. Pakistan Mission Southern Baptist Convention
    4. CARITAS East Pakistan
    5. Christian Organization for Relief and Rehabilitation

6. East Pakistan Christian Council
7. League of Red Cross Societies
8. Uncle Erik's Help Children
9. Save the Children Fund
10. International Union for the Child
11. HELP
12. Service Civil International Pakistan
13. Service Civil International (Asian Secretariat)
14. CARE
15. OXFAM
16. Bread for the World (Germany)

20. Figures derived from *Bangla Desh Documents,* 446
21. *The Guardian* (London) 15 May 1971; Ibid., 497.
22. *Bangladesh Documents,* 536-7.
23. See statements of the UNHCR dated 5 May, 23 June, and 30 June; ibid., 612-18, 628-35.
24. Text of the statement of 12 May, ibid., 618-23; Also see *Pakistan Horizon,* vol. XXIV, No. 2, 76 which noted that India was not a member of the ECOSOC and had raised the question of refugees on humanitarian grounds.
25. *Pakistan Horizon,* vol. XXIV, No. 2, 76.
26. Text of Sen's statement of 17 May in *Bangla Desh Documents,* 623-5.
27. Ibid., 612-16.
28. Text of Yahya's statement in *Pakistan Horizon,* vol. XXIV, No. 2, 110-11.
29. Robert Jackson, *South Asian Crisis* (London: Chatto & Windus, 1975) 60.
30. The statement is based on my personal experience and conversations with senior army, civil, and police officers, serving at the time in East Pakistan.
31. Immediately after the explosion I happened to be passing by the Hotel and saw the fire brigade extinguishing the fire inside, and a gathering of the residents, including some West Pakistani politicians who were staying there, on the lawn. Much later in 1978, Kaiser Rashid, who was at one time in the foreign service, told me that his daughter had placed the bombs in the bathroom on the ground floor when she was visiting someone in the Hotel. He himself, of course, was quite ignorant of the act.
32. *Bangla Desh Documents,* 628-32; also see Jackson, *Crisis,* 61.
33. Ibid., 633-41.
34. Ibid., 642.
35. Ibid.
36. Ibid., 643-9.
37. Ibid., 650.
38. The account of the Fifty-first session of the ECOSOC is based on the Provisional Summary Record of the one thousand seven hundred and eighty-third meeting dated 20 July 1971, E/SR 1783, GE 71-16151.

Chapter 9

1. See Ashok Raina, *Inside RAW: The Story of India's Secret Service* (New Delhi: Vikas Publishing House, 1981) 53-4 for an account of the activities of the

Indian intelligence agency, Research and Analysis Wing (RAW), in East Pakistan in early 1971. In the first week of March, it says, a message was sent from Dhaka by a RAW operative to Calcutta about the imminence of an army crackdown on Awami Leaguers. This was supported by reports of movement of troops from Karachi to Chittagong, and armour from the border to Dhaka. On receiving these reports, New Delhi ordered, '. . . advise Menon . . . to bring in our friends'. The Indian intelligence operatives tried to convince Mujib to leave Dhaka, but he refused. He, however, relented in respect of other Awami League leaders a few hours before the crackdown, and they made their way to India in various disguises.

2. See L. F. Rushbrook Williams, *The East Pakistan Tragedy,* (London: Tom Tacy) Appendix 4 which reproduces the government press release dated 20 April of the findings of the judicial commission set up by the Pakistan government to inquire into the hijacking of the Indian Airlines plane to Lahore. The commission has quoted public statements of the leaders of Indian-held Kashmir about the patronage of the hijackers by the Indian intelligence agencies. By implication, the commission's findings also highlight the inept handling of the affair by the Pakistan government in not dealing firmly with the hijackers and not ascertaining their antecedents. The rumour in Islamabad in those days was that President Yahya was not available, during the critical stage of negotiations with the hijackers, for instructions.
3. This is borne out by various attempts by the Awami League to prevent reinforcement of the army. The ship M.V. *Swat* which had arrived in Chittagong with arms, ammunitions, and other military supplies at the end of February was not allowed to be unloaded until 24 March; the Pakistani troops had to fight their way through with the consignments from the ship to the cantonment. Similarly, in the first week of March, transport of petrol and other oil products from company storages at Narayangunj by the army was obstructed. Supplies of provisions to the cantonments by the local contractors were also blockaded by the Awami Leaguers during the same period.
4. *Bangla Desh Documents,* 671.
5. Ibid., 669-70.
6. Ibid., 672.
7. Ibid.
8. *Pakistan Horizon,* vol. XXIV, No. 2, 64.
9. Mohammad Ayoob and K. Subrahmanyam, *The Liberation War* (New Delhi: S. Chand & Co., 1972) Chapter 9, 'The Genocide and the Refugees', argues at length the threat to India's security by the influx of refugees from East Pakistan. It criticizes the Indian army for not meeting 'a challenge to its security from a nation one-fourth India's size and resources without a response time of nine months.'
10. Major-General D. K. Palit, *The Lightning Campaign* (New Delhi: Thomson Press, 1972) 63–4.
11. Quoted in Pakistan's *note verbale* of 7 April 1971 to the UN Secretary-General in response to the Indian Note circulated as a press release on 31 March; text of Pakistan's Note given in *Pakistan Horizon,* vol. XXIV, No. 2, 124.
12. See Jackson, *Crisis,* 45. Also Kissinger, *White House,* 856-7, 'In May 1971 we learned . . . that Mrs Gandhi had ordered plans for a lightning "Israeli-type"

attack to take over East Pakistan. . . . The Indian commanders insisted, at a minimum, on waiting until November when weather in the Himalayas would make Chinese intervention more difficult.'

13. Palit, *Campaign,* Chapter II; he defends the army's reluctance to attack East Pakistan in April–May. He also implies that the threat to India had arisen from its own support to the rebels, and not from any action taken by Pakistan against India as such.
14. Text of the Heath statement in *Pakistan Horizon,* vol. XXIV, No. 2, 141-2.
15. Ibid.
16. Quoted in Mehrunnisa Ali, 'East Pakistan Crisis: International Reactions', ibid., 50.
17. Quoted ibid.
18. Quoted ibid.
19. Text of the statements of the State Department issued on 2, 5, and 7 April in *Pakistan Horizon,* vol. XXIV, No. 2, 145-7.
20. The account of the developing US policy and the quotations in this and the succeeding six paragraphs, except where otherwise indicated, are from Kissinger, *White House,* 851-6.
21. Choudhury, *Last Days,* 120,168 describes the hostile activities of the US consul-general, and the group of US economists financed by the Ford Foundation, at Dhaka; USAID was also generally sympathetic to the East Pakistan 'cause'. Ambassador Farland, however, according to the author, had made it clear to Mujib in a meeting in early 1971 that the US would not support secession. This was reiterated by Farland in March in another meeting with Mujib. Farland was a former FBI agent; in West Pakistan he conjured up the conventional image of CIA cloak-and-dagger operations to undermine the established orders in Third World countries. The influential Lahore Urdu daily, *Nawa-i-Waqt,* in an editorial on 2 April called Farland's activities, before and after the general elections, 'dubious', referred to his secret meetings with certain political leaders, and asked for his recall by the US government. Also see *The New York Times* 1971, *Index,* 1288, for Pakistanis' suspicions of American activities in general and of Farland's in particular.
22. Text of Podgorny's letter datelined Moscow, 2 April 1971 in *Bangla Desh Documents,* 510-11; slightly different text in *Pakistan Horizon,* vol. XXIV, No. 2, 149-50 is dated 3 April and indicated as a translation from the Russian.
23. Choudhury, *Last Days,* 120.
24. Text of Yahya's reply to Podgorny in *Pakistan Horizon,* op.cit., 150-2.
25. Extracts from the Note of the People's Republic of China to the Government of India, dated 6 April 1971, ibid., 153.
26. Text of Zhou Enlai's message, ibid., 153-4.
27. Jackson, *Crisis,* 41.
28. Ibid., 41-2. Clare Hollingworth reported in *The Daily Telegraph,* London, of 21 April 1971 that each day more than a hundred Chinese military lorries were bringing military and other supplies from China through the all-weather Karakoram Highway to West Pakistan.
29. *Pakistan Horizon,* vol. XXIV, No. 2, 156.
30. Ibid., 140.
31. Interview with Agha Shahi. Statements attributed to him are throughout from it.

32. *Pakistan Horizon,* vol. XXIV, No. 2, 73.
33. Government of Pakistan, *White Paper on the Crisis in East Pakistan,* 5 August 1971.
34. *Dawn,* 16 June 1971.
35. Ibid., 18 June 1971.
36. *Bangla Desh Documents,* 511-12.
37. *Dawn,* 12 June 1971.
38. *Bangla Desh Documents,* 514-15.
39. Ibid., 505.
40. Heath's statement that on aid the British policy was to deal regardless of certain political aspects of the country; *Dawn,* 6 May 1971.
41. *Kessing's Contemporary Archives*—7-14 April 1971, 24759.
42. Ibid.
43. Ibid.
44. *Bangla Desh Documents,* 451; also see *Kessing's Archives.,* ibid.
45. *Kessing's Archives,* op cit.
46. *Bangla Desh Documents,* 508.
47. Ibid., 508-9; also *Kessing's Archives,* op. cit.
48. *Kessing's Archives,* op. cit. Particular exception was taken in the protest note of 5 July on the agreed statement of 21 June on the conclusion of the visit of Indian Foreign Minister; the statement had called for a political settlement acceptable to the people of East Pakistan.
49. *Pakistan Horizon,* vol. XXIV, No. 3, 80.
50. *Dawn,* 16 June 1971; Swaran Singh hinted at the possibility of military measures by India against Pakistan during his briefings of the Soviet Russian, West German, and French government officials on India's stand on East Pakistan crisis.
51. *Pakistan Horizon,* vol. XXIV, No. 3, 75.
52. *Dawn,* 8 August 1971.
53. Arnold Smith, *Stitches in Time* (London: Andre Deutsch, 1981) 136-8.
54. Kissinger, *White House,* 860.
55. Ibid., 862.
56. Ibid., 863.
57. Christopher Van Hollen, 'Tilt Policy', *Asian Survey,* vol. XX, No. 4, April 1980.
58. Kissinger, *White House,* 862.
59. Van Hollen, 'Tilt Policy', 346.
60. Kissinger, *White House,* 860.
61. Norman D. Palmer, *The United States and India* (New York: Praeger Publishers, 1984) 47.
62. Seymour M. Hersh, *The Price of Power* (London: Faber and Faber, 1983) 451-2.
63. Kissinger, *White House,* 862.
64. Text of *aide-mémoire* in *Pakistan Horizon,* vol. XXIV, No. 3, 126-7.
65. Government of Pakistan, *Press Information Handout,* E. No. 1540-R, 4 August 1971.
66. *Kessing's Archives,* September 4-11 1971, 24802.
67. Text of the Secretary-General's Memorandum in *Pakistan Horizon,* vol. XXIV, No. 3, 127-30.
68. *Pakistan Times,* Rawalpindi, 28 July 1971.

69. Ibid., 5 August 1971.
70. *Dawn,* 29 July 1971.
71. *Bangla Desh Documents,* 708.
72. *The Times,* 7 August 1971; dispatch by Peter Hazelhurst.
73. Yahya made a similar gaffe at the first Islamic Summit at Rabat. Yousuf J. Ahmed related the incident to me at Ambassador Shahryar Khan's house in London in 1987. Both of them, as directors in the Foreign Office, were members of the delegation to the Summit. Yahya called on the Shah of Iran, King Faisal, and the King of Morocco, all of whom mentioned India's request to join the Islamic Organization; Yahya gave the impression of acquiescing in the proposal. When S. M. Yousuf and Agha Shahi came to know of this, they felt unhappy but Yahya had already committed himself; at the first informal summit in the morning, the Shah of Iran proposed inviting India, and the King of Morocco or the King Faisal seconded the proposal. The murmurings in the delegation increased. At lunch Tyabji, the outspoken Pakistan ambassador in Morocco, barged into Yahya's suite and strongly objected to India's joining the Organization. Yahya then registered the point and was angry that he had not been properly advised. Later, in the formal session Pakistan opposed the proposal when India was invited to take the seat which was kept for it. This threw the conference into pandemonium, because the matter had been taken as settled. Eventually, Pakistan's objection prevailed. On his return to Pakistan, Yahya was hailed as *Hadi-i-Islam*.
74. Quoted in Zubeida Mustafa, 'USSR and Indian Action in East Pakistan', *Pakistan Horizon,* vol. XXIV, No. 4, 72.
75. Ibid., 73.
76. Ibid.
77. Jackson, *Crisis,* 71.
78. Full text of the Treaty and Extract from the Indo-Soviet joint statement in *Pakistan Horizon,* vol. XXIV, No. 4, 163-9.
79. Hersh, *Price of Power,* footnote 452-3; the author adds that the CIA director was agitated about the publication of the story blowing off the cover of his source in the Indian government; he was Morarji Desai, the Indian deputy prime minister.
80. Kissinger, *White House,* 866–8.
81. Van Hollen, 'Tilt Policy'.
82. See, for example, *The Economist,* 14 August 1971; *The Times* editorial, 10 August 1971; and *Daily Telegraph,* 10 August 1971.
83. Ayoob and Subrahmanyam, *Liberation,* 66.
84. *The Observer* London, 15 August 1971; dispatch by Sunada Datta-Ray from Calcutta.
85. Palit, *Campaign,* 66.
86. Kissinger, *White House,* 867.
87. *Morning News,* 13 August 1971.
88. *Dawn,* 13 August 1971.
89. *Pakistan Horizon,* vol. XXIV, No. 3, 88.
90. Text of the protest note to the Secretary-General, ibid., 87-9.
91. Kissinger, *White House,* 868-9.
92. Sajjad Hyder, who was High Commissioner in India 1971, says in an article in

daily Urdu *Jang* Rawalpindi of 13 June 1983 that the Indo-Soviet treaty was discussed at the Geneva meeting, and the consensus was that it did not necessarily mean war with India; the ambassador in Moscow did not disagree with this analysis. Sajjad Hyder says that he disagreed with the majority view. It is not clear whether he expressed this view in the formal sessions to bring it on record or merely mentioned it in informal chats.

93. *Pakistan Horizon,* vol. XXIV, No. 4, 167-9.
94. Ibid, 104.
95. Zubeida Mustafa, 'USSR and Indian Action', ibid., 66-67.
96. Ibid., 67; *Dawn,* 28 October 1971.
97. *The Memoirs of Richard Nixon* (New York: Crosset & Dunlop, 1978) 525-6.
98. Hersh, *Price of Power,* 456.
99. Van Hollen, 'Tilt Policy', 351-2.
100. *Pakistan Horizon,* vol. XXIV, No. 4, 118.
101. Ibid., 110.
102. Ibid., 152-3.

Chapter 10

1. Bhutto, *Tragedy,* 51.
2. *Pakistan Times,* 17 April 1971; statement of Maulana Kausar Niazi, Information Secretary, Pakistan People's Party.
3. *Dawn,* 6 May 1971, statement of Qayyum Khan, President Pakistan Muslim League (Qayyum group); *Dawn,* 13 September 1971, statement of Mumtaz Daultana, President Pakistan Council Muslim League.
4. *Dawn,* 7 June 1971.
5. *Dawn,* 10 May 1971; this was one of the early statements calling for transfer of power; in the later months it was Bhutto's constant theme.
6. See, for example, *Dawn,* 6, 13, and 22 May, for the statements of Qayyum Khan, Nurul Amin, and Tufail Muhammad respectively, all urging Yahya not to transfer power until normalcy was restored in East Pakistan.
7. See Herbert Feldman, *Revolution in Pakistan: A Study of the Martial Law Administration* (London: Oxford University Press, 1967), Appendix VI, 226-30, for a description of the role of the Pakistan Press during and after the martial law of 1958.
8. 'Islamabad's Blind Alley', *Far Eastern Economic Review,* 15 May 1971, 5.
9. *Dawn,* 5 May 1971.
10. *Dawn,* 10, 21 May 1971; *Pakistan Times,* Rawalpindi, 12 June 1971
11. Text of the broadcast in *Pakistan Horizon,* vol. XXIV, No. 3, 111-23.
12. Appendix 15. I am grateful to M. I. Karim for this document.
13. *Jang,* 6, 9, July 1971.
14. Ibid., 10, 19, 22 July 1971; 2 August 1971.
15. Ibid., 16 July 1971.
16. Ibid., 17 July 1971.
17. The People's Party delegation comprised of J. A. Rahim, Mahmud Ali Kasuri, Abdul Hafeez Pirzada, and Rafi Raza. The President's team consisted of

Cornelius, Hasan, and Shafqat on 25 August 1971, and on subsequent days included M. M. Ahmed also.

18. *Dawn,* 26 August 1971.
19. Text of the statement in *Pakistan Horizon,* vol. XXIV. No. 4, 147-8.
20. Ibid., 146.
21. A West Pakistani subdivisional magistrate in Chittagong division was beaten up in his own jurisdiction by the local army commander, for resisting the latter's orders. The West Pakistani commissioner, S. K. Mahmud, strongly protested to the martial law authorities, and demanded action against the army officer but to no effect.
22 *Dawn,* 8 August 1971.
23. Ibid., 20 August1971 .
24. Ibid., 4 September 1971.
25. Election Commission of Pakistan notification No. F. 14 (3)/71-Els. II. dated 21 September and No. F.14(3)/71-Els. II(2), of the same date, called on the electors to elect 78 members of National Assembly; 76 to the vacancies caused by disqualifications, and 2 on account of deaths. The same notification fixed the programme for elections to 104 seats of the East Pakistan Assembly vacated due to disqualifications and one by death. By another notification No. F. 14 (3)/71-Els.II(1) dated 3 October, the Commission announced the election schedule for filling another 87 Provincial Assembly seats vacated due to disqualifications and one due to death. The Awami League position that emerged in the two Assemblies from these notifications was as follows:

	National Assembly	Provincial Assembly
Original Awami League membership	160	288
Disqualified	76	191
Deaths	2	2
After by-elections	82	95

According to the official announcement of 8 August, 88 National Assembly members of the Awami League were allowed to retain their seats, which meant 72 were disqualified. Apparently, on further scrutiny, four more were removed from membership.

26. The following few selections from *Dawn* (date of issue given against each) give an indication of the West Pakistan support to Yahya's policies.
    (i) Bhutto was anxious that the list of disqualified Awami League members should be published. 1 August.
    (ii) Maulana Maudoodi 'was at a loss to understand how the membership . . . of the Awami League [in the Assemblies] . . . would be retained . . . (in the light of) the White Paper read with . . . (Yahya's statement) that the victory of Awami League was due to intimidation, terror and malpractices'. 7 August.

(iii) Resolution of the Council Muslim League appreciated various pledges of Yahya and asked the President to announce the Constitution at an early date, followed by fair and free elections. 13 September.
(iv) Daultana demanded that the Constitution be given by the President. 17 September.
(v) Convention Muslim League Working committee requested the President to make public the Constitution. 8 October.
(vi) Asghar Khan announced his party would not participate in East Pakistan elections but it should not be construed to mean boycotting them. 12 October.
(vii) Qayyum Khan, president Muslim League (Qayyum group) asked all patriotic parties to support the government and stand behind the armed forces. 24 October.
(viii) Editorial of 14 October—Yahya's political plan (announced in the radio broadcast of 12 October) 'points unmistakably to his [the President's] resolve to fulfil his pledge to transfer power at the earliest moment feasible.'

27. *Dawn,* 13 October.
28. Ibid., 20 October. The six parties in the electoral alliance had actually distributed amongst themselves 88 National Assembly seats of East Pakistan as against 78 notified by the Election Commissioner. Of these, 5 were later given to the People's Party. The relative party positions after the division of spoils at this time emerged somewhat as given below. The figures will not add up to the total membership because the bargaining process among the parties was still going on.

	West Pakistan	East Pakistan	Total
Awami League	–	82 (160)	82 (160)
People's Party	81	5 (Nil)	86 (81)
Muslim League (Total three factions)	18	9 (Nil)	27 (18)
Jamaat-i-Islami	4	50 (Nil)	54 (4)
Pakistan Democratic Party (Nurul Amin)	Nil	23 (1)	24 (1)
Nizam-i-Islam	Nil	6 (Nil)	6 (1)

(Figures within brackets show the seats obtained in the 1970 elections).

29. Ibid., 24 September.
30. Another 13 women members (7 from East Pakistan, 6 from West Pakistan provinces) were to be elected by the members of the respective provinces. Given the new composition, the women members were likely to belong to the

rightist parties. Moreover, even the former Awami League members attending the Assembly would not be inimical to the regime.

31. Out of 193 vacancies in the East Pakistan Assembly, agreement had been reached in the alliance on 156 by 20 October; by 28 October, compromise had been reached on 178, leaving 13 to be decided later. *Dawn,* 20, 28 October.
32. *Dawn,* 11, 14, 18 October.
33. *Dawn,* 23 October, Dhaka statement of Kasuri; *Dawn,* 24 October, Bhutto's statement.
34. *Dawn,* 3 November.
35. *Dawn,* 30 October.
36. Ibid., 16 November.
37. Ibid., 22 November.
38. This was Article 16 of the Constitution which Yahya had proposed to announce on 20 December; it was ordered to be deleted on 18 December though the Constitution itself was never announced.
39. Choudhury, *Last Days,* 195.
40. Kissinger, *White House,* 871.
41. Jackson, *Crisis,* 80.
42. Kissinger, *White House,* 869-73.
43. Lifschultz, *Unfinished Revolution,* 113-16, 158-60. The book is mainly based on the research material collected for a study of US policy on the Bangladesh crisis in 1971, commissioned in 1973 by the Carnegie Endowment for International Peace, a US research foundation. One hundred senior officials of the concerned agencies of the US government were interviewed. The final report, Lifschultz says, was never published because of difference of opinion within the project staff.

Chapter 11

1. Palit, *Campaign,* 72.
2. Ibid., 74.
3. *The Gazette of Pakistan Extraordinary,* Rawalpindi, 23 November 1971.
4. Muqeem, *Leadership,* 109-13.
5. Kissinger, *White House,* 894; text of Article I of the 1959 bilateral agreement between the United States and Pakistan given on 1488 reads 'The Government of Pakistan is determined to resist aggression. In case of aggression against Pakistan, the Government of the United States of America, in accordance with the Constitution of the United States of America, will take such appropriate action, including the use of armed force, as may be mutually agreed upon and as is envisaged in the Joint Resolution to Promote Peace and Stability in the Middle East, in order to assist the Government of Pakistan at its request.'
6. Palit, *Campaign,* 78.
7. Muqeem, *Leadership,* 240.
8. Kissinger, *White House,* 896.
9. The text of resolutions and the proceedings of the Security Council meetings held between 4 and 16 December 1971, mentioned in this chapter, are based on the following volumes of United Nations Security Council Official Records:

S/PV. 1606-8, S/PV. 1611-13 S/PV. 1614 and Add. 1, S/PV. 1615-17. Texts of some of the draft resolutions of the period also given in *Pakistan Horizon,* vol. XXV, No. 1, 1972, 149-55.

10. Kissinger, *White House,* 901.
11. Jackson, *Crisis,* Appendix 14. Minutes of WSAG Meeting of 6 December, 222-3.
12. Ibid., Memo on 8 December WSAG Meeting, 226-8.
13. Ibid., 227.
14. Kissinger, *White House,* 901. Hersh, *Price of Power,* 452–3, 459, says that as described by Kissinger, the source of this information could only have been Morarji Desai who was working for the CIA. Hersh discounts the report on the ground that Mrs Gandhi 'relied on a small subcabinet committee into which the CIA was not likely to penetrate', implying that Desai, even as the deputy prime minister, did not have access to state secrets. On the other hand, Hersh gives full credence to the same source when it reported that the Soviet Union had signed the friendship treaty to prevent India from recognizing Bangladesh and that it was not intended against Pakistan.
15. Muqeem, *Leadership,* 212-13.
16. There is some evidence that the Chinese had agreed to activate the borders and also start air activities on them. But this was to be on a very limited scale, due to bad weather conditions. The airfields in Tibet were frozen. More than that, perhaps the Russian military manoeuvres on the Chinese border deterred the Chinese from any intervention in the subcontinent. In any case there was no commitment from them and the hopes given to Dhaka were unwarranted.
17. Muqeem, *Leadership,* 213.
18. Palit, *Campaign,* 125-6.
19. Kissinger, *White House,* 903-4.
20. Palit, *Campaign,* 110. The Indian army officers whom we met, after the surrender, were generally full of praise for the valour of Major-General Nazar Hussain Shah. Unlike other army commanders, there were no allegations of atrocities and violation of human rights against him.
21. Salik, *Surrender,* 179-80.
22. Palit, *Campaign,* 125.
23. Salik, *Surrender,* 162.
24. Ibid., 197.
25. Conversation with Muzaffar Husain.
26. Kissinger, *White House,* 905.
27. Ibid., 906.
28. Ibid., 905-6.
29. Reconstructed from conversations with Ghulam Ishaq Khan and Roedad Khan.
30. Salik, *Surrender,* 188, 201.
31. Palit, *Campaign,* 128-9.
32. Muqeem, *Leadership,* 213.
33. Kissinger, *White House,* 907-8.
34. Ibid., 908.
35. Ibid., 909-11.
36. Text of the speech of the US permanent representative in the Security Council in *Pakistan Horizon,* vol. XXV, No. 1, 1972, 165-8.
37. Kissinger, *White House,* 912. During a lecture by Kissinger at the National

Defence College Rawalpindi on 20 January 1985, I asked him two questions with references to his memoirs of the India-Pakistan crisis of 1971: first, being convinced after 25 March that East Pakistan could not remain in Pakistan, why did the White House continue to support Yahya's policies? and second, what was the purpose of sending the Task Force to the Bay of Bengal? On the first Kissinger was not very explicit; to the second, he said it was to save West Pakistan.

38. Van Hollen, 'Tilt Policy', 356.
39. Palit, *Campaign,* 130–1.
40. Muqeem, *Leadership,* 217.
41. Conversation with Ijlal Haider Zaidi, the then director-general Radio Pakistan.
42. Muqeem, *Leadership,* 215.
43. Ibid., 217.
44. *Pakistan Horizon,* vol. XXV, No. 1 1972, 166; speech of the US permanent representative in the Security Council.
45. Kissinger, *White House,* 892.

Epilogue

1. Yahya's 'Undelivered Address to the Nation', dated 17 December, giving an outline of the Constitution is given in Feldman, *End & Beginning*, Appendix B, 194–201. It was not actually Yahya's speech; the document was to have been published as the 'Salient Points of the Constitution'. Yahya had already addressed the nation on 16 December.
2. The account of the mutiny has been reconstructed from Feldman, *End & Beginning,* 184-9, and, like other dark corners of the period dealt with in the book, by conversations and interviews extending over a period of twenty years with those who were involved in these events or had knowledge of them, and from unpublished documents.
3. Anthony Mascarenhas has given an account of the arrival and short stay of Mujib in London, on his way to Dhaka, on 8 January 1972 in *Bangladesh, A Legacy of Blood* (Hodder and Stoughton, 1985). 5. According to Mascarenhas Mujib, soon after his arrival in a London hotel, told him, 'I have a big scoop for you. We are going to keep some link with Pakistan but I can't say anything more till I have talked it over with others.' Apparently, the author says, Mujib and Bhutto had arrived at some understanding on a 'link' of Bangladesh with Pakistan. Mujib, however, seemed to have given up any such notions, even before he arrived in Dhaka, after he was told what had happened since his arrest.

List of Important Persons Involved in the Management of the East Pakistan Crisis in 1971

Armed Forces

General A. M. Yahya Khan, President, Chief Martial Law Administrator and Commander-in-Chief, Army

General Abdul Hamid Khan, Chief of Staff, Army.

Lieutenant-General S. G. M. M. Peerzada, Principal Staff Officer to the President.

Lieutenant-General Gul Hassan Khan, Chief of General Staff.

Lieutenant-General Sahibzada Yakub Khan, Commander Eastern Command up to March.

Vice-Admiral S. M. Ahsan, Governor East Pakistan up to March.

Lieutenant-General Tikka Khan, Governor and Martial Law Administrator East Pakistan, March-September; commanded 4 Corps during the war.

Lieutenant-General A. A. K. Niazi, Commander Eastern Command.

Major-General Ghulam Umer, Secretary National Security Division.

Major-General Rao Farman Ali, In Charge Civil Affairs, Martial Law HQ Dhaka.

Brigadier Ghulam Jillani, Chief of Staff to the Commander Eastern Command until the middle of the year when promoted as Major-General and posted as head of the Inter-Services Intelligence; later Lieutenant-General.

Air Marshal Rahim Khan, Commander-in-Chief Pakistan Air Force.

Brigadier M. I. Karim, CMLA Secretariat; in June promoted Major-General and commanded 6 Armoured Division.

Brigadier Rahim Khan, CMLA Secretariat; in June promoted Major-General and posted to Dhaka on martial law duties, commanded 14 Division in East Pakistan during war.

Brigadier A. R. Siddiqui, Director-General Inter-Services Public Relations.

Colonel (later Brigadier) Siddiq Salik, of the Inter-Services Public Relations Directorate at Dhaka; spokesman of the military administration of East Pakistan.

Lieutenant-Colonel M. A. Hasan, Legal and Constitutional Adviser of the CMLA Secretariat; belonged to the office of the Judge-Advocate General GHQ.

Civil Officials

Dr A. M. Malik, Governor East Pakistan, September–December.

M. M. Ahmed, Adviser Economic Affairs (Minister In Charge of Economic Ministries).

G. W. Choudhury, Adviser Communications; he was the principal constitutional adviser of Yahya in the framing of the Legal Framework Order 1970.

Justice (Retd.) A. R. Cornelius, Adviser Law, former Chief Justice of the Supreme Court of Pakistan.

S. Ghiasuddin Ahmed, Adviser Defence.

Ghulam Ishaq Khan, Cabinet Secretary.

A. G. N. Kazi, Secretary Ministry of Finance.

Muzaffar Husain, Secretary National Assembly; in charge of East Pakistan Cell created in April until September when appointed Chief Secretary East Pakistan.

Sultan Muhammad Khan, Secretary Ministry of Foreign Affairs.

Qamarul Islam, Secretary Ministry of Industries.

Roedad Khan, Secretary Ministry of Information and National Affairs.

Vaqar Ahmed, Secretary Establishment Division.

A. Rab, Secretary Planning Division.

V. A. Jaffery, Secretary Ministry of Commerce.

S. S. Iqbal Hossain, Secretary Economic Co-ordination and External Assistance Division.

S. M. Shafiul Azam, Chief Secretary East Pakistan until September when posted Secretary Ministry of Communication in the central government.

M. Qayyum, Secretary to the President.

A. M. S. Ahmed, Chairman Planning and Development Board East Pakistan.

Q. J. Ahmed, Secretary Transport Department East Pakistan.

M. A. K. Choudhury, Inspector-General Police East Pakistan.

S. K. Mahmud, Commissioner Chittagong Division.

Syed Alamdar Raza, Commissioner Dhaka Division.

M. A. Alvie, Additional Secretary Ministry of Foreign Affairs.

N. A. Rizvi, Director Intelligence Bureau.

Zafar Iqbal, Joint Secretary Economic Affairs Division.

S. Munir Husain, Director-General Pakistan Television.

S. Ijlal Haider Zaidi, Director-General Radio Pakistan.

A. Hilaly, Ambassador to the USA until the middle of 1971.

Agha Shahi, Permanent Representative at the United Nations New York.

Niaz Naik, Ambassador to the UN Agencies, Geneva.

Major-General (Retd) N. A. M. Raza, Ambassador to the USA in the latter part of the year.

Index

21-Point Programme 34, 39
Abdul Qayyum Khan, 68, 71, 124, 330, 499(n), 501 (n)
Abdul Hamid Khan, Gen., 108, 112, 120, 122, 136, 141, 148, 371, 422, 429, 430
Abdul Haroon, Sir, 5
Abul Hashim, 8-12, 13, 25
Afzal Qadir, Dr, 5
Agartala Conspiracy, 98, 102
Ahsan, Vice Admiral S. M., 107, 108, 141, 143, 487(n)
Akhtar Mahmood, 266, 267
Alec Douglas-Home, Sir, 277
All Pakistan Jinnah Awami Muslim League, 20
Altaf Gauhar, 104, 476(n), 485(n)
Alvie, M. A., 314,
American Connection, 72, 73
Amir Abdullah Khan Niazi, Lt. Gen., 148, 335, 336, 363, 364, 367, 368, 371, 372, 377-9, 381-4, 387, 390, 394, 395, 401, 402, 404, 405-7, 409, 412, 413, 415, 432
Army, 12, 34, 38, 48, 54; interaction with political leadership, 58-68; 70, 71, 73, 74, 76, 101, 104-7; takeover March 1969, 108-16, 121, 125, 130, 135-7, 142, 143, 145-9, 158, 159; action March 1971, 163-77, 178-183, 185, 186, 188-94, 196, 199, 202, 204, 205, 208, 212, 215, 218, 220, 230, 234, 237, 239, 241, 247, 250, 257, 261, 263, 266, 267, 273, 274, 276-81, 283, 285, 286, 288-91, 296, 297, 301, 304, 306, 310-12, 317, 320, 321 322-8, 335, 336, 338, 341-3, 345-7, 349, 352; war and surrender 353, 354, 357-62, 364, 367, 373, 375, 376, 378, 379, 381, 382, 388, 389, 391, 394, 395, 397-9, 402, 405-7, 409-12, 415, 417-19, 426, 428-32; 488-90(n), 494-6(n), 502-3(n)
Asghar Khan, Air Marshal (Retd), 99, 100, 431, 501 (n)
Awami League, 16, 20, 25, 26, 30-4, 38-46, 56, 65, 68-71, 73, 75, 76, 81, 82, 84, 86, 92, 96-100, 103, 104, 119, 123, 125-8, 130-2, 134, 135, 138-40, 142-4, 146, 148, 149-59 163-7, 172-4, 178-84, 190, 191, 234, 265, 273, 274, 276, 290, 296, 299, 308, 314-16, 322, 324, 326-30, 332, 335, 337, 340, 341, 345-7, 349-51, 365, 390, 393, 403, 409, 420, 475(n), 476(n), 478(n), 480(n), 482(n), 487(n), 488(n), 495(n), 500-2(n)
Ayub Khan, Field Marshal Mohammad Defence Minister 38, 48; C-in-C, 62, 63, 65, 68, 68, 71-4, 76; elected President 77, 79-88; inter-regional economic and other issues, 90-2, 96, 97; fall of, 99-107, 108, 112, 114, 115, 121, 123, 124, 126, 131, 214, 289, 304, 358, 478-85(n)
Baghdad Pact, 67
Basic Democracy Order, 76
Basic Principles Committee, 24, 29-33, 35, 40, 63, 477(n)
Basic Democracies, 76, 86
Beijing, 98, 175, 126-8, 180, 183, 279, 287, 293-6, 298, 299, 302
Bengali Hindus, 14, 261
Bengali language, 8, 24, 326
Bhashani, Maulana Abdul Hamid, 9, 19, 20, 25, 33, 38, 40, 40-6, 69, 75, 85, 96, 98, 100-2, 116, 124, 125, 128, 131, 181, 183, 340, 489(n)

Bhutto, Z. A., 99-104, 116, 123, 132, 133, 135-43, 147-9, 152, 153, 157, 158, 317, 322-4, 327, 328, 330-4, 336, 338, 340-4, 380, 389, 390, 395-400, 402, 403, 410, 412-4, 416, 419, 426-8, 431-3, 487(n), 488(n), 499(n), 500(n), 502(n), 504(n)
Cargill, I. P. M., 220-4
Casey, R. G., 11, 473(n)
Cease-fire, 321
Chaudhry Khaliquzzaman, 19
China, 85, 18, 183, 201, 238, 246, 247, 279, 280, 282, 283, 285-7, 293, 295, 297-9, 302-7, 313, 317, 318, 320, 350, 357, 365-7, 369, 370, 372, 373, 375, 382, 390, 399, 412, 413, 496(n)
Chittagong, 32, 128, 169-72, 174, 175, 177, 178, 179, 181, 186, 187, 189-91, 198, 199, 206-13, 219, 238, 242, 267, 335, 340, 354, 357, 361, 377, 379, 397, 495(n), 500(n)
Choudhry, G. W., 328, 427, 477(n), 486(n)
Choudhury Muhammad Ali, 39, 41, 43, 72, 77
Chundrigar, I. I., 39, 65
Combined Opposition Parties, (COP), 86, 87, 483(n)
Comilla, 169, 170, 175, 179, 211, 213, 361, 379, 381, 383, 393
Communist Party of Pakistan, 15, 61
Communist Party of India, 15
Confederation, 5, 32, 57, 155-7, 393
Congress, Indian National, 4, 11, 12, 26, 32; East Pakistan National, 180; US, 241, 242, 251, 278, 279, 282, 294, 310, 380, 420
Constituent Assembly Order 1955, 38
Constituent Assembly, 10, 18, 26; constitution-making 28-41; 49, 62, 65, 70, 72, 82, 140, 179, 332, 473(n), 475(n), 477(n), 478(n); Constitution Commission 77, 482(n)
Constitution, 4-7, 10, 20, 24; by first Constituent Assembly, 28-37; by second Constituent Assembly, 39-46, 58, 59, 65, 69, 74; by Ayub, 76-80, 82, 86, 92, 93, 103, 106, 108, 109, 116-23, 129, 131, 133-40, 142, 143, 145, 150-2; negotiations on Awami League's proposals, 154-8, 178, 324; Yahya's proposals, 327-34, 342, 343, 410, 427, 428, 431, 500-2(n)
Convention Muslim League, 85, 124, 501(n)
Cornelius, Justice A. R., 328, 329, 331-4, 345, 500(n)
Council Muslim League, 84-6, 100, 499(n), 501(n)
Daultana, Mumtaz Muhammad Khan, 63, 116, 124, 153, 330, 331, 499(n), 501(n)
Democratic Action Committee, (DAC), 100-4
Democratic Youth League, 14
Devaluation, 52, 53, 57, 217, 218
Dhaka, 3, 13, 14, 21-5, 27, 40, 46, 80, 81, 83, 86, 91, 99-102, 107, 111, 116, 121, 126, 127, 130, 132, 134, 136, 138, 139, 142, 143, 148, 149, 150-2, 157-9, 166, 167, 169, 171-7, 178, 181, 185, 189, 191, 195-200, 203, 208, 209, 211, 213, 244-6, 252, 255, 257, 259, 261, 265-7, 269, 271, 272, 279, 283, 288, 291, 322, 325, 330, 337, 340, 341, 358, 359, 363, 364, 367, 370-3, 377, 379-81, 383, 386-9, 393-5, 397, 401, 404-6, 408, 411, 412, 415, 417, 419, 427, 431, 432, 475(n), 476(n), 480(n), 482(n), 487-92(n), 494-6(n), 502-4(n)
Disparity, 84, 88, 90-5, 98, 129
East Bengal Rent Control Act, 14
East Bengal State Acquisition and Tenancy Act, 14
East Pakistan Students Union, 100
East Bengal (Emergency) Requisition of Property Act, 14
East Pakistan Awami Muslim League, 19, 20
East Pakistan Student League, (EPSL), 21, 126
East Pakistan Student Union, (EPSU), 126
East Pakistan Provincial Assembly, 337

Election, of Nazimuddin, 18; East Pakistan by-election, 31, 44, 69, 71, 76, 86, 87, 102, 118, 119, 122-8; of 1970, 130, 131, 134, 140, 142, 144, 156, 273, 283, 295, 327, 337, 339, 481-2(n); October 1971 by-election, 341-3, 421, 500-2(n)
Elective Bodies (Disqualification) Order, (EBDO), 75, 76, 81, 84
Emergency Committee, 355-8, 362, 368, 372, 385, 391, 395, 407, 408, 416, 423, 426-8, 430
Establishment of West Pakistan Act, 39
Farland, Joseph, 250, 315-7, 347, 348, 351, 372, 421, 422, 424, 426, 496(n)
Farman Ali, Maj. Gen., 113, 121, 138, 159, 167, 173, 185, 254, 336, 337, 340-2, 350, 351, 364, 377, 386-9, 395, 397, 398, 401, 402, 404-6, 408, 412, 416, 419, 420, 432, 488(n), 505
Fatima Jinnah, 86, 483(n)
Fazlul Huq, A. K. M., 3-6, 8, 19, 26, 31, 33-5, 38-42, 69, 70, 472(n), 473(n)
Fazlur Rahman, 12, 21, 24, 53, 54
Finance Commission, 89, 91-3, 483(n), 484(n)
Firoz Khan Noon, 24-6, 35, 65
First Five Year Plan, 55, 90, 480(n), 484(n)
Gandhi, Mrs Indira, 236, 351, 354, 358, 373, 375, 417, 418, 495(n), 503(n)
Ghiasuddin Ahmed, 356
Ghulam Muhammad, 36, 37, 50, 51 57, 72, 479(n)
Ghulam Ishaq Khan, 110, 147, 235, 354, 357, 391-3, 395, 409, 410, 426, 492(n), 503(n)
Government of India Act 1935, 3, 477(n)
Gul Hassan, Lt. Gen., 360
Hamidul Haq Choudhury, 11, 25
Hasan, Col. M. A., 111, 116, 120, 143, 149-53, 157, 158, 328, 341, 345, 360, 431, 485(n), 505
Heath, Edward, 277, 278, 289, 292, 314, 496(n), 497(n)
Hilaly, Agha, 243, 244, 250, 254, 266
Indo-Soviet Treaty, 303, 307-10, 312, 318, 498(n)
International Committee of Red Cross, (ICRC), 248, 407, 432
Iskandar Mirza, Maj. Gen., 39, 47, 48, 58, 59, 64-6, 68, 69, 72, 479(n), 481(n)
Jamaat-i-Islami, 44, 82, 84, 86, 116, 123, 124, 324, 339, 343, 501(n)
Jha, L. K., 298
Jinnah, M. A., 3, 4, 9-11, 20, 86, 87, 472(n), 473(n), 483(n)
Joint Electorate, 30, 44
K. Subrahmanyam, 274, 301, 490(n), 495(n), 498(n)
Kamal Hossain, 150, 157, 487(n), 488(n)
Karim, M. I., Maj. Gen., 24, 106, 107, 111, 114-16, 120-2, 127, 129-32, 137, 143, 144, 346, 428-30, 485(n), 486(n), 488(n), 499(n)
Kashmir, 5, 59-62, 66, 67, 96, 146, 304-6, 361, 375, 383, 399, 411, 420, 495(n)
Kazi, A. G. N., 222, 225, 226, 409, 484(n), 492(n)
Khan of Kalat, 69
Khawaja Shahabuddin, 3
Khondkar Mushtaque Ahmed, 132, 133
Kissinger, Henry, 247, 278-82, 294-9, 302, 307, 309, 310, 314-17, 320, 344, 347, 348, 351, 364, 366, 376, 375, 382, 383, 390, 391, 395, 396, 399, 400, 412, 418-21, 493(n), 495-8(n), 502-4(n)
Kittani, Ismet, 252, 253, 258, 493(n)
Kosygin, A. N., 283, 284, 289, 303-5, 310-13
Krishak Proja Samity, 3
Krishak Sramik, 33, 39, 41, 69, 82, 84
Lahore Resolution, 5-7, 9-12, 29, 30, 34, 146, 472(n)
Language Agitation, 14, 23, 24
Legal Framework Order, (LFO), 117, 118, 119-23, 127, 134, 136, 139, 140, 143, 154, 329, 330, 486(n), 506
Liaquat Ali Khan, 18, 19, 21, 28, 29, 31, 51, 60, 62, 67, 472-4(n)
M. M. Ahmed, 115, 120, 129, 146, 151, 153, 157, 199, 232, 241, 251, 289, 324, 328, 331-3, 409, 410, 416, 423, 424, 485(n), 500(n)

Madras Resolution, 29

Malik, H. R., 253, 255, 259, 260, 272

Malik, Dr A. M., 334-336, 359, 386, 388, 389, 407, 408, 412, 419, 420, 432

Maudoodi, Maulana Syed Abul Ala, 324, 500(n)

Mian Iftikharuddin, 18, 32, 33, 46

Monem Khan, 83, 177

Mountbatten, Lord, 10, 11

Muhammad Shah Nawaz Khan of Mamdot, 5

Muhammad Ali (Bogra), 22, 23, 33, 35, 37, 65, 477(n)

Muhammad Munir, 37, 64

Muhammad Toaha, 128

Mujibur Rahman, Sheikh, 19-21, 33, 38, 42, 43, 45, 53, 75, 76, 81, 84, 96-9, 101-5, 111, 116, 121-3, 125-8, 130-9, 141-3, 147-53, 157-9, 163, 164, 166-8, 178, 179, 184, 278, 283, 289, 290, 292, 294, 297, 306, 309, 310, 312-16, 323, 329, 338, 344-52, 382, 414, 418, 432, 433, 478(n), 482(n), 485(n), 487(n), 488(n), 495(n), 496(n), 504(n)

Muslim League All-India, 4-11 13, 15; Pakistan, 17-20, 23, 24, 26, 27, 31-5, 38, 39, 41, 43, 44, 47, 51, 64, 65, 68, 69, 71, 72, 82-6, 100, 116, 123; Qayyum, 124, 140; 327, 329-31, 339, 472(n), 473(n), 475(n), 499(n), 501(n)

Muslim Homeland, 7, 8, 29

Muzaffar Ali Qizilbash, 74, 124

Muzaffar Husain, 194, 377, 378, 386

National Democratic Front, (NDF), 82-5, 87, 98

National Awami Party, (NAP), 46, 74, 81, 82, 84-6, 97, 98, 100, 180, 340, 482(n)

Nawab of Kalabagh, 83, 479(n), 482(n)

Nazimuddin, Khawaja, 3-5, 8, 9, 11, 13, 18, 22-4, 31-3, 36, 63, 64, 68, 85, 475-7(n)

Nixon, Richard, 220, 247, 251, 278-82, 289, 293-7, 302, 310, 314-17, 320, 351, 361, 366, 374, 382, 392, 396, 399, 418, 419, 421, 424, 426, 427, 493(n), 499(n)

Nizam-i-Islam Party, 33, 86, 481(n), 482(n)

Nur Khan, Air Marshal, 108-10

Nurul Amin, 11, 49-51, 87, 98, 116, 124, 340-34, 364, 387, 410, 411, 431, 476(n), 482(n), 499(n), 501(n)

One Unit, 43, 46, 47, 59, 65, 71, 75, 79, 82, 85, 86, 103, 116-20

Operation Close Door, 65

Osmany, Col. M. A. G., 130, 164, 165, 179, 180, 182, 350

Pakistan Resolution, 10, 29, 97

Pakistan Democratic Movement, (PDM), 98, 100

Pakistan Democratic Party, (PDP), 116, 339, 340

Pakistan People's Party, (PPP), 116, 499(n)

Palit, Maj. Gen. D. K., 309, 362, 383, 495(n), 496(n), 498(n), 502-4(n)

Peerzada, Lt. Gen. S. G. M. M., 106, 109-12, 114, 115, 119, 120, 122, 123, 129, 130, 133, 134, 136, 140, 141, 143, 146, 148-150, 153, 155, 157, 158, 164, 327, 328, 331, 332, 334, 338, 345, 349, 409, 410, 423, 427, 428, 431, 485(n), 488(n), 505

Polish Resolution, 373, 414-16

Public and Representative Offices (Disqualification) Act, (PRODA), 36, 75

Qayyum, M., 112, 114, 130, 402, 485(n), 506

Quaid-i-Azam, 12, 18, 21-4, 38, 49, 50, 86, 473(n), 475(n), 476(n), 478(n)

Rab, A., 115, 230

Rawalpindi Conspiracy, 48, 60

Raza, Maj. Gen., N. A. M., 350, 351, 372, 380, 390, 395, 396, 506

Refugees, 87, 236, 237, 248-51, 255, 258, 261-72, 274, 275, 282, 289-94, 296, 299, 300, 311, 365, 366, 370, 376, 494(n), 495(n)

Rizvi, N. A., 337, 486(n), 506

Roedad Khan, 167, 311, 346, 355, 356, 360, 362, 391-3, 395, 409, 410, 417, 424, 427, 430, 489(n), 503(n), 506

Round Table Conference, (RTC), 102, 104, 105, 107, 485(n)

Rowlands, Sir Archibald, 38, 49, 478(n)
Sadruddin Aga Khan, Prince, 258, 264-71
Sarat Chandra Bose, 11
Second Five Year Plan, 88, 90, 483(n), 484(n)
Security Council, 112, 296, 300, 301, 310, 314, 319-21, 357, 365-7, 369, 370, 372-5, 378, 385, 388, 389, 393, 396-400, 403, 404, 411-16, 418-21, 480(n), 502-4(n)
Shah of Iran, 287, 288, 304, 312, 318, 319, 363, 374, 393, 429, 430, 498(n), 503(n)
Shahi, Agha, 252, 255, 256, 258, 263, 270-2, 288, 311, 314, 319, 320, 380, 388-90, 395, 496(n), 498(n)
Sikandar Hayat Khan, Sir, 5
Sisco, Joseph, 243, 254, 261, 374, 380
Six Points, 31, 49, 92, 97, 98, 102, 103, 119, 122, 125, 127, 132, 134-8, 141-4, 146 147, 152, 154, 155, 156, 164, 344, 347, 486(n), 487(n)
Soviet Union, 127, 181, 270, 283-6, 289, 290, 293, 299, 301-8, 311-14, 316-20, 348, 351, 362, 365-7, 369, 370, 372-5, 393, 399, 400, 403, 404, 412-16, 420, 421, 423, 424, 503(n)
Suhrawardy, H. S., 3, 5, 8-12 13, 18-20, 23, 33, 37-9, 41-8, 56, 68, 69, 72, 73, 76, 81-4, 96, 119, 473-6(n), 479(n), 481-3(n)
Sultan Muhammad Khan, 250, 264, 265, 287, 289, 295, 309, 311, 316, 350, 351, 356, 402, 409, 421-3
Swaran Singh, 273, 274, 290, 292, 300, 303, 307, 497(n)
Syed Zafarul Hasan, Dr, 5
Sylhet, 169, 170, 175, 179, 182, 190, 208-11, 213, 217, 219, 340, 354, 357, 397, 476(n)
Tajuddin Ahmed, 133, 135, 303, 350, 488(n), 490(n)
Tamaddun Majlis, 14
Tashkent Declaration, 96, 97, 303
Third Five Year Plan, 94, 484(n), 485(n)
Tikka Khan, Lt. Gen., 122, 148, 172, 174, 175, 200, 201, 203, 205, 266, 267, 282, 292, 334-6, 376
U Thant, 248, 249, 288, 293, 309, 319, 320, 388, 389, 493(n)
Umer, Maj. Gen. Ghulam, 112, 113, 115, 121-3, 129, 130, 132, 142, 146, 159, 163, 164, 264, 310, 311, 388, 345, 347, 349, 350, 485(n)
United States, 30, 34, 66, 67, 72, 239, 279, 294, 302, 307, 308, 313, 374, 399, 400, 480(n), 497(n), 502(n)
United Front, 33, 34, 37-41, 57, 477(n), 478(n)
USAID, 239, 240, 243, 244, 246, 247, 496(n)
V. A. Jaffery, 506
Van Hollen, Christopher, 247, 296, 308, 315, 316, 400, 493(n), 497-9(n), 504(n)
World Bank, 199-201, 204, 215, 218, 220, 251, 257, 491(n)
Yahya Khan, General, 105, 106, 108-25, 127, 129-43, 146-53, 157-9, 163, 166, 181, 183, 194, 204, 214, 220, 230, 235, 243, 244, 246, 248, 250, 251, 264, 266, 275, 278-89, 291-7, 299, 301, 304-6, 308, 310-21, 322-4, 326-8, 330-2, 334, 336, 338, 339, 341-9, 351, 352, 355, 356, 359-63, 365, 367, 368, 374, 379, 380, 386, 388-90, 392, 395-8, 402, 403, 405, 408-11, 415-25,426-31, 433, 486-8(n), 490(n), 492(n), 494-6(n), 498-502(n), 504(n)
Yakub Khan, Lt. Gen. Sahibzada, 122, 123, 138, 148, 487(n), 490(n)
Zafar Iqbal, 200, 201, 491
Zhou Enlai, 284, 285, 287, 297, 298, 496(n)